Mastering Unix

Mastering™ Unix

Kate Wrightson and
Joe Merlino

SYBEX®

San Francisco • London • Paris • Düsseldorf • Soest

Associate Publisher: Dick Staron
Contracts and Licensing Manager: Kristine O'Callaghan
Acquisitions and Developmental Editor: Diane Lowery
Editor: Ronn Jost
Production Editor: Lorrie Fink
Technical Editor: Patrick Ramseier
Book Designer: Kris Warrenburg
Graphic Illustrator: Richard Whitaker/Seventeenth Street Studios
Electronic Publishing Specialist: Seventeenth Street Studios
Proofreader: Kevin Stoffel/Seventeenth Street Studios
Indexer: Nancy Guenther
CD Technician: Keith McNeil
CD Coordinator: Kara Eve Schwartz
Cover Designer: Design Site
Cover Illustrator: Jack D. Myers

Library of Congress Card Number: 00-106460

ISBN: 0-7821-2817-3

Manufactured in the United States of America

10 9 8 7 6 5 4 3 2

For TW,
whose world was a different one
but who was proud of us anyway

ACKNOWLEDGMENTS

A large group of people worked to bring this book to you. Although Joe and Kate get their names on the cover, there are many other folks whose hard work and effort made this book possible. We appreciate their diligence and patience with us over a long and bumpy period of time. We're especially grateful to Sybex and Seventeenth Street Studios for their understanding; during the last part of this book's writing, Kate's father died unexpectedly. Our team accommodated our transcontinental travels and made finishing the project as easy as possible under the circumstances.

In addition to the people whose names follow, we'd like to thank our agent, David Fugate, and Waterside Productions. David and the Waterside team keep us going and keep us working, and we love being part of their team. Kate also thanks the usual suspects, especially Mason Kramer, who won the lucky random drawing to be named here.

Sybex

Sybex people made the project possible and kept it going, from the first contact to the final printing. We'd especially like to thank the following people:

- Roger Stewart initially brought us into the project.
- Diane Lowery shepherded the first quarter of the book.
- Colleen Strand managed administrative details of the full project.

Editing Team

We have had good luck in our careers in being able to work with fine editors who understand what we're trying to say and who catch all the places where we've said it poorly. This project was no different, and we'd like to thank the two editors who reviewed each chapter as it came past:

- Ronn Jost fixed our prose and ensured that we made sense, with the greatest of good humor and friendly e-mail.

- Patrick Ramseier checked the technical validity of our work and kept us from giving you bad information.

Seventeenth Street Studios

The folks at Seventeenth Street Studios did most of the dirty work involved in getting the book organized and arranged into a far more attractive package than the original documents ever promised. In particular, we'd like to thank the following people:

- Lorrie Fink, our production coordinator, kept track of the schedule and tried valiantly to keep us on target despite our wildly erratic lives over the past year.

- Kevin Stoffel proofread everything that went into the book and caught all the errors before they hit the page.

- Richard Whitaker and Bob Giles laid out the pages as they appear here, composing them into readable and appealing form; Richard also redrew our extremely amateur line drawings into more professional images.

CONTENTS AT A GLANCE

CONTENTS

B Documentation and Resources   799

INTRODUCTION

Call us evangelists, street corner preachers, radical partisans, or just plain junkies: We love Unix and all its derivatives. When we were offered the chance to write this book, we thought it was a tremendous opportunity to showcase this fine operating system and help those new to the OS learn how to use it to its fullest. Unix is a powerful and robust operating system that rarely fails and that offers even the most casual users the ability to manage individual accounts at a level far surpassing the options offered by other operating systems.

Recently, we saw a Web banner that proclaimed Unix to be "The Original Alternative." This isn't quite right: Unix is much closer to being the Original Operating System than it is to being an alternative of any sort. In fact, Microsoft Windows and the Macintosh Operating System (MacOS) were initially designed as alternatives to Unix, not the other way around! Unfortunately, the marketing and PR for the personal operating systems such as Windows and MacOS has been successful, and now most computer users either don't know Unix exists or think that they are too stupid to use it because "Unix is for geeks and computer science majors."

That's where this book comes in. Neither of us were computer science majors (English and economics), and we've learned most of what we know about Unix in a hands-on fashion—or, in the traditional manner, by pestering our more knowledgeable friends until they taught us what we needed to know. We used books like this one to lay the base for further experimentation, and we still refer to those old friends when we need a jogged memory. If we can do it, you can do it, too.

Unix doesn't have to be expensive; in many cases, you can get free copies of Unix variants from the Internet or pay just the cost of the CD and shipping to get a Unix variant on a disc. Unix doesn't have to be hard; you don't start out with programming, and with graphical user interfaces, Unix is eerily similar to those other operating systems you've used. Unix doesn't have to be an either/or choice; we use a variety of operating systems in our daily work and recreation.

We hope that after you have read this book, you will feel comfortable and capable when confronted with a Unix machine. Whether or not you delve into the world of administering your own Unix-variant system—and we hope you do—you will have the skills necessary to work with Unix at your school or workplace. If you decide to run your own system, you'll be able to manage your users, your files, and any services you choose to run. Unlike the users of other operating systems, you won't be shielded from the actual operation of your computer; we hope this gives you a sense of power and accomplishment that is hard to equal in the computing world.

Learn Unix, and new worlds open to you.

What the Book Contains

Because we wrote this book intending it to be useful for a wide variety of readers, there is a lot of information here. Some of it is quite basic, while other chapters contain complex and advanced material. However, there should be nothing here that is beyond the average reader's understanding, even if you never plan to use Unix.

The book is divided into nine major parts, with 43 chapters distributed among those parts. We begin with a basic introduction to Unix and its history, move into basic Unix commands and concepts, and then move into discussion of the various components of a working Unix-based system. You'll find separate sections devoted to graphical user interfaces, text editors, basic and advanced system administration, networking, and the various services used by networks across the Internet.

TIP   You can find a complete listing of the chapters and their contents in the expanded table of contents, which precedes this introduction.

In each chapter, you'll find real-world examples and sample output from a variety of Unix commands. We show you how things work and give you the tools to try each concept out on your own system. Where pictures would be helpful, we've included them; however, because so much of this book is written about text-mode work, we thought you'd prefer to see the output in the main text, instead of in a shot of a terminal window containing some tiny text that's barely readable.

Whom the Book Is For

We've written the book so that absolute beginners and longtime system administrators should both find some use in it, though the latter will probably also need more-specific books designed to answer hardcore questions. If you have never seen Unix before, you will learn most of what you need to get going in the early chapters of the book. If you've worked with Unix, but don't quite understand how it does what it does, you'll find the information you need here as well. If you're comfortable as a user, but find yourself in possession of a new Unix system (or you've just been hired as a system administrator), we show you what to do, too.

We do make some assumptions about you, dear readers. We have based the book on the following "typical reader," so if you don't actually meet one of our assumptions, you'll need to make adjustments for your own circumstances. Here are the basic assumptions we've made:

- We assume that you have access to a computer running some variant of Unix. It can be one of the three Unices covered in the book (Linux, Solaris, or FreeBSD) or another variant, but you should know that we have targeted our discussion of *how Unix works* to those three Unices.

- We assume that, on that computer, you have a valid user account and access to shell functions. If your system administrator has devised a menu system, you should be able to break out of the menu and get to the regular shell prompt; if you use a graphical user interface, you should be able to open a terminal window.

- We assume that you do not have any restrictions on what you can do in your user account, within reason. By restrictions, we mean the ability to execute shell commands, write basic shell scripts, change file permissions, and the like. We do not mean file size limitations, connection time restrictions, or other user-policy functions.

- We assume that, if you are interested in running your own Unix variant system, you have obtained a suitable computer and have installed your preferred Unix variant already. Whatever Unix-based operating system you buy should have clear installation directions and, in most cases, an auto-installation program.

- We assume that you are interested in maintaining a secure system and that you will take the appropriate precautions to keep your system secure, especially if you have other users or if you connect to the Internet from the system.

How to Use the Book

You can read straight through or find each chapter as you need it, but regardless of how you use the information in the book, you'll find consistent formatting to help you identify particular kinds of information. We use special conventions to highlight commands you need to type at a shell prompt, commands that are accessed with a mouse, lines of code, and key combinations. We also use margin icons to identify bits of information that might be dire warnings, helpful material beyond what's in the text, or unique pieces of knowledge that should either give you a chuckle or help you understand more about the Unix world.

Formatting in the Text

As you read along, you'll see that the text on each page is not necessarily all the same. Those different fonts and the layout indicate a particular type of information. Most frequently, you'll see text conventions that indicate something you should type, as written, at a shell prompt to perform a particular task. For example, if we ask you to issue the command that brings up the documentation for the `ls` command, you'll see the sentence "Type `man ls` at the shell prompt." Note that `man ls` is in a different typeface, indicating it is the actual command to be typed. The same typeface is used for directory paths, the way in which file locations are noted in Unix. If you're looking for a log file, we'll tell you that logs are usually located in `/var/log`. Individual filenames also use this font.

However, if we're showing you a particularly long command (or if we think the command is important enough not to be buried in a block of text), we'll use a different convention. So, you'll sometimes see the command set off on its own line, using a monospace font, like this:

```
man ls
```

or

```
cp /var/log/mail maillog
```

This convention is also used for excerpts from files, or for complete files, as well as for shell scripts and other programming examples.

TIP   If you see a line that ends in an arrow, that arrow indicates that the line was so long it had to be broken up into two lines. The arrow will look like this: ➡.

Words in italics are new terms, which are usually defined in the next sentence. You can also find italicized terms in the Glossary. We've added other important terms to the Glossary, but it also contains all the important new concepts from the main text of the book. Commands introduced throughout the book are also listed in Appendix A, a Unix command compendium. In that appendix, we've shown you the command, its syntax, and some of the most important options or flags it can use.

If we describe a process that uses mouse clicks instead of text commands, the command is written using arrows like this: ➤. That is, we might say, "From the menu at the top of the screen, select File ➤ Save." This convention saves time and space, because we can use the arrow instead of saying, "Select the File menu. In the drop-down list that appears, click the Save option."

Finally, we show you some key combinations in various places throughout the book. A key combination requires that you press two or more keys simultaneously. Usually, one of those keys is a *metakey*: Ctrl, Alt, or Esc. When you see the command "Press Ctrl+c" you need to press the Ctrl key and the c key at the same time. Key combinations are usually found in graphical programs, though the Ctrl+c combination will stop any active process in a Unix shell, and the Ctrl+z combination will suspend the active process so that you can perform another action at the prompt without ending the initial process. (Resume the process by typing fg at the prompt.)

Margin Icons

You'll see many special icons in the outer margins of this book's pages. These icons are used to indicate particular pieces of information we felt were so important they should be flagged. There are three types of icons used in the following chapters:

WARNING   A Warning is the most important thing to read on any page where it appears. We use Warnings to flag security risks and tell you about commands or habits that might damage your hardware or cause you to lose files and data. If you read nothing else in the book, at least read the Warnings.

NOTE Notes are extra information that didn't quite fit into the main text. We use Notes to provide commands or concepts that are a bit more advanced, or that point out some feature of Unix history or the Unix community that might be useful to readers.

TIP Tips are shortcuts or handy hints that will speed up some of the work you need to do when you use Unix. We also use Tips to tell you about programs or Web pages that will make your Unix life easier or that will shed some light on a difficult concept.

PART I

Introducing Unix

CHAPTER
ONE

History and Background of Unix

- What Is Unix?

- Creation and History of Unix

- The Unix Philosophy

- Summary

Welcome to *Mastering Unix*! As we explained in the introduction, we've written this book with a variety of users in mind. You might be an old hand at using Unix systems and you've picked this book up (heavy, isn't it?) to serve as a reference guide. You could be an intermediate user of Unix or Unix-based operating systems who's looking for that extra information that will take you to the next skill level. You may be someone who knows enough about Unix to get around your shell Internet account, reading mail and news, but not doing much else. You might even be completely new to Unix and its derivatives, and have picked this book up out of idle curiosity. No matter who you are, you'll find something of use in this book. Both of us have been using Unix or Unix-based operating systems for over a decade now, and we learn something new about this magnificent beast almost every day.

If you're reading this book because you've been told, or have decided, that you need to learn how to use a Unix system, odds are that you already know at least a little bit about Unix. If you picked up this book because of its striking cover or size, or because you've heard the term *Unix* and you're wondering what it's all about, it's possible that you might not have any idea whatsoever what Unix actually is—and how it's different from the other operating systems you're probably familiar with.

One position that we hold strongly is that computer users should know the background of the software they are using. In many cases, all that's really necessary is a bit of basic history; everyone seems to know that Microsoft Windows is the brainchild of the Microsoft Corporation. Microsoft is in the news so frequently that even people who don't use computers know about Windows. The Macintosh is slightly less well-known, but it has a reputation of being user-friendly, easy to learn, and the challenger to Microsoft and the personal computer (PC).

So, you might ask, what's the point of knowing all that? Well, there are several points. If you know that Microsoft is responsible for your operating system, your integrated office suite, and your Internet Web browser, you have some idea of where that software came from. There's a company you can point to. With Unix, it's a little different—and with all the operating systems that have grown out of the original Unix, it's even more different.

To give you an understanding of Unix and where it fits into the world of computing, we've decided to start the book with Part I: "Introducing Unix." This part of the book contains information about Unix: the history of the operating system, the various Unix variants, an introduction to the concept of Free Software, and some basic Unix concepts that you should know before reading further.

In this chapter, we provide a brief introduction to what Unix is and explain a little bit about its development, history, and philosophy. Chapter 2: "Which Unix?" introduces the wide variety of Unix variants now available and covers in more detail the three variants we've selected for this book: Linux, FreeBSD, and Sun Solaris. In addition, we will present a brief history of the Free Software movement, which affects Unix users in a significant manner. Finally, we give the opportunity to start building your Unix skills in Chapter 3: "Some Basic Unix Concepts." We've designed this part of the book to help you to understand why Unix is what it is and how that affects the concepts, skills, and programs that we describe in the rest of the book.

What Is Unix?

In the simplest terms, Unix is an *operating system*. An operating system is the software that runs behind the scenes and allows the user to operate the machine's hardware, start and stop programs, and set the parameters under which the computer operates. Modern operating systems also do a lot of other things, such as controlling network connections, but in the strictest sense, these can be thought of as extra capabilities. The most basic requirement of an operating system is that it permits the user to operate the computer.

Anyone who has used a computer in the past 10 or 15 years has used an operating system. The most common personal operating systems in use today are Microsoft's Windows family (Windows 95 and Windows 98) and Apple's MacOS. These systems were developed for use with the new generations of low-cost, personal-use computers that became available in the 1980s. As these desktop computers became more powerful and more popular, these personal operating systems saw a commensurate increase in popularity.

However, the popularity of personal operating systems such as Apple's and Microsoft's is only part of the operating-system story. Well before these systems existed, academics and computing professionals were using a variety of operating systems. Most of these are now extinct, but a few—especially Unix—survived and continued to evolve.

What we now know as *Unix* is actually an entire family of operating systems. From IBM's AIX, Xerox's Xenix, and Hewlett Packard's HP-UX to the publicly licensed Linux and FreeBSD, versions of Unix are produced by a variety of companies and organizations. All of these versions have slight differences, but it is what they have in common that makes them important.

All Versions of Unix Are Multiuser

Unix was originally designed to be used on large mainframe computers with many users. Consequently, Unix has support for user accounts and varying levels of file security, allowing users to keep their files private from one another. Even if you install a Unix-based operating system on a standalone computer and you are the only person who will ever use the computer, you will still create at least two accounts: the root account and a personal user account. Many administrators set up accounts for nonexistent people so that they can test configurations or programs under different account settings.

All Versions of Unix Are Multitasking

Unix systems can perform many tasks at once. Unix does this by means of *time slicing* (also called *true* multitasking), which means that each running process gets to use the computer for a specific period of time. This behavior is in contrast to *task switching,* which is the "multitasking" system used by personal operating systems. Task switching means that each running process gets to use the computer until it has completed a particular task; it's not really multitasking in the true sense of the term, so we've put quotation marks around it. When we talk about multitasking in this book, we are talking about time slicing, the true form of multitasking.

All Versions of Unix Can Use the Same Commands

It doesn't matter what kind of Unix-based operating system you're using, whether it's Linux, FreeBSD, Solaris, or some commercial Unix. When using a Unix-derived operating system, users can issue commands to the system by means of a *command shell.* The command shell is separate from the operating system; in fact, the shell acts as a translator between the commands you enter with the keyboard and the operating system itself. A multitude of shells is available to the Unix user. These shells can be run on any version of Unix, so that the same commands will work on any machine using that shell. We've devoted an entire part of this book to the bash shell, which is one of the most commonly used command shells.

What Does This Mean to the End User?

To the user, then, all versions of Unix look pretty much alike. With only some minor differences, a user will use one given Unix machine in the exact same way as she would use any other Unix machine. The display might be a bit different, and the exact syntax of commands might be altered (if a command shell different from her regular shell is installed), but she can still perform her regular tasks with the same commands. The differences between the various *Unices* (the plural of Unix) come into play when you reach the level of programmers and system administrators. These are the people to whom the nuts and bolts of different systems become critically important.

If you are wondering whether it's better to use Unix A or Unix B, or if you're caught in the Linux vs. FreeBSD dilemma, don't worry. Pick one and get to know it. When you're comfortable with that one, you might want to explore another. However, you will never find that learning one particular Unix makes all other Unices incomprehensible; Unix just doesn't work that way.

When non-Unix people hear Unix people talking about command languages, shell environments, and so on, they often get the idea that Unix is an obscure and old-fashioned operating system that makes computing difficult by requiring the user to memorize complicated command syntaxes. Although it is true that Unix can be operated entirely from a command-line interface, it may come as a surprise to some of these folks to learn that Unix has a windowing system that is both older and more sophisticated than the ones that form the basis of the personal operating systems. Hundreds of graphical applications, including word processors, spreadsheets, image manipulation software, and others, can be run on Unix machines. With the continuing development of applications for Unix platforms and the transfer of popular Windows-based programs to Unix, the popularity (and ease-of-use) of this powerful operating system is bound to blossom.

So what is Unix? Unix is a powerful multiuser, multitasking family of operating systems. Unix is mature technology, having its genesis in the late 1960s, but it is thoroughly modern—it runs on just about any computing hardware you can think of.

Creation and History of Unix

Once upon a time, every computer came with its own operating system and cost thousands of dollars. The idea that an operating system could be independent of the hardware had not been developed. How is that different from today? Today, the computer you buy at Best Buy has an operating system preinstalled, but you can change that operating system if you want. For example, the Windows operating system is not integrated into the hardware of your new Compaq.

In the very earliest days of computing, of course, there were no operating systems. Computing was done by human operators on *bare machines.* This meant that for every computing task that needed to be done, the computer would have to be configured for that specific task. This was a very cumbersome way to do computing tasks, and computer scientists were always looking for ways that the machine itself could take over more of the work of processing data.

As hardware got more powerful, and the computers' internal switches were further automated, programmers began writing programs that could reconfigure the machine on the fly. Each computer manufacturer would write operating programs that were specific to the particular hardware they'd designed. This was more or less the state of affairs until the late 1970s and early 1980s, when the popular personal operating systems were first conceived and developed. Apple, for example, wrote its operating systems specifically for the hardware they'd designed, while Microsoft developed its system specifically for Intel's processors.

The Story of C

Meanwhile, others were looking for ways to use operating-system software to get the same behaviors from different types of hardware, so that a new operating system didn't need to be written for each new computer. In 1965, two computer scientists at Bell Labs, now known as Lucent Technologies, wrote the first incarnation of Unix, which ran on a Digital Equipment Corporation (DEC) PDP-7. When they acquired a PDP-11/20, the scientists (Dennis Ritchie and Ken Thompson) decided to *port* Unix to the new computer. (To port a piece of software is to rewrite it for a different platform.) The experience they gained in this exercise resulted in Ritchie's conception and design of the C programming language, still one of the most useful programming languages for Unix users.

The idea behind C was to create a programming language suitable for creating an operating system. Once C was usable, programmers could then create *compilers* for the various hardware devices; the compilers would translate C instructions into the machine's native command language, no matter what that language was. C turned out to be very successful, because it filled a need that everyone had. In fact, it was so successful that in 1973, Ritchie and Thompson completely rewrote Unix in C.

In the meantime, Bell Labs' parent company, AT&T, had been declared a monopoly by the United States Federal Trade Commission. As a result of this declaration, AT&T was subject to certain restrictions on its behavior. Partly because of these new requirements, Bell Labs began making Unix available to universities, free of charge. This was quite popular, and Unix became widely used in the academic environment. It subsequently began to propagate into the private sector when students began to graduate or leave school, taking their knowledge and affection for Unix with them.

The Rise of Unix Derivations

In 1978, AT&T announced that they would begin charging everyone, including academic institutions, for the Unix source code. In response, computer scientists at the University of California at Berkeley announced that they would create their own Unix-like system, to be called BSD (Berkeley Software Distribution) Unix. BSD was released under a very permissive license and has gone on to form the basis of many other Unix variants.

In 1987, around the same time that version 4.3 of BSD was being released, AT&T and Sun Microsystems agreed to cooperate on a plan to reintegrate the AT&T and BSD versions of Unix. Other vendors who had created their own Unices in the intervening years, such as IBM and Hewlett Packard, felt threatened by this plan and formed an organization called the Open Software Foundation. Although OSF-1, the Foundation's 1991 version of Unix, was never a major hit, parts of it managed to find their way into other distributions.

The Internet and Unix

In the mid to late 1980s, other events were occurring that would affect the growth and development of Unix. The Internet began to establish a real presence in universities and research labs. This rapid access to information and colleagues made possible a new type of software development. In previous years, programmers and developers worked in laboratories together. The physical proximity of other team members and the computers fueled innovation and hard work; this method of development was typified by MIT's Research Lab, home of many of the inventions we take for granted today.

However, the Internet changed everything. Programmers were no longer required to be in the same building or city. With instant communication via e-mail and the ability to share code files with negligible cost, programmers soon realized that they could work on software projects with colleagues thousands of miles away or on different continents. The result of this realization was that Unix variants began appearing that were free for the downloading. Anyone with a yen to hone their programming skills could work on these distributions and contribute their work back to the project.

These free Unices had the effect of reenergizing enthusiasm for Unix on college campuses, because students could download them for free and install them on their personal computers. The result was that computer science students now had the same programming environment in their dorm rooms or apartments as they used in their classes—no more fighting for time on a mainframe computer or waiting in line for a computer in the campus-research laboratory. The additional time has meant that college students are now as involved in the Unix community as those who are professional Unix administrators or programmers.

Unix Today

All the developments of the last 40 years have brought us to the vibrant Unix community of today. Linux and FreeBSD, two free Unices, are very popular on college campuses, and Linux is beginning to make inroads into business and the popular consciousness. CNN's online news site, http://www.cnn.com, even runs regular columns on Linux in their Technology section.

Although nowhere near as popular as Microsoft's operating systems, Linux and FreeBSD are beginning to establish a toehold in the personal-computer market, as consumers are beginning to learn that they can have a full-power, industrial-strength operating system at low cost. Businesses are beginning to take advantage of Linux and FreeBSD to save money on small servers for their internal use.

Meanwhile, Unix and Unix-derived operating systems are the de facto standard for large servers. AIX, HP-UX, and Sun's Solaris are extremely popular for serving large Internet sites and databases. We've heard several reports from system administrators at large corporations who use a Unix-derived operating system on their Web and e-mail servers to provide reliability and lengthy up-times, even if the majority of the company's computers are managed with Windows NT so that Windows software programs can be used.

The Unix Philosophy

We've covered the history of Unix, but is that what makes Unix special? Not completely. From the very beginning, a number of assumptions have been built into the design of Unix. Over time, these ideas have proven themselves as valid and have taken on the quality of an entire philosophy. Some of the main ideas of this Unix philosophy are explained below; you'd probably get quite a few suggestions for other main components of the concept, were you to ask around, but these seem to be the core of everyone's idea of Unix.

Keep things small: Each component of the system should be as small and simple as possible. Each component may not be especially powerful by itself, but small components can be combined into powerful and flexible complex objects. Small programs are easy to understand and maintain, and simple programs can often be adapted to unforeseen uses. Small modules can be used to affect the kernel's behavior, so that only one action or setting is controlled by each module.

Everything is configurable: The behavior of any particular program or command can be configured in as many different ways as imaginable. Users can configure their individual accounts as they like, while administrators can configure general system settings or regular routines to save time and effort. If you find a Unix program that isn't configurable, it's an anomaly.

Everything is consistent: Every aspect of a Unix system is represented as a file. Text documents, executable programs, system features, hardware devices, and just about anything else you can think of are represented by the system as a file. A set of consistent ways of dealing with system features has been developed based on this idea. We explain this concept in more detail in Chapter 3: "Some Basic Unix Concepts."

Captive user interfaces are avoided: The more popular personal operating systems, such as MacOS and Windows, are based on the assumption that the user of a program is always a human. This ignores the fact that the user of a program might be another program. In those operating systems, the user interface is therefore captive to the human user; if you don't click the button in a dialog box, the operating system patiently waits until you do. This can take hours or days. Unix avoids this problem wherever possible by allowing programs to function in noninteractive modes. These modes allow programs to be chained together to perform complex tasks without any intervention from the user.

Automation is possible: Many aspects of the Unix interface allow for automation. The Unix shells, in addition to being simple command interpreters, are also program interpreters. Anything that can be done from the keyboard can also be done from within a program. This means that you can write scripts that will call certain programs automatically at a given time or system state. Most system administrators automate routine tasks, such as backups, to avoid having to do such jobs by hand. Unix is powerful enough to handle most of its administration tasks by itself, with the only human intervention required being a check of the results.

Summary

Unix is an operating system with a long and rich history, as computer history goes. Since Unix's roots are found in mainframe computers, the operating system includes support for multiple users, wise allocation of system resources through multitasking, configurability and flexibility for user and administrator preferences, and the ability to use the same commands regardless of the Unix variant being used.

The underlying Unix philosophy keeps the operating system flexible. Unix is small and modular, effectively organized, responsive to user needs yet able to run multiple automatic processes, and consistent in its operation and output. With Unix, you can perform simple tasks or complicated programming operations. Whatever you choose to do with a Unix computer, Unix will be able to keep up.

CHAPTER
TWO

Which Unix?

- The Fragmentation of Unix

- Differences between Unices

- Unix Versions Used in This Book

- We GNU, Do You?

- Getting to know GNU

- The Free Software Foundation

- If GNU's Not Unix, What Is It?

- The Free Software Explosion

- The Meteoric Rise of Open Source

- Summary

As we mentioned in the previous chapter, *Unix* can be thought of as a family of operating systems. When AT&T Unix and BSD Unix diverged, that event set into motion a chain of subsequent events that led to the genus *Unix* diverging into multiple species. Although each retains the essential nature that makes Unix *Unix*, each also has its own idiosyncrasies. These peculiarities might not affect the user much, but they have important consequences for the system administrator and the programmer. People with such responsibilities must make sure they understand how things operate when they move to a version of Unix with which they've never worked.

The Fragmentation of Unix

Historically speaking, the granddaddy of all current Unix versions is the Sixth Edition of the original AT&T Unix. This version was released around 1975 and was the first Unix widely available outside of AT&T. (The Sixth is the Unix version that first found favor in universities.) It was this edition that formed the basis for the first BSD release as well as for several other variants. Two of these variations, PWB (Programmers' Workbench) and UNIX/TS, were the ancestors of System III, which would turn out to be the beginning of a very influential line. The Sixth Edition eventually became the Seventh Edition, which itself formed the basis of Xenix, one of the first versions of Unix to run on an Intel x86-series processor.

If all of this seems a little complicated, that's because it is. The diagram in Figure 2.1 shows a somewhat simplified version of the Unix family tree.

For most purposes, we can think of almost all Unix variants as being the descendants of either some version of BSD or System V (a descendant itself of System III), or some combination of the two. Solaris, for example, was originally a descendant of 4.1BSD, but eventually inherited some features from the fourth release of System V (usually abbreviated SysVR4). Even if a particular version can't trace its lineage directly to either family, the influence of these two branches is such that it probably has significant features drawn from one or the other or both.

FIGURE 2.1:

The Unix family tree is a dense and bushy one.

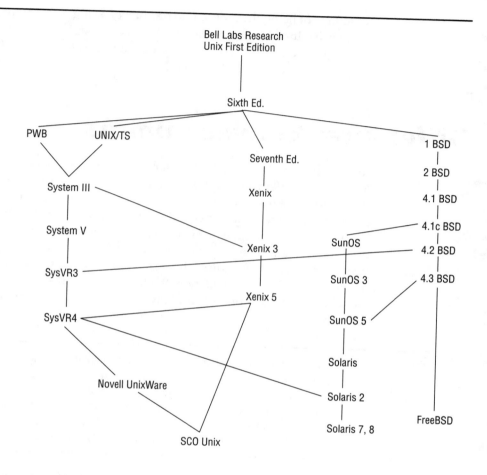

Linux is something of a special case. Although it does draw features from both SysV and BSD, Linus Torvalds did not use any existing Unix code when he began to write the first Linux kernel.

An unfortunate consequence of this fragmentation was that Unix's position in the marketplace began to suffer. Although Unix continued to dominate in universities and research laboratories, corporate information technology managers faced a bewildering assortment of hardware and software choices, and Unix was not always their first selection. As Microsoft emerged as a real force in the 1990s, its Windows NT operating system began to challenge Unix. Windows NT had the advantage of being the monolithic product of a single company, and it ran on inexpensive Intel hardware. Although Unix was still widely used, the general public grew to believe that *computers* meant *personal computers* (PCs) and *operating system* meant Microsoft Windows.

Differences between Unices

As we mentioned in Chapter 1, different versions of Unix have a lot of similarities. This doesn't mean they're the same—far from it. Although the commands, shell environments, and basic design may be similar, there are significant differences in such crucial elements as the start-up procedure, the directory structure, the names of devices, the installation procedure, and so on. Versions of Unix also differ in how they handle the internal functions involved in moment-to-moment operation. This can include such decisions as how network functions are implemented, how data is moved, how the filesystem works, and how processor tasks are scheduled. Many of these low-level functions depend on the hardware upon which a particular version of Unix is designed to run.

NOTE Although Unix was designed to be portable, there is a limit to exactly how portable something can be. This is especially critical in regard to an operating system, where the software needs to interact with the processor and memory in a very finicky, low-level sort of way. In theory, anything written in C is completely portable, provided you have a compiler for the new system. In practice, a good deal of work is required to port an operating system from one type of hardware to another.

To the user, most of these differences go unnoticed. To the administrator or programmer, though, differences in directory structure or device names can become very important. Imagine trying to maintain a large number of *heterogeneous* machines, meaning that your network is composed of computers running different versions of Unix. You need to install a piece of software on all of them, but the files that configure and run the software need to go into different directories on each machine. It's easy to see how such differences can cause major headaches. Fortunately, most versions of Unix are similar enough that an experienced administrator can pick up the differences fairly quickly.

This book, naturally enough, tends to focus on the common features of the various *Unices*. Although Unices is the usual plural of Unix, it's not clear whether this is grammatically correct—but it is certainly common usage. We used three different versions of Unix as we wrote this book. In those places where procedures or descriptions diverge between the three, we make a note of it. These mentions are not a suitable substitute for reading documentation specific to those operating systems. We hope, though, that by the time you reach the end of this book, you will be familiar enough with the Unix way of doing things that any idiosyncrasies in the particular version of Unix you use will seem less troubling.

Unix Versions Used in This Book

As we said above, three Unices were used in the writing of this book. They were chosen because they are the most popular versions of Unix available for the PC platform. In this context, when we say *PC*, we mean Intel x86-series processors and those compatible with the x86 architecture. The Unices we selected are described below; although we personally use Linux for most of our daily work, we don't recommend it over either FreeBSD or Solaris if you find one of those to be more suitable for your tastes.

Linux

The bulk of our recent Unix experience is with Linux. Linux is a rather unique beast in the annals of operating-system history, because it is the first one that was developed openly. What does that mean? It means that Linux exists because of a group effort. When he began to develop the Linux kernel, Linus Torvalds (the originator of Linux) made the source code for it available on the Internet. He invited anyone interested in the project to contribute code or fix code that had already been contributed. Although there is now a central core of Linux developers, they regularly evaluate volunteer contributions for inclusion in the formal releases. Even those who aren't interested in contributing to kernel releases can write, maintain, and distribute a patch that fixes a known problem or adds a new bit of functionality to the operating system. The Linux license requires public release of all source code for patches written to the operating system, making it an Open Source project.

Linux is not the first or only such Open Source software project, but it is the one that has attracted the most attention. We discuss Open Source software in more detail in the section "We GNU, Do You?" In a way, the Open Source methodology shares quite a bit with the academic and scientific way of doing things. Work is done by diverse individuals and evaluated by the community. If it works, it's accepted. If someone comes up with a better way of doing it, the better way will be adopted. Readers who are familiar with academic behavior will find an analogue in the concept of peer review.

Because no one owns Linux in the way that AT&T owns Unix, anyone is free to package and distribute the source code. A number of companies and organizations have done just that. The version of Linux used in the creation of this book is distributed by the Red Hat Corporation, a publicly traded company headquartered in Durham, North Carolina. Another popular distribution is produced by the Corel Corporation of Ottawa, Canada. Both of these are for-profit corporations who derive revenue from the sale of packaged versions of Linux. Because of Linux's license, however, it is also possible to download these distributions from the Internet or purchase them at a discount from independent distributors.

Another popular distributor is not a company, but an organization. Software in the Public Interest produces the popular Debian GNU/Linux distribution. Their goal in creating their distribution was to maintain a 100-percent public-domain operating system, and the Debian distribution has proved to be popular. In addition to the distributions listed here, there are a number of other distributions—some for general use and some for niche uses. The last time we counted, there were over 100 Linux distributions available. In addition to PC platforms, Linux has also been ported to Sun's Sparc platform, DEC's Alpha, and Apple's Macintosh.

FreeBSD

FreeBSD is a direct derivative of the original BSD Unix. Like Linux, it is available for download over the Internet, complete with source code. Unlike Linux, FreeBSD is developed and maintained by a formal group of developers (although it is possible to contribute code if you want to). The license under which FreeBSD is distributed differs from Linux's in that it does not require redistributors to make their changes public.

FreeBSD is known as a very fast and reliable operating system and is often preferred by hardcore computer science types. There is some friendly rivalry between adherents of FreeBSD and Linux, though both are united in their preference for a Unix-derived operating system and the flexibility it gives to the user. FreeBSD runs on Intel or Intel-compatible processors as well as the DEC Alpha platform.

Solaris

In contrast to both Linux and FreeBSD, Solaris is a fully proprietary system. It is produced by Sun Microsystems and was originally developed for use on Sun's Sparc line of processors. As Intel's x86 chips became more popular for use on higher-end systems (instead of running solely on consumer-level computers), Sun ported Solaris to that platform, as well. While Sun does provide downloads of Solaris, the software license limits use of the software to personal use, and redistribution is not permitted. Solaris has the most restrictive license of the three Unices we used in this book.

Solaris became a popular platform based on the power and performance of the Sparc platform. Many businesses like to use Sparcs as a relatively low-cost server solution, and some academic environments have adopted Sparcs as desktop machines for researchers who run statistical software that produces significant system loads. Sparcs are compact, yet powerful, machines. Solaris has gained some popularity among the Intel-hardware crowd, but its limited license has kept it from becoming as widely used as Linux or FreeBSD.

We GNU, Do You?

No discussion of Unix would be complete without mention of the Free Software Foundation and the GNU project. GNU stands for GNU's Not Unix and is pronounced like the name of the animal. The Free Software Foundation and the GNU project have been two of the major forces in Unix and Unix-based operating-system development over the past 30 years, and their contributions are critical components of the Unices that we all use today.

In this chapter, we explain the background of the Free Software movement and its founder, Richard Stallman. We also describe the Open Source revolution of the late 1990s, which shared many of the characteristics of the earlier Free Software movement, yet was targeted more at corporate adoption of Open Source software than the earlier wave's reliance on personal users and their adoption of Free Software packages.

Getting to Know GNU

The story of the GNU project begins in the Artificial Intelligence Laboratory at the Massachusetts Institute of Technology in 1971. A young computer scientist named Richard Stallman was working there at the time, and he and the rest of the lab's programmers had hacked together an operating system for the PDP-10 computer they were using. This was a routine task; as we described in Chapter 1, computers each had an individualized operating system that allowed them to run, but the operating systems weren't interchangeable.

At this point in history, nobody thought of software as a possession. When others asked how a certain task had been accomplished, the programmers told them and even shared the software they had written to do the job. To programmers of this era, code was just a set of instructions, and it had never occurred to anyone that instructions should be considered property. True to the academic environments in which many programmers were working, code was shared with colleagues just as any other research findings were shared. This attitude began to change in the 1980s. As a new generation of more powerful computers was making the PDP-10 and its like obsolete, the manufacturers began to require nondisclosure agreements before they would provide licenses for their operating systems to users.

To Stallman, the idea of a nondisclosure agreement was abhorrent. It meant that the first step in using technology was to agree not to help others. As proprietary software became the rule, Stallman found himself at a crossroads. On the one hand, he could wave the white flag and join the crowd. This would likely mean a well-paid job in the software industry. On the other hand, he could use his skills to write and distribute software that could be redistributed freely. To Stallman, this was nothing less than a "stark moral choice"; he believed that he had an ethical duty to help stem the tide of proprietary software.

Stallman decided that the first thing he should write was an operating system, because without an operating system, other software would be useless. He decided to pattern his operating system after Unix, which was growing in popularity. Showing his wry sense of humor, he called his operating system GNU (GNU's Not Unix). (Such acronyms, called *recursive* acronyms because they contain the acronym in the definition, are common in the software world.)

Creating an entire operating system is a huge job. Stallman felt that the first thing he needed was a good text editor, because that would make the rest of the coding process easier. The editor that he wrote is called GNU Emacs and is still in use today. In fact, it is the subject of Chapter 18: "GNU Emacs." Before he could distribute it, though, he had to come up with a way to make sure that Emacs would remain free.

NOTE
When Stallman (and others following his lead) use the word *free*, they do so in a very specific way. *Free* for Stallman means that anyone may use, distribute, or modify the software, that the producer or distributor must provide the source code, and that all derivative products must also be free. *Free* in this context does not necessarily mean *free of charge*. Nothing in this definition prohibits charging for the software. (However, given the freedom for anyone to redistribute it, the net effect is often that the price will soon drop to the cost of distribution.) Stallman likes to say that, when he says *free*, he means it in the sense of *free speech* rather than *free beer*.

Stallman crafted a license that would codify this free status and called it the GNU General Public License (GPL). Emacs and all subsequent products of the GNU project are licensed under the GPL, and most Open Source software released today uses some variation of the GPL, if not the GPL itself.

The GNU General Public License

Because we refer to the GNU General Public License, or GPL, throughout this book, we thought it would be a good idea to acquaint you with the terms of the GPL before we go much further. You can read the full text of the license in Appendix F, which contains all the software licenses for the CD-ROM; many of the programs contained on the CD are released under the GPL. However, we reprint the Preamble of the license here, so that you

Continued on next page

can get a quick overview of the GPL terms and conditions, which will help as you read on through the book and learn more about Free Software.

Preamble to the GNU General Public License:

"The licenses for most software are designed to take away your freedom to share and change it. By contrast, the GNU General Public License is intended to guarantee your freedom to share and change free software—to make sure the software is free for all its users. This General Public License applies to most of the Free Software Foundation's software and to any other program whose authors commit to using it. (Some other Free Software Foundation software is covered by the GNU Library General Public License instead.) You can apply it to your programs, too.

"When we speak of free software, we are referring to freedom, not price. Our General Public Licenses are designed to make sure that you have the freedom to distribute copies of free software (and charge for this service if you wish), that you receive source code or can get it if you want it, that you can change the software or use pieces of it in new free programs, and that you know you can do these things.

"To protect your rights, we need to make restrictions that forbid anyone to deny you these rights or to ask you to surrender the rights. These restrictions translate to certain responsibilities for you if you distribute copies of the software or if you modify it.

"For example, if you distribute copies of such a program, whether gratis or for a fee, you must give the recipients all the rights that you have. You must make sure that they, too, receive or can get the source code. And you must show them these terms so they know their rights.

"We protect your rights with two steps: (1) copyright the software, and (2) offer you this license which gives you legal permission to copy, distribute, and/or modify the software.

"Also, for each author's protection and ours, we want to make certain that everyone understands that there is no warranty for this free software. If the software is modified by someone else and passed on, we want its recipients to know that what they have is not the original, so that any problems introduced by others will not reflect on the original authors' reputations.

"Finally, any free program is threatened constantly by software patents. We wish to avoid the danger that redistributors of a free program will individually obtain patent licenses, in effect making the program proprietary. To prevent this, we have made it clear that any patent must be licensed for everyone's free use or not licensed at all."

The Free Software Foundation

As the GNU project began to pick up steam and people began using its products, it began to attract other programmers. Since the source code for any item was freely available, it was easy for programmers to browse the code and suggest improvements, extensions, or even complete revisions. This was, of course, exactly what Stallman had in mind when he created the GPL: a community of programmers who could create better software together and share it with the world.

In 1985, issues of funding and project management had become sufficiently complex that it was evident some sort of formal structure was needed to handle the management of the GNU project. Stallman and his co-conspirators created an organization called the Free Software Foundation as a tax-exempt charity, using the U.S. Internal Revenue Service definition. The Free Software Foundation can now raise money through donations or the sale of packaged distributions of Free Software, and can employ people to work full time on creating more Free Software for distribution.

If GNU's Not Unix, What Is It?

The GNU operating system was originally intended to be an alternative to commercial versions of Unix. Stallman's idea was that GNU would comprise a complete system from top to bottom that could completely replace proprietary operating systems. (This hasn't happened—yet—although Stallman and others continue to work on it.) Ironically, however, the GNU project's first successes were as adjuncts to proprietary Unices. GNU components, such as GNU Emacs, GCC (the GNU C Compiler), and bash (a free replacement for the Bourne Shell), began to be included in commercial Unices.

These days, it's unusual to run across a Unix system that doesn't include GNU Emacs, bash, or some chunk of GNU software. If GNU components aren't installed by default on a particular Unix or Unix-derived system, fans of the programs often install them directly. The rather perverse fact is that GNU *is* Unix or at least part of it.

The Free Software Explosion

The people of the Free Software Foundation, of course, were not the only people doing this sort of work. The BSD people were working on their own Unix variant, and once the GNU General Public License began to become better known, a number of independent projects also began using it. Such projects really began to take off as the Internet came into widespread use in the late 1980s and early 1990s. The Internet made it possible for people who might be separated by thousands of miles, oceans, or national borders to collaborate on projects in a way that was impossible only a few years earlier.

Not surprisingly, some of the most successful Free Software projects have been Internet tools. `sendmail`, an e-mail server, and Apache, a World Wide Web server, are two of the most frequently used programs of their type, and both are licensed under the GNU GPL. We cover both `sendmail` and Apache later in this book.

Free Software really took off, however, when Linus Torvalds made the early versions of his Linux operating system available under the GNU GPL. Once Linux was developed to the point where it was a completely usable system, it was possible for the first time to build a complete system using nothing but Free Software. The addition of the Linux *kernel* (the operating system's core component) to the suite of existing GNU tools completed the system. In fact, what most people refer to as Linux is more properly referred to as GNU/Linux, because the Linux part is actually only the kernel.

Stallman continues to work on his own kernel, called the Hurd, but it will probably be some years before the Hurd is ready for widespread adoption. Unlike Torvalds, who patterned his kernel after existing Unix kernels, Stallman's design is based on some rather advanced theory. Consequently, the progress on Linux has been much faster than on the Hurd.

The Meteoric Rise of Open Source

In this chronological tale, we've now reached 1997. By this point, Linux had become a very advanced system and was a reasonable alternative to commercial Unix systems. It was also arguably superior to the Microsoft Windows NT systems that had come to dominate the corporate world. Apache and `sendmail` were firmly established in their niches, and a growing number of users were becoming curious about Linux, whether because of irritation with Microsoft's software or because of the low cost of the Linux operating system. Companies, such as Red Hat, and organizations, such as Debian, were busily producing Linux distributions that contained the Linux kernel and a variety of useful software. These distributions were also easy to install.

Nevertheless, Free Software was getting little respect in the marketplace. Despite its robustness and stability, Linux was regarded as something of a hacker's toy by information technology professionals, and Free Software advocates were having a difficult time making their case. The gulf between the programming community and the corporate world seemed unbridgeable, and there was some concern that it might never be crossed.

One Free Software advocate, Eric Raymond, wrote a monograph called "The Cathedral and the Bazaar" in an attempt to explain the concept of Free Software more clearly. In the essay, he contrasted the process of developing Free Software with that of its proprietary counterpart. He wrote that commercial software was developed in a cathedral style, insulated from the vast majority of users and independent developers, while Free Software was developed in a bazaar style, providing a meeting place for anyone who wanted to be there. Raymond argued that the bazaar model was superior because a large number of users and programmers would tend to produce better code faster. With anyone who wanted to contribute code to the project being allowed to do so, code would be produced quickly, and the best code would tend to stick to the project.

As support for his argument, Raymond offered a case study. He had written a program called `fetchmail`, which would download e-mail from a server and deliver it to Linux computers. He recounted the development process of `fetchmail` and how contributions from others had helped the program develop quickly in a classic example of bazaar-style development.

"The Cathedral and the Bazaar" turned out to be a very influential document. It prompted officials at Netscape to release the source code for their popular Web browser, Netscape Navigator, in the hopes that independent developers would help to improve it. Netscape even went as far as to consult with Raymond about the best way to go about bringing their code into the Free Software mainstream.

In early 1998, buoyed by the Netscape announcement, Raymond met with a few other Free Software advocates to discuss what they could do to encourage this sort of behavior among other software companies. They decided that part of what was holding Free Software back was an implied confrontational attitude inherent in the term *Free Software*. Whether the implication was intentional or not, they felt that the term sounded antibusiness, and they decided to introduce the term Open Source as a replacement. Netscape used the term *open software* in their press release announcing the release of their source code; O'Reilly and Associates, a computer book publisher, adopted the term for use in their promotional materials. With these two major players on board, the *Open Source* term got a huge boost.

Although the extent of the Open Source initiative's influence is debatable, 1998 was a banner year for Free Software. The Linux user base increased by 212 percent, and major software companies such as Corel and Oracle announced support for Linux. Torvalds, Raymond, and Stallman were in demand as the subjects for interviews and magazine articles. This trend continued well into 1999, with Red Hat and VA Linux Systems successfully going public and other Linux-based corporations not far behind.

At the time we wrote this book, in the spring of 2000, Linux was being credited with a resurgence of interest in Unix. Although Richard Stallman might not be happy about *Open Source* replacing *Free Software,* the repercussions of the GNU project are being felt in a big way. Everyone using Linux or a Unix-derived system is probably using some components that were created on the Free Software model and released under the GPL or one of its derivatives. In this book, we focus on a variety of programs that use Open Source licenses or are released under the GPL; we believe strongly in the power of community software development and hope that you'll share our opinion—as well as both Richard Stallman's and Eric Raymond's opinions—that many eyes and minds make stronger software.

Summary

The thought of selecting a particular Unix variant can be overwhelming because there are so many variants available. No matter which Unix variant you choose, though, the core of the operating system will be shared, and you can use most familiar commands or programs on any Unix variant. Unices differ because they've been ported to different hardware platforms, because they were released under different licenses, or because they've been adapted for particular needs. Still, different Unices are pretty similar when you get down to the business of working with them.

In this book, we focus on three Unix variants: Linux, FreeBSD, and Sun Solaris. These three versions are extremely popular and are available for a very low price (or for free if you download the code from the Internet).

The Free Software movement has been extremely influential upon Unix and its development over the last 20 years. With their unlimited and completely open attitude toward code sharing, Free Software advocates have built a number of robust and useful programs and tools that have bolstered Unix's usability for a variety of purposes. The development of the GNU General Public License has left these programs open to the programming community, so there is no danger that Free Software will somehow become proprietary software as it evolves.

Although Free Software is still the guiding force behind the movement, an alternative name for the concept has risen in the past few years: Open Source. The term was developed to make Free Software a more palatable option for businesses, who don't necessarily see profit as a bad thing. We use the terms interchangeably in this book, because we are hard-line adherents of neither Stallman nor Raymond. We think both are visionaries and have done a great deal to further the cause of Unix and its variants.

CHAPTER
THREE

Some Basic Unix Concepts

- Structure of a Unix System

- Files and Directories

- Users

- Commands

- Summary

So far in this part of the book, we've talked a lot about the background and development of Unix, but we haven't talked much about Unix systems themselves. In this chapter, we provide a basic introduction to the parts of a typical Unix system and how they work together to provide the operating functions that make a Unix computer run. Although this may seem simplistic if you've had some Unix experience before, those of you without much time spent on Unix systems will find this to be a useful overview of the remainder of the book. In the rest of the book, we will assume that you have this knowledge and build on it to explain more complicated concepts.

Structure of a Unix System

One of the basic ideas behind Unix is that of *modularity*. By keeping functions separate, a great degree of flexibility can be achieved. Also, improvements and additional functions can be added incrementally, just by replacing a small module or adding a new module, without having to revamp the entire system. The modular structure of Unix means that problems are usually contained within a sector of the system, but won't necessarily shut down the system completely because of one small error. The computer's administrator can then do whatever is necessary to that particular process or sector, without affecting the entire system more than needed.

The major modular components of Unix are the kernel and the command shell. The command shell interprets user commands for the kernel, which executes the desired process. Although you could probably run a computer with just those two elements, it would be neither simple nor interesting. To keep track of everything, Unix uses a precise filesystem structure. When you combine the filesystem with your choice of command shells, you're starting to configure your Unix system to your own tastes.

The Kernel

The *kernel* is a set of functions that constitute the guts of the operating system. It comprises a number of extremely low-level functions that control many aspects of the way in which the computer operates: the way data moves around the system, the way tasks are scheduled in the processor, the way memory is allocated, and so forth. In a sense, the biggest task of the kernel is to direct traffic within the operating system. When a new version of a Unix variant is released, it is usually a new version of that variant's kernel.

Most Unix users will not have any direct experience of the kernel. Rather, the user tends to interact with the shell or desktop environment. It is the kernel's job to interpret the things that happen in those environments and translate them into instructions to the hardware. The kernel operates very much behind the scenes. Although it is a program like any other, it's not something a user can run, and it won't show up in any list of running processes.

In fact, the notions of *users, running,* and *processes* are abstractions that don't mean anything to the hardware. These are purely conceptual constructs that exist for the convenience of humans. (Remember that the computer itself is just a big collection of interconnected switches.) It is the function of the kernel to make these concepts meaningful to the computer. For this reason, it is necessary for the kernel to exist outside of these ideas.

To understand the role of the kernel more clearly, it helps to know what happens when you run a program on your computer. When you decide to fire up your word processor, for example, a complex chain of events is set into motion. The requested program needs to be identified, and the particular file containing the program needs to be found on the system's storage medium (usually a hard-disk drive). A space must be made in the system memory to contain the program, and then the program has to be read off the disk and loaded into memory. Then, time must be scheduled in the processor to actually run the program. Finally, input to and output from the program must be directed and managed.

If the program operates peripheral devices such as printers or network devices, input and output to those devices must also be managed and formatted in a way that the device can understand. It is the kernel's job to direct and coordinate all of this activity. Keep in mind that, on a Unix system, there may be dozens of users, each running multiple programs. Managing all these processes is no trivial undertaking; luckily, Unix systems are designed to handle these kinds of loads without problems.

The Shell

If the user has no direct communication with the kernel, how does the kernel know what it needs to do for the user? Communicating with the user is the job of the *shell*. When you first log into a Unix machine, you automatically start a shell. The shell then translates the commands you give it into *system calls*, commands that the kernel understands. System calls are not directly available to the user, because they are a programming construct. That is, the system calls are a set of functions designed to be integrated into programs. They are not designed to be used interactively by users. This layer of abstraction, in addition to reflecting the modular construction of Unix, prevents users from having direct access to the kernel in ways that could be destructive to the system.

The shell serves as a *command interpreter;* whatever command is given to the shell is interpreted by the shell into the proper system action. For example, if you open a file for editing, the shell tells the kernel to start the editor, find and load the file into memory, and set up communication between the editor and the file. Then, the kernel handles the nuts and bolts of actually doing these things.

The shell is more than just a command interpreter, though. Shell commands comprise an entire programming language. You can write programs, often called *scripts*, composed of multiple shell commands. You're then able to run the entire script as a single unit. In fact, shell scripts are used to control most of the operations of the system, from start-up to shut-down. Anything that can be configured or customized is usually handled with shell scripts. The shell also handles certain aspects of the user environment, such as identifying the user and keeping track of the location of certain files, among other functions. We teach you how to write scripts in Part VI: "Shell Programming."

Which Shell?

Although it is common to talk about *the* shell as if it were a singular entity, there are, in fact, a variety of shells, each slightly different from each other. The most common shell is called the *Bourne Shell*, named after its creator. The Bourne Shell, known as sh to the system, is the mainstay of interactive shells. It is basic but reasonably flexible and powerful. As an alternative to the Bourne Shell, there is the *Bourne Again Shell*, or bash. bash is a replacement for the Bourne Shell that was developed as part of the GNU project. Some minor differences exist between sh and bash, but for most practical purposes, the two are interchangeable. We concentrate on the bash shell in this book.

Two other shells, the *Korn Shell* (ksh) and the *Z Shell* (zsh) are popular alternatives to sh and bash. Although quite similar in their command syntax, ksh and zsh have attempted to make up for some of the Bourne Shell's known weaknesses, particularly in the way they handle mathematical functions and variables. Most users should not need these extended functions, though people doing complex shell programming often find them useful.

The *C Shell* (csh or tcsh depending on the operating system being used) is a shell that imitates the C programming language. People who are used to writing programs in C can write shell scripts using a syntax that is familiar to them. A similar project has been undertaken to create a shell based on the Perl programming language. Although still in its infancy, the *Perl Shell* (you guessed it—psh) shows great promise.

The File System

It may seem surprising to think of the set of files stored on the computer as part of the operating system, but this is the case. In addition to being the home of the programs that make up the operating system, the filesystem itself provides important functions. This is especially true of Unix systems, because Unix represents every part of the system as a file: Every program is a file, every directory is a file, every piece of hardware is represented as a file. Because Unix views everything as a file, the structure and format of the filesystem are integral to the operation of the computer.

Some files are program files. In the case of programs such as the kernel and the shell, these files are clearly part of the operating system. Other system files are less obvious. For example, there are a large number of configuration files. These are nothing more than text files that are read by programs and used to control certain aspects of the program's behavior. Other file constructs, such as links and pipes, are used to provide basic operating functions by connecting the various system files in the proper way.

The kernel, shells, and filesystem together make up the major components of a Unix system. It should be noted that a system made up of just these things wouldn't be terribly useful. There are a huge number of additional programs that, although not actually part of the operating system, are so closely associated with it that most people would find a system without them to be practically unusable. We will describe many of these programs throughout the book, and quite a few of them are included on the CD-ROM.

Files and Directories

Now that you have a basic understanding of the structure of the Unix system itself, it's time to talk about some of the practical aspects of running and using a Unix system. The bread-and-butter of a Unix system is its files and directories. As a user, the data you store on your computer will be kept in files, and the vast bulk of the work you do will consist of editing and manipulating files in one way or another.

Unix files are contained within *directories*. A directory is just a file that has the ability to contain other files. On popular personal operating systems, directories are represented as *folders, briefcases,* or something similar. Directories can also contain other directories, called *subdirectories*. The Unix filesystem is arranged like an upside-down tree. At the top of the hierarchy is the *root* directory. All other directories are subdirectories of the root directory. We explain the directory structure further in Chapter 5: "Navigating the File System."

Users

Unix is, and always has been, a multiuser operating system. That is, it is designed to be used by more than one person. This is one of the main things that distinguishes it from the personal operating systems such as Windows and MacOS. Not only is Unix designed to be used by more than one person, it is designed to be used by more than one person *at the same time*. Using multiple terminals or network connections, any number of users can be connected to a single Unix machine, all happily working without being much affected by the others.

To achieve this happy situation, Unix uses the concept of *user accounts*. Each user is assigned a username, a password, and some personal directory space, and each user has access to certain system resources and has direct control over the files that he or she creates. The operating system manages the distribution of such resources as memory and processor time between users and systems processes. We explain the concepts behind user accounts in Chapter 29: "Managing Users And Groups."

The Superuser

With a multiplicity of users comes a need for some type of governance and management. Unix solves this problem in the most efficient way possible: dictatorship. On every Unix system, there is one user who has absolute power over the system. This user is called the *superuser*. The superuser has access to every file, function, and process on the system—even those owned by other users. The reason for this is twofold. First, the superuser needs to be able to manage the user base. This means that the superuser needs to have this power to enforce the policies set in place for the users. Second, if something goes wrong with the system, the superuser needs to have total access to the system to fix the problem and make the system usable again.

The superuser is also known as *root* because the superuser's login name is always *root*. We will discuss superuser functions in depth throughout the rest of this book, particularly in Part VII: "Basic System Administration."

Commands

Although it is becoming possible to use Unix entirely with graphical tools, most serious Unix users would agree that it would be foolish to do so. One of the great strengths of Unix is a powerful and flexible command syntax, only a small subset of which is available through graphical tools. Consider the following command line:

```
ls /etc > /home/phil/etc-list | mail john
```

(This may look arcane, but trust us, by the end of this book, you'll be rattling things like this off without thinking about it.)

This is actually a combination of three commands. What this line says is, "list the contents of the directory named /etc, dump the list into a file called etc-list in the user phil's home directory, and mail a copy of it to the user john." Using graphical tools, this command would involve at least three programs and probably take 10 times as long to accomplish. The other advantage to the command line is that it is available even if graphic functions are not functioning because of a problem with the X Window Server. You can always get to a command line, but you may not always be able to get to a graphical environment.

Because each Unix command is a program, each command can have its own syntax. In practice, however, the great majority of commands follows the same general format:

```
command [flags] [options] source destination
```

Here's how this works. For purposes of this example, we will deconstruct this command:

```
cp -i /home/phil/etc-list /home/john
```

This breaks down as follows:

```
cp
```

This is the *command*. cp is the command that launches the copy function. In other words, you're going to make a copy of a file.

```
-i
```

This is a *flag*. It will control some aspect of the command's behavior. In this case, the -i flag means that cp should run interactively. The computer will prompt you to confirm your decision if this command would replace another file.

```
/home/phil/etc-list
```

This is the source, or the file, that is to be copied.

```
/home/john
```

This is the destination, or the location, of the copy to be made.

So, we could translate this command into English like this: "Make a copy of the file /home/phil/etc-list in the /home/john directory. If a file called etc-list already exists in /home/john, alert me, and give me the option of whether to proceed."

At this point, don't worry about memorizing all of this. We just want to get you used to the types of things you'll be seeing later in this book. We also include a large appendix of common Unix commands at the back of the book. One of the most comforting things we've ever heard was years ago, when someone told Kate, "Don't worry about learning all the commands. No two Unix people know the exact same set of commands, and everyone performs common tasks using slightly different methods."

Summary

Unix works differently from other operating systems you may have used that are targeted at the individual user. Unix systems are designed with a modular approach, so that each component of the operating system is self-contained and interacts with other components as a unique module. Modularity leads to flexibility and an easier way to solve system problems. Part of that modularity is displayed within the kernel, the set of code instructions that control the behavior of the computer; the kernel is constructed with modules. In addition, you can select various modules to run at the kernel level if you desire.

Unix is organized modularly as well. Each item—whether a file, a program, or a piece of hardware—is represented as a single file in the larger filesystem. Various directories store the files so that they are easily accessible for modification, if necessary. Because Unix permits machine use by multiple users at the same time, the superuser can use the filesystem to determine what belongs to each user and monitor the system demands that each user's processes are generating.

PART II

Getting Started

CHAPTER
FOUR

Logging In and Looking Around

- Getting Access to Unix

- Logging In for the First Time

- Changing Your Password

- What Are These Files

- Logging Out

- Summary

This part of the book is intended for readers who have never used a Unix machine. Readers who already have Unix accounts or who can get around their account with some basic skill can skip ahead to the next part of the book. Rest assured, we will reach a more advanced level soon enough.

In this chapter, we explain the basic process used to log into a Unix account and log out after you've finished your work. If you haven't used this kind of system before, the login procedure may be quite different from that of other operating systems you've used. Navigating through your files may be even more mystifying. In this chapter, we'll walk you through some of the basic things you'll experience and see as a beginning Unix user.

Getting Access to Unix

The very first thing you need to do is to get an account on a Unix machine. There are a number of ways to go about this:

- You can install Linux, FreeBSD, Solaris, or some other personal-computer version of Unix on a PC and have your own system.

- You can find a friend who has installed a Unix variant on a personal computer and who will give you an account on that machine.

- You can obtain a *shell account* with an Internet service provider (ISP). Shell accounts are rare these days, because most people don't want text-based access to the Internet. You'll have the best luck finding a shell account with a local ISP rather than with one of the huge, megalithic ISPs such as Earthlink or America Online.

TIP   If you already have one, you can use a PPP account with your Unix computer as well. In the next part of the book, "Unix Desktop Environments," we explain how to set up a graphical interface. Once you have a graphical user interface (GUI), you can use a PPP account to serve your Web needs as well as other functions made easier with a PPP account.

- You can find a public-access system. These are no longer as common as they used to be, but you may have a local library that offers Unix accounts to local residents.

- You can get access through your school or work. We assume that people new to Unix without a system of their own have been confronted by a Unix system at work or have enrolled in a school that uses Unix for its campus computing needs.

For the remainder of this chapter and most other chapters not relating specifically to administering a system, we will assume that you have access to a machine that you do not administer. When we talk about the *system administrator,* we mean the person who actually controls the computer: the person who "has root," as we explained in Chapter 3. If you run your own Unix system, you will be the system administrator.

Every business, school, organization, or other entity that runs a Unix system has a different procedure for granting accounts. You need to find out who's in charge of doing this and contact that person or department to see what you need to do. If you're trying to get a shell account with an ISP, you'll need to contact the ISP and sign up. (Search the Web—the last time we checked, there were still some free shell accounts available.)

When you do this, you will probably be asked to read, and possibly sign, the organization's Acceptable Use Policy (AUP); this may also be called the *Terms of Service.* This is a document that sets out exactly what kind of behavior is expected of users on the system. Read this document carefully because you are using a shared resource, and you need to know the rules for doing so. In general, AUPs require users to behave politely, not to abuse resources, and to refrain from running programs that may damage the system. Some sample AUP terms are provided in the sidebar, "What's Acceptable Use?"

What's Acceptable Use?

Acceptable Use Policies state the terms under which subscribers may use the Internet via a given Internet service provider. Although the terminology changes from ISP to ISP, the prohibited actions are usually the same. We read through more than 50 AUPs while writing this chapter and provide here the most commonly stated parts of an AUP. If you plan to do

Continued on next page

any of these things while on the Internet, you'll be acting against the "gentlemen's agreement," which keeps the Internet functioning without undue interference, so please don't!

Illegal use of the system: Using the ISP's computers to pass material that violates any known law, regulation, or rule, whether local, national, or international.

Threatening behavior: Using the ISP's computer to pass materials that threaten or encourage destruction of property or bodily harm. This clause usually includes stalking.

Harassing behavior: Related to the previous point, using the ISP's computer to pass materials that harass another individual (as defined by the laws governing harassment).

Fraud: Using the ISP's system to pass materials with the intent of fraud. This clause covers pyramid schemes, chain letters (even if not financial), and other fraudulent offers to sell or buy products, services, or items.

Forgery: Using the ISP's system to pass materials with an intentionally false return address or other tracing mechanism.

UCE/UBE: Using the ISP's system to send Unsolicited Commercial E-Mail or Unsolicited Bulk E-Mail. This is usually called the *spam clause*.

Cracking: Using the ISP's system to gain illegal or unauthorized access into another computer system. May include prohibitions on unfriendly activity such as Denial of Service attacks.

Copyright infringement: Using the ISP's system to pass material that violates the author's or creator's legal copyright. This includes digitized images and sound files.

Other clauses may include a ban on multiple logins at the same time, long connections with no activity, or using the ISP to cause harm to minors.

Whatever the AUP stipulates at your particular service provider, workplace, or school, please adhere to it. We do not knowingly provide any information in this book that will cause you to violate a specific AUP, but it is your responsibility to know the terms of your particular agreement with your service provider.

When your account is created, you will usually choose (or be assigned) a login ID, or *username,* and a password. On many large systems, the initial passwords are randomly generated and appear to be gibberish. You can—and should— change your password to something that is easier to remember. We explain how to change your password later in this chapter.

Logging In for the First Time

Armed with your new username and password, it's now time to log in. We assume that you are either logging in at a terminal directly connected to the Unix system or using a terminal emulator program from a PC to log in over the Internet. If the latter is the case, you will need to open the terminal program and enter the name of the machine you're logging into. Once you have successfully connected to the system, you should see a prompt that looks something like the one shown in Figure 4.1.

To enter the system, make sure that the cursor is blinking right after the line that reads

    Login:

(If the cursor isn't blinking, it may not be set to do so on this screen. Just follow directions and don't worry.)

FIGURE 4.1:

Most Unix shell accounts will have a login screen resembling this one.

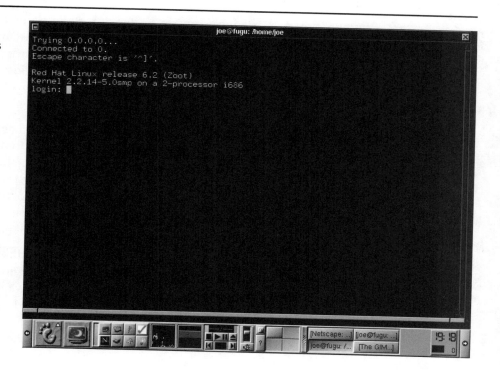

Type your username after the colon and press the Enter key. You should then see a prompt that says

```
Password:
```

Enter the password that was given to you when the account was created. You will not see your password printed on the screen.

WARNING   When you enter your password, depending on the system configuration, you will see either a row of asterisks or nothing at all. For this reason, it's important that you type your password exactly as it was given to you. You won't get any visual feedback when you type it.

Remember that Unix is *case sensitive*. This means that whether a letter is typed in uppercase or lowercase characters makes a difference. If you type **John** instead of **john**, your login will fail.

If your login does fail, it's no big deal—just start again. Some systems have a security feature that disconnects you if you make bad login attempts more than a certain number of times. This is designed to prevent people from trying to crack into a system by just guessing at passwords. If this happens, just reconnect and try again.

Once you've logged in successfully, you should see some sort of message, as shown in Figure 4.2. This is often a welcome message, but in many cases, it is a news item. This message is called the *MOTD*, which stands for Message of the Day. If the system's administrators need to communicate something to all users, they will usually put the information in the MOTD. Typically, this might be a notice that the system won't be available for a certain period of time or a reminder to delete your unneeded files to free up disk space. Whatever it is, don't ignore the MOTD. Read it when you log in and, if necessary, make a note of the news.

After the MOTD, you will see a shell prompt. This is an indication that you have logged in and a shell process has started to handle your commands. The shell prompt can be configured to appear in any number of ways, so we can't tell you exactly what it will look like. It may contain the current date and time, it may contain the name of the machine you're logged into, or it may contain your username. It will, however, almost always end with one of the following characters: $, >, %, or #.

FIGURE 4.2:

Read the Message of the Day for important information about the system.

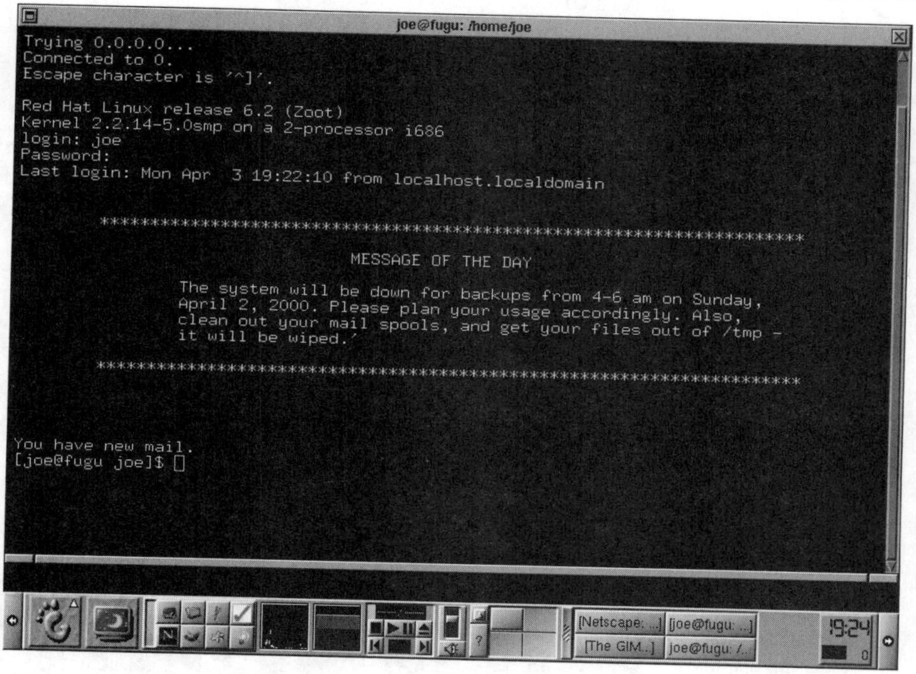

```
                                    joe@fugu: /home/joe
Trying 0.0.0.0...
Connected to 0.
Escape character is '^]'.

Red Hat Linux release 6.2 (Zoot)
Kernel 2.2.14-5.0smp on a 2-processor i686
login: joe
Password:
Last login: Mon Apr  3 19:22:10 from localhost.localdomain


   ***************************************************************************

                        MESSAGE OF THE DAY

             The system will be down for backups from 4-6 am on Sunday,
             April 2, 2000. Please plan your usage accordingly. Also,
             clean out your mail spools, and get your files out of /tmp -
             it will be wiped.'

   ***************************************************************************



You have new mail.
[joe@fugu joe]$ 
```

For example, when Joe logs into our Linux machine, the shell prompt looks like this:

`[joe@fugu joe]$`

You can see this in Figure 4.2, just under the MOTD. This prompt shows his username, joe, the name of the machine, fugu, and the current directory, /home/joe. The prompt shows only the last few segments of the full directory path so that you have the maximum space available on each command line.

Once you're at this prompt, nothing else will happen until you give a command. The prompt is the shell's way of saying, "Okay, I'm ready to do something for you." At this point, you're ready for just about anything, but take the time instead to look around a little.

Try typing **ls** at the prompt. ls is the command that lists the files in a directory. You may or may not see any files, depending on how your system administrator has the system configured. Now, type **pwd**. This command prints out the name of the current directory. It will probably print something like /home/harry, if your login name is harry. Next, type **echo $SHELL**. This will output the name of the shell you're using, probably /bin/bash or /bin/sh. Figure 4.3 shows the screen after these three commands have been given.

NOTE   If you're using a shell different than bash, you'll need to find documentation for that shell. We cover only bash in this book. However, most basic shell commands are usable regardless of the specific shell being used.

These are just a few of the commands that you can use to get information about your working environment. Again, don't worry about memorizing them now; we just want you to get a feel for what you're doing. You can always consult Appendix A of this book, which contains a variety of shell commands, if you forget the one you need.

FIGURE 4.3:

Your screen should resemble this one after you've issued the 1s, pwd, and echo $SHELL commands.

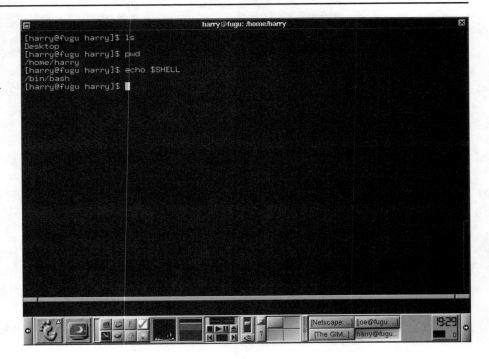

Changing Your Password

Now that you've gotten your feet wet, it's time to do something useful. Remember that awful, gibberish-like password you got assigned? You're never going to remember that, and it's a terrible security risk to write down your password and leave it lying around. So, it's time to change your password to something a little more memorable.

Choosing a password is something you should think about before you do it. There is something of an art to good passwords. A good password needs to be both easy to remember and hard to guess, and a good password is not a word found in the dictionary. One of the ways that crackers try to gain illegal access to systems is by using software that tries word after word until it gets one right. This is not a particularly elegant method of gaining access, but thanks to the poor security habits of many users, it remains effective. A good password should also not be any part of your name.

Here are some password do's and don'ts:

Do:

- Choose a password that you can remember. About the only thing worse than having a password that's easy to guess is having a password that is so hard to remember you end up taping it to your monitor.

- Mix up the case and type of characters that you use. Use capital letters and lowercase letters, and throw in a few numbers for good measure: *m0TH3r* is a better password than *mother.*

- Make a habit of changing your password periodically.

Don't:

- Choose a password that might be easily guessed by someone who knows you. Your spouse's name, your dog's name, or your birthday are all obvious choices that should be avoided.

- Tell *anyone* your password. Ever. Not even your spouse. Really. We mean it.

- Use a password that you've used on another system. Those of us who seem to accumulate Unix accounts are often tempted to use the same password on all our accounts to limit the amount of remembering we have to do. This is a bad idea, because once one of your passwords is known, the others are immediately known, as well.

When you've decided what your new password is going to be, type **passwd** at the shell prompt. You will be prompted to enter your old password; do so. Then, you will be prompted to enter your new password. Type in your new password exactly as you want it. Remember that you won't be able to see it, so type carefully.

When you're done, hit the Enter key. You will be prompted to enter your new password again, so be sure to type it exactly the same way you typed it the first time. The two instances of the new password must match, or your password won't be changed. If they do match, your password will be changed. The next time you log in, you will have to use the new password. You can see the full sequence of prompts—though not the passwords we entered—in Figure 4.4.

FIGURE 4.4:

Changing your password is easy enough to be done on a regular basis for security's sake.

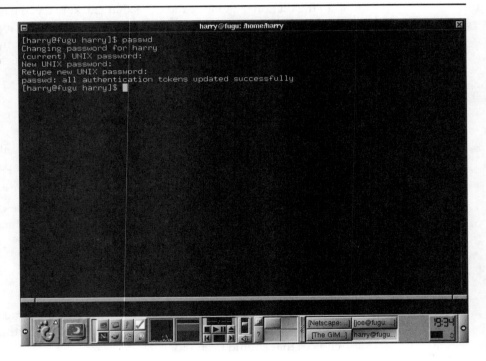

What Are These Files?

Earlier in this chapter, we told you to type **ls** to see whether there were any files in your home directory. Now, you're going to do that again, only this time you'll do it a little differently. This time, type **ls -a**. You will almost certainly see some files listed this time, and if you did see files before, you will see more of them now. Some sample `ls -a` output is shown in Figure 4.5.

What happened? The `-a` flag is a directive to the `ls` command to show all files, including hidden files. The astute reader will have noticed that all of the files not visible before have filenames that begin with a leading dot. This dot means that the file will not normally be seen by the `ls` command. Why? The `ls` command assumes that the reader doesn't want to see these files. These are almost all some sort of configuration file and are not normally of interest for the purposes of day-to-day work.

FIGURE 4.5:

List the files in your current directory with the `ls -a` command.

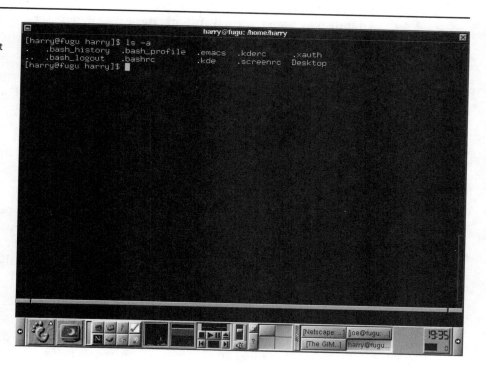

However, we're interested in them, because these *dot files* are the files that determine how information is presented to you and what it feels like to work in your account. So what are these mysterious files? Here are some of the most common:

`.bashrc`: This is a configuration file for `bash`, the Bourne Again Shell. You may also see `.bash-profile` and `.bash-logout`. These files control various aspects of `bash`'s behavior, such as what the prompt looks like, where it looks for your mail, what happens when you log out, and other basic operations.

`.emacs`: This is a configuration file for the GNU Emacs text editor.

`.Xdefaults`: This file is a configuration file for the X Window System, Unix's graphical user interface.

If you check this listing periodically, you may notice that these dot files tend to accumulate. As you use various programs, configuration options are usually stored in a new dot file for each program. That way, when you start a program you use frequently, the program can remember certain things about you, such as your display preferences. By placing these files in the user's home directory, each user can have a different configuration.

Most of the time, you shouldn't have to bother with these files. Sometimes, however, the best way to elicit a particular behavior from a program is by editing a dot file. This is usually fairly simple, and we explain the art of configuration files in later chapters.

Logging Out

When your Unix session has come to an end, it's time to log out. This is done, simply enough, by typing **logout** at the shell prompt. However, not all Unix systems have a `logout` command, so if `logout` doesn't work, try `exit` or Ctrl+d. The successful command will close your session and return the machine to the `Login:` prompt.

WARNING   Under *no* circumstances should you turn off the power to a Unix machine after you log out. Unix machines do not need to be turned off except by intention. If you turn the power off to a Unix machine without running the proper shut-down procedures, you run the risk of damaging data.

Summary

Although it may look very different from other operating systems you've used before, Unix becomes more familiar with practice. You may already have access to a Unix computer through your school, work, or a friend. You may have to locate a system where you can purchase an account or install a Unix variant yourself, if you can't find one that's a free alternative.

Once you have obtained an account, logging into the system is straightforward. You'll need to change the password you were given when the account was created, using the `passwd` command. With a few other simple commands, you can view your files and learn a bit more about the directory and shell you're using. In many cases, once you know the command that launches a program, the program itself will prompt you for the required information; the password program, `passwd`, is a good example.

CHAPTER
FIVE

Navigating the Filesystem

- Where Are You?

- Moving Around

- What's Where?

- Summary

To work effectively with Unix, it's important to have a good conceptual grasp of the filesystem so that you will be able to navigate through it more easily. As in other operating systems, Unix uses directories to organize files. The ability to know what directory you're using is an important skill, and it's also important to know what directories hold what types of files.

To explain the Unix directory concept, we—and many others who talk about Unix—use a location metaphor. That is, we think of the filesystem as being *a place* and various directories as being *unique locations* within that place.

NOTE   This idea did not originate with us. It's something that we've picked up from years of working with Unix and from dealing with other Unix users and administrators. The idea of a filesystem as a *space* is so fully ingrained into Unix culture that it goes almost unnoticed.

This may seem a bit high-concept at first, but as you become used to it, you'll find that you really can visualize the filesystem space and move from directory to directory with the same familiarity with which you move from room to room in your house.

Where Are You?

When you first log into your Unix system, you will be in your home directory. You can think of this as home base. This directory has been specifically designated for your personal use. If you worked through the previous chapter, you typed **pwd** at the command prompt to get the computer to tell you the current directory. (pwd is the command for *print working directory*.) If you do this when you first log in, you should see /home/melinda, /usr/home/melinda, or something similar—assuming your username is melinda. This line of text is called the *path*, and it's worth taking a moment to examine.

In common Unix notation, directory names end with a slash (/) character. When you see a path name (e.g., /usr/home/harry), you can interpret it as meaning that the directory on the far right—harry—is a subdirectory of the directory home/, which is a subdirectory of the directory usr/, which, in turn, is a subdirectory of the root directory /. In other words, / contains usr/, which contains home/, which contains harry.

NOTE

> Astute readers will probably be wondering whether the harry directory should have a slash after it, as well. The answer is yes, it should. /usr/home/harry/ is an equally valid (and probably more semantically correct) way of representing that directory. It is a common convention, though, that the slash for the term on the far right may be omitted.

The term *path name,* then, is quite apt. The path name shows the path from the root directory to the current directory. If you're trying to invoke a program that you don't use very often or that's in a new directory, you may need to type the full path name to start the program or find the file. In Chapter 13: "Customizing the Shell Environment," we show you how to create shortcuts for frequently used directories, so that you don't have to remember and type full path names all the time.

Absolute vs. Relative Path Names

A path name like /home/harry is an *absolute* path name, because it shows the full path from the root directory to the current directory. It is also possible to specify a *relative* path name. Assume that you are in the /home directory. (We'll show you how to get there in a moment.) If you want to specify the harry directory, you can simply type harry. The specification harry is assumed to be relative to the current directory. Now, suppose that there is a subdirectory in harry called mail. If you are in /home, you can specify that subdirectory as harry/mail.

Moving Around

Now that you know how to find out where you are, how do you move between directories? It's a simple task. Moving is done with the cd command; cd stands for *change directory*. If you are in /home/harry and you want to change to the / (root) directory, you can issue the command cd /. If you wanted to move into the /usr directory, you would type the command cd /usr. Arguments given with cd

can also be relative path names. If you are in /usr and you want to move to
/usr/home/linda, you can give the command cd home/linda.

Now that you know how to move around the directory structure, we suggest
that you take a few minutes to explore your system. Move to the root directory by
typing cd / and look at a directory listing by issuing the ls command. Note the
subdirectories. Move to one of them and do another listing. A few sample directory listings are shown in Figure 5.1. Use this process to get an idea of the layout
of your system.

FIGURE 5.1:

Learn more about your
filesystem by moving
through the directories and
issuing an ls command in
each.

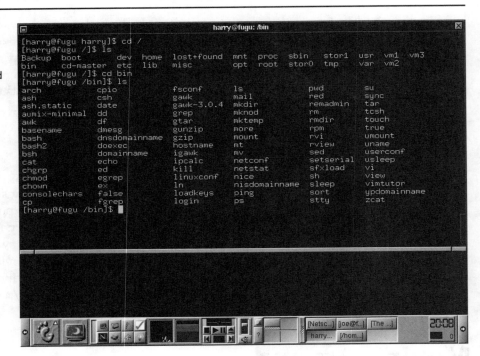

What's Where?

Now that you're comfortable with changing directories, it's time to take a look at
what other directories are out there in your filesystem. As we mentioned earlier,
the Unix filesystem is arranged like an upside-down tree, with the root directory
at the top, and all other directories branching out toward the bottom. A representation of this arrangement is shown in Figure 5.2.

FIGURE 5.2:

A Unix filesystem resembles an upside-down tree or plant.

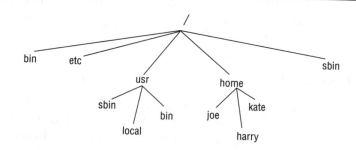

In the remainder of this chapter, we explain the function of the major system directories. Chapter 12: "Manipulating Files and Directories" and Chapter 30: "Disks and Filesystem Management" contain further discussions of system directories and the Unix filesystem in general.

> **TIP**
>
> Different Unix systems have slightly different filesystem arrangements, but certain conventions are followed fairly closely from one system to another. If the directories on your system don't quite seem to match up with what we describe here, don't worry. Simply move around the structure until you find the directory that contains the kinds of files described and pencil that directory name on the page. (You may run other Unices later, so crossing out the printed directory names may be annoying to you when you need this chapter again.)

/bin

The /bin directory contains the program files for the various system commands, such as the ls and cd commands you've already used, that are routinely used in the course of a typical Unix session. This is also the directory that contains the program files for the various shells and common Unix utilities. Originally, the /bin directory was intended to house all of the system's program files, but eventually there got to be so many different program files that some sort of additional organization was needed. Now, only system commands go in /bin, and regular applications go in other directories.

/etc

The /etc directory contains system configuration files. A good number of the programs that run on a typical Unix system require some sort of configuration file to direct their behavior. Most programs will put these files in the /etc directory. We will cover the files in /etc in great detail later in the book, in Part VII: "Basic System Administration."

/home

/home is the repository for users' home directories. /home is occasionally put under a different directory or subdivided to organize groups of users (this is especially true on large systems with many users), but as a rule, if you can find a directory named *home*, you should be able to find users' home directories. Some varieties of Unix use *users* instead of *home*, so if you're having trouble finding the /home directory, try looking for /users instead.

/tmp

As the name implies, /tmp is a place for temporary storage. Some programs create temporary files as a byproduct of their operation, and these files are usually dumped into the /tmp directory. This is also a convenient place for users to put files temporarily if they don't have enough room in their home directories, though they need to exercise some caution when they do this.

TIP   Many system administrators delete everything in the /tmp directory at regular intervals, and no one should get the impression that /tmp is a convenient solution for long-term storage. If you administer your own system and have other users, we suggest that you implement a site policy against using /tmp as extra storage space.

/usr

The /usr directory contains program files for software applications. Any program that is not a Unix system utility will go in /usr. Despite its name, the /usr directory is not designed for individual user directories. Those all go in /home.

/usr/local

A subdirectory of /usr, /usr/local contains application programs that are intended to be protected from any upgrades or changes to the system. By making a program local, it is taken out of the way of any systemwide changes. This is important primarily for computers that are attached to a network, but it's still a good habit to establish even if you're running a standalone machine.

/var

/var is intended as a holding area for files that may vary in size or number. /var is usually the home of mailbox files, log files, and anything else that appears and disappears or grows and shrinks. If you administer your own system, you may want to check /var regularly to prune outdated files and logs.

All of these directories may (and usually do) have subdirectories that serve specific purposes. For example, on Linux systems, the /etc directory usually contains a subdirectory called X11 that contains various configuration files for the X Window System. In addition, there may be other directories under /. On our machine, for example, there are a couple of large storage directories called /stor0 and /stor1 that Joe created when he added a second hard drive. Despite being on the first level of the directory tree, these are not the sort of directories that one would find on any other system; they're just an example of the enormous configurability of Unix. Your system may have similar quirks depending on your or your organization's needs.

Summary

Once you have logged into your Unix account, you can use the cd command to move around the directories contained in the filesystem. All your personal files will be kept in your personal home directory, called something like /usr/home/*yourusername*, depending on your system configuration. There may be subdirectories in that directory, especially the subdirectories used for e-mail or USENET news, but the main files you create will be stored in your home directory until you move them somewhere else.

If you start to explore the directories outside of your home directory, you'll find a variety of system directories in the overall filesystem. The most important of these system directories are /bin, /etc, /home, /tmp, /usr, /usr/local, and /var. Your computer may have some additional directories as well, which were installed by the system administrator or by certain programs that create their own directories upon installation.

PART III

Unix Desktop Environments

CHAPTER

SIX

The X Window System: An Overview

- What Is the X Window System?

- Desktops and Window Managers

- The Structure of X

- Installing and Configuring X

- Summary

If you are new to Unix or have not used it in many years, you may have the idea that Unix is limited to the command-line interface and that you need to know a plethora of weird commands to accomplish anything on the Unix computer. Although this is certainly true for some people, you do not have to rely on the command line if you do not want to. Most current Unix distributions, including the ones we cover in this book, ship with a *graphical interface* called the X Window System.

The X Window System, sometimes called X Windows or just X, makes it possible for Unix computers to use the same kind of windowed interface that is familiar to you from Macintosh and Windows computers. In fact, the X Window System is as old as both of those operating systems, having been developed in 1984 (the year the first Macintosh was sold, and several years before the Windows operating system was released). The three windowed systems share quite a few similarities, which is not surprising, because they were all built around a concept first developed at the Xerox Palo Alto Research Center in the 1970s.

What Is the X Window System?

The X Window System is not something that you work with directly. If you log into a Unix computer and see windows and fancy backgrounds, you're not looking at X—you're looking at a *window manager* or *integrated desktop*. We explain both those terms later in this chapter. Rather than being a user-level program, the X Window System is a sort of middle manager. In the most concise terms, the X Window System provides the basic graphic capabilities that your computer needs to produce graphical displays on the monitor.

Think of your computer like this: At the heart of its operation lie the operating system and its kernel. What you see when you interact with the computer is the user interface, and we're going to assume that you have a graphical interface because most users do have one available. X Windows lies between the operating system and the user interface. X Windows is the mechanism through which the operating system can construct the graphical images that you work with on the desktop, even though Unix itself does not "do graphics." We've used the term *GUI sandwich* to describe this before—where Unix and the user interface are the pieces of bread, X is the peanut butter.

We should clarify something here. We have used the term *X Window System* somewhat imprecisely. The X Window System is not a program. X is, instead, a *standard*. This means the X Window System is actually a set of rules, administered by a neutral body called the X Consortium, which all graphical display functions must obey and incorporate if they are to work smoothly with Unix. X has gone through many changes over the years; the current version is X11R6, meaning that it is the 6th revision of the 11th version. Any particular program that implements the X standard is referred to, somewhat confusingly, as *an X Window System*. One of the more familiar X implementations is XFree86, discussed later in this chapter. There are also commercial X implementations, such as MetroX and AcceleratedX. Most X implementations run on Unix, but a few run on Windows as well.

Desktops and Window Managers

Because X is a standard and not a single program, you can run any kind of *window manager* or *desktop environment* on top of it. These terms seem interchangeable, and to a certain extent, they are. In general terms, a window manager is simply a set of functions that controls how windows appear on the monitor, how various items such as icons or menu bars are shown, and how the mouse works with all the items on the monitor screen. X makes these things possible, but the window manager handles the specifics of each action.

NOTE Regardless of whether you select a desktop or window manager, it will work closely with the *display manager*. The display manager is the program that actually handles data transmission between the X Window System and the graphical user interface. The default X display manager is called **xdm** (logically enough, for X Display Manager). You may find that your desktop or window manager uses a specialized display manager instead of **xdm**; KDE, for example, uses **kdm** (KDE Display Manager).

You may hear people express strong affinity for, or objection to, particular window managers or desktops. This is probably not because of any particular flaw or function of the program in question, but because of the unique feeling that program generates from its blend of graphical elements, peripheral behavior, file management, and so on. Even if you don't think much about how your computer handles these functions, they are an integral part of your computing experience. If you try a window manager or desktop and it just doesn't feel right, try another one. You'll eventually find something that works for you and that you're comfortable configuring until it's just perfect.

Window Managers

A wide variety of window managers is available for the Unix platform, some designed specifically for certain Unix-derived distributions and some globally available for all the various versions of Unix. For example, some of the window managers available for Linux include fvwm, BlackBox, AfterStep, and Enlightenment. Each window manager has a slightly different feel, and the choice of a window manager is an extremely personal one. Once you've selected a window manager program, you can configure it to your heart's desire with wallpaper, unique icons, and so on, at least as much as the window manager will let you. (Some let you change anything you want, while others—such as BlackBox—let you configure only very basic options.)

The thing to remember about window managers is that their name is literal. You can run multiple windows at the same time, with a different shell session or program running in each, but you can't drag and drop from one window to another (or any other integrative function). Window managers simply make it easier to run multiple sessions at once and provide an attractive backdrop while doing so. You can see a sample window manager in Figure 6.1.

This is where it gets confusing. In a global sense, any program that handles multiple sessions in a graphical environment is a window manager. However, in recent years, the Unix community has begun to produce *integrated desktop environments,* which function like Windows or MacOS. These environments may look like window managers, but they are fully integrated and have additional functions that X Windows simply doesn't provide (and thus won't be found in plain window managers). So, when we talk about desktops vs. window managers, we are talking about integrated environments such as KDE or Gnome vs. simple multiple-session interfaces such as Enlightenment or fvwm.

NOTE   We go into greater detail about several popular window managers in Chapter 8.

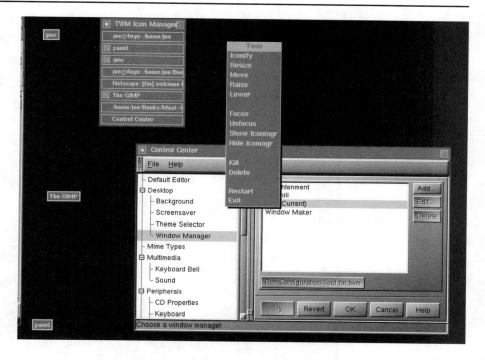

FIGURE 6.1:

The window manager called *twm* manages multiple sessions in a pleasing graphical manner.

Desktop Environments

Desktop environments are like window managers on steroids. Not only do desktop environments allow you to run multiple sessions, they also integrate those sessions. This means that you can drag and drop elements from one session to another, click and drag files from one folder of a directory manager to another, and so on. You can't work between windows in a regular window manager because X doesn't offer those functions.

The other major appeal of a desktop environment is that it incorporates a complete set of programs that make your computing life easier. The two main desktop environments, KDE and Gnome, both offer a panel that contains icons for frequently used programs such as a terminal window, Netscape, and a graphical file manager. Integrated desktops also let you start programs from an applications manager, which bears an uncanny resemblance to the Start menu in Windows 95/98. Figure 6.2 shows the Gnome integrated desktop. Note that it resembles the `twm` window manager shown in Figure 6.1. The differences between window managers and desktops are quite small at the cosmetic level—it's the actual operation of the programs that makes the difference.

FIGURE 6.2:

The Gnome integrated desktop offers both multiple sessions and a complete suite of user-interface programs.

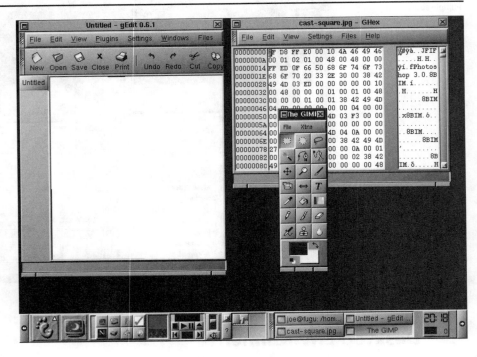

NOTE   We cover KDE in Chapter 9 and Gnome in Chapter 10.

Which to Use?

If you're confused at this point, don't worry. It's a confusing topic, complicated by a lot of similar terms that are often used imprecisely. We recommend that you concentrate on integrated desktop environments, where available. That is, we suggest that you choose between KDE and Gnome. Read Chapters 9 and 10 to learn more about each environment, but don't feel that you'll lose too much if you pick one over the other. The two programs are moving closer together in terms of integration and available functions, and there's no real reason to prefer one over the other.

That said, if you have a fairly slow computer or are concerned about system resources, you might find a window manager more to your liking. They place less strain on your computer because they don't have the overhead of a complete array of user-assistance programs; X places enough of a load on system memory—adding an integrated desktop can bring less robust systems to a crawl. If you decide to go with a window manager, read Chapter 8 to learn more about your options. We prefer the more feature-laden managers such as Enlightenment and AfterStep, but it all depends on how much of your system resources you want to devote to graphical interfaces and how much you want to save for programs.

TIP

Remember that you don't have to use a graphical interface at all. You'll lose out on graphical programs, including Netscape, but you'll gain a lot in terms of system speed and power. Many people, including us, often log directly into the shell instead of loading the graphical interface. You can choose to do the same, loading Gnome or Enlightenment only when necessary. This may be easier for you than purchasing more RAM or a faster chip.

The Structure of X

As described earlier in this chapter, the X Window System is part of neither the operating system nor the user interface. X has several unique characteristics that make it quite different from the MacOS and Windows interfaces.

- The X Window System stands apart from the operating system, which means that if you don't need a graphical interface, you don't need to run X. Machines that operate as servers, for example, can save the system overhead of X and apply that overhead to faster turnaround of service requests.

- The X Window System is designed for networks, not for standalone computers. You can use X to display graphical applications, running on Computer A, on the monitor of Computer B. Other operating systems, such as Windows NT, are starting to do this, but X has done it all along.

- The X Window System is not actually part of the user interface. As described in the previous section, X makes it possible for window managers and desktops to work, but you do not interact directly with X. This generic approach means that you can customize the actual appearance of your screen, without having to settle for some components that are part of X itself.

Because X is a standard instead of a single program, you may find different versions of X on different Unix computers. For example, a computer running Linux or FreeBSD will probably be using XFree86. XFree86 is an implementation of the X standard designed for Intel x86-series hardware (386, 486, and Pentium-class chips) and is usually used by people working with Free and Open Source software. Sun Solaris, in contrast, uses a proprietary X server that also meets the X Consortium's requirements. Most commercial Unices use their own X servers; as long as the server matches the requirements of the X Window System standard, it's fine.

How Does X Work?

The X Window System utilizes a *client-server architecture*. This is a common way of handling traffic across a network or even within a single computer. When you look at a Web page, for example, your computer requests the page data from a Web server; in this case, your computer is the client. Servers usually handle incoming requests from a large number of clients. Popular Web sites may receive as many as 12 or 15 client requests per second. Figure 6.3 shows a basic image of the client-server architecture.

FIGURE 6.3:

A client-server architecture is useful for a variety of services, including the X Window System.

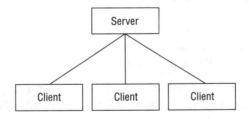

When it comes to X, though, things seem a little different—even though they're not. When you installed X on your computer (or when it was installed while you installed a Unix variant), X was installed as a server. So, when you use a program that requires X, such as a desktop or window manager, you are actually running a small X Window System server within your computer. The desktop or window manager acts as a client, requesting particular operations from the server, which feeds back that data and allows the client to draw a particular graphic image on your monitor. No matter what program you're running—a user interface, Netscape, or a game—they all act as clients to the X server.

It may seem odd that you would need a client-server setup within a stand-alone computer. Indeed, it is a bit strange, but it works very well for a couple of reasons. First, it mirrors the way an actual network would operate, if you were using X on a larger network. Because X is designed as a networked program, it makes sense to treat the local machine and its applications as clients, just as they would be clients if they requested X services from a different computer. Second, it brings an immense amount of stability to the system. If X crashes, your Unix operating system probably won't. This means that you can go in and fix what's wrong with X without having to reboot, which could possibly cause even more damage. The client-server architecture lets X work separately from both your client applications and the operating system itself, which is the most secure and reliable method.

Installing and Configuring X

In the vast majority of cases, the X Window System was installed when you installed your Unix-based operating system. Most new distributions have a graphical installation program, which requires the use of X during installation itself. It used to be the case that installing and configuring X was one of the worst parts of using Unix; there is a lot that can go wrong, and the X configuration process is quite arcane. However, due to a lot of hard work on the part of programmers and developers over the years, much of the troublesome work has been automated.

For example, most X Window System installations now auto-detect your video hardware. This is important because X must be installed with the components that match your hardware exactly. If the wrong components are installed, X will not work.

WARNING If X does not start when you start your computer, especially if you have just installed the server, the likely culprit is your video card. Although most implementations of the X standard provide specific drivers for the vast majority of video cards on the market, it's possible that you have one of the few that isn't supported. This is especially likely if you bought a cheap card online that isn't from a major manufacturer. Unfortunately, there's not a lot you can do if your card isn't supported under X. You will need to buy a new card or possibly shell out the cash to buy a commercial implementation of X (buying a new card is cheaper).

If you're using Linux, you can save yourself some headaches by checking the Linux Hardware Compatibility FAQ at `http://www.linuxdoc.org/HOWTO/Hardware-HOWTO-6.html`. If you're using XFree86 with either Linux or FreeBSD, check the XFree86 FAQ at `http://www.xfree86.org/FAQ` for important compatibility information.

Basic X Configuration

If your Unix-variant installation went smoothly, your X server should be working fine. Basically, if you can see graphical images such as login screens or a colorful desktop, you probably don't have a problem with X. If your keyboard and mouse are working properly, you're home free.

You should check your monitor, though. Be sure that you've selected the appropriate screen resolution for the monitor. Sometimes a bad display is blamed on X when it's actually the hardware causing the problem. We also suggest that you use the positioning wheels to pull the display all the way to the edges of the monitor glass. For some reason, we see a lot of monitors where the users leave a black band around the display that's an inch or more in width, and this is one of our pet peeves. Why waste monitor real estate that you paid for? Monitors are designed so that you should get no image distortion if you go to the edge of the glass. If you do get distortion, you're due for an upgrade to a classier monitor.

If X appears to freeze up once in a while or leaves you hanging without a way to continue your work, this is not unusual. It's caused by a wide range of reasons, none of which is particularly critical. If you get stuck, try pressing Ctrl+Alt+Backspace. This command stops and restarts the X server, and usually clears up whatever was bothering X and causing it to hang.

X Window System Problems

Apart from the infrequent freeze, you shouldn't have too much trouble with X. If you do experience significant trouble with the X Window System, the answer is probably neither simple nor quick. X is so complex that it requires a series of manuals more than 10 volumes long, so you can imagine how complicated it is to fix significant problems.

> **WARNING**
>
> The single most common cause of X problems is something that the user did. Do not mess around with X configuration files unless you know what you are doing or were told explicitly what to do by someone who is a guaranteed expert. In particular, do not install configuration files that were given to you by someone trying to be helpful. These files are probably incorrect for your particular hardware situation and may cause physical damage to your computer. Seek expert help for X woes.

For those people using XFree86, we suggest that you check out the resources available through the XFree86 Web site at `http://www.xfree86.org`. There are several critical FAQs there, including a Configuration FAQ that is quite helpful. Those using other X servers, including proprietary servers such as the one used by Sun Solaris, should consult their manuals or the developers of the X server in question.

Remember that, unlike almost any other part of your operating system, the X Window System can harm the hardware of your machine if something goes wrong. We believe that the average user can fix Unix problems with a bit of thought, but we do not think this is true about X. You could cost yourself a lot of money if you dive into X repair without assistance.

Summary

The X Window System is the intermediary between the operating system and the graphical user interface. X provides the information needed to translate graphical actions, such as using check boxes or a mouse, into commands understood by the operating system and the computer itself. Although the X Window System is referred to as a single entity, it is actually a collection of rules, or a standard, that have been used to build multiple versions of X server software. Those using Linux or FreeBSD are probably using the X server called XFree86, while those using Solaris or another commercial Unix are likely using a proprietary X server written specifically for that operating system.

The X Window System makes it possible to use graphical user interfaces, such as window managers and integrated desktop environments. Regardless of what interface a user selects, X will work with the interface using a client-server architecture to handle requests for data. Because X runs independently of both the operating system and the user interface, X is stable and fast. Other operating systems integrate their windowing software directly with the operating system, causing a greater opportunity for crashes or other malfunctions.

CHAPTER
SEVEN

Advanced X Techniques

- ■ Using X Applications over a Network

- ■ Fonts

- ■ Colors

- ■ Security

- ■ X and Users with Disabilities

- ■ Summary

In Chapter 6: "The X Window System: An Overview," we covered the basics of X. We also alluded to the fact that the X Window System is a flexible and easily networked system. In this chapter, we show you some of the other things that X can do, with a focus on the visual components, such as font and color, that make some graphic displays preferable to others. We also address the security issues of running the X server.

NOTE Some of the topics that we cover in this chapter assume basic knowledge of material that we haven't covered yet, such as networking. If you see something in this chapter that doesn't make sense, odds are that it's covered in another part of the book. In particular, we suggest that you read Part VIII: "Network Administration," especially Chapter 34: "Introduction to Unix Networking." Once you have a feel for basic networking theory, the specific details of networking with X will make more sense.

Using X Applications over a Network

From its earliest development, the X Window System was designed to be networkable. In practical terms, this means that it is possible to run a program on one computer in a network and have the program display on a second computer's monitor. Indeed, some computers are even sold as *X Terminals*, which are simply a processor, some memory, and a network connection; no hard drive is needed because the machine is designed to do nothing other than make connections to a central user host. Once the connection is made, the remote host's filesystem can be mounted via the network, and applications are displayed on the X Terminal's monitor using networked X functions.

X via the Internet?

Although it may seem like a conundrum, it is possible to open an X Window System session over the Internet, through a Web browser. (Yes, those people running Web browsers on a Unix system already have open X sessions.) This is especially interesting for those who

Continued on next page

use Windows or Macintosh computers, but need or want to use X-dependent programs, hosted on Unix machines, on their remote computers.

This new concept is handled by the Broadway project. Broadway was the initial nickname for the project, which has now been incorporated into the latest release of X (6.11). You'll hear Web-based X session technology referred to by the Broadway name or as *X Web*. The protocol includes a low-bandwidth option for those users with limited-speed connections (such as dial-ups). This protocol integrates the X Window System protocol and the HTTP protocol to take advantage of both protocols' strengths. The alternative is Java, which offers lower-quality transmissions and requires that any program delivered over the Internet be rewritten in Java; with X Web, programs don't need to be rewritten because they're being delivered in their original format.

One of the best things about the Broadway project is that it has focused on security issues as part of the general development. If you run X Web, you can choose to implement a variety of security features. For example, you can distinguish between secure and insecure applications; determine individual client configurations and watch those clients as they make requests of the X server; and implement firewall compatibility. You can even specify that applications must run remotely without any host access. These new options override some of the troubles inherent in the X protocol that make it insecure.

Learn more about Broadway at the project's site, `http://www.broadwayinfo.com`.

As we explained in Chapter 6: "The X Window System: An Overview," when you run the X Window System on your computer, you're actually running an X server (also called a *display server*). Any X-based program that you run, whether it's running on the same computer or on another machine in your network, acts as a client to the X server. The client takes advantage of the various services offered by the server to draw program elements on the screen of the client computer. Other than some slight delay caused by the transfer of signals between the local and remote machines, it's usually not possible to tell which programs are running locally and which are running from the remote machine. If you're using high-speed networking hardware, you probably won't get enough delay to be noticeable.

The DISPLAY Variable

One of the ways in which Unix controls the user environment is through the use of *environment variables*, which are tags that programs use to make decisions about how to perform certain tasks. To use an X-based program over a network, the DIS-PLAY variable must be set properly on both the server and the client computer.

NOTE

We cover environment variables in Chapter 13: "Customizing the Shell Environment." If you're unfamiliar with the concept, we suggest that you review that chapter before continuing with this section.

To see the current value of DISPLAY, type the following line at the shell prompt of the client machine:

```
echo $DISPLAY
```

The output should resemble one of these two lines:

```
:0
```

or

```
localhost:0
```

If the output on the client computer is fine, you can then check the server's settings. Log into the remote server computer using telnet, rlogin, or ssh (see Chapter 43: "Remote Access (inet) Services" for more information on these programs). When you've reached the remote machine's shell prompt, type the following command:

```
export $DISPLAY="/local machine\:0
```

This command causes the remote machine's output to be displayed on the local machine's monitor. Once the command is executed, you can run the X-based program that you want to work with, and the data from the server computer will show up on your client computer's screen.

If you get an error message after the previous command, you may need to make an additional adjustment. The error most commonly seen is output like this:

```
cannot connect to X-server
```

If you see this, log out of your connection to the server. On the client computer, issue the command

```
xhost +<remote machine>
```

You can use either the machine's IP address or its name. Now, log back into the server computer and reissue the command

```
export $DISPLAY="/local machine\:0"
```

It should work properly.

Fonts

One of the joys of working with a graphical interface is the ability to use different fonts for different purposes. A font can be as simple as regular Courier, a graceful handwriting style, or a set of pictographs. Regardless of the kind of font you want, somebody has probably created it as an X-friendly font.

Installing fonts on Unix, however, is more complicated than installing fonts on Windows or MacOS. We cover the basic process of installing single fonts for the X Window System here, but nothing replaces reading material intended for your specific operating system. X configuration can be tricky, and it's easy to miss a step. Be careful whenever you're working with X configuration files, and don't delete anything that you didn't put there yourself and know to be a mistake.

Installing Fonts

The first step in installing new fonts is to locate new fonts to install, of course. You can find a wide variety of X fonts on the Web; try your favorite search engine to see what the latest releases are. Once you have obtained a font package or two, installing them is quite simple. Just unzip the packaged fonts into the correct directory, adjust the format, compress the fonts, and restart the X server.

The basic font process is shown here, with addenda for various Unices below:

1. Once the font is downloaded, uncompress and untar it using the `tar -xvfm` *packagename* command.

2. Convert the format. Fonts are usually distributed in the BDF (Binary Distribution Format), but X cannot use this format. Use the `bdftopcf` program, included with the X Window System, to convert the format by issuing the command `bdftopcf -o` *packagename*`.bdf` *packagename*`.pcf`.

3. Change to the appropriate directory; the usual location is `/usr/libs/X11/fonts`.

4.   Create a subdirectory for the font type you're working with. The font types currently available are 75dpi, 100dpi, Type 1, Speedo, and Cyrillic.

5.   (Optional) If disk space is a concern—and fonts can be large files—you can now compress the font. You will notice some drag on system resources as X unpacks fonts on the fly, but the drag is more than compensated by the saved disk space.

6.   Build the fonts directory, `fonts.dir`, which tells X how to relate a given font name to the associated font properties. You will need a separate `fonts.dir` file in each subdirectory of `/usr/lib/X11/fonts/`. Create the file by issuing the command `mkfontdir`.

From this point, follow the specific directions for your Unix variant.

Linux

For Linux installations, follow the six steps above and then perform these two steps.

1.   Set the font path using the `xset` command, used to configure X preferences. Issue the following commands:

```
xset +fp /usr/lib/X11/fonts/newsubdirectory/
xset fp rehash
```

2.   Configure XFree86 to recognize the new font path. Locate the configuration file, which is usually stored as `/usr/X11/lib/X11/XF86config`, and open it in a text editor. Find the `FontPath` variable in the configuration file and add a new line (don't delete anything):

```
FontPath "/usr/lib/X11/fonts/newsubdirectory/"
```

The next time you run the X Window System, the new paths will be loaded. If you need the new fonts right away, kill the X server process and restart it.

FreeBSD

FreeBSD users should use the six steps given above, substituting the path `/usr/X11R6/lib/X11/fonts/` for the directory named in step 3. Create new subdirectories in this directory. Then, follow the additional steps listed under Linux. Because FreeBSD users usually run the XFree86 X server, the steps are the same.

Solaris

Solaris users should follow the six steps given above, substituting the path /usr/openwin/lib/X11/fonts for the directory named in step 3. Create your subdirectories in this directory. Then, perform the following additional steps to complete the font installation and ensure that the new paths will be added each time X is started:

1. Copy the configuration file at /usr/dt/config/Xconfig to the file /etc/dt/config/Xconfig.

2. Open the /etc/dt/config/Xconfig file in a text editor and add the following line:

   ```
   Dtlogin.fontPathTail: /usr/openwin/lib/X11/fonts/newsubdirectory
   ```

3. (Optional but recommended) Add this line as a comment before the line inserted in the previous step:

   ```
   # Add fontname font directory
   # /usr/openwin/lib/X11/fonts/newsubdirectory to FontPath.
   ```

4. Save and exit the file.

5. Restart your current X session by issuing the command /etc/init.d/ dtlogin reset. The new configuration file will be read during the start-up process, and the new path will be included.

X Font Servers

A new development in X font technology for Linux-based operating systems is the X Font Server (xfs). The server divorces font management from general X Window System functions, which means that you could have X installed on every computer in your network, essentially as a standalone installation. However, even if each computer has X, you don't have to give a complete set of fonts to each computer. Rather, you can install a font server, and each client computer can connect to the font server when the client needs a new font for its display.

The problem with xfs is that it doesn't quite have all the bugs shaken out of it yet. If you're using only a few fonts, you might prefer to install them on each machine as single fonts. However, if people on your network require a variety of fonts for their daily business, a font server might be the most efficient solution. It certainly saves disk space on individual machines.

NOTE If you run a network where several people use non-English fonts, such as those used for Russian, Chinese, Korean, or similar Cyrillic or ideographic languages, a font server is an ideal solution. These fonts are generally very large and would swamp a workstation's hard drive. Placing them on a separate machine used as a font server is an elegant and economical solution.

Building a Font Server

This is the general process for installing a font server under Linux. Note that this may not work for every Linux distribution; it is best to check your documentation and the Web to see whether there is something specific you need to do, depending on the distribution you run. In addition, before you decide to run a font server, we suggest that you spend some time reading through current information on xfs. There are known bugs and problems, so you should be aware of them before you attempt this process.

To establish an X Font Server, use this simple procedure:

1. Create a new file called /etc/conf.xfs.

2. Open the new file in a text editor and enter the following text:

   ```
   catalogue=/usr/X11R6/lib/X11/fonts/misc,
   /usr/X11R6/lib/X11/fonts/75dpi,
   /usr/X11R6/lib/X11/fonts/100dpi,
   /usr/X11R6/lib/X11/fonts/Speedo,
   /usr/X11R6/lib/X11/fonts/Type1,
   /usr/X11R6/lib/X11/fonts/cyrillic
   ```

3. Save and exit the file.

4. Start the font server by issuing the command
   /usr/X11R6/bin/xfs -config/etc/conf.xfs &

The server will now run until you kill the process. You can check to see whether the server is running by looking at your ports; the font server usually listens for requests on port 7100.

Using a Font Server

To use the font server, make sure that the server is listed in your font paths. You can configure this on Linux and FreeBSD with the xset command:

```
xset +fp fontserver:port
```

To speed up font access, you may want to check the font paths by hand and make sure that the font server entry comes before any hard-coded font paths. If the font server entry comes first, X will always check the server for the most updated files; if the desired font isn't there, X will then check the other font path entries.

Using International Fonts

We mentioned non-English fonts in the previous discussion of font servers. One of the main font concerns for many X administrators is the administration and use of fonts for languages that do not use the standard Roman alphabet, or for characters in certain Romance or European languages that are not used in English. For example, French and German use specialized characters that are not always found in the normal character sets installed with X.

To use an *international font,* the term used for all non-English sets of characters, the administrator must install the font as any other font would be added to the system. The problem comes in using the font. Each item in a particular font is identified by a particular number, defined by the ISO standard for that language's fonts. These numbers are then mapped to the keyboard, which may or may not have key mappings for that particular language's characters. The identification numbers are also used for programs such as word processors or the toolkits that draw windows and provide icon labels on the desktop.

The font needs to be specified in the X configuration files if it is to be used as the default for a particular X-based program. For the font to be made available as the default font for X terminal windows, for example, the administrator must configure the `.Xresources` file with this line:

```
xterm*font: font-identification
```

Thus, if you wanted your Xterms to start with a small-point-size Arabic font, for example, you'd use the entry

```
xterm*font:  yarb20
```

NOTE

If you use a specialized or international font as your default font, you may need to use different hardware. There is a wide variety of international keyboards that support different character sets; if you plan to use an international font, you may want to have an appropriate keyboard on hand.

NOTE   Ideographic languages, such as Chinese, Japanese, and Korean, face a particular problem with their fonts. Although the ASCII standard defines a character as 7 bits, these languages use 8-bit encoding for their characters. Some programs, mostly older ones, don't recognize 8-bit characters and thus cannot display these fonts. Luckily, there are patches and revised versions of most of these programs (one of the most notorious offenders was the mail server `sendmail`). An administrator whose users need to use Asian language fonts should research the available fonts; there are a number of fonts for each language, in various formats.

Colors

One of the advantages of using the window managers or integrated desktops that we discuss in the remainder of this part of the book is that you don't have to deal with color at the X Window System level. Window managers and integrated desktops handle display colors in a much friendlier manner, though their sophistication varies, with the integrated desktops KDE and Gnome having the most sophisticated color management. With these interfaces between the user and the graphic display, you can select color *themes*, suites of colors selected to work well together, or you can tailor specific colors for specific items. Using a window manager or desktop to handle X display colors is much like using the Control Panel in Windows.

With that said, you may not want to use a window manager or an integrated desktop all the time, or you may have chosen a display program that doesn't handle colors particularly well. In such cases, it's good to know how X handles colors itself, without the intermediary of a windowing program.

Default Colors

The X Window System defines default colors for the various components of the graphic display. For example, there's a default color for window title bars, a default color for icon labels, and a default color for text within a terminal window. The defaults are contained within a file called `.Xdefaults`, which is stored in your home directory.

You may not have such a file if you've never changed X's default colors. You can find a template in the file /etc/skel/.Xdefaults, which should have been installed when you installed X. Copy this file to your home directory and use it as the basis for your own set of X color defaults.

Various programs have different resources available for X to manage. You can see which resources are available for configuration by issuing the command appres *programname* at the command prompt. The output, shown in Figure 7.1 as the output for the xterm program, will show all the configurable resources and their current settings. In general, such output is easy to read, and you can get a pretty good idea of the default color from its name.

FIGURE 7.1:

Using the appres command will show you the various X resources associated with the named program.

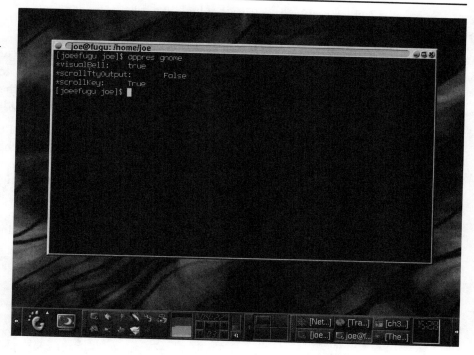

NOTE   If you administer a network, you can set color defaults systemwide by configuring another file. Look in your X directories for a subdirectory named **app-defaults**. In this file, you can store individual files for each program that you want to configure; name the file with the program's name and use the syntax of the **.Xresources** file to define the colors. These will become the new default colors for every user on your system. (Of course, the users can override your settings by creating their own individual **.Xresources** files in their home directories.)

Once you've established an **.Xresources** file, you can edit it to change your default settings. All you need to do is to open the **.Xresources** file in a text editor and change the values that need to be changed. However, don't change the settings randomly. The entries in **.Xresources** use the syntax

    *programname*settingColor: *colorname*

which results in entries that look like this:

    netscape*textColor: blue

The values in the *colorname* section of the entry are usually written as actual color names. These names vary from the prosaic, such as *red,* to the fanciful, such as *papayawhip.* You can't just make up color names, because the names are preassigned, but chances are good that a basic color name will produce a color value.

Color names are used as nicknames for the more complex RGB value, a number that represents the actual mixture of red, green, and blue in the resulting color. You can fill the *colorname* variable in three ways: color text name, RGB value, or hex value. See the sidebar "RGB and Hex Value Color Naming" for more information on computerized colors. Just determine the color you want to use, insert it in the proper line in **.Xresources**, and save the file. The next time you start the affected program, it will read from the file and use the new default colors.

RGB and Hex Value Color Naming

The X Window System relies on RGB values as the method it uses to produce screen colors. RGB stands for Red-Green-Blue, and the value represents the combination of three separate values for each of those colors. That is, the RGB value **rgb:FF/FF/FF** equals white. The individual values can range from 00 (no presence of that color at all) to FF (the highest possible value).

Continued on next page

Once you understand that on a computer screen all colors are an RGB mixture, it becomes easier to figure out RGB values. Of course, most people can't visualize an exact color from an RGB value. It's easy enough, though, to look at a value and figure out its general place on the spectrum. For example, consider the value `rgb:00/104/139`. Just from its construction, you can tell that this color is primarily blue, with an almost equal value of green, and that there is no red. You might guess aqua or some other shade of light blue (the actual color name is SkyBlue4), but you'd be on the right track even if you didn't guess sky blue.

If you've ever worked on Web page design, you may think that these values look familiar. Web designers use *hexadecimal notation* for color values. Because values produced from such notation are always six characters long, it's a convenient standardization. Some RGB values transfer directly into hex; for example, `rgb:00/00/00` is the same thing as #000000 (black). Other RGB values, when converted to hex, don't look anything like their original values. Purple is `rgb:160/32/240`, but its hex value is #A020F0. X understands both hex and RGB, so it's your choice.

We suggest using hex, mostly because it's useful to be familiar with hex values if you ever plan to work with Web design software, which relies on hex values instead of RGB values. However, you can stick with RGB—or even with X color names—as long as you have a handy cheat sheet with all the correlating values listed. Our favorite site for this is `http://users.rcn.com/giant.interport/COLOR/1ColorSpecifier.html`. This site contains a large table that shows the X color name, the actual color, the RGB value, and the hex value. It is an invaluable resource. There are many similar charts on the Web, but most focus only on hex value for Web designers. If you don't like the site listed above, you can find others with a quick search-engine check.

Because we encourage the use of integrated desktops or window managers, we suggest that you use those tools to handle display colors. Individual programs often have color configuration options as well, though you may need to search through several layers of menus to find them. However, understanding how X addresses colors is an important part of comprehending how graphical displays work, and it's also a good way to figure out what colors you can have on your monitor.

TIP Make a note of any default settings before you change them. You may find your-self with a truly horrendous setting and, if you don't remember what it was before, some time ahead of you spent setting it right. Also, try to avoid *tonal displays* where you might have lavender text on an orchid background against a pur-ple desktop. If your monitor isn't up to the task, or the colors are too close together, you may not be able to see the individual elements on the screen; this can make it really hard to make any changes if you don't know where the cursor is or which line to change in `.Xresources`.

Security

The X Window System is not a secure system, and X's own documentation acknowledges that. Although the chance of X exploitation is less than that of, say, an open SMTP port, it is still important for users and administrators to be aware of X's vulnerability. You can take some simple steps to ensure that X is as secure as possible. For obvious reasons, in this section of the chapter, we address those readers who are their own system administrators.

We recommend treating the X Window System as any other service accessed remotely, even though X is usually accessed only within a local network. How-ever, X was not originally designed as a secure server, so it is quite easily cracked. Unauthorized access to X can lead to several malicious activities:

- Viewing screen content, including passwords

- Viewing and altering content of the Clipboard or buffer

- Changing X Window System settings, sometimes with scripts that cause system damage when X is invoked from a remote client

- Destroying active X windows while they are being used by other clients

How can you deal with the issue of X security? The remainder of this section offers some suggestions on securing your X server. We don't recommend deleting it altogether, which would be overkill in the worst way. Because X is critical for most currently popular software, it's best to make some adjustments to the server and then run it normally. Keep an eye out for odd happenings; if you follow our suggestions, though, you probably won't have a problem unless it's coming from within your network. (Another good reason to know your users.)

Using ssh

As security exploitations become more and more sophisticated, many system administrators have decided to stop permitting the use of `telnet` and `rlogin` connections to their machines. `telnet` and `rlogin` have some well-known weaknesses that make them suitable targets for crackers. In place of these programs, administrators now recommend or require the use of `ssh`.

NOTE   We cover the use and administration of `ssh` in Chapters 38: "Network Security" and 43: "Remote Access (inet) Services."

Fortunately, `ssh` forwards X connections, so there is relatively little work necessary to make `ssh` and X coexist nicely. To invoke an X-based program from a remote server, simply issue this command at a shell prompt:

```
ssh <remote server machine> <command>
```

If X forwarding is properly configured, you will be prompted for your password on the server machine. Once the password is verified, the remote X-based program will display on your client computer's monitor. If this process doesn't work for you, it's possible that your system administrator has turned off X forwarding for security reasons. Check with this person to see whether that's the case, or whether you need to use a different command or syntax.

Securing Ports

The easiest way to secure the X Window Server is to make it accessible only from within your network. This limits the number of people who can connect to the server, whether for routine use or for malicious reasons. If you run a very large network, you may still be dealing with more people than you can actually know, but it's still easier to trace attacks from inside the network than it is to track down users from other parts of the world who are targeting your computers.

X is primarily associated with port 6000, but can use ports ranging from 6000 to 6063. If you restrict access to these ports so that they are open only to computers within a specified IP number range, you will limit potential abuse with a simple block.

TIP   To learn how to restrict access to these ports, see Chapter 38: "Network Security."

You can then double up the security by using the Xhosts file to restrict access to domain names within your network, as described in the next section. The combination of the Xhosts file and restricted port access should be enough to stop most external attacks.

The /etc/X0.hosts File

Located in the /etc directory, the /etc/X0.hosts file contains the domain names of the systems that are allowed to access the X Window Server in your network. This file is not created by default when you install X, so you need to build it yourself. Use a regular text editor to create the file.

NOTE   We use the zero character in the filename because most people will run only one local X Window System server. If you use more than one, and you want to allow different sets of machines to contact different X servers, you must replace the zero with the appropriate number for the local server.

Once you've created /etc/X0.hosts, enter the names of the machines that will be able to access the X server. Although you don't need to use complete domain names for machines on the local network (and, if you followed the directions in the previous section, no other machines should be requesting access), it's a good habit to develop. If your network's domain name is funkbands.com, for example, your /etc/X0.hosts file might look like this:

```
commodores.funkbands.com
parliament.funkbands.com
earthwindfire.funkbands.com
```

Any machine not explicitly listed in the /etc/X0.hosts file will receive the following error message if the machine tries to connect to the X server:

```
Xlib: connection to "machinename:0.0" refused by server
Xlib: Client is not authorized to connect to Server
Error: Can't Open display
```

WARNING   Using this file does not make your X server secure. Although it does limit access to the machines named in the `/etc/X0.hosts` file, it permits access by any user on one of those machines. You are still vulnerable to attacks from within your network. We suggest that you combine this method with some sort of user-based authentication, such as the `xauth` program described a little later in this chapter.

Using the xhost Client

X ships with a client called `xhost` that makes editing the `/etc/X0.hosts` file a bit simpler. However, `xhost` requires that you be sitting at the server machine itself, as a security precaution. If you issue the command `xhost +machine.domain.name`, the named domain will be added to the `/etc/X0.hosts` file. You can also remove names from the file by issuing the command `xhost -machine.domain.name`. Learn what names are currently in the file by simply typing `xhost` at the prompt.

In general, we don't recommend using this client to add and subtract machine names from the `/etc/X0.hosts` file. It's just as simple to work with the file directly, using a text editor; because you can't run `xhost` remotely, but you can access a text file remotely, `xhost` has limited usability in a large network. It's best suited for use in shell scripts, where you might want to grant access to a certain machine name, wait a given amount of time, and then deny access to that machine. The machine will still be able to use the server as long as that initial connection is maintained, but won't be able to set up additional server connections.

The xauth Program

User-based authentication with X is based on a unique identifier called MIT-MAGIC-COOKIE-1. The cookie is generated when a user logs into the server using the `xdm` command (to open the X display manager). The cookie is a string of characters that is stored in a file in your home directory, named `.Xauthority`. Once you have established a connection and obtained a cookie, you will be able to access the server from that account as long as the `.Xauthority` file is retained.

If everyone in your network uses a shared home directory, nothing further needs to be done with the cookie. However, many networks are made up of computers with their own home directories that do not share common files across the network. This is where the `xauth` program comes into play.

xauth is a program that copies the cookie from one user machine to another. xauth locates the authorization on the initial user machine, copies the authorization to the new user host, and builds a new .Xauthority file containing the cookie. The user can then access the X server from the new host without having to request a new permission code. Note that you are working from user machine to user machine here; xauth never contacts the X server itself. Therefore, you need to run xauth against a machine from which you have already successfully contacted the X server, because a cookie will be stored in your account on that user host for xauth to obtain.

The syntax of xauth is a bit complicated, though you shouldn't need to run it too often unless you must access the X server from a variety of computers throughout your network. xauth uses two major functions, extract and merge. The extract function searches the remote host for the X cookie, and the merge function takes the cookie and places it into the .Xauthority file on the local machine. Issue the xauth command like this:

```
xauth extract - $DISPLAY | ssh machine.domain xauth merge -
```

This complex command must be issued on the machine from which you have successfully logged into the server; here, we'll call the machine User1. The command extracts the value of the $DISPLAY variable, or your MIT-MAGIC-COOKIE-1, and sends it to the standard output (signified by the dash). In the second component of the command, an ssh connection is made to the remote machine from which you wish to access the X server (User2). You will probably be prompted for your ssh password at this point. Once access has been granted, xauth takes the value of $DISPLAY from the standard output and merges it into the .Xauthority file on User2. Once the command has completed successfully, you will be able to access the server from User2.

Why does copying the cookie matter? After all, you could just log in from User2 and obtain a new cookie. In some cases, it doesn't matter at all. However, in large networks, administrators often allocate resources or access to particular programs to certain users, while other users have access to different programs and resources. Using xauth to copy the cookie means that you will retain access to your particular profile, regardless of the machine you're working on.

WARNING   xauth and xhosts are attempts to solve known security problems with the X Window System. They are better than nothing, though they do not make X wholly secure. The best solution is to limit access to the X server and track down any untoward activity from your own user base.

X and Users with Disabilities

The advent of X was of some concern to disabled Unix users. The original text-only appearance of Unix was easily piped through various adaptive programs that made commands and output accessible to people regardless of their ability to see the screen. However, with the invention of a graphical interface, many of these earlier adaptive programs were no longer usable under X. (Many of these same concerns have risen again with the popularity explosion of the Web.)

What can be done to make X more accessible to users? Several adaptations have been built into the X standard, as well as programs written to take advantage of those adaptations. Users can install adaptive programs on their individual machines, and administrators can develop a systemwide policy that makes system resources available to all users regardless of their abilities.

There are three major areas in which X accessibility efforts have been concentrated. First, users with low vision need adaptive mechanisms such as screen magnification. Second, blind users need to use *screen readers,* programs that translate the screen contents into either Braille or spoken output. Regardless of the level of visual impairment, such users need keyboard-based input instead of mouse input, because mouse use depends heavily on the ability to track a small and rapidly moving screen image. Finally, users with limited mobility need different options for using the keyboard and mouse.

Mobility issues have been addressed not only in X, but in many of the window managers and desktops built for Unix users. For example, in Gnome and KDE, you can configure the keyboard so that it prints a given character only once, no matter how long the key is held down. Users who cannot release keys quickly enough often struggle with deleting unwanted characters, so this function solves a persistent problem. In other cases, those who must use a pointer held in the mouth or attached to a headband cannot press simultaneous key combinations, such as Ctrl+s. The StickyKeys X option allows these users to press the keys in sequence, not at the same time.

Visual issues are not as easily handled as mobility issues, which often center on time needed to complete a task or the difference between gross motor ability and fine motor ability. In contrast, users with visual disabilities use a wide array of adaptive technologies that each have particular requirements concerning how data is passed to the adapter and through to the user. How a Braille interpreter parses a particular window display may be quite different on the data level than how a speech recognition interpreter parses that display. The response has been to incorporate particular *hooks* into the X protocol, so that screen interpreters can be written that use those hooks as a predictable way to interpret particular screen images or events.

It is surprising to realize an advance that is so useful to so many users can be immensely frustrating to others. The traditional text-based Unix interface was much more accessible than the more advanced graphic interface made possible by the X Window System. If you have a visual or motor impairment, or if you administer a system whose users have such disabilities, it's worth the time to do some research. There are programs available, based on adaptive strategies implemented in the X protocol, that can make it easier for you to use an X display regardless of your disability.

NOTE   A visually impaired user may find it easiest to use a shell interface as her primary interaction with a Unix computer. Plain text can be parsed through one of several text interpreters more easily than a graphic display can. Though it is one of the major reasons for using a graphic display, the World Wide Web can be accessed through a text Web browser such as **lynx** without the need for X.

Summary

Those who administer their own Unix machines or networks should have some understanding of the X Window System's complexity. X can be used either on a standalone computer or over a network. If you intend to serve X-based applications to remote machines, you'll need to work with the value of the DISPLAY environment variable to display the graphic application on the remote screen. Those users who plan to use X over a network should pay special attention to security issues, and implement both host-based and user-based security precautions.

Among the most widely used and configured functions of X are fonts, screen colors, and security issues. X permits the use of a wide variety of fonts, including True-Type and Cyrillic fonts, as long as their directory paths are known to X. You can also use a font server, which will feed fonts to individual machines from a central location. Colors are controlled by setting individual or networkwide configurations and can be determined through RGB value, hexadecimal value, or color name. Finally, anyone using X should be aware that it is not a secure system and that certain precautions should be taken to lessen the chances of unauthorized access.

CHAPTER
EIGHT

Window Managers

- Graphic Interfaces

- twm

- IceWM

- BlackBox

- fvwm

- AfterStep

- WindowMaker

- Enlightenment

- Summary

Choosing a window manager is usually a matter of deciding which manager feels right to you. You may want a basic window manager that doesn't offer a great number of features, but runs quickly and uses a small slice of system resources. Someone else might want a manager that permits the use of desktop themes or that has a particularly elegant menu system. Some window managers meet both extremes; others occupy various plots of the middle ground. We cover the more basic window managers first in this chapter, including twm, IceWM, and BlackBox. We end the chapter with a discussion of the more configurable managers: fvwm, AfterStep, WindowMaker, and Enlightenment. Because of their high level of functional integration and configurability, these latter window managers are a good transition to the integrated desktops covered in Chapters 9 and 10: "KDE" and "Gnome."

If you're used to the integrated desktops such as KDE or Gnome (or Windows 98 and MacOS), you may find window managers a bit frustrating. They are not as fully featured, and some tasks that are common in an integrated desktop can't be performed in a window manager. The most common example is probably drag-and-drop between open windows; although you can cut and paste text between windows in most window managers, you can't select text in one window and drag the text into another. You can do that in KDE and Gnome, however.

NOTE   Both KDE and Gnome have window managers. Users don't work with the window managers directly, though, because the desktops are set up so that the user works directly with the desktop itself. Still, both KDE and Gnome use a regular window manager to handle the various parameters for windows, icons, and other graphic elements. These window managers, though, are not designed for independent use. Sure, you could use KWM or Sawfish as a window manager, but why not use a program specifically designed as an independent manager instead of an ancillary program for an integrated desktop?

TIP   If you don't like the default window manager for your integrated desktop, most of the managers described in this chapter can be used as a replacement with minimal fuss.

In this chapter, we review seven of the most popular window managers for Unix operating systems. Some are still being developed, while others are drifting into the past because nobody is coding for the projects. None of them are obsolete, though; all of them are being run on large systems throughout the world, and all have unique features that make them desirable for one type of installation or another.

Graphic Interfaces

In the previous two chapters: " The X Window System: An Overview" and "Advanced X Techniques," we explained the X Window System and its various features. Although you must run X to get a graphical display on the monitor, X itself does not create or manage that display. X is merely a program that makes such displays possible.

The display that you see on your screen is built and controlled by some sort of *graphic interface*. There are two basic types of graphic interfaces: window managers and integrated desktops. This chapter covers the various window managers available for use with Unix, while Chapters 9 and 10 cover the two dominant integrated desktops available at the time this book was written.

As we explained in Chapter 6, a *window manager* is a set of functions that control how various elements of a graphical interface appear on the monitor. Window features, icons, menu bars, colors, fonts, and other such components are all controlled by the window manager, which works in conjunction with the *display manager*. The display manager is the conduit between the X Window System and the window manager, but users don't generally work directly with the display manager, especially if a window manager or integrated desktop is being used.

Most graphic interfaces are quite configurable. You can choose the colors, the window behavior, the fonts, and many other items that contribute to the interface's look and feel. Some managers are designed to feel like other operating systems, especially Windows; the most significant Windows-like configuration has to do with window behavior. In Windows, you must click a window to make it active; in many window managers, the default action is to make a window active when the mouse pointer is over that window. This can get confusing if you like to leave many windows open and move your mouse around a lot. However, you can change this easily in your window manager's configuration files (look for an item called ClickToFocus or something similar).

At its most basic, a window manager simply helps you keep a series of terminal windows organized. Most window managers are capable of far more, however.

We suggest that you try several window managers and desktops before you settle on one; we've included one window manager, WindowMaker, on the CD-ROM included with this book. Resources for downloading other window managers described in this chapter are listed in Appendix B: "Documentation and Resources."

NOTE   Most of the window managers described in this chapter (as well as the integrated desktops KDE and Gnome) support the use of *themes.* A theme is a collection of display configurations and image files that provide a coherent and consistent visual appearance for your display; themes range from abstract geometrical and color concepts to themes built around photographs of popular actresses or scenes from video games. The biggest archive of window manager and desktop themes for Unix operating systems can be found at `http://www.themes.org`; if you enjoy creating your own themes, you can upload them to `themes.org` and share your creations with other users.

---

twm

twm has been around for years. It used to be one of the most widely available window managers, especially in a distributed X Window System environment that used *X Terminals* (monitor-and-keyboard-only systems connected to a central server, as described in Chapters 6 and 7). twm is a simple window manager that offers a basic windowing system and a minimal menu configuration, as shown in Figure 8.1. twm is especially useful in situations where there is relatively little system memory, because it has a reasonably small memory footprint. Other window managers and desktops with more features will commandeer a significant portion of system resources, making them unavailable for other programs.

twm has been supplanted on many systems by flashier window managers, which are both more configurable and more fully featured. However, it's possible that you'll run across twm if you use Unix in an environment that's been around for 5 or 10 years. We know of several universities that still use twm as a default or an optional window manager.

FIGURE 8.1:

twm is a good basic window manager without many additional features.

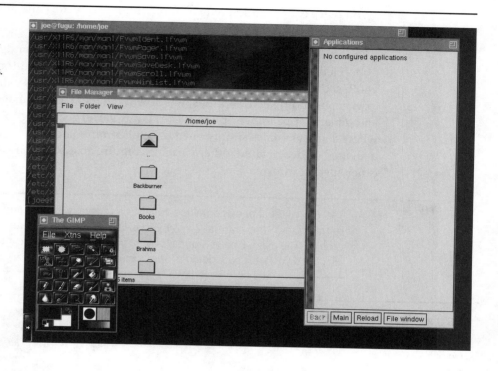

TIP

twm is useful for those who prefer not to use a mouse. Because twm's roots are in an earlier Unix world, its developers did not assume that everyone had a mouse. You can use keyboard shortcuts in twm to perform any functions that you might otherwise use a mouse to perform. However, some system administrators may have configured twm to work primarily with mouse commands; the keyboard shortcuts won't be disabled, but you might find that the documentation refers to mouse buttons, pointers, and clicks where you need information about control keys and key combinations. Consult your system administrator if you're having trouble figuring out key combinations.

Configuring twm

Configure twm by creating a file in your home directory called .twmrc. This is the usual location for user configuration files and is where twm will look at start-up.

If you place configuration data in another home directory file, it's unlikely that the data will be found by twm.

The .twmrc file handles a variety of variables that are either defined by default or defined by the user. If you open the .twmrc file in a text editor, as in Figure 8.2, you'll see variables at the top of the file. There are nearly 100 valid variables for .twmrc, including color options, window movement and management options, and general appearance options. The syntax varies according to the variable; where some variables simply need to be uncommented or commented out to be activated or deactivated, other variables require an additional string of data or other specific information.

TIP   The twm manual page contains a full list of .twmrc variables and their required syntax. Open the manual page by issuing the command man twm at a shell prompt. The manual page is quite long, so you may wish to pipe it to a text file for printing if you anticipate doing a lot of twm configuration.

FIGURE 8.2:

Configure twm with the .twmrc file, which offers many variables.

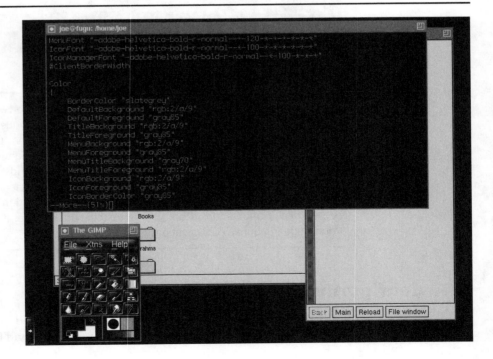

After all the variables are listed, the .twmrc file also contains a set of functions that determine how windows are drawn and a set of instructions that create the menu system. (twm menus are invoked by pressing mouse buttons instead of clicking a toolbar button.) The window function variables take the form f.*variable*, as in f.beep. As with the display variables, some of the window functions take specific arguments, detailed in the twm manual page. The menu variable syntax is somewhat complicated, and includes configurations for foreground and background colors as well as the names of programs to be contained in the menus.

NOTE   We don't recommend that you tinker with the window functions. If you make an error in these variables, you may freeze twm because it can't perform the actions you required or your changes conflict with other X functions.

IceWM

One of the newer window managers is called IceWM. This manager is especially useful for those who have minimal system resources, because Ice works very well with a minimal amount of RAM. It also integrates keyboard shortcuts into every feature and is completely usable without a mouse.

If you're trying to migrate from Windows, or you are migrating a full network of users to Unix, IceWM may be the best solution for you, because its default appearance and feel is quite similar to that of the Windows desktop. Figure 8.3 shows the default IceWM interface. If you don't like the default, IceWM also handles themes quite nicely; we suggest that you try Gnome themes first, because the manager is more compliant with Gnome than with KDE at this point.

Many IceWM users feel that the manager's limited configurability is a positive feature. With a limited set of options, the user does not have to spend a great deal of time configuring every aspect of the interface before using the manager. Others find this to be limiting and may prefer more completely configurable managers such as Enlightenment. However, we do not want to imply that IceWM is difficult to configure or that it has few configurable items. In fact, there are multiple configuration options for the manager; the preferences file (one of four configuration files) has 300 configuration settings alone. If you're looking for a window manager that is streamlined while still permitting you to manage its look and feel, IceWM is worth a try.

FIGURE 8.3:

IceWM is a newer alternative to basic window managers and has a friendly interface.

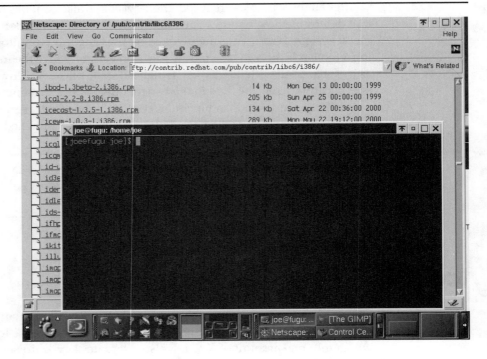

Configuring IceWM

IceWM can be configured by editing the various configuration files related to the manager. Though there are at least two graphic interfaces to the manager's configuration files, the interfaces are still under development and may not incorporate all the features of the current release version of IceWM (1.0 at the time we wrote this chapter). You can learn more about these graphic interfaces at the IceWM site, `http://www.icewm.org`.

NOTE   Look for the IceWM configuration files in the directory /usr/local/lib/X11/icewm/. Note, though, that individual variants may place these configuration files, and the IceWM directory, in different locations. Check through the various X Window System directories on your machine if you can't find the files in /usr/local/lib/X11/icewm. However, changing the files in this directory will affect all IceWM users systemwide. If you want to configure only your own IceWM preferences, copy the configuration files to an .icewm subdirectory in your home directory before you edit them.

The four configuration files are named menu, preferences, toolbar, and winoptions. Their functions are fairly obvious: menu contains information about the Start menu's contents; preferences controls the general user experience; toolbar determines the various icons in the Taskbar; and winoptions handles specific application behaviors. Open the desired configuration file in a text editor to make changes.

The syntax of the IceWM configuration files is reasonably self-explanatory. There are more than 300 configuration options in the preferences file (shown in Figure 8.4), for example, using the syntax

```
# Setting description
# SettingName=1 # 0/1
```

The first line is usually just an explanation of the setting, while the second line of the pair is the actual command. To activate a particular command, remove the hashmark at the beginning of the line. Then, set the command to the value you want to use. As with other Unix scripts we've covered elsewhere in this book, 0 equals false, and 1 equals true. Thus, to set a setting's value to 0 means that the setting definition is false, while using the value 1 means that the setting definition is true and will be used.

You can also define keyboard shortcuts in the IceWM preferences file. There are several predefined shortcuts already in place at the end of the file, but you can add your own. However, make sure that you select keys that aren't already set to other functions; if you try to define the Ctrl+Esc combination as the command to close an active window, for example, you might crash IceWM, because that key combination is already assigned to opening the menu system.

TIP

The Alt+F4 key combination closes the active window in IceWM.

Although all four configuration files are reasonably easy to edit, you will probably find the most useful to be the preferences file and the menu file. The menu configuration file lets you place certain programs and folders into the main menu (analogous to the Windows Start menu). The menu syntax is

```
menu <foldername> <icon>(
prog <programname> <icon> <command>
)
```

You can also add a <separator> element on its own line to display a line between items in the menu.

FIGURE 8.4:

IceWM configuration files use a simple syntax that makes configuration easy.

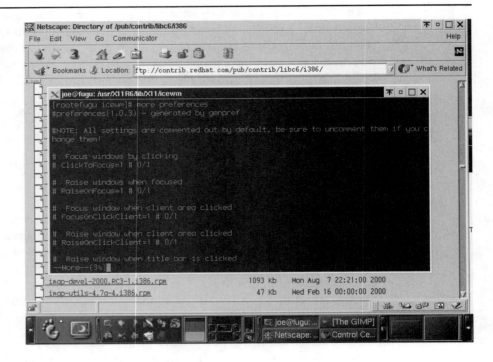

In practice, the menu configuration syntax will look like this:

```
menu <Internet-apps>(
prog Pine tree pine
prog Netscape netscape netscape
)
<separator>
```

In this example, we've created a menu folder labeled Internet-apps. All the programs between the parentheses will be stored in the Internet-apps folder. The first application is Pine, the e-mail program. We've chosen a generic icon named tree to represent Pine in the menu, and IceWM will invoke the program by issuing the command pine when this item is selected from the menu. The second item in the folder is Netscape, for which we used an icon named netscape. The program is started with the command netscape. At the end of this entry, we used the <separator> element. In the menu itself, there will be a horizontal line below the Internet-apps folder.

BlackBox

Like IceWM, the BlackBox window manager is designed as a small and efficient manager without a large amount of extraneous options. It has an unusually attractive user interface without requiring a lot of work from the user; in fact, although BlackBox themes are available on the Web, this is one of the window managers that may feel more attractive without any additional graphic display.

Call up the system menu with a right-click on the desktop. BlackBox defaults to text for all menus and toolbars, saving resources because icons don't need to be drawn. If a program has an icon as part of its own source code (for example, Netscape), the icon will be displayed, but BlackBox doesn't create or associate icons from external icon libraries.

TIP

If you prefer a window manager that doesn't use a lot of keyboard shortcuts, we suggest BlackBox. You can use keyboard combinations in BlackBox, but very few are created by default. Define your own for shortcuts that you'll actually use, or rely on the shortcuts defined in individual programs.

BlackBox has the advantage of being very small. The source code takes up only about 50KB of disk space, making it sleek and fast; its memory footprint is similarly small. BlackBox is a great alternative for server machines or for workstations with limited system resources because it requires so little from the machine. As Brad Hughes, the creator of BlackBox, has put it, "It's not meant to be Eye Candy, nor the most Featureful, nor the most Adorned for emulating the Widely acclaimed NeXT interface. It is just meant to be **fast**."

Configuring BlackBox

As you can probably guess by now, BlackBox configuration is controlled by the .blackboxrc file kept in your home directory. You can also control menus and visual styles through files contained in unique subdirectories. BlackBox creates the .blackboxrc file itself upon the first invocation of the program, and you probably won't need to deal directly with this file because there is so little configurable material in this window manager.

If you do want to work with .blackboxrc, you'll find that it uses the same kind of syntax as other configuration files that we've covered in this chapter.

However, BlackBox configuration entries tend to require additional strings of data after the option name; the option name is followed by a colon, and then the value's definition follows the colon. For example, the entry

```
session.menuFile: ~/.blackbox/menu
```

tells BlackBox that the menu configuration file is found in the user directory `~/.blackbox/menu`. If you want to keep your files in nonstandard locations, you'll need to define those locations in `.blackboxrc` so that BlackBox can find them upon boot-up.

The `menu` and `style` configuration files are far more complex than the `.blackboxrc` file. We don't recommend going into the `menu` or `style` files if you aren't sure of what you're doing; note that these files should be kept in their original locations unless you explicitly edit the `.blackboxrc` file to contain the new locations, lest BlackBox be confused at start-up and not be able to load the requisite configuration files. BlackBox display styles can be manipulated simply by downloading and applying one of the many themes found at `http://bb.themes.org`; these themes will edit the `style` configuration file automatically and ensure that there are no unforeseen conflicts between individual entries in the file.

Menu configuration is slightly easier, using a simple syntax, though the individual components of each entry in the `menu` configuration file can be somewhat obscure. Consult the BlackBox manual page (issue the command `man blackbox` at a shell prompt) and scroll down to the "Menu File" section for more detailed information on menu configuration.

fvwm

Because `twm` is somewhat limited in its scope, `fvwm` was initially developed as an expanded version. `fvwm` demands less memory than `twm` and offers a more attractive graphic interface. It also allows the user to manipulate and configure the window manager with keyboard shortcuts instead of mouse commands. This is more useful for those coming from a text-only environment, but can be handy for those who don't like the mouse or whose hardware setup doesn't permit mouse use. Mouse users can work with ease as well, using the features in the `fvwm` button bar to manage their windows and desktops.

`fvwm` was one of the first window managers to work toward a level of extreme configurability, in which the user can use all sorts of special modules and configure just about every single component of the manager. The integrated desktops are the natural outcome of this trend, but other window managers besides fvwm tend to this direction, including AfterStep, WindowMaker, and Enlightenment. One of the unusual features of fvwm is the large virtual desktop, which occupies more space than the monitor offers. That is, when using the virtual desktop, you can scroll up and across the desktop to see additional portions of the desktop that may contain icons or open windows.

If you find this unappealing or strange, you might prefer the multiple-desktop option. With this feature, you can have multiple identical desktops that are unrelated. You might run a Web browser on one, be logged into a terminal window as root on another, and play a game on the third. (This is similar to the *virtual desktops* offered by KDE.) Though the default number of virtual desktops is usually set at 6 or 8, fvwm permits the default to be set as high as 256.

Other features include a window list, accessed by right-clicking the desktop. This brings up a small window that contains the titles of all open windows whether minimized or not. Click a particular window title to activate that window. The window list is especially useful if you like to use multiple virtual desktops, because you can see whether you've left any programs running before you log out.

TIP	If you want a window manager that resembles Windows 95, try the fvwm variant fvwm95. You can find it in most online Unix software archives. It works much like regular fvwm, but the graphic display is closer to the Windows 95 display.

Configuring fvwm

As with many other window managers and Unix programs, fvwm is configured with the dot file .fvwm2rc (assuming that you're using the fvwm2 variant, the current version). .fvwm2rc contains configurations for colors, key and mouse-button bindings, window display options, and other miscellaneous configuration options. The syntax used in .fvwm2rc is similar to that used by twm; the syntax varies from variable to variable and may need only the variable name, or may require the variable name plus a defined set of options or flags.

fvwm handles configuration variables and built-in functions identically. That is, if you want to configure a regular fvwm function, you simply need to add it to the .fvwm2rc file and make any necessary edits to its default configuration. A variety of built-in functions can be called in the .fvwm2rc file, and they are all described in the fvwm manual page, accessible by typing man fvwm or man fvwm2 at a shell prompt. The fvwm manual page is unusually well-written and provides complete information about each possible configuration in the section "Built-In Commands."

NOTE   If you feel it necessary to change the default settings of fvwm, we recommend that you familiarize yourself with the manual page first, because it is a clear and complete reference for fvwm configuration options.

AfterStep

AfterStep is a window manager designed to emulate the display of the late (and often lamented) NeXT operating system. The NeXT display was clean and easy to use, and AfterStep has been built to offer the same feeling to its users. AfterStep falls into the category of highly configurable window managers, with many options for the user's personal preferences and configurations.

Unlike most of the window managers described in this chapter, AfterStep is *modular*. A modular program is one that has a main program that is quite small and sleek, while individual characteristics are handled by individual modules. The main program loads particular modules at start-up, as defined by the user. This means that unused programs simply don't get loaded and aren't available to the user, and don't take up system resources even if they're idle. This can save quite a bit of strain on system memory and CPU processes, especially if graphics-intensive modules are not loaded automatically. Thus, AfterStep itself has quite a small footprint; it's the various modules that take up a lot of space and resources. A fully loaded AfterStep with all available modules can be quite bloated, but it's fair for the AfterStep developers to call their product streamlined and quick.

AfterStep loads with three modules, by default. These modules provide flexibility and ease of use to the user. The WinList module allows you to see a small list of the titles of all open windows; the Pager module shows a small graphic representation of all virtual desktops; and the Wharf module provides a panel into which various program icons can be docked for quick access. (The Wharf is equivalent to the panel in both KDE and Gnome.) You can add additional modules, including those designed to control window behavior. Most users will want to use a significant number of modules to create a powerful and flexible window manager that meets their needs.

Configuring AfterStep

Unlike the window managers described so far in this chapter, AfterStep does not handle its configurations in a single file. Instead, AfterStep configuration files are divided into a number of smaller files contained in the ~/GNUstep/Library/ AfterStep/directory in your home directory. To get these files into your home directory, create the directory named above. Then, copy the systemwide configuration files from the /usr/local/share/afterstep directory and edit them as necessary. If you have files in a personal ~/GNUstep/Library/AfterStep directory, AfterStep will use those configurations as the default for your account, regardless of systemwide defaults set by the system administrator.

> **NOTE**   Older versions of AfterStep, prior to release version 1.8, used a configuration file called .steprc. If you have a version of AfterStep that uses .steprc, we suggest that you upgrade to the newest version (available at http://www.afterstep.org). You will find a number of changes as of the 1.8 release, including a complete change in the way that configuration is handled.

There are 18 AfterStep configuration files, listed in Table 8.1. You may never touch some of these files; you might want to edit others extensively. The syntax is straightforward, with each entry starting with the variable name, followed by the particular definition for each variable. Look through the particular file you want to edit for examples of how individual variables are handled in that file. You can find a full list of variables for each configuration file in the AfterStep manual pages, accessible by typing man afterstep at a shell prompt. Note that the man page for AfterStep is extremely long, but that individual modules have their own manual pages as well.

TABLE 8.1:   AfterStep Configuration Files

Filename	Configuration Effect
animate	Defines animation settings used when windows or other programs are minimized or iconified
asetroot	Configures the asetroot module, which controls the background appearance of AfterStep
asmail	Configures the applet asmail, used to handle mail more efficiently

Continued on next page

TABLE 8.1 CONTINUED: AfterStep Configuration Files

Filename	Configuration Effect
audio	Configures the audio module so that you can use sound effects with particular actions or use plug-in modules that require audio enhancement
autoexec	Defines what programs and modules are automatically loaded when AfterStep starts
base.xxbpp	Defines the directory path for modules, graphical pixmaps, cursor icons, and AfterStep script files
clean	Manages the Clean module, which automatically closes or minimizes windows after a defined idle period
compatibility	Determines whether AfterStep configuration files from earlier versions of the program (i.e., .steprc files) will be used when AfterStep 1.8 and later are started
database	Defines the configuration of various applications, including their window behavior and appearance
feel.name	Configures the feel of the window manager, including window behavior and other mechanical functions (used in consort with look.name, described below)
forms	Contains information on any forms used by AfterStep
ident	Defines the variables of the Ident module, which controls basic information about every open window
look.name	Configures the look of the window manager, including color and gradient shading (used in conjunction with feel.name, described above)
pager	Defines the variables of the Pager module, used to show the various virtual desktops and their contents
scroll	Defines the variables of the Scroll module, which determines how individual windows on the desktop will scroll from top to bottom or side to side
wharf	Defines the variables of the Wharf module, including docked icons and other applets plugged into the desktop display
winlist	Defines the variables of the WinList module, which shows information for all open windows
zharf	Defines the variables of the Zharf module, which is a text version of the Wharf module

WindowMaker

Like AfterStep, WindowMaker is a window manager based on the NeXT display. The resulting desktop, shown in Figure 8.5, is a clean and usable interface. WindowMaker is a product of the GNU project, so it is Free Software and is designed to work well with other GNU programs. We have included WindowMaker on the CD-ROM provided with this book. WindowMaker offers a sophisticated menu system, with detachable menus that can be left open by "sticking" them to the desktop; WindowMaker also has a feature called the Dock, which serves the same function as the AfterStep Wharf or the KDE and Gnome panels.

WindowMaker is not the fastest window manager available, nor is it the smallest in terms of system use, nor does it have the most bells and whistles. However, it has a nice balance of all these components and is a good choice for the user who

FIGURE 8.5:

WindowMaker, like After-Step, is based on the NeXT display, and has a clean and simple interface.

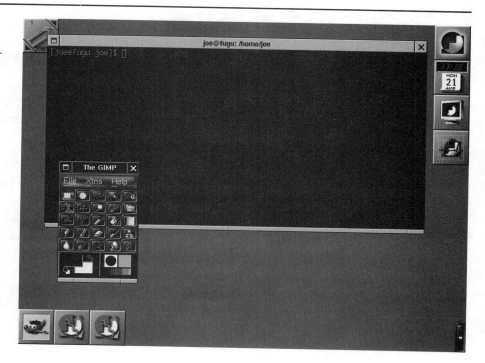

wants a fully featured window manager without the overwhelming system demand of an integrated desktop and a window manager that handles multiple tasks easily without the bare-bones appearance of the more basic window managers. WindowMaker has a large number of configurable features, without tipping over into configuration overload as is sometimes the problem with Enlightenment.

The decision between WindowMaker and AfterStep is difficult, because the two managers appear almost identical. The major difference between the two is that WindowMaker integrates more functions into its core binary code than AfterStep and does not rely on modules to the extent that AfterStep does. This difference doesn't matter to the majority of window manager users, though, so you should try them both out and make your decision based on how they feel to you.

Configuring WindowMaker

Like AfterStep, WindowMaker uses a multiple-configuration-file system instead of a single file, as with BlackBox or IceWM. WindowMaker configuration files are divided into a number of smaller files contained in the ~/GNUstep/ directory and its various subdirectories in your home directory.

NOTE   To get these files into your home directory, create the directory named above. Then, copy the systemwide configuration files from the `/usr/local/share/windowmaker` directory and edit them as necessary. If you have WindowMaker configuration files in a personal `~/GNUstep` directory, WindowMaker will use those configurations as the default for your account, regardless of systemwide defaults set by the system administrator.

There are five WindowMaker configuration files, listed in Table 8.2. You may never touch some of these files; you might want to edit others extensively. However, WindowMaker offers a configuration utility, described below, that handles some of the editing that you might otherwise do by hand. The syntax in these configuration files is straightforward, with each entry starting with the variable name, followed by the particular definition for each variable. Look through the particular file you want to edit for examples of how individual variables are handled in that file.

TABLE 8.2: WindowMaker Configuration Files

Filename	Configuration Effect
~/GNUStep/WindowMaker /WindowMaker	Sets the majority of WindowMaker configuration variables, including window behavior, fonts, keyboard shortcuts, and other such items.
~/GNUStep/WindowMaker /WMWindowAttributes	Contains individual configurations for various applications installed on the computer. Each program may have a different set of attributes, and those are all defined in this file.
~/GNUStep/Defaults /WMState	Contains information for the Dock's current settings, including graphical buttons and program launch information. Do not edit this file; it is automatically generated.
~/GNUStep/Defaults /WMRootMenu	Defines the file that serves the root menu. In versions of WindowMaker newer than 0.19, this file should be replaced by ~GNUStep/Defaults/ plmenu if the configuration application Wprefs.app is to be used for menu configuration.
~/GNUStep/Library /WindowMaker/Menu	Handles menu configuration for WindowMaker versions older than 0.19.

You can find a full list of variables for each configuration file in the WindowMaker manual pages, accessible by typing man windowmaker at a shell prompt. Note that the man page for WindowMaker is extremely long.

NOTE If you are using a newer version of WindowMaker (any version 0.62 and later), you can sidestep much of the configuration-file process by using Wprefs.app, a program designed as a graphical interface to the WindowMaker configuration files. Wprefs.app is shown in Figure 8.6. Along the top of the Wprefs.app window, there are 16 square icons. Each icon opens a separate window in which you can set various configuration options for that particular set of variables; for example, you might open the Window Preferences tab to define your preferred window styles or the Appearance Preferences tab to define the overall display.

FIGURE 8.6:

WindowMaker configuration is made simple with the Wprefs.app program.

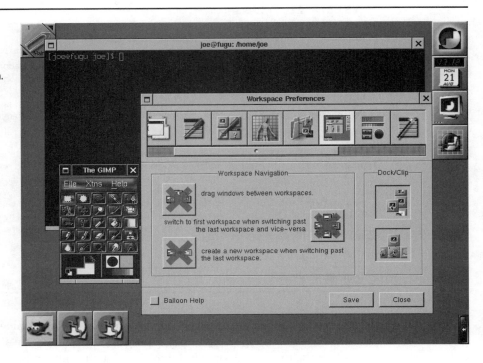

Enlightenment

Of all the window managers covered in this chapter, Enlightenment is the most configurable. Almost every single element of the display can be altered to meet the user's needs. Although some people find this overwhelming, many Enlightenment users choose this window manager precisely because of its flexibility and power. With Enlightenment, shown in Figure 8.7, you aren't even limited to the graphical files that are included in downloaded themes; if you have access to a graphical design program such as The GIMP (included on the book's CD-ROM), you can create your own files and add them to the display.

Enlightenment is still very much under development. The programmers on this project hope that, eventually, Enlightenment will function as a standalone shell environment with seamless integration of applications and non-Enlightenment programs already installed on the hard drive. For now, these details are covered by configuration files, but the dream is to have Enlightenment handle many of

FIGURE 8.7:

Enlightenment is the most configurable window manager available.

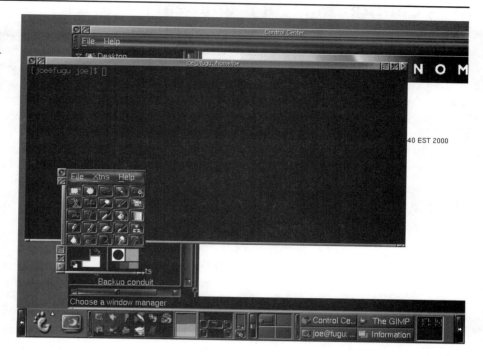

these tasks automatically without the need for hand configuration. Some features most commonly associated with integrated desktops, such as a file manager and drag-and-drop capability, are also planned for Enlightenment. It's easy to see, from the list of features, that Enlightenment started as part of the Gnome project. Though no longer associated with Gnome (which now uses the Sawfish window manager), Enlightenment offers—or plans to offer—much of the same functionality found in the desktop.

You can certainly use Enlightenment if you aren't thrilled by the idea of editing multiple configuration files. If you prefer a window manager that you can use out of the box, though, you may prefer BlackBox or even WindowMaker. For those who love tinkering and want the most cutting-edge window manager, however, Enlightenment is for you. Readers who want to program for the display environment will be especially happy with Enlightenment, because the project's development philosophy is to accept and integrate most patches submitted for consideration.

Configuring Enlightenment

Enlightenment configurations are usually grouped by theme. That is, if you want to configure a particular element of the Enlightenment display or behavior, you edit the configuration files for the theme that you're using. These changes don't carry over when you change themes. The default theme's configuration files are located in /usr/local/enlightenment/config, and configuration files for alternate themes are located in /usr/local/enlightenment/themes. There are three basic configuration files for each theme:

- usr_main.cfg controls user preferences.

- theme_pre.cfg controls various class definitions for the given theme.

- theme_main.cfg controls the graphical display of windows within the given theme.

You can change basic user preferences by editing the user_main.cfg file; you will probably never need to edit theme_pre.cfg or theme_main.cfg. Open the file in a text editor and change the appropriate setting. There are several user-preference entries at the top of the file, which are mostly variables for window behavior. Display variables, such as color, font, and background image, are usually changed by installing a different desktop theme instead of editing a configuration file. Sound options are also contained in this file.

> **NOTE**   The default settings in user_main.cfg should be the same from theme to theme, though the file is created anew each time a new theme is developed. However, individual programmers may not want to use the default settings; if you come across a theme that has an unusual set of button functions or keystroke combinations, chances are that the developer has chosen not to adhere to the general user-preference standards.

Installing Themes

Because so much of Enlightenment's power and flexibility is concentrated in themes, you'll probably want to download and install a variety of themes to see what they can do. The largest archive of Enlightenment themes, as with the other theme-enabled window managers and the integrated desktops, is found at themes.org: specifically, at http://e.themes.org. The themes are stored as tar-balls, meaning that you'll need to unpack them once they're downloaded.

Download into the /usr/local/enlightenment/themes directory. Unpack the theme by issuing the command

```
tar zxf filename
```

(being sure to include any extensions such as filename.tar.gz). The package will unpack itself and sort its files into newly created subdirectories. You can then select the new theme in the Enlightenment configuration tools. If you are running Enlightenment with the Gnome desktop, for example, click the main Gnome menu button and select Window Manager ➤ Enlightenment. Click the button marked Run Configuration Tool for Enlightenment, select the Themes tab, and pick the new theme from the list, as shown in Figure 8.8. Click OK to set the new theme on the desktop. Theme selection works in the same way whether you are using KDE or just straight Enlightenment.

FIGURE 8.8:

Change themes easily with Enlightenment's built-in configuration tools.

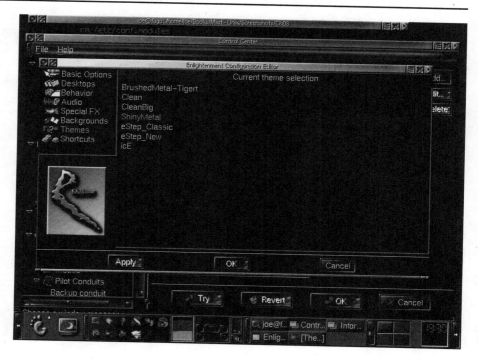

Summary

Window managers, at their most basic, offer the Unix user the ability to manage multiple terminal sessions. However, most window managers now available offer far more. Window managers may have features such as a complex menu system, icon-based management tools, or the ability to use graphic themes to control the display's appearance and behavior. A multitude of window managers are available for all Unix variants; as long as you are running the X Window System, you can use a window manager. Window managers can be used as standalone programs or in concert with an integrated desktop environment.

Window managers can be divided into two major camps. One camp is focused on developing window managers that are lean and sleek, requiring relatively little portions of system resources for their operation. Some window managers in this category include twm, IceWM, and BlackBox. The other camp is focused on developing window managers with a high level of configurability, which inevitably leads to a higher demand on system resources, though the end result is a more detailed and feature-rich program. Window managers in this category include fvwm, AfterStep, WindowMaker, and Enlightenment.

CHAPTER
NINE

KDE

- What Is KDE?

- Getting and Installing KDE

- The KDE Panel

- The KDE File Manager

- The KDE Control Center

- Desktop Themes

- Summary

In Chapter 8: "Window Managers," we described one kind of program that works with the X Window System to provide a graphical user interface. Although window managers provide a basic windowing system, permitting you to open multiple Unix sessions on one desktop, window managers are limited in their scope. When compared to other operating systems such as Windows or MacOS, the window managers described in Chapter 8 come up a bit short: no drag-and-drop, no cutting and pasting between windows, and a somewhat awkward method of managing programs and monitoring system activity. Window managers are a good step beyond plain command-line interface sessions, but they're not the most current graphical interface technology, either.

What *is* the current graphical user interface technology? The integrated desktop environment. These desktop environments combine the functions of regular window managers with a new level of features, including drag-and-drop, better graphics management, and a suite of integrated features that make normal system and account administration easier. For system administrators, integrated desktop environments even provide an array of graphical administrative tools that can replace arcane command-line methods.

In this chapter and the next, we describe the two major integrated desktop environments currently available for Unix and Unix-derived operating systems: KDE and Gnome. We don't recommend one over the other. Although we've written a book about KDE, we use Gnome on many of our machines, and we don't see a significant reason to prefer one of the two. Try them both out (we've placed both on the CD) and see which you like best.

What Is KDE?

KDE (the K Desktop Environment) was the first integrated desktop environment to be released for Unix and Unix-derived platforms. The KDE project is based in Germany and is one of the most multinational volunteer groups we've seen in Open Source development. (More than 100 people work on the KDE translation projects alone.)

NOTE   Despite any rumors you might have heard, KDE is Open Source software. KDE was developed with a particular software library called Qt, which used a software license more restrictive than the GNU Public License. In particular, the Qt license had a loophole for developers who wanted to write commercial software with Qt and who did not want to release their code publicly (one of the core tenets of the GPL). Qt's developers permitted such use as long as a license fee was paid. The issue has now been resolved, and KDE is true Open Source software. If this is ethically problematic for you, flip to the next chapter and learn more about Gnome, which has been Free Software from the beginning.

KDE is designed to work with the KWM window manager, a manager native to KDE and integrated tightly with the desktop. As the first integrated desktop to hit the Unix community, KDE brought Unix users a new level of ease with a complete menu system, integrated help documents, and native graphical administration and configuration tools. KDE also gave users the ability to design their own desktops, whether basic or deeply complex, and to share desktop themes with other KDE users.

Getting and Installing KDE

KDE is easy to find. In fact, we've put all the packages you'll need on the CD that comes with this book. We do recommend that you check out the KDE home page at http://www.kde.org, though. We went to press before KDE 2 was ready for release, but the development team promises some big changes in the new version. If there's an upgraded version on the Web site and you'd rather use that, just download the packages recommended there and install as instructed.

You should experience few, if any, problems when you install KDE. (If you're using Corel Linux, you won't even need this section, because KDE is the default desktop for that distribution.) KDE should run smoothly on most Unix-derived operating systems, even the more obscure distributions. Certainly, it will run just fine on the systems covered in this book.

On its Web site, KDE provides download packages in six different formats, including .rpm and .deb files for the Red Hat and Debian Linux package managers; regular source code tarballs for those not running Linux; and packages for Solaris 2.6 and 2.7. Regardless of your Unix flavor, you should be able to compile and run the source code packages; if you can use .rpm or .deb formats, or you run an appropriate version of Solaris, try those specialized formats first. We concentrate on the source code in this chapter and provide the source packages on the CD.

Downloading KDE

In this section of the chapter, you will locate and download the appropriate packages to install KDE. If you're using the KDE packages from the book's CD, insert the CD into a mounted CD drive and move these packages to the appropriate directory, as explained in the "Unpacking the Source Code" section. If you're downloading packages from the KDE Web site, point your browser or FTP client to `ftp://ftp.kde.org`.

You'll need to download quite a few packages to get KDE working properly. We base the lists in this section on KDE 1.1, the current release at the time we wrote this chapter. These package names are for the source code packages, not for .rpm, .deb, or Solaris packages.

> **WARNING** If KDE 1.1 is not the current version at the time you are reading this book, see the KDE Web site to learn which packages you will need to install the desktop.

Base Package Downloads

The first two base packages listed below are required to install and run KDE.

> **WARNING** If you do not already have Qt installed on your system, you must obtain that as well and install it before you install anything else. Get Qt at `http://www.troll.no/dl` and make sure you download version 1.42 or higher. Do *not* download Qt 2 or higher, because those versions will not work with KDE 1.1. That may be different with KDE 2, but we do not know that for sure.

kdelibs: This package contains the various software libraries that KDE applications require to run.

kdebase: This package contains the basic KDE applications, such as the Window Manager, the File Manager, the Panel, and so on.

kdesupport: This package is not technically required to run KDE, but it certainly doesn't hurt to install it. It contains various software libraries that aren't produced by the KDE team, but are needed to run the software.

NOTE

If you are running Debian Linux, you must install the kdesupport package. It is required for Debian users.

Recommended Package Downloads

These packages are not required for KDE to run, but if you don't install them, you won't get many of the advantages of an integrated desktop. We suggest that you install them the first time, to see what a complete KDE installation looks like, and then uninstall anything you don't need or want.

kdeadmin: This package contains graphical programs for system administration. The current package contains a graphical user manager and a runlevel editor.

kdegames: This package contains a variety of games built for the KDE desktop, including several versions of Tetris, strategy games, and card games.

kdegraphics: This package contains several viewers for various graphic formats, including PostScript, .dvi, and others. It also includes a drawing program.

kdemultimedia: This package contains utilities that help you use the multimedia capabilities of your computer, such as an audio CD player, a sound mixer, and the like.

kdenetwork: This package contains various KDE-specific Internet applications, such as Kmail (an electronic mail client) and Krn (a USENET news client).

korganizer: The korganizer package contains an electronic organizer, similar to Microsoft Outlook, that will manage your schedule and contact information.

kdetoys: This package contains a variety of games and other entertainment programs designed for the KDE desktop.

kdeutils: The kdeutils package contains several basic desktop utilities, such as a calculator and Knotes, which are electronic versions of sticky notes. This package also contains KEdit, a graphical text editor covered in Chapter 20: "Graphical Editors."

Unpacking the Source Code

First, locate the packages that you've downloaded. If you're using the packages on the CD, copy them to a location on your hard drive; you can't install directly from the CD. Unix users generally move packages to the /usr/src or the /tmp directories before beginning an installation; /tmp is especially good if you've developed the habit of deleting old files from /tmp on a regular basis. We usually use /usr/src, often creating a new subdirectory such as /usr/src/kde for KDE packages.

WARNING   You need to be logged in as root to install these packages.

Once you have moved the KDE packages to the appropriate directory, you'll need to unpack them before they can be installed. You must install the kdesupport and kdelibs packages first, because all the other packages depend on the software libraries contained in those two packages. To unpack kdesupport, issue the command

```
tar xvfz kdesupport.tgz
```

at a shell prompt. As the package unpacks, it will create its own subdirectory in your current directory. If, for example, you followed our lead and created the directory /usr/src/kde, this command will create the subdirectory /usr/src/kde/kdesupport. Next, unpack the kdelibs package by issuing the command

```
tar xvfz kdelibs.tgz
```

at the command prompt.

Once you've unpacked those two packages, you can continue to unpack the other packages you downloaded. You will need at least kdebase, which contains the basic KDE distribution, but we recommend that you install all packages. Continue to repeat the tar xvfz command, ending it with the specific package name, until all packages have been unpacked and have their own subdirectories.

NOTE   Once you've unpacked everything, you can scan the various subdirectories to see what's included. Most of it is code, of course, but each package will also have a README file. You should always read the README files, because they contain important information about installing the specific files in each package. Sometimes they even include platform-specific help.

Compiling and Installing the Source Code

After all the packages are unpacked, you can begin to install the software. Move back to the directory containing all the subdirectories, if necessary; then, move into the subdirectory housing the kdesupport package by issuing the command

```
cd kdesupport
```

Configure the kdesupport package by issuing the command

```
./configure
```

at the shell prompt. The `configure` command determines your hardware configuration so that KDE can install cleanly.

Next, issue the command

```
make
```

at the shell prompt. The `make` command starts the compiler, which builds the actual binary package used to execute the KDE program. While `make` is working, a number of messages will scroll up your screen. You need not scrutinize these messages, because a serious error will halt the flow and wait for your response.

When the messages finally stop scrolling, type

```
make install
```

at the prompt. This command moves all the newly created binary packages into their permanent directories of residence.

Return to the previous directory (use the `cd ..` command) and move into the `kdelibs` subdirectory. Repeat the three-step procedure described above—`./configure`, `make`, and `make install`—for this package. When finished, return to the previous directory and move into the `kdebase` subdirectory.

NOTE

The kdebase package has some special configuration options. Before you begin the configuration process, issue the command `./configure - help` at the prompt to display the options available for your installation. If you choose to use one of these options, follow the directions on the screen. Then, continue with the three-step process described above.

After you have installed kdesupport, kdelibs, and kdebase (in that order), you can use this process for all the remaining KDE packages. It does not matter which order you use, as long as those three packages are installed first and in the proper order.

NOTE
If you had a problem that resulted in the shut-down of the configuration or installation process, the odds are overwhelming that you're missing a library or required program somewhere. This is why we recommend that you install the libraries first, then the base package, and then the optional packages. Scroll back through the error messages and try to determine what's missing. Find the package containing that element, install it, and then try to reinstall the failed package again.

When you have finished installing all the packages, log out of the root account and log back into your user account.

Configuring X for KDE

Once you've logged back into your user account, issue the command

    usekde

at the command prompt. You will see a few system messages appear on the screen as your computer sets KDE to be the default user interface. When the messages stop, you can test your installation and configuration by typing

    startx

at the prompt. The X Window System will boot up—you should see the KDE splash screen and, eventually, the KDE desktop, as shown in Figure 9.1.

NOTE
If you are already running X for some reason (perhaps you are using a window manager or Gnome as your current graphical interface), you must log out of your current session before you can test KDE. Exit your session and log back in at the text prompt. KDE should start as the graphical interface at that point.

The KDE Panel

The heart of KDE's user interface is the KDE Panel, a long set of icons that runs along the bottom of the screen, as shown in Figure 9.2. The Panel contains icons that represent frequently used applications or commands, but it can be configured to show only the icons for items you use frequently. You can also move the default position of the Panel, or collapse it and open it only when needed. The remainder of this section describes each of the Panel's default items.

FIGURE 9.1:

The first time you run KDE, you will see the default desktop configuration.

NOTE   Once you've installed KDE, you may see some of the buttons described here, but not others. If your monitor is too small for the screen resolution you're using, the Panel automatically layers icons to fit. We recommend that you remove icons you don't use much to get the Panel neatly located on your desktop.

FIGURE 9.2:

The KDE Panel contains icons that launch frequently used applications with a single click.

Panel Collapse Bar

Located at the left and right ends of the Panel, these textured bars collapse the Panel or reopen it to its full size. When you click the bar, the Panel slides behind the bar and will remain there until you click it again.

> **TIP** Use these bars if you like to work in full-screen mode, so that the Panel doesn't obscure what you're working on.

Application Starter

The Application Starter icon launches a menu, which works like the Windows 95 and Windows 98 Start menu. You can launch programs, navigate files, or execute commands via this menu. Click the Application Starter icon to open the menu and then continue with your selections from that point. Figure 9.3 shows the Application Starter menu and some of its sub-menus.

File Manager

In the "KDE File Manager" section of this chapter, we describe the KDE File Manager, a graphical interface to your computer's directory system. Use this icon to launch the File Manager with a single mouse-click. If you are logged in as a user, the File Manager will show you the contents of your home directory; if you're logged in as root, File Manager will display the computer's entire directory structure.

Terminal Emulator

Throughout this book, we ask you to work with a command prompt so that you can work directly with the shell environment. Although KDE is a graphical interface, you can still launch shell sessions with this icon. Click it to open a window containing an independent shell session. Figure 9.4 shows a KDE session with an open shell session on the desktop.

FIGURE 9.3:

The Application Starter menu works like the Start menu in Windows.

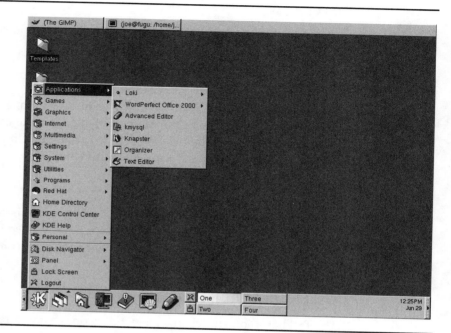

FIGURE 9.4:

Even though KDE is a graphical interface, you can use KDE tools to work directly in the shell.

Text Editor

Click this button to launch KEdit, a graphical text editor. We cover KEdit in some detail in Chapter 20: "Graphical Editors."

Help

Click this icon to launch your default Web browser, which will show the opening pages of the KDE online help system. KDE help is quite good, though there is not yet a comprehensive index of help pages. To get the help you need, you'll need to move through the various documents until you find the correct help file.

Pager

Although it appears to be a single icon, the Pager icon is actually composed of four tiny icons that take up the space of a regularly sized icon. The Pager controls the KDE virtual desktops, which we explain in the "Virtual Desktops" section of this chapter.

Taskbar and System Tray

The Taskbar's contents change, depending on what you're currently doing with your Unix session. The Taskbar contains an icon for each window that is currently open, whether or not it is active. (The *active window* is the window in which you're currently working.) The icons are labeled with the window's name, which is usually the name of the application running in that window. In some cases, KDE will label the Taskbar buttons with sequential numbers if it cannot determine the application name.

The System Tray is the item in the final section of the Panel. The tray shows icons for programs that are running in the background. Such programs are active and consume system resources, but aren't usually used directly by users. The System Tray also contains the Date and Time icon; when no background programs are active, you'll see only date and time information in the System Tray.

Clock/Date

The final item on the Panel shows the date and time, drawn from your system settings. You should ensure that the operating system has the correct date and time so that various files get the proper timestamps; that your KDE clock will be correct is simply a useful side effect.

Virtual Desktops

Virtual desktops are a KDE feature that are somewhat difficult to describe. In essence, KDE's virtual desktops provide you with four individual computer desktops while still requiring you to log in only once. Virtual desktops are a useful way to distribute application windows if you like an uncluttered desktop; they're also a good way to divorce your fun applications, such as Netscape or a session of Tetris, from work applications, such as Corel WordPerfect or a graphical administration tool.

Virtual desktops are controlled by the Pager. You can use the four tiny icons of the Pager to move among the desktops, or click the small arrow to the left of the Pager buttons. This arrow opens a miniature graphical pane that shows all four desktops at once; then you simply need to click the appropriate pane to open that desktop. Figure 9.5 shows the Pager's graphical display.

TIP

Those who like virtual desktops can configure up to eight of them; those who dislike them can configure only two. The minimum is two, so we suggest just ignoring the second virtual desktop. You can remove the Pager from the panel if it is distracting.

FIGURE 9.5:

The Pager helps you manage up to eight virtual KDE desktops in the same user session.

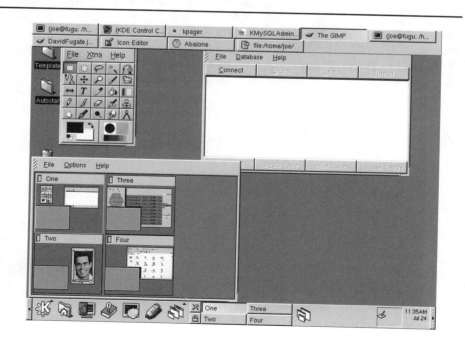

The KDE File Manager

If you have worked with Windows 95 or 98 before starting your Unix experience, you're probably familiar with the Windows Explorer. The KDE File Manager works in much the same way—it's a graphical interface to the computer's directory structure. The KDE File Manager is more than just a visual display, though; it offers you a number of ways to handle your files without having to memorize arcane commands. Open the File Manager in one of two ways:

- Click the File Manager icon in the Panel.

- Open the Application Starter menu and select File Manager from the menu that appears.

Whichever method you use, the File Manager will open. The default mode is *simple view,* as shown in Figure 9.6. We prefer to use *tree view,* which you can turn on by selecting View ➢ Show Tree from the menu bar. The next time you open File Manager, it will look like the screen shown in Figure 9.7. Note that, in tree

FIGURE 9.6:

The KDE File Manager uses a simple tree display to show your computer's filesystem.

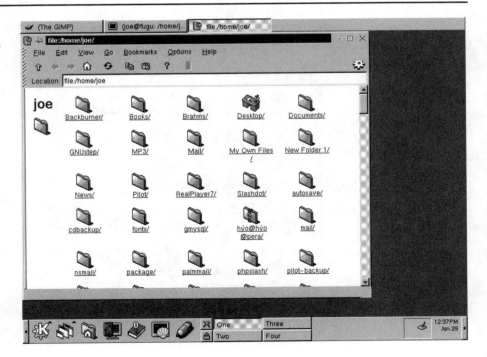

view, the File Manager window is separated into two panes. On the left side, the computer's full directory structure is shown. This type of display is commonly called a *file tree*, because directories branch out as they become more specific. On the right side, the selected directory's contents appear.

NOTE

If you come to Linux from Windows 95 or Windows 98, this is all familiar. Feel free to skip to the next section of this chapter if you have used Windows Explorer confidently in the past.

FIGURE 9.7:

Use tree view to see the entire directory system at once, in two panes.

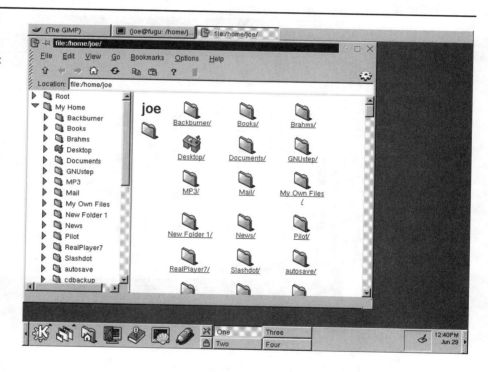

When File Manager opens, one directory in the left pane is highlighted. By default, this is your home directory. The right pane shows the files and subdirectories contained in your home directory. If you click another directory in the left pane, that directory's contents will appear in the right pane. In other words, the right pane contains all the files contained in the directory selected in the left pane.

Note that some directories have small arrows to the left of their names, while other directories have none. An arrow pointing to the right indicates that the directory contains subdirectories. Click the arrow to expand the directory tree and show those subdirectories in the left pane. Just as with the main directories, click a subdirectory to display its contents in the right pane. When you've expanded a directory tree in this manner, the right arrow changes to a downward-pointing arrow. Click that arrow to collapse the branch back to the parent directory. Expanded and collapsed branches are shown in Figure 9.8.

FIGURE 9.8:

File Manager can be collapsed or expanded to show all directories and subdirectories, or to limit the view.

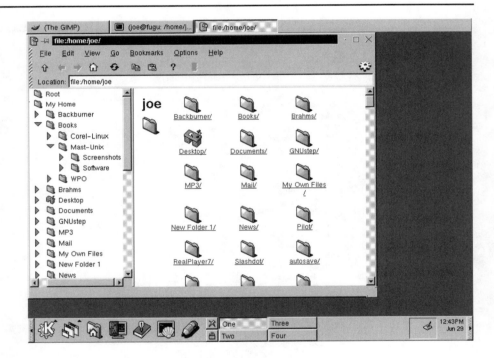

In addition to providing an efficient manner of moving through the filesystem, File Manager provides a single location for performing a number of basic operations on your files. In particular, you can use File Manager to copy files from one directory to another, delete files, rename files, and set file permissions.

The KDE Control Center

One of the benefits of using KDE as your integrated desktop is that almost every aspect of KDE is configurable. Most of these changes are done with the KDE Control Center, a tool that contains configuration options for 10 categories: Desktop, Information, Input Devices, Keys, Network, Sound, Windows, Password, Date & Time, and Printers. Most of these categories have sub-options as well.

Open the KDE Control Center by clicking the Application Starter icon and selecting Control Center from the menu that appears. The Control Center will open, as shown in Figure 9.9. As you can see in the illustration, the Control Center has two panes. The left pane contains a tree structure, similar to the structure used in File Manager. When an entry is selected in the left pane, a set of controls for that category is displayed in the right pane.

FIGURE 9.9:

The KDE Control Center holds multiple configuration options.

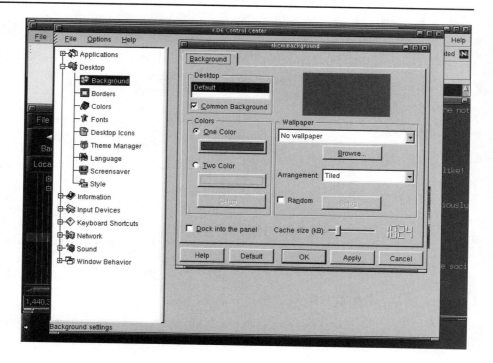

> **NOTE**
> You may never use some of these KDE Control Center options. We provide basic information on each category here, but if you need more specific information, we suggest consulting the online help or the KDE Web site at `http://www.kde.org`. In general, if you want to change something about KDE's appearance, you'll start at the Control Center.

Desktop

The Desktop category of the KDE Control Center contains control sets for most of the popular desktop configurations. With this category, you can configure the desktop background, window borders, display options, fonts, desktop icons, language, screensavers, and other desktop styles. Many KDE users find that they use this category most frequently in the Control Center.

Background

In the Background category, you can set the appearance of the desktop itself. Windows and Macintosh users will recognize this as the wallpaper setting. The background can be a solid or gradient color, or you can use an image file.

> **NOTE**
> To set a background with matching icons and colors, see the "Desktop Themes" section of this chapter.

There is a preview window at the bottom right of the Control Center screen, where you can see how changes will appear on your desktop. Click the Apply button to make changes on your actual desktop without closing the Control Center. Click the OK button when you're finished, and wish to save your changes and exit the Control Center.

Borders

The Borders category controls the way in which individual windows behave on the KDE desktop. There are two types of border control sets: active and magic.

- *Active borders* are used in conjunction with virtual desktops. With active borders, you can switch between virtual desktops simply by moving your mouse to the edge of the screen that borders the desktop you want to switch to. After a defined period (the default is 5 milliseconds), the desktop will change. To enable this feature, click the Enable Active Desktop Borders check box.

- *Magic borders* activate the desktop's *snap zone,* a region around the edge of the entire desktop. When you drag an application or program window toward the edge of the screen, and the snap zone is active, the window will snap to the edge of the screen.

Display

As with the Background option, you can use the Display control set to change the colors of various KDE desktop components, such as window title bars, text, and similar items. Select one of the predesigned schemes or create your own; your selections will be displayed in the preview window. Click the Apply button to see the new colors on your actual desktop, and click OK to save your changes and exit the Control Center.

Fonts

The Fonts category allows you to define the various fonts used on the KDE desktop. You can set font choices for Panel icons, window titles, and other KDE components, as well as systemwide default preferences for a proportional and a fixed-width font. To change a font, select the category and the font you want to use, and click the Apply button. When you are ready to save your changes and exit the Control Center, click OK.

Desktop Icons

This category affects the way in which icons are displayed on the desktop itself, rather than in the Panel. You can control the spacing between icons and the manner in which an icon's text label is displayed. Click the Apply button to see your changes on the actual desktop, and click OK to save your changes and exit the Control Center.

Language

By default, KDE uses English for all its actions. If you want to change the language that KDE uses, select the new language from the drop-down menu. Click OK to save your changes and exit the Control Center. The new language will apply only to programs started after you exit the Control Center; if you want everything to be shown in the new language, including windows already open, you must log out of KDE and back in again.

NOTE   This setting does not affect the keyboard input. If you want to use a different (non–American English) keyboard with your computer, you must set it in the International Keyboard sub-category of the Input Devices category, described below.

Screensaver

If you want to use a screensaver with your KDE desktop, set it in this category. The various screensavers are visible in a preview window. You can also configure certain settings, such as the time idle before the screensaver is activated and whether to require a screensaver password. Several of the screensavers have individual configurations that you can set by clicking the Setup button and making your selections. Click OK when you've finished to save your changes and exit.

Style

The Style category is one that is infrequently used. Choices in this category control how window elements are drawn on the desktop: select from Windows 95 or MacOS. You can also determine whether your display choices will be applied to non-KDE applications as well as KDE programs.

Information

The Information category is not open to configuration. Instead, you can learn a lot about your hardware setup with the various options in this category. As with other Control Center options, select an item in the left pane to display its contents in the right pane. You can see information about input/output devices, DMA channels, interrupts, I/O ports, memory, partitions, PCI slots, processor data, SCSI devices, Samba status, sound card data, and your computer's X Server.

Input Devices

This category contains configuration options for the input devices attached to your computer: keyboard and mouse. You can define the language used by your keyboard, and configure several settings for speed of input and how KDE will react to different types of input.

> **NOTE**
>
> If you are using a different kind of input device, such as a graphic tablet or a joystick, we assume you have a driver for it and know how to use it.

International Keyboard

KDE offers support for a wide variety of keyboards designed for various character sets. There are KDE drivers for Cyrillic and ideographic language keyboards, as well as for accented Roman-alphabet language keyboards or Roman-alphabet language keyboards that use non-English characters. Select the appropriate driver in the drop-down box, click the OK button, and attach the new keyboard to the keyboard port.

Keyboard

In the Keyboard category, you can configure keyboard repeat and volume. Keyboard repeat determines whether a keystroke will print multiple times to the screen if it is depressed for a period of time, while keyboard volume creates a clicking noise each time KDE senses a keystroke. Click the OK button to save your changes and exit this window.

Mouse

The Mouse category controls mouse behavior, which is a very personal choice. You may need to work with these controls until you find the perfect blend between physical mouse movement and on-screen behavior. This category contains settings for acceleration, threshold (nearness of mouse pointer to item), and mouse button mapping. Click the OK button to save your changes and exit the Control Center.

Keys

The Keys category is where you can define various keystroke combinations that act as shortcuts for frequently performed actions. For example, the familiar keyboard shortcut Ctrl+O executes the Open command just as if you'd used the menu system to navigate to the Open command. The Keys category contains two types of key patterns: Global Keys (system commands) and Standard Keys (application commands).

Global Keys

Global Keys combinations perform KDE system functions, such as changing desktops or selecting desktop icons. The various Global Keys combinations already defined are shown in the right pane; check them out before you duplicate an existing combination. To define a new Global Keys action, follow these steps:

1. Choose the action you want the combination to perform in the Action window of the left pane.

2. Select a *metakey* in the Choose a Key for the Selected Action window at the bottom of the right pane. A metakey is a key that needs to be pressed as part of the keystroke combination: KDE metakeys are Shift, Ctrl, and Alt.

3. Press the key on your keyboard that you want to use in combination with the metakey. The key combination appears in the Action window.

4. Click OK to save your new keystroke combination.

Standard Keys

Standard Keys combinations control the functions used when working with text. Cut, Paste, Copy, Save, and other familiar functions all have Standard Keys shortcuts. The various predefined Standard Keys combinations are listed in the right pane. To define a new Standard Keys combination, follow these steps:

1. Choose the action you want the keystroke combination to perform in the Action window of the right pane.

2. Select a metakey in the Choose a Key for the Selected Action window at the bottom of the right pane. A metakey is a key that needs to be pressed as part of the keystroke combination: KDE metakeys are Shift, Ctrl, and Alt.

3. Press the key on your keyboard that you want to use in combination with the metakey. The key combination appears in the Action window.

4. Click OK to save your new keystroke combination.

Network

The Network category contains various configuration options for Ethernet and Samba networking. We cover networking in Part VIII: "Network Administration."

Sound

In the Sound section, there are two options. The first allows you to control the properties of the *bell*. This is the "beep" sound that you hear if, for example, you try to do something that you're not allowed to do. Using the sliders, you can control the volume, pitch, and duration of the sound. We recommend that you pick something easy on the ears, because this sound has the potential to be really annoying. Click the Test button to hear the sound.

The second option allows you to enable certain system sounds. These are sound effects that may be associated with certain events, such as the opening and closing of windows. These are often "bing" or "whoosh" sounds. Some people enjoy them, and some do not. These sounds are disabled by default. To enable them, click the check box marked Enable System Sounds. In the two panes below the check box, you can associate the events shown in the left pane with sound files in the right pane. Use the Test button to preview the sound files. When you have made your selections, click OK.

Windows

In the Windows category, you can configure the appearance and behavior of desktop windows. There are five sub-categories: Advanced, Buttons, Mouse, Properties, and Titlebar.

Advanced

The Advanced sub-category lets you define how the Alt+Tab key combination will affect desktop windows. This sub-category also contains a control set that defines window styles based on window title or class (window *class* is an X Windows function that tells the computer the window type and how to display it). You will probably not need to work with these control sets unless you are doing specific X Window System configurations.

Buttons

The Buttons sub-category defines the placement of window control buttons in the window title bar. These buttons are the familiar minimize, maximize, and close buttons that usually appear at the right of the window title bar.

Mouse

The Mouse sub-category determines how the mouse buttons affect window behavior. You can assign any of four window attributes to any of three mouse buttons: window raise, window lower, window activation, and window operations menu. Depending on your assignments, a single mouse click can control desktop window behavior.

Properties

The Properties sub-category contains control sets for several miscellaneous window behaviors. You can determine whether windows will open at their full vertical height by default; how content will be displayed in a scrolling or resizing window; where new windows will be placed on the screen as they are opened; and how windows become the active window.

Titlebar

The Titlebar sub-category determines how any given window's title bar will appear and behave. You can configure title alignment, title bar appearance, title bar animation, and how mouse buttons will affect the window when clicked in the title bar.

Password

The Password category is a graphical password-change tool. In the Change Password window, type your old password and your new password. You need to enter your old password to verify that you are the appropriate account user. (This window can be used in place of the shell command passwd.)

Date & Time

The Date & Time category displays a clock and calendar that you can use to adjust your system time. Be sure that you check this regularly, especially if you live in a country or region that observes seasonal clock changes. It's also good to check this category in leap years.

Printers

The Printers category is used to configure and select printers attached to the computer. Despite its name, this category cannot be used to send documents to the printer; that must be done from within an application that issues print commands, such as an editor or word processor. Use this category to check whether your printers are working correctly before you try to print something.

Desktop Themes

Although all the configurations of the KDE Control Center make working with the KDE desktop easier, most people will focus on another sort of desktop configuration for daily changes. KDE permits the application of various *themes* to the desktop; a theme is a suite of stylistic elements that are designed to work together to create a certain look and feel. For example, you might choose a theme that applies various natural woodgrains to different parts of the window: cherry on the window title bars, beveled blocks of birch for desktop icons, and an expanse of bird's-eye maple on the desktop. Other users might prefer one of the dark, moody themes that use a lot of gray, black, and bright neon to create a different feeling.

Themes are easy to apply with KDE's Theme Manager, shown in Figure 9.10. Open the Theme Manager by clicking the Application Manager icon in the Panel and selecting Control Center ➢ Desktop ➢ Theme Manager. When the Manager appears, select a theme from the list at the left. The theme will appear in the preview window; when you find one you like, click the Apply button to see how it appears on your actual desktop. Click OK to save your selected theme and exit the Theme Manager.

You can also use Theme Manager to select parts of a given theme, even if you don't want to use the entire theme. With Theme Manager open, click the Contents tab. On this tab, shown in Figure 9.11, all the elements that compose the currently selected theme are displayed. Check the boxes next to the elements you want, and deselect the boxes next to elements you don't want on your desktop. Click the OK button to save your changes and exit.

FIGURE 9.10:

Use the KDE Theme Manager to apply different graphic themes to your desktop.

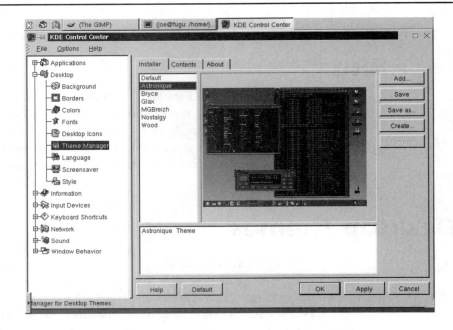

FIGURE 9.11:

The Theme Manager can also be used to apply portions of a theme to a different desktop.

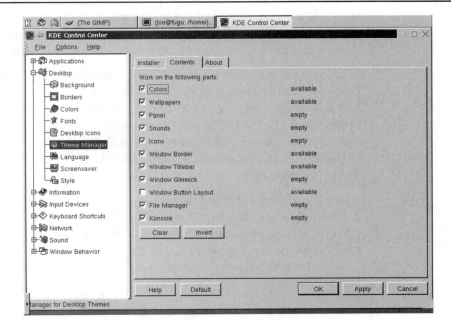

NOTE

If you like playing with themes, we suggest that you check out `http://kde.themes.org`, where you will find a frequently updated set of user-created themes.

Summary

The KDE integrated desktop environment offers a variety of tools to make your Unix experience easier, as well as a high level of configurability. KDE is an Open Source project and can be downloaded free of charge (or installed from the CD-ROM included with this book). KDE has a useful graphical file manager and a menu system that will be familiar to anyone experienced with Windows or MacOS.

The heart of KDE is the Panel, which runs along the bottom of the desktop; various icons are located on the Panel, providing shortcut access to frequently used programs. As with almost all other aspects of KDE, you can alter the Panel's icons and appearance to fit your needs. Configure KDE in the KDE Control Center, a set of tools that offers detailed control over the entire KDE environment.

CHAPTER
TEN

Gnome

As we explained in Chapter 9: "KDE," an *integrated desktop environment* is a different animal than a *window manager* (covered in Chapter 8: "Window Managers"). KDE is one of the two major integrated desktops available for Unix-derived platforms. The other desktop is called GNOME, an acronym standing for *GNU Object Model Environment.* Because GNOME is also a regular word in English, the desktop is usually referred to as Gnome, though the fully capitalized version is frequently seen as well.

Gnome is part of the GNU project described in Chapter 2: "Which Unix?" One of the main attractions of Gnome is that all of its components are released under the GNU Public License. This is not the case with KDE, which was built with a proprietary software library called Qt. Although the Qt developers recently changed their license so that the library is essentially Free Software now, many Free Software advocates have chosen Gnome because it has always been Free.

NOTE   Although Gnome and KDE are often cast as competitors in the press and by their advocates, this isn't really the case. Developers from both teams have collaborated in the past, and the two desktops are growing closer in functionality. It is possible, for example, to run KDE applications under Gnome and vice versa. Sure, it looks kind of odd, but the programs work. We would not be completely surprised if the two desktop development teams brought their programs even closer together in the next few years; although we're not predicting a merger, we think the line between KDE and Gnome will become fuzzier still.

The major difference between Gnome and KDE is that Gnome is at an earlier stage of development than KDE, which means that some of the Gnome components may still be somewhat unstable or may have spaces in menus for features that haven't been written yet. To get past this problem, we recommend that Gnome users check frequently for updates and bug fixes, and install them as needed. In general, Gnome is usable, and most instabilities should not affect the average user much.

What Is Gnome?

So, what makes Gnome a viable alternative to KDE even though it's younger and less developed? Gnome brings a slick, integrated appearance and an extreme degree of configurability to the Unix desktop. Gnome simply looks great, and appearance is a large part of the reason many people choose integrated desktops over window managers.

Gnome is based on a software library called The GIMP ToolKit (GTK). This library was designed to draw various screen elements, called *widgets,* in an easily modifiable manner. The Gnome team took this concept of *visual plasticity* and extended it throughout the entire desktop system, so that almost every element of Gnome can be configured or modified.

> **TIP**
>
> The GIMP is a Free Software graphics program that is nearly as fully featured as Adobe's PhotoShop or Corel's CorelPAINT and CorelDRAW. If you are interested in graphics manipulation or creation and you're running a Unix-derived operating system, you owe it to yourself to pick up The GIMP. Try the project Web site at `http://www.gimp.org`. You can also find The GIMP on the CD-ROM included with this book.

In addition, Gnome is usually used in tandem with a window manager that also supports individual configuration, such as Enlightenment. Recent releases of Gnome have been issued with the Sawfish window manager, a new program that has been the focus of much recent development by Red Hat. The final result is an integrated desktop that can be controlled by the user in almost every aspect of appearance and function.

Getting and Installing Gnome

Gnome is easy to find and install for almost all Unix-derived operating systems. Linux users should have no problem at all installing Gnome; in fact, it is the default desktop on several major Linux distributions, most significantly Red Hat and Debian. Gnome may be an installation option on other distributions, so check the installation screens carefully. Those people with Linux distributions without Gnome can download either *.rpm (Red Hat package format) or *.deb (Debian package format) files from the Gnome team.

Solaris users who are using Solaris 2.7 on an UltraSparc hardware platform can also download precompiled binary packages of Gnome.

> **WARNING** If you are running Solaris on any other platform than an UltraSparc, you cannot use the precompiled Solaris Gnome packages. You must download and compile the source code.

Users of any other form of Unix (including FreeBSD, Solaris on non-UltraSparc computers, and minimalist Linux distributions) will need to download the source code and compile it. This is not as complicated as it sounds, and we walk you through the process in this chapter.

Downloading Gnome

To download the proper Gnome packages for your computer and operating system, fire up your Web browser and go to http://www.gnome.org/start/installing/. Gnome is a complicated system, and therefore you'll need to download quite a few individual packages that will eventually form the complete Gnome program. At the time of this writing, Gnome 1.2 has just been released, so we base the lists in this section on the 1.2 requirements.

These lists are for the source code download. If you are planning to download the *.rpm, *.deb, or Solaris packages, just follow the directions on the Gnome Web page to download and install the proper versions.

> **WARNING** If Gnome 1.2 is not the current release at the time you are reading this book and installing Gnome, follow the directions on the Gnome Web site to obtain the proper packages.

Base Library Downloads

These are software libraries that Gnome requires to operate at all. Different libraries are required for different components of the desktop, so be sure to download all these packages:

- audiofile-0.1.9.tar.gz
- esound-0.2.18.tar.gz
- glib-1.2.8.tar.gz

- `gtk+-1.2.8.tar.gz`
- `imlib-1.9.8.1.tar.gz`
- `gtk-engines-0.10.tar.gz`
- `ORBit-0.5.1.tar.gz`
- `gnome-libs-1.2.0.tar.gz`
- `libgtop-1.0.9.tar.gz`
- `libxml-1.8.7.tar.gz`
- `libghttp-1.0.6.tar.gz`
- `libglade-0.13.tar.gz`
- `gdk-pixbuf-0.8.0.tar.gz`

Core Application Downloads

These packages are the core of the Gnome system and are the actual software that forms Gnome itself. You will need all four of these:

- `control-center-1.2.0.tar.gz`
- `gnome-core-1.2.0.tar.gz`
- `gnome-applets-1.2.0.tar.gz`
- `mc-4.5.49.tar.gz`

Additional Source Downloads

These packages are optional, but we recommend that you download and install them. They contain most of the programs that make Gnome fun and useful, including audio and multimedia applications, games, and a multitude of utilities:

- `bug-buddy-1.0.tar.gz`
- `glade-0.5.9.tar.gz`
- `gnome-python-1.0.53.tar.gz`
- `users-guide-1.2.tar.gz`
- `gnome-utils-1.2.0.tar.gz`
- `gnome-pim-1.2.0.tar.gz`

- gnome-media-1.2.0.tar.gz
- gnome-audio-1.0.0.tar.gz
- gnome-print-0.20.tar.gz
- gnome-games-1.2.0.tar.gz
- ee-0.3.9.tar.gz
- gnumeric-0.54.tar.gz
- gtop-1.0.9.tar.gz
- ggv-0.95.tar.gz
- gdm-2.0beta4.tar.gz
- xchat-1.2.1.tar.gz

Unpacking the Source Code

Before you unpack anything, create a directory into which you will put the source code files. If you have a directory called /usr/src or /src or something like that (/src is the general shorthand for directories containing source code), create a subdirectory called /usr/src/gnome or one similarly named. Move all the files you just downloaded into that directory.

TIP   If you're reading this before you download, download the files directly into the new subdirectory and save yourself some time.

Each of the files that you downloaded from the Gnome Web site is a *compressed archive file,* which means that each file contains several files that, taken together, make up a unique software program. Before you can compile the packages and make the Gnome program run, you need to unpack the compressed archives. (If you've ever used StuffIt! on a Macintosh or WinZip on a Windows computer, you've used archiving programs designed to mimic the Unix tar program.)

To unpack the packages, move into the subdirectory containing the files you just downloaded. At the shell prompt, issue the command

```
tar xvfz <packagename>
```

where *<packagename>* is the name of one of the packages you have just down-loaded (do not include the angle brackets). For example, one of the packages you'll need to unpack is gnome-core-1.2.0.tar.gz, so you'd issue the command

```
tar xvfz gnome-core-1.2.0.tar.gz
```

As soon as you press the Enter key at the end of the command, you'll see a bunch of filenames scroll up the screen as tar unpacks the archive. These filenames represent the individual files that were compressed into the downloaded file.

When the list stops scrolling, issue the command ls at the command prompt to see a directory listing. You should see a new subdirectory called gnome-core-1.2.0. If you change into that subdirectory, you'll see all the files that were just unpacked. Continue to unpack all the files you downloaded from the Gnome Web site.

TIP

If you downloaded all the files into a single directory or moved them into one after they were downloaded, you can unpack all the files with a single command. Issue the command **tar xvfz *.tar.gz** at the command prompt. The * character is a wild card that refers to *any combination of characters,* so *.tar.gz will match any filename ending in .tar.gz.

Compiling and Installing the Source Code

Once all the packages are unpacked and the various subdirectories have been created, you can begin to install the code itself. This is a reasonably straightforward procedure, which will become repetitive after you've done the first few packages.

WARNING

This section is not meant to be a substitute for reading the documentation that comes with each package, usually found as a README file in each package subdirectory. Anytime you install software, you should read the documentation for the program. Any peculiarities that are involved in installing a particular version of a given package will be explained in these documents.

For each package that you unpacked in the previous step, you will have a corresponding subdirectory bearing the name of that package. Move into one of these subdirectories by issuing the command

```
cd <directoryname>
```

With Gnome, it doesn't matter what order you use to configure the code, though other programs require that you configure certain libraries first. In general, it's a good idea to deal with software libraries before you begin working with programs. That way, if a program requires a particular library to install, the libraries will already be present.

NOTE Some of these required libraries may be ones that aren't part of the Gnome distribution, such as the libraries used by the C or C++ programming languages. If your Gnome compilation fails, it may be that you are missing one or more of the standard C libraries. Look at the error messages generated by the failure for a clue to what the problem might have been.

When you have moved into a subdirectory, issue the command

```
./configure
```

Some messages will scroll up the screen. If all goes well, the last line of these messages will read "Created Makefile" or "Makefile successfully created" or some other message telling you that a Makefile has been built. Once you see that message, type

```
make
```

Again, you'll see a series of cryptic messages. If none of them were error messages (you'll be able to tell error messages from other types of messages), type

```
make install
```

After completing these three steps, you have installed that particular package. Repeat the process for every package you downloaded.

NOTE If you had a problem that resulted in the shut-down of the configuration or installation process, the odds are overwhelming that you're missing a library or required program somewhere. This is why we recommend that you install the libraries first, then the core packages, then the optional packages. Scroll back through the error messages and try to determine what's missing. Find the package containing that element, install it, and then try to reinstall the failed package again.

Configuring X for Gnome

Now that you've unpacked, configured, and installed each downloaded package, you need to let the operating system know that you want to use Gnome as your desktop upon start-up. To do this, you'll have to change the configuration files used by the X Window System so that X knows Gnome is present. This may seem intimidating—and we know that we warned you against monkeying around with X in Chapter 6: "The X Window System: An Overview"—but it's necessary. Just follow the directions to get X set to go.

Check your home directory for the files .Xclients, .xsession, or .xinitrc. If any of these files exists, open it in a text editor to see whether it contains a line similar to

```
exec startkde
```

This line is the automatic key for the KDE desktop. Obviously, you don't want your computer to try starting both KDE and Gnome, because you'd have a traffic jam.

If you find that line in the file, close the text editor. You will need to change the executable bit on that file so that the KDE line does not start KDE automatically. Do this by issuing the command

```
chmod -x <filename>
```

where *<filename>* is the name of the file containing the exec startkde line. Then, restart your X session by pressing Ctrl+Alt+Backspace to kill the current session, then typing **startx** to open a new session. You can also do this by logging out of your current session to the beginning prompt and logging back in again.

If X continues to boot up with a desktop or window manager that isn't Gnome, you'll need to do some configuring. Create the file .xsession in your home directory by issuing the command

```
touch .xsession
```

TIP

The **touch** command is designed to update timestamps carried by each file, which are used by the kernel to determine various allocations. However, you can use **touch** to create new files quickly; simply issue the command **touch** *<newfilename>* to create a new file with the specified name. This is a fast and simple way to add new files without having to open text editors and save buffers.

Open the `.xsession` file in a text editor (see Part V: "Using Text Editors" for more information on these programs). Enter the following line into the file:

```
exec gnome-session
```

Save the file and set the executable bit on it so that your operating system will run the file automatically. Do this by issuing the command

```
chmod +x .xsession
```

Then, restart your X session as described above.

At this point, if everything has gone properly, you should see the Gnome desktop, as shown in Figure 10.1. Obviously, with a procedure that involves this many variables, there are a lot of places where something can go wrong. If you don't see the Gnome desktop, the only thing you can do is to track down the problem and fix it. Use the documentation distributed with each package to guide your search or look through the Gnome Web site at `http://www.gnome.org` for some clues about frequently encountered problems and their solutions. When in deep despair, the final solution is always to download everything again and reinstall, paying close attention to each step of the process as you go.

FIGURE 10.1:

The default Gnome desktop will appear after bootup if you have configured X correctly.

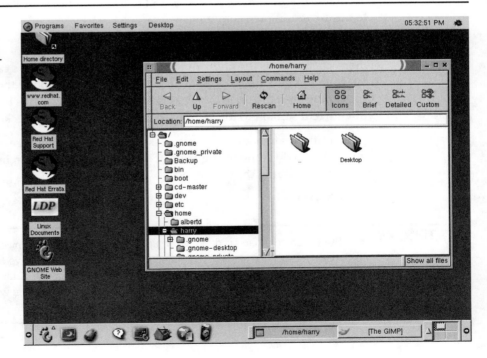

Using Gnome

Now that you have Gnome installed and working, it's time to explore. The Gnome interface centers on the Gnome desktop; we explain its individual components in detail later in this section. The desktop is comprised of a suite of applications, such as a menu system, icons, and so on, that all handle regular account administration tasks with a few simple mouse clicks instead of arcane commands typed at the prompt. Once you've toured the desktop and are familiar with the default appearance of Gnome, you're ready to begin working with the Gnome Control Center, in which you can use Gnome's flexibility to build a unique desktop just for you.

The Gnome Panel

The most important part of the Gnome desktop, from a user's perspective, is the panel, shown in Figure 10.2. Think of the panel as the control box for Gnome, because just about all of Gnome's major functions are controlled from this element. The panel stretches across the bottom of the Gnome screen by default, though you can move it to the left or right side, or across the top, if you wish.

The panel contains the main menu system, any user-defined menus that you might create, application launchers, docked *applets* (small programs that run entirely within the panel), and special items such as a logout button. As with everything else in Gnome, the panel is fully configurable. Not only can you change its location, you can change the buttons and launchers that it contains. You can change the look, behavior, and placement of the panel itself or of its elements; add and remove most of the objects docked into it; or even create multiple panels—each with its own unique look and set of functions.

FIGURE 10.2:

Use the Gnome panel to streamline your regular Unix habits.

The Main Menu

If you've used Windows or Macintosh computers before, you'll find the menus of Gnome (and KDE) to be familiar analogues. The Gnome main menu is accessed from the panel. The button at the furthest left end of the panel has the image of a footprint, which is the Gnome logo; this button launches the main menu (it's like the Windows Start menu).

Click the footprint button to open the main menu. Many of the menu items have sub-menus, indicated by small arrows at the end of the menu entry. If you click one of these entries, another menu will open, and you can navigate through the various sub-menus, as in Figure 10.3, until you find the item you want to select. Table 10.1 shows the default options of the Gnome main menu. Note that if you configure the menu yourself, some of these options may disappear or additional ones may be available.

FIGURE 10.3:

The Gnome main menu is a quick way to launch programs and utilities.

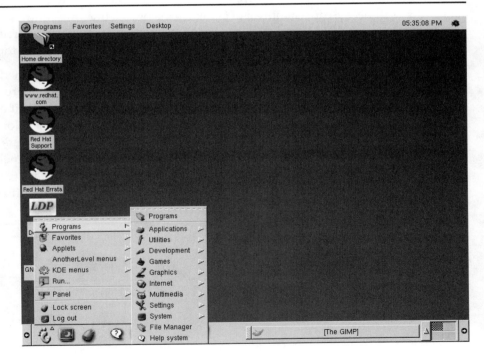

NOTE

Click a main-menu entry, and the menu will stay open until you make a final selection. Each final entry—one without an arrow—represents a particular program that can be launched by selecting that menu item.

TABLE 10.1: Gnome Main-Menu Items

Main Menu	Sub-Menu	Function
Applications	gEdit	A text editor (see Chapter 20)
	Calendar	An electronic appointment book
	Address Book	An electronic address book
	Time Tracking Tool	Tracks time spent on an individual project
	gnotepad+	A minimal text editor
	Gnumeric	A basic spreadsheet
	Gnu Cash	Tracks your bank account balances
	GnomePGP	A graphical interface to PGP and GNUpg encryption packages
	AbiWord Personal	A basic word processor
	Dia	A diagramming tool that uses vector graphics
	Emacs	An advanced text editor (see Chapter 18)
Utilities	Gdict	A searchable dictionary
	Simple Calculator	A simple calculator
	Gnome Character Map	Allows you to use special characters not found on your keyboard
	Color Browser	Helps you find hex values for a particular color
	gfloppy	Formats a floppy diskette
	Font Selector	Organizes installed fonts for easy retrieval
	Gnome Search Tool	Finds a single file rapidly

Continued on next page

TABLE 10.1 CONTINUED: Gnome Main-Menu Items

Main Menu	Sub-Menu	Function
	IDE Device Tool	Manages installed IDE devices (must be used as root)
	Startup Hint	Displays a tip when Gnome is started
Development	Glade	An integrated programming environment
	Memprof	A tool that locates memory leaks
Games	FreeCell	Solitaire on steroids (highly addictive)
	Gnibbles	Battle snakes to the death
	GnobotsII	Robot attack!
	Gnome Stones	Find the diamonds and escape the mine
	Gnome Mines	A logic game
	Gnotravex	A number puzzle
	GTali	A dice game
	gTuring	A Turing machine simulator
	Iagno	Similar to the board game Othello
	Mahjongg	Tile-matching game
	SameGnome	Eliminate colored balls to win points
	Aisle Riot	A solitaire variant
	gataxx	A variation of Iagno
	Glines	A game with colored lines
	Gnotski	A spatial relations puzzle
	Gnome xBill	Stop Bill from installing Windows on every computer in the world
Graphics	Electric Eyes	A basic graphic-tweaking program
	GQview	An organizer for graphics files
	gPhoto	A digital photography program

Continued on next page

TABLE 10.1 CONTINUED: Gnome Main-Menu Items

Main Menu	Sub-Menu	Function
	Eye of Gnome	A graphics viewer
	PostScript File Viewer	A PostScript file viewer
	The GIMP	The GNU Image Manipulation Program (the Cadillac of Free imaging software)
	GNOME Icon Editor	A bitmap editor
Internet	gFTP	A graphical FTP client
	GnomeICU	An ICQ-compatible messaging client
	X-Chat IRC Client	An IRC client
	Gnome Napster	A Napster client
	Gaim	An AIM-compatible (AOL Instant Messenger) client
	Gnapster	Another Napster client
	Netscape	The popular Web browser
	Lynx	A basic text-mode Web browser
	Pan	A USENET newsreader
Multimedia	Extace Waveform Display	A graphical sound analyzer
	Audio Mixer	An interface for your sound card
	CD Player	A basic CD player
	ESD Volume Meter	A graphical volume control and display
	Sound Recorder	Records files with a microphone plugged into your sound card
	grip	Rips *.mp3 files from your CDs
Settings	Gnome Control Center	Starts the Gnome Control Center (see instructions later in this chapter)
	Desktop	Controls desktop appearance
	Multimedia	Controls sound files

Continued on next page

TABLE 10.1 CONTINUED: Gnome Main-Menu Items

Main Menu	Sub-Menu	Function
	Peripherals	Configures peripheral devices
	Session	Controls session properties
	User Interface	Controls various aspects of Gnome's look and feel
	Imlib Configuration Options	Controls certain display properties
	Menu Editor	Customizes menus
	Sawfish Window Manager	Configures Sawfish
	Document Handles	Associates file types with installed programs
System	GnoRPM	A graphical interface to the RPM package manager
	Eterm	A terminal emulator
	Regular Xterm	Another terminal emulator
	Color Xterm	A third terminal emulator
	GNOME Terminal	Yet another terminal emulator
	Gnome DiskFree	Shows disk usage
	System Info	A variety of useful information
	User Listing	Lists system user accounts
	System Log Monitor	Shows process, CPU, and memory logs
File Manager		A graphical file manager
Help System		A help-file browser
Favorites		A user-customizable menu
Applets	Amusements	Fun and games in the panel
	Monitors	CPU load, memory usage, etc.
	Multimedia	CD player, etc.
	Network	Mail monitors and other network tools

Continued on next page

TABLE 10.1 CONTINUED: Gnome Main-Menu Items

Main Menu	Sub-Menu	Function
	Utility	Miscellaneous applets
	Clocks	Time-tellers
Run		A miniature command-line window
Panel	Add to Panel	Adds an item to the panel
	Create Panel	Creates a new panel
	Remove This Panel	Removes a panel
	Properties	Panel properties
	Global Preferences	Controls panel behavior
	Panel Manual	Basic panel documentation
	About the Panel	Shortened informational file
	About Gnome	Gnome documentation
Lock Screen		Screensaver that requires a password
Log Out		Exits Gnome

Application Launchers

Launchers are panel objects that launch a particular program when clicked. For example, you might have a panel launcher that bears the Netscape logo. Start Netscape just by clicking the launcher, rather than using the menu system or issuing a command from a shell prompt. Launchers are extremely useful for programs that you use all the time, because saving just a few mouse clicks or keystrokes each time will add up over the day or month. Add a launcher to the panel with this process:

1. Click the Gnome logo button to launch the main menu.

2. Find the entry for the desired program in the menu.

3. Click the menu item, but don't release the mouse button.

4. Drag the item over the panel and release the mouse button.

5.   A new generic launcher will appear.

6.   Right-click the new launcher.

7.   Select Launcher Properties from the pop-up menu that appears.

8.   In the Launcher Properties window, seen in Figure 10.4, you can set various properties for this launcher, including the icon that will appear in the panel and the specific command that Gnome issues to start the program (especially useful if you want particular flags to be used when the program is started).

9.   Set the properties you wish to use.

10. Click OK.

The Launcher Properties window closes, and the new settings are applied to the new launcher. You can now use the panel icon to start the associated program.

FIGURE 10.4:

Configure a new launcher button with the Launcher Properties window.

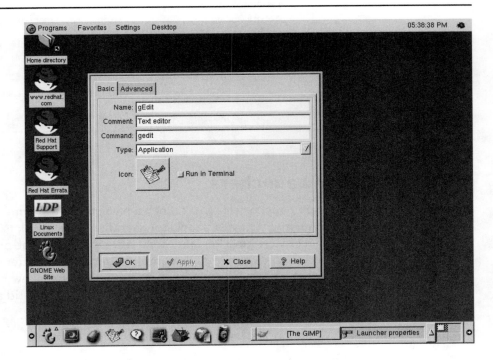

Applets

Applets are small programs that run entirely inside the panel. For example, you may have a clock applet that sits in the panel and always displays the current time. Another popular applet changes to indicate that you've received e-mail. There are even applets that control your CD player or tell you the weather conditions outside. Applets are a convenient source of information, as well as a good way to handle certain low-level functions. Just be careful—it's easy to load up your panel with so many neat applets that there isn't room for anything else.

Applets can be added to the panel in one of two ways. The first way is to right-click a blank area of the panel and select Panel ➤ Add to Panel ➤ Applet ➤ *<category>* ➤ *<applet>*, replacing the last two elements with the actual applet category and applet name from the sub-menus. The other way is to select Applets ➤ *<category>* ➤ *<applet>* from the main menu; this option will dock the applet into the first available space in the panel.

Once you've gotten a new applet into the panel, right-click it and select Properties from the pop-up menu. Most applets can be configured in their Properties screen, though this is not an option for all applets. To move the applet, right-click it and select Move from the pop-up menu; you can then slide the applet from right to left in the panel until you find the proper location. To set the applet's new location, click it once.

The File Manager

If you've used the Windows Explorer in Windows 95 or 98, or similar programs in other operating systems, you already have a basic idea of how the Gnome File Manager works. The File Manager is a graphical representation of the computer's filesystem, showing directories as file folders and individual files with an icon representing their file type. Start the File Manager by selecting its entry from the main menu.

TIP

We suggest that you put a launcher into the panel for the File Manager. It's a useful tool and one you'll probably use frequently.

When you start the File Manager, it will open as a two-paned screen, seen in Figure 10.5. In the left pane, you will see a directory tree. By default, your home directory is displayed at start-up. In the right pane, you'll see a list of all subdirectories and files contained in that directory. If a directory folder in either pane contains subdirectories, a small plus (+) sign will be shown to the left of its entry. Click the plus sign to expand the directory tree, showing the subdirectory folders and files as well; an expanded view is shown in Figure 10.6. The plus sign will also change to a minus (–) sign; if the minus sign is clicked, the directory tree will collapse back to the short view.

FIGURE 10.5:

The Gnome File Manager uses a two-paned screen to display the computer's directories.

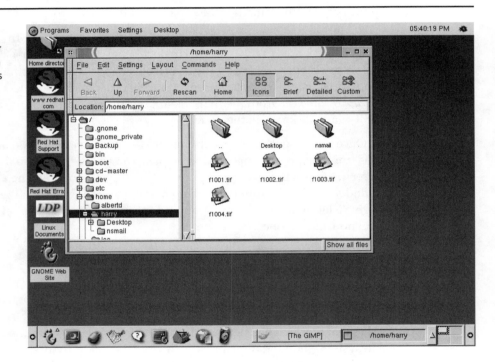

You can move files between directories by clicking and dragging them to the new directory. Further file manipulations can be achieved by right-clicking the filename and selecting an option from the pop-up menu. Options include Delete, Copy, Rename, and so on.

FIGURE 10.6:

The File Manager's expanded view lets you see all the files in all directories on the disk.

The Gnome Control Center

The Gnome Control Center is a one-stop shopping center for all the Gnome configuration options. The Control Center, seen in Figure 10.7, can be accessed by selecting Settings ➤ Gnome Control Center from the main menu. Once the Center is open, you can use it to set your selections for various categories of configuration, which are described in Table 10.2.

FIGURE 10.7:

Configure Gnome to your liking with the Control Center.

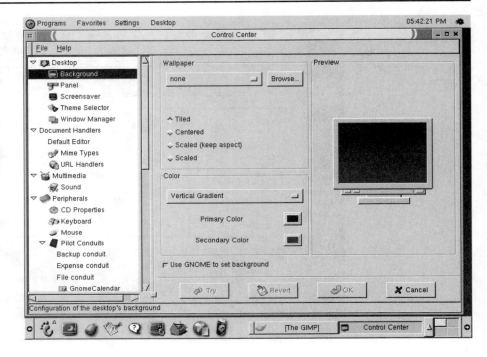

TABLE 10.2: Gnome Control Center Categories

Category	Function
Desktop	Options to control the look and feel of the desktop
Document Handlers	Options to associate various file types with particular programs
Multimedia	Options to control system sounds
Peripherals	Options to control various peripheral devices such as the CD-ROM drive, the keyboard, or a portable computer such as a Palm Pilot
Sawfish Window Manager	Configuration manager for the window manager
Session	Controls options that execute upon login
User Interface	Controls the behavior of dialogs and menus

The astute reader will have noticed that the categories shown in Table 10.2 are the same as those under the Settings sub-menu in the main Gnome menu. If you select an option from the main menu, the control module for that option will run independently of the Gnome Control Center. These methods have the same end result, but with the Control Center, you can make multiple changes to the user environment without having to open multiple modules. (More precisely, when you open the Control Center, all the modules open at the same time.) As a rule, the Control Center is best for a full-scale reconfiguration of Gnome, while the individual modules are best for making a quick tweak to a single aspect of the integrated desktop.

Themes and the Desktop

One nice feature of the Gnome desktop is the ability to apply *themes,* collections of graphical elements that give the various aspects of the desktop a consistent look. The default theme is shown in the first image of this chapter, Figure 10.1. The GTK library, which is responsible for drawing the screen widgets, leaves options open for other programs to alter the look and behavior of those widgets.

Many Gnome users have risen to the challenge and created a multitude of themes (archived at `http://gtk.themes.org`) that can be downloaded and installed. These themes range from the very basic to the beautiful, and include several that are downright painful to look at. (We think this was intentional, but with user-created art, we're just never sure.)

A set of stock themes is included with the basic Gnome distribution. Access these by using the Gnome Control Center. Open the Control Center by selecting Programs ➢ Settings ➢ Gnome Control Center from the main menu; under the Desktop category, click Theme Selector. The Theme Selector appears, as shown in Figure 10.8. The top pane of the Theme Selector window, labeled Available Themes, contains the names of all the themes that are currently installed on your system.

FIGURE 10.8:

Use the Theme Selector to
change the look of your
Gnome desktop.

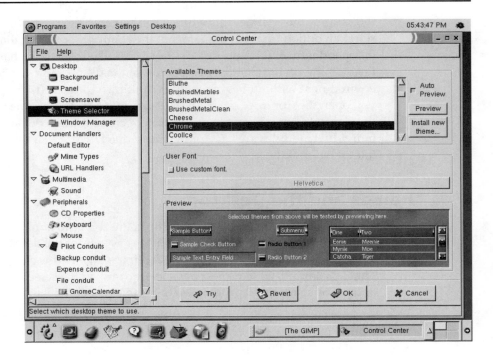

If you want to check out some new themes, scroll through that list and find the
name of one that sounds intriguing to you. Click the name to highlight it, and the
various widgets in the Preview pane will change to show you what that theme
looks like. If that theme is something you'd like to see on your desktop, click the
Try button.

TIP   It's our experience that themes often don't look as good on your actual desktop as
they might in the Preview window. If you decide that you don't like the theme you
have just selected, click the button marked Revert, and you will be returned to the
previous theme.

Once you've decided on a theme, click OK to close the Theme Selector and
make the desktop change permanent. You can go back and change themes at any
time. If you download themes from various Web archives, make sure to download them into the directory that holds the default Gnome themes. This will make

it possible for Theme Selector to pick up the new themes that you got from the Web or other users.

> **TIP**
>
> The right desktop background goes a long way toward making a theme look right. If you find a theme that you like, but that doesn't quite seem to work, click the Background option in the Gnome Control Center and try out some different colors. Often, finding the right background color can really pull the desktop together.

Summary

The Gnome integrated desktop environment is a Free Software graphical user interface that can be installed on a variety of Unices and Unix-derived operating systems. You can download Gnome packages for some Unix-derived systems or install the software from source code. Once the code is installed, you will need to configure the X Window System to recognize Gnome and start it automatically.

The Gnome interface centers on the desktop. The desktop is comprised of a background, various icons, a menu system, and a panel containing application launchers and applets. Every element of Gnome is configurable, so you can tinker with it until it meets your standards. You can also use a configuration shortcut by installing one of the many graphical themes available for download; these themes provide new icons, panel items, and backgrounds centered on a unified concept or image. No matter how you configure Gnome, you will be able to take advantage of its full integration and ease of use.

PART IV

Using the Shell

CHAPTER
ELEVEN

Introduction to the Bourne (Again) Shell

- Why Bourne Shell?

- Some Common Shell Commands

- Summary

This part of the book, Part IV: "Using the Shell," covers the command shell that you use to interact with the kernel—and, by default, with the computer itself. In the chapters that make up Part IV, we focus on the Bourne Shell, because it is the shell most likely to be installed as the default on any Unix account you might have. Although we are nominally writing about the Bourne Shell as our standard for these chapters, almost all of what we say will also apply to the Bourne Again Shell (bash). As we move into chapters on shell programming, we focus on the bash shell.

We can't guarantee, of course, that you'll have the Bourne Shell as your default shell. The default is determined by the system administrator, and it is entirely possible that the administrator has chosen the C Shell, the Korn Shell, or some other shell to be the default. Type echo $SHELL at a command prompt to see what shell you're using. If you are in the Bourne Shell, echo will print sh to the screen; if you're in the bash shell, echo will print bash to the screen. If you get any other answers, you have three choices:

- Ask your administrator to change your default shell.

- Consult Chapter 13: "Customizing the Shell Environment" to change the default shell yourself.

- Start the preferred shell manually.

TIP   To start the Bourne Shell manually, type **sh** at the shell prompt. This will move you into the Bourne Shell; you should get some sort of Bourne Shell prompt that looks different from your default prompt. When you are done using the Bourne Shell, type **exit**, and you will be returned to your original shell. You can configure your user environment to use the Bourne Shell or the bash shell if you prefer; see Chapter 13 for more information on setting environment variables.

Figure 11.1 shows the difference in prompts between the tcsh shell and the Bourne Shell, to give you an idea of what to look for.

Why Bourne Shell?

Why have we chosen to go into detail on the Bourne Shell and not some other shell? We've chosen Bourne because it is the de facto standard for shell environments. In the three Unices we describe in this book, the Bourne Shell is the default shell for FreeBSD and Solaris; with Linux, the default environment is the bash shell, which is essentially the same thing for most practical uses. The odds, therefore, are greatly stacked in favor of your having the Bourne Shell available on your system, if not already installed as the default shell environment.

FIGURE 11.1:

Different shells produce subtle differences at the command prompt.

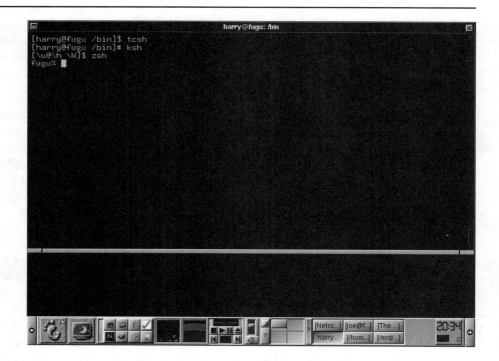

The fact that the Bourne Shell is the general standard shell environment has other implications, as well. The vast majority of *systems programming* (that is, the writing of programs that configure the operation of the system itself) is done with the Bourne Shell. Thus, to understand the fundamental operations of a Unix system, it's quite important to have a good grasp of Bourne Shell commands and scripting. Even if you choose to use another shell for your daily environment, you'll still need some familiarity with Bourne or bash and their various functions.

TIP   If you decide that you really dislike Bourne or bash, see Chapter 15: "Other Shells." We describe some of the common Unix shells that many people use instead of Bourne or bash, including ksh, csh, tcsh, and zsh. We also provide some information on newer shells that haven't quite become as popular as those listed above.

Bourne Shell vs. Bourne Again Shell

In the opening paragraphs of this chapter, we mentioned the bash shell and said that, for most practical purposes, it was much the same as the Bourne Shell. If that's true, why are there two different shells? The Bourne Again Shell was written as part of the GNU project. It was originally intended to be a Free Software clone of the Bourne Shell, but the developers added a few twists as they worked on the new shell.

For most practical purposes, sh (the Bourne Shell) and bash are identical; there are, however, a few important differences. bash features include the ability to move the cursor around the command line with key combinations derived from GNU Emacs; the ability to remember previous commands and browse the command history; and the ability to recognize file and directory names from a few characters and then to complete the name by using the Tab key. bash also has a few features that affect the writing of scripts.

We've used a variety of shell environments over the years, but we really like bash. Because we think it's a good all-around shell, we use bash for examples throughout this book. We do, however, attempt to avoid bash-isms, so the examples that we give should work on the regular Bourne Shell as well. In fact, they're probably worth trying in other shells. The only place where we've written something that truly depends on bash is in Part VI: "Shell Programming," where we use bash programming conventions. You may also notice some differences with shell environment variables or the way in which particular shells handle output, but these differences should be minor.

As with anything Unix-related, there may be differences in your user environment depending on what version of a particular program or shell you're running and how it is configured on your system. Most of the things in this section, as well as throughout the book, should work regardless of versions or shells (unless you're running truly dinosaur Unix); if something doesn't work the way we indicate that it should, consult with your system administrator to see whether there is some idiosyncrasy that you need to be aware of.

Some Common Shell Commands

If you read Part II: "Getting Started," you've already learned a few commonly used *shell commands:* ls, pwd, passwd, cd, and others. In this section of the chapter, we review these commands, and a few others, more closely. We show you what each command does and how to expand the command's function with various options and flags. We also provide a few examples of how these commands are used in practice.

NOTE   The term *shell command* is something of a misnomer. Most of the commands we're about to discuss are their own individual programs, and the program file for each can usually be found in the /bin directory. Most of these are not functions that are built into the shell. They are called shell commands because they are run from the shell.

Although these are some of the most basic shell commands, we provide a plethora of commands in Appendix A: "A Unix Command Reference." If you're interested in what the programmers themselves have to say about their commands and programs, type man command at a shell prompt; that is, for the ls command, you'd type man ls. This brings up the *man page,* a document stored on the system that is the official way to run the program, as written by the developer. Some man pages are very clear and easy to understand, while others are quite confusing. However, man pages are the best resource if you're looking for a complete listing of command options.

TIP   Interested in shell commands beyond what we've provided here or in Appendix A? You might need an encyclopedic command reference. We get a lot of use from *The Unix and X Command Compendium,* by Alan Southerton and Edwin C. Perkins, Jr. (John Wiley & Sons, 1994).

Before you jump into these command descriptions, here is a quick set of vocabulary terms that are used to discuss shell commands:

Syntax: The way in which a command is issued, or typed, at the shell prompt.

Flags: The various options that can be appended to a command to get more precise output. Flags are usually preceded by a hyphen, such as –a, but some commands do not use hyphens for flags.

Output: The result of the command. Most commands will print output to the monitor, but for some commands, you'll have to request the output.

Argument: Any additional components issued with the command that will modify the basic command behavior. For example, a flag is an argument. Arguments must be given following the command's syntax.

Arguments and syntax are case sensitive.

ls

ls is the command that generates a list of files. No matter how you plan to use Unix, ls is one of the commands that you'll use most frequently. Whether you're looking for a file or simply browsing directories, ls is a reliable companion.

If you just type **ls** at a command prompt with no other options, it lists the contents of the current directory. Here is an example of the ls command being run in the directory that Joe was using to make the notes for this book:

```
[joe@fugu Mast-Unix]$ ls
ch01-notes.txt   ch03-notes.wpd   ch05-notes.wpd   ch12-notes.wpd
test.wpd         ch02-notes.wpd   ch04-notes.wpd   ch06-notes.wpd
test.html
```

Filenames are printed to the screen; usually they print in alphabetical and numerical order. This is the simplest way to list a directory.

NOTE On some systems, the names of subdirectories will have a slash (/) after them, such as Mail/, and the names of executable programs will have an @ character after them, such as emacs@. We show you below how to make this happen if it's not set by default on your system.

If you want to find out more about the files listed by ls, you can do a long-form listing by using the -l flag:

```
[joe@fugu Mast-Unix]$ ls -l
total 156
-rw-rw-r- 1 joe  joe     11558 Mar 14 09:59 ch01-notes.txt
-rw-rw-r- 1 joe  joe     18419 Mar 24 16:41 ch02-notes.wpd
-rw-rw-r- 1 joe  joe     16655 Mar 25 10:14 ch03-notes.wpd
-rw-rw-r- 1 joe  joe     20608 Mar 27 13:28 ch04-notes.wpd
-rw-rw-r- 1 joe  joe     20468 Mar 27 18:00 ch05-notes.wpd
-rw-rw-r- 1 joe  joe     13774 Mar 28 12:10 ch06-notes.wpd
-rw-rw-r- 1 joe  joe      8003 Mar 29 11:41 ch12-notes.wpd
-rw-rw-r- 1 joe  joe     15078 Mar 17 11:59 test.html
-rw-rw-r- 1 joe  joe     18118 Mar 17 11:58 test.wpd
```

This output may seem a little arcane, but it actually tells you a good deal about each file.

The first entry for each file looks like this:

```
-rw-rw-r-
```

This entry shows that this is a normal file and not a directory. If it were a directory, the first character would be a *d* instead of an *r*. The entry also shows the *file permissions*. That is, it explains who is allowed to have access to the file and for what purpose. We cover file permissions in detail in Chapter 12: "Manipulating Files and Directories."

The second entry, the 1, tells you how many files are *symbolically linked* to the file; a symbolic link is a way of associating more than one filename with a single file. Unless you've created a link intentionally, most normal files should have only one filename linked to them. However, it is not uncommon to see higher numbers on entries for directories, because symbolic linking is also used to associate subdirectories with their parents.

The third and fourth entries show you the user and group that own the files. In this example, each file is owned by user joe and group joe; because user joe is the only member of group joe, it amounts to the same thing. User and group ownership are attributes that are used to determine file permissions. As the owner of the files, Joe will have the right to determine who has access to them except for the superuser, who has access to everything. We explain user space in Chapter 29: "Managing Users and Groups."

The fifth entry tells you the size, in bytes, of each file. This is the amount of space the file takes up in memory or on a disk. The sixth and seventh entries show the date and time the file was last accessed. Finally, the eighth entry is the filename.

There are other flags for ls as well:

- -d lists only directory entries.

- -h lists the file size in human-readable format: e.g., 23M or 15k (works only in combination with the -l flag described below).

- -a lists all files, including hidden files.

- -F shows a character that indicates the type of file: that is, / for a directory or @ for an executable program.

TIP You can combine flags to get multiple types of output in the same printing. To do so, group them together after a single dash, as in ls -lh. This example will issue the -l flag and the -h flag at the same time.

Besides using it with flags, ls can be used on a different directory, other than the current one you're in. To do so, issue the name of the desired directory as an argument. Thus, the command ls -l /etc/rc.d/init.d will give you a long-form listing of the /etc/rc.d/init.d directory.

pwd

The pwd command outputs the full path name of the working (current) directory. It's a very simple command and has no interesting options.

cd

The cd command allows you to move into a new directory. It takes the name of the desired directory as an argument. For example, cd /etc/rc.d changes the current directory to /etc/rc.d.

If no argument is given, cd takes you directly to your home directory. This can be quite useful if you've somehow gotten lost in the filesystem. Arguments can be given either as absolute (e.g., /usr/local/bin) or as relative paths from the current directory (e.g., local/bin if the current directory is /usr). cd has no flags or other options.

mv

The mv command allows you to move a file or subdirectory from one directory to another. It takes the name of a source file or directory and a target file or directory as arguments. For example, the command mv /etc/foo /home/joe moves the file named foo from the /etc directory to the /home/joe directory. If foo is a directory rather than a file, all files and subdirectories contained in foo will be moved as well.

mv can also be used to rename files. If you have a file named foo in the current directory and want to change its name to bar, simply issue the command mv foo bar.

mv has several flags:

* -b makes a backup copy before moving the file.

* -i causes mv to prompt the user before overwriting a file (in case the target filename already exists).

* -v gives *verbose* output; that is, the command explains what's being done as it does it.

cp

The cp command copies a file from one directory to another. Suppose that you have a file named /home/harry/foo, and you want to make a copy in the /tmp directory for someone else to look at. You just have to give the command cp /home/harry/foo /tmp. Once the command has executed, there will be both the original /home/harry/foo file and a new file in the /tmp directory called /tmp/foo.

cp has several flags:

* -b makes backup copies of each file copied.

* -f causes cp to overwrite any files with the same name as the destination file without prompting the user. *Use with caution.*

* -i is the opposite of -f. If a file with the same name as the target exists, -i causes cp to alert the user and prompt for confirmation before taking any action.

- -v causes cp to operate in *verbose* mode, meaning that the command will produce more output than usual. The additional output explains what the process is doing while it's working.

cat

The cat command outputs the contents of a file, with the desired file's name given as an argument. The syntax of cat is cat *filename*. Use the -n flag to cause each line to be numbered. Sample cat output, the first without the −n flag and the second with −n, is shown in Figure 11.2.

more and less

The more and less commands both do the same thing, only in slightly different ways. Each command outputs the contents of a file one page at time. The syntax is the same for both commands: more *filename* or less *filename*.

FIGURE 11.2:

See the contents of a file with the cat command and add optional line numbers.

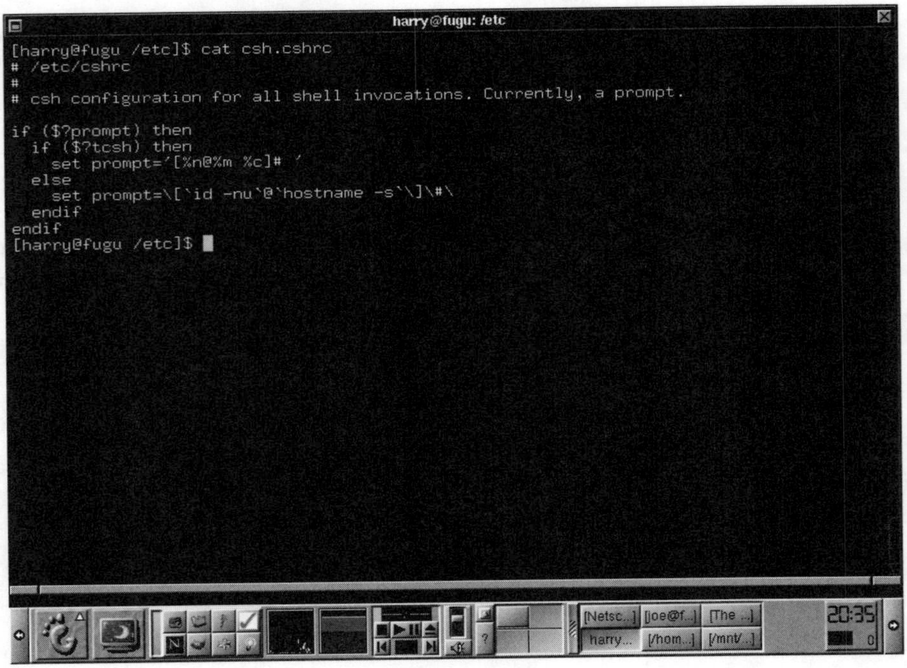

```
harry@fugu: /etc
[harry@fugu /etc]$ cat csh.cshrc
# /etc/cshrc
#
# csh configuration for all shell invocations. Currently, a prompt.

if ($?prompt) then
  if ($?tcsh) then
    set prompt='[%n@%m %c]# '
  else
    set prompt=\[`id -nu`@`hostname -s`\]\#\
  endif
endif
[harry@fugu /etc]$ 
```

Why use this instead of cat? If a file is longer than one screen, reading it with cat can be impractical. more and less make long files more manageable. Reading a file with more or less makes the output stop after one page (screenful). To advance to the next page, press the spacebar. To go back a page, press the *b* key.

There are many differences between the two programs, but they are identical in these basic functions, and most people will never use the advanced functions of either program. Which one you use is a matter of preference. Read the manual pages (man more and man less) to get a full rundown of each.

echo

The echo command prints out whatever is given to it as an argument. For example, if you give the command echo hello, you will see hello print to your screen. echo is primarily useful for providing output in shell programs and printing out the values of variables; we'll discuss these topics in later chapters. You've used echo to determine the shell environment you're using, by typing echo $SHELL.

grep

grep is a program that searches for a particular pattern of characters in a file and prints the lines that contain that pattern. The syntax is grep [pattern] [file(s)].

The pattern can be a simple word or a complex *regular expression.* A regular expression is a pattern wherein certain special characters can represent more than one character. By using groupings of these special characters, it is possible to create conditions that will match certain types of character strings, even though certain characters within the strings may differ.

For example, the ? character can represent any single character, while the * character can represent any combination of zero or more characters. In other words, * matches everything. Here are some of the most commonly used special characters:

- * matches everything (any combination of zero or more characters). An example is St*; grep would match any string that began with the *St* characters, regardless of what followed.

- ? matches any single character.

- ^ matches the beginning of a line. That is, ^more matches the word *more* only if it appears at the beginning of a line.

- $ matches the end of a line. That is, more$ matches the word *more* only if it appears at the end of a line.

We will talk more about regular expressions in Part VI of this book, because they can be used quite effectively in shell programming.

Summary

To use the Unix kernel, you need to use a command shell to interpret your commands for the kernel so that it can perform the tasks you want to do. In this book, we focus on the Bourne Shell, known as sh, and the Bourne Again Shell, known as bash. There are other shells available, and we describe them later in Chapter 15.

Although there are thousands of shell commands, each executing a different program or function, most Unix users have a core command vocabulary of far fewer commands. Some of the most frequently used commands are listed in this chapter, including mv, cp, ls, grep, and more. Even more commands are contained in Appendix A. You don't need to memorize every command you'll ever see; keep a few commonly used commands in your mind and use a reference for the rest.

CHAPTER
TWELVE

Manipulating Files and Directories

- Creating and Editing Files

- Copying Files

- Moving Files

- File Ownership and Permissions

- Deleting Files

- Managing Directories

- Summary

In Chapter 11: "Introduction to the Bourne (Again) Shell," we talked briefly about some of the commands that can be used to manipulate files and directories. We discussed basic tasks, such as changing directories and copying, moving, and renaming files. In this chapter, we expand on that discussion. We show you how files are created and edited, and how to deal with file permissions and ownership.

TIP   File management is a subject you'll want to spend some time getting to understand. Manipulating files and directories is at the very heart of using Unix, especially if you're planning to use Unix as an administrator. Many, if not most, of the problems you'll face will be file-access problems.

If you're new to Unix, you may find this topic a little overwhelming. The concepts of file ownership and file permissions are not ones found in personal operating systems, such as Windows or MacOS. Remember, though, that Unix was designed to be a multiuser system, and these features are essential to the security of systems that could have dozens, or even hundreds, of users logged in at any given time.

Creating and Editing Files

As we've said repeatedly, everything in Unix is considered to be a file. Files can represent system hardware components, programs, or data collected by a program. Files that you create when you use a program, such as word processor or graphic files, use the same kind of organization as do the other types. It's likely that you'll start creating files almost as soon as you log into your first Unix account.

TIP   If you find that you keep referring to the same pages of this book for help, or if you need to write down a particular sequence of events so that you can execute a certain process, we recommend that you enter that data into a file in your user directory. That way, you can call up the file and see the work sequence on the screen as you type—far easier than trying to remember a complicated sequence.

Files can be created in a number of different ways. They can be created intentionally by using an editor, they can be created as a byproduct of other operations, they can be downloaded from a network, or they can be created as copies of other files. For most practical purposes, the most common way of creating a file is by using an editor.

There is a plethora of text editors available for Unix. The most common are vi and GNU Emacs, which are *text-mode editors*. Text-mode editors are those designed to run in text mode and not under X Windows. There are also *graphical editors*, such as NEdit, xedit, and others, that are designed to take advantage of graphical mode. There is even a version of GNU Emacs that has been altered to run in graphical mode, though we're not quite sure whether that's a benefit or a drawback. As if that weren't a broad enough array, there are also noninteractive editors, such as sed and awk, that can be used in script programming. Figure 12.1 shows a document in progress using the GNU Emacs text-mode editor, and Figure 12.2 shows a document in progress using the NEdit graphical editor.

We cover some of the most common editors in detail in Part V: "Using Text Editors." For now, you can think of these editors as stripped-down word processors. Although they contain a lot of text-editing functions, they don't contain any of the

FIGURE 12.1:

For the fastest work pace, use a text-mode editor for your text files.

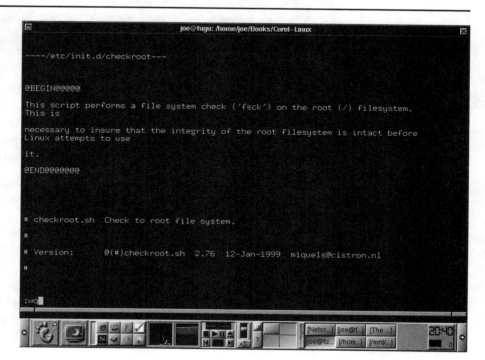

FIGURE 12.2:

If you prefer to use the mouse while you write, you might prefer a graphical editor.

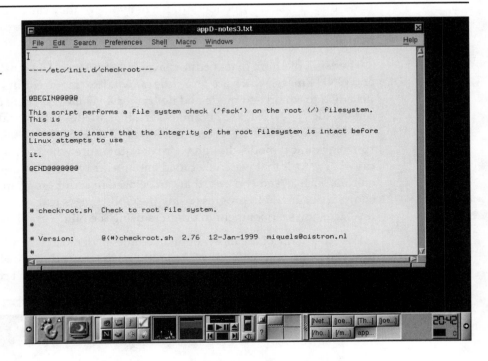

advanced formatting or publishing features that you would find in a word processor such as WordPerfect or FrameMaker. Creating files with the editors we describe here is a simple matter of running the editor, typing and editing the file, and then saving it under a particular filename. Once saved, the file will persist until it is altered (again, by using an editor or as a byproduct of a program) or deleted.

> **TIP**
>
> WordPerfect and FrameMaker are now both available for the Linux platform and may be ported to other Unices by the time you read this. Even though we think full-featured word processors are indispensable, we use text editors for system administration tasks and save the processors for letters and other documents that need to be formatted.

One other way of creating files is to use the `touch` command. This command is used to update the *timestamp* of a file, which shows the date and time that a file was last accessed. However, `touch` has the useful side effect of creating a new file if the file specified in the command doesn't exist. Thus, the command `touch myfile` creates an empty file named `myfile`. This method of creating files is most commonly used in programming, but it can be quite useful when you need to make a file quickly, but don't feel like firing up a text or graphical editor.

Copying Files

As we explained in Chapter 11, files are copied using the `cp` command. For example, the command

```
cp original copy
```

makes a copy of the file named `original` and names the new file `copy`.

> **NOTE** You can copy only files that you have permission for. If the file is not yours, it will need to have either world or group permissions set so that you can access it for copying purposes.

Use `cp` to place multiple copies of files in multiple directories, as well. If, for example, you have a Web page in your home directory's WWW subdirectory and want to place a copy of that page into a shared directory so that others can see it, you might issue the command

```
cp WWW/recipes/soups.html shared/recipes/SusieSoups.html
```

With this command, you have placed a copy of the page into the `shared` directory's `recipes` subdirectory. Note that you have also changed the name of the copied file, from plain old `soups.html` to `SusieSoups.html`. If you don't want to change the name of the file, you can simply issue the command

```
cp WWW/recipes/soups.html shared/recipes/
```

The file will appear in the `shared/recipes` directory as `soups.html`.

Moving Files

Moving files is as simple as copying them; the only difference is that when you move a file, a copy does not remain in the original directory location. To move a file, use the mv command with the syntax mv *filename newlocation*. For example, the command

    mv /dir1/snacks /dir2

will move the file named snacks from the /dir1 directory to the /dir2 directory. You can move files from any directory to any other directory, regardless of the directory that you're in at the moment. Simply put the full path names of the file and the destination into the command, as in

    mv WWW/recipes/snacks.txt /tmp/storage/snacks.txt

You can also issue the mv command with a full path name, but no destination, as in mv /dir1/snacks. This will move the file into the current directory.

If you do not specify directories but use filenames alone, you can use mv to change the name of a file. Thus, the command

    mv soup nuts

will change the file's name from soup to nuts.

A Note on Naming Files

Unix gives you a lot of freedom in choosing the names of your files. However, there are certain rules you need to follow for Unix to handle the filenames correctly; not following these rules may cause trouble when you try to work with the files.

- Filenames can be built from any combination of letters or numbers as well as the characters - (hyphen), _ (underscore), or . (period). A period is usually called a *dot* in Unix parlance.

- As a rule, the first character of a filename should be a letter or a number. A dot at the start of a filename has special significance to the operating system, and dot files are usually not displayed with a regular ls command. Other characters should not be used in the first character position at all, because Unix doesn't parse them well.

- Try to keep your filenames to 14 characters or less. This rule is not absolute, because the precise number varies from system to system, but some older systems will not recognize anything beyond 14 characters. It's best to keep it on the safe side.

- Make your filenames descriptive. This is not a technical requirement but rather a suggestion that will keep you happy in the long run. When your home directory becomes filled with files—and it will—you'll have a much easier time finding a particular file if it is named descriptively. JonesLetter is much better than letter1, letter2, and so on.

File Ownership and Permissions

Because there is potential for a number of users on a single Unix computer, the operating system has a structured way of handling files so that they can be kept private or public, as necessary. In the Unix world, each file is owned by someone, whether it's the person who created it or someone who was given control of the file. Each file also has a set of *file permissions* attached to it; these permissions determine who can read or edit the file. If the file is a program, the permissions determine whether a given user can actually run the program.

Who Owns the File?

Every file has an owner. The owner of the file is usually the user who created or downloaded the file, or otherwise caused the file to be on the system. (There are exceptions to this, but as a rule, it's true.) The owner of any particular file can be seen in the output of the `ls -l` command:

```
[joe@fugu Mast-Unix]$ ls -l
total 188
-rw-rw-r-- 1 joe    joe      11558 Mar 14 09:59 ch01-notes.txt
-rw-rw-r-- 1 joe    joe      18419 Mar 24 16:41 ch02-notes.wpd
-rw-rw-r-- 1 joe    joe      16655 Mar 25 10:14 ch03-notes.wpd
-rw-rw-r-- 1 joe    joe      20608 Mar 27 13:28 ch04-notes.wpd
-rw-rw-r-- 1 joe    joe      20468 Mar 27 18:00 ch05-notes.wpd
-rw-rw-r-- 1 joe    joe      13774 Mar 28 12:10 ch06-notes.wpd
-rw-rw-r-- 1 joe    joe      24816 Mar 30 11:31 ch12-notes.wpd
-rw-rw-r-- 1 joe    joe       9517 Apr  2 10:48 ch14-notes.wpd
-rw-rw-r-- 1 joe    joe      15078 Mar 17 11:59 test.html
-rw-rw-r-- 1 joe    joe      18118 Mar 17 11:58 test.wpd
```

The third column of this output shows the user ID of each file's owner. The fourth column shows the group ID of the file's owner; we talk more about groups in Chapter 29: "Managing Users and Groups." Groups are a way for a system administrator to organize users into groups who may need particular file-access privileges or other group-specific settings. For now, you simply need to be aware that groups exist and that users can be assigned to groups.

Ownership of a file is changed with the chown command. The syntax of chown is straightforward:

```
chown user filename
```

In this command, *user* is the name of the file's new owner, and *filename* is the name of the file. Only the current owner of a file or the superuser can change a file's ownership. Why do you care who owns a particular file? Ownership of files is important, because it is a file's owner who has the sole right to set the permissions on a file.

Who Can See the File?

A file's set of permissions is a symbolic description of the level of access that a particular class of users can have to that file. This description is shown by the rather arcane-looking 10-character string in the first column of the `ls -l` output:

```
-rw-rw-r-
```

The first character in this statement indicates the type of file:

- **-:** Ordinary file

- **b:** Block device; disk drives and the like

- **c:** Character device; keyboards, modems, etc.

- **d:** Directory

- **l:** Link; a file that points to another file

- **p:** Named pipe; programming tool

The next nine characters are the permissions proper. They can be broken down into three groups of three. The first, or leftmost, group represents the owner of the file. The second class represents the file's group. Every member of the group that owns the file (shown in the fourth column of the `ls -l` output) falls into this class. The final, rightmost, class is the class of all users on the system.

For each class, you can define three levels of access, denoted by the letters `r`, `w`, and `x`. These stand for read, write, and execute. A user who has only read permission to a given file may access that file for reading, with a command such as `more` or `less`, but may not alter the file in any way. If the file is a program, a user with read permission only may not run it.

Look again at the example:

```
-rw-rw-r-
```

Now that you have read the material above, you can see that this is an ordinary file. The file's owner has read and write permission, as do the members of the file's group. All other users have read permission only.

Permissions are set using the chmod command. This is a very unintuitive name for this command, so the best thing to do is simply commit it to memory. The chmod command syntax works like this:

```
chmod [class(es)] [+ or -] [permissions] [filename]
```

Classes are u for the file's owner (user), g for the group, and a for all users. Permissions are r for read, w for write, and x for execute. Permissions are granted using the plus sign (+) and revoked using the minus sign (–).

So, if a user wanted to grant read and write access to all users for the file soups, she would issue the command

```
chmod a+rw soups
```

Later, if she wanted to revoke write privileges, she could issue the command

```
chmod a-w soups
```

NOTE   Permissions can also be set using an octal (base 8) number instead of the symbol system described above. We find the octal system to be quite cumbersome and difficult to remember, but some folks really like doing their file permissions in octal. If you are interested in this system, read the manual page for chmod (type man chmod at the shell prompt).

Mastery of the chmod command does take a little practice, but file permissions are an important part of system security, and we recommend that you take the time to learn to manage them. It will pay off in the long run.

Deleting Files

To keep your filesystem clean and neat, you should junk old files that you don't use any more. Files are deleted with the rm (remove) command. The syntax is simple:

```
rm filename
```

In this command, *filename* is the name of the file to be deleted. Only a file's owner may delete it.

You can also use *wildcard* symbols to speed up file deletion if you have a number of files with the same file type or initial characters. If you type rm *.doc, for example, all files with the extension .doc will be deleted. Type rm June* to remove all files with names that begin with *June,* regardless of the rest of the name or the file type.

WARNING   Use wildcards with rm only with extreme caution. Depending on how your system is configured, you may or may not get a prompt asking you whether you want to delete individual files. On many systems, the computer will assume you meant to delete everything that fits that string and will do so without asking permission.

WARNING   *Under no circumstances* should you ever type rm *.*. That will remove every single file in your account, including configuration files. If you are the system administrator and issue that command, every single file on your entire system will be wiped. Believe us—you do not want this to happen to you.

Managing Directories

For most practical purposes, directories can be treated just like files. Directories can be moved with the mv command; ownership of directories works just as it does with files; and permissions are very similar. The differences are largely a matter of context.

Creating Directories

Directories are created using the mkdir command. The syntax is very simple:

    mkdir *dirname*

In this command, *dirname* is the name that you want to give the directory. This can be either a full path name or a name relative to the current directory. To create a directory, you must have write permission to the directory in which you wish to create your new directory.

Directory Ownership and Permissions

Directory ownership works exactly the same way as it does for files. Ownership of a directory confers the right to set permissions, and ownership can be transferred with the chown command.

Directory permissions are almost exactly the same, except for a couple of contextual differences. Read permission gives a user the right to list the files in a directory. Write permission gives a user the right to create and alter files in a directory. Execute permission gives a user the right to access files and subdirectories contained in that directory. Directory permissions can be changed using the chmod command, just as file permissions are changed.

Deleting Directories

Directories are commonly deleted with the rmdir (remove directory) command, as in

    rmdir *dirname*

This requires, however, that the directory be empty of all files and subdirectories. This can be quite cumbersome when you want to delete a directory containing a large number of subdirectories, all with files and subdirectories of their own.

In such instances, you'll want to use

    rm -rf *dirname*

By using the -r and -f flags with rm, you force the deletion of everything contained in that directory. You must use care when doing this, because the command will not ask you to confirm the removal of any files. This can include important system files or crucial data. Files and directories deleted in this way cannot be recovered.

WARNING   It is very easy to cripple your system if you use this command when logged in as the superuser. This command should be thought of as a nuclear weapon.

Summary

With a few simple commands, you can create, move, edit, and delete files in your user directory or systemwide. If you are the superuser, you can do all those things to any file on the system, even if you aren't the actual owner; such are the powers of the superuser. Good file-management habits mean that you'll always be able to put your hands on the precise file that you need and that you can take in the state of your system with a single glance.

One of the biggest changes for those new to Unix is the concept of file permissions and ownership. Every file has a unique set of permissions that determine whether anyone can read the file, edit it, or run it if it's a program. System security is affected by file permissions, so it's a good idea to keep permissions as restricted as possible for each file; that is, if it's a program, figure out who needs to run it. If only you are going to run the program, don't make it world-executable. On the other hand, if you don't make your Web pages world-readable, nobody will be able to see them. Make your permissions decisions on a file-by-file basis.

CHAPTER
THIRTEEN

Customizing the Shell Environment

- Elements of Shell Configuration

- Run Control Files

- Environment Variables

- Summary

As with most other components of the Unix operating system, there are many options for customization of the shell environment. For most people and most purposes, the default shell configurations should be fine. However, some users may have special needs or preferences that they would like to have incorporated into their shell environment.

What do we mean by *shell environment* anyway? Think for a moment about your *work environment*. If you're in an office, you have a desk, a chair, some drawers or cabinets to hold your files and supplies, a phone nearby, and so on. You might have a picture of your partner, a vase of flowers, or your bike tucked behind the door waiting for your ride home. If you are at home, you probably have many of the same elements, along with your own personal things such as a game console or your favorite fluffy slippers next to your computer chair. No matter where you're working, you've probably customized the environment to make your time there easier, more comfortable, and more pleasant.

As humans, we change our environments to suit ourselves so naturally and unconsciously that we usually aren't even aware of what we're doing. If you move your phone so you can answer it without having to get up, that's a modification of your environment. Although this seems logical for a physical space, it's not so obvious to look for an analogue in the functions of a computer and its operating system.

The building blocks of your physical environment are the objects and conditions of the physical space around you; the building blocks of the computer's shell environment are the qualities of the shell's interaction with you. What does the prompt look like? How are commands handled? What syntax do you use when writing a script? All these elements can be configured or completely changed, depending on the shell you're using. You may want to pound away on bash until it meets your needs, or you might want to change to another shell that will give you the same results with less work on your part.

NOTE   We describe several different shells in Chapter 15: "Other Shells." In this chapter and Chapter 14: "Input and Output Redirection," we focus on the bash shell. Most of this material should transfer to other shells, however.

Elements of Shell Configuration

There are four types of shell environment configuration. You can use just one of these types, or all four, to make your shell environment perfect for your needs. The various combinations possible within these four categories can result in quite a wide array of configuration possibilities, so try new combinations until you find something that works for you.

Run Control Files

Run control files are files that control the behavior of the shell for a particular user. You have run control files in your personal account, as does every other user on the machine; however, your files control only your settings and not the settings of other users. With the bash shell, run control files are .bashrc, .bash_profile, and .bash_logout. Other shells have analogous files that are used to control the shell's behavior. We discuss run control files more in the "Run Control Files" section of this chapter.

Environment Variables

As we explain in the "Environment Variables" section later in this chapter and in Chapter 22: "Variables," *environment variables* are particular elements of the shell environment that can be configured by the user. If a shell element is controlled by a variable, you can change the value of the variable to change how the shell reacts. For example, the environment variable $EDITOR determines which text editor will be used as the default editor. If you don't like the editor that runs by default (set with a systemwide variable by the system administrator), you can change the value of $EDITOR to reflect your favorite text editor instead.

TIP   By convention, environment-variable names are always written in full capitals.

Aliases

An *alias* is a user-defined synonym for a common command. That is, if you have a long command that you type frequently, such as ls -la /usr/home, you can create an alias, such as lshome. That way, you have to issue only the alias at the command prompt to run the full command. Aliases are an excellent way to create shortcuts for particular command configurations that you use routinely.

Options

There are several aspects of the shell's behavior that don't need to run all the time. You can choose whether to run these optional configurations by turning them on or off. Here are some examples of shell options; note the dash at the beginning of the option name, which often denotes a command-line option:

-norc: .bashrc will not be read upon login.

-noprofile: .bash_profile will not be read upon login.

-rcfile *filename*: Another specified file will be read upon login and used as the substitute for .bashrc.

-nolineediting: Line editing will not be used for this session.

-posix: Features that do not conform to the POSIX standard will not be implemented during this session.

Run Control Files

A run control file is a file that is executed as soon as the shell begins to operate when you log in. As soon as you enter your account, the default shell environment starts up; it could be the default environment created with systemwide settings made by your system administrator, or it could be your personal default environment configured with your own choices. When the shell starts up, all the instructions contained in the various run control files are carried out.

> **NOTE**
> The run control files also kick into operation when you start a new instance of the shell or run a *shell script,* a program made up of shell commands. We will talk much more about shell scripts in Part VI: "Shell Programming."

The main run control file used in bash is the file /etc/bashrc. This file controls the default configuration of bash for the entire system and all its users. As a regular user, you should not try to modify this file in any way, because you will affect all other users and possibly even important system processes.

WARNING

The `/etc/bashrc` file should have appropriate file permissions set on it so that you couldn't modify it if you wanted to. If you are, in fact, able to edit this file without being the system administrator, alert the sysadmin at once; this is an error that needs to be fixed. If you are the administrator of this machine, make sure that you've set `/etc/bashrc` to read-only access for everyone but the root account. Otherwise, things could get severely messed up.

Instead of using `/etc/bashrc` to affect your personal shell environment, you can use the following files, located in your home directory: `.bash_profile`, `.bashrc`, and `.bash_logout`. If you don't have these files in your home directory already, create them; they should work just fine.

TIP

You can create files quickly with the **touch** command; just type **touch .bash_profile** at the command prompt to create that file. Repeat for the other two if necessary. Remember that these filenames begin with periods—do not omit the dots, because they are necessary for these files to function properly.

We describe `.bash_profile` and `.bashrc` in detail in the following sections. When you exit from your login shell, `bash` runs `.bash_logout`. With this file, you can automatically execute a few commands just prior to logging out. This is especially useful if you like to clean out log files or other temporary files as you close out for the day.

.bash_profile

Of the three files mentioned above, the most important is the `.bash_profile` file. Every time you log into your Unix account, this file is read, and the commands in it are executed before you ever type a letter (assuming you're using the `bash` shell). A typical `.bash_profile` file may be somewhat confusing if you don't know what the various elements stand for. Here's a sample `.bash-profile`:

```
# .bash_profile

# Get the aliases and functions
if [ -f ~/.bashrc ]; then
. ~/.bashrc
fi
```

```
# User specific environment and startup programs

PATH=$PATH:$HOME/bin:/sbin:/usr/sbin
BASH_ENV=$HOME/.bashrc
USERNAME=" "
MAIL="/var/spool/mail/mnt/joe"

export USERNAME BASH_ENV PATH MAIL
```

These lines set up some important parameters for this account. In this case, the parameters are set through definitions for a few environment variables; we'll explain how to set these definitions in the next section of this chapter. It is not important at this point that you know exactly how this file works, as long as you understand how .bash_profile fits into the general scheme of your account. You should also know that if you need to add additional configuration options later, you can just add them onto the end of this file. Finally, you should be aware that *rc files*, such as .bashrc, environment variables, and aliases, are all interrelated; as with most other parts of the Unix operating system, you can choose from several options to perform a single configuration.

You might have noticed that this sample .bash_profile makes several references to the .bashrc file. There's a good reason for that: These two files are closely related. .bash_profile is executed only when you log into your account, but .bashrc is executed every single time you start a *subshell* process. A subshell is a second (or third or fourth) instance of the bash shell and is started from the original shell. You could start a subshell by hand, by typing bash at the command prompt, or by executing a script that issues the bash command. Certain processes spawn subshells as they work, as well.

All these subshells use the .bashrc file, and not .bash_profile, to set their operating environments. This method is used because it makes it possible to separate any commands or parameters necessary at login from those you might want to use only in a subshell. In the example above, .bashrc is run as part of .bash_profile; thus, .bash_profile includes everything configured in .bashrc as well as a few extras needed only at login.

NOTE   If you don't normally run bash as your login shell, but you call it by executing the bash command, it is possible that you won't have a .bash_profile file in your home directory. As a fail-safe mechanism, bash allows two other files to substitute for .bash_profile or act as synonyms for it. If bash doesn't locate .bash_pro-file, it looks for a file called .profile. This is the run control file for the plain Bourne Shell and the Korn Shell. If you defined operating parameters for either of those shells in .profile, bash will use those settings. If neither .bash_profile nor .profile is found, bash will look for .bash_login, which is derived from the C Shell's .login file. (That covers most of the shells in wide use.)

Environment Variables

Now that you have an idea of how run control files are constructed, it's time to take a look at what's contained in the file. At this point, it's time to introduce a programming concept that we'll use throughout the remainder of the book: the environment variable. A variable, as you learned in math class many eons ago, is a name to which a value can be attached. The variable is an abstraction that allows us to use a piece of information *without actually knowing what that piece of information is.* As long as that variable has been defined somewhere prior to its being used, that definition (or value) is substituted for the name of the variable when it's used. Some variable values are static, while others can be changed and updated routinely.

Here's an example, taken out of the .bash_profile context to show you how environment variables work:

```
DINNER=steak
```

In this example, the name of the variable is DINNER, and the value of the variable is steak. If you were to write a script that included a sentence making reference to the variable name, such as

```
echo At 7:00, I will eat $DINNER.
```

the computer would parse that as

```
At 7:00, I will eat steak.
```

Granted, it's a silly example (and the sentence alone would not function as a valid program), but you can see the principle at work. The existence of the variable DINNER lets you talk about a food, without knowing what specific food is being discussed. Say that you wanted to change the value of DINNER to falafel.

You need to change only the value, and the computer will parse the original sentence as

```
At 7:00, I will eat falafel.
```

So, how do you change the value of a variable? In the shell environment, there are two ways to note the value of a variable. When you're assigning a value, you simply use the name of the variable, as in

```
BIKE=diamondback
```

In this case, the name of the variable is BIKE, and the value is diamondback.

When you want to use the value of an already defined variable, you need to prefix the variable's name with a dollar sign ($). So, if you want to use the BIKE variable in an expression but have the actual value of the variable appear in the sentence, you might do it like this:

```
echo I want to ride my $BIKE.
```

The value of the expression then becomes

```
I want to ride my diamondback.
```

Take another look at the run control file shown in the previous section. You'll see several environment variables defined in that file. Each of those variables tells the shell something specific about your user environment. For example, the $MAIL variable tells the shell which directory holds your incoming mail. When you use a shell mail program, such as Pine or Elm, to read your e-mail, the program will use the $MAIL variable to locate the new mail.

By now, you might be wondering what the difference is between an environment variable and a regular variable. Good question. Most shell variables exist only within the script that defines them. Programs external to those scripts usually don't have access to the variables defined within the scripts, so certain variables might have to be defined and redefined several times.

If you look in the run control files, though, you'll see that the definitions of environment variables are followed by an **export** command, like this:

```
PATH=$PATH:$HOME/bin:/sbin:/usr/sbin
BASH_ENV=$HOME/.bashrc
USERNAME=""
MAIL="/var/spool/mail/mnt/joe"

export USERNAME BASH_ENV PATH MAIL
```

When you export a variable, you make it available for use outside of the script that defines it. There are two ways to do this:

```
NAME = "value"
export NAME
```

or

```
export NAME = "value"
```

Both syntaxes do the same thing. The first is generally better if you want to define a number of variables all at once and export them all, while the second is easier if you want to make sure that you're exporting only particular variables.

TIP   Want to see a full list of all environment variables currently defined for your user account? Type **set** at the command prompt. If you have a lot of variables defined, you might want to pipe the output of **set** into a text file or pipe the output to the **more** command, so you can look at the output more closely. See Chapter 14: "Input and Output Redirection" for the way to do this.

Common Environment Variables and What They're for

Once you have a basic understanding of the environment-variable concept, you can start to review some of the more common environment variables and learn their function in your shell environment. In this section, we review a few of the most basic environment variables and explain their purpose, as well as some possible configurations.

$USER

The $USER variable contains your login ID. That is, if your username is mountainbiker, the following entry will be in your .bash_profile:

```
$USER = "mountainbiker"
```

The $USER variable is particularly useful for system administrators, who might want to use programs that will function differently for different users. The $USER variable is also helpful for defining variables that may differ for different users.

$USER brings up an important point about environment variables. You can define variables in terms of other variables, not just with unique and specific values. For example, you might define the variable $MAIL as

```
export $MAIL = "/var/spool/mail/$USER"
```

With this definition, each user gets his or her own individual mail path based on the value of $USER.

$MAIL

As shown in the previous section, the $MAIL variable contains the directory that holds incoming electronic mail. This variable is usually defined by the system administrator with something similar to the example shown under the "$USER" section. If, for some reason, you want to point your mail reader to a different directory, you'd do so by changing the value of $MAIL.

$PS1

The $PS1 variable determines the format of the *shell prompt*, the small bit of information to the left of your cursor at the command line. If you define $PS1 as

```
export PS1 = "bash\$"
```

the shell prompt would appear as

```
bash$
```

NOTE The backslash before the dollar sign is an *escape character*, which tells **bash** that the dollar sign is to be interpreted literally in this case, not as an indicator that the value of a variable should be used in the expression.

$PS1 is commonly defined in terms of *escape sequences*. These sequences are small combinations of characters that are interpreted by the command shell to mean something specific. For example, on our Red Hat Linux system, $PS1 is defined as

```
$PS1 = "[\u@\h \W]$"
```

This arcane little string translates into the following when Kate logs into her account on the computer named fugu:

```
[kate@fugu kate]$
```

This works because the shell interprets \u as $USER, \h as $HOSTNAME, and \W as the name of the current directory. So, the prompt says that user kate is logged into machine fugu in directory /usr/kate. Table 15.1 contains a list of bash escape sequences so that you can use them to construct your own combinations.

TABLE 15.1:   bash Escape Sequences

Sequence	Function
\t	The current time in HH:MM:SS format
\d	The date in *Weekday Month Date* format (e.g., Tue May 26)
\n	New line
\s	The name of the shell, the basename of $0 (the portion following the final slash)
\w	The current working directory
\W	The basename of the current working directory
\u	The username of the current user
\h	The hostname
\#	The command number of this command
\!	The history number of this command
\$	If the effective UID is 0, a #; otherwise, a $
\nnn	The character corresponding to the octal number nnn
\\	A backslash
\[	Begins a sequence of nonprinting characters, which could be used to embed a terminal control sequence into the prompt
\]	Ends a sequence of nonprinting characters

TIP

You can also define subordinate prompts by setting definitions for the environment variables $PS2, $PS3, $PS4, and so on. You won't see these too often, however, unless you're doing interactive shell programming—and if you're that advanced, you probably don't need this book.

$HOSTNAME

The $HOSTNAME variable contains the name of your computer. If you're running your own Unix system, you can name your computer anything you want. If you have an account on another person's machine, or on a corporate or school system, you won't be able to edit this variable.

$PATH

The $PATH variable contains a list of directories, separated by the colon character (:), in which the shell will look automatically for executable programs. These directories are usually those like /bin, /usr/local/bin, and other directories that often contain executables. Because of the way in which Unix systems start up, the path is often defined in several different scripts, each adding directories to the previous path. For this reason, you'll often see $PATH defined in terms of itself, as in

```
export PATH="$PATH:/usr/bin:/usr/sbin"
```

This line says, in effect, that the new value of $PATH is equal to the old value (however it was defined in a previous script), except that the /usr/bin and /usr/sbin directories are now appended to its value.

$PATH is the source of some of the most common problems you might encounter when you're trying to install and run a new piece of software. If the directory containing the executable file is not contained in $PATH, your shell won't know to look in that directory for executable files. So, when you type the command that starts the program, your shell will report that no such program exists. To get the program going, you'd need to type the entire directory path name of the program, such as /usr/sbin/traceroute, instead of simply typing traceroute at the prompt. If this happens to you, edit your .bash_profile or .bashrc files and add the new directory to your $PATH variable's definition.

We cover other environment variables in Chapter 22: "Variables."

Summary

Although many users never need to change their shell environment from the default settings, you can create different configurations to provide the most personalized experience possible. In Unix shells, configurations are made using one (or more) of four basic tools: run control files, environment variables, aliases, and options. Run control files control personal account settings; environment variables allow you to change the value of particular elements used by the shell; aliases are shortcuts for common commands; and options can be turned on or off as necessary.

Although these four tools are different in nature, they rely upon each other to work properly. Environment variables are used in run control files, while options affect whether certain run control files are used instead of others, and aliases may rely on variables or run control files to execute. You can make very precise changes in the shell's behavior with these tools, and they are worth exploring.

CHAPTER
FOURTEEN

Input and Output Redirection

- Standard Input and Output

- Introducing Redirection

- Redirection Operators

- Pipes

- Command Substitution

- Combining Operators

- Summary

In the preceding chapters, we've introduced you to several basic shell commands. These commands can be divided between commands that produce output and those that do not. For example, cp and mv do not produce output; they simply execute the desired action and return you to the shell prompt. ls, however, does produce output, which can be customized by the particular flags that you append to the command when you issue it.

There is no general rule about which Unix commands produce output and which do not. Most of the commands that do not produce output do have a *verbose mode* that, if invoked by a flag or other argument, will cause the command to produce output even if it does not normally do so.

TIP   You can check to see whether a command has a verbose mode by consulting the command's man pages. Although not all man pages are easy to understand, they usually contain a thorough listing of flags and arguments that control the command; scan through this listing to see whether a verbose-mode flag exists. Call up a particular man page by typing **man *command*** at the shell prompt, replacing *command* with the actual command you're looking for.

For most commands more complex than cp or mv, though, people tend to expect output. It helps the user to understand what's happened or confirms that the desired process has been completed. Output is tremendously useful.

Standard Input and Output

As useful as output is, though, there are some underlying concepts that you might not have considered. Why does output print to your screen, anyway? It seems to be the logical place, sure, and in most cases it is. Likewise, most people assume that input logically comes from the keyboard in a shell situation (in a graphical environment, the keyboard and mouse both provide input).

"Duh," we hear you think. "That's glaringly obvious." Keep in mind, though, that just because the keyboard/screen combination is the most common and obvious way of dealing with input and output, it is not the only way. In some cases, that combination is not even the best way to handle input and output.

Why is this important? We bring this topic up to introduce the concept of *standard input* and *standard output*. Most programs, including shell commands, take their input from the keyboard by default. Thus, we can say that the keyboard device is that program or command's *standard input*. Likewise, when the program prints its output to the monitor screen, we can say that the monitor is that program's *standard output*.

NOTE

The keyboard/screen combination is not, of course, standard input or output for every program. If, for example, you issued a print command such as `lp`, the standard output would be the printer. Standard inputs and outputs are fairly obvious; consider the context of the commands you issue to determine the input and output devices.

Introducing Redirection

Now that we've established the concept of standard input and output, it might seem that we've finished the chapter. Not quite: We now step into one of the features that makes Unix so powerful—and, quite frankly, timesaving and fun. Assume that you're issuing a command that normally outputs data to the screen in a big blob of text. However, for some reason, you don't want the data sent to the screen—you need it in a text file. What do you do?

Well, you could copy the data by hand; send a screen dump to the printer and reenter the data; or cut and paste. Any of these options takes nearly forever and introduces the possibility of error. Instead, why not use Unix to do the work for you? It's simple to redirect standard output into a file or use the output as the input for another command. Similarly, instead of typing a complex command input, you might pull the input from a file or from the output of another command.

This process of modifying the input and output streams is called *redirection*. It is accomplished with several distinct *redirection operators,* which we describe in the next section of the chapter. Throughout the remainder of this chapter, we show you increasingly complex ways to redirect input and output; once you master these skills, you will find yourself using them to save time, enhance accuracy, and let your machine use the power that it has on your behalf.

Redirection Operators

Unix doesn't know automatically that you want to redirect output or input. To alert the system that you're combining commands or shunting output to another nonstandard location, you have to use a specialized character set. These characters are called redirection operators, and when used in a specific way, they are the keys to getting Unix to do what you want.

Output Redirection Operators

The most common use for output redirection is when a user wants to redirect a command's output into a text file so that the data can be saved or edited. This is especially useful when you want to run complex sets of commands; checking the output is the best way to confirm that you got the results you wanted. When you redirect output into a file, you don't have to deal with screens upon screens of data scrolling past at a fast pace. All you have to do is check the redirect file when the operation has finished, and the output will be waiting patiently for you.

To redirect the output of a command, you need to use one of the two output redirection operators: > or >>. The single angle bracket and the double angle bracket give much the same result, but they get that result by performing in slightly different ways. The main difference between the two bracket operators is that the single bracket may cause data loss if used improperly, while the double bracket will not.

To show how the angle brackets work, we can use the output of ls. Assume that you want to call up the contents of the /etc directory and redirect the output of ls into a file so that you can edit it later. To do so, issue the command

```
ls /etc > listing
```

This command creates a new file called listing in the current directory and then dumps the output (all the files and directories in /etc) into that new file. You can edit the listing file, save it, or delete it.

Now, assume that you want to check the contents of the /usr directory. So, you issue the command

```
ls /usr > listing
```

Check the listing file. Ack! What happened? The files from /etc have disappeared from the text file. You have just discovered the problem with the single angle bracket: When you use the single angle bracket to redirect data into an already existing file, the command *overwrites* the data in that file, erasing the data and replacing it with the new data. This is where the double angle bracket redirector comes in handy.

Keep the `listing` file intact and issue the command

```
ls /etc >> listing
```

Then, check the `listing` file again. You'll see the files from `/etc` shown below the files from `/usr`. The double angle bracket *appends* data to the listed file, tacking the data on at the end of whatever other data is already in the file. The easy way to remember which redirector to use is this: > always creates a new file, even if that means erasing the data in an existing file; >> always adds to an existing file, but does not harm the existing data.

NOTE   If you're using a double angle bracket redirector and the specified file doesn't already exist, >> will behave like > and create a new file with that specified name. If you want to use extreme caution and make sure that data is never destroyed, always use >>.

Input Redirection Operators

The title of this section is somewhat misleading. Although input redirection works much like output redirection, there is only one input redirection operator: <. Having only one input redirection operator makes sense, because you don't have to determine whether to overwrite or append data to a particular command input.

To use the input redirection operator, you simply need to provide the source of the input, and the command will execute with the data in the input source. Here's an example:

```
sort < names
```

In this example, `names` is a file that contains a list of (naturally) names. Assume that the list is unsorted; maybe you've just downloaded the top 10 baby names for 1998, for both boys and girls. In its unsorted state, the file looks like this:

```
Kaitlyn
Emily
Sarah
```

```
Hannah
Ashley
Alexis
Brianna
Samantha
Madison
Taylor
Michael
Jacob
Matthew
Nicholas
Joshua
Christopher
Brandon
Zachary
Austin
Tyler
```

The list is usable as it is, but it would be easier to work with if it were alphabetized. (Given the trend toward unisex names, mixing up the boys' and girls' names might not even matter.) Instead of spending precious time figuring out the alphabetization yourself, why not use the handy Unix command **sort** to do the work for you?

Issue the command we showed at the start of this section:

```
sort < names
```

The command uses the data in the names file as its input. When the operation is finished and you are returned to the shell prompt, check the names file again. You should see a list that looks like this:

```
Alexis
Ashley
Austin
Brandon
Brianna
Christopher
Emily
Hannah
Jacob
```

```
Joshua
Kaitlyn
Madison
Matthew
Michael
Nicholas
Samantha
Sarah
Taylor
Tyler
Zachary
```

Combining Input and Output Redirection Operators

As useful as input and output redirection are as single commands, they are even more powerful when used together. Continuing with the example from the previous section, assume that you want to alphabetize that list of baby names, but you want to keep the original list in its original order as well so that you can keep track of popularity as well as have the names in alphabetical order. You could do this by copying the names file before you issued the sort command, but that's an extra set of keystrokes and an extra step.

Instead, issue the command

```
sort < names > names-alpha
```

Pretty simple! This command causes sort to take the data from the original names file as its input and then redirect the output of the sort into a new file called names-alpha. The original order of the names file is preserved, while you also have the alphabetized list in its own file.

Think about the work that this saves. Without redirection, you would have had to issue the sort command, type in the list of names to be sorted, and then press Enter. Then, when you got the output, you'd have had to create a new file and type the output into the new file. This is not too big of a deal with a list of 20 names, but what if you were dealing with the 100 most popular names for boys and girls in 1998, or the 100 most popular names for every year in the 20th century? Imagine the number of keystrokes that would take. Instead, with redirection, you can accomplish the task with only 27 keystrokes.

Pipes

The angle brackets are not the only input and output redirection operators. One of the most frequently used redirection operators is |, called a *pipe*.

NOTE   The pipe's location is not standardized, because it is not a common touch-typing key. It's usually combined with the backslash (\\); on some of our keyboards, it's in the row above the Enter key, while on others it's near the apostrophe key or even on the left side of the keyboard by the 1 key. It's well worth finding, wherever it appears on the keyboard.

Think of the pipe as a sort of combined input/output redirection operator. That is, the pipe channels the output from one command into the input of another command.

To show you how pipes actually work, here's an operation that we do all the time that uses pipes to do its job. Assume that you want to list the contents of a particular directory with ls. However, this directory has so many files in it that when you issue the ls command, the filenames just scroll off the top of the screen before you can see them. You could dump the ls output into a text file, but that just creates another file in the directory. Wouldn't it be nice to be able to page through the file listing just as you would if you were using the more command to read a text file?

With pipes, you can do that. Issue the command

```
ls /usr | more
```

This command takes the output from the ls /usr command and *pipes it through* the more command. The result is that you can see the ls output one screen at a time, tapping the spacebar to move to the next screen, but you don't have to deal with an additional file containing temporarily interesting information.

Another convenient use of pipes is with the grep command, which searches a given input source for a particular text string. Suppose that you are looking for a particular set of files in that large directory and want only the ones with *unix* as part of the filename.

To do this, pipe the output of the ls command through grep, providing the correct text string to grep. The command is

```
ls /usr | grep unix
```

The output printed to the screen will contain only those files in the /usr directory with *unix* in the filenames.

You can also chain several pipes together for even more complex operations. If, for example, the output of the previous command were more than one screen long, you could combine the two pipe commands we've shown in this section for a command like this:

```
ls /usr | grep unix | more
```

With that command, you can page through the output one screen at a time.

Command Substitution

Although it is not technically input or output redirection, the concept of *command substitution* fits well alongside those concepts. As we explained in Chapter 13: "Customizing the Shell Environment," the $ character is used by the command shell to access the value of a shell variable. (We develop this concept further in Chapter 22: "Variables.")

Command Substitution Syntax

The $() construction that we use for command substitutions in this section is probably the most common way of doing these operations, but it is not the only way. There are other popular ways to do command substitutions, and some of these methods produce slightly different results and behavior.

If you issue the command ls $(pwd), the pwd command is executed in a *subshell*. A subshell is a new shell process that is started specifically for this command and that shuts itself down after the command is finished. The subshell is spawned by the operation, the command is executed, the output of the command is piped back to the original shell, and the subshell exits. You can get the same effect by using the backtick character (`), as in ls `pwd`.

Continued on next page

However, if, instead of parentheses, you use curly braces ({}), the command inside the curly braces will be executed in the current shell, as in `ls ${pwd}`. This has some important implications.

Remember that, in `bash`, the `.bash_profile` file defines the environment for the login shell, while the `.bashrc` file defines the environment of the subshells. This means that if you're giving a command that depends on an environment parameter defined in `.bash_profile`, you need to use the curly braces instead of the smooth parentheses when you use command substitutions.

The $ character can be used in a similar way to access the output of a command directly without actually running the command itself. For example, the command

```
ls $(pwd)
```

lists the contents of the current directory, regardless of what directory you are in.

NOTE   In this construction, the parentheses enclosing the command are necessary to indicate that it is a command substitution rather than a variable named *pwd*.

The effect of that command is the same as if you had issued the command

```
pwd | ls
```

which would pipe the output of the `pwd` command through `ls`. (The command would print the working directory with `pwd` and then use that directory name as the input for `ls`.)

This concept illustrates one of the fundamental tenets of the Unix philosophy: There is more than one way to do it. Which construction you use to execute a particular operation is a matter of personal preference. In this example, we think that the `ls $(pwd)` command is a bit more semantically coherent than `pwd | ls`, but there is no particular increased value in doing it our way if you prefer the second construction.

As with chained pipes, it is possible to have multiple substituted commands in one operation. For example, if you wanted to use the `wc` command (word count) to find out the number of words in each file in the current directory, you could issue the command

```
wc $(ls $(pwd))
```

Combining Operators

By now, you should be getting an idea of the power and flexibility possible with these operators. Just as you can combine input and output redirection operators to consolidate multiple commands into one operation, you can also add pipes and command substitutions to the mix to create operations of almost unlimited complexity.

> **TIP**
>
> There are practical limits to these combinations, of course. You might find that overly complex commands are confusing, difficult to read or remember, and difficult to explain to others. In many cases, it's probably better to break up a complex operation into several less complex commands just for the sake of clarity. You don't have to, but there is a point where a command becomes much less comprehensible to humans for the sake of clarity to the computer. If you get flustered by complex commands, take the time to reduce each operation to a set of commands at the level you're happy with.

To show you the kind of complex problem that can be solved in a jiffy with these techniques, we've developed an example. Assume that you have a friend called Nevada who works for the fictional Baby Naming Standards Bureau. Nevada's e-mail address is nevada@babyname.gov. Nevada, for some odd reason, has asked you to e-mail her a list of the file sizes of all the files in your /etc directory that have filenames containing the string *name*; she doesn't care whether you send it in kilobytes or megabytes.

To get Nevada what she wants, you'll need to use the ls command to get the list of filenames, the grep command to find the character string, and the du -h command to get the file size. Then, you'll need to mail the output to Nevada using the mail command. To do all this, you simply need to create and use the complex command

```
du -h $(ls /etc) | grep name | mail nevada@babyname.gov
```

Just imagine how much time it would have taken to get that information if you'd checked each file size and name by hand. Now Nevada has the data she needs, and we need worry no more about the reasons for her request.

> **NOTE**
>
> If you laughed at the Baby Naming Standards Bureau example, you might find it interesting to learn that Norway actually has a governmental list of approved personal names, and selecting a name not on the list for your baby will result in a stiff fine.

These complex commands can get somewhat complicated as you add new elements. Be sure that you aren't inadvertently changing the syntax of the command as you add new components. Note that the syntax of the command

```
du -h $(ls /etc) | grep config
```

is not the same as the syntax of the command

```
grep config $(du -h $(ls /etc))
```

or the syntax of the command

```
du -h $(grep config $(ls /etc))
```

The syntaxes are different because of the way in which the initial commands operate on their input. That is, in the first case, grep works directly on the output of the ls command, which is individual filenames; in the second and third cases, grep works on the contents of the files named by the output of ls, not the filenames themselves. Pipes and redirection operators are simple things, but they can trip you up if you're not paying attention as you build complex operations.

Summary

Any interaction with Unix requires some sort of input (a keyboard or mouse, for example) and some sort of output (the monitor or a printer). Unix commands use input consisting of the command itself and perhaps some additional arguments or data. Commands usually output to the monitor, though some commands do not provide output unless you specifically request that the command operate in verbose mode.

Input and output can be redirected, either to make dealing with the output simpler by sending it to a text file or to build complicated sequences of operations where one command's output functions as the input for another command. Modifying the input and output streams is called redirection, and it is done by issuing commands along with redirection operators, characters that direct the operating system to handle input and output in a particular way. You can also use the concept of command substitution to pull the value of certain shell variables into your complex operations. All of these concepts can be combined in different orders to produce different results.

CHAPTER
FIFTEEN

Other Shells

- The Bourne Shell

- The Korn Shells: ksh and pdksh

- The C Shells: csh and tcsh

- The Z Shell

- Other Shells: scsh, rc, es, psh

- Summary

In this part of the book, we have covered a lot of material about using the Bourne Again Shell (`bash`). `bash` isn't the only option, though; there are several other shells in wide use and quite a few more that are either specialized or growing in popularity. In this chapter, we present some of these shells, and explain their features and capabilities. We don't go into exhaustive detail, because we've selected `bash` as our main shell for this book, but we do show you what else is out there and how it differs from `bash`.

TIP

If you're interested in using a shell other than `bash`, we recommend that you consult one of the many good books available for particular shells and that you find shell-specific resources on the Web to help you decide which shell to use.

The Bourne Shell

The original Bourne Shell is the default on most commercial versions of Unix (e.g., Solaris, HP-X, and other closed-source distributions). Some Open Source versions of Unix also ship with the Bourne Shell to maintain compatibility with the commercial versions, and users of Open Source Unices may want the Bourne Shell because they learned Unix with a commercial version.

NOTE

If you're trying to run a machine that is 100-percent Free Software, you may not want to use the Bourne Shell. Bourne is released under the BSD license, which is *semifree* according to the GNU project. However, if you have your heart set on using the Bourne Shell on a 100-percent Free Software box, you can use the Free Software replacement, `ash`. (`ash` stands for *a shell*, which is about as generic of a name as is possible.) `ash` is almost identical to the Bourne Shell and can be used as a replacement if you prefer not to use `bash`. We've put `ash` on the CD for your convenience.

The Bourne Shell, invoked with the `sh` command, was the original Unix shell. It was developed by Steve Bourne at Bell Labs, hence the name. Given the wide array of shells and features now available to Unix users, the Bourne Shell may seem a touch old-fashioned to you; it will certainly seem pared-down if you are familiar with more complex shells such as `bash`. Bourne does not have some of the features that many users take for granted, especially the ability to edit directly on the command line and the ability to move through the history of previous commands issued in a particular session.

Despite its drawbacks in an age when more-featured shells are standard, the Bourne Shell serves a distinct purpose. Some users prefer a stripped-down shell without a great deal of bells and whistles, while others find that script programming in the Bourne Shell is particularly responsive. If you use Solaris or another commercial Unix, you will have Bourne as your default shell, so it's good to know a bit about it to use those systems. However, we recommend that you upgrade your shell if you plan to do a lot of command-line work. (Those who plan to use integrated desktops, such as KDE or Gnome, can probably stick with Bourne, though we still recommend installing bash or another newer shell.)

NOTE bash was written as a revision of the Bourne Shell, which is why bash is called the Bourne Again Shell. To create bash, its developers pulled components from the Korn and C Shells and patched them into the standard Bourne program. The result is a shell with the power of the Bourne Shell, with the increased flexibility of later shells.

The Korn Shell

The Korn Shell, usually called ksh, is second in user base only to the Bourne Shell. In fact, if bash hadn't adapted the Bourne Shell and gotten a bit of a ride off of Bourne's popularity, ksh would probably have eclipsed the Bourne Shell's user base by now. Like bash, ksh features the ability to edit commands directly on the command line, and it can be configured to emulate either the vi or the emacs text editor.

NOTE The Korn Shell is not Free Software; for an Open Source alternative, see the "pdksh" section of this chapter.

In addition to command-line editing, the Korn Shell features include the ability to work with a number of processes at the same time. You can even alter the order in which processes gain access to the kernel. To do so, suspend the current top process by pressing Ctrl+z; you can then move the suspended process into the background with the bg command. Then, use fg [*jobnumber*] to bring the desired process into the foreground. With this kind of detailed control, ksh brings a new level of system management to the shell user. (This process is so useful that it's found its way into other shells, including bash.)

The Korn Shell also features built-in integer arithmetic. This is a significant improvement over both the Bourne Shell and the Bourne Again Shell. In sh and bash, you must use the expr command to evaluate mathematical expressions, because the shell treats every mathematical value as a string instead of as an integer. The Korn Shell, however, uses various parenthetical operators (both parentheses and square brackets), along with the let command, to provide a good number of mathematical operations directly on the command line.

Programmers like the Korn Shell because it provides a second type of variable. *Array variables* are indexed lists of values that can be quite useful in shell programming. Arrays and mathematical functions are good shortcuts for shell scripts, and save quite a few keystrokes over the methods necessary for accomplishing the same tasks in bash or sh.

A final feature of the Korn Shell is the ability to create menus easily. If you are writing a shell program that will run interactively, you might want to add a menu so that users will have an easier time running the program. With the Korn Shell, building these menus of possible responses is a quick and helpful option.

Korn Shell Run Control Files

Like bash and sh, ksh uses several specific run control files:

.profile: This file works the same in ksh as it does in sh and bash. It controls the login environment.

.kshrc: The .kshrc file controls the basic shell environment and is similar to .bashrc.

.sh_history: This file stores the most recent commands issued. The default number of stored commands is 100, but you can change that number to reflect your habits.

Environment Variables

Like other shells, ksh uses environment variables to control the user environment. The environment variables used by ksh are shown in Table 15.1.

TABLE 15.1: Korn Shell Environment Variables

Variable	Function
CDPATH	Sets the search path for the cd command.
COLUMNS	Defines the width of the edit window for the shell edit modes.
EDITOR	Specifies which editor is used as the default text editor.
ENV	If set, parameter substitution is performed on the value of this variable to generate the path.
ERRNO	A value set by the most recently failed subroutine.
FCEDIT	The default editor name for the fc command.
FPATH	The search path for function definitions.
HISTFILE	The path name of the file that stores the history of commands issued (by default, .sh_history).
HISTSIZE	The number of commands stored in the history file.
HOME	The subdirectory that becomes current upon login and that is used as a default for cd.
IFS	Characters to be used as internal field separators.
LANG	Determines the location to use when LC_ALL does not specify one.
LC_ALL	Determines the location to be used to override any previously set values.
LC_COLLATE	Defines the collating sequence to use when sorting.
LC_CTYPE	Determines the location for the interpretation of a sequence of bytes.
LC_MESSAGES	Determines the language in which messages should be written.
LINENO	The line number in the current line within the script or function being executed.

Continued on next page

TABLE 15.1 CONTINUED: Korn Shell Environment Variables

Variable	Function
LINES	Determines the column length for printing select lists.
MAIL	The path name of the file used by the mail system to detect the arrival of new mail.
MAILCHECK	The number of seconds that the shell lets elapse before checking for new mail.
MAILMSG	The mail notification message.
MAILPATH	A list of programs separated by colons; if new mail arrives while you are using these programs, the shell will notify you of new mail.
OLDPWD	The previous working directory set by the `cd` command.
OPTARG	The value of the last argument processed by the `getopts` special command.
OPTIND	The index of the last option argument processed by the `getopts` special command.
PATH	The search path for commands separated by colons.
PPID	The process number of the parent of the shell.
PS1	The string to be used as the primary system prompt.
PS2	The value of the secondary prompt (when the shell finds a new-line character).
PS3	The value of the selection prompt string used within a select loop.
PS4	This value precedes each line of an execution trace.
PWD	The present working directory.
RANDOM	Generates a random number between 0 and 32767.
REPLY	Set by the `select` and `read` special commands when no arguments are given.
SECONDS	The number of seconds since the shell was invoked.
SHELL	The path name of the shell (should be exported by the `$HOME/.profile` script).
TMEOUT	The number of minutes the shell remains inactive before it exits.

pdksh

If you'd like to try the Korn Shell's features, but you prefer an Open Source version of the shell, you might enjoy pdksh, the Public Domain Korn Shell. pdksh is a clone of the Korn Shell, released under a public-domain license that permits the user to download, use, redistribute, and alter the shell as needed or desired. There are no significant differences between pdksh and the regular Korn Shell, ksh.

The C Shells

Although the casual user probably won't notice it, the C-based shells (csh and tcsh) are quite a bit different from the Bourne-derived shells such as bash and ksh. The C Shells are based on the C programming language; although the same commands work in the C Shells as work in the Bourne-derived shells, the syntax used for more complicated processes is quite different. One way in which the casual user will find the C Shells different is in the way environment variables are set; we explain this difference in the "Environment Variables" section below.

csh and tcsh are appealing to users who are already familiar with C and prefer to use the C syntax when programming in the shell. Those users who don't use C may like these shells as well; you certainly don't have to be a C expert to use them. (For example, Kate is certainly not a C wizard, yet she likes to use tcsh.)

C Shell Run Control Files

csh and tcsh use these files for run control:

.login: This file controls the login environment; it is similar to .profile.

.cshrc: This file, used in csh, controls the basic user environment; it is similar to .bashrc.

.tcshrc: This file, used in tcsh, controls the basic user environment; it is similar to .bashrc.

.logout: This file executes the commands included in the file when the login shell is exited.

Environment Variables

Unlike other shells, the C Shell uses the setenv command to set the value of various environment variables. The syntax of setenv is

```
setenv NAME value
```

If, for example, you wanted to set your EDITOR variable's value to emacs, you would add the line

```
setenv EDITOR emacs
```

to the appropriate run control file (either .cshrc or .tcshrc, depending on which C-based shell you are running).

You can set a variety of environment variables using the setenv command. C Shell environment variables are shown in Table 15.2.

TABLE 15.2: C Shell Environment Variables

Variable	Function
ARGV	This variable controls the argument list or list of command-line arguments supplied to the current shell session.
CDPATH	This variable contains a list of directories to be searched by the cd, chdir, and popd commands. The CDPATH variable is used for directories that are not a subdirectory of the current directory.
CWD	This variable contains the full path name of the current directory.
ECHO	This variable causes the shell to print commands to the screen just before executing the operation.
FIGNORE	This variable contains a list of filename suffixes that the shell will ignore when filename completion is used. The value of FIGNORE is typically the single word .o.

Continued on next page

TABLE 15.2 CONTINUED: C Shell Environment Variables

Variable	Function
FILEC	This variable controls the filename completion feature, which will automatically complete partial filenames. If filename completion is enabled, typing a partial filename and pressing Ctrl+d will print a list of all filenames that begin with that partial character string. If filename completion is enabled, typing a partial filename and pressing the Esc key will complete the filename with the longest unambiguous extension that appears in the file listing of that directory.
HARDPATHS	This variable toggles symbolic links. If it is turned on, symbolic links in directory path names will not work.
HISTCHARS	This variable's value is always a two-character string, and the default is !^. The first character replaces ! as the history substitution character. The second replaces the carat for quick substitutions.
HISTORY	This variable's value determines the number of lines saved in the history list. Although you can set it to any number, large numbers will occupy a big portion of the shell memory. If this variable has no value, the C Shell will save only the most recent command.
HOME	This variable defines the user's home directory. Note that you can use the shorthand ~ to represent the value of this variable.
IGNOREEOF	This variable toggles the End Of Field sensitivity. If turned on, the shell will ignore all EOF messages from the terminal, so you won't accidentally shut down a C Shell process by pressing the Ctrl+d key combination.
MAIL	This variable contains a list of directories where the C Shell will check for incoming electronic mail. If the first word of the variable's value is a number, it specifies a mail-checking interval in seconds. Otherwise, the shell will check for mail every five minutes.
NOBEEP	This variable toggles a system beep when filename completion is requested from the shell.
NOCLOBBER	This variable controls output redirection to prevent inadvertent file deletion. See Chapter 14: "Input and Output Redirection."
NOGLOB	This variable limits filename completion to the first match. It is mostly used in shell scripting to save time and limit the amount of processor cycles invested in filename searching.
NONOMATCH	This variable substitutes an echo of the filename completion request for an error message if the pattern is not matched by an existing filename.
NOTIFY	This variable toggles immediate notification from the shell as soon as a job is completed. If this variable is not turned on, the shell will wait to notify you until a prompt is returned to the screen.

Continued on next page

TABLE 15.2 CONTINUED: C Shell Environment Variables

Variable	Function
PATH	This variable contains a list of directories in which the shell will normally search for commands and programs. It's a good idea to check the default setting and see whether there are directories you commonly use that should be added to the path. Commands that execute programs resident in PATH directories can be issued with just the command; programs that reside in non-PATH directories must be executed by issuing the full path name of the program. That is, you would have to type /usr/sbin/traceroute instead of traceroute if the /usr/sbin directory was not in the PATH variable.
PROMPT	This value sets the string that constitutes the shell command prompt. The default prompt reads the HOSTNAME variable and ends it with a % character for regular users and a # character for root.
SAVEHIST	This variable sets the number of lines in the command history list that are saved in the .history file at logout. Large values for this variable will slow down the login process.
SHELL	This variable defines the file where the C Shell resides. You should not change this location; this variable is used for system-level functions.
STATUS	This variable contains the status code returned by the most recently completed operation.
TIME	This variable controls the automatic timing of commands. It can use either one or two values: the first is the reporting period defined in CPU seconds, while the second is a character string that determines the resources to be reported on.

What's the Difference?

If you're new to the C-based shells, you may be wondering what makes csh different from tcsh. As with the Bourne Shell and bash, tcsh is usually described as an *enhanced* C Shell, meaning that tcsh has a few features that the regular C Shell doesn't. These features include the following:

- A command-line editor that can use Emacs or vi-style key bindings
- Interactive word completion and listing
- Spell-checking of filenames, commands, and variables
- Editor commands that can be inserted into complex command operations to perform certain functions during the operation
- Timestamps for events stored in the history file

- Enhanced directory parsing and directory stack-handling commands

- Improved file-inquiry operators and a new file-test function that uses these operators

- An increased number of automatic, periodic, and timed events that save administrative work; these events include scheduled events, automatic logout and terminal locking, command timing, and tracking of logins and logouts

- Expanded terminal management tools

- More commands built into the shell

- New variables that provide useful information to the shell

- A new prompt-string syntax

- Read-only variables that cannot be altered and therefore cannot harm the system by being inadvertently changed

The Z Shell

We round out this discussion of the popular Unix shells with the Z Shell (zsh). Of these shells, zsh is the new kid on the block, as the most recently developed of the five. Like the Korn Shell, the Z Shell is a derivative of the Bourne Shell with some new enhancements. The Z Shell also borrows features from the Korn Shell and the C Shell; so, as you can imagine, it is a complex and fully featured environment.

The Z Shell has an enormous number of configuration options, contained in no fewer than five run control files: .zprofile, .zlogin, .zshrc, .zlogout, and .zshenv. The man page for the Z Shell is so long, it had to be split into eight parts. (As a comparison, we can't think of more than one or two other man pages that are even split into two parts.)

Obviously, a shell this complex is far too elaborate to be dealt with in this small space, whether just for description or for actual skill-building. If you are interested in learning more about the Z Shell—and we recommend that you take a look, once you're familiar with Unix shell environments in general—we suggest you read one of the many Web pages or books devoted to the shell. A good place to start is at http://www.zsh.org, the home page of the Z Shell development project.

Other Shells

Although the shells already reviewed in this chapter are the most popular shell environments for Unix, there are other shells with small but devoted followings. Four of them are described in the remainder of this chapter; if you're interested in using a unique shell, you might try out one of these.

scsh

scsh is a shell based on the Scheme programming language. Scheme is a very elegant programming language with a devoted following. As with the C shells, the main advantage to using a shell like scsh is that script programming follows the same syntax and argument requirements that the Scheme language uses. If you're a Scheme devotee, scsh might be the appropriate shell for you.

rc and es

rc and es are attempts to bring more modern programming techniques to the shell environment; the programming techniques in the Bourne derivatives and the C-based shells are based on program languages that are 30 years old or older. There have been many advances in programming-language development since Ritchie and Thompson developed C, and the rc and es shells try to incorporate some of those new features. The es shell, for example, represents command substitution, pipes, and input/output redirection as *function calls*. Although function calls exist in all programming languages, rc and es are unique in *what* they represent with function calls.

The Perl Shell

Over the past few years, the Perl programming language has become very popular. It was originally created as a Unix "glue" language that could make common system administration tasks easier, but Perl has also found homes in Web design, database administration, and other types of programming. Perl's adherents can be somewhat fanatical (there are programmers who write poetry in Perl), so it was probably only a matter of time before someone tried to make a Unix shell with a Perl-like syntax. Currently, the Perl Shell (yes, psh) is in a very early stage of development.

Summary

There are many shell alternatives to bash. The most popular are the original Bourne Shell, the Korn Shell, and the C Shell variants. There are also several shells with less, but growing, popularity. The main differences lie in the way that the shell environment handles scripting and environment variables. There are also some minor differences in the user interface itself, but these differences are merely issues of personal preference and not of substantive significance to the general user.

PART V

Using Text Editors

CHAPTER
SIXTEEN

The ed Editor

- What Is ed?

- Starting ed

- Reading a File

- Editing a File

- Saving and Quitting

- Editing by Content

- Summary

It is unlikely that you will ever use the ed text editor to any great extent. We (Joe and Kate) have over 20 years of combined Unix experience, and neither of us have ever used ed for any practical purpose. Furthermore, we don't know anyone who uses it regularly and know only a few who have ever used it at all. So, if ed is so unpopular, why are we bothering to include an entire chapter about it?

We decided to cover ed because—though we are not Scouts—we agree with the motto "Be Prepared." You never know when you might find yourself in front of a Unix computer that doesn't have any of your favorite programs: no graphical interface, no fancy text editors with convenient keystroke shortcuts, nothing but the pure basics. Even if the system is completely bare-bones, the chances are pretty good that you'll have ed available.

| NOTE | We know that a lot of people find more advanced editors, such as vi and emacs, to be unintuitive and complicated. (We cover vi in Chapter 17: "The vi Editor" and emacs in Chapter 18: "GNU Emacs.") Learning how to use ed will give you a greater appreciation for these editors and will give you a glimpse into the technical innovations that both vi and emacs represented when they were released. |

What Is ed?

ed is a *line editor*. There are two major types of text editors in the Unix world: line editors and full-screen editors. (We discuss full-screen editors in Chapter 17: "The vi Editor.") When you edit a file with a line editor like ed, you must do so one line at a time. In contrast, when you use a full-screen editor, you can work on multiple lines at once. Although line editors are extremely cumbersome, they are better than nothing. There is enough functionality in a line editor to get your work done; it's simply not as easy as it would be with more advanced tools. You can see the simplicity of ed's commands in Table 16.1.

TABLE 16.1: Basic ed Commands

Command	Function
ed	Invokes the **ed** line editor
r *filename*	Reads the named file into the buffer
p	Prints the named line's contents to the screen
a	Switches **ed** into input mode and adds new text at a specified line location
d	Deletes specified lines from the buffer
m	Moves text from one specified line to another
j	Joins specified lines on one line
w	Writes (saves) the current buffer to a file on the disk
q	Quits **ed** (will fail if the current buffer has not been written to the disk)
Q	Quits **ed** without saving the current buffer

ed operates in two modes: input mode and edit mode. (ed also has a command mode, which is used to manipulate the program until you are ready to work with text.) As their names imply, *input mode* is used to insert text into a file, and *edit mode* is used to alter the entered text. In later chapters of this part of the book, you'll see other editors that use the input and edit mode concepts, even though they are not line editors.

Starting ed

To start **ed**, simply type **ed** at a command prompt. If you want to start **ed** to work on a particular file that's already been saved, you can issue the command **ed** *filename*, where *filename* is the actual file's name. If you choose to open **ed** with a particular file, you will see a number print to the screen. This number is the total number of characters in the file. Regardless of the method you use to open ed, you will then see the cursor at the beginning of the first line, doing nothing, as in Figure 16.1. This indicates that ed is now ready for input.

When you start ed, you are in *command mode* by default. Anything you type at this point will be interpreted by the program as a command. If you didn't open a file when you started ed, type r filename and press Enter (substitute an actual name for *filename*). This command reads a new file into ed's *buffer*. A buffer is a temporary workspace in the computer's memory. The file on the disk will not be created or altered until you give ed the command to save your work.

NOTE   You will not see a prompt when you use ed. You'll only see the cursor sitting at the beginning of a line. Considering that most interactive programs, including text editors, have a prompt of some kind, this can be a bit unnerving. It's normal for ed, though.

FIGURE 16.1:

The text editor *ed* works on each line individually, rather than on the entire document.

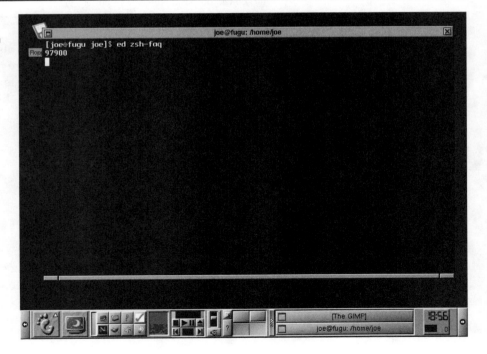

Reading a File

Now that you have a particular file open in **ed**, it's time to take a look at the contents of the file to see what you're working with.

TIP

We recommend that you work with an existing file in this chapter so that you have some text to play with. Don't use a file that's quite important, but do use one with 10 or 20 lines of data.

The p command will print the file's contents to the screen. However, first you must tell **ed** precisely what it is that you want to print to the screen. Do this by specifying the line numbers you want to print. Thus, the command 1,3p will print lines one through three to the screen, while the command 2,4p will print lines two through four.

We assume that you don't know how many lines your file has, so you can use the wildcard symbol $ to represent the last line of the file. That is, the command 1,$p will cause **ed** to print the entire file to the screen, no matter how many lines the file has. Issuing a single number before the p will cause that single line to print, while using the p command by itself will print the current line to the screen.

The *current line* concept is a bit slippery in **ed**. If, immediately after opening a file, you issue the command 1,$p, there is no current line. To set a current line with **ed**, just type the line's number. Typing 2 will set the current line to the second line of the document. If, after setting a current line, you then type p, the second line will be printed to the screen.

TIP

The current line can also be represented by the dot (.) character. The dot character has some other special uses. For example, assume that you have a buffer open with a file in it that you've named **crocodile1**. If you set the current line to five in that file and then issue the command .r alligator1, the contents of the alligator1 file will be inserted into the **crocodile1** file after that file's fifth line.

Editing a File

Once you have a handle on opening and reading files with ed, you're ready to move on to creating and editing text. There are four main categories of activity in ed: inputting text, deleting text, moving text, and saving the file. To add text, you'll need to be in input mode, while to edit text, you'll need to be in edit mode.

Inputting Text

At this point, you are still in command mode. Enter input mode by issuing the command a. (Think of *a* for *add*.) After you type a and press the Enter key, anything you type will be interpreted by ed as text to be inserted into the buffer. ed will stay in input mode until you type a period on a line by itself, which will cause ed to switch back to command mode.

In this section of the chapter, we show you how to start a new blank file and insert some text into it. Take a look at the example given below:

```
bash$  ed
a
Now is the time for all good men
to come to the aid of the party.
.
1,$p
Now is the time for all good men
to come to the aid of the party.
1p
Now is the time for all good men
```

Given what you've learned already in this chapter, this example should be easy to understand. The first line shows the shell prompt, bash$, and the command that invokes the ed editor. The a command switches ed into input mode, and the next two lines are the text we entered into the file.

The period, or dot, on a line by itself signifies that the input has ended. It signals ed to switch back into command mode. At that point, the command 1,$p is issued, which causes ed to print the entire file to the screen. The 1p command causes ed to print the first line of the file only.

At this point, the buffer contains the two lines of text only. Anything typed after the period on a line by itself was not added to the buffer. Assume that you want to add a new line to the file, following the existing text. Remember that the $ character represents the last line of the file (no matter what that line's actual number might be). So, to input text after the last line, you would need to issue the command $a. Thus, the next part of the session might look like this:

```
$a
This is a patriotic sentiment indeed.
.
```

Now that you've added the text and returned to command mode, you can look at the whole file:

```
1,$p
Now is the time for all good men
to come to the aid of the party.
This is a patriotic sentiment indeed.
```

True, it's a fine sentiment. But doesn't it need some updating for modern sensibilities? Suppose that you want to insert a line between the first and second lines of the buffer file. Do this with a command that forces new lines at the end of a named line, as in this example:

```
1a
and women
.
```

Issue the 1,$p command to get this output:

```
Now is the time for all good men
and women
to come to the aid of the party.
This is a patriotic sentiment indeed.
```

NOTE

The inserted text can be more than one line. ed will continue to read and add input until it reaches a line that contains only the dot character. The new material will be inserted after the line named in the initial command.

TIP

Just as $ represents the last line of the file and . represents the current line, you can use 0 (zero) to represent the beginning of the file. Issuing the command 0a will cause your new text to be inserted at the very start of the buffer file.

Deleting Text

Although it's useful to know how to add text to the buffer, it's equally important to know how to delete text. ed has a very simple delete mechanism that uses the d command. The d command follows the same rules as the other commands we've explained.

Use line numbers to delete specific lines, or use the various wildcard characters to delete sequences of lines. For example, issuing the command 3d will delete the third line from the file, while 2,4d will delete the second through fourth lines of the buffer, and 3,$d will delete everything from the third line to the end of the file.

NOTE Once you have issued a delete command, ed will renumber the remaining lines to reflect the disappearance of the now-deleted lines. You cannot get back text that you've deleted with the d command.

Moving Text

Although it is certainly possible to move text by deleting it from one location and retyping it in another, this can get tedious quite quickly. A more convenient way to move text is to use ed's m command. The m command's syntax is a bit different from the other commands you've seen so far in this chapter. m takes the syntax

```
line number(s)mnew line number(s)
```

So, the command 1m3 will move the complete first line of the buffer to the third line. The old second line will become the new first line, and the old third line will become the new fourth line.

You can also move ranges of lines. Thus, the command 1,25m$ will move the first 25 lines of the file to the very end of the buffer.

Joining Lines

Lines can be joined together with the j command. This is especially useful if you have several short lines that would all fit nicely onto one line. The j command uses the standard ed syntax described for all other commands but m in this chapter. Thus, the command

```
1,2j
```

would join the first and second lines together into one line. The old line three would then become the new second line.

Return for a moment to the example we used at the start of the chapter, where the inserted second line was quite a bit shorter than the other lines. As we left it, the buffer read

```
Now is the time for all good men
and women
to come to the aid of their party.
This is a patriotic sentiment indeed.
```

To join lines one and two, issue the command 1,2j. The result is this:

```
Now is the time for all good men and women
to come to the aid of their party.
This is a patriotic sentiment indeed.
```

The appearance of the text is much more pleasant without the short second line.

You can use the j command to join larger ranges of lines, as well. For example, the command 1,10j would join the first 10 lines together into one long line. This is not usually a good idea, though there might be times (as when coding in HTML) where having a single long line is preferable to several short lines.

NOTE   When you use the j command, no spaces are inserted between the joins. If you want spaces, you'll have to insert them manually.

Saving and Quitting

All this time, you've been working in the buffer and not with a file that's actually saved to the disk. As everyone knows, working on an unsaved file is an invitation to disaster. (Just ask us—we recently worked on a book about some word-processing software that was in the beta stage at the time. It routinely ate Joe's notes as he worked. The ironic thing is that issuing the Save command usually triggered the program crash.)

To save your buffer to an actual file on the hard drive, use the w command (think *w* for *write*). If you haven't named the buffer yet, add the new filename after the w. For example, if you want to save the buffer we've been working on to a file called `patriot`, you'd issue the command

```
w patriot
```

To quit ed, simply type q. If you haven't saved your work yet, or if you've changed the file since the last time it was saved, ed will not let you quit. Instead, it will print the ? character to the screen. To quit without saving your work, type Q instead, and ed will let you quit anyway. (We don't particularly recommend this, but there are certainly times when you just want to get rid of a file without committing it to the disk.) If you do want the file to be saved, use the w command to write the revised version to the disk and then issue the q command again.

Editing by Content

ed is most useful with short files. With a large file, or one that you've already done a number of edits on, you will probably find it difficult to remember actual line numbers. Listing the entire file to find a single line can be unwieldy, especially if the file is longer than your screen can hold. There are several ways to edit by using the content of each line, including matching and substitution.

Matching

The programmers who developed ed knew that there had to be a way to work with a file that relied on each line's content instead of its line number. Therefore, they included a tool that matches strings of characters to locate a particular line when the line number is unknown.

To find the next line containing a particular character string, enclose the desired string between slashes, as in

```
/string/
```

Press Enter, and ed will locate the next line containing that string. Note that the search starts with the line immediately following the current line. If you are looking for matches prior to the current line, substitute question marks for the slashes, as in

`?string?`

It is possible to use certain wildcard characters in these strings so that you get more than one possible match. For example, the * (asterisk) character will match zero or more occurrences of any character. Basically, * will match any character or set of characters in that space. If you wanted to search for the next occurrence of any word ending in the suffix *-ing,* you'd issue the command

`/*ing/`

Where the asterisk can represent any number of characters, the dot character represents any single character. Issuing the command

`/.ing/`

would result in ed finding words such as bing, ming, or ping; to find thing, string, or bring, you'd need to use the asterisk.

If you are actually looking for an asterisk or a dot character, you need to suppress their wildcard functions. Do this by preceding the special character with a backslash (\), as in

`/\*ing/`

Substitution

In addition to simple matching as described in the previous section, the slash characters can be used to perform substitutions as well. For example, assume that you have a file that describes Linux behavior for a particular program. Because the program operates the same way in all Unix-derived operating systems, you want to change every occurrence of *Linux* to *Unix* so that you can use the file with a broader audience.

To make this change, use the slash characters in combination with the s command, as in

`s/Linux/Unix`

This command operates in a fairly specific manner. The command shown above will substitute the string *Unix* for the first occurrence of the string *Linux* on the current line. If you want to replace all occurrences on the current line, you need to add the g (global) suffix to the end of the command, as in

```
s/Linux/Unix/g
```

If this is not enough and you want to apply these changes to more than one line at once, prefix the command with a range of line numbers. Thus,

```
1,10s/Linux/Unix/g
```

will replace all occurrences of the word *Linux* with the word *Unix* in the first 10 lines of the document. Of course, as described earlier in this chapter, you can apply the substitution to the entire document with the command

```
1,$s/Linux/Unix/g
```

WARNING   If you decide that you've just made a mistake with a substitution, you can undo it by simply typing **u**. If this was a substitution that affected more than one line, only the last line in which the substitution was made can be restored. You will have to redo the substitution for all other lines.

Summary

Because **ed** is a line editor rather than a full-screen editor, its utility for most users is limited. However, it is important to understand how **ed** works, if only as an emergency backup to your regular text editor. Almost all Unix systems will have **ed** installed, regardless of any other editors that may or may not be found on that computer.

ed uses a simple set of commands to control the insertion and editing of text. With **ed**'s commands, you can move through the file and join or delete lines; search for strings of characters; or substitute certain strings for other character sets. We don't think you'll use **ed** as your full-time editor, but many of the commands and concepts found in more advanced editors can trace their beginnings to **ed**.

CHAPTER
SEVENTEEN

The vi Editor

- The One True Editor

- vi's Modes

- Basic Editing in Command Mode

- Using the Shell within vi

- Abbreviations

- Macros

- The set Command

- The .exrc File

- Saving and Exiting

- Summary

In Chapter 16: "The ed Editor," we described a *line editor*. With the advent of more advanced text editors, line editors have become relegated to emergency use and are interesting primarily for historical reasons. If you find yourself on an archaic Unix machine, ed may be your only option for editing files; however, after reading Chapter 16, you may have come to the conclusion that using ed is a very cumbersome way to edit a file—you'd get no argument from us on that point.

Almost all modern Unix systems ship with at least one *full-screen text editor*. A full-screen editor is one that, unlike line editors such as ed, operates on entire files at once, using the full area of the screen (or of the terminal window if you're working in an X Window System environment). Full-screen editors allow you to move around within a file and make changes in various locations during the same session. To a generation of computer users raised with word processors, which basically means anyone under 35 or anyone who learned to use a computer after 1980, using the full-screen text editor is a much more intuitive way to handle your files.

The One True Editor

As you enter into the world of Unix text editors, you get a bonus—your very first "holy war." (And believe us, there are quite a few more to await.) Unix enthusiasts can be quite vocal in the advocacy of their favorite things, including text editors. Debates on the relative merits of a wide variety of editors rage almost nonstop on USENET newsgroups, mailing lists, and Web sites, and even during in-person social events and meetings.

NOTE   You need not participate in these debates if you don't care to, nor should you feel compelled to defend your choice of editor. Just be aware that these debates exist, and they can sometimes get kind of heated. Don't take it personally if someone calls you a weenie because you favor a particular editor; just ignore it, or toss the insult back and get on with your life.

Our choice for the One True Editor is vi. (That's pronounced *vee-eye*, not *vye*.) This is not an arbitrary choice on our part. We are not vi partisans at all—in fact, neither of us use vi very much, preferring pico or one of the newer graphical text editors such as KEdit. Rather, our choice of vi is based on a single fact: It is pretty darn hard to find a Unix machine that isn't running vi. This cannot be said about any other text editor, except perhaps ed. If you're trying to fix a crashed Unix system, many *rescue kits* (diskettes with a few critical Unix utilities) contain vi and no other text editor.

WARNING   Even if you decide not to use vi for your day-to-day file editing, it is crucial that you know at least the basics of the editor. There's nothing worse than being in a situation where vi is your only editor and having no idea how to use it.

---

vi also has history on its side; it was the very first full-screen editor. In fact, vi is short for *visual editor.* In this advanced day, with so many editor choices available, it may seem trivial to use a visual editor, but if you took a look at ed during the last chapter, you'll have some idea of the advances in computing that vi represents.

NOTE   When you start vi by issuing the vi command, you might notice that the name of the program that actually starts is not called vi. It might be vim or vile. These programs are clones of vi that have improved features. Whatever the actual flavor of vi you use, the techniques in this chapter should work.

---

vi's Modes

Before you start working with vi, you need to understand one very critical concept. vi has two modes of operation: *command mode* and *insert mode.* When you first start vi (by issuing the command vi at the prompt), vi will be in command mode; in this mode, everything you type is interpreted by the editor as a command. This can get really confusing, because people generally expect that they'll be able to begin typing once they enter the editor. With vi opening in command mode, there is no text available for the commands to act on, so you may see a stream of error messages. Do not become discouraged.

To get out of command mode and into insert mode, type the letter i. Once you type i, you should see a cursor appear at the beginning of the screen's first line. Now, you can begin typing. For now, type anything—type this paragraph if you're stuck for text. To move the cursor around in your block of text, use the arrow keys. The Backspace key will erase the character to the left of the cursor position, while the Delete key will erase the character directly underneath the cursor. Type for a while, until you have a few lines of text.

When you're done typing, it's time to return to command mode. You do this by pressing the Esc (escape) key. At this point, you can use vi's built-in commands to edit your file, as described in the next section of this chapter.

TIP   If you don't know whether you're in command or insert mode, hit Esc a few times. This won't harm anything, and you'll know for sure that you're in command mode.

Basic Editing in Command Mode

Insert mode is straightforward and self-explanatory; there just isn't a lot to say about insert mode other than "type your text." vi's real power becomes clear in command mode, where you have a number of options and commands to deal with the text you entered in insert mode. The biggest problem with vi is that some of the commands seem arcane and hard to remember. Therefore, in this section, we've provided a series of tables that contain the most commonly used vi commands. Don't worry too much about memorizing these commands; it will happen naturally as you use vi more and more. If you've memorized a few Ctrl key combinations for use in other word processors (Ctrl+s for save, Ctrl+o for open, and so on), you'll be fine with vi's commands as well.

NOTE   If you really get into the vi experience, or you need more information than we've provided in this chapter, we suggest that you locate a copy of *Learning the vi Editor,* by Linda Lamb and Arnold Robbins (O'Reilly & Associates, 1998). This book will teach you vi like none other; when you've worked your way through this book, you will know vi tricks that few other people know. Who knows, vi may even become your favorite editor.

Moving the Cursor

As with word processors or other full-screen text editors, the easiest way to move the cursor around the vi screen is to use the arrow keys on your keyboard. However, this isn't the only way to move around vi. In the 1970s, when vi was developed, keyboards often had no arrow keys, so an alternative cursor movement strategy was implemented. Even today, some vi users prefer these alternate keys, because they don't have to move one hand off the main keys to press the arrows and thus lose momentum in their writing or editing.

As Table 17.1 shows, you can move the vi cursor around the document by pressing the appropriate key for the direction in which you want the cursor to move.

TABLE 17.1: vi Cursor Movement Keys

Command	Action
h	Left
j	Down
k	Up
l	Right

NOTE

This works only in command mode. If you are in insert mode, you will simply type the letters *h*, *j*, *k*, or *l* into your document. To get into command mode, press the Esc key a few times.

Although using the keys is a rapid way to move through the document, you can make the cursor move even more precisely by adding a number to the instruction. For example, if you issue the command 3h, the cursor will move three spaces directly to the left.

NOTE

If you are issuing precise space commands to the left or right with the h or l keys, you won't be able to go beyond the left or right end of the current line. To go up or down to a different line, use the j or k keys.

Table 17.2 shows two similar commands that allow you to move up or down through the document with precision (replace the character *n* with the actual number of lines you want to move).

TABLE 17.2: vi Line Movement Commands

Command	Action
n+	Moves the cursor down n lines
n-	Moves the cursor up n lines

In addition, it is possible to move the cursor to specific locations within the text with the commands shown in Table 17.3, replacing any n characters with a specific number.

TABLE 17.3: vi Cursor Movement Commands

Command	Action
0	Moves to the beginning of the current line
$	Moves to the end of the current line
n$	Moves the cursor to the end of the line, n lines below the current line
w	Moves to the beginning of the next word
nw	Moves the beginning of the word n words from the current word
nG	Moves to the beginning of line n
n|	Moves to the beginning of column n
G	Moves to the last line of the file
^B (Ctrl+b)	Scrolls back one page
^D (Ctrl+d)	Scrolls forward one-half page
^F (Ctrl+f)	Scrolls forward one full page
^U (Ctrl+u)	Scrolls back one-half page

Deleting Text

One of the most important components of editing is deleting, sad to say. It would be a lousy editor indeed that did not allow the writer to delete characters, lines, or entire sections of text that are wrong or unnecessary for the document at hand. vi has a set of deletion commands that will speed your removal of unwanted text; although you can just use the Backspace or Delete keys to get rid of individual characters, the vi commands can take out more characters at once to move the process along. Table 17.4 shows the basic deletion commands; note that some commands have identical results. You can use whichever command is more comfortable for your typing habits.

TABLE 17.4: vi Text Deletion Commands

Command	Action
x	Deletes the character under the cursor
dd	Deletes the current line
D	Deletes everything from the cursor to the end of the line
:D	Deletes the current line (same as **dd**)
:D$	Deletes to the end of the line (same as **D**)
esc u	Undoes the last command
:U	Undoes the last deletion

Pattern Matching and Replacing

One of the features that really distinguishes vi from line editors such as **ed** is vi's ability to search for a given pattern in a document and replace that pattern with another text string if desired. Suppose that you're writing a letter about your running plans for the year, and you've inadvertently typed *10K* instead of *5K* for all the shorter races you want to run. One way to solve the problem would be to page through the document, manually correcting each race distance, but that would take some time (and you might not catch them all).

A better solution is to use the vi match and replace tools. Simply issue the command

```
:s/10K/5K
```

within vi, and the editor will locate the first occurrence of 10K and replace it with 5K. If you want to replace all the 10Ks with 5Ks, you could issue the command

`:s/10K/5K/g`

WARNING   This pattern matching can be extremely helpful, but it can also cause problems if you don't want to replace every single occurrence of the string—even if it occurs in the middle of another word. To be safe, use the command syntax without the /g component at the end. Use the /g only if you are certain that you want to replace that string everywhere it occurs, and be sure to do a thorough proofreading when the process is done.

Table 17.5 contains the vi pattern matching and replacement commands.

TABLE 17.5: vi Pattern Matching and Replacement Commands

Command	Action
/pattern	Searches forward for *pattern*
?pattern	Searches backward for *pattern*
:s/pattern1/pattern2	Replaces first instance of *pattern1* with *pattern2*
:s/pattern1/pattern2/g	Replaces all instances of *pattern1* with *pattern2*

Using the Shell within vi

Although we assume that most people will work with vi inside a terminal window while running X Windows, there are times (and preferences) that call for working in plain text mode. In text mode, the current operation takes up the entire screen, and you can't switch between your vi session and another command prompt to run operations while you're editing in vi.

This can be kind of a hassle, especially if you're working on a lengthy document at the same time as you're performing system administration tasks. Many people probably save the vi document, exit vi, do their shell business, restart vi, and work some more on the document until another command needs to be run, and the whole process starts over again. However, you don't have to do this. vi allows you to run shell commands from within vi itself, which is an incredibly helpful feature.

To run a shell command from within vi, issue the command

`:!unix command`

(replacing *unix command* with the actual command, of course) and press the Enter key. The command will run outside vi, and you can continue your vi session.

You can use some shorthand for shell commands within vi as well. The % character stands for the file currently being edited; # stands for the last file that was edited; and ! stands for the previous command. Thus the command

`:!cp % edit.txt`

will copy the file currently being edited to the file edit.txt. The command

`:!!`

will rerun the last command you gave.

> **NOTE**
>
> The first ! character (called a *bang* in Unix terminology) is required. If you want to issue a second bang to call the previous command, you need to type two bangs.

If you need to perform shell operations that are interactive and require your input while they're running, you'll need to suspend your vi session and exit to the shell. You can do this with the :sh command. When you issue the :sh command, your vi session will disappear, and you will see the shell as you left it, along with the message [No write since last change]. This is a reminder that your text file has changed since the last time you saved it. Do what you need to do in the shell, and when you're ready to return to your vi session, press the Ctrl+d key combination. Your vi session will reappear just as you left it.

Abbreviations

There are many kinds of documents where a certain phrase or word is repeated multiple times. It can become boring or tedious to type the repeating characters over and over, especially if it's a long phrase or uses a mix of characters and numbers. Luckily, you can use the abbreviations feature of vi to save yourself some keystrokes.

With the abbreviations tool, you can create a shorthand string of characters that will automatically call up the full word or phrase as you type it. For example, if you're writing an article about Sun computers, you probably don't want to type *Sun Microsystems* every time you mention the company. Simply set an abbreviation by issuing the command

```
:abbr sunx Sun Microsystems
```

Now, every time you type *sunx* while you are in insert mode, vi will automatically substitute the phrase *Sun Microsystems*.

WARNING Do not use a real word as a vi abbreviation, such as using *sun* as your abbreviation in the example above. If you do, you might find your document containing sentences like "During a solar eclipse, you should never look directly into the Sun Microsystems." Instead, use character combinations that you know you won't type in the document, and clean out old abbreviations after you're finished.

TIP To remove an abbreviation, use the **unab** command: `:unab sunx` (substituting your abbreviation for **sunx**, of course).

Macros

Abbreviations aren't the only shorthand you can use in vi. A *macro* is a type of shorthand that substitutes for a command string, instead of a text string. To create a macro in vi, use the map command.

For example, assume that you want to use the mail command while you're in vi to see whether anyone has sent you e-mail while you've been editing. You could use the shell command sequence described above, or you could create a macro that maps the mail command to a key combination. One possible macro command would be

```
:map <Ctrl>+q :!mail
```

This command maps the Ctrl+q keystroke combination to the `mail` command. Now, when in `vi`, you have to press only Ctrl+q, and the `mail` command will be issued.

NOTE   Obviously, this is a very short example. Macros work most effectively when they are used to map sequences of commands to a single keystroke or keystroke combination.

The set Command

Although `set`'s configurations are not as extensive as those of a word processor, you can set `vi` to meet your personal likes with the `set` command. This command determines various environment settings while you're in `vi`: how the editor handles indentations, letter case, tab width, and so on. Indicate these settings with the `set` command, which uses the syntax

   `:set argument=value`

where *argument* is the name of the parameter, and *value* is the setting. Table 17.6 contains some common `vi` parameters that you can set to configure your `vi` environment.

TABLE 17.6: Common `vi` Parameters

Parameter	Action
autoindent	Each line is indented to match previous line.
autowrite	Automatically saves the file after certain commands.
directory	Specifies the directory of the edit buffer.
ignorecase	Ignores upper- and lowercase in pattern matching.
list	Displays tabs as ^I and end-of-lines as $.
mesg	Toggles e-mail write permission.

Continued on next page

TABLE 17.6 CONTINUED: Common vi Parameters

Parameter	Action
number	Shows line numbers.
shell	Specifies shell that is escaped to during :! commands.
shiftwidth	Sets tab width.
wrapmargin	Sets the maximum line length.

There is an alternative format for options that are toggled on or off, rather than having a specific value. For example, if you want to turn on auto-indenting, you can simply use the syntax

```
set autoindent
```

If you want to turn it off, use

```
set noautoindent
```

The .exrc File

Like the various shells described in Part IV: "Using The Shell," vi also has a run control file that the program uses to determine settings and user configurations. The vi run control file is called .exrc, and it lives in your home directory.

> **NOTE**   If your system has the vim program (a clone of vi) instead of regular vi, your run control file is called .vimrc instead of .exrc. .vimrc should look much the same as the .exrc file that we describe here.

> **TIP**   Remember that the dot files (those whose names begin with a period, or dot) won't show when you do a plain ls command. To see your dot files, add a few flags to the command, such as ls -la. That will show your dot files, as well as their size and file permissions.

The .exrc file will contain any parameter settings that you made with the set command, as well as macros made with map and abbreviations made with abbr. If you want to create a whole slew of set, map, or abbr functions at once, you can edit .exrc directly (with a text editor such as vi). A sample .exrc file might look like this one, which contains some of the settings we've shown in this chapter:

```
set list
set noautoindent
set wrapmargin=80
abbr sunx Sun Microsystems
map ^z :!mail
```

NOTE
Reviewing your .exrc file regularly is a good habit. You can locate old abbreviations or macros that you don't use any more and clean them out of the file. Because vi runs the .exrc file every time vi starts up, a slim and trimmed-down .exrc will make vi boot more rapidly.

Saving and Exiting

We suspect that there are several readers who have turned directly to this section of the chapter because they can't figure out how to get out of vi. We share your pain. In her early days with vi, Kate was known to suspend the process and kill vi with the job number (this is not a very good idea), because she couldn't remember how to quit the program. We hope to save you this indignity; however, if you don't know how to exit vi, you could find yourself just as stuck as she was.

The simplest way to exit vi is to get into command mode (tap Esc a few times) and type the command :q. Note the colon; simply typing q will not get you out of vi. However, there is a bit of danger in using the :q command, because vi is capable of quitting without saving your file—thus losing all your work from the last save. To save the file, issue the command :w in command mode.

TIP
To do both at the same time, develop the habit of issuing the command :wq. This command will both save your file and exit vi. Remember this with the phrase *w for write, q for quit;* thus, :wq both writes and quits.

Table 17.7 shows some other options for saving and quitting.

TABLE 17.7: vi Saving and Quitting Commands

Command	Action
:w	Saves (writes) file
:q	Quits vi
:wq	Saves file *and* quits vi
:q!	Forces a quit (allows you to quit on an unsaved file)
ZZ	Saves and quits (same as :wq)

Summary

Many Unix adherents argue that vi is the most useful and powerful text editor available. Although there are other candidates for the position, it is certainly true that vi holds a large share of the text-editor market and that it is the editor you are most likely to find on the widest variety of Unix computers. Even if you do not choose to use vi as your permanent text editor, it's wise to familiarize yourself with it.

vi has two modes of operation: command mode and insert mode. Text must be entered in insert mode, while command mode is used for editing and other tasks performed after text has been added to the file. vi's commands are all keyboard-based, so it can be quite fast once you learn the basic keystroke combinations. It is also an effective editor for matching patterns, constructing macros, and executing shell commands from within the editor.

CHAPTER

EIGHTEEN

GNU Emacs

- What Is GNU Emacs?
- Running emacs
- emacs Peculiarities
- Getting Started with emacs
- Dealing with Buffers
- Dealing with Windows
- The GNU Emacs Window
- Getting Help
- Backups and Auto-Save
- Killing and Yanking Text
- Searching and Replacing
- Saving and Editing
- Doctor
- Summary

In Chapter 17: "The vi Editor," we declared that vi is the One True Editor. In this chapter, we proclaim GNU Emacs to be the Other One True Editor. Although it is not as essential to know emacs as it is to know vi, emacs is nearly as popular and has more features than vi. emacs also inspires a level of devotion (some say fanaticism) among its adherents that is rivaled only by that of some religious sects.

NOTE
We refer to this program both as GNU Emacs, its proper name, and as emacs, the command used to invoke the program. If you are going to use the proper name when discussing the editor, be sure to keep the GNU component in the name. See Chapter 2: "Which Unix?" for more information on the GNU project.

What Is GNU Emacs?

In addition to having a host of standard editing tools, GNU Emacs has several unique features. With this editor, you can work on more than one file at a time, as well as use the built-in newsreader and mailreader. emacs also has a built-in macro scripting language and even its own psychiatric help.

emacs has many adherents among programmers, who like the elegant way that the editor interacts with gcc (the GNU C Compiler) and gdb (the GNU Debugger) to form a full software development environment. GNU Emacs is such a feature-rich program that it is possible to use it as your entire operating environment. We actually know a couple of people who do this, and, although we would never do it ourselves, it's kind of cool to think about an editor having that much power.

All of these features come with a price. GNU Emacs is a very large program, both in terms of the hard-disk space it occupies and the amount of memory it requires to run effectively. This isn't too much of a problem if you're running emacs on a powerful workstation, but if you're using an old 386 running Linux, or if you have multiple users on multiple workstations pulling emacs from a central server, you might notice some serious system lag, because all those emacs processes start adding up.

GNU Emacs also has a pretty hefty learning curve. We tell you this up front so that you won't be discouraged when you run into a wall, and you probably will.

Although we can give you the basics in this chapter, it is the sort of program that warrants entire books, and it takes some practice before you can use it effectively without referring to cheat-sheets every time you need to do something. emacs isn't very intuitive (unless, we suppose, you're Richard Stallman), but once some basic emacs habits have become ingrained, the editor really does make many common editing tasks an absolute breeze.

> **NOTE**
>
> Many Unix systems do not include emacs in their basic distributions. If you need to get it, check the CD-ROM included with this book. You can also get a copy of the latest version (recommended) from the Free Software Foundation at http://www.fsf.org. For this chapter, we assume that you have obtained a copy of GNU Emacs and have installed it successfully.

Running emacs

Start GNU Emacs simply by issuing the command emacs at a command prompt. Alternatively, you can issue the command emacs *filename* to start the editor with the named file already loaded and ready for work.

Once you have the editor open, as seen in Figure 18.1, you're ready for work. However, we suggest that you read through the rest of this chapter before beginning to learn more about the many peculiarities of the emacs editor and pick up some tips that may make your emacs session less confusing and annoying.

emacs Peculiarities

One of the reasons why GNU Emacs seems so hard to learn is that it approaches common editing tasks in an unusual way. The two main peculiarities unique to emacs are the way in which it structures data and the way in which it interprets keyboard input. Although these functions are found in other editors, emacs is unique in that it forces the user to confront these mechanisms while working on a file; other editors often camouflage this material behind a friendlier user interface.

FIGURE 18.1:

The GNU Emacs editor runs in single-window mode by default.

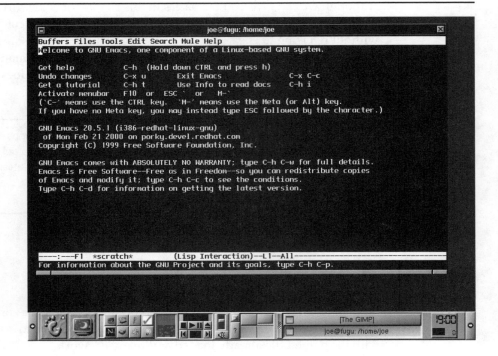

Data Structures

It is crucial to note that when you work on a file in emacs, you are not actually working on the file itself. As with ed (see Chapter 16: "The ed Editor"), you are working in a buffer, a copy of the file held in system memory. Any changes you make to the file in emacs will not be permanent until you save them back to the real file. This is true of many other editors, not just ed and emacs, but emacs makes this process explicit.

emacs contains a number of functions reserved specifically for working with buffers, so you need to be aware of this when working in the editor. During an emacs session, it is possible to have multiple buffers open with different files—or different views of the same file—in each. Most of the time, this level of complexity is not necessary, but should the need arise, the capability is there.

In addition to offering files and buffers, emacs also offers *windows* as a feature. These are not windows in the Microsoft or X Window System sense, but are rather individual views of a given buffer. It is possible to split the screen vertically or horizontally into multiple windows, as shown in Figure 18.2, and have separate buffers (or separate views of the same buffer) in each window. This allows you to view and edit multiple buffers simultaneously.

FIGURE 18.2:

GNU Emacs lets you view multiple buffers within windows on the desktop.

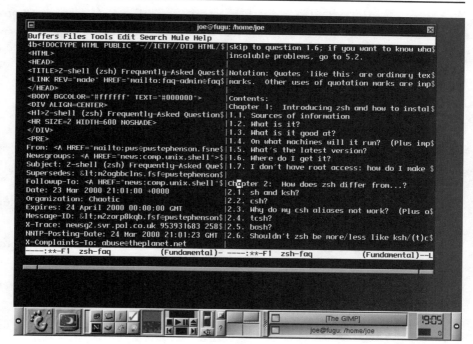

Key Bindings

Because of the way emacs was written, each keystroke you type is actually a command to the editor. For example, if you type the letter **A**, you are issuing a command for emacs to insert the A character into the buffer. For the letters and numbers that appear on your keyboard, this has no interesting practical applications, but there are a couple of keys for which this concept becomes very important.

When you want to use the native command functions in GNU Emacs, you will usually do so with the Ctrl key and the metakey.

NOTE   If you are running `emacs` on a PC, the metakey is the Alt key. However, if you are using a terminal or a terminal emulator program over a network, the Alt key may not work for this. In that case, you'll have to use the Escape key instead.

The Ctrl and metakeys are an integral part of using `emacs` properly. GNU Emacs documentation, and most other documents about `emacs`, makes use of a particular notation to describe `emacs` command sequences. To maintain consistency, we also use the same notation in this chapter (as opposed to the notation used throughout the rest of the book). Here's how it works:

C-x: For any character *x*, C-x means *hold down the Ctrl key and type the character*. So, if we say C-d, you would hold down Ctrl and type **d**.

M-x: For any character *x*, M-x means *hold down the metakey and type the character*. So, if you see M-d, you would press the metakey (probably Alt) and type **d**.

C-M-x: For any character *x*, hold down both the Ctrl key and the metakey, and type the character.

Note that you should not think of these key combinations as modifying that particular character, but rather as issuing a command with a keystroke combination.

Getting Started with emacs

For this section of the chapter, we assume that you have already started `emacs` by issuing the `emacs` command, but that you have not loaded any buffers yet. To read a file into the buffer, use the command C-x C-f. The C-x combination is a *prefix* indicating that a command intended to manipulate a file, buffer, or window will be typed next.

After you type C-x C-f, you will see Find file: ~/ appear on the bottommost line of the screen. The ~/ indicates your home directory. Anything you type at this point will be entered in a path relative to your home directory; if you want to use a file in your home directory, you simply need to type the filename. If you want to specify a file above the home directory, just backspace over the ~/ and type the full path name of the desired file. When you've entered the correct filename, press Enter. The text of the file will appear in the main window (remember that this is an `emacs` window and can be moved or divided).

At this point, you can begin to edit the file. You can use regular editing techniques, such as using the arrow keys to move the cursor around the file and using the Backspace or Delete keys to get rid of characters. In addition to the basic techniques common to almost every editor (Unix or not), the C-a command will move the cursor to the beginning of the current line, and the C-e command will move the cursor to the end of the current line. Other cursor movement commands are shown in Table 18.1.

TABLE 18.1: Other GNU Emacs Movement Commands

Command	Function
C-b	Moves cursor back one character
C-f	Moves cursor forward one character
M-b	Moves cursor back one word
M-f	Moves cursor forward one word
M-a	Moves cursor to beginning of current sentence
M-e	Moves cursor to end of current sentence
M-	Moves cursor to beginning of current paragraph
M-"	Moves cursor to end of current paragraph
C-v	Scrolls to next screen of document
M-v	Scrolls to previous screen of document
M-<	Moves cursor to beginning of buffer
M->	Moves cursor to end of buffer

Dealing with Buffers

As we said in the previous section, the command C-x C-f reads a file into the buffer. It is possible to have more than one buffer open if you want; just use the C-x C-f command again to create a second buffer, and read another file into it. You can then use the C-x b command to switch between buffers.

The name of the second buffer will already be given as the default value for the C-x b command, so all you need to do is press Enter. If you have more than two buffers open and don't know the names of all of the buffers, use the C-x C-b command to see a list of all available buffers.

To close a buffer, issue the C-x k command. You will be prompted for the name of the buffer to be closed. If that buffer contains unsaved changes, you will be asked whether you want to save the changes before closing the buffer. Remember that changes will not be saved automatically to the file on the disk.

Dealing with Windows

If you want to have more than one window, or buffer view, open at the same time, you have a couple of options. The command C-x 2 will split the current window in half horizontally, while C-x 3 will split it in half vertically. Figures 18.3 and 18.4 show both options. When you have opened a second window, you can move the cursor into the new window with the C-x o command. Other window commands are shown in Table 18.2.

FIGURE 18.3:

Split the emacs window horizontally to view two buffers at once.

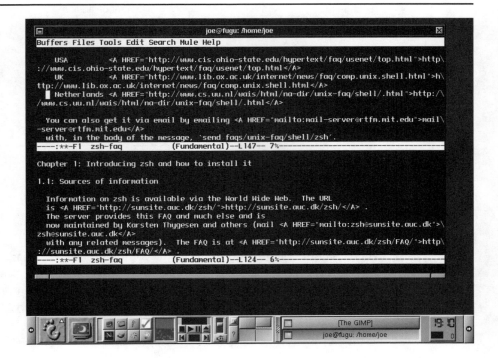

FIGURE 18.4:

If you prefer, you can split the emacs window vertically.

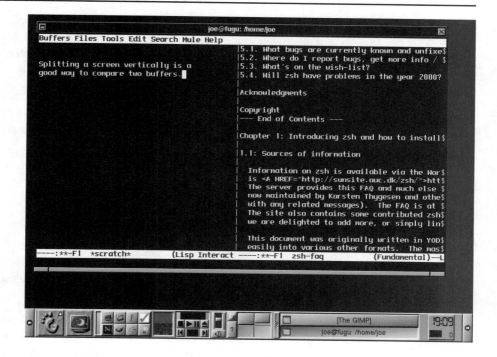

TABLE 18.2: Other GNU Emacs Window Commands

Command	Function
C-x 0	Closes the current window
C-x 1	Closes all windows but the current window
C-M-v	Scrolls the other window to the next screen of the buffer
M-x shrink-window	Shrinks the current window vertically
C-x ^	Makes the current window grow vertically
C-x -	Shrinks the current window horizontally
C-x "	Makes the current window grow horizontally
C-x 4 b	Selects the buffer in the other window
C-x 4 C-o	Displays the buffer in the other window
C-x 4 f	Finds a file in the other window

When you first create a new window, the current buffer will appear in both windows. You can switch to another buffer using the method described in the previous section, or you can open a new buffer in the new window. If you prefer, you can even work on the same buffer in both windows. This is often useful if you're editing a large file and want to check out two parts of the file simultaneously.

Remember that there is nothing in particular that ties a given window to a given buffer. If you close a window, you do not close the buffer that is displayed in that window. To close the buffer, you must issue a separate command.

The GNU Emacs Window

Now that you have an understanding of emacs windows, buffers, and commands, there are only two elements of the emacs window that you need to know about before you can begin to work. These elements are found at the bottom of the screen and are called the mode line and the mini buffer. They are labeled in Figure 18.5. Use these tools to manage your document and issue the commands that let you control emacs and its behavior.

FIGURE 18.5:

The mode line and mini buffer let you control GNU Emacs in command mode.

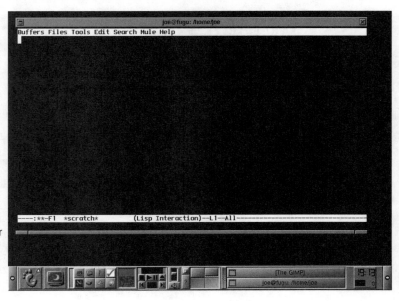

Mode Line

Mini Buffer

The Mode Line

When you edit a buffer in emacs, the entire area of the screen is given over to the text of your file, with the exception of two lines at the very bottom of the screen. The upper of these two lines is the *mode line.* The mode line is the line that is highlighted in reverse color (white on black instead of black on white, if you use a black/white display).

The mode line contains various bits of information about your buffer, such as its name and what part of the file you're currently viewing on the screen. You cannot directly edit the information that appears in the mode line, but it will change as the attributes of your buffer change.

The Mini Buffer

The line at the very bottom of the screen is called the *mini buffer.* The mini buffer is where messages from emacs are displayed, where you enter your commands, and where the command keystrokes are echoed. You can watch what you're doing in the mini buffer, which can be quite helpful if you find yourself mistyping command sequences.

Getting Help

If you find yourself flustered by GNU Emacs, you can consult the extensive online help. Table 18.3 shows the five commands that access the help files. We especially recommend the tutorial, which is excellent for emacs beginners and also may teach a tip or two to those who've been around emacs for a while, but have never run the tutorial. emacs help is accessible in a variety of ways, so you can get context-specific help or more generalized help indices.

TABLE 18.3: GNU Emacs Help Commands

Command	Result
C-h a	Prompts for a keyword and then lists all commands containing that word
C-h k	Prompts for a keystroke and then describes the command bound to that key
C-h i	Enters the hypertext documentation reader
C-h p	Opens a browser, in which you can search the help files by subject
C-h t	Runs the tutorial program

Backups and Auto-Save

If you've ever lost a lot of work because you closed a file without saving it, or realized after you saved a file that you made a mistake that's deleted a lot of your hard work, you'll appreciate the backup and auto-save features of GNU Emacs. These features are part of the reason that emacs is so favored, because it is hard to lose a file when your editor is quietly keeping copies as you work.

Every time you save a file, emacs creates a second backup file that is a copy of the previous version. That is, the backup file is one version older than the current file version, which is very helpful indeed if something happens to the current file. The backup file is named with a trailing tilde (~). That is, if the filename is wallaby, the backup file will be called wallaby~.

If GNU Emacs, or your entire system, crashes before you can save your changes, an auto-saved file should be available for you when the system comes back up. If you are looking for the auto-saved copy of the wallaby file, check for a file called #wallaby#. This is the auto-saved new version of your files. Auto-saving occurs every 300 characters or so, or when a system error is encountered.

WARNING Do not let auto-saves and backups replace frequent saving by hand. These are meant as emergency measures, not as regular habits.

Killing and Yanking Text

In the unique language of emacs, *killing* text and *yanking* text are roughly analogous to the terms *cutting* text and *pasting* text in other programs. To cut a line of text, use the C-k command. This kills all the text from the cursor position to the end of the line. If you want to cut the full line, you'll need to position the cursor at the beginning of the line; refer back to Table 18.1 for cursor movement commands. Note that the C-k command will not kill the invisible *new-line* character at the end of the line. You must issue the C-k command a second time if you want to delete the new-line character and close up the whitespace in the document.

Once you've killed a chunk of text, you can *yank* it back into the buffer by issuing the C-y command. If you killed several lines of text in one go, without any nonkill commands in between, all of those lines will be treated as one object and will all be pasted back into the buffer.

You can also use the M-y command to scroll back through previous killed text. To scroll, issue the C-y command first, and then M-y. The previous kills will appear at the cursor position. When you see the kill you want, simply leave it there and continue editing.

You can move text by killing it, moving the cursor to a new position, and yanking the kill back in. To copy text, kill it, immediately yank it back in, move the cursor to a new position, and yank it in again. This may seem a bit complicated, but it will quickly become second nature.

Searching and Replacing

To search for a given character string in the text, issue the C-s command and then type your search string when prompted. As you type, emacs searches incrementally for the next character, which speeds up the search process quite a bit. This means that emacs will often locate the string you're looking for before you even finish typing it. Find the next match of the same string by typing C-s again. You can search backward from the cursor position by typing C-r.

To search for a pattern and replace it with another string, use the M-% command. This is an interactive function that will prompt you for the string to be found and the string with which it will be replaced. When a match is found, you will have six options, described in Table 18.4. You will need to begin replacement searches from the start of the document.

TABLE 18.4: GNU Emacs Search and Replace Options

Option	Result
Spacebar	Performs the replacement
Delete	Doesn't perform the replacement
Enter	Terminates the search-and-replace without having performed this replacement
Esc	Same as Enter
.	Terminates the search-and-replace after having performed the replacement
!	Performs the replacement for all matches in the current buffer

Saving and Exiting

As with vi, exiting emacs is not the most intuitive process in the world. The command to exit is C-x C-c. If you have unsaved buffers open when you issue this command, emacs will prompt you to save them before quitting. To save a file without exiting emacs, use the command C-x C-s. If you have multiple buffers that need to be saved, use the command C-x s to save them all at one time.

Doctor

One of the more amusing features of GNU Emacs is the Doctor program. Based on the pioneering interactive psychological program Eliza, the emacs Doctor will respond to your statements in a nondirective and calm manner based on the therapy ideals of Rogerian analysis.

Start the Doctor by issuing the command M-x doctor. Explain your problem in a single sentence and press Enter twice. The Doctor will respond and will continue to respond as long as you enter more statements. Let the conversation flow naturally. You might become extremely frustrated, highly amused, or actually aided by the Doctor's responses. A sample session is shown in Figure 18.6.

Summary

Although it is complicated and somewhat hard to learn, GNU Emacs is a text editor that offers a great deal of flexibility and power to its users. emacs has a wide variety of functions, including tight integration for programmers and an effective multiple-window interface. The editor is controlled through a series of Ctrl and Alt (meta) key sequences.

With emacs, you can work on multiple files at one time. You can also take advantage of strong backup and auto-saving features, as well as a quick and accurate cut-and-paste system. emacs performs strongly in searching and replacing text strings, as well. If you are willing to put in a bit of time to learn how to use the editor, GNU Emacs will reward you with a powerful editing toolkit and a well-built interface.

FIGURE 18.6:

GNU Emacs even provides built-in psychological help.

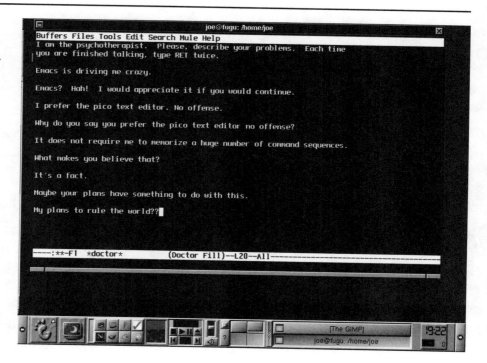

CHAPTER
NINETEEN

pico, joe, and jed

- pico
- joe
- jed
- Summary

Although vi and emacs are certainly the "Big Two" of Unix text editors, they are not the only choices you have. Thank heavens! Other alternatives might be the proper selection for you and the way you like to work with text. Each of these editors has its own features and its own way of doing things; some are quite simple, while others are much less so—though none are as complex as emacs. Some of these editors run in text mode, while others require a graphical X Windows interface.

In this chapter, we provide a brief introduction to three of the more popular text-mode editors: pico, joe, and jed. Of these three, pico is the most widely used, but joe and jed have a general feel similar to that provided by other editors such as emacs. As with almost everything else in the Unix environment, your decision about a text editor can be made based on what feels right for you.

pico

Let's get this out of the way up front: We love pico. It's our preferred editor, and we make sure it's available on all the machines we run or use. However, this affection causes some consternation among our most geekish friends, who think that pico is not a particularly serious text editor (there is a suspicious overlap in this group with the folks who think everyone should use emacs as an operating system). Luckily, we've never really felt that seriousness was a criterion for text editors, so we happily use pico to generate tons of data.

We'll admit that pico is not the best choice for serious programmers. It does lack some of the features of the more powerful editors, such as emacs, but in return, it's small, lightweight, and a snap to use. It's also perfect for folks who are generating text files (like us), rather than programs. We assume that serious programmers probably don't need this book, though, so you might want to give pico a try.

TIP   pico was developed at the University of Washington as part of the Pine e-mail client, but the editor can be installed and run as a separate text editor for those who don't want to use Pine.

Starting pico

To start pico, just type pico at a command prompt. If you want to open pico with a particular file already available for editing, type pico filename (where *filename* is the name of the particular file you want to work on). You can begin entering text as soon as the pico screen appears, as shown in Figure 19.1.

FIGURE 19.1:

The basic pico screen contains a text-entry area and a brief command reference.

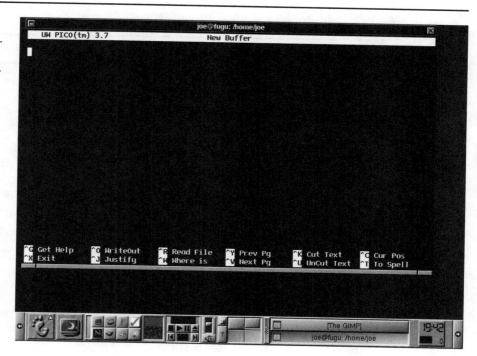

Editing Text in pico

Unlike either vi or emacs, pico has only one mode of operation. By default, anything that you type on the keyboard will be interpreted by pico as text to be inserted into the open file. The exception is any keystroke combination that uses the Ctrl key, because Ctrl key sequences are pico's command language.

While working in a pico file, you can use the arrow keys to move around the document. Deleting text is done with the Backspace key. More complicated editing functions can be done with the Ctrl key sequences described in Table 19.1. The most frequently used combinations are always visible along the bottom of the pico screen in a two-line bar; cycle through the context-sensitive commands with the Ctrl+o key combination.

TABLE 19.1: pico Ctrl Key Sequences

Command	Function
Ctrl+a	Moves to the beginning of the current line
Ctrl+e	Moves to the end of the current line
Ctrl+f	Moves forward one character
Ctrl+b	Moves backward one character
Ctrl+n	Moves to the next line
Ctrl+p	Moves to the previous line
Ctrl+v	Scrolls forward one page
Ctrl+y	Scrolls backward one page
Ctrl+k	Deletes (kills) the current line of text
Ctrl+u	Undoes the last deletion
Ctrl+j	Justifies (reformats paragraph)
Ctrl+w	Searches for a text string
Ctrl+r	Inserts the contents of another file at the current cursor position
Ctrl+o	Outputs the current buffer to a file (effectively saving the file to the disk)
Ctrl+x	Exits pico—you will be prompted to save the buffer
Ctrl+g	Gets help
Ctrl+t	Spell-checks the document (this function requires that you have ispell, a Unix spell-checking program, installed and operating)

Although pico lacks some of the features that make vi and emacs appealing to programmers, pico's consistent and intuitive interface makes it a natural for tasks such as e-mail (in the Pine e-mail program) and other tasks that require dealing with big text files. pico is quite easy to learn, and we find it simple to teach new Unix users how to handle the program.

Setting a Default Editor

Many Unix programs, such as e-mail readers, newsreaders, and the like, will call on the *default editor* to handle any text-editing needs. The default editor is not a particular editor; rather, it's whatever the system administrator has set as the systemwide setting. The default editor is usually—though not always—vi.

If you want to set a different default editor, such as pico or emacs, you can do this by changing the value of the $EDITOR environment variable (assuming you're using the bash shell). Put the following line in your .bashrc file:

```
export $EDITOR="pico"
```

If you want to use something other than pico, of course, substitute its name. If you're using a shell other than bash, use that shell's procedure for setting environment variables. See Chapter 22: "Variables" and Chapter 13: "Customizing the Shell Environment" for more details.

joe

The joe editor is sort of a cross between emacs and pico. Like pico, joe has only one mode. As with emacs, joe's commands and procedures are controlled with various combinations of Ctrl key sequences and regular keystrokes. Also, as with emacs, you can split the joe screen into multiple windows. Figure 19.2 shows joe in single-window mode, while Figure 19.3 shows joe split into two windows, each showing a different buffer.

To begin working with joe, just type joe at a shell prompt. Enter text as you would with pico. Because joe is a single-mode editor, you don't have to worry about getting into the correct mode before you enter text. As with pico, you can use the arrow keys to move around the document, and you can backspace over text to delete unwanted characters. Unlike pico, though, joe has more Ctrl key sequences, giving you more flexibility and precision in your editing tasks. Tables 19.2 to 19.7 display the various Ctrl key combinations used in joe.

FIGURE 19.2:

The joe editor runs in a single-window mode by default.

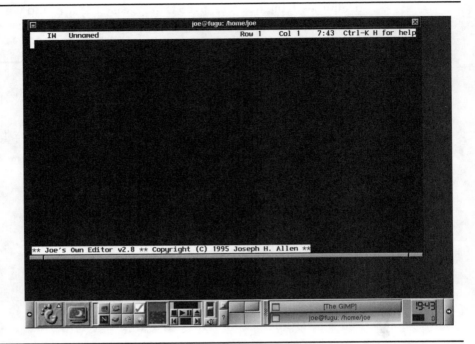

FIGURE 19.3:

Like emacs, joe can run multiple windows within one session.

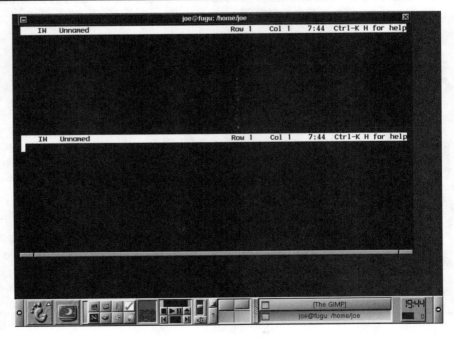

TABLE 19.2: joe Cursor Movement Commands

Command	Function
Ctrl+b	Moves cursor one space left
Ctrl+f	Moves cursor one space right
Ctrl+p	Moves cursor up one line
Ctrl+n	Moves cursor down one line
Ctrl+z	Moves cursor to the previous word
Ctrl+x	Moves cursor to the next word
Ctrl+a	Moves to the beginning of the current line
Ctrl+e	Moves to the end of the current line

TABLE 19.3: joe Page Movement Commands

Command	Function
Ctrl+u	Scrolls back one screen
Ctrl+v	Scrolls forward one screen
Ctrl+k,u	Goes to the beginning of the file
Ctrl+k,v	Goes to the end of the file

TABLE 19.4: joe Deletion Commands

Command	Function
Ctrl+d	Deletes character at current cursor position
Ctrl+y	Deletes the current line
Ctrl+w	Deletes word to the right of cursor
Ctrl+o	Deletes word to the left of cursor

Continued on next page

TABLE 19.4 CONTINUED: joe Deletion Commands

Command	Function
Ctrl+j	Deletes from cursor position to the end of the line
Ctrl+_	Undoes last deletion (this sequence is Ctrl+Shift+dash/underscore key)
Ctrl+^	Redeletes last undone deletion (this sequence is Ctrl+Shift+6/caret key)

TABLE 19.5: joe Search Commands

Command	Function
Ctrl+k,f	Finds a text string (you will be prompted for the string)
Ctrl+l	Finds next occurrence of previously searched text string

TABLE 19.6: joe Window Operation Commands

Command	Function
Ctrl+k,o	Splits the window in half
Ctrl+k,g	Makes the current window bigger
Ctrl+k,t	Makes the current window smaller
Ctrl+k,n	Goes to the window below the current window
Ctrl+k,p	Goes to the window above the current window
Ctrl+c	Kills current window
Ctrl+k,e	Loads a specified file into the current window
Ctrl+k,l	If multiple windows are open, shows only one window; otherwise, shows all windows

TABLE 19.7: joe Miscellaneous Commands

Command	Function
Esc+y	Yanks previously deleted text back into buffer at current cursor position
Ctrl+k,'	Escapes to shell prompt
Ctrl+k,!	Executes shell command
Ctrl+k,j	Reformats paragraph
Ctrl+k,r	Inserts contents of a named file at the cursor position
Ctrl+k,h	Displays help file
Ctrl+k,x	Saves file
Ctrl+c	Exits joe

jed

jed is an interesting text editor with a small but loyal following. The program is named with the initials of its developer, John E. Davis. The most interesting thing about jed is that it can be made to emulate other editors. By default, it is configured to emulate GNU Emacs, as shown in Figure 19.4, but it can also emulate EDT, one of the first Unix editors, and WordStar. (Those readers who, like us, remember early DOS word processors, will probably feel a twinge of nostalgia at that.) One advantage of using jed over other text editors is that there are versions of jed for both Unix and MS-DOS, which is handy if you work in a mixed operating-system environment.

jed's Run Control Files

jed's emulation modes are controlled from the program's various run control files. The systemwide run control file for jed is usually located at /usr/lib/jed/lib/jed.rc. If you run jed without any personal environment customization, this file will be loaded automatically. However, if you want to customize your own jed environment, you must create a file named .jedrc in your home directory and place your personal configurations in that file. Any options you put in the .jedrc file will override options selected in the global file (/usr/lib/jed/lib/jed.rc).

FIGURE 19.4:

By default, jed emulates the GNU Emacs text editor.

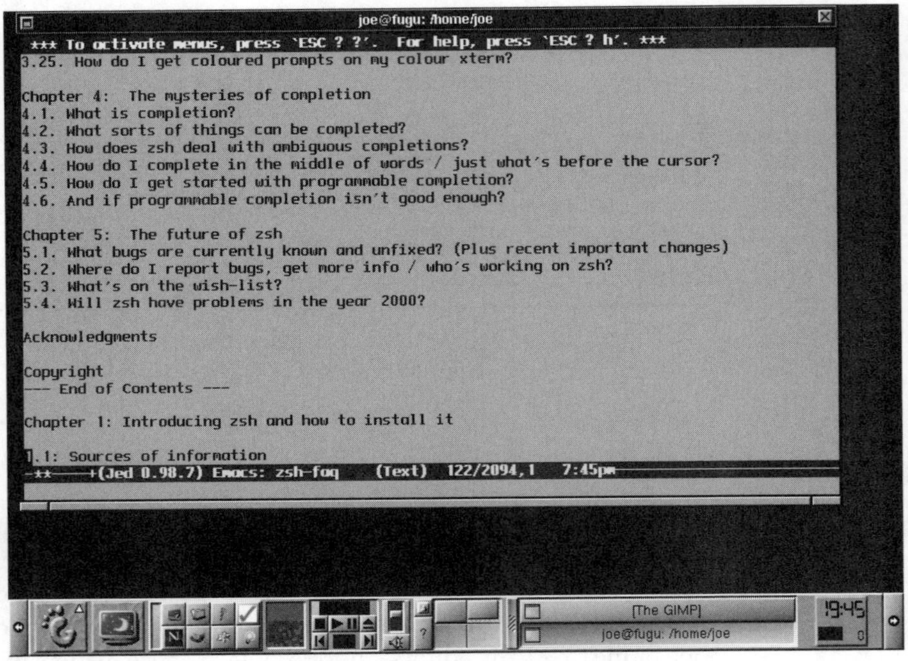

The easiest way to accomplish personal customization of jed is just to copy the systemwide file into your home directory and save it as .jedrc. You can do this with the command

```
cp /usr/lib/jed/lib/jed.rc .jedrc
```

Once the file has been copied, you can make the changes you want for your personal jed use. For example, if you want to switch jed from emacs emulation to WordStar emulation, you would locate the line

```
() = evalfile("emacs");      % Emacs-like bindings
```

and put a percent symbol in front of it, so that it looks like this:

```
%() = evalfile("emacs");      % Emacs-like bindings
```

jed treats the percent symbol as a comment marker and ignores anything on a line that begins with the percent symbol.

Then, locate the line

```
% () = evalfile("wordstar");     % Wordstar
```

and delete the first percent symbol. Now, when you start jed, it will start in WordStar mode, as seen in Figure 19.5.

There are many other configuration options in this file, and the comments in the file explain the options fairly well. We encourage you to browse through this file to learn what you can do with jed.

Running jed

jed is started just like any other editor, by typing jed or jed filename at a shell prompt. Once in jed, type Esc+?,? to see a menu of functions across the top of the screen. These functions can be activated by typing their assigned number. There are functions for windows, buffers, shell commands, spell-checking, and so on, which should all be familiar if you have worked in other editors, especially emacs.

FIGURE 19.5:

jed can also emulate the MS-DOS editor WordStar.

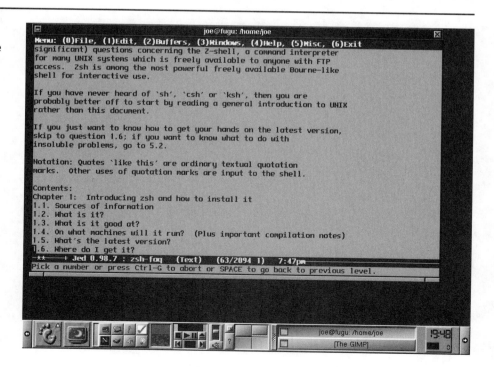

Move around the jed screen with the arrow keys, and the Page Up and Page Down keys. Further keyboard functions will depend on the emulation mode that you choose. To exit jed, use the exit option in the menu or use the exit command for the editor that jed is emulating.

Summary

There are several choices for a text editor, beyond vi and emacs. Whether you are looking for an editor that is easy and fast to learn, or for one that operates like another editor without its size or complexity, you can find a program that will work for you. Three of the most popular text editors are pico, joe, and jed.

pico is a small but powerful text editor that relies on a small number of easily remembered keystroke combinations to do its work. joe is also small but powerful, and uses keystroke combinations similar to those in emacs. Finally, jed has the ability to emulate several different editors, using the key bindings and screen layout of those programs.

CHAPTER
TWENTY

Graphical Text Editors

- Why Graphical Editors?

- NEdit

- KEdit

- gEdit

- Summary

With the growing availability of attractive graphical user interfaces for Unix systems, such as the integrated desktop environments described in Part III of this book, it is becoming more common to use graphical editors for text manipulation instead of the text-mode editors described in the other chapters of this part of the book.

As their name implies, *graphical editors* are designed to be used with a window manager or desktop environment running under the X Window System. They constitute a sort of middle ground between the ultra-spare text-mode editors such as vi and a full-blown word processor such as Corel's WordPerfect 9. If you've ever used the Notepad in Windows or Simpletext on a Macintosh, you have a general idea of what graphical text editors are like.

Why Graphical Editors?

Whether you view graphical editors as stripped-down word processors or fancied-up text-mode editors has more to do with your computing experience than it does with the editors themselves. Those who come to Unix and graphical editors from a word-processing environment will tend to regard graphical editors as word processors lacking certain features, while people who come to graphical editors from a pure command-line Unix environment tend to regard them as unnecessary overkill.

Personally, we like graphical editors. In fact, the preliminary notes for this book were mostly written in NEdit, a graphical editor we'll describe in the next section of this chapter. Graphical editors offer most of the features of text-mode editors, while adding the convenience of being able to use the mouse, cut and paste easily, control the appearance of the document on-screen, and use drop-down menus instead of memorizing keystroke combinations. These may seem like trivial considerations, but unless you've ingrained a text-mode editor's commands so thoroughly into your mind that you don't even need to think about them, these "trivialities" can make your work go a lot faster.

There is, of course, a downside to all this convenience. Most graphical editors use more system memory than most text-mode editors (GNU Emacs being the exception). If you need to allocate your precious memory carefully, vi or pico might be a better choice from a performance standpoint. Also, you can't use graphical editors over a network unless you've set up the X Windows display forwarding function, which seems like an awful lot of work just to edit a file.

The general rule of thumb we use is that for quick and dirty file editing such as tweaking a configuration file, text-mode editors are easier and faster. For extended composition, such as correspondence or the notes for a book, a graphical editor is probably a better tool.

NOTE   Remember that graphical editors are still text editors. That is, graphical editors are designed to edit text in a file, not words on a page. Although it is possible to configure the look of a graphical editor in any number of ways, the page you see on the screen may not bear any resemblance to what you see if you print the document. If you want to do advanced formatting such as layout, fonts, line spacing, and the like, you'll need to use an actual word processor such as WordPerfect, Abiword, StarOffice, or something similar, or a typesetting program such as LaTeX or FrameMaker.

NEdit

NEdit is a solid graphical text editor with a clean, spare look and a lot of useful features. It happens to be Joe's favorite graphical text editor, because it doesn't clutter up its screen with a lot of graphical elements such as buttons, and because it's fast and solid. NEdit has a very small memory footprint; for regular text editing, NEdit's drain on resident memory clocks in at just under 3MB.

As seen in Figure 20.1, NEdit has a large composition window with a single menu bar at the top. Each menu-bar item activates a drop-down menu with a number of functions, some with sub-menus. This is similar to how regular word processors work, but is a feature that text-mode editors don't have.

To begin working with NEdit, simply open it by typing nedit at a command prompt. If you're working in a desktop environment, such as that of KDE or Gnome, you will probably be able to launch NEdit from the application starter or by clicking an icon in the panel if you've created one. Type your data into the main text-entry screen. To save the file, select File ➤ Save from the menu bar or press Ctrl+s, and name the file at the prompt.

FIGURE 20.1:

NEdit is a clean, uncluttered graphical text editor.

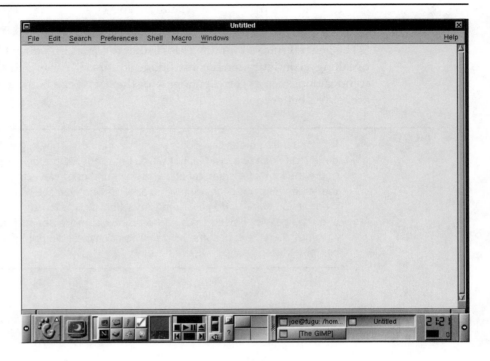

FIGURE 20.1:

NEdit is a clean, uncluttered graphical text editor.

Tables 20.1 to 20.7 show the various menu functions of NEdit. We cover menu options thoroughly in this chapter because, as we mentioned above, having menu alternatives is something relatively new for Unix text editors. Menu commands also offer the ability to integrate more features and functions into the editor, so that a program such as NEdit offers more flexible editing tools than most text-mode editors can.

TABLE 20.1: NEdit File Menu Commands

Command	Function
New	Creates a new buffer
Open	Opens a file in the current buffer
Open Selected	Allows a programmer to open an #include file when working in C
Open Previous	Allows you to open a recently worked-on file

Continued on next page

TABLE 20.1 CONTINUED: NEdit File Menu Commands

Command	Function
Close	Closes current buffer
Save	Saves buffer to file
Save As	Saves buffer under new name
Revert to Saved	Discards all changes since last save
Include File	Inserts a specified file at the current cursor position
Load Macro File	Loads a macro (predefined sequence of actions) file
Load Tags File	Loads an index file of tags (a programming feature)
Unload Tags File	Unloads the tags file
Print	Prints the current document
Print Selection	Prints only the selected text
Exit	Closes NEdit

TABLE 20.2: NEdit Edit Menu Commands

Command	Function
Undo	Discards previous edit
Redo	Repeats previous edit
Cut	Cuts the selected text and stores it in the cut-buffer
Copy	Copies the selected text to the cut-buffer
Paste	Inserts text in cut-buffer at the current cursor position
Paste Column	Allows you to paste a vertical selection
Delete	Deletes the selected text
Select All	Selects all text
Shift Left	Shifts line one space to the left

Continued on next page

TABLE 20.2 CONTINUED: NEdit Edit Menu Commands

Command	Function
Shift Right	Shifts line one space to the right
Lower Case	Makes all selected characters lowercase
Upper Case	Makes all selected characters uppercase
Fill Paragraph	Removes all new-lines within a paragraph
Insert Form Feed	Inserts a form-feed character at current cursor position (acts as a page break for printing)
Insert Control Code	Inserts a specified ASCII character

TABLE 20.3: NEdit Search Menu Commands

Command	Function
Find	Finds a regular expression
Find Again	Repeats previous find operation
Find Selection	Finds next instance of selected text
Find Incremental	Every character typed triggers a new search (Incremental searching is generally the quickest way to find something in a file, because it gives you the immediate feedback of seeing how your search is progressing.)
Replace	Replaces one text string with another
Replace Again	Repeats the last replacement
Goto Line Number	Moves cursor to a specified line number
Goto Selected	Moves cursor to the selected text
Mark	Sets a marker in the text
Goto Mark	Moves the cursor to a previously set mark
Goto Matching ()	Moves the cursor to the start or end of an expression in parentheses
Find Definition	Works with a tags file to find the definition of a function

TABLE 20.4: NEdit Preferences Menu Commands

Command	Function
Default Settings	Allows you to set defaults for various features
Save Defaults	Saves current settings as the default
Statistics Line	Shows a line containing the filename, line number, column number, and size of the file (in bytes)
Show Line Numbers	Prints a sequential number before each line
Language Mode	Highlights the syntax in a file in an appropriate manner for a number of different programming languages—e.g., may show comments, functions, etc.
Auto-indent	Sets the way in which text is indented
Wrap	Sets the way in which lines wrap
Tabs	Sets the style and width of tabs
Text Font	Specifies the font to be used when displaying the text
Highlight Syntax	Attempts to guess the programming language you're using and highlight the syntax accordingly; similar to language mode, but automatic
Make Backup Copy (.bck)	Automatically makes a copy of the file in its state previous to the current Save operation and appends the .bck suffix to the filename
Incremental Backup	Makes automatic backups of buffer at scheduled intervals
Show Matching (..)	Whenever the cursor is at a parenthesis character, its mate will be shown with a red background if this option is selected
Overtype	Switches NEdit from insert mode to overtype mode
Read Only	Does not allow you to save changes to buffer

TABLE 20.5: NEdit Shell Menu Commands

Command	Function
Execute Command	Executes a particular shell command
Execute Command Line	Same as above, but lets you give options
Filter Selection	Prompts you for a Unix command to use to process the currently selected text—the output from this command replaces the contents of the selection
Cancel Shell Command	Self-explanatory

TABLE 20.6: NEdit Macro Menu Commands

Command	Function
Learn Keystrokes	Keystrokes and menu commands are recorded, to be played back later, using the Replay Keystrokes command, or pasted into a macro in the Macro Commands dialog of the Default Settings menu in Preferences
Finish Learn	Stops recording
Cancel Learn	Cancels the recording
Replay Keystrokes	Replays learned keystrokes
Repeat	Repeats last replay
Complete Word	Attempts to deduce the word you're typing and complete it
Fill Sel. w/char	Fills the selected area with a character that you specify
Quote Mail Reply	Precedes each line of selected text with a > character
Unquote Mail Reply	Removes > characters

TABLE 20.7: NEdit Windows Menu Commands

Command	Function
Split Window	Splits window in two allowing you to see different parts of the buffer simultaneously
Close Pane	Closes the selected pane's open buffer(s) (In this menu, you will see the names of files being worked on in various buffers. By clicking the name of the file, you will bring that window to the foreground.)

KEdit

KEdit is the graphical text editor included with the KDE integrated desktop environment. Although it is not as full-featured as NEdit, KEdit is more than adequate for most basic editing tasks. In addition to editing text, KEdit has a simple interface that works with your computer's mail program, so that you can edit and send e-mail directly from KEdit.

Although KEdit is distributed as part of the KDE package, you don't necessarily have to run KDE to use it. You do, however, need to have the Qt library installed on your computer. Qt is the *widget set* (a set of instructions that define the basic building blocks of a graphical program) upon which KDE is built. As long as you have Qt installed, KEdit should work. In fact, when making the notes for this chapter, Joe was running KEdit under Gnome, KDE's main competitor.

The default KEdit screen, shown in Figure 20.2, has a menu bar; a toolbar containing various icons; a status bar showing the mode (either *insert* or *typeover*), and line and column position of the cursor; and a main text area. As with NEdit,

FIGURE 20.2:

The KEdit screen is straightforward and easy to use.

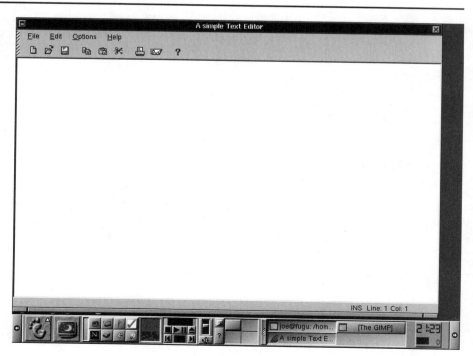

all you need to do when you start KEdit is to simply click in the text area and begin typing. Your text will appear in the window as you type. Use the mouse or the arrow keys to move the cursor to various locations within the text.

The KEdit Toolbar

The toolbar contains various icons that are linked to frequently used functions. From left to right, they are as follows:

- New Document
- Open Document
- Save Document
- Copy
- Paste
- Cut
- Print Document
- Mail Document
- Help

The Menu Bar

The menu bar is similar to that used in many other graphical programs, such as NEdit. Since the commands are so similar, we suggest that you consult the tables in the "NEdit" section of this chapter to see what the basic command functions are. The menus available in KEdit are as follows:

- File
- Edit
- Options
- Help

gEdit

Just as KEdit is the graphical editor that ships with the KDE desktop, gEdit is the editor that ships with the Gnome desktop. It is not as full-featured as NEdit, but gEdit has more features than KEdit. gEdit does, however, have one feature not found in either KEdit or NEdit: a bar along the left side of the screen, as shown in Figure 20.3, that allows you to manage a number of open documents simultaneously. This is similar to NEdit's windows feature, but the bar is always on-screen, and creates an attractive and intuitive way to manage multiple documents.

FIGURE 20.3:

gEdit is the Gnome graphical text editor, which is similar to NEdit and KEdit.

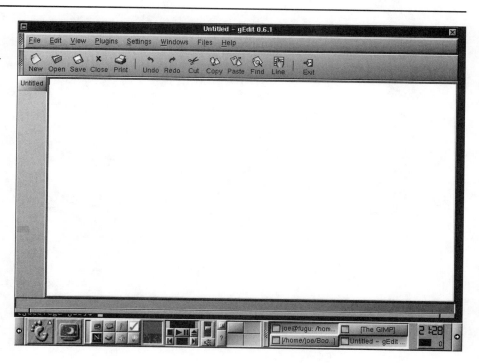

Like KEdit, gEdit has a toolbar with icons linked to commonly used functions. The gEdit toolbar icons are listed below:

 • New

 • Open

 • Save

 • Close

 • Print

 • Undo

 • Redo

 • Cut

 • Copy

 • Paste

 • Find

 • Line

 • Exit

The menu options in gEdit are much the same as those in KEdit and NEdit, so we will not repeat that information here. We will, however, note that gEdit has a number of *plug-ins* that are found, usefully enough, in the Plugins menu. These are fairly simple utility programs, most of which are primarily helpful to programmers. These programs include utilities that convert numbers from decimal to hexadecimal, octal, or binary notation; open Unix manual pages; encrypt or decrypt documents; and so on. It is easy to add new plug-ins when they are created. If you're interested, keep an eye on http://www.gnome.org for announcements of new utilities.

Summary

Graphical text editors function much like the text-mode editors described in other chapters in this part of the book. Unlike those text-mode editors, however, graphical editors have some added functions, such as the ability to use the mouse, drop-down menus, and a more pleasing appearance on the screen. There are several popular graphical editors, both those that are shipped as part of an integrated desktop package and those that are standalone programs.

NEdit, KEdit, and gEdit are three of the best graphical text editors. NEdit is a standalone program, while KEdit and gEdit are part of the KDE and Gnome integrated desktop environments, respectively. All three have more functions and features than most of the text-mode editors, with NEdit being the most-featured and KEdit the simplest. Although graphical editors place some additional memory load on your computer, the intuitive surroundings and the ability to use your mouse make graphical editors a useful addition to the text-editing arsenal.

PART VI

Shell Programming

An Introduction to Shell Programming

- Why Program the Shell?

- What Is a Script and What Is a Program?

- Parts of a Program

- Summary

In the preceding chapters, we have shown you the various tools that make up the complete Unix environment. Windowing systems, shells, and text editors form the basic toolbox from which you can draw to make Unix work for you. Many users need not go any farther than these programs, because they can be configured and used in a multiplicity of ways to meet your unique needs; with the combination of graphical programs and shell commands, a casual user can easily accomplish any number of common tasks. However, if that was all there was to Unix, the operating system would never have acquired the popularity and loyal following that it has today.

Starting with this part of the book, we begin to exploit the real power of Unix. In earlier chapters, we alluded to the near-infinite configurability of Unix. In this chapter, and those that follow, we begin to show you how this configuration actually happens. *Shell programming* forms the basis of the Unix operating system. When a Unix system boots up, it executes a series of shell scripts that initiate various services. It is these shell scripts that determine how a particular computer functions, whether it is a workstation, a Web server, a mail server, or any of the multitude of roles that a Unix computer can play.

NOTE   Some of the examples in this part of the book require the use of **bash** version 2 or later. Not all Unix systems have this version installed as the default **bash**. If your system does not, install the **bash** version included on this book's CD-ROM. It is capable of handling all the examples constructed in the shell programming chapters.

Why Program the Shell?

At its most basic, a *shell program* is simply a series of shell commands executed sequentially and automatically. At first glance, this may seem like a pedestrian sort of thing: Couldn't you just do that by hand? Consider the implications, though. Any program can be run from the shell, and input and output for those programs can be redirected by the shell. This means that a sufficiently skilled shell programmer can automate an enormous range of tasks, simply by creating shell scripts.

By happy coincidence (or maybe not), the tasks that are most amenable to automation are usually the most tedious and repetitive tasks to be found in Unix system administration. Properly applied, shell programming can turn any Unix computer into a true labor-saving device. In this part of the book, we give you the tools you will need to begin shell programming, show you how to use them, and turn you loose to figure out how shell scripts will best fit your system administration needs.

The scripts we develop in these chapters, though, will probably seem trivial and useless at first. Certainly, they're not related to system administration in any clear or obvious manner. In some ways, that's an accurate impression; what these scripts do is not system administration, and quite often they're just silly. However, we designed these scripts to illustrate the techniques involved in shell programming. If we gave you a bunch of scripts that did everything you needed, you could run them and be fairly happy. However, if we show you how to come up with your own scripts, you'll be able to build shell programs that do exactly what you need without adaptation. We think it's a worthwhile trade-off.

NOTE   If you're really searching for practical scripting solutions, go ahead and turn to Part VII: "Basic System Administration." The chapters in that part of the book, especially Chapter 28: "System Programming," explain how these techniques can be applied to the practical tasks of running a Unix system.

So, the answer to the question "Why program the shell?" is this: Programming the shell can save you a lot of time and tedium, and it can also teach you a lot about the inner workings of your Unix system. We think that learning the basics of shell scripting is one of the bridges between beginner and intermediate Unix proficiency, and that doing it well puts you well into advanced territory.

What Is a Script and What Is a Program?

We use the terms *shell script* and *shell program* interchangeably. The distinction between the two—to the extent that there is a distinction at all—varies depending on whom you ask. This is one of those small issues that is very important to some people and completely beside the point for others; we don't think there's much to be gained by insisting on one term over the other, but be aware that some people do care quite a bit.

Some Unix folk like to distinguish between programs and scripts on the basis of the programming language used. In Chapter 1: "History and Background of Unix," we described the C programming language and how programs in C need to be compiled before they can be run. For people who adhere to a strict definition, *programs* are written in compiled languages such as C, whereas *scripts* are written in interpreted languages such as bash's native scripting language or Perl.

NOTE   An interpreted language is one where the program's instructions are converted to machine code language on the fly as the program is being executed. A compiled language is one where the entire program is converted before it is run.

For other people, the distinction between program and script comes in the size and/or scope of the file. The term *program* is reserved for large, multifunction pieces of software such as Netscape or The GIMP, while *scripts* tend to be short and single-function, and are often called *one-offs* because they do only one thing. Still other people reserve *script* for something that the user or system administrator writes for use on her own machine, while a *program* would be something written by someone else.

In any case, we think the distinction is based on semantics and not on any easily definable factual basis. Both scripts and programs are sets of instructions that the machine must execute to perform a particular task or set of tasks. Scripts can have all the functions of programs, and vice versa. We think they're pretty much the same. That said, we tend to use the phrase *shell script* more than we say *shell program*. This is largely a matter of habit and nothing more. Do not be confused into thinking that we are talking about two different things.

Parts of a Program

In this section of the chapter, we introduce the various parts of a shell program. In the remaining chapters of this part of the book, we go into far greater detail about each of these components. For now, we simply want to familiarize you with the terms so that you'll be able to follow the remainder of this part of the book, in which we build upon these concepts.

Statements

The basic unit of programming is the *statement*. A statement, in the `bash` context, can be any valid shell command. Thus,

```
ls /etc
```

can be a statement, as can any of the other commands that we showed you in earlier chapters.

There are also some types of statements that we haven't introduced yet. These statements are not generally used as interactive commands; rather, they are statements that serve almost entirely as programming constructs. These constructs help the finished program make decisions about how to execute itself when necessary.

In general, statements fall into one of three major categories:

Directive: *Directive statements* instruct the computer to perform a particular action. The `ls /etc` example shown above is an example of a directive statement.

Declarative: A *declarative statement* is one that, in human language terms, makes a statement of fact. For example, the instruction A=1 is a declaration of the fact that the value 1 has been assigned to the variable A.

Conditional: *Conditional statements* are those that mark sections of the program to be executed only if a particular circumstance is true. For example, you might include a section of code that runs only if the user enters the answer Yes to a particular question.

NOTE   The example used for the declarative statement, A=1, is directive in the sense that it instructs the computer to equate the two elements, but because the statement sets a condition rather than performing an action (from the user's point of view), it is easier to think of it as a declarative statement.

Operators

Operators are special characters that indicate to the program that a particular action is to be taken or that a particular condition is to be set. Most people are familiar with a certain set of operators called *arithmetic operators*. The symbols

+, −, *, and / stand for addition, subtraction, multiplication, and division, respectively. In addition to these basic arithmetic operators, there is the assignment operator (=), comparison operators such as < and >, and several others.

In the shell scripting context, operators are used as a consistent way to alert the computer of particular actions. Because scripting syntax is quite precise, the use of operators means that different script authors will be able to get the same results, because they don't have to figure out how to tell the machine to perform a particular task. Rather, they can simply use the appropriate operator and move on to the next line of the script.

Regular Expressions

Regular expressions are a text-matching mechanism. With regular expressions, it is possible to construct a set of conditions within which one or more text strings will be matched as part of the action of the script. Once the strings have been identified, the script can then search a stream of text for matches to those strings. That text stream can be either a preexisting file or the output from another operation that produces a certain amount of text. We discuss regular expressions in great detail in Chapter 25: "Regular Expressions."

Variables

If you recall your earliest algebra classes, you'll remember that a *variable* is a name to which an arbitrary value can be assigned. For example, using the assignment operator (=), we can make the statement

```
NAME = "Joe"
```

This statement assigns the value Joe to the variable NAME. Later, if we need to change the value for whatever reason, we simply need to make another statement that reassigns the value:

```
NAME = "Kate"
```

In shell scripts, variables are most often used to designate bits of information whose exact value is unknown or whose value changes based on circumstances. With the use of variables, you don't have to rewrite the script every time a variable's value is altered. You just need to reassign the variable value and proceed. We discuss variables in detail in Chapter 22: "Variables."

Comments

Last, but not least, there are *comments*. A comment is a statement that does not serve a specific programming purpose. Rather, comments are included in programs to help human beings understand what a particular section of code is designed to do.

In bash scripts, comments are designated with the hashmark operator (#). Anything from the right of the hashmark to the end of the line is ignored by the command interpreter. Here is a sample comment:

```
# This is a comment.
```

Comments that span multiple lines must have a hashmark at the beginning of each line.

```
# This script alphabetizes the contents of a named file
# It was written in July 1987.
# E-mail me if you have any questions about it.
```

You can also insert a hashmark in the middle of a line, causing the command interpreter to execute the operations at the beginning of the line and ignore everything after the hashmark.

```
ls /etc  # This is a really basic statement.
```

It may seem that comments are unimportant, because they don't contribute to the program's function. Nothing could be further from the truth. Programming instructions are written for the computer to execute and are sometimes hard to understand from a human language perspective. If you intend to share your work with others, or you plan to use this script for some time, comments are invaluable in explaining what you were trying to do with a particular section of code.

TIP

Because you never know when you might want to revisit a given script, you should include comments even if you think it's a one-off. It is amazing how quickly one can forget how a given section of code was supposed to work. We urge you to get into the commenting habit and place explanatory comments liberally through your scripts. Trust us—you'll be glad you did.

Summary

Shell scripts are programs written to automate certain system activities. They are written in a language native to the shell environment preferred by the user; although we use the bash shell language in this book, scripts can be written for any available Unix shell. Shell scripts can be used to run any shell commands, even those that require the output of other commands as their input. Although a shell program can be very simple, it can also be a lengthy and complex file that takes many minutes to run.

Shell scripts are created from some basic programming elements. The basic unit is a statement, which can be any valid shell command. Statements can be extended with operators, special characters that define a particular action. Variables allow the script writer to use a name with an arbitrary value. Because the value is set outside the script, the value can be changed without affecting the script. Regular expressions allow the script to incorporate text-matching elements. Finally, good scripts include comments, which provide some extra information to future users about blocks of code, without interfering in the script's execution.

CHAPTER

TWENTY-TWO

Variables

- What Is a Variable?

- Assigning Values to Variables

- Special Variables

- Summary

As we explained in Chapter 21: "Introduction to Shell Programming," one of the major components of a shell script is the use of variables. Variables are an essential part of shell programming. Without their use, it would be quite difficult to create a program with any kind of flexibility. If this were the case, shell programs really would be scripts—they would perform the same actions in the same manner every single time they were run, rather than adapting to the current situation.

Variables allow programmers to build a certain level of uncertainty into a script or program. When programmers use variables, they direct the computer to make decisions about information that the programmers don't currently have. That is, the programmer writes the program knowing what *type* of information is to be used, but without knowing the exact *value* of that information. The advantage of this should be obvious: The value of the information described by a variable can be supplied by a user, a calculation, another program, or another part of the same program. This flexibility allows the script to behave differently under different circumstances, which, when you get right down to it, is what modern computing is all about.

So, are variables inevitably abstract and high-concept? Not really. Once you understand that the use of variables means that scripts really do save system administrators time because they don't have to write separate scripts for each possible value of a given piece of information, you have the basic concept. For the remainder of this chapter, we'll step back and provide some practical terms and framework around this central concept.

NOTE It is difficult to discuss a single element of programming, such as the variable, without making references to other elements, such as operators. As we describe these concepts, we will explain the concept and give some idea of what that element does in the programming environment. However, we also cover most of the elements more fully in other chapters of this part of the book. If you see something you don't understand, chances are that you'll be able to figure it out by looking elsewhere in this book.

What Is a Variable?

Simply put, a variable is a name. If you read Chapter 13: "Customizing the Shell Environment," you might recall the discussion of shell variables. Shell variables are used to associate a general setting, such as EDITOR, with a specific value, such as "pico". In the bash shell, variables are set with a command such as

```
export EDITOR="pico"
```

For now, ignore the export command, because it has a specific shell function.

> **NOTE**
>
> The export command makes the variable available to programs outside the one in which the variable is defined. This is important for shells, because the shell itself is a program. If you don't export the variable's value, it won't be reflected anywhere but in bash itself; you wouldn't get your preferred text editor when you run your newsreader, for example.

Without export, then, the core of the statement is

```
EDITOR="pico"
```

The variable here is simply the word *EDITOR*. The value of EDITOR could be anything: vi, emacs, or even something completely senseless like flibnert. The variable is just a tag or handle, something that the actual value will be attached to. The variable itself has no intrinsic meaning except as an association for the value; just be sure your variables are named clearly so that you remember them.

> **NOTE**
>
> flibnert, of course, would be meaningless from a functional point of view. There is no text editor called flibnert currently in existence (though if someone were to write one, this section suddenly becomes moot). Even though it's meaningless, there is nothing prohibiting you from using it as a value. You just wouldn't have access to a default text editor whenever the value EDITOR is consulted by another program. This isn't so terrible for text editors, but imagine the problems if you were trying to use a nonsensical value in a crucial system administration script.

Variable Names

You can name a variable anything you want, as long as you stick to letters for the name. Numeric characters and other symbols often have special meanings in the shell programming context. You can use numbers if it's really necessary, but keep them to the end of the variable name; VARIABLE3 would be okay, but 3VARIABLE might cause problems in unforeseen ways.

WARNING   Naming a variable 0, $, or _ will almost certainly cause the failure of scripts using that variable. Stay away from nonalphanumeric characters in general.

By convention, environment-variable names are written in capital letters. Variables that are used only within a particular script can be written in lowercase, but it's a good idea to get into the habit of using uppercase for variable names. Why? It distinguishes the variable name from the variable value. Remember the earlier example?

```
EDITOR="pico"
```

With the capitalization, it's clear that EDITOR is a different beast than "pico", even if you don't know what EDITOR or "pico" actually mean. This means that if you start to read a script where the variables are unfamiliar to you (perhaps they were named poorly), you can still pick out the variables and their values.

Name your variables with terms that mean something. USERNAME is a better variable name than UN, because you are more likely to remember the purpose of the USERNAME value when you revisit the script later. The best variable names are the ones that describe the function of the variable.

Variable Types

By default, variables in bash are *strings*. That is, they are sequences of characters. Thus, if you were to assign the value of "1" to the variable VAR, the shell would interpret the value as the text character 1 and not the mathematical value of 1. This can cause some confusion for beginning shell programmers, if they expect to do mathematical calculations without understanding the difference between text characters and mathematical values. (The value of var+1 turns out to be the string 1+1, not the mathematical value 2.)

In the regular Bourne Shell, sh, you are limited to variable values as text strings. To do mathematical computations, you will need to use the expr command or one of the several command-line calculator programs that are available for this purpose. It's not simple, but it's a good solution for situations that require the use of sh instead of another, more fully featured, shell environment.

TIP

If you're writing scripts that might be moved to another system that doesn't use **bash**, you will probably want to stick to the limitations of the regular Bourne Shell. Because **sh** is so stripped down, scripts that work under **sh** will work better with other shells than will scripts written to take advantage of **bash** functions.

bash, however, gives you the ability to assign a *variable type* to each individual variable. The variable type lets the shell know what the purpose of that variable is before it's executed. Assign variable types with the **declare** command, along with one of its flags. For example, if you wanted to use the variable VAR to work a mathematical calculation, as we tried to do in the first paragraph of this section, you could declare that the value of VAR should always be parsed as an integer.

NOTE

If **declare** doesn't seem to work on your computer, check the version of **bash** that you're using. **declare** is not available in **bash** versions earlier than **bash** 2. (See the book's CD for a version of **bash** that supports **declare**.)

Do so with this command:

```
declare -i VAR=1
```

The **-i** flag tells **bash** that VAR is an integer. Now, the value of VAR will be parsed as the mathematical value 1, not as the text character 1. Table 22.1 contains the flags for **declare** in **bash**.

TABLE 22.1: Variable Types Defined with declare

Flag	Variable Definition
-a	Variable is an array (a list of multiple values).
-f	Variable is limited to function names only.
-i	Variable is an integer.
-r	Variable is read-only (value cannot be changed).
-x	Variable is exported (same result as that of the **export** command).

Typing `declare` on a line by itself displays the value of all variables in the shell environment, as shown in Figure 22.1. If you use the `-f` flag with this command, the output will be limited to function names and definitions, as shown in Figure 22.2.

Arrays

An *array* is a special type of variable that holds more than one value. An array actually holds a list of values that can be accessed by using an index number that corresponds to the position of the value in the list. Here's an example of an array declaration:

```
cars=(ford,gm,chrysler)
```

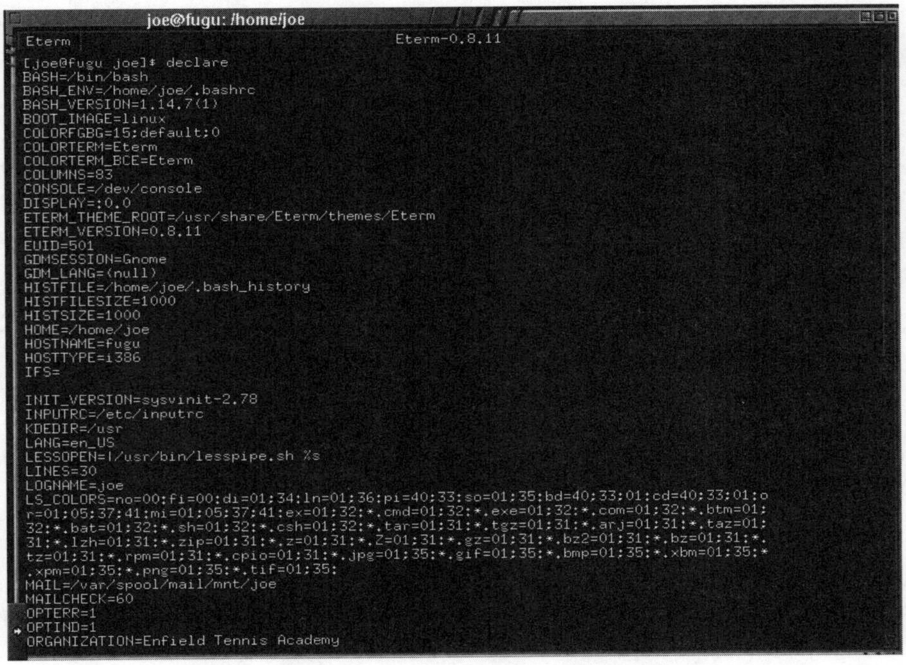

FIGURE 22.1:

Use the `declare` command to list the values of all defined variables in the shell.

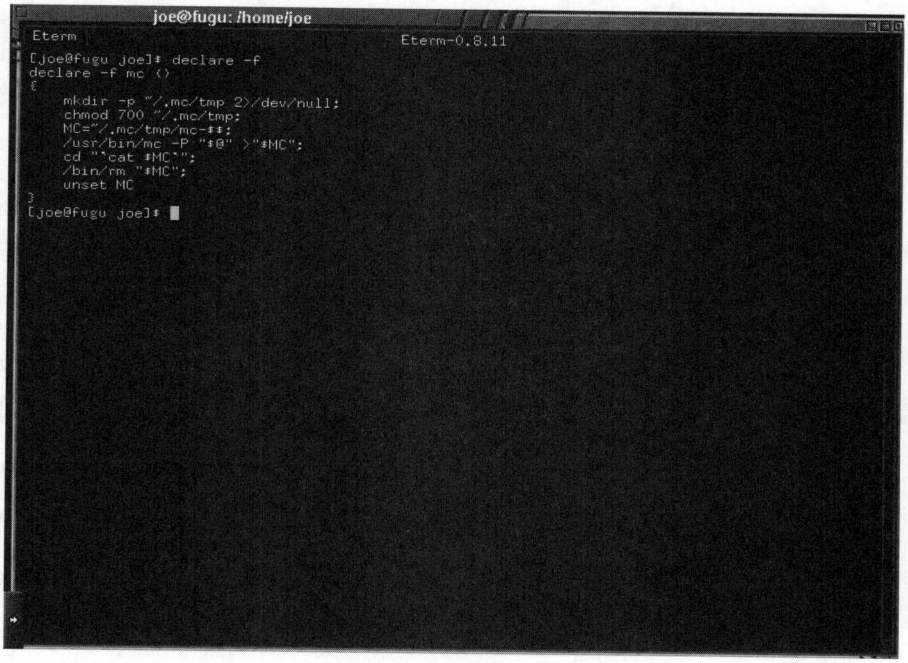
joe@fugu: /home/joe
Eterm
Eterm-0.8.11
[joe@fugu joe]$ declare -f
declare -f mc ()
{
mkdir -p ~/.mc/tmp 2>/dev/null;
chmod 700 ~/.mc/tmp;
MC=~/.mc/tmp/mc-$$;
/usr/bin/mc -P "$@" >"$MC";
cd "`cat $MC`";
/bin/rm "$MC";
unset MC
}
[joe@fugu joe]$

FIGURE 22.2: Limit `declare`'s output to function names and definitions with the `-f` flag.

When you want to access a particular value from that array, simply use an index number that is placed in square brackets immediately to the right of the variable name, as in

```
cars[0]=ford
cars[1]=gm
cars[2]=chrysler
```

NOTE Remember that in the Unix world, we always start counting from zero and not one.

Integers

An *integer* is any positive or negative number that doesn't have a fractional component. Zero is also an integer. The numbers 1, 5, –42, 42, 0, and –1052 are all integers, but 1.1, 0.5, and –3.75 are not. Declaring values as integers (using the `-i` flag for the `declare` command, as shown above) makes it possible to do simple arithmetic in shell scripts. However, more complicated calculations, such as floating-point-oriented arithmetic, cannot be done via the shell. You'd need to install a separate calculator program to handle more complex equations.

The $ Operator

As you start to read more and more shell scripts (trust us, you will), you will start to notice that some variable names are preceded by a dollar-sign character ($). This is an operator that permits you to access the value of a variable, rather than the variable's name. Why is this important? Think of it this way: Suppose that you have a variable named CLOWN. The word *CLOWN* is just the name of the variable, but the expression $CLOWN represents the actual value of the variable.

To see how this works, run through this example. At a command-line prompt, type

```
CLOWN="bozo"
```

When you press the Enter key, you'll see the shell prompt again. Now, type

```
echo $CLOWN
```

The word *bozo* will print to the screen. However, if you were to type

```
echo CLOWN
```

instead, the word *CLOWN* would print to the screen, and you would get no information about the actual value of the CLOWN variable. This exercise is shown in Figure 22.3.

NOTE   You can combine literal character strings and variables in the same statement. For example, in the example above, you could have issued the command `echo "I am usually scared of clowns, but I don't mind $CLOWN."`. When the command is executed, you'd see `I am usually scared of clowns, but I don't mind bozo.` printed to the screen. (Variable values are context-sensitive.) This blend of actual text and variables is called *variable substitution*.

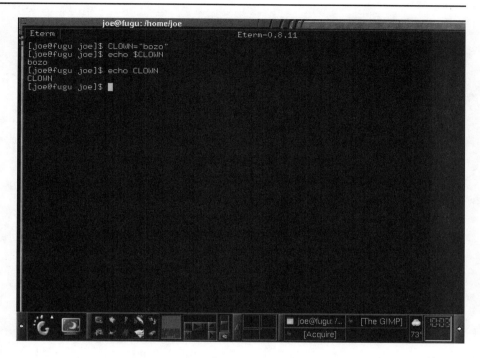

The $ operator allows you to distinguish between the variable's name and its value.

Assigning Values to Variables

Variables wouldn't be much use if you couldn't assign values to them. In fact, in the previous sections of this chapter (and in Chapter 13), you've seen several examples of variable-value definition. Value assignment is done with the *assignment operator* (=). (The = character can also be a *comparison operator* in some contexts, but it's usually obvious when it's being used in that manner.)

Here's an example of a simple value assignment:

```
VAR="hello"
```

When the shell sees the = character, the shell interprets whatever is to the left of the character as the variable name and whatever is to the right as the value assigned to that variable name. You can change the value of the variable at any time, just by reassigning the value:

```
VAR="goodbye"
```

Taking Input from the Keyboard

In many scripts, you'll want to let a user define the value of a variable while the script is running. This is done with the read command, as in

```
read var
```

When the bash interpreter sees a read statement, the interpreter pauses the execution of the script and waits for input from the keyboard. The user must enter something and then press the Enter key. When the computer receives the signal from the Enter key, the interpreter resumes the script, entering whatever was typed as the variable's value.

For example, suppose that you had this script:

```
echo "What is your name?"
read NAME
echo "Hello, $NAME".
```

When executed, this script prints the question *What is your name?* to the screen. The script then takes the keyboard input and uses it as the value of the variable NAME, and inserts that value into the next line of the script after the word *Hello*.

NOTE The shell makes no judgment about whether the input from the keyboard makes any sense. If a user were to input the character string *qwertyuiop123* at the request for a name, the script would echo the line *Hello, qwertyuiop123* to the screen. However, you can limit scripts to respond only to certain answers, and we show you how in Chapter 23: "Flow Control, Part I: Conditional Flow Control."

Special Variables

Earlier, we cautioned you about using certain numbers and symbols in variable names. Some symbols shouldn't be used, because they are reserved for use as operators. These include the *mathematical operators* +, -, *, and /; as well as < and >, which are used as *comparison operators*; !, which is used as a *negation operator*; and, of course, =, which is used both as an assignment operator and as a comparison operator.

However, there are some characters that shouldn't be used, because they comprise a set of variables that have predefined meanings. For example, the ? character, when used as a variable, reports the success or failure of the previous command in the script. This is referred to as the previous command's *exit status*. If you were interested in knowing whether a particular command in your script had executed successfully each time, you could just make the next line of the script read like this:

```
echo $?
```

If the previous command exited successfully, the output of the echo statement will be 0. An output of any other value, usually 1, means that the previous command failed.

NOTE

The meaning of a particular exit status can be defined by the programmer. Sometimes programmers use exit status to report certain information about the command that was executed. In that case, the value might be something other than 1 or 0. To find out exactly what a particular exit status means, you'll need to read the documentation for that command.

The value of the ? variable changes after each command in the script to reflect the exit status of the most recently executed command. This is a built-in function of the bash shell programming environment, and there is no need for you—the scriptwriter—to define the ? variable. In fact, most of the special variables are already defined as *read-only* by default, so that you wouldn't be able to redefine them even if you wanted to. Table 22.2 shows a partial set of bash's special variables; you cannot use these as names for your own variables, but you will probably want to use their functions in your own scripts as you learn to build more complex programs.

TABLE 22.2: Special Variables in bash Shell Programs

Variable	Function
?	Exit status of the previous command
$	Process ID of the current shell
!	Process ID of the last background command
-	Options given to the shell on start-up
0	Name of the current script
1–9	First through ninth command-line arguments to the current script (that is, $1 is the value of the first command-line argument, and so on)
_	Last argument to previous command

Summary

There's a lot to absorb with the concept of variables. However, you need to understand the main concepts before you can use variables in your own shell scripts. Variables are names that you create that can be associated with particular values. The value contained by a variable can change, so the variable name is used as a placeholder for the actual value in scripts. The value of a variable is accessed by prefixing the variable name with the $ character.

Some variables are predefined by the shell environment. You can use the predefined values of these variables in your scripts without any additional work. For variables that are not predefined, the value can be set either by using the assignment operator (=) or by using the read command to take the value from the keyboard. Variables are always considered to be character strings, unless you specify otherwise by using the declare command. If you plan to use your scripts in a shell environment that is not the one in which you're writing them, we suggest that you limit yourself to commands and variables that are executable in the Bourne Shell (sh) so that your script will run in as many shell environments as possible.

CHAPTER
TWENTY-THREE

Flow Control, Part I:
Conditional Flow Control

- The if-then Statement

- Evaluating Variables

- Evaluating Non-Variables

- Evaluating Multiple Conditions

- Building an Example

- Extending the if-then Statement with else

- The elif Statement

- The case Statement

- Summary

In Chapter 22: "Variables," we explained how variables work in a programming context and how values are assigned to variables outside a script or program. Although variables are a mildly interesting topic in themselves, the previous chapter probably prompted you to think, "So what? Okay, so I get variables. What am I supposed to do with them?"

One of the main uses of variables in programming is to give your programs the ability to determine how to execute themselves. That is, you can use variables to mark certain sections of code, so that those sections will execute—or not execute—depending on certain conditions. This ability is called *flow control*, because it is used to control how the program flows from one instruction to the next.

There are two types of flow control: *conditional flow control* and *iterative flow control*. Conditional flow control involves the creation of code sections that will execute, or not, depending on whether a given condition is true. Iterative flow control involves marking certain code sections so that they will execute repeatedly until a certain condition is met. The distinction between conditional and iterative flow control is rather subtle, because it can be argued that both types involve setting and meeting conditions. In practice, however, the difference is fairly clear, because the two types use distinct commands to obtain the desired results.

> **NOTE**   We discuss conditional flow control in this chapter and iterative flow control in Chapter 24: "Flow Control, Part II: Iterative Flow Control."

How do variables fit into this picture? Remember that a variable is composed of two parts: a name, which is static (it doesn't change), and a value, which is dynamic (it does change). Using the static component—the name—we can define a condition against which we can test the dynamic value. As the program executes, the value of the variable may be changed. Depending on how it changes, the variable's value may or may not meet the test conditions, and the program may either succeed or fail.

In this chapter, we cover the main components of conditional flow control. These components are called *statements* and are the building blocks of shell scripts. As we show you each statement, we provide examples that show how the statement works. At the end of this part of the book, we'll construct a new script that uses all the components introduced in this chapter, and in Chapters 24 and 25.

The if-then Statement

The heart of conditional flow control is the *if-then statement*. The general form of this statement is

```
if <condition>
then
    <something happens>
fi
```

The *<condition>* in the first line is a statement. This statement can return a value of either *true* or *false*. (Actually, the statement can return a value of 0 or 1, where 0 equals *true* and 1 equals *false*.) If the condition evaluates as true, the *<something happens>* part of the program executes. If the condition evaluates as false, the *<something happens>* part is skipped, and the program's execution continues at the line immediately following the `fi` statement.

> **TIP**
>
> `fi` is just *if* spelled backward. It is a convention used to mark the end of a conditional section.

The 0 and 1 values that represent true and false are the *exit status* of the expression. Remember that, in Chapter 22, we discussed exit status in reference to the special variable ?. The same concept applies here: If an evaluative expression is successful—that is, if the variable being evaluated meets the condition—the expression is said to have *evaluated successfully,* and thus it exits with a status of 0. If the condition is not met, the evaluation fails, and a status of 1 is produced. This may seem like an overly complicated way of looking at success or failure, but if you comprehend that success/failure, 0/1, and true/false all represent the same thing, you have reached a significant point in your understanding of shell programming.

> **NOTE**
>
> The expression being evaluated by an `if` statement doesn't have to be a variable comparison. Any expression that returns an exit status of 0 or 1 will work. In fact, it's fair to say that exit status is the only thing that `if` actually tests. Variable evaluations are the easiest way to see this at work, however, so that's how we've chosen to introduce the concept.

Indentation

You'll notice that the code sections of this chapter, and throughout the book, are indented on certain lines. Indentation is used for the sake of readability; it's not technically necessary, because programs will run if not indented, but it is required as a matter of programming style. Indentation makes the program much easier to read for human eyes, and easier to read means easier to debug. It is far easier to find the beginning or end of a particular block of code if it is indented correctly. Plus, when programs become complex (like the scripts you'll see in Chapter 26), they commonly embed entire blocks of code into other blocks of code, in a practice called *nesting*.

When you begin to write your own scripts, please use indentations. If you don't indent your code, you will have a hard time understanding it the next time you read the scripts. Plus, indenting your code will make your programs much more readable to others if you share your scripts at a later time or need to ask for help. Professional programmers indent their code, and if they do, so should amateurs.

Evaluating Variables

So, if if-then statements evaluate variables, how is the evaluation done? Evaluating variables is done using *comparison operators*. Comparison operators are divided into two general categories: string comparison operators and arithmetic comparison operators. Tables 23.1 and 23.2 show some common operators in each category and their functions.

TABLE 23.1: String Comparison Operators

String	Function
string a = string b	String a is the same as string b.
string a != string b	String a is not the same as string b.
string a > string b	String a is greater than string b.
string a < string b	String a is lesser than string b.

TABLE 23.2: Arithmetic Comparison Operators

String	Function
a –eq b	a is equal to b.
a –ne b	a is not equal to b.
a –gt b	a is greater than b.
a –ge b	a is greater than or equal to b.
a –lt b	a is less than b.
a –le b	a is less than or equal to b.

Here's an example using comparison operators. Suppose that you had a script with a code block like this:

```
MY_VARIABLE="walnut"
if [ $MY_VARIABLE="walnut" ]
then
    echo "Success!"
fi
```

In the first line of this block, the = functions as an *assignment operator,* assigning the value "walnut" to the variable MY_VARIABLE. In the second line, the context provided by the if statement changes the function of the = character to that of a comparison operator. The square brackets around the $MY_VARIABLE="walnut" expression identify it as the expression to be tested.

Because, in this case, the value of the variable does match the condition set in the second line of the block, the result of 0, or true, is returned to the if command. Because the test was true, the line between the then and fi statements will be executed. If you were to run this script, the word *Success!* would be printed to the screen.

Now, assume that you have a similar block of code that looks like this:

```
MY_VARIABLE="pecan"
if [ $MY_VARIABLE="walnut" ]
then
    echo "Success!"
fi
```

Because the value of MY_VARIABLE is now "pecan" and not "walnut", the test expression in the second line will not evaluate successfully. Because the test returns an exit status of 1, or false, the script will skip to the line immediately following the fi statement, whatever that line may be. In this case, there is no line after fi, so the script would simply end without printing anything to the screen.

The test Command and Square Brackets

The square brackets used in our if-then examples are actually commands themselves. The bash shell regards the [*<expression>*] construct as a synonym for the test command. Thus, the statement

```
if [ MY_VARIABLE="walnut" ]
```

is exactly the same as

```
if ( test $MY_VARIABLE="walnut" )
```

Earlier in this chapter, we noted that the expression used in conjunction with an if-then statement need not be a variable evaluation, but could be any statement that returns an exit value of 1 or 0. This is exactly what the test command does. If the variable matches the condition, test exits successfully and returns a value of 0. If not, it returns a value of 1.

Be aware that the square brackets and the test command are synonyms only in the bash shell. You can't use the square brackets in this manner with the regular Bourne Shell—or with any other shell environment—because this is one of bash's features. You'll have to use the test command explicitly if you wish to test expressions while programming for other shells.

Evaluating Non-Variables

If your script requires evaluation of items that are not variables, there are several ways to handle this need. You can use the test command to check components of the computer's filesystem, and you can use the if-then statement to determine whether a given command has executed successfully. Both of these functions provide additional flexibility in shell scripts, which makes scripting an even more useful skill to learn.

The test Command

In addition to evaluating variables, the `test` command has other functions. (Because we are working with the `bash` shell in this book, the `test` command is synonymous with square brackets, [], as explained in the sidebar "The `test` Command and Square Brackets." If you are programming in another shell, you will need to use `test` alone.) Through the use of various flags, it is possible to use `test` to determine the existence and status of files and directories.

For example, suppose that you want to write a script that will take a certain action only if a particular file exists. You might write a code block like this:

```
if ( test -e <filename> )
then
    <something happens>
fi
```

The `-e` flag causes `test` to exit successfully only if the file in question exists.

You can also use these flags with the [] construct in the `bash` shell. An equivalent to the previous code block would be

```
if [ -e <filename> ]
then
    <something happens>
fi
```

Table 23.3 shows the various flags used by `test` when working with files and directories.

TABLE 23.3: test Flags

Flag	Function
-e	The named file exists.
-d	The named file exists and is a directory.
-f	The named file exists and is a regular file (i.e., it is not a directory or any other kind of special file).

Continued on next page

TABLE 23.3 CONTINUED: test Flags

Flag	Function
-s	The named file exists and is not empty.
-r	The user has read permission on the file.
-w	The user has write permission on the file.
-x	The user has execute permission on the file.
-O	The user is the file's owner.
-G	The owner's group ID matches the file's ID.
-nt	The file is newer than another file (usage: *<file1>* -nt *<file2>*).
-ot	The file is older than another file (usage: *<file1>* -ot *<file2>*).

NOTE   The –nt and –ot flags compare the *timestamp* on the named files, which is updated any time the file is accessed or modified. Thus, file1 could have been created a month earlier than file2, but if file1 were modified or accessed more recently, the –nt and –ot flags would report file1 as being a newer file than file2.

Commands

The if-then statement can also be used to create conditional code, based on whether a given command has been executed successfully. For example, suppose that your script's action needs to operate within a particular directory. You need to move into that directory before the script executes, and you don't want the script to execute if—for some reason—you can't move into that directory. In that event, you might write conditional code that looks like this:

```
if ( cd <directory> )
then
    <something happens>
fi
```

In this case, the conditional code will execute only if the `cd` command was successful.

In this example, there is no test. Thus, the square brackets do not appear. In fact, the parentheses are not strictly necessary, but they improve the readability of the code. See the sidebar "Indentation" for more about code readability.

Evaluating Multiple Conditions

Although single-condition statements are extremely common in shell scripts, it is often the case that two or more conditions must be met simultaneously before a code block will execute. There are two ways to build a multiple-condition evaluation into a script: using multiple if-then statements and using logical operators.

If you choose to use multiple if-then statements for the evaluation of multiple conditions, your code might look like this:

```
if <condition1>
then
    if <condition2>
    then
        <something happens>
    fi
fi
```

This is understandable, but it's also kind of bulky. If you were to impose a third or fourth condition in this block, the indentations alone would be difficult to follow.

The easier method is to use a *logical operator*. The logical operators are &&, which stands for *and*, and ||, which stands for *or*. Table 23.4 shows the function of these operators.

TABLE 23.4: Logical Operator Functions

Statement	Function
<condition1> && <condition2>	<condition1> AND <condition2> are both true.
<condition1> || <condition2>	Either <condition1> OR <condition2> is true.

So, the example used at the beginning of this section could be rewritten more simply as

```
if ( if <condition1> && <condition2> )
then
    <something happens>
fi
```

There may be times when the first construction, with multiple if-then statements, is preferable. As a rule, good programming style dictates that you shouldn't use nested conditional expressions (one conditional expression embedded inside another) unless it's absolutely necessary. The logical operators create more elegant and streamlined code, which is generally the goal.

Building an Example

Now that we've explained the concepts of conditional flow control, it's time to begin building an example that will show you how this material works in practice. The first example is a very simple program that asks a user to guess a secret word. Fire up your favorite text editor (see Part V: "Using Text Editors" if you don't have a favorite yet) and enter the following code into an empty file:

```
#!/bin/bash

# SECRET WORD version 1
#
# This program invites the user to guess a secret word
# from a list of choices.

SECRET_WORD="telephone"

echo "What is your name?"
read NAME
echo
echo "Hello, $NAME. Please guess the secret word. Your"
echo "choices are iguana, telephone, or slurp."
read GUESS

if [ $GUESS=$SECRET_WORD ]
then
```

```
        echo "Congratulations, you are correct!"
fi
```

Save this file with the name `secword`. Exit the editor and change the new file's permissions so that it is executable by issuing the command

```
chmod u+x secword
```

at the command prompt. Once it is saved and executable, run the program by typing `./secword` at the prompt. You will be prompted to guess the secret word from the list; because this is the first time you have run the script, type `telephone` and press Enter. You should be congratulated.

Hash Bang Slash Bin Slash Bash

The first line of the sample program given above reads `#!/bin/bash`. The hashmark character (#) might lead you to believe that this line is a comment (i.e., a line that is not executed as code), but it isn't. A hashmark followed immediately by an exclamation point (called a *bang* in Unixese) tells the computer that this program is to be executed using the named shell: in this case, the **bash** shell.

If you're already running the program from within **bash**, the line is redundant, but it doesn't hurt anything. If you're using another shell, though, the line ensures that a **bash** session will be opened to handle the script, which is necessary if you're using **bash**-specific shortcuts such as the square brackets described earlier. If the line is not included and someone tries to run the script in a shell other than **bash**, the script will not run. We encourage the use of the `#!/bin/bash` line as the first line in all your scripts if you're using the skills learned in this book, because we are working explicitly with **bash** mechanisms and shortcuts.

As you can see in the script, we've defined the value of the variable SECRET_WORD to be `"telephone"`. The user's input is assigned to the variable GUESS. If the two match, the user has guessed the secret word, so the congratulatory message will print to the screen. If the user guesses incorrectly, the program exits. Run the program again, but guess *slurp* or *iguana* this time. You should see just the command prompt appear, instead of a message.

Extending the if-then Statement with else

By itself, the if-then statement is somewhat limited. It can define only single sections of code that are conditionally executed. If you wanted to allow choices with multiple alternatives and wanted to use if-then statements to do that, you'd need to construct entire chains of if-then statements. Needless to say, that would become cumbersome and confusing. Fortunately, bash provides some extensions to the if-then construct that make setting up multiple conditions much more elegant and readable.

The first of these extensions is the else statement. else works like this:

```
if <condition>
then
    <something happens>
else
    <something else happens>
fi
```

Using else is roughly equivalent to a second if-then statement where the condition is equal to *everything that isn't the first condition.*

Now that you know about else, reopen the secword file. It's time to edit that program and see how you can improve it with an else statement. Edit the file so that it looks like this (the changes are in the final code block):

```
#!/bin/bash

# SECRET WORD version 1
#
# This program invites the user to guess a secret word
# from a list of choices.

SECRET_WORD="telephone"

echo "What is your name?"
read NAME
echo
echo "Hello, $NAME. Please guess the secret word. Your"
echo "choices are iguana, telephone, or slurp."
read GUESS

if [ $GUESS=$SECRET_WORD ]
```

```
then
    echo "Congratulations, you are correct!"
else
    echo "Sorry, $GUESS is not correct."
fi
```

Save and exit. You can run the program again by typing ./secword at the shell prompt. In this new program, if the user guesses incorrectly, an informative message will print to the screen before the program exits. Note that the two blocks making up the if-then-else construct are exclusive of one another; that is, if one executes, the other does not.

The elif Statement

Using the else statement is not the only way to extend the if-then statement. Another bash extension is the elif statement. elif is sort of a cross between if and else. It allows the programmer to add further conditions to a basic if statement, as in this example:

```
if <first condition>
then
    <something happens>
elif <second condition>
then
    <something happens>
elif <third condition>
then
    <something happens>
else
    <something else happens>
fi
```

Each elif statement acts as a separate if statement, and the block that is defined under each elif is a separate alternative. You could achieve the same effect by chaining multiple if statements, like this:

```
if <first condition>
then
    <something happens>
fi
```

```
if <second condition>
then
    <something happens>
fi

if <third condition>
then
    <something happens>
fi
```

However, using elif is far more elegant. Also, using elif lets you use an else statement to provide an alternative outcome, which will execute if none of the conditions are met.

Open secword once again, to revise the program and take advantage of the elif construct. The edits are at the end.

```
#!/bin/bash

# SECRET WORD version 1
#
# This program invites the user to guess a secret word
# from a list of choices.

SECRET_WORD="telephone"

echo "What is your name?"
read NAME
echo
echo "Hello, $NAME. Please guess the secret word. Your"
echo "choices are iguana, telephone, or slurp."
read GUESS

if [ $GUESS=$SECRET_WORD ]
then
    echo "Congratulations, you are correct!"
elif [ $GUESS="iguana" ]
then
    echo "Why would the secret word be iguana?"
elif [ $GUESS="slurp" ]
then
    echo "No, it's not slurp."
else
```

```
echo "$GUESS is not even in the list."
fi
```

Save the file and exit the editor. You can run the edited program by typing `./secword` at the prompt. In this new version, there is a special message for each option in the given list of choices. If the user guesses something that isn't on the list, there is a message for that choice after the `else` statement.

The case Statement

In some cases, using `if-then-elif-else` statements can be a bit cumbersome. `bash` provides yet another way of setting up multiple conditionals with the `case` statement. The `case` statement uses this syntax:

```
case <expression> in
    <pattern 1> )
        <something happens>
    ;;
    <pattern 2> )
        <something happens>
    ;;
    <pattern 3> )
        <something happens>
    ;;
esac
```

TIP

Like `fi` is just *if* spelled backwards, `esac` is just *case* spelled backwards. It indicates the end of that particular **case** code block.

As you have done with the other `bash` extensions, open the `secword` file to edit it by incorporating the `case` statement:

```
#!/bin/bash

# SECRET WORD version 1
#
# This program invites the user to guess a secret word
# from a list of choices.
```

```
SECRET_WORD="telephone"

echo "What is your name?"
read NAME
echo
echo "Hello, $NAME. Please guess the secret word. Your"
echo "choices are iguana, telephone, or slurp."
read GUESS

case $GUESS in
    $SECRET_WORD )
        echo "$SECRET_WORD is correct!"
    ;;
    "iguana" )
        echo "Iguana is incorrect."
    ;;
    "slurp" )
        echo "Slurp is incorrect."
    ;;
    * )
        echo "$GUESS wasn't even a choice."
    ;;
esac
```

As before, save the file, exit the editor, and run the script. In this version of the program, the final option * serves the same function as the else clause in an if-then statement. The asterisk character, in this context, means *anything else.*

Taking Arguments from the Command Line

One task that the case statement is especially helpful for is the processing of *command-line arguments.* Command-line arguments are options that you give to the script at the command line. Flags to a command, as in ls -la, are an example of command-line arguments. Using case statements, you can define various behaviors in response to certain command-line arguments.

How do you get your program to realize that the arguments are even there? This is done with special variables, $0 to $9. Each of these variables corresponds to an element on the command line, moving from left to right. So, for example, $0 would be the name of the program itself (or whatever abbreviation is used as the command), because $0 is the first thing typed at the prompt. The first argument to the program is $1, the second is $2, and so on.

This is one of the few instances in the Unix environment where counting from one is actually a better way to visualize enumerated objects than the traditional count from zero.

To illustrate this final element of conditional flow control, open the `secword` file yet once again and make the following edits:

```
#!/bin/bash

# SECRET WORD version 1
#
# This program invites the user to guess a secret word
# from a list of choices.

SECRET_WORD="telephone"

case $1 in
    $SECRET_WORD )
        echo "$SECRET_WORD is correct!"
    ;;
    "iguana" )
        echo "Iguana is incorrect."
    ;;
    "slurp" )
        echo "Slurp is incorrect."
    ;;
    * )
        echo "$1 wasn't even a choice."
    ;;
esac
```

Once again, save the file, exit the editor, and run the script. In this case, the user needs to know something about how the program works before she can use it. This is required because, to make a guess at the secret word, she will have to specify her guess on the command line by issuing a response like this:

```
prompt%  ./secword iguana
```

As you can see, her choice is the second item on the command line, which is parsed by the script as $1.

A command-line argument probably isn't the best selection for an interactive game script such as the one you've worked with in this chapter. However, command-line arguments have many uses in the Unix programming world. Perhaps your script is a utility intended to be run noninteractively. In such a case, command-line arguments might be a good way to specify a given behavior or pass the value of certain variables on to other code blocks in the script. System administration has lots of situations where scripts with command-line arguments may be the best solution.

Summary

Flow control is the mechanism that is used to control how scripts move from one instruction to the next. There are two types of flow control, conditional and iterative. Conditional flow control, the subject of this chapter, works by determining whether given conditions are true. If the conditions are true, one set of instructions executes; if they are false, another set of instructions executes.

There are several types of conditional flow control statements. The basic statement is an if-then statement, which determines that if a given condition is true, then a specified action will happen. if-then statements can be used to evaluate variables and their values, or can be used to evaluate non-variables. Conditional flow control can also be used to evaluate multiple conditions at one time, though if-then statements are an inelegant solution to that task. In the case of multiple conditions, the else, elif, or case statements are better suited to the job.

CHAPTER
TWENTY-FOUR

Flow Control, Part II: Iterative Flow Control

- The for Statement

- The select Statement

- The while Loop

- The until Loop

- Nesting Loops

- Summary

In the previous chapter, we discussed the concept of conditional flow control. That is, we described how to set aside sections of code that are executed only if a particular condition is true. In this chapter, we describe a second kind of flow control. *Iterative flow control* means marking sections of text that will be executed repeatedly until—or unless—a certain condition is true.

TIP   Although the two concepts might be easily confused because they both rely on the existence of a particular true condition, the important thing to remember is that iterative flow control causes a code section to repeat (*iterate*).

Three different statements are used in iterative flow control: the `for` statement, the `until` statement, and the `while` statement. These statements are also called *loops,* and we use the terms interchangeably. In this chapter, we explain each type and then build examples using the various statements.

The for Statement

The `for` statement causes a given section of code to repeat one time for each value in a list of values specified by the programmer. The list of values is most commonly an array. The general form of the `for` statement is

```
for <name> [in <list>]
do
    <something>
done
```
Consider the following block of code:

```
#!/bin/bash

declare -a NAMES
NAMES=(tom dick harry)

for name in "${NAMES[ @]}"
do
    echo $name
done
```

This script simply takes and prints the value of each element in the array NAMES (i.e., tom, dick, and harry).

As you can see, this script declares the variable NAMES to be an array, using the -a flag to the declare command. (The flag is not technically necessary, because the way in which the variable was assigned makes it clear to the bash shell that the variable is an array, but we use the flag to be explicit.) We have assigned the values tom, dick, and harry to be the elements of the array. Individually, these values would be referred to as $NAMES[0]=tom, $NAMES[1]=dick, and $NAMES[2]=harry.

Once the for loop begins, it creates a new variable; in this case, the new variable is named name. This new variable is called a *loop variable,* and it can be used within the loop to access the value of that particular element of the array. Note that the loop variable is created and assigned a value implicitly by the for statement. There is no need to declare or assign this value manually.

Each time the script executes this loop, the value of the loop variable is assigned to be whatever the value of the next element in the array is. So, the first time that this loop executes, the value of $name is $NAMES[0] (*tom*). The second time through the loop, the value of $name is $NAMES[1] (*dick*), and so on.

When you make reference to the array that contains the individual values as you work on scripts like this, you need to use the construct "${<arrayname>[@]}". Because of the way in which bash handles arrays, the quotes and curly braces are required to access the value of a particular element. The [@] component is the *positional parameter,* in which the @ character is used to track which element is currently being referred to. It starts at zero, in traditional Unix counting style, and increases incrementally by one each time the loop repeats.

Command-Line Processing

One of the great strengths of the for construct is with command-line processing. Recall that, in Chapter 23, we used the special variables $0, $1, and so on to access the various elements of the command line. You can do much the same thing with the special variable $@. $@ is a variable containing all of the command-line arguments, which can then be iterated by the for statement.

For example, you might change the previous code block to look like this:

```
#!/bin/bash
```

```
for name in $@
do
    echo $name
done
```

and invoke the script using this command at the shell prompt:

```
prompt% ./names tom dick harry
```

You will get this output:

```
tom
dick
harry
```

Indeed, the $@ variable is so integral to the idea behind the for construct that it can be omitted entirely. As long as nothing else is specified, for will assume that $@ is intended to be the list. The following block of code will do exactly the same thing as the block above:

```
#!/bin/bash

for name
do
    echo $name
done
```

Building an Example with for

Now that you have some exposure to the for construct, you can create a script that will take a list of files at the command line and return output that defines the file type and what the file's permissions are in regard to the user running the script. Here's an example of such a script:

```
#!/bin/bash

# Checkfile. Checks type, ownership, and permissions of
# a file or list of files.

for file in $@
do

    # Test file type
    if [ -d $file ]
    then
```

```
        echo "$file is a directory"
    elif [ -f $file ]
    then
        echo "$file is a regular file"

            if [ -s $file ]
            then
              echo "$file is not empty"
            else
              echo "$file is empty"
            fi

else
    echo "$file not found"
fi

# check ownership

if [ -O $file ]
then
    echo "You are the owner of $file"
else
    echo "You are not the owner of $file"
fi

# check permissions

if [ -r $file ]
then
    echo "You have read permission for $file"
fi

if [ -w $file]
then
    echo "You have write permission for $file"
fi

if [ -x $file ]
then
    echo "You have execute permission for $file"
fi
done
```

The meat of this script is a series of if statements that use the file-attribute testing functions of the test command to test various attributes of a given file. If these statements are not clear to you, review Chapter 23: "Flow Control, Part I: Conditional Flow Control." If you look past all the if statements, however, you can see that all the script really uses is a simple for loop. If you execute this script with the names of multiple files on the command line, information will be produced for each file in the order in which the file appears on the command line.

It should be clear from this example that the for loop is a powerful construct. Whether used for command-line processing or in combination with an array, a for loop allows you to iterate over a range of values and process each value in turn.

The select Statement

The select statement is similar to the for statement, but select has a special use. Syntactically, it is identical to for:

```
select <name> [in <list>]
do
    <something>
done
```

The difference between select and for is that, instead of iterating a list of values and processing each one in turn, select generates a menu based on the list, with numbers for each item. The user is then prompted to select one item from the list. For example, assume that you were to rewrite the Checkfile program given in the previous section to use a select statement:

```
#!/bin/bash

# Checkfile. Checks type, ownership, and permissions of
# a file or list of files.

select file in $@
do

    # Test file type
    if [ -d $file ]
    then
        echo "$file is a directory"
```

```
        elif [ -f $file ]
        then
           echo "$file is a regular file"

           if [ -s $file ]
           then
              echo "$file is not empty"
           else
              echo "$file is empty"
           fi


        else
           echo "$file not found"
        fi

        # check ownership

        if [ -O $file ]
        then
           echo "You are the owner of $file"
        else
           echo "You are not the owner of $file"
        fi

        # check permissions

        if [ -r $file ]
        then
           echo "You have read permission for $file"
        fi

        if [ -w $file]
        then
           echo "You have write permission for $file"
        fi

        if [ -x $file ]
        then
           echo "You have execute permission for $file"
        fi
done
```

The initial output of this program, if invoked on the command line with the names of two files as arguments, would look like this:

```
$ checkfile file1 file2

1) file1
2) file2
#?
```

The #? prompt is the user's cue to enter one of the listed choices: 1 or 2. The program then runs the loop for the file that corresponds to the user's numerical choice. When the loop is finished, the program presents the menu and prompt again, letting the user choose another option.

This will continue forever, unless either the user presses Ctrl+d or Ctrl+c to stop the script, or you add a break statement to your select loop to stop the infinite repeat. A break statement would edit the first code block like this:

```
select <name> [ in <list>]
do
    <something>
    break
done
```

When the program reaches the break statement in its execution, it will exit the select loop.

Most people find the default value for the prompt, #?, to be unattractive—let alone less than helpful. You can remedy this problem by using the special variable PS3. You may recall from our discussion of bash environment variables in Chapter 13: "Customizing the Shell Environment" that the value of PS3 is the third-level bash prompt. It is also the value of the select statement's prompt. So, you can rewrite the Checkfile program to take advantage of that variable:

```
#!/bin/bash

# Checkfile. Checks type, ownership, and permissions of
# a file or list of files.

PS3="Select a file to check: "
select file in $@
do

    # Test file type
    if [ -d $file ]
```

```
then
   echo "$file is a directory"
elif [ -f $file ]
then
   echo "$file is a regular file"

   if [ -s $file ]
   then
      echo "$file is not empty"
   else
      echo "$file is empty"
   fi

else
   echo "$file not found"
fi

# check ownership

if [ -O $file ]
then
   echo "You are the owner of $file"
else
   echo "You are not the owner of $file"
fi

# check permissions

if [ -r $file ]
then
   echo "You have read permission for $file"
fi

if [ -w $file]
then
   echo "You have write permission for $file"
fi

if [ -x $file ]
then
   echo "You have execute permission for $file"
```

```
        fi
    done
```

When the script is run, the output will now show the amended prompt:

```
prompt% Checkfile file1 file2

1) file1
2) file2
Select a file to check:
```

Much better, don't you think?

The while Loop

Another type of iterative flow control uses the `while` command. The `while` command causes a section of code to repeat as long as a certain condition holds true. The general form of this statement is

```
while <condition>
do
    <something>
done
```

As with the `if` statement, the *<condition>* can be any statement that evaluates as true (0). For example, consider the following code block:

```
#!/bin/bash

echo "Guess the secret word: telephone, iguana, gallon"
read GUESS

while [ $GUESS != "iguana" ]
do
    echo "Incorrect - guess again"
    read GUESS
done

echo "Correct."
```

As long as the value of $GUESS is *not* equal to `iguana`, the program will continue to loop, prompting the user for input.

Remember that the exclamation-point character is a *negation operator.* It reverses the value of whatever comes immediately after it. So, != means *not equal to.*

As soon as the user enters the word *iguana,* however, the condition will fail, generating the exit status of 1, and the script's execution skips to the next line following the done statement.

A common use for the while statement is to cause a section of code to iterate a specific number of times. Consider this code block:

```
#!/bin/bash

declare -i i
i=0

while [ $i -lt 5 ]
do
    echo $i
    i=$i+1
done

echo "done"
```

In this example, the variable i has been declared to be an integer. The script's programmer then assigns the value of 0 to the variable $i. In the while statement, the programmer has defined the condition to be true if $i is less than 5. (Remember that the -lt operator is the *less than* comparison for integers.) Because 0 is less than 5, the loop will iterate.

In the course of executing the conditional block, the integer 1 will be added to the value of $i. Now, the value of $i is 1. Because 1 is less than 5, the loop iterates again, and again adds the integer 1 to the value of $i, which now has the value of 2. The process continues until $i is equal to 5. At that point, $i is no longer less than 5, and the conditional block is skipped. If you were to run this script, the output would look like this:

```
0
1
2
3
4
done
```

The until Loop

Remember the word-guessing game script that we used earlier in this chapter?

```
#!/bin/bash

echo "Guess the secret word: telephone, iguana, gallon"
read GUESS

while [ $GUESS != "iguana" ]
do
    echo "Incorrect - guess again"
    read GUESS
done

echo "Correct."
```

The negative comparison in the while statement, while [$GUESS != "iguana"], seems inelegant and counterintuitive to many. Is there a way to reconstruct that statement so that it is a positive comparison?

You can use the until loop to recast that statement. The until statement does almost exactly the same thing as the while statement, except that until addresses the equation from the opposite direction. That is, the until loop iterates a section of code as long as a given condition is *not* true. The general syntax of this statement is the same as that used for the while construct:

```
until <condition>
do
    <something>
done
```

So, if you wanted to rewrite the word-guessing script with a positive condition, you might come up with something like this:

```
#!/bin/bash

echo "Guess the secret word: telephone, iguana, gallon"
read GUESS

until [ $GUESS = "iguana" ]
do
    echo "Incorrect - guess again"
```

```
        read GUESS
done

echo "Correct."
```

This version of the script functions in exactly the same way as the other version using `while`, but the code is easier to understand because the condition is positive. Negative comparisons, although sometimes necessary, are much more likely to cause confusion in the reader, whether that reader is someone else or is you reading the script at a later time.

Nesting Loops

A common programming technique, *nesting loops* can yield fairly powerful results. Nesting loops is the practice of inserting one loop into another loop. This requires the `inner` loop to execute all of its iterations before the `outer` loop can execute once.

> **NOTE**
>
> In the previous chapter, we suggested that you avoid nesting `if-then` statements wherever possible. To a certain extent, the same admonition holds true here. If you can accomplish a task more simply and elegantly without nesting loops, then by all means do not nest them. However, nesting iterative loops can often yield such robust benefits that it has become a standard technique of programming.

The general form of a nested loop looks like this:

```
while <condition>
do
    while <condition>
    do
        <something>
    done
done
```

The loops need not be `while` loops; `until`, `for`, or `select` statements will work as well. Also, the loops need not be of the same type. There is no reason that you couldn't embed a `for` loop inside a `while` loop, or vice versa. The permutations are limited only by the programmer's imagination.

To show nested loops in a practical setting, we can return to the Checkfile program used earlier in the chapter:

```bash
#!/bin/bash

# Checkfile. Checks type, ownership, and permissions of
# a file or list of files.

PS3="Select a file to check: "
select file in $@
do

    # Test file type
    if [ -d $file ]
    then
        echo "$file is a directory"
    elif [ -f $file ]
    then
        echo "$file is a regular file"

        if [ -s $file ]
        then
            echo "$file is not empty"
        else
            echo "$file is empty"
        fi

else
    echo "$file not found"
fi

# check ownership

if [ -O $file ]
then
    echo "You are the owner of $file"
else
    echo "You are not the owner of $file"
fi

# check permissions
```

```
    if [ -r $file ]
    then
        echo "You have read permission for $file"
    fi

    if [ -w $file]
    then
        echo "You have write permission for $file"
    fi

    if [ -x $file ]
    then
        echo "You have execute permission for $file"
    fi
done
```

Before you make any amendments to this script, note that you already have some nested conditional constructs. In this case, there are if statements inside other if statements, and all of them are inside a select statement. Suppose, however, that instead of wanting to report on a single file, you wanted to generate a report for every file in a specified directory.

NOTE

The following example uses the construct $(<*command*>). This construct uses the output of <*command*> as the expression upon which the rest of the statement operates. Thus, in this case, LIST=$(ls $dir) assigns the output of the ls command to the value of the LIST variable.

You can rewrite the script to incorporate further nesting, as in this example:

```
#!/bin/bash

# Checkfile. Checks type, ownership, and permissions of a
# file or list of files.

PS3="Select a directory to check: "
select dir in $@
do

    # Test file type

    if [ ! -d "$dir" ]
```

```
then
    echo "$dir is not a directory"
else
    declare -a LIST
    LIST=$(ls $dir)

    for file in ${LIST[@]}
    do

    # Check Ownership

    if [ -O $file ]
    then
        echo "You are the owner of $file"
    else
        echo "You are not the owner of $file"
    fi

    # Check permissions

    if [ -r $file ]
      then
      echo "Read permission for $file"
    else
        echo "No read permission for $file"
    fi

    if [ -w $file ]
    then
        echo "Write permission for $file"
    else
        echo "No write permission for $file"
    fi

    if [ -x $file ]
    then
        echo "Execute permission for $file"
    else
        echo "No execute permission for $file"
    fi
done
```

```
fi

done
```

With this script, you can see that there are a number of if statements nested inside a for statement, inside another if statement, inside a select statement. In skeletal form, the script would look like this:

```
select <name> in <list>
do
    if <condition>
    then
        for <name> in <list>
        do
            if <condition>
            then
                <something>
            fi
        done
    fi
done
```

This type of nesting is typical of more complex programs. This does not imply that complexity cannot be achieved without four levels of nesting, only that these levels are sometimes necessary to perform a complex task. In fact, once we write a script like this, our first impulse is always to go over the finished script and see whether there is another way to get the desired result without nesting so deeply.

By this time, you should have a good idea of the sorts of things it is possible to accomplish with bash shell programming. The kicker here is that bash is a language designed to do simple things. Imagine what is possible—both in accomplishment and in headache—with a "real" programming language such as C++ or Java.

Summary

As described in the previous chapter, flow control is the mechanism that is used to control how scripts move from one instruction to the next. Iterative flow control, the type covered in this chapter, marks certain code blocks in a given script so that those blocks will be repeated until—or unless—a particular condition is true.

There are several types of iterative flow control statements, including the for statement, the select statement, the while loop, and the until loop. These statements can be issued independently of each other, or they can be nested within each other (or combined with conditional flow control statements). The combination of conditional and iterative flow statements makes it possible for the programmer to build shell scripts of some complexity, even though the bash scripting language is intended for relatively simple processes.

CHAPTER
TWENTY-FIVE

25

Regular Expressions

- How Regular Expressions Work

- sed

- awk

- Summary

Frequently in shell programming, many programmers find there is a small piece of text they want to identify and use. This is not a problem if the piece of text is a literal one: that is, if it is always the same text and always appears in the same way regardless of situation or context. Sometimes, though, the text you need to find is not a literal sequence of characters, but rather a type of text. You might know, for example, that the text will have certain qualities or that it will appear in a particular place in a particular file, but you don't know what the text will say until it appears.

Many Unix tools let you work with vague pieces of text like this, using a mechanism called *regular expressions*. Regular expressions are constructions that may match any number of literal text strings, but will match those strings only if they conform to certain characteristics. Unfortunately, many of these tools differ in the specifics of how their regular-expression-matching mechanisms work. It is therefore important for the shell programmer to be aware of the individual tool that you're using for any particular situation and how that tool handles regular expressions.

Regular Expressions: grep/sed/awk or Perl?

If, after reading this chapter, you decide that regular expressions are the greatest technique you've ever encountered, we suggest that you take a look at the Perl programming language. Like the shell environment, Perl is an interpreted language; thus, Perl programs don't need to be compiled before they are run.

Perl has a comprehensive and powerful way of handling regular expressions, as well as some programming features that make manipulating those expressions very easy. Perl is especially good for writing short programs that perform operations on strings of text. For example, there are Perl programs that will download a page from a Web news site—say, `http://www.cnn.com`—and then extract a certain subset of the headlines for quick reading. This kind of task is quite simple in Perl, and such a program would be no more than 20 or 30 lines.

Learn more about Perl at `http://www.perl.org` for a start. If you do find yourself interested in Perl, you must have the requisite Perl "Bibles": *Learning Perl*, by Larry Wall and Randall Schwartz (second edition, O'Reilly & Associates, 1997), and *Programming Perl*, by Larry Wall (third edition, O'Reilly & Associates, 2000). Anyone you talk to about Perl will assume that you have these books and have read them.

How Regular Expressions Work

So, you are probably wondering, how can you identify a piece of text if you don't know what it is or what it's likely to be? This particular conundrum is solved by the use of *metacharacters*. Metacharacters are characters that can match more than one other character, depending on how they're implemented. You've seen examples of metacharacters elsewhere in the book in places where we've talked about *wildcard characters*.

For example, if you issue the command

```
ls *.txt
```

at the shell prompt, the `ls` command would print out only those filenames that contain the suffix `.txt`. The `*` metacharacter in this context—and indeed in most others—means *any combination of zero or more characters.* In other words, `*` matches everything. When you combine that metacharacter with the literal string `.txt`, the operating system understands the combination as *match any combination of zero or more characters that ends in* `.txt`. Similarly, the `.` character is usually used to represent *any single character.*

In addition to these wildcard characters, there are other types of metacharacters that match certain types of *non-characters.* For example, the `^` character (called a *circumflex*) matches the beginning of a line. Thus, the regular expression `^Joe` would locate and match the word `Joe` only if it appeared at the beginning of a line. `Joe` anywhere else in a line would go unnoticed. Similarly, the `$` metacharacter matches the end of the line. If you were to append that to the previous expression, as in `^Joe$`, you'd get matches only if the word `Joe` were the only text on any given line because the word would have to be at both the beginning and the end of the line.

There is a final metacharacter that doesn't fit into either of these categories; this metacharacter is the backslash character (`\`). This character is also known as the *escape character* because it is used to "escape" the normal pattern-matching behavior of regular expressions. For example, if you wanted to match a literal dollar-sign character, you'd need to use the combination `\$`. This pairing tells the interpreter that you're really looking for a dollar sign, not for something at the end of a line.

TIP   To match a literal backslash, you'd use the construction `\\`.

Table 25.1 contains a summary of the most common metacharacters. However, it is important to note, as we mentioned above, that not all metacharacters are used in the same way by all programs. Thus, this summary should serve only as a guide and not as a definitive reference. Check the documentation for the program or language in which you're using metacharacters to search for text strings.

TABLE 25.1: Pattern-Matching Metacharacters

Character	Function
*	Matches any combination of zero or more characters.
.	Matches any single character.
[. . .]	Matches any of the characters enclosed between the brackets. For example, [aeiou] will match any vowel, [a-z] will match any lowercase letter, and [a-zA-Z] will match any upper- or lowercase letter.
^	Matches given string if it appears at the beginning of a line.
$	Matches given string if it appears at the end of a line.
\	Escapes pattern-matching behavior of the following character.

Using Metacharacters

Now that you've seen some common metacharacters, how do you use them to identify strings of text? Suppose that you're dealing with a document that contains the prices of various items. You know that, in the document, the prices take the form $XX.XX; that is, a literal dollar-sign character followed by two digits, a literal decimal point, and then two more digits. You want to find text strings that contain this construction and every occurrence of this sequence in the document.

To do this, you need the grep command.

TIP

grep is an acronym for Get Regular Expression Print, but it's usually used as a verb, as in "I grepped the log to find times when Steve sent print jobs to the laser printer."

The syntax for `grep` is

```
grep <expression> <file>
```

Thus, if the file you're searching is called `prices.txt`, you could construct your `grep` request like this:

```
grep \$[0-9][0-9]\.[0-9][0-9] prices.txt
```

Notice that we've used the backslash to indicate that the dollar-sign and decimal characters are to be treated as literal characters and not as metacharacters. Also, we have defined the allowable range of each digit as anything from zero to nine.

Alternative grep Syntax

Although the way we've used `grep` above is perfectly permissible, we often find it easier to think of `grep` as a type of filter. Another way of writing the command above, under the filter concept, would be

```
cat prices.txt | grep \$[0-9][0-9]\.[0-9][0-9]
```

If no filename is given to `grep` on the command line, it will use the standard input.

This alternative method causes the operating system to print the file `prices.txt`, piping it through the `grep` command. There isn't a real advantage to doing it this way, but if you find it to be more comprehensible, it's certainly another way to use this flexible and powerful command to find the data you need. We find that this method fits our conception of Unix logic a bit better, but—as with all things Unix—whatever works best for you is the way to go.

More about grep

There are two characteristics that make the regular expression in the previous section less than ideal for its purpose. First, it is possible for a price higher than $99.99 to be contained in the `prices.txt` document. Second, the expression [0-9] is repeated four times. Although the second concern is more aesthetic than practical, the two characteristics are structurally related. Wouldn't it be helpful if you could specify the number of times a particular expression, or a component of an expression, would be repeated?

You can do this by using the `grep` syntax called \{n,m\}. This syntax works under the following rules:

1. The expression \{*n*\} will match *n* occurrences of the designated character.

2. The expression \{*n*,\} will match *n* or more occurrences of the designated character. (Note the inclusion of the comma.)

3. The expression \{*n*,*m*\} will match at least *n*, but not more than *m*, occurrences of the designated character.

NOTE   The reason that the curly braces have backslashes in front of them is to prevent the curly braces from being interpreted as literal curly braces. This is the reverse of using a backslash to invoke the literal meaning of a metacharacter. Instead, in this case, you're using a backslash to turn a regular character into a metacharacter.

The \{n,m\} construct is placed immediately after the expression it is to modify. Thus, you could rewrite the `grep` expression used in the previous section as

```
\$[0-9]\{2,\}\.[0-9]\{2\}
```

Note that, to the left of the decimal point, you're seeking at least two numerical characters, while to the right of the decimal point, you're requiring exactly two numerical characters.

Now, suppose that there are prices in the `prices.txt` document that are less than $10. To pick up those prices, you need to tweak the `grep` command a bit more:

```
\$[0-9]\{1,\}\.[0-9]\{2\}
```

This method makes it possible to match only one character to the left of the decimal point. So, the final `grep` command looks like this:

```
grep \$[0-9]\{1,\}\.[0-9]\{2\} prices.txt
```

NOTE   Complicated regular expressions can often look like a forest of backslashes. You need to be careful when reading and writing these expressions, because every character matters, and a misplaced backslash can wreak havoc—while being extremely difficult to notice. The thing to remember is that a backslash always modifies the character immediately to its right.

---

sed

sed is a close relative of the line editor ed, which we introduced in Chapter 16: "The ed Editor." The difference lies in the fact that, whereas ed is a line editor that makes its changes one line at a time, sed is a *stream editor*. This means that sed operates on an entire file in one pass or on a stream piped to it through the standard input (usually the keyboard, unless you've defined standard input differently for some reason). This stream editing is quite handy for making standardized changes in a file or a group of files.

A simple way of using sed is to make a simple substitution in a given file. Suppose that you have a file that makes multiple use of the abbreviation etc., and you want to replace that abbreviation with the full term et cetera throughout the document. You can do such a thing very simply with sed, by issuing the command

```
sed 's/etc\./et cetera/g' filename.txt
```

This example uses sed's s// substitution construct. Very simply, this construct works like this:

```
s/<target>/<replacement>/
```

where *<target>* is the expression you want to replace, and *<replacement>* is the string with which you want to replace the first expression. In addition, in the previous command, we appended the g option to the end. g is the global flag that tells sed to replace all occurrences of *<target>* with *<replacement>* without asking your permission first. In the example, the *<target>* is the expression etc\..

NOTE

Note that we need to use the backslash to escape the period character so that it will be interpreted as a literal period and not as a metacharacter.

The *<replacement>* is the string et cetera.

The s// construct is only one of several commands that can be used with sed. Moreover, you can arrange for multiple commands to be run on any one given page or document by writing a sed script. If, for example, you have several substitutions that you want to make to a particular file, you could write a quick script called sedscript that might contain the following entries:

```
s/etc\./et cetera/g
s/i\.e\./that is/g
s/e\.g\./for example/g
```

You would then invoke sed with the following command:

```
sed -f sedscript filename.txt > outputfile.txt
```

The −f flag tells sed that its commands will be coming from the file named next on the command line. Here, *filename*.txt is the name of the input file, and *outputfile*.txt is the name of the file that will collect the output after editing.

WARNING Although it is possible to direct the output back to the original file, it is not recommended that you do so. If you made a mistake in your sed script, it would be easy to mess up the original file to the point where you might not be able to retrieve the original data. Saving the output to a new file ensures that you can always tweak your sed script and run it again without damaging the original data.

Writing sed Scripts

Before you begin to write sed scripts of your own, it's wise to learn a bit more about the general command syntax used with sed, and then learn some of the individual commands used with sed. The basic concepts used in other kinds of scripts are found in sed as well, such as comments and markers used by the scripts to define particular locations. With the proper syntax, sed can be quite useful, but if you try to use sed without knowing how it works, you may cause changes that were not what you intended (and that could even be detrimental depending on what you were trying to do). Despite the cautionary tone of this paragraph, if you've read the other chapters in this part of the book, you'll do fine with sed scripts.

Comments

As with other types of scripts in the shell environment, you can add comments to your sed scripts. A hashmark (#) at the beginning of a line denotes a comment.

TIP Remember to comment your scripts thoroughly and liberally so that you will remember what the script does and how it does it. Whether you revisit your own scripts at a later date or you share them with others, good comments make the difference between a usable script and a pointless curiosity.

Line Addresses

Any command can take, as a prefix, a line number or range of line numbers. These numbers are simply added to the beginning of the command. For example, if you want to change etc. to et cetera in only one place in your file, on line 42, you can use the command

```
42s/etc\./et cetera/g
```

If you wanted to do the same substitution on the 42nd through 58th lines, the appropriate command would be

```
42,58s/etc\./et cetera/g
```

It is also possible to prepend a line address to a group of commands. This is done by grouping the commands inside curly braces, like this:

```
42,58 {
    s/etc\./et cetera/g
    s/i\.e\./that is/g
    s/e\.g\./for example/g
}
```

Note that ranges of lines don't work for all commands. Some commands will generally be useful only on a single line, and, as a rule, those commands can take only a single line as an address.

sed Commands

As with other types of editors, sed uses standard commands for text substitution, deletion, and other tasks. These commands use the same slash-based syntax that we've already shown you for the substitution operator, s///. In this section of the chapter, we introduce commands that you can use to delete text, append or insert new text, or change existing text.

Substitution Commands

You have already seen the substitution operator, s///, earlier in this chapter. The general format of this operator is

```
[address]s/<target>/<replacement>/[flags]
```

We've used one of the possible flags already, the g flag, which is used to indicate that the substitution is to be applied to every instance of the match throughout the entire file. A few other flags are shown in Table 25.2, and you can learn even more by consulting the sed manual page, by issuing the command man sed at a command prompt.

TABLE 25.2: sed Flags

Flag	Function
n	n is a number between 1 and 512. This flag indicates that you want to match the nth occurrence of the string.
p	When the pattern is matched, the matched string will print to the standard output (usually the monitor).
w <file>	When the pattern is matched, the matched string will be written to the named file.

Deletion Commands

Instead of substituting one string for another, you might want to delete a matched pattern once it is found. For example, assume that you want to delete all strings beginning with the string CAN from the document you're working with, because those prices would be in Canadian dollars and not relevant to a US audience. The general format for the delete function is

```
/<pattern>/d
```

Thus, you'd use the command

```
/CAN/d
```

Commands for Appending, Inserting, and Changing

You can also use various sed commands to handle how text is appended to a line, inserted into a line, or changed altogether. These commands use much the same syntax as other sed commands already introduced in this section.

Append

The append command is used to place text after a designated line. Its syntax looks like this:

```
[address]/<pattern>/a\
<new text>
```

Note the backslash at the end of the first line. This indicates that the line is to be continued. You must put a backslash at the end of each line of new text as well, except for the last line. For example, assume that we wanted to add a line of text immediately after the section header for this section. We could do it with the command

```
/-Append*/a\
This is the new text. It may\
span several lines.
```

Insert

The insert command places the new text on the line above the matched line. It uses the syntax

```
[address]/<pattern>/i\
<new text>
```

Change

The change command replaces the matched line with the new text specified. Its syntax is

```
[address]/<pattern>/c\
<new text>
```

A sed Script Example

Now that you know some of the basics of **sed** scripting, it's time to build a sample script. Assume that you have a document that contains basic information about a company and some of its senior managers. The name of the company is MassiveCo, and the officers are Ms. Smith, Dr. Jones, and Mr. Green. However, between the time the document was written and the time it was published to the Internet, the company was bought out by another company. The company's name was changed to Massive & Associates, Inc. In addition, Mr. Green quit, and Mr. Rose was hired to replace him. Ms. Smith was fired, Dr. Jones was promoted to her position, and nobody has been hired to replace Dr. Jones. It's your job to update the document to reflect the current status of the company and its officers.

You could use the following script to make all the required changes quickly:

```
s/MassiveCo/Massive & Associates, Inc./g
s/Mr. Green/Mr. Rose/g
```

```
/Dr. Jones/d
s/Ms. Smith/Dr. Jones
```

You can then run the script by issuing the following command at a shell prompt:

```
sed -f <scriptname> <document> > <newdocument>
```

The file *<newdocument>* will contain the text of the original document, but with all the correct edits made. You can now save the original file as document.old and save the new document under the old document's name if you like.

Using sed on the Command Line

Although we have shown you some ways in the previous sections to use sed from the command line, these methods don't really capture the essence of sed as a *stream editor*. The greatest thing about sed is the way that you can use it as a filter to edit things on the fly. If no input file is specified, sed will take its input from the standard input as defined in your environment variables. This means that you can pipe the output of other commands through sed for on-the-fly processing.

Let's take an example. Suppose that you want to capture the output of a particular server program's log, but you want to work certain substitutions on that output. In our example built below, the process logs the IP number of everyone who connects to the mail server on your network. However, you hate reading straight IP numbers, so you want to convert the IP numbers to the machine names before you read the log. You know that the IP numbers on your network correspond to the following machine names:

```
192.168.0.1     alaska
192.168.0.2     arizona
192.168.0.3     california
192.168.0.4     connecticut
```

So, you can set up your sed script like this:

```
s/192.168.0.1/alaska/g
s/192.168.0.2/arizona/g
s/192.168.0.3/california/g
s/192.168.0.4/connecticut/g
```

Then, you can run the logfile watcher script with the following command:

```
tail -f /var/log/ourserver | sed -f sedscript >➡
/var/log/ourserver.edited
```

Here, you've piped the output of the `tail -f` command through the `sed` script filter.

TIP

The `tail` command shows the last few lines of a file, and the `-f` flag means that `tail` will print the new lines as they are created.

Once the output is piped through the filter, it is placed into a new file with the name `ourserver.edited`. When you look at the new file, you'll see the same log that the server generated, but it will show the machine names instead of the IP numbers.

Using sed in Shell Scripts

In shell scripts, you can use `sed` in much the same way as you use it at the command line. However, you can also use all your previously learned scripting techniques to tweak `sed`'s behavior when you use it in a shell script.

Consider the following script:

```
#!/bin/bash

case $1 in
    -a )
        SCRIPT="sedscript1"
        ;;
    -b )
        SCRIPT="sedscript2"
        ;;
    -c )
        SCRIPT="sedscript3"
        ;;
esac

sed -f $SCRIPT $2
```

This script takes a flag of either –a, -b, or –c and the name of a file as the command-line arguments. Depending on what the flag is, the script will cause `sed` to use a different script as a source of commands.

Another way to use `sed` in a script might resemble the following excerpt from a longer script.

```
#!/bin/bash

for file in "$@"
do
    sed -f sedscript $file

done
```

This segment would apply the set of commands in sedscript to multiple files, as indicated by the array $@, appearing on the command line.

Tips for Using sed Effectively

There are a few guidelines that will make using **sed** in your shell scripts more effective. Although you can use **sed** without following these tips, you'll probably find it easier to use as long as you keep these things in mind (in fact, these tips are applicable to more kinds of scripts than just **sed** scripts).

1. Know your input. Understanding the pattern that you're looking for, and how it might appear in the input stream, makes it a lot easier to devise the regular expressions that will catch those patterns.

2. Make sure to identify any metacharacters appearing in your input file, and escape them using the backslash character. Characters that need to be interpreted literally will mess up your programming if they are interpreted as metacharacters instead.

3. Test. Before you put your script to work, test it out. Make sure that it's catching everything that it should be, and—perhaps more importantly—make sure that your script isn't catching anything that shouldn't be caught in the regular-expression net you've woven.

awk

Like sed, the awk program can take input either from a file or from the standard. awk can also use commands given either on the command line or in a file. awk also works its operations on each line as it works its way through the input stream. With all these similarities, it's reasonable to wonder what the difference is between `sed` and `awk`, especially because the programs are often named in the same breath as *sed-and-awk*.

The difference between `sed` and `awk` lies in the types of commands that are handled by each program. Where `sed` is concerned with pattern matching and editing, `awk` is more useful for formatting output into a particularly desired pattern. `awk` handles these formatting tasks through the use of fields.

In `awk`, a *field* is any subsection of a line that is delimited by a particular character. The default field delimiter is *whitespace* (i.e., a space or a tab character), so that each word on a line is a separate field. However, the field delimiter can be changed with the –F flag.

WARNING   Do not confuse the –F flag with the –f flag, which—as in `sed`—specifies the script file to be used in a particular command.

The fields in an `awk` command are identified by the dollar-sign character ($) and the field number. Thus, if the input line reads

```
This is a line of input
```

the fields are identified like this:

```
$1 = This
$2 = is
$3 = a
$4 = line
$5 = of
$6 = input
```

NOTE   You'll need to exercise some caution while working with `awk` so that you don't confuse these $-delimited fields with shell command-line variables, which also use $ as a delimiter.

If the above line were contained in a file called `input.txt`, you could use `awk` to determine the fields in a particular line of the file. Assume that you want to see only the third field in that line (because it's the only line in the document, you don't have to supply a line number). Issue the following command:

```
awk '{print $3}' input.txt
```

Note that the command is enclosed in curly braces, which are themselves enclosed in single quotes. The curly braces are part of the awk command syntax, and the single quotes are there to protect the curly braces from being interpreted by the shell instead of by awk. If you give this command at the shell prompt, you'll get the following output:

a

Not very complex, is it?

Let's look at a more complicated example. Suppose that the file input.txt contains the output of the ps command and looks like this:

```
1      ?      00:00:30 init
2      ?      00:00:10 kflushd
3      ?      00:00:49 kupdate
4      ?      00:00:00 kpiod
5      ?      00:00:08 kswapd
6      ?      00:00:00 mdrecoveryd
49     ?      00:00:00 khubd
348    ?      00:00:29 syslogd
358    ?      00:00:00 klogd
373    ?      00:00:00 portmap
389    ?      00:00:00 lockd
390    ?      00:00:00 rpciod
400    ?      00:00:00 rpc.statd
454    ?      00:00:00 identd
455    ?      00:00:37 identd
457    ?      00:00:00 identd
458    ?      00:00:00 identd
459    ?      00:00:00 identd
473    ?      00:00:00 atd
504    ?      00:00:00 xinetd
539    ?      00:00:00 lpd
583    ?      00:00:09 sendmail
599    ?      00:04:59 gpm
631    ?      00:00:03 crond
636    ?      00:00:00 safe_mysqld
657    ?      00:00:00 mysqld
667    ?      00:00:39 mysqld
668    ?      00:00:00 mysqld
690    ?      00:00:16 xfs
721    ?      00:00:00 rhnsd
```

```
733   ?      00:19:48 _upsd
758   tty1   00:00:00 mingetty
759   tty2   00:00:00 mingetty
760   tty3   00:00:00 mingetty
761   tty4   00:00:00 mingetty
762   tty5   00:00:00 mingetty
763   tty6   00:00:00 mingetty
764   ?      00:00:00 gdm
10380 ?      00:00:28 fetchmail
10892 ?      00:00:04 sshd
30321 ?      00:03:58 X
30322 ?      00:00:00 gdm
30692 ?      00:00:01 gnome-session
30725 ?      00:00:00 gnome-smproxy
30725 ?      00:00:00 gnome-smproxy
30737 ?      00:01:09 magicdev
30745 ?      00:00:00 gnome-name-serv
30747 ?      00:00:04 sawfish
30821 ?      00:00:00 gmc
30823 ?      00:00:01 panel
30827 ?      00:00:00 gpilotd
30829 ?      00:00:14 cdplayer_applet
30831 ?      00:00:00 quicklaunch_app
30833 ?      00:00:01 deskguide_apple
30835 ?      00:00:05 mixer_applet
30838 ?      00:00:00 tasklist_applet
30841 ?      00:00:04 clockmail_apple
30847 ?      00:05:01 multiload_apple
30850 ?      00:00:04 gnome-terminal
30851 ?      00:00:00 gnome-pty-helpe
30852 pts/0  00:00:00 bash
30884 ?      00:03:11 netscape-commun
30897 ?      00:00:00 netscape <defunct>
30898 ?      00:00:00 netscape-commun
31011 ?      00:00:11 nedit
31063 pts/0  00:00:00 ps
```

This is a long and thorough list of processes. However, you're probably not interested in all of them. If you want to view only the process ID numbers of the currently running processes, you can issue the command

```
awk '{print $1}' input.txt
```

You can also use pattern-matching operations in awk. Suppose that you want to view the process ID numbers of only those processes that have an associated tty. Issue the command

```
awk '/tty/ {print $1}' input.txt
```

to get the following output:

```
758
759
760
761
762
763
```

Here, you have matched any line that contains the string tty and printed the first field of that line. Of course, you can eliminate the need to have a separate input.txt file by simply piping the output of the ps command directly into awk, as with the following command:

```
ps -a | awk '/tty/ {print #1}'
```

awk Metacharacters

In addition to the metacharacters introduced earlier in this chapter, awk uses some extended metacharacters of its own. Table 25.3 shows the most useful of these characters.

TABLE 25.3: awk Metacharacters

Metacharacter	Function
\b	Backspace
\n	New-line
\t	Tab

To use these metacharacters, assume that you have a file full of lines delimited by tab characters. You could use awk to split the fields based on the tabs, simply by using the −F flag and the t metacharacter, as in the command

```
awk -F\t '<commands>' <input>
```

This command will prevent awk from splitting the fields based on spaces, as is awk's default behavior.

Printing in awk

When using the print command under awk, you are not limited to printing the values of individual fields. Assume that, with the above example, you want to note any instance where a process is running with a tty, but you don't need the process ID number. You could issue the command

```
ps -a | awk '/tty/ {print "Found one! \n"}'
```

to get a report whenever an active tty is found.

> **NOTE**   The trailing new-line character (\n) is used so that each **Found one!** will appear on a separate line.

Summary

When you are writing shell programs, you may need to know the value of a particular text string to accomplish the task you want to perform. However, the value of the given text string may vary from time to time, especially if it is part of the output of another command. If you can't know the value of the text string before you write the script, you cannot include that specific value in the script. The solution is to use regular expressions, which enable you to use pattern-matching techniques to identify the value of a text string that follows a particular pattern.

The major programs that are used for pattern matching are sed and awk. Perl, a popular programming language, also uses pattern matching and may be a more elegant solution to some scripting needs. sed and awk are stream editors, meaning that they can perform pattern-matching actions on a streaming set of data or an inanimate file. Both sed and awk use metacharacters to handle the patterns for which the script will search, and both can report individual strings or a full set of matched patterns. The main difference between sed and awk is that awk works in a field-delimited manner, whereas sed is less concerned with formatting. Although you will probably not use either sed or awk on a frequent basis, pattern-matching tools such as the popular utility grep are fast and highly useful tools for the system administrator.

CHAPTER
TWENTY-SIX

Signals and Status

- Exit Status

- Managing Status

- Signals

- Unique Identifiers

- Managing Signals

- Summary

In the previous chapters of this part of the book, we introduced basic concepts of shell programming. Although you can write some complex scripts and accomplish some wonderful feats with those tools, there are elements of shell programming that open whole new worlds of potential script-managed automation. In this chapter and the one that preceded it, we expand on the basic shell programming structure and show you how to harness the power of your Unix computer at a level higher than that usually attained by the average Unix user.

This chapter addresses the concepts of exit status and signals. These terms are used to describe the means by which a particular process can know what is happening with another process, without human intervention. These mechanisms also allow individual processes to tell other processes how to behave, to generate a desired result. Such techniques are part of the general practice of *interprocess communication* and form a valuable part of the programmer's toolbox.

NOTE   In Chapter 25, we introduced *regular expressions,* tools used to match text patterns without having to type each affected item's name individually. Both regular expressions and the concepts covered in this chapter are commonly used shell programming techniques, but they fall into the category of *intermediate* rather than *basic* techniques. Adding regular expressions, exit status determination, and signal processing to your shell scripts will make it possible for you to attack increasingly larger and more complex system administration tasks with your programs.

Although most shell scripts are not complex enough to warrant huge amounts of interprocess communication handling, it's well worth knowing about these techniques. If you download scripts or receive them from other sources, you may find sections containing these mechanisms. In addition, though you may be writing small, straightforward scripts right now, in the future you might need to write lengthy and complicated scripts that can function only with the help of such techniques. In either case—and even if neither case holds true—knowing a bit about exit status and signals will expand your capability as a script programmer.

Exit Status

In various places throughout Part VI: "Shell Programming," we have made references to *exit status.* The exit status of a command or program is a numerical value that represents whether the command or program exited successfully. By default, an exit status of 0 represents the successful completion of a command or program, and an exit status of anything else represents failure.

Interpreting Exit Status

Some programs define success and failure in ways that might seem to be counterintuitive. For example, the `diff` command (which compares two files and reports the differences between them) returns an exit status of 0 if it doesn't find any differences. Because the program is designed to find differences between the files, it may seem strange that actually finding those differences constitutes a failure. However, it does make sense in a convoluted way. If two files are identical, and you run a `diff` on them, you get no output. If there are differences, you will probably need to do something to evaluate those differences and possibly process them somehow. So in a sense, having no differences is success because that's all you need to know. This may seem counterintuitive at first, but if you think about it from a usefulness standpoint, it makes perfect sense.

When using exit status in a script, you need to be aware of those idiosyncrasies. Not every Unix program handles exit status in the same way. Luckily, the manual page for any given command usually details the various exit status possibilities so that you can configure your script properly.

Though 0 and 1 are the standard exit status values, they can be customized. Although we don't recommend that you mess around with the 0 exit status (it's far too useful as it is), you might want to assign particular values of 1 or greater to the myriad ways in which a program can fail. These individual values can tell you a lot more about the failures than can the standard value of 1; if different values are assigned to different outcomes in the script, you'll be able to tell exactly what went wrong when the script failed.

For example, consider the case of a program that sends its output to a log file. If you've assigned the exit status of 1 to the case where the program fails to produce output and the exit status of 2 to the case where the program fails to open the log file for writing, you can then write a script that monitors the exit status of that particular program. Your script can take appropriate action based on the exit status of that program, whether it is to halt some other process or continue based on the nonexistence of any output.

Exit status is sometimes referred to as *return value*. It is common to hear, for example, the statement that *command X returns 0 for success and 1 for failure.*

Managing Status

To use the exit status of a particular program, your script must be able to tell what that status is. There are several ways to do this. You can use the `exit` command to cause the script or program to report a particular exit status based on parameters that you define. You can also use one of two methods to determine the exit status of a particular program and then have another action performed, based on whatever the exit status is reported to be. Each method has its place, but you'll probably find one to be more useful than the others depending on the circumstances of the particular situation.

Reporting Status

Exit status is reported through the `exit` command, which takes the number of its status as an argument. That is, to report an exit status of 1, you would use the command

```
exit 1
```

The `exit` command is a somewhat unusual command. By itself, it really doesn't do all that much, and it doesn't do much good at the command prompt. The key to using this command effectively is to place it in a strategic location within a script or in a block of code and then write other code that takes advantage of the information that `exit` provides.

For example, consider this small program (which is written more for the example than for any particular function):

```
if <first type of failure>
then
   exit 1
elif <second type of failure>
   exit 2
```

```
   elif <third type of failure>
      exit 3
   else
      exit 0
   fi
```

Aside from terminating the execution of the program, all that the `exit` command needs to do here is to report a particular piece of information. An exit status of 1, 2, or 3 indicates the particular kind of failure that you have defined here; of course, the status of 0 indicates success. The effect of this information, however, lies only in how you choose to use it later in the script.

Accessing Status

There are two different ways to find out the exit status of a given process. The first method is the explicit method, which involves using the ? variable; the second is the implicit method, which involves using the command itself as the expression in the conditional statement. Both methods are described below, with examples of code blocks that might appear in shell scripts.

The Explicit Method

The explicit method of determining exit status uses common variables. As the script runs, the exit status of the most recently executed program is assigned to a variable, which can then be used later in the script. A skeleton example of this method might look like this:

```
<execute some command>
if [ $? -eq 0 ]
then
   <normal processing>
else
   <error processing>
fi
```

The ? variable contains the exit status of the most recently executed command. Because this variable's value changes every time a command is executed, the programmer needs to exercise some caution about how it is used. For example, if you want to preserve the exit status of a command so that it can be used even after other commands are executed, you need to assign its value to a more permanent variable. Thus, you might amend the basic example shown above into a script component like this:

```
<execute some command>
status = $?
<execute some other command>
if [ $status -eq 0 ]
then
    <normal processing>
else
    <error processing>
fi
```

The Implicit Method

The implicit method uses the command itself as an expression, rather than resorting to the use of variables, as in the explicit method. Because the command itself is used in the conditional statement, the code block can be a bit shorter. A skeleton example of the implicit method might be

```
if <some command>
then
    <normal processing>
else
    <error processing>
fi
```

Remember that the if statement considers a value of 0 to represent *true*. By putting the command directly into the if statement, you can use the command's exit status as the value that the if statement will evaluate. If the command executes successfully, the if statement will interpret that value as a *true expression*.

NOTE   In this situation, the reason for the alternate term *return value* becomes more clear. The if statement evaluates the value, not the status.

If that explanation seems a bit abstract, that's because it is. The implicit method is a bit more difficult to understand because it is based on evaluation of a value that you don't actually call in the script; instead, the if statement evaluates a value that is the by-product of an action explicitly called. Here's a code block that will help clarify the action of the implicit method of evaluating exit status:

```
if cd $1
    then
       <do something>
    else
       <echo "Directory not found.">
    fi
```

In this example, we assume that the name of a directory is passed from the command line as the value of the variable $1. If the directory exists, the cd command works; if the directory doesn't exist, the cd command fails, and the if statement then directs the program to the code in the else clause. The message "Directory not found." will print to the screen and inform the user that a mistake has been made.

NOTE
In the process of evaluating the cd command's success or failure, the command is executed. Thus, you can kill two birds with one stone and make subsequent commands based on the assumption that the working directory has been changed with cd. This kind of sequential chain can be a bit confusing if you're not used to it, but it is a very common programming practice and can be quite useful once you've mastered it.

Building an Example

Now that you have some familiarity with the function of exit status, and the different ways to evaluate and use it, it's time to build an example that shows how exit status can be used effectively in your own shell scripts. In this example, we've constructed a basic script that takes the name of a directory as an argument at the command prompt. If the directory exists, the script lists the contents of the directory to the screen. If the directory does not exist, the script prints a warning message instead. (Yes, this is an expanded version of the skeleton code block shown above in the discussion of implicit exit status evaluation.)

```
#!/bin/bash

# Define a function that checks for the existence
# of a specified directory
```

```
checkdir () {

    # Using the explicit exit status of 'test',
    # assign an appropriate exit status to the
    # function

    test -d $1

    if [ $? -eq 0 ]
    then
        exit 0
    else
        exit 1
    fi

}

# Set the variable $dir to the value passed on
# the command line

dir=$1

# Using the implicit exit status of the 'checkdir'
# command, list the directory or report an error

if checkdir($dir)
then
    ls -l $dir
    exit 0
else
    echo "Directory not found."
    exit 1
fi
```

This sample script does essentially the same thing as the ls command, except the sample script requires the explicit checking for the directory's existence. (Of course, ls does it much better and faster than this script does.) The point here is not to duplicate the function of ls, but to show that the exit status of the checkdir() function is used to determine implicitly whether the named directory exists before the program attempts to list it. In addition, the checkdir() function itself uses a redundant and explicit exit status test to determine how to set its own exit status.

NOTE
The astute reader has, no doubt, noticed the staggering amount of redundancy in the script shown above. Without a doubt, this is one of the most unnecessary and inefficient scripts ever written, and we're willing to acknowledge that. However, it does make the uses of exit status quite clear, with both the explicit and implicit methods.

Signals

Another species of interprocess communication is the *signal*. Signals are a function of the operating-system kernel, though they are uniform across all Unix variants. Signals tell a particular process, or program that is running, that the operating system wants it to do something. That *something* is usually to stop running, though it can be other functions as well (there are even multiple ways in which stopping a process can be handled).

To use a signal, three unique items must be present:

- A unique identification for the process that is to receive the signal
- A way of sending the signal
- A *signal trap,* which is a bit of code in the recipient process that describes what should happen when a particular signal is received

Unique Identifiers

To send a signal to a given process, there needs to be a way to identify that process with a unique label. In most cases, you'll use the *process identification number (PID)*. Each process that runs on your system is given one of these numbers, and each number is unique and incremental.

To see the process identification numbers of the processes currently running on your system, issue the command ps at the command prompt. ps will return a list of all running processes that belong to your user ID, which usually means programs that you've started (including the shell you're using).

TIP

To see a list of all running processes, regardless of who's running them, use the −a flag. Thus, the command would be **ps** −a. Other useful flags and options can be found in the **ps** manual page, invoked with the command **man ps**.

When Joe issues the **ps** −a command on his machine, he usually gets a list that looks like this:

```
[joe@fugu joe]$ ps −a
PID    TTY           TIME    CMD
7644   tty1       00:00:00   bash
7862   tty1       00:00:00   su
7683   tty1       00:00:00   bash
2951   pts/0      00:00:00   ps
```

In this list, there are four processes. The process identification number is listed in the first column, and that PID will serve as that process's identifier as long as the process is running. The program that is using the PID is listed in the final column.

The PID of any given shell process can also be accessed with the shell variable $. If you issue the command

```
echo $$
```

at a shell prompt, you'll see that shell's identification number. This can then be used to kill the shell or used in other scripts; you might find that command to be a useful component of a shell program that requires a shell to start, run a process, and then kill itself after the task has been completed. Because the shell process's identification number will change each time the shell is spawned, the script needs to determine the shell process's PID before it can be killed. This command makes it easy to do so.

One way in which the $ variable is used frequently is to echo its value into a file. You'd do so by adding a line into a script that looks like this:

```
echo $$ > /var/run/myprogram.PID
```

Why would you do this? Well, if you need to kill off the shell later by using the **kill** command, you can simply issue a command like

```
kill -9 `cat /var/run/myprogram.PID`
```

(This is the entire *raison d'etre* for the /var/run directory.)

Why would you do something like this? Well, this method offers the benefit of not needing to know the exact process identification number of the shell to kill it. Because the process identification number is different every time you start a new shell, you can't set an absolute value as the PID. Similarly, you could set an environment variable containing the PID with a command like this:

```
export MYPROGRAM-PID=$$
```

However, we are not aware of this method being used. It's probably more efficient memory-wise to use a file instead of an environment variable, and it's certainly more congruent with actual scripting and administrative habits.

Managing Signals

To use signals most effectively, you need to know two things: the type of signal you want to send and the unique process identification number of the process you wish to affect. The second part is easier to determine than the first. Simply use the ps command to obtain the listing of all processes currently operating on your system, find the correct one, and use that number when you issue the signal. The first part is more complex in theory than in reality because—though many signals are available, and the list varies depending on your Unix variant—most people use just a few signals over and over again.

Using signals for hand-performed tasks is a straightforward and basic operation. When you begin to use signals and signal management in your scripts, things become a bit more complex. You may find yourself using more esoteric signals in scripts than you would in a hand-issued command, because you can create a complicated series of events and what-if statements that vary depending on the criteria you select. When using signals in your scripts, you can rely on signal traps to perform the desired functions automatically. These traps can save you a lot of coding time and provide an extra level of function to your programs.

Sending Signals

Signals are sent using the kill command. Because signals are most often used to terminate a process, the *kill* name is appropriate and easy to remember. Assume that you have issued the ps ─a command as shown earlier in this chapter and that you've received the following output:

```
[joe@fugu joe]$ ps ─a
PID   TTY             TIME   CMD
7644  tty1        00:00:00   bash
7862  tty1        00:00:00   su
7683  tty1        00:00:00   bash
2951  pts/0       00:00:00   ps
```

If you then issue the command

```
kill 7644
```

you would end the first process in that list, an open bash process.

Because you didn't specify the particular kind of signal to be sent, the default signal was used. The default signal is called *signal 15* or the *SIGTERM signal*. SIGTERM is the termination signal, and it causes the process to exit in an orderly way, closing down any tendrils it may have sent into other programs or other processes that may depend on the process being closed.

If something is going wrong, however, SIGTERM may not be able to exit cleanly, and the kill command will fail. In that case, you'll have to use a stronger signal: *signal 9,* called the *SIGKILL signal.* SIGKILL causes the process to exit immediately without any attempt or time to clean up after itself.

WARNING When you use SIGKILL, you may experience some trouble with other processes still running, if the process being killed does not shut down cleanly. Although using signal 9 usually doesn't cause trouble, if you sense instability in the system after using it, you may need to shut down all processes and log in again. In rare cases, you may even need to reboot.

To specify the signal that kill will use, simply place the signal number on the command line. You can use either the signal's name or its identification number, though the numbers are far more commonly used. For example, you might issue the command

```
kill ─9 7644
```
or
```
kill ─KILL 7644
```

You don't have to use the SIG segment of the signal's name, because that segment is implied when you use the suffix.

To see the various signals that are available to you with your particular Unix variant, use the −1 flag with the `kill` command. When we issue this command on one of our machines, we get the following output:

```
[joe@fugu joe]$ kill -1
1) SIGHUP      2) SIGINT     3) SIGQUIT    4) SIGILL
5) SIGTRAP     6) SIGIOT     7) SIGBUS     8) SIGFPE
9) SIGKILL    10) SIGUSR1   11) SIGSEGV   12) SIGUSR2
13) SIGPIPE   14) SIGALRM   15) SIGTERM   17) SIGCHLD
18) SIGCONT   19) SIGSTOP   20) SIGTSTP   21) SIGTTIN
22) SIGTTOU   23) SIGURG    24) SIGXCPU   25) SIGXFSZ
26) SIGVTALRM 27) SIGPROF   28) SIGWINCH  29) SIGIO
30) SIGPWR    31) SIGSYS
```

Note that all the signal names begin with the prefix SIG to indicate that they are signals. You can use whatever is easiest for you to remember and type, and you'll hear these signals referred to by both their full names and just their suffixes.

TIP
As we mentioned above, the `kill` command is configured so that you can omit the SIG prefix if you want to issue a signal by its name; `kill -TERM` is the same as `kill -15`.

The most commonly used signals are SIGHUP (1), SIGINT (2), SIGKILL (9), SIGSEGV (11), and SIGTERM (15). These signals work in slightly different ways, but how they behave is determined largely by the kinds of signal traps that are used to handle and invoke them.

NOTE
The exception is signal 9, SIGKILL, which always kills the specified process.

If you want to find out how the signals differ from each other by learning each signal's technical specifications, you'll have to read the section of the kernel code that defines them. Under Linux, signals are defined in the file `/usr/include/linux/signal.h`, but the comments are very sparse—if you don't know the C programming language already, you probably won't get much enlightenment from reading the kernel. Those who use Unices that don't make kernel code accessible to users may not be able to learn the technical specifications of their signals directly.

However, don't fret: You don't need to know how they work to use them. You'll be using `kill -9` for the vast majority of your `kill` commands anyway.

Signal Traps

As we mentioned earlier in this chapter, a *signal trap* is a way of defining how a particular program will behave when it receives a particular signal as it operates. When writing a script, you can include a signal trap by using the `trap` command. `trap` uses this syntax:

```
trap <command> <signal> [<signal> <signal> … ]
```

You can stack up as many signals as you need within the square brackets, though for the sake of simplicity, you shouldn't try to cover every signal operation in a single signal trap. Thus, if you want to trap the SIGINT signal and cause the script to print out a message when the signal is received, you might place a line in the script that looks like this:

```
trap "echo 'caught a SIGINT'" INT
```

To understand more about signal traps, let's take a look at a more complex script that uses them to perform actions automatically. Consider this small script:

```
#!/bin/bash
while true
do
    sleep 60
done
```

This script doesn't do much. `true` is an expression that will always return an exit status value of 0; thus, the loop will always execute. If you decide to run this script, it will loop indefinitely until you stop it with a signal or kill it with `kill -9` *processnumber* at another shell prompt.

NOTE   You can send a signal to stop this script by pressing Ctrl+c, which is defined as the key combination that sends the SIGINT signal. This should work regardless of Unix variant, because it is a very common expectation on the part of programmers.

The script as it stands now does not have a signal trap. So, amend the script and add a trap at the start of the program:

```
#!/bin/bash
trap "echo 'caught a SIGINT'" INT
```

```
while true
do
    sleep 60
done
```

If you run the script now, it will loop infinitely just like the first one. However, if you press Ctrl+c while the script is running, you'll now see a message printed to the screen that reads "caught a SIGINT." (The program will continue to run after the message is printed.)

TIP To kill a running process when you have only one shell session available to you (for example, if you're not running X and you can run only a single terminal session), press Ctrl+z to put the running process into the background. Then, issue the `ps` command to get a list of process identification numbers, and use the `kill -9` command to kill the running process.

At this point, you have a script that runs indefinitely, though it will alert you if an interrupt signal has been received. That's helpful, but the purpose of SIGINT is usually to stop the process and not just to alert you that something has happened. To make this script work a bit more usefully, amend the signal trap so that the script will exit when it notices the Ctrl+c key combination producing a SIGINT:

```
#!/bin/bash
trap "echo 'caught a SIGINT'; exit 1" INT
while true
do
    sleep 60
done
```

In this version, you have added an *exit statement* as part of the signal trap. The exit statement sets the condition under which the program will shut itself down. Now, when you hit Ctrl+c while the script is running, you'll see the message, and the program will shut down. It will also return an exit status of 1, letting you know that something untoward has happened; remember, an exit status of 1 indicates that the program ended because of an error or other incorrect situation.

TIP The semicolon in the signal trap signals the end of a line to the shell. Thus, the trap line appears as two separate lines to the shell interpreter. Programmers use the semicolon to keep several short commands on the same line for easier reading and to keep the various components of a complex command together.

If you want to add more complex behavior than can fit into a single trap line, even with semicolons, you can pull that behavior out into its own function, as in this variation on our example script:

```
#!/bin/bash
croak () {
    echo "Ugh! I'm ….. dying….."
    sleep 3
    echo "klunk"
    exit 1
}


trap "croak" INT

while true
do
    sleep 60
done
```

With the croak function added, the script will now produce a little soliloquy while it shuts down. You can probably think of more useful ways in which to use a function in a shell script than to turn your computer into a bad imitator of Shakespeare, but the process is illuminated here.

WARNING Some readers may think that signal handling and functions are the answer to their prayers, permitting incredibly complex behavior in a simple construction. Don't go overboard. If you're just writing shell scripts, most of the tasks you'll write scripts for are not complex enough to warrant a huge amount of signal handling. You'll eat up valuable processor resources to execute the various responses, taking that time away from the actual tasks you're trying to complete.

Ignoring Signals

Although it's not all that common, there may be times when you want your program to ignore certain kinds of signals. For example, you may be a system administrator who needs to run particular scripts in your users' directories to clean out dead files or programs that aren't permitted by your Acceptable Use Policy, such as files over a stated size. However, you might have a user who Ctrl+c's any process he doesn't recognize, so your scripts keep dying before they have a chance to work.

> **TIP**
>
> You'll find some ignore traps in the most system-critical scripts, though. It would be disastrous if these programs were ended abruptly before they finished their work, so programmers embedded ignore traps so that the scripts wouldn't shut off without authorization.

Luckily, it's easy to ignore particular signals. (You should never set a program to ignore SIGKILL, though. You'd have to reboot to stop a runaway process that ignores −9.) To ignore a particular signal, just add an empty command line in your signal trap, as in this example:

```
trap "" INT
```

This line makes the script trap the SIGINT signal, but specifies that nothing is to be done about it and that the program should continue as normal.

Summary

Exit status and signals are two useful identifiers that can be used to expand the functionality and precision of your shell scripts. Exit status is the value returned by a particular process as it finishes; the status is either 0, in which case the process has finished cleanly, or another number (usually 1), which indicates failure or some other nonideal conclusion. You can use the exit status number in an `if-then` construction to cause subsequent action based on the value of the exit status.

Signals are used to manage active processes (those that have not yet produced an exit status value). Signals are used with the unique process identification number assigned to each ongoing process on the system; for example, the `kill` command can be issued only with a specific process identification number passed as the argument. Signals are generally used from the command line only to end running processes. However, in scripts and programs, a wider variety of signals can be used to affect running processes and then perform particular tasks based on the outcome.

PART VII

Basic System Administration

CHAPTER
TWENTY-SEVEN

What Is System Administration?

- The Administrator's Job

- Administering a Small System

- Professional System Administration

- Basic System Administration Tasks

- Summary

The first parts of this book dealt with subjects relevant to all Unix users, whether administrators or simply account-holders; the remainder of the book focuses on tasks unique to the system administrator.

- Part VII: "Basic System Administration" introduces the concept of administration and explains the basic tasks that are required of every administrator, whether on a network or a standalone machine.

- Part VIII: "Network Administration" introduces networks and covers the physical devices that make up networks of computers, both the machines themselves and the cabling and cards that connect them.

- Part IX: "Administering Services" deals with the various programs that handle external requests to the local network, such as Internet services like e-mail or Web.

The subjects covered in the remaining chapters are those that truly distinguish Unix computers from computers running other operating systems. Readers who run their own Unix machines will find help here both for the basic tasks of administration and for the more advanced concepts involved in working with multicomputer networks and providing services to external networks. Any Unix computer can perform these tasks; you do not have to purchase a special version of Unix to handle networking and administrative functions. The only barrier is hardware power, especially RAM and hard-disk space.

In this chapter, we introduce the chapters that complete this part of the book. We also spend some time discussing the concept of *system administration* itself: Who is a sysadmin? Who is not? Are you? Even if you are not sure whether you will ever run your own Unix machine, we encourage you to read Part VII. At the least, it will give you a fuller understanding of the tasks your own system administrator performs; at the most, it will give you the information you need to run your own system if you decide to do so. Readers who are already root on some system can use Part VII as a refresher, before tackling the networking and services topics in Parts VIII and IX.

The Administrator's Job

At its most basic, the term *system administrator* is self-explanatory. A system administrator (sysadmin) is a person who administers systems, usually computer systems. System administration involves maintaining hardware, installing and updating software, and dealing with users. It requires specific knowledge in a variety of disparate areas, from programming to dispute resolution, and the ability to learn quickly and on the run.

In the term's more habitual use, a system administrator is a person who is in control of one or more computer networks, usually for an organization, whether corporate or nonprofit. System administration requires long and irregular working hours, often at the beck and call of a pager. The system administrator is responsible for dealing with a plethora of requests and demands that often are contradictory, enforcing network policies and standards, and managing a budget. It is an unenviable job.

Luckily, in most situations, system administration is a shared job. Larger organizations will have several sysadmins to handle general network operation, while other employees will handle specific tasks such as Web administration or mail management. There may be 100 or more people at a particular organization who are, in the whole, responsible for system administration, while their individual tasks are small slices of the complete job.

Although there is no semantic difference between the system administrator of a large network and the system administrator of a single home machine, there is a practical difference between the professional and the amateur. If you run a single Unix machine, you are a very different kind of system administrator from someone who's responsible for 100 machines. Don't insist on being called a sysadmin, especially by people who are professionals; there's a pecking order in the Unix world, and upward movement is based on demonstrated skill and ability.

That said, in this book we use the term to cover all sorts of people. If you have root on a Unix machine, we consider you to be a system administrator and refer to you as such. The skills you'll learn in the remaining chapters are those used by professional sysadmins, and they are crucial tasks that need to be performed by anyone in charge of Unix computers, whether beginners or wizards.

Administering a Small System

We assume that most readers will be administrators of single computers or of networks containing fewer than five computers. If you are in this category, you have a lot to learn because you will be responsible for every aspect of your system. You'll have to handle maintenance, upgrades, services, and users.

The advantage of a small system is that it's possible to familiarize yourself with everything that's going on within the network. (We use the network example in this chapter because it's the larger of the two options; if you are a single-computer administrator, just reduce all the examples to concern only one computer.) You probably know all your users personally, and are familiar with the kind of traffic and system load they tend to generate. It's easier to know when something's wrong, intuitively, because you know your system so well.

WARNING As a small-system administrator, you need to be very conscious of security. Because you're in charge of everything, you don't have the luxury of a person whose sole job is to keep your system intact. Keep up with security news and help yourself out by installing software that will monitor your system even when you're not there.

Even though you're running just a few computers—or even just one—it's a good idea to set up basic policies if you have users other than yourself. Your policies can be as simple as "Don't do anything illegal" or as detailed as "Uploads and downloads larger than 3Mb are permitted only between 8:00 P.M. and 6:00 A.M." Inform your users of your policies, and enforce them. It's probably your name on the Internet connection, and you don't want to lose access because one of your users decided to join a pyramid scheme that's distributed by unsolicited e-mail.

Your job will be simplified if you review Part VI: "Shell Programming" and learn at least the basics. Shell scripts will automate a lot of your daily tasks and can keep you from giving up the Unix enterprise because of the busywork. You'll learn more about shell programs in Chapter 28: "System Programming."

Finally, don't be afraid to experiment. If you have a small network or single computer, you don't have a lot of responsibilities to other people who rely on you for all their computing needs. You can try out shell scripts, install and test new services, or learn about kernel management on your own system. (Back everything up first, though.) The Unix world is filled with people who taught themselves from scratch, so you're upholding a long tradition of autodidactery.

Professional System Administration

To those readers who are professional system administrators, welcome. Because this book covers a spectrum of abilities, you'll find much of the material in these remaining chapters to be information you already know. However, in the grand tradition of Unix, there are probably things here that are new to you, especially if you are a specialist.

As with the small-system administrators, we recommend that professional sysadmins maintain a high level of security awareness. Security risks and successful exploits are constantly in the news, and the cracking isn't just for fun anymore (if it ever truly was, despite the romantic myths). Especially if you work for a major corporation, your data is vulnerable to loss or compromise, which can lead to legal trouble or profit losses. You probably have a commercial security package installed on your networks; even if it isn't your direct responsibility, take some time to familiarize yourself with it. At the least, you'll have a new skill for your next job search.

We encourage you to skim through this part of the book to check your basic system administration skills, though you probably perform many of these tasks in your daily work. Some of the material covered in these chapters may not be part of your job, especially print services or kernel management, or you may not be familiar with the Unix variants we describe here.

Basic System Administration Tasks

In this part of the book, we review the tasks common to system administration at all levels. No matter how many computers there are in your network or how many users you manage, you will find these tasks to be the basic components of your system's work. Whether you become proficient in all of the tasks or you choose to specialize, it's a good idea to become familiar with all these skills. It is likely that you'll be called upon to use them all at some point in your time as a Unix system administrator.

System Programming

Chapter 28: "System Programming" expands on the skills presented in Part VI: "Shell Programming." The chapters of Part VI explained the basic theory of programming for the shell environment; Chapter 28 shows you how those theories translate into system administration. You'll need to understand the concepts behind shell programming to take advantage of this streamlining technique.

You can use shell scripts to manage almost any system administration activity, whether it's user management or routine hard-drive cleaning. If it can be done with a shell command, it can be done with a shell script. This chapter also presents the useful commands `cron` and `at`. When used in combination with shell scripts, these commands will relieve you of even the most basic part of shell programming: remembering to run the program so it will do its work.

Managing Users

Even if nobody else will ever log into your Unix computer, you'll need to manage your user base because you will have a personal user account as well as the root account. You may want to have multiple user accounts as easy ways to test new scripts or commands, as well. Chapter 29: "Managing Users and Groups" introduces the various Unix user commands and tasks, and offers some useful tips on user management.

WARNING   Never use the root account to perform personal activity, especially if it's Internet activity. Save the root account for root activity and use your personal account for everything else.

User management encompasses a range of tasks. Creating a new user is only the first step. Users can be divided into groups, which makes it easier to manage various administrative details. Special attention should be paid to the `/etc/passwd` file, which contains encrypted passwords for every user on your system. Finally, when you no longer have a particular user, the user should be fully removed from your system.

Managing Disks and Filesystems

Unix handles disks differently from other operating systems. In Chapter 30: "Disks and Filesystem Management," we introduce this concept and explain how disks can be partitioned to provide even more flexibility. We also explain the differences between physical media (the hard drive itself, or CD-ROMs and floppy disks) and the Unix filesystem itself, though management of both is similar.

Chapter 30 then explains the concept of *mounting* various filesystems, including local and remote drives. To use a drive, such as the CD-ROM, it must be mounted and made available to the filesystem as a whole. With Unix, you can't just shove a disk into a drive and have the disk be usable. We show you the subtle differences between using local filesystems and remote ones, a concept that underlies the Internet as a whole.

Managing Software

In Chapter 31: "Installing and Managing Software," we show you how to install software from *source code*, the basic packaging you'll find for Unix software in every program archive you visit. If you can compile from source code, you can install every Unix program that's available, as long as it's been ported for your operating system.

We then introduce *package management systems*, which are interfaces used by certain Unix variants (most notably the Linuxes offered by Red Hat and Debian) to simplify the software installation process. Package managers use a specialized code format, and handle much of the installation and configuration process without requiring your input or constant vigilance. Finally, we discuss how best to keep on top of your software, find upgrades and patches, and make software maintenance a routine task.

Managing the Kernel

Chapter 32: "Getting to Know the Kernel" introduces the core of the operating system. The Unix kernel, far from being a mysterious jewel hidden beneath layers of code designed to hide it from unqualified eyes, is something that you can manage and change with a modicum of knowledge. Although you should be careful with the kernel (an error can really cause trouble), there's no reason to avoid working with it altogether.

We explain the differences between modular and static kernels, showing you the uses of each type. We then explain how to compile the kernel and how to recompile it when you want to add a new function or module. Knowing how to work with the kernel is one of the skills that distinguishes between casual and skilled Unix users, and it's not that hard to learn.

Managing Print Services

The final chapter in this part of the book focuses on a frequently used function that can be problematic for many. Chapter 33: "Managing Print Services" explains how Unix handles print requests and printer devices. We show the difference between local printers (those attached to the machine being used) and network printers (shared resources for all computers attached to the network).

We then explain the mysteries of the /etc/printcap file, which is the heart of printer management. Finally, we show you how to set up and maintain a print queue, the method by which networked printers handle printing requests. The queue is a simple concept that can cause quite a few problems in administration, and we offer some tips for smooth queue management.

Summary

No matter how you use your Unix computer, if you have access to the root account, you are a system administrator. There are as many kinds of system administrators as there are kinds of computer users, so it is possible to make a statement about system administrators that applies to no more than 20 percent of the total pool of sysadmins. However, some general duties are common to all system administrators: They are responsible for maintaining and upgrading computer systems, whether hardware or software, and must keep the system working and available to users. Most readers of this book will administer single computers or small networks and need not be concerned with the issues that face the administrator of a massive network, but the jobs each administrator does are often the same.

System administrators should define a set of policies for their network or computer that will affect all users. These policies should cover security, file management, and permissible use of system resources. Users who abide by such policies make the sysadmin's life easier. Administrators can streamline much of their work by learning some basic system programming skills, and by maintaining open and effective communication with their users. Most other system administration tasks will be easy to pick up as necessary, including software maintenance, disk management, and printer administration. The chapters in this part of the book and in Part IX: "Administering Services" provide much of the basic information needed to get you started in your system administrator role.

CHAPTER
TWENTY-EIGHT

System Programming

- Automating Common Tasks with Shell Scripts

- Case Study: A Simple Backup Script

- Executing Scripts with cron and at

- init Scripts

- The Initialization Process

- Summary

In Part VI: "Shell Programming," we showed you how to create programs using the bash shell's built-in programming language. In this chapter, we put those skills to work and show you how to use shell scripts to your advantage. You can use shell scripts to handle many of the common tasks that take up a lot of administrative time, as well as the repetitive chores that you may want to avoid because they're boring.

At the same time, we provide some insight into the way Unix works. Many of the functions that Unix performs, whether at boot-up or at regularly scheduled intervals, are controlled by shell scripts. An administrator can arrange these scripts so that any given machine on a network is configured to do only the tasks assigned to it, or so that all machines on the network perform their regular actions in a particular sequence to relieve demands on network connections or system resources.

We also show you how to use Unix's built-in scheduling functions so that you can have certain tasks executed automatically. This is an excellent way to deal with some of the tedious tasks that have to be performed regularly, and it eliminates the chance that a task might be overlooked or ignored. The computer never forgets, so it's a good solution to let the computer handle these jobs. However, automatic scheduling is not a panacea. Some tasks can be performed only by a human making conscious decisions, but a sufficiently creative system programmer can make basic Unix administration much less irritating.

Automating Common Tasks with Shell Scripts

It's been said—though not usually in front of the boss—that the best system administrators are the laziest ones. This doesn't mean that the best administrators are the folks who show up late and spend most of the day playing Solitaire or Quake, but rather that the best sysadmins find creative ways to shift some of their duties to the computer. After all, what is a computer intended to do if not to automate certain complex tasks? In fact, getting the computer to do more and more of its own work has been at the heart of computer science since the earliest days, and is a big part of the reason that operating systems were invented in the first place.

Here's a real-life example. One of the most common system administration chores is to make backups of certain branches of the filesystem. This is usually done with the `tar` command, which makes a compressed archive file of a specified directory and any files stored beneath that directory, whether simply as files or within a subdirectory.

Assume that you want to back up the /home filesystem so that your users don't lose their valuable files, or at least so that you'll have a copy in case the files are lost. You probably want to store the archive in another directory called /backup, which is remotely mounted across the network and resides on another machine.

> **WARNING**   It's never a good idea to leave backup files on the same computer where the backed-up files live. If the computer goes down, so does the backup file. You can put backup files on another computer or store them on removable media such as Zip disks or writable CD-ROMs; just don't leave the files on the same machine. It defeats the whole purpose of backups.

To create this archive, you'd issue the command

```
tar cvfz /backup/may20-mymachine-home.tgz /home/*
```

This command creates an archive file named `may20-mymachine-home.tgz`, saved in the /backup directory. The name indicates the date, machine name, and filesystem being recorded in the backup file; adopt a similar system to name your own backup files so that you can select the correct one if it's needed.

Unfortunately, you can't run this simple command every day and consider your backups done. The filename changes from day to day as the date changes, and you may want to back up other directories as well as /home on some days. Also, you may not have the remote /backup directory mounted on the local machine every day; if the operating system can't find the specified directory, the command will fail, and the backup won't be made.

Case Study: A Simple Backup Script

This is where shell programming can really help out. Remember that any command that can be issued at a shell prompt can also be executed from a shell script, as we explained in Chapter 21: "An Introduction to Shell Programming." So, in this case, you need to write a script that will check whether /backup is mounted remotely (and alert you if it isn't available), create the backup archive, and give the archive a unique name based on your naming system for backup files.

Such a script can be quite simple:

```
#!/bin/bash
# backup - a program to back up a directory

BACKUP_DIR="home" # directory to be backed up

STORAGE_DIR="backup" # directory to store the archive

DATE=$(date+%b%d) # today's date in month/day format

if [ -d /$STORAGE_DIR ] && [ -s /$STORAGE_DIR ]
    then

    tar cfz /$STORAGE_DIR/$DATE-$HOSTNAME-➡
    $BACKUP_DIR.tgz /$BACKUP_DIR/*

    else

    echo "Storage directory may not be mounted."

fi
```

As you can see, this script is pretty straightforward. We've defined some of the parameters as variables, used to identify the files and directories affected by the backup. We then use the variables to construct the naming system for the individual backup files.

There are two [...] constructs, linked by a logical AND operator (&&), that ensure the /backup directory exists and is not empty. If the directory were empty, it would be unmounted; all mounted directories contain at least two files. If the /backup directory does not exist, or if it's empty, the script returns the statement "Storage directory may not be mounted", and you have the opportunity to mount the directory by hand before you run the script again.

The DATE variable is defined as the output of the command date +%b%d. The second component of that command is a group of individual formatting macros: + indicates to the operating system that macros are about to follow, while %b indicates the name of the month in a three-letter abbreviation, and %d indicates the day of the month. This data is pulled from system settings, another reason to ensure that your system date and time are accurately set.

By chaining the $DATE, $HOSTNAME, and $BACKUP_DIR variables, we create an individual name for the archive that unmistakably identifies that file in a list of backup files. We don't need to define the $HOSTNAME variable because it's already defined in the global environment variables. All other variables need to be defined within the script for the value needed in performing the script's commands.

Adapting the Script for Multiple Backups

Although this script is quite useful as it stands, there's no reason not to expend a bit more effort. The script can be rewritten so that it's a bit more flexible, incorporating more directories. With an adapted script, you won't have to write a different script using the previous model to back up directories other than /home.

The rewritten script might take this form:

```
#!/bin/bash
# backup - a program to back up a directory

  STORAGE_DIR="backup" # directory to store the archive

DATE=$(date+%b%d) # today's date in month/day format

for BACKUP_DIR in "$@"

do
    if [ -d /$STORAGE_DIR ] && [ -s /$STORAGE_DIR ]

    then

    tar cfz /$STORAGE_DIR/$DATE-$HOSTNAME-➡
    $BACKUP_DIR.tgz /$BACKUP_DIR/*

    else
```

```
        echo "Storage directory may not be mounted."

    fi

done
```

This version of the script will accept a list of directories as arguments and will make backup archives for each specified directory. For example, you could issue the command

```
backup etc home usr
```

The script will then create backup archives for the /etc, /home, and /usr directories, naming each archive with a particular identifying name. Note that you don't need to give the leading slash as an argument when invoking the script because the script is written to provide those slashes itself. Using the slash in the invocation will cause the script to fail.

Adapting the Script for Future Flexibility

This second version of the script is certainly more useful than the preceding version, because the second version can be expanded to create multiple directory backups with one command. However, it's still a bit clumsy. To make it more elegant (an issue both of style and of making the code easier to process by the operating system), you might rewrite it once again, like this:

```
#!/bin/bash
# backup - a program to back up a directory

STORAGE_DIR="backup" # directory to store the archives

DATE=$(date +%b%d) # today's date in month/day format

dobackup () {

    if [ -d /$STORAGE_DIR ] && [ -s /$STORAGE_DIR ]

    then

        tar cfz /$STORAGE_DIR/$DATE-$HOSTNAME-➡
        $BACKUP_DIR.tgz  /$1/*
```

```
        else

            echo "Storage directory may not be mounted."

            exit 1

        fi

        exit 0

    }

    for BACKUP_DIR in "$@"
    do
        dobackup $BACKUP_DIR
    done
```

In this version of the script, we've moved the commands that make the backup file into a new function called dobackup. The main part of the script (the part that iterates the list of arguments) now calls the function as needed. Granted, this is more a matter of programming style than anything else, but this version is certainly more elegant than the previous versions.

Note that, in this version, we had to change $BACKUP_DIR to $1, because the value of $BACKUP_DIR is passed to the new function as $1, just as if it were a regular command-line parameter. Although it's not critical at this point, it's a good idea to take care of that change now. In the event that we change the script again (as we will momentarily), we can add subsequent places where the dobackup function will get called again.

Adapting the Script to Include Logs

Administrators are often responsible for keeping logs of their activities. It would be quite helpful if this script could generate a log of its backup activity so that its work could be recorded and tracked. This is an easy modification, because all we need to do is add the line

```
echo "$DATE : Wrote backup archive for $BACKUP_DIR" >>➥
/var/log/backup
```

to the main part of the program, like this:

```
for BACKUP_DIR in "$@"
do
    dobackup $BACKUP_DIR

    echo "$DATE : Wrote backup archive for $BACKUP_DIR"➥
    >> /var/log/backup

done
```

However, this line will generate the confirmation message whether or not the backup was successful, which is not very useful if you're relying on the logs to tell you what happened.

The dobackup function returns an exit status of 0 if it is successful, so we can use that as a condition to report success in the log. (We cover exit status in Chapter 26: "Signals and Status.") Instead of using the previous block of code, we can use the following block to handle log reporting accurately:

```
for BACKUP_DIR in "$@"
do
    dobackup $BACKUP_DIR

    if [ $? -eq 0 ]

    then
        echo "$DATE : Wrote backup archive for➥
        $BACKUP_DIR" >> /var/log/backup

    else
        echo "$DATE : Unsuccessful backup for➥
        $BACKUP_DIR" >> /var/log/backup

    fi

done
```

The script can now handle log report entries whether the backup was successful or not, and the administrator can tell the difference with a quick scan of the /var/log/backup file.

Once the new block is integrated, we have yet another revision of the script:

```
#!/bin/bsh
# backup - a program to back up a directory

STORAGE_DIR="backup" # directory to store the archives

DATE=$(date +%b%d) #today's date in month/day format

dobackup () {

    if [ -d /$STORAGE_DIR ] && [ -s /$STORAGE_DIR ]
    then

        tar cfz /$STORAGE_DIR/$DATE-$HOSTNAME-➡
        $BACKUP_DIR.tgz /$!/*

    else

        echo "Storage directory may not be mounted."

        exit 1

    fi

    exit 0

}

for BACKUP_DIR in "$@"
do

    dobackup $BACKUP_DIR

    if [ $? -eq 0 ]
    then

        echo "$DATE : Wrote backup archive for➡
        $BACKUP_DIR" >> /var/log/backup

    else
```

```
        echo "$DATE : Unsuccessful backup for➡
        $BACKUP_DIR" >> /var/log/backup

    fi

done
```

As the script has moved through several revisions, it has incorporated new functions and actions into its operation. Although the initial script was useful, it was limited. The final version is much more flexible and also provides important feedback to the administrator. Now, the administrator doesn't have to look through the /backup directory to see whether backups were made; instead, all that's needed is a quick check through the /var/logs/backup file to see what the latest entries say.

There is a place for both kinds of scripts. Most system administrators are comfortable with whipping up a quick script to solve a particular problem. Whether that script is ever revisited is another issue. We tend to favor scripts that perform multiple functions at one time; it saves both disk space and system stress, because there are fewer scripts on the system and thus fewer calls on system resources to run the scripts.

That's not to say that you should try to combine every script you have ever written into two or three huge scripts. Rather, look through your script library and see what sorts of tasks you like to automate. Are any of the scripts for similar tasks? Can they be combined? More importantly, do your scripts have some sort of outcome reporting entry? A line or two that causes the script to report its success or failure to a log file can be invaluable in later use. The final version of the backup script may still be simple, but it combines several tasks and a reporting function into one short shell script.

Executing Scripts with cron and at

Once you've put a certain amount of work into creating a script, it may seem like a waste of time if you have to run that script by hand every time you want to perform those actions. (We are reminded of the old joke, "What do you mean it's automatic? I have to push a button!") Wouldn't it be nice if the script could run automatically so that the only time you have to interact with it is to check the logs?

Although saving time is an important reason to consider automation, there is another significant reason to do so. Many of the processes that are normally executed by scripts are disk- and processor-intensive. Running your backup script, or scripts like it, at a time when many users need to share system resources can be crippling to everyone's work because the processor must switch back and forth in tiny timeslices until all the processes are complete.

Backups, in particular, should be done only when none of the files to be backed up are in use. Backing up the /home directory while your users are all at work and actively using their accounts, for example, would result in a faulty backup, if the process succeeded at all. It's much better to do things like backups late at night, when hardly anyone is using the system; you can kick one or two people off the system before you do backups, but it is much harder with 10, 20, or 100 users.

The cron Command

We aren't particularly fond of getting up at 2:00 in the morning and doing sysadmin things, and we suspect you aren't either. Luckily, Unix has a solution: using the system utility cron. The magic command is

```
crontab -e
```

crontab is the command that lets you schedule processes to be run automatically with the cron utility. When you issue the crontab -e command, the file crontab will open in whatever editor you've defined with the EDITOR environment variable. Once the file is open, add a line that looks like this:

```
0 2 * * *  /path/to/backup <list of directories>
```

where /path/to/backup is the full directory path of your script file—in this case, the backup script—and <list of directories> is the list of directories that you want backed up each time the backup script is run.

TIP   You can omit full directory paths in crontab if the script file is contained in one of the directories named in your PATH environment variable.

Save the file and exit the editor. You should see a message that says something like Installing new crontab, though the exact message will differ from Unix variant to variant. That's all you need to do. With the entry shown above, the backup scripts will run every day at 2:00 A.M. and back up the directories listed in the <list of directories> component.

crontab Syntax

To use `cron` to automate your system tasks, you need to make an entry for each task in the `crontab` file. Entries in `crontab` use a particular syntax:

```
<minute> <hour> <day> <month> <day of week> command
```

You don't have to fill out every field of the entry; you can substitute the * character if you want to include every possible value in the field. Thus, the time value 0 2 * * * means "zero minutes after 2 A.M., every day of the month, every month, every day of the week." The time value 0 2 * 2 would mean "zero minutes after 2 A.M., every day of the month, in February only."

Because we wrote the `backup` script with `crontab` in mind, we can set up varying backup schemes just by making different entries in `crontab`. For example, we could set up some `crontab` entries like these:

```
0 2 * * *      backup home root
0 3 * * 0      backup etc usr/local
0 4 1,15 * *   backup bin sbin usr
```

These entries tell `cron` to back up `/home` and `/root` every day; `/etc` and `/usr/local` every Sunday; and `/bin`, `/sbin`, and `/usr` on the 1st and 15th of every month. This is a reasonable schedule for backups, and they will now be done automatically.

TIP   You can specify multiple values for a given field in a `crontab` entry by using a comma-separated list, as in the third entry shown above. There are also other ways to specify ranges or multiple values, all of which are shown in the manual page for `crontab`. Issue the command `man crontab` at a shell prompt to learn more.

The at Command

You can also set up one-time script executions if you have a script or command that you want to run automatically, but not repeatedly. For this purpose, you need to use the `at` command instead of `cron`. `at` is extremely flexible in the way in which it handles time specifications, more so than `cron`. For example, the most basic syntax for `at` would be

```
at 14:30 command
```

which would run the specified command at 14:30 (2:30 P.M.) (at uses military time.) If it's already past 14:30 when you issue this command, at assumes you mean 14:30 tomorrow.

at handles less-explicit time statements as well. You can use common time references such as noon, midnight, or teatime (16:00, or 4:00 P.M.) with the syntax

```
at teatime command
```

You can also specify relative times, as in noon + 4 hours, or give a specific date and time, as in 02/21/01 + 08:15.

TIP

There are quite a few variables for at. See the at manual page for more details and ideas about using this utility to handle one-time automatic command performance.

---

init Scripts

Understanding system programming can open up a whole new level of understanding about how your system works. When you first boot up the computer, a number of initialization scripts (init scripts) are run automatically. These scripts are responsible for starting up almost all the basic functions of the operating system. Exactly how these scripts are set up varies from Unix variant to variant, but they are all fairly basic examples of the type of system programming we introduced above by building the backup script.

As an example, consider the syslog file used by Red Hat Linux version 6.2. This file starts the system logging functions and runs at boot-up so that all subsequent system actions are logged.

```
#!/bin/sh
#
# syslog         Starts syslogd/klogd.
#
#
# chkconfig: 2345 30 99
# description: Syslog is the facility by which many
# daemons use to log messages to various system log
# files.  It is a good idea to always run syslog.
```

```
# Source function library.
. /etc/rc.d/init.d/functions

[ -f /sbin/syslogd ] || exit 0

[ -f /sbin/klogd ] || exit 0

RETVAL=0

# See how we were called.
case "$1" in
   start)
      echo -n "Starting system logger: "
      # we don't want the MARK ticks
      daemon syslogd -m 0
      RETVAL=$?
      echo
      echo -n "Starting kernel logger: "
      daemon klogd
      echo
      [ $RETVAL -eq 0 ] && touch /var/lock/subsys/syslog
      ;;
   stop)
      echo -n "Shutting down kernel logger: "
      killproc klogd
      echo
      echo -n "Shutting down system logger: "
      killproc syslogd
      RETVAL=$?
      echo
      [ $RETVAL -eq 0 ] && rm -f /var/lock/subsys/syslog
      ;;
   status)
      status syslogd
      status klogd
      RETVAL=$?
      ;;
   restart|reload)
      $0 stop
      $0 start
      RETVAL=$?
      ;;
```

```
    *)
        echo "Usage: syslog {start|stop|status|restart}"
        exit 1
esac

exit $RETVAL
```

As you can see by reading through it, this is a simple script, little more than a `case` statement, as introduced in Part VI: "Shell Programming." Each `case` contains a few functions that start or stop the system logger.

As a piece of programming, the `syslog` script is not particularly fascinating or innovative, but it does what it needs to do. The important thing to get from this script is the concept that, by creating rather simple shell scripts and invoking them in the right places, you can exercise a great deal of control over the configuration of your system.

The Initialization Process

Organizing and invoking system scripts is all part of the initialization process that occurs at boot-up. There are two main flavors of initialization; as with other Unix processes, such as printing, System V (AT&T) Unix and BSD Unix have different ways of handling initialization. The System V style is used by Solaris, most Linux distributions (the Slackware distribution being the notable exception), and some commercial Unices, while the BSD style is used by all the variants in the BSD family and the commercial Unices that don't use System V. In this section of the chapter, we cover both System V and BSD initialization.

In addition, the "System V Initialization Process" section introduces a new concept: *runlevels*. Runlevels are collections of functions that define a particular mode of operation. There are normally seven runlevels, numbered 0 through 6 in the traditional Unix numbering scheme. Runlevels 0 and 6 are considered special, because they designate *shut-down* and *reboot* respectively. Runlevel 1 is also special, because it designates *single-user mode*, a special mode most often used for emergency system repairs. Runlevels 2 through 5 are configurable, though the configuration may be predetermined by the developers of your Unix variant. We refer to runlevels elsewhere in the book, but they are most commonly used in initialization scripts, which is why they're introduced here.

The System V Initialization Process

When you boot up a System V–based Unix system such as a Solaris or Linux machine, one of the first things that happens is that a program called init is run. init has a unique responsibility: It starts all the other processes. Therefore, if you know how to control init, you can force a number of system configurations immediately upon boot-up, saving work later.

The first thing that init does, once invoked, is to read the file /etc/inittab. This file uses a special syntax for its entries, which define the various processes run at each runlevel. A sample /etc/inittab configured for Red Hat Linux (and with excellent comments from its author) looks like this:

```
# inittab   This file describes how the INIT process
# should set up the system in a certain run-level.
#
# Author:      Miquel van Smoorenburg,
# <miquels@drinkel.nl.mugnet.org>
# Modified for RHS Linux by Marc Ewing and Donnie Barnes


# Default runlevel. The runlevels used by RHS are:
#   0 - halt (Do NOT set initdefault to this)
#   1 - Single user mode
#   2 - Multiuser, without NFS (The same as 3, if you do
#   not have networking)
#   3 - Full multiuser mode
#   4 - unused
#   5 - X11
#   6 - reboot (Do NOT set initdefault to this)
#

id:5:initdefault:

# System initialization.
si::sysinit:/etc/rc.d/rc.sysinit

l0:0:wait:/etc/rc.d/rc 0
l1:1:wait:/etc/rc.d/rc 1
l2:2:wait:/etc/rc.d/rc 2
l3:3:wait:/etc/rc.d/rc 3
l4:4:wait:/etc/rc.d/rc 4
```

```
l5:5:wait:/etc/rc.d/rc 5
l6:6:wait:/etc/rc.d/rc 6

# Things to run in every runlevel.
ud::once:/sbin/update

# Trap CTRL-ALT-DELETE
ca::ctrlaltdel:/sbin/shutdown -t3 -r now

# When our UPS tells us power has failed, assume we have
# a few minutes of power left.  Schedule a shutdown for
# minutes from now. This does, of course, assume you
# have powerd installed and your UPS connected and
# working correctly.
pf::powerfail:/sbin/shutdown -f -h +2 "Power Failure;➥
System Shutting Down"

# If power was restored before the shutdown kicked in,
# cancel it.
pr:12345:powerokwait:/sbin/shutdown -c "Power➥
Restored; Shutdown Cancelled"


# Run gettys in standard runlevels
1:2345:respawn:/sbin/mingetty tty1
2:2345:respawn:/sbin/mingetty tty2
3:2345:respawn:/sbin/mingetty tty3
4:2345:respawn:/sbin/mingetty tty4
5:2345:respawn:/sbin/mingetty tty5
6:2345:respawn:/sbin/mingetty tty6

# Run xdm in runlevel 5
# xdm is now a separate service
x:5:respawn:/etc/X11/prefdm -nodaemon
```

Most of this file is made up of basic initialization commands. The script starts the various getty programs so that users can log in; getty and its variants are the programs that listen for terminal connections. If a UPS (Uninterruptable Power Supply) is connected to the system as in this example, power management needs to be started. In the event of a power failure, the UPS will supply electricity until the system can shut down cleanly.

However, a few lines in this script are of particular interest. For example, the line

```
id:5:initdefault
```

determines the default runlevel. In this case, the default is runlevel 5. On a Red Hat Linux system, runlevel 5 is a full graphical user mode with full networking support. Because this is defined as the default, the system will always start at runlevel 5 when booted up. The default runlevel can be changed, if desired, simply by changing the value 5 on that line to the value representing the desired default runlevel.

The other interesting entry in the Red Hat `syslog` initialization script is the line

```
si::sysinint:/etc/rc.d/rc.sysinit
```

This line tells the system to run the script located at `/etc/rc.d/rc.sysinit`. The `rc.sysinit` script does a number of routine tasks, such as mounting filesystems and loading kernel modules, but it also initializes a particular runlevel by running all of the scripts located in a specified directory. In this case, that directory is `/etc/rc.d/rc5.d`, because the default runlevel is 5.

If you change into that directory and issue the `ls` command to see a listing of the files kept there, you'll see an output like this:

```
K10xntpd         K55routed        S10network      S25netfs
S45pcmcia        S80sendmail      S90vmware       K20nfs
K83ypbind        S11portmap       S30syslog       S50inet
S85gpm           S90xfs           K20rstatd       K92ipchains
14nfslock        S35identd        S55sshd         S90cdwrite
S99linuxconf     K20rusersd       S05kudzu        S16apmd
S40atd           S601pd           S90fonttastic   S991ocal
K20rwhod         S09net-setup     S20random       S40crond
S75keytable      S90mysql
```

Notice that some of these entries begin with an S, while others begin with a K. Entries that begin with S are services to be initialized, easily remembered with the mnemonic *S for Service*. Entries that begin with K are services to be shut down, easily recalled with the phrase *K for Kill*. K entries are always performed first, and then the S entries are started.

NOTE   The number that follows the S or K designates the order in which services are started or stopped. The lower numbers are handled first. If two services have identical numbers, they are processed in alphabetical order based on the letters following the identifying number.

A longer-form listing of the files in this directory would show that these entries are not actual files, but symbolic links to various scripts kept in the directory /etc/rc.d/init.d. The scripts in that directory are simply initialization scripts like the one for the system logger that we showed you earlier in this section. In fact, the entry S30syslog in the file listing above is the symbolic link to that script.

Runlevels can be customized by adding or removing these symbolic links in the appropriate directory. The directories have names that correspond to their runlevels. Thus, /etc/rc.d/rc5.d corresponds to runlevel 5, while /etc/rc.d/rc3.d corresponds to runlevel 3, and so on.

NOTE These directory locations are not standardized. The examples in this section are correct for Red Hat Linux, in keeping with the use of a Red Hat initialization script as our example. Other Unix variants—and indeed, other distributions of Linux—put these directories in different locations. Debian Linux, for example, omits the rc.d component of the path, so that initialization scripts are kept in /etc/init.d, and the runlevel directories are in /etc/rcX.d, where X is the number of the runlevel. If you're using a Unix variant with System V–style initialization, you'll need to do a little investigating to find the exact location of the initialization files. They'll almost always be somewhere under /etc, though.

By convention, the various runlevels have evolved to take on different functions. Runlevel 3 is usually command-line mode with networking (but no X Window Server), while runlevel 5 is usually full graphical mode with networking. However, these conventions aren't etched in stone. Corel's version of Linux, for example, uses runlevel 2 for almost everything. If you look in the /etc/inittab file, you'll usually find a comment that defines the runlevels' default configuration, as in the /etc/inittab file shown earlier in this section:

```
# Default runlevel. The runlevels used by RHS are:
#   0 - halt (Do NOT set initdefault to this)
#   1 - Single user mode
#   2 - Multiuser, without NFS (The same as 3, if you do
#   not have networking)
#   3 - Full multiuser mode
#   4 - unused
#   5 - X11
#   6 - reboot (Do NOT set initdefault to this)
```

You can cause your system to change runlevels by issuing the command `init` *X*, where *X* is the new runlevel number. Thus, if you're currently in runlevel 5, but you want to change to runlevel 3, you can just issue the command

```
init 3
```

and the system will shift to runlevel 3 and the functions associated with that level. This makes it very easy to set up runlevels so that they reflect the various functions you might need at different times on your computer, and then to use the `init` command to shift levels when appropriate.

NOTE
Depending on your Unix variant, you may also have a graphical runlevel management tool that works by creating and destroying symbolic links in a specified directory. This can be a handy way to deal with runlevels without working directly with `/etc/inittab`.

The BSD Initialization Process

BSD-style initialization is a bit different from the System V method. Instead of using `/etc/inittab` and `/etc/rc.d/rc.sysinit`, BSD uses two main configuration files called `/etc/rc` and `/etc/rc.conf`. These serve more or less the same purpose as `/etc/inittab` and `/etc/rc.d/rc.sysinit` in the System V method, though, so learning about one system does assist you when working with the other style.

The `/etc/rc` file contains all of the configuration parameters for the system. If you're using a BSD-based system, it's well worth looking through `/etc/rc` to see how your system is configured. The `/etc/rc.conf` file, meanwhile, contains values for a number of basic system variables. The commands to start any services you need should be placed in the file `/etc/rc.local`, which is run from `/etc/rc`.

As you can see from this description, BSD initialization does not use the concept of runlevels. There is only one mode of operation; if you need to start or stop any service, you must do it by hand. This is a much simpler way of handling system functions than that used by System V, because the BSD way greatly reduces the number of files that you have to deal with. However, it achieves this simplicity at the cost of some flexibility.

We won't go so far as to say that one method of initialization is better than the other. It's mostly a question of which tool is more appropriate for the job and for the system administrator. If you prefer to have predetermined collections of functions, a System V Unix variant may be the best solution for you. If you prefer to make case-by-case decisions about services, a BSD-based variant may be best.

Summary

The `bash` programming skills introduced in Part VI can be used not only to combine certain tasks or commands into one script, but to streamline system administration. Shell scripts are at the heart of the Unix initialization process, and additional shell scripts can be written to encompass many routine administrative jobs. These scripts can be run by hand or started automatically. Running the scripts automatically ensures that tasks will be carried out at specified intervals and won't be forgotten due to human error. The Unix utilities used for command automation are `cron` and `at`. `cron` is controlled by the file `/etc/crontab`, while `at` is managed with commands given at the shell prompt. With a judicious use of complex shell scripts and `cron`, a system administrator can reduce the daily workload quite a bit and transfer most of that work to the computer itself.

Some of the most crucial shell scripts are those run at initialization (boot-up). These scripts are often called `init` scripts because they are run by the `init` process. The way in which these scripts work for System V–based Unix variants, such as Solaris and Linux, is different from how they work for BSD variants, such as FreeBSD. System V–based Unix has a more complicated initialization process involving runlevels, which are collections of functions and services that are started at the same time when the computer is booted into that runlevel. BSD-based Unix does not use runlevels, preferring to control services and other system functions individually.

CHAPTER
TWENTY-NINE

Managing Users and Groups

- The Root Account

- Adding New Users

- Alternate Password Schemes

- Removing Users

- Groups

- Summary

One of the primary jobs of the system administrator is managing users. The administrator creates accounts for each person using the system, deletes accounts for users no longer on the system, and ensures that every user has access to the files and programs that are appropriate for that user. To streamline these various processes, some small Unix programs have been developed. However, knowing how to manage users with shell commands is a critical system administration skill.

One Unix concept of which you should be aware is the way in which user space is apportioned on the machine. On a Unix machine, each individual user's account exists on a completely separate portion of the hard drive; the size of that portion is allocated by the system administrator. Because each of these user accounts has its own space, users can configure their own account appearance and behavior without affecting the configuration of other users' accounts. The only account that can view or affect other users' accounts is the *superuser* (or *root*) *account*.

WARNING   If you are used to working with MacOS or Windows 95/98, you may have a different understanding of user accounts. Though both those operating systems use a form of user accounts, they are primarily designed to affect desktop appearance and multiple user passwords for networking. There is no real division of the filesystem as there is under Unix.

In this chapter, we explain the central importance of the superuser account and how best to manage your system's users. We show you how to add and remove users, and how to use user groups to make particular system resources available to some users but not others. In addition, we provide information about password schemes and some useful ways to boost password security on your system.

The Root Account

Unix is not a democratic system. Rather, it is best compared to a dictatorship or other single-leader system. On the Unix machine, the superuser (or root) is the sole authority. Whatever root wants, root can do. Root can change the filesystem, add or delete users, install systemwide programs, set system defaults, and perform every other administrative task required on the machine. In fact, many of the administrative commands and tools that you may use will require that you be logged in as root to use them. No passwords or file permissions are binding on the superuser, because the superuser can view any file and run any program on the system.

The superuser's power is systemwide precisely because there needs to be one person who has authority over all activity on the system. If a user is being destructive, root can revoke their access to the system or to particular programs. Programs can be modified by root so that only certain options are available to users or so that they are available only to certain users. For the very reason why the superuser is so necessary, you should be sure to keep the root password closely guarded. If someone unauthorized gets access to superuser powers, you may return to your system and find that you are no longer able to use it. If you do share the password with someone, make sure it is someone who is reliable and who will follow the same guidelines and policies that you have established for your system.

Because the root account has such power, it can be quite destructive if the wrong person has root access. Those who are inexperienced with Unix should not have root access on any machines containing critical files; practice your superuser skills on a single-user machine or a personal network that isn't used for work or other important purposes. That way, if you (or your inexperienced friends) make a mistake, it won't damage anything that might cause you distress. For example, if you issue the command `rm -rf /` in your user directory, you'll erase everything in your user directory irretrievably. If you issue that command as root, however, you'll erase *every single file on your system,* regardless of what it is. Obviously, don't issue that command!

WARNING   One concept that isn't always mentioned when the powers of the superuser are discussed is the idea of ethical root behavior. You have the potential to view all the files in your users' directories and trace their behavior on your system. Although there is a certain level at which you are permitted—and in fact encouraged—to keep an eye on what your users are doing, don't go through their files or e-mail just to see what they're up to. You can run a secure system without compromising your users' privacy or their individual files.

As soon as you install your Unix variant on your system, log into the root account. (It will have been created automatically at installation.) Change the root password immediately, and don't tell anyone what it is. Don't write it down and leave it lying around, and don't make it so obvious that it's easily guessed. The root password is the most important piece of information on your system, so make it hard to get. Once you've logged in and changed the password, you may never need to log in as root again. There are commands that you can use to access superuser powers without logging into the root account.

WARNING   You don't have to avoid the root account. If you feel that using the root account will help you distinguish between actions you take as root and actions you take as a user, it's fine to log into the root account and do your administrative work there. Just don't get into the habit of doing personal tasks, such as writing e-mail or working on files, while you're logged in as root.

Accessing Superuser Powers

As we mentioned above, you can get access to superuser powers without having to log into the root account. There are several ways to do this: some require knowing the root password, and others do not. If you choose to use the latter method, you will need to create a list of users who can have access to superuser powers; if you use the former method, you will need to provide the root password to the users whom you want to have superuser powers.

Superuser Powers with the Root Password

If you want to give others access to the root account, one way to do it is to give them the root password. This is the most basic way to handle the issue, but it's also the least secure. You really shouldn't share the root password unless the person with whom you're sharing it is completely trustworthy. If someone has the root password, they can just log in as user root at the regular login prompt.

Some integrated desktop managers, such as KDE and Gnome, have a graphical administration tool that users can use to gain access to the root account. For example, if you have KDE installed and you select Start ➤ Applications ➤ System ➤ File Manager, a small window will pop up and prompt you for the root password. Once you supply that password correctly, you will have access to all root functions on the machine. Your users can do this, too, if they have the root password.

Superuser Powers without the Root Password

The most common way to access superuser powers is through the su command. With su, a command-line utility, you can move into other user directories across the system as long as you know the other user's password. For example, if you have multiple user accounts called elizabeth and betsy, one for work and one for personal use, you can switch between them by issuing the command

```
su accountname
```

and providing the correct password when prompted.

However, if you don't provide an account name and simply issue the command su, the operating system will assume that you want to change into the root account. The operating system will thus prompt you for the root password. When the password is supplied, the command prompt changes to show that you are now in the root account.

If the password is required, how can you use su as a tool that works without the root password? The answer lies in the su configuration file, which is stored at /etc/suauth. A sample /etc/suauth file might look like this:

```
#  /etc/suauth - secure-su control file. See suauth(5)
#  for full documentation.

#  Uncommenting this line will only allow members of
#  group root to su to root.
#  root:ALL EXCEPT GROUP root:DENY


root:elizabeth:OWNPASS
root:ALL EXCEPT elizabeth:DENY
```

Each entry in this file configures the behavior of the su command.

Entries in /etc/suauth use the syntax

```
to-id:from-id:action
```

The to-id is the username of the account that the entry is configured to access; the from-id is the username of the account whose access is being configured; the action is the way in which su will behave when the from-id account attempts to access the to-id account. There are three possible actions: DENY, NOPASS, and OWNPASS.

- DENY means that the `from-id` account will not be able to access the `to-id` account, even if the password is known.

- NOPASS means that the account in `from-id` will be able to enter the `to-id` account without entering a password.

- OWNPASS means that the account in `from-id` will be able to enter the `to-id` account by supplying the account password for the `from-id` account.

Therefore, entries that use NOPASS will not be prompted for any password, while entries that use OWNPASS will require the password of the originating account.

For security reasons, we recommend that you keep the following two lines in your `/etc/suauth` file:

```
root:yourusername:OWNPASS
root:ALL EXCEPT yourusername:DENY
```

This will limit access to the root account to just your account, and you will need to supply your user account password and not the root password when you `su` into the root account.

WARNING Even though it may be tempting, never set yourself as NOPASS to the root account. In fact, don't use NOPASS at all. It's a terrible security risk; if someone gets access to a user account that has NOPASS privileges to another account, you might end up with an awful mess on your hands. Be safe and use OWNPASS for those whom you want to permit to use `su` on your system.

Once you've configured your access to the root account using `su`, you can change into that account anytime you'd like by issuing the command `su` at the command prompt. If you're set for OWNPASS, just enter your user account password at the prompt. When you get into the root account, you can do anything you need to do, including regular everyday functions such as reading e-mail. Just be aware that you are acting as root, not as yourself. Check root's e-mail regularly; some processes generate e-mail to root as part of their operation, while other people may send e-mail with a cc: to root so that someone will be guaranteed to see the message. (Of course, this kind of e-mail usually means that someone on your system is causing trouble in e-mail or on USENET, so don't be overjoyed to see these messages.)

When you've finished doing your superuser tasks, issue the command `exit` at the command prompt to leave the root account and return to your own user account. Get in the habit of entering the root account to perform specific tasks and leaving as soon as you're done. You don't need to spend any more time as root than absolutely necessary. It may seem like we're belaboring that point, but only root has the ability to cause significant system damage without too much thought. Be careful and use root powers only when you need to.

WARNING   If you need to issue only one command as root, you can use a handy shortcut to get that command executed without even logging into the root account. Simply issue the command `su -c "command"` at the shell prompt in your user account. You'll be prompted for the password, and when it's entered correctly, the command will execute with superuser privileges. You never leave your user accounts; when the prompt returns, it will be your normal user prompt. This is quite handy for situations when you just need to do one quick thing; it is far faster to use `su -c "command"` than it is to `su` into root, issue the command, and exit the root account.

Adding New Users

Though there are easier ways to add new users, it's important for administrators to understand the basic way in which Unix handles new accounts. The easier methods are generally front-ends for this process, though they may incorporate elements of other commands as well. Not many people use the basic method any more, because it's somewhat complex and there are other ways to do it, but we include it here to show you what actually happens when a new user is added.

When a new user is added to a system, the following tasks must be completed:

1. Create an entry in the `/etc/passwd` file for the user.

2. Create the user's home directory.

3. Set an initial password for the account.

4. Create all the start-up files for the user.

5. (Optional) Set disk quotas.

6. Create the user's mail directory.

7. Perform whatever other record-keeping tasks need to be done.

These may not seem like overly complicated tasks, but imagine having to go through all of this every time you wanted to add a new user, especially if you had more than 100 accounts to add. Why, you might ask, couldn't this be automated?

Luckily for all of us, these tasks have been automated. Almost every Unix variant has a standard utility called either useradd or adduser. Often, you'll find both commands on your system, though one of the commands will be a symbolic link to the other program. useradd and adduser are basically identical, but agreement on the final name for the program hasn't been reached yet. To simplify things, we'll use useradd from this point forward; if you have adduser on your system instead, just change the terminology you use to invoke the program.

The useradd syntax is simple:

```
useradd [options] <username>
```

For example, if you want to add a user named robin and use all the default settings, you could simply issue the command

```
useradd robin
```

and Robin's account would be created. Note that you'll still have to create the initial password for the account by hand, because neither useradd nor adduser handle initial passwords. This is a good thing, from a security perspective.

If you want to create accounts with a bit more precision, you can use the various options offered by useradd. Table 29.1 shows the available options and their functions. Be sure to check documentation on your own Unix variant to see whether these options will work for you or whether there are additional features that you can use.

TABLE 29.1: Options for `useradd`

Option	Function
`-d <homedir>`	Specifies the path for the new user's home directory.
`-e <expire date>`	Sets a date upon which the account becomes inactive. Date must be in the format YYYY-MM-DD, as in 1964-12-13.
`-g <primary group>`	Sets the user's primary group identification (see the section "Groups" later in this chapter).
`-G <group list>`	Sets the user's membership in multiple groups. Group numbers must be separated by a comma, but with no space between the comma and the next group number.
`-p <password>`	Sets the user's initial password.
`-s <shell>`	Sets the user's default shell environment.
`-u`	Sets the user's login ID number. Each user has a unique number. As a rule, lower user IDs are reserved for administration use, while higher numbers are for regular users.

If you choose to add some of these options when you work with `useradd`, you'll build commands that look quite complex. Consider the command

```
useradd -g staff -G projA,projB -u 721 -s /bin/bash steve
```

This command creates a new account for the user `steve`, which will have the user ID number 721. Steve's primary group is the `staff` group, but he is also a member of the `projA` and `projB` groups. His default shell environment is `bash`, called with the actual path name of `bash` on the system.

If you don't like working with `useradd` or `adduser`, check your window manager or integrated desktop program. Some of these programs have graphical user management tools, which act as a front-end to the `useradd` or `adduser` programs. Figure 29.1 shows the KDE user management tool. All you have to do is enter the username for the new account, fill out the form, and click OK, and the new account will be created automatically. Solaris has a similar tool.

FIGURE 29.1:

Simplify the user management process with a graphical tool, such as this one from KDE.

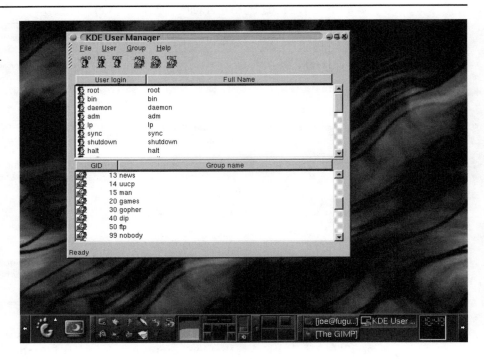

Creating Accounts with Linux and FreeBSD

The Linux system's main repository for user information is the file found at /etc/passwd, while the FreeBSD file is located at /etc/master.passwd. We'll use /etc/passwd in this section, but if you're a FreeBSD user, substitute /etc/master.passwd. Each user has an entry in this file, and the entry contains a variety of data about the user. Information included in /etc/passwd includes username, group membership, default shell environment, and password (in encrypted format).

WARNING   Because of the sensitive nature of this data, it is extremely important to keep the /etc/passwd file secure. Make sure that its file permissions are set so that nobody but root may write to the file; the file needs to be world-readable so that it can be used. Yes, the passwords are encrypted, but it's easy for crackers to run the file against a de-encryption program and break the code. /etc/passwd does not use a highly sophisticated encryption method.

A typical `/etc/passwd` entry looks like this:

```
harry:Inlo0i908jklk8kjbJjj:503:503:HarryUser:/home/harry:/bin/bash
```

This entry contains seven separate fields, each separated by a colon. Table 29.2 shows the various fields and their contents.

TABLE 29.2: Components of an `/etc/passwd` Entry

Component	Contents
Username	The user's login name.
Password	The user's password, in an encrypted format.
UID	The user's unique user ID number.
GID	The user's primary group ID number.
GCOS	Any particular information you'd like to record about the user. Typically, this includes the user's full name. (The `finger` utility parses the contents of this field into several comma-separated fields, such as name, address, phone number, and so on. However, most systems don't run `finger` any more because it is a terrible security risk.) The name of this field is a historical artifact, stemming from the days when the field's data was used with a program called GCOS.
Home directory	The full path of the user's home directory.
Shell	The user's default shell environment.

Creating Accounts with Solaris

Rather than use `adduser` or `useradd`, Solaris simplifies the user addition process with a graphical tool called `admintool`. `admintool` is available only to root, so you must log into the superuser account with the `su` command to access `admintool`. To start `admintool`, issue the command `admintool &` at the shell prompt.

When the `admintool` window appears, select Edit ➤ Add from the menu to see the Add User screen. Fill in the information requested on the screen; at the minimum, you'll need to provide the username and ID number, and a primary group. Other fields, such as shell environment and home directory location, are filled with the default settings, but you can select alternatives from the drop-down menus. Click OK when you're finished, and `admintool` will automatically build the new account.

Alternate Password Schemes

From a security point of view, password information is the most sensitive information on the system. An unauthorized person who gets access to a trusted user's password has a golden key into the system. Although the passwords are encrypted in `/etc/passwd`, the encryption scheme is fairly weak by today's robust standards. At the time the `/etc/passwd` encryption process was developed, it may have been quite strong, but advances in processor speed and cryptographic technology have made many formerly strong ciphers obsolete.

Because of this danger, a number of Unix administrators use alternate password schemes. `/etc/passwd` cannot be done away with; it has become so integrated into various Unix processes that it needs to be there and needs to have correct entries in proper syntax. However, the password field in the entry—the second component—can be altered to work in a different way, because the only legitimate use for that field is user authentication.

One popular password scheme under Linux is the *shadow password* method. In this process, the password in an `/etc/passwd` entry's second field is replaced with the character *x*. The real password is kept in the file `/etc/shadow`, which has its permissions set so that it is accessible only by root. Shadow passwords are usually enabled when you install Linux. If you want to install shadow passwords on a system that's already in operation, you will need to make a number of modifications, and it may be easier to reinstall. See the Shadow Passwords HOWTO document at `http://www.tscnet.com/sysop/mhjack/SHADOW-HOWTO/SHADOW-HOWTO.html` for a full explanation of how the system works and how to install it.

FreeBSD handles alternative password management a little differently. FreeBSD supports one-time password generation through a program called S/Key. With S/Key, which operates independently of the regular login program, you can require your users to generate a new password each time they log in. They still have regular Unix passwords, but those passwords are used in conjunction with a second, secret password to generate a single-use password that will grant entry to their FreeBSD account. This process is a bit convoluted, but it's a great way to thwart `/etc/master.passwd` crackers who just run de-encryption programs against the stolen file. Learn more about S/Key in the FreeBSD Handbook, at `http://www.freebsd.org/handbook/skey.html`.

Solaris offers PAM (Pluggable Additional Modules). These modules, when integrated into Solaris, strengthen the regular password and login structures of the operating system. With PAM, administrators can use security programs such as

Kerberos without changing any of the regular programs (and thus possibly confusing users who are used to the traditional telnet, FTP, login, and so on). PAM works on the stacking method, requiring a series of authentications from the user before the user's identity is verified. Learn more about these modules from Sun, at `http://www.sun.com/solaris/pam/`.

NOTE Although FreeBSD and Solaris have their own ways of handling alternative password schemes, they can both use the `/etc/password` and `/etc/shadow` method described for Linux in this section. FreeBSD and Solaris users have the option to use either the native method or the `/etc/password` and `/etc/shadow` method to handle their passwords more securely if they want to do so.

Removing Users

Now that you know how to add users, the next thing to learn is how to get rid of them. There are many reasons to get rid of users: The user no longer has the right to use your system (graduating, leaving a job, closing an account); the user has violated a system policy; or the account's security has been compromised. In the first type of case, deleting the account is the best solution. The user isn't going to come back, so the directory space associated with that account might as well be reclaimed and the username released.

In the second and third types, though, you may not want to delete the account right away. If a policy has been violated, for example, you may want to disable the user's access temporarily while you inform the user about the infraction and offer a second chance. Disabling an account is quite simple. Simply open the `/etc/passwd` file (or its equivalent in your system) with a text editor and replace the password section of that user's entry with an asterisk (*). The asterisk is not permissible in passwords or in any password encryption scheme and will not be matched by any password that any person tries to use to gain access to the account. (This is contrary to the asterisk's usual function as a wildcard character.)

NOTE Solaris users can disable an account by opening `admintool` and selecting Edit ➤ Modify. In the Password drop-down menu, select Account Is Locked. You can restore the account by selecting Normal Password or Cleared Until First Login (the user will have to change the password while logged in for the first time).

WARNING Never leave the password field empty. If you do, absolutely anyone can access that account without providing any attempt at a password. Simply pressing the Enter key will suffice. You are leaving your metaphoric key ring stuck in the front door's outside lock if you leave the password field empty.

Removing Users with Linux and FreeBSD

Removing users is even easier than adding them. If you use a graphical user administration tool such as those in KDE or Gnome, just open the program, select the user you want to remove, and press the Delete key. (Various programs behave in various ways.) Some administrative programs offer the option to remove associated files and directories; you'll have to do that by hand if you're using other graphical administrative tools.

If you prefer command-line tools, use the `userdel` program. As you might guess, `userdel` is the opposite of `useradd`. Unlike `useradd`, however, `userdel` has only one option. You can add the `-r` flag to `userdel` if you want the program to delete the user's home directory and its contents at the same time as the user account is removed.

NOTE Most user removal programs, including graphical user administration tools, offer the option of deleting the user files or keeping them around. If the user had files that you want to use, such as good configuration files or other information that might be useful later, you can remove the user while retaining the files. However, be aware that users' personal files are their own property. You can't use someone else's documents or e-mail without their explicit permission unless you have previous permission to do so.

If, for some reason, you don't have a `userdel` program available on your system, you'll have to remove the user by hand. This is quite simple; all you need to do is to remove their entry line in the `/etc/passwd` file (or its equivalent in your Unix variant). If you want to delete the user's home directory, you can do that as well. You may need to check program scripts or other system records to see whether that user's account is referenced anywhere, because the loss of the account may cause the script to fail.

Removing Users with Solaris

Deleting users from a Solaris system is very easy. Open `admintool` and select the account from the list of users in the User window. Select Edit ➤ Delete from the menus. A window appears with the account name at the top; click the check box if you want the user's home directory and all files to be deleted as well. Click OK, and `admintool` takes care of the rest.

Groups

The concept of *user groups* is one that is original with Unix and can be somewhat confusing to the Unix newcomer. Groups are a convenient way to make directories, files, and programs available to some users on a single system and not to others. A very common use for groups, for example, is to allow some administrative users to have access to various system functions while preventing ordinary users from running those programs. In this way, specified users can perform certain tasks without having full root access to the system.

Assume that you run a system in which you have a staff of junior administrative personnel who need to access a variety of administrative tasks, while you are the head administrator and have full root access. You can use groups to organize this. Similarly, if some subset of your users consists of programmers who are working together on a particular program, you might want to give them their own group so that they can share files, while keeping the files away from regular users who might cause trouble if they attempt to run half-written software. With a bit of imagination, it's easy to come up with a whole list of uses for groups.

The main configuration for groups in Linux and FreeBSD is the `/etc/group` file. Each existing group has an entry in this file, which looks like this:

```
harry:x:503:
```

These entries are similar to those in `/etc/passwd` and `/etc/master.passwd` in that they are divided into fields separated by colons. The first field is the name of the group. In this case, the group's name is `harry`, corresponding to the user `harry`; in many versions of the `useradd` program, a group is created for each user. The second field, containing the `x`, is a historical artifact and isn't used, but can't be deleted lest it cause trouble in other programs. The third field is the group's unique ID number. In the fourth field, empty in this example, you'll find a list of any additional users in the group.

Here's a more concrete example. Suppose that you have a group of programmers working on some files for a development project. Their names are Smith, Ramirez, and Afiz. As their system administrator, you need to set up a group so that they can share files easily. Create an entry in `/etc/group` that looks like this:

```
programmer:x:1001:smith,ramirez,afiz
```

With this entry, you've assigned the three programmers to the `programmer` group and given the group the unique ID number 1001.

Users can get a list of all the groups they are in by typing the command `groups` at the shell prompt. For example, if Afiz issues this command, she will get output like this:

```
$ groups
afiz programmer
```

This shows that user `afiz` is a member of both the `afiz` group and the `programmer` group. She will be the only member of the `afiz` group, because it was created when her user account was built.

Now, suppose that Afiz creates a file as part of the programming project and names it `program.c`. (The `.c` suffix identifies files written in the C programming language.) She wants the other programmers to be able to use this file, but doesn't want any nonprogrammer users to see it because it isn't finished. The programmers have created a directory called `/usr/local/programs`, where they can put files that they want to share with each other, so Afiz moves the file there. When she issues the command

```
ls -l /usr/local/programs/program.c
```
she receives the output

```
-rw----  1  afiz  afiz  26366423  Aug 1  12.22 program.c
```

There are two interesting features of this output. One is that the file has been created with only read and write permissions for Afiz. The other is that the file's group owner is still the `afiz` group.

Afiz changes the file's group ownership with the `chgrp` (change group) command:

```
chgrp programmer /usr/local/programs/program.c
```

Now, if she runs the `ls -l /usr/local/programs/program.c` command again, she'll see the following output:

```
-rw----- 1 afiz programmer 26366423 Aug 1 12.22 program.c
```

You can see that the file's group owner has changed, but that the permissions are still set for Afiz alone. She can change that with the `chmod` command, issuing the command

```
chmod g+rw /usr/local/programs/program.c
```

Running the `ls -l /usr/local/programs/program.c` command one more time generates the output

```
-rw-rw-- 1 afiz programmer 26366423 Aug 1 12.22 program.c
```

Now, both Afiz and the `programmer` group have read and write permission for the file. At this point, any of the other members of the group (i.e., Smith or Ramirez) can read and edit the file. Note that Afiz is still the file's owner. If Smith or Ramirez decided to make the file available to other users, they would not be able to. Only Afiz has that power.

Groups with Solaris

As with the other tasks described in this chapter, Solaris uses the `admintool` utility to handle groups. You can create, modify, and delete groups with `admintool`, and you can place users into different groups with the program as well.

Adding a Group

To add a group, open `admintool` and select Browse ➤ Groups from the menus, then select Edit ➤ Add. A small window will appear, in which you need to enter the group name and ID number. If you already know the users who will be placed in this group, enter their names, separated by commas, in the Members List field. Click OK to create the group.

Modifying a Group

If you created a group, but did not add members to it at the time of creation, you'll need to either add the users individually or modify the group. To add users individually, select Browse ➤ Users from the menus, pick the user you want to add from the list of users, and then choose Edit ➤ Modify. When the user's information screen appears, type the new group's ID number into the Secondary Groups field and click OK. To add users in batches, select Browse ≻ Groups from the menus, select the group from the list, and then choose Edit ≻ Modify. Enter the usernames of the new group members in the Members List field, separated by commas, and click OK.

Deleting a Group

To delete a group, choose Browse ≻ Users from the menus, select the group from the list, and then select Edit ≻ Delete. You will be prompted to confirm your deletion of the group; click OK if you really want to delete the group. The window will close, and the group will be erased. User records will be automatically edited to remove references to the deleted group's ID number.

Summary

Although it is a significant part of any system administrator's duties, user management does not take up much time. The process has been automated, and several programs are available that reduce the steps involved in adding a new user to a single command or mouse-click. With Linux, FreeBSD, and other Unix variants, adding a user can be done either with the adduser or useradd programs, or with a graphical user administration tool such as those found in the integrated desktop environments Gnome and KDE. Those using Solaris can handle their user management tasks with the comprehensive admintool utility. Modifying individual user profiles, or deleting users altogether, can be done with similar tools. However, in lieu of deleting a user completely, an administrator can choose to block that user's access to the system temporarily, simply by editing the password file usually stored at /etc/passwd (or /etc/master.passwd in BSD variants).

Once user accounts have been created, they can be assigned to various groups. These groups permit the administrator to control access to system resources, programs, files, and other shared resources. Resource allocation is streamlined by granting access to a particular group of users instead of to individual users. Users can be moved in and out of groups as the groups are created or deleted, but can always learn which groups they belong to by issuing the groups command at the system prompt. Group creation and deletion is handled with programs similar to those used for user administration; Solaris uses the same tool, the admintool utility, to handle both.

CHAPTER
THIRTY

Disks and Filesystem Management

- What Is a Disk?

- Disk Partitions

- Physical Media vs. Filesystems

- Mounting Local Partitions

- Automatic Mounting

- Mounting Remote Partitions

- Summary

No matter what kind of computer you use or what kind of operating system you've selected, you must deal with filesystems. The major operating systems differ in how they organize their filesystems and in how the filesystems are represented to the user. However, without some sort of filesystem management—no matter how rudimentary—the data on a disk or any other kind of storage medium would not be comprehensible or usable. The data must be organized before it can be used.

Today, there is hardly a computer in use that doesn't use some kind of disk mechanism to store data. True, there are diskless machines, but they tend to be either dumb terminals that are attached to a disk-using computer or specialized equipment, such as a router, which is constructed for a particular purpose that doesn't involve users. If you use any of the common personal-computer hardware, such as the PC or Macintosh, you are certainly familiar with your computer's hard disk, diskette drive, and probably a CD-ROM or DVD drive as well. Not surprisingly, other types of computer hardware, such as mainframes and servers, also make use of disk drives.

What Is a Disk?

At its most basic, there isn't much to a disk. A *disk* is generally a circular piece of plastic coated with a material that reacts easily to magnetic fields. This coating is similar to the material used to make magnetic tapes, such as cassette tapes or video tapes. The substance will record any magnetic field that is close enough to cause a reaction; a rough analogue can be seen in the way that a steel needle will take on a magnetic field if you rub the needle with a magnet. When the intensity of the magnetic field is varied in particular patterns, the coated surface of the disk can be made to retain information encoded in those patterns.

| **WARNING** | The coating's reaction to magnetic fields is indiscriminate. If you place a magnet against a video tape, the data encoded on the tape will be degraded or lost. The same is true for computer disks. Never put magnets anywhere near your CPU or diskettes, because you risk losing data from your disks. This can be especially harmful if the data you lose was part of the operating system. We've seen people decorating their CPU cases with magnets, which is a terrible idea. Use stickers or tape if you want to create an artistic computer, not magnets. |

Hard and Floppy Disks

The two most common types of disks used today are *fixed disks*, also known as hard disks, and *floppy disks* or diskettes, which are removable and portable. Like so much in the computing world, these names are holdovers from an earlier time. The first hard disks were indeed hard. They were made of a rigid substance unlike today's flexible plastics and were quite large. Although these hard disks could be removed from their drives, the portability factor was very low. (The earliest computers filled entire rooms.)

In response to this problem, hardware manufacturers began to work on a removable disk. The technology used in the removable disk involved a lighter and thinner plastic, which created an object quite different from the hard disks. Thus, the removable disks began to be called *floppy* because they were so flexible. Floppy disks are encased in a more rigid shell to protect the delicate disk itself; as technological skill has increased, the size of floppy disks has shrunk. Initially, floppies were as large as 12 inches or 14 inches across. The term *diskette* arises from the size difference between the original hard disks and floppy disks, because—even at a foot across—the removable disk was smaller than the stationary disk.

Today, the physical characteristics of hard and floppy disks have converged. Both types of disks are made from the same thin, light, and flexible material. The difference between the two is now solely that hard disks are permanently attached to their drives, while floppy disks are removable.

Although the disks themselves are physically similar, there is a great deal of difference in the way that the disks are constructed. This difference reflects the different purposes of each type of disk: The hard disk is designed to maximize storage capacity, while the floppy disk is designed to be portable and stand up to frequent handling. The common 3.5-inch floppy diskette can hold 1.44MB of information, while hard disks can hold many times that amount. Indeed, it seems that the storage capacity of hard disks takes a quantum leap every other week. Kate's first computer had a 512KB hard drive, and that was quite sufficient, while she's now straining a 10GB disk at the seams. Despite its vast capacity, the average hard disk is only a bit bigger than the average floppy diskette.

Optical Disks

In addition to hard and floppy disks, there are other types of storage media available to the computer user. CD-ROM and DVD-ROM disks are both a type of storage medium called an *optical disk.* An optical disk uses light, specifically laser light, to encode data on the disk instead of the magnetic fields used by hard and floppy disks. A CD or DVD disk contains millions of embedded prisms so small that the human eye has no chance of seeing them. When the disk is placed into a drive, a laser shines onto the surface of the disk; the information encoded on the disk is read by an optical eye that translates the way in which the light refracts from the prisms into machine-readable data. Information is recorded on an optical disk by another laser, which changes the optical properties of the prisms as it encodes the data.

Optical disks have the advantage of holding far more data than a portable magnetic disk, while being only marginally less portable—and certainly less susceptible to damage. The drawback is that optical drives are more expensive than diskette drives; a diskette drive can be had for as little as $15, while a writable CD-ROM drive can cost upward of $200. Optical-drive cost is directly related to the speed at which the disk rotates in the drive; the faster the disk rotates, the faster data can be decoded. Recording or *burning* a CD is also a more involved and time-consuming process than recording information to a floppy diskette. It is, however, a good option for the administrator who wants to make a permanent backup of certain files. Writing backups to CDs is not the best method for daily or weekly maintenance, but if you have a set of files that you really want to keep in a pristine format, consider burning them to a CD.

Other Types of Disks

In addition to the magnetic and optical disks, there are other types of disks being developed. The most familiar are the disks built by the Iomega Corporation, including the Zip and Jaz disks. Both the Zip and Jaz are portable high-capacity storage disks, with the Zip having either 100 or 250MB storage capacities and the Jaz having a 1GB capacity. These disks combine the floppy's ease of use with the hard disk's volume, and are especially effective with modern files and programs that can easily exceed a magnetic floppy's 1.44MB capacity.

Zip disks are especially useful for the system administrator on a small network or single computer, because they are good storage devices for small backups. You might back up your personal home directory or certain configuration files to a Zip disk, which come in a variety of colors for easy organization. Larger backups can be done to Jaz disks, which may hold an entire backup of a small system. The advantage of using Jaz or Zip disks is that they're reusable, unlike a CD-ROM, and are more durable than an open reel of tape. Jaz drives can also be used as a second hard drive, because they have enough storage capacity to hold applications that can then be run directly from the Jaz drive.

Regardless of the format, all of these disk devices do the same thing: store information. Not surprisingly, once the details of running the disk-drive hardware are ironed out, all of the media storage devices are dealt with in a similar manner by the operating system. It's good to have a variety of disk types, because the various types carry different kinds of information. We recommend a floppy drive and a CD-ROM drive at the minimum, and suggest that you add a Zip drive and a writable CD-ROM drive when possible.

Disk Partitions

One of the interesting things that you can do with disks under Unix is to subdivide them into a number of smaller *partitions*.

NOTE   The word *partition* is Linux terminology. BSD uses the term *slice*, and Solaris uses the word *volume*, but they all mean the same thing. We use the term *partition* in this section because it is the clearest explanation of what a disk segment really is.

When you create a partition, you are essentially putting up a metaphorical high wall between various areas on the disk. The operating system then treats these areas as separate disks, even though they are physically housed on the same disk. Although partitioning is possible in most, if not all, operating systems, it's not a common practice among Windows and Macintosh users. Creating and managing multiple partitions in these operating systems is often difficult, and there's no compelling reason to do it.

The case is different with Unix. It is very common to partition the hard drive if you're using a Unix variant. Perhaps the biggest reason for this is to separate system files from user files. For example, assume that you have a user who writes a new program. That program's output creates new files. If there's a bug in the program that causes it to go haywire and start creating new files nonstop, sooner or later the disk will crash because there is no remaining disk space for critical system processes.

If the user's directory is in a separate partition, though, the system will not crash no matter how many files the program generates. The runaway processes can't spill over into the other partitions because the operating system sees the other partitions as separate disks. It's a fairly simple task for the administrator to step in, kill the runaway processes, delete the extra files, and return the system to normal operation, but that wouldn't be possible if the rogue program were on the same partition as the critical administrative functions.

The idea of a user creating such a program may not be terribly realistic, but running out of disk space is a normal occurrence on many systems. Systems with a large number of users, or systems that run mail or news servers that generate unpredictable amounts of information, are especially vulnerable to disk-space concerns. On a heavy e-mail day, for example, a mail server may run out of space several times on the partition allotted to the /var/spool filesystem. If the administrator has not allocated a separate partition for /var/spool, it would be very easy for the mail flood to take the entire machine down.

How to Create Disk Partitions

In most cases, disk partitions are created when you install the operating system. The installation process for Unix variants is usually interactive, and you will be prompted for your decision about partitions so that the installer can set up the filesystem accordingly. At the minimum, we suggest that you create a partition called /home in which you'll store user directories.

Partitioning the disk after the operating system has been installed is a different matter. It's useful to know how to do it, though, because it's not too far-fetched to think that you might want to add another partition at a later date. You don't have to reinstall your operating system to add a new partition. However, if you do plan to reinstall your operating system or change to a different Unix variant, you might save your partitioning tasks for that time and do it all at once. We explain the process of disk partitioning in Linux, FreeBSD, and Solaris in the remainder of this section.

WARNING   Partitioning a disk is not something to be undertaken lightly. In almost all cases, partitioning a disk destroys all the data on the disk. Some partitioning programs claim to be nondestructive, but even these will destroy data if you don't perform each step perfectly. This is not such a big deal if you are partitioning a new or blank disk, but if you are partitioning a disk that already has data on it, you are *strongly advised* to back up your data before you start. Proceed with the assumption that all data on the disk will be lost and plan accordingly.

Disk Partitions under Linux

Creating disk partitions with Linux is done with the cfdisk program. This program allows you to edit the partition table that controls how the disk is divided. To create a partition, follow these steps, in which we've assumed that you're adding a second hard drive to the computer:

1. Connect the disk to the machine. In this example, you've connected the new disk to the second slot on your primary IDE controller, so that the new disk will be known as /dev/hdb (device hard-disk B). You must unplug machines before adding new components lest you electrocute yourself or cause irreparable damage to the computer.

2. Reboot the machine. Linux should see the new drive, but won't do anything with it because you haven't identified it in the operating system yet.

3. Log in as root. You must be root to create partitions.

4. Start cfdisk by issuing the command cfdisk /dev/hdb. The cfdisk window will appear, as shown in Figure 30.1.

FIGURE 30.1:

Configure a disk partition in Linux with the cfdisk program.

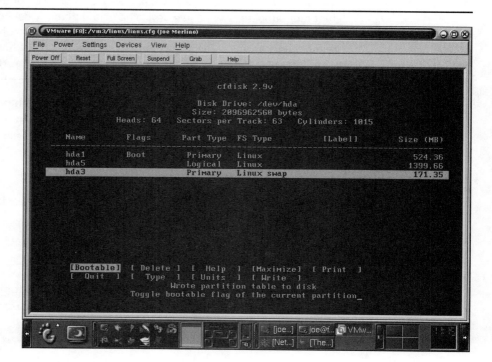

5. Configure the partition table using the options shown along the bottom of the cfdisk screen.

6. For each partition you create, select the partition size in MB and the type of partition. Note that the amount of available free space shrinks as you continue to create partitions. The type depends on your needs: Linux supports a variety of filesystem types. Assuming that you need just a regular Linux partition, select type 83, which is the normal filesystem type, also called ext2 or the *second extended filesystem*.

7. When you have finished creating all the partitions you need, select the Write option. This will commit your changes to the partition table.

NOTE   Each partition you create will be named by the cfdisk program. The first partition will generally be called **hdb1**, the second **hdb2**, and so on. These names are the same as the names of the corresponding devices. That is, the first partition will be known to the operating system as **/dev/hdb1**, the second as **/dev/hdb2**, and on through all the partitions. The use of **/dev/hdb*** varies from computer to computer, even if they're running the exact same operating system. Device naming depends to some extent on the actual hardware configuration of the system. Different motherboards will handle device naming differently depending on how their CMOS is organized. If you are not sure how your computer handles device naming, check through the **/dev** directory to get an idea of how preexisting devices were named on your system.

After you have finished with cfdisk, you must format each partition for its corresponding filesystem. For a standard Linux filesystem using the ext2 (type 83) filesystem type, this is done with the mke2fs command. Issue the following command at the shell prompt:

```
mke2fs /dev/hdb1
```

This will format the first partition. Repeat the command for each subsequent partition, substituting its name for /dev/hdb1.

Disk Partitions under FreeBSD

In BSD variants, disk partitions are called *slices*. The process for creating slices is very similar to the process for creating partitions in Linux. To create a new slice on a FreeBSD computer, follow these steps (as in the Linux example, we assume you are adding a second hard drive to an existing computer):

1. Connect the disk to the machine.

2. Reboot the machine.

3. Log in as root. You must be root to create new slices.

4. To invoke the `sysinstall` program, shown in Figure 30.2, issue the command

   `/stand/sysinstall`

   `sysinstall` uses the `fdisk` program to handle disk slices. `fdisk` is an older version of `cfdisk`, the program used to edit the Linux partition table.

5. Select Configuration ➤ Partition from the `sysinstall` menu. A list of hard disks installed in your system will appear on the screen. The disk you just installed should appear, with the name da1 or higher (the highest number is the newest drive).

FIGURE 30.2:

Create disk partitions under FreeBSD with the `sysinstall` program.

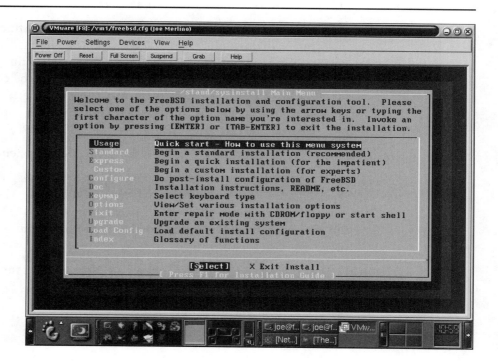

6. (Optional) If your new disk does not appear, check the file /var/run/dmesg.boot to see whether there is an error message from the boot process. If no error message appears, turn off the system and check the physical connection, then restart this process.

7. Select da1 (or the name of the new disk if it is different). The fdisk partition editor opens.

8. Select A if you want the entire new disk to be used with the FreeBSD operating system.

9. When the program asks you to decide whether you want the new drive to remain cooperative with any future possible operating systems, answer Yes.

10. Select W to write the new changes to the disk.

11. Select Q to exit the partition editor.

12. When the program asks whether you wish to make changes to the master boot record, select None. You are adding a disk to an existing system, so no changes need to be made to the boot record.

13. Select the Disk Label Editor to create the actual disk partitions. FreeBSD disks can be divided into eight or fewer partitions, named a–h. The a partition is always used for the root partition, so only the main disk should have an a partition. The b partition is a swap partition, and the c partition is used for dedicated mode. You may use the d, e, f, g, and h partition labels for whatever purpose you like. sysinstall defaults to the e partition label for new nonswap partitions.

14. Select C in the Disk Label Editor to create a single filesystem.

15. When the program asks whether this will be a filesystem or swap partition, select FS and define the filesystem's mount point. The mount point you define here doesn't have to be permanent. sysinstall will modify the /etc/fstab file for you and define the actual mount point, so don't panic if you don't know it.

16. Select W to write the new label to the disk. Note that sysinstall may return several error messages. Ignore them.

17. Select Q to exit the Label Editor.

18. Select Exit to leave sysinstall.

Disk Partitions under Solaris

To create new disk volumes under Solaris, you must use the Solaris formatting utility. As with the other examples, we assume that you are adding a second hard drive to an existing system.

When working with disk partitions under Solaris, it's important to understand the *free hog slice* concept. (No, it has nothing to do with sausage pizza.) The free hog slice is a default disk volume created by the `format` utility and contains all the disk space not committed to other volumes. When you add disk space to a new volume, the free hog slice *frees* the space from its own capacity; when you make a partition smaller or delete it, the free hog slice *hogs* that space into its capacity. The free hog slice becomes important in step 8 of the process shown below.

Follow this process to create a new volume:

1. Connect the disk to the machine.

2. Reboot the machine.

3. `su` into the root account. Only root may run the `format` program.

4. Issue the command `format` at the shell prompt. You will be dropped into the `format` utility's own shell environment, which has a prompt that looks like this:

   ```
   format>
   ```

5. Enter partition mode by issuing the command `partition` at the prompt. You should see the prompt change to

   ```
   partition>
   ```

6. (Optional) If you want to print the current volume table to the screen, do so by issuing the command `print`.

7. Issue the command `modify` to begin working with new partitions. The prompt should now look like this:

   ```
   Choose base (enter number) [0]?
   ```

   At this point, you will need to notify the free hog slice that it must free up some disk space for the new partition.

8. Type **1** at the prompt and press Enter. You will see the following confirmation message:

   ```
   Do you wish to continue creating a new partition table based on
   above table[yes]?
   ```

9. Answer yes or press Enter. The program now prompts you to create new partitions. Answer each question as it is presented. As each volume is created, you will see the new partition table and the question

   ```
   Okay to make this the current partition table[no]?
   ```

10. Answer no until you have finished creating all the partitions you want to make.

11. When you have finished creating volumes, answer yes. You will see a new prompt:

    ```
    Enter table name (remember quotes):
    ```

12. Enter the table's name, enclosed in quotation marks, as in

    ```
    "partition-table"
    ```

    You will see a new prompt:

    ```
    Ready to label disk, continue?
    ```

13. Answer yes.

14. Issue the command q to exit the partition mode. You will be returned to the format> prompt.

15. Issue the command verify to see the new partition table and check that it is accurate.

16. If there are no problems, issue the command q to exit the Solaris format utility. You should now be able to see and use the new volumes.

Physical Media vs. Filesystems

So far in this chapter, we have talked about the particulars of the physical media: the disks, the drives, and the partitions. We have not talked about how these items work together as a usable filesystem to manage data in the computer. In this section, we explain how the Unix filesystem works.

A Unix filesystem includes a top directory, and all the subdirectories and files contained within that directory. The / directory is a filesystem, as are the /usr and /usr/bin directories. Each filesystem is subordinate to the filesystems above it and is included in those filesystems, though they are not included in it. Everything in Unix is a file, whether it is a text file, directory, program, graphic image, or any other item contained on the system. An average Unix system contains thousands of individual files; thus, a method for dealing with those files, and for preventing them from causing trouble for each other, has been developed over the years through the various permutations of Unix.

As you now know, Unix represents physical drives and partitions as entries in the /dev directory. Exactly how each drive or device is named varies greatly among Unix variants. Under Linux, for example, the first partition on the primary hard drive is represented as /dev/hda1. If there is a second hard drive, it will be represented as /dev/hdb.

> **NOTE**
>
> If you read this book after the 2.4 version of Linux is released, the device naming structure will be somewhat different.

With FreeBSD, the same first partition would be represented as /dev/rda1; under Solaris, the partition might be called /dev/c0d0s1. Cryptic as the device names may seem, there is some logic to them. The documentation for your particular operating system should help you decipher the correct names.

> **TIP**
>
> Device names usually identify the device controller, the disk, and the partition, in that order.

The inquisitive reader may now be confused. If you know that the files on your hard drive have names like /home/*filename*, how do those filenames correlate with the fact that the files are stored on a device with the name /dev/hda1? Shouldn't the proper name be /dev/hda1/home/*filename*? It's a reasonable question. The answer is simple, though. The entries in the /dev directory are there only to give the operating system access to the hardware. To use the files stored on these devices, the devices must be *mounted* (made available for use).

Mounting is the process by which a disk partition is "grafted" onto the system's overall directory structure. For example, the device file called /dev/hda6 may house the partition that holds your /home filesystem. You can express this idea by saying that /dev/hda6 is *mounted on* /home.

Mounting Local Partitions

Mounting a partition is a fairly easy process. To mount a partition, you must first create a *mount point.* A mount point is simply an empty directory that has the name of the filesystem to be mounted. For example, if your /dev/hda6 filesystem contains your users' home directories and you want it on /home, /home would be considered the mount point.

There is nothing particularly special about a mount point. You can create it in the same way that you'd create any other directory, by using the mkdir command with the syntax:

```
mkdir /mountpoint
```

For example, to create the mount point discussed in the previous example, you'd issue the command

```
mkdir /home
```

You have now created a directory named home that resides below the / directory. To mount /dev/hda6 on this new mount point, use the mount command. mount uses the syntax

```
mount [options] <device> <mount point>
```

Options for mount vary from operating system to operating system, so check the manual page for mount (type man mount at a shell prompt) to learn about the version of mount used on your system.

If you were mounting a standard partition on a Linux machine, you might issue the command

```
mount /dev/hda6 home
```

On some systems, you'll need to specify the filesystem type, as in the command

```
mount -t ext2 /dev/hda6 /home
```

where ext2 is the standard filesystem type used by Linux variants. FreeBSD's use of mount is similar.

Once you've used a particular filesystem, you may want to unmount it so that you can remove media from the drive (in the case of a floppy or CD-ROM drive), or simply to reduce the number of available filesystems. Unmount drives with the umount command, which uses the syntax

```
umount filesystem
```

This is less complicated than mounting the drive, because you need not specify the filesystem type or the location of the filesystem to be mounted. You simply need to tell the operating system which filesystem to unmount, and the operating system will take care of the rest.

> **NOTE** There is only one *n* in **umount**. If you type **unmount**, you'll get an error message. There is no **unmount** command in Unix.

> **WARNING** Never remove a disk from a drive that has not been unmounted. You may cause damage to the drive or the operating system. Make a habit of unmounting drive-based filesystems when you have finished using them.

Automatic Mounting

You probably have a number of partitions that you want to have mounted as soon as the computer boots up. It's a pain to mount a set of partitions by hand every time you boot the computer. Luckily, you can set up a series of partitions to be mounted automatically, which saves you some time.

Automatic Mounting under Linux and FreeBSD

Automatic mounting is controlled in FreeBSD and Linux systems by the /etc/fstab file. The Linux and FreeBSD partition programs will edit /etc/fstab automatically as part of the partition creation process. A typical /etc/fstab file looks as follows:

```
/dev/hda1      /          ext2    defaults      1 1
/dev/hda6      /home      ext2    defaults      1 2
/dev/hda7      /misc      ext2    defaults      1 2
```

```
/dev/hda9      /tmp        ext2     defaults          1 2
/dev/hda5      /usr        ext2     defaults          1 2
/dev/hda8      /var        ext2     defaults          1 2
/dev/hda10     swap        swap     defaults          0 0
/dev/hdb1      /vm1        ext2     defaults          1 2
/dev/hdb2      /vm2        ext2     defaults          1 2
/dev/hdb3      /vm3        ext2     defaults          1 2
/dev/hdb5      /cd-master  ext2     defaults          1 2
/dev/hdb6      /stor0      ext2     defaults          1 2
/dev/hdb7      /stor1      ext2     defaults          1 2
none           /proc       proc     defaults          0 0
none           /dev/pts    devpts   gid=5,mode=620    0 0
```

You can see that the system covered by this file has a large number of partitions: 13. The general form of an /etc/fstab entry is

```
device        mount point     type      options       df  pn
```

The first three elements are obvious. The last three elements introduce new concepts:

options: Mounting options that complement the options used directly with the mount command

df: *Dump frequency* (how often the filesystem specified in that entry should be backed up using the dump command). 1 means every day, 2 means every two days, and so on.

pn: *Pass number* (indicating the order in which these filesystems will be checked with the fsck command, a process that happens when the system boots up). The root filesystem must have a pass number of 1. If you want to specify an order for the remaining partitions, use ordinal numbers: 2, 3, etc. If you don't care which order the filesystems are checked in, make the / partition 1 and the remaining partitions 2. fsck will then check the partitions in alphabetical order.

Automatic Mounting under Solaris

Under Solaris, the relevant file for automatic mounting is /etc/vfstab. Entries in this file use a slightly different format than that in the FreeBSD and Linux /etc/fstab file

```
device      device      mount    FS     fsck    mount     mount
to mount    to fsck     point    type   pass    at boot   options
```

The individual elements are somewhat similar to those in /etc/fstab, but there are differences in terminology.

device to mount: The name of the device.

device to fsck: Also the name of the device.

mount point: The name of the mount point.

FS type: The filesystem type.

fsck pass: Same as the *pass number* (pn) described in the previous section.

mount at boot: The value is yes if the partition should be mounted at boot, no if it is to be mounted by hand.

mount options: Various options that will be passed to the mount command as the /etc/vsftab file is run at the time of boot-up.

Thus, a typical entry in /etc/vfstab might look like this:

```
/dev/dsk/c0t3d0s7 /dev/rdsk/c0t3d0s7 /files1 ufs  2  yes  -
```

These file paths specify the partitions to be mounted at boot-up. You can also mount all the partitions named in the /etc/vfstab file by using the -a flag with the mount command, as in mount -a.

Mounting Remote Partitions

True to Unix's highly networkable nature, a partition does not need to be on a disk physically attached to a particular computer to be mounted. A local machine can mount partitions from a remote machine using a service called NFS (Network File Service), provided the local machine has permission to do so.

TIP   Some systems use remote partitions to handle user directories. The user directories are kept on a central machine; when a user wants access to her directory, she logs into a local workstation and mounts her home directory from the remote machine.

Mounting Remote Directories under Linux and FreeBSD

To mount a filesystem from a remote machine, where both machines are using Linux or FreeBSD, you use the mount command as you would for a local filesystem. However, you must specify the file type in the FS field as nfs, and you must specify the name of both the remote machine and the filesystem you wish to mount. A typical networked mount command might thus look like this one:

```
mount -t nfs fido:/export /import
```

where fido is the name of the remote machine.

Before you can issue this command, however, you must set up the /export filesystem on the machine fido so that the filesystem can be exported. There are two steps to this process: First, ensure that fido's NFS server is running; second, place an entry in the /etc/exports file on fido that shows which machines have permission to mount the /export filesystem remotely.

Your entry in /etc/exports might take this form:

```
/export          bowser
```

where bowser is the machine that has permission to mount the exported directory. Generally, entries in /etc/exports use the syntax

```
directory          remotemachine (options)
```

The options for /etc/exports entries are numerous, and you can learn more about them by consulting the exports manual page, by typing man exports at a shell prompt.

Once the /etc/exports file is set up and the NFS server is running successfully, issue the command exportfs on the machine fido. Now, you should be able to go to the local machine, bowser, and mount the exported directory.

Mounting Remote Directories under Solaris

Solaris, of course, has a different way of handling remotely mounted directories. Under Solaris, you must use the file /etc/dfs/dfstab instead of /etc/exports. Entries in /etc/dfs/dfstab use a unique syntax:

```
share -F nfs -o ro /export/ftp
```

Here, the /export/ftp directory is the directory being shared. The ro option indicates that the filesystem will be given to the local machine as *read-only*. The full list of options for these entries can be found on the manual page for the share_nfs command (type man share_nfs at a shell prompt).

Once the /etc/dfs/dfstab entries are configured correctly on the remote machine, you can return to the local machine and mount the remote directory as you would a local directory.

Summary

Computer disks can be divided into two categories: magnetic and optical. Magnetic disks are those that use a thin, flexible base coated with a substance that records data through impulses from magnetic fields; hard disks are all magnetic disks, as are floppy diskettes. Optical disks use a laser to read microscopic prisms etched onto the underside of a plastic disk; CD-ROM and DVD disks are optical disks. Most computer systems today have both magnetic and optical disk drives.

Unix regards all devices, including hard drives, floppy drives, and optical drives, as individual filesystems. In fact, hard drives can be partitioned into multiple filesystems, so that an individual hard drive might be treated by the operating system like as many as eight different filesystems. These divisions are called partitions under Linux, slices under FreeBSD, and volumes under Solaris, but they all act in much the same way. You may wish to partition your drive so that system files and user files are in different partitions, or you might want to make some partitions available to be mounted from remote locations. No matter how you handle partitions and drive devices, Unix requires you to mount them to empty local directories before they are usable. Once mounted, the files and data contained in the partition are freely available for use.

CHAPTER
THIRTY-ONE

Installing and Managing Software

- Software Formats

- Compiling Software from Source Code

- Software Management for Unix Variants

- Keeping Up with Upgrades

- Summary

Although you could run a Unix computer without ever adding new software beyond that installed when you built the machine, there isn't really a point in doing so. Even the most minimal Unix machines, or those running the most non-interactive software, need to be upgraded at some point. All machines should have security software installed or upgraded regularly.

Software management is slightly more complicated under Unix than it is with other operating systems. Actually, it's just as complicated in other operating systems, but attractive and easy-to-use front-ends have been developed to streamline the process. Unix variants have begun to incorporate these front-ends as well. In this chapter, we explain the basic software installation process using the most universal software format, source code. We also introduce other forms of software and the programs used to install them on each Unix variant covered in this book.

Software Formats

When you visit a Unix software archive on the Internet, you may be amazed by the variety of programs available. Not only is the scope of programs and their functions quite broad, but there are also several versions of the same program available for download. It can be confusing to decide which copy of the program you want, let alone to figure out why they all exist.

The various versions that you might find in an archive are all copies of the same program, but they're configured for different Unix variants. They are *ports* of the basic software, configured to make them easier to install on one particular variant; some ports are even designed to work with one particular distribution of a given variant. So, how do you pick the correct package to download and install?

NOTE The term *package* has two related definitions when used in the software context. At its most basic, a package is a suite of files related to one program: source code, documentation, and configuration files. These basic packages are usually source code packages. However, *package* is also used to describe source code packages that have been configured for a particular Unix variant or package manager program. These specialized packages won't install on Unix variants other than the one for which the packages are designed, whereas source code should work on almost all Unix computers.

No matter which Unix variant you are using, you probably have an alternative to commercially packaged software. Noncommercial Unix programs are almost always released in plain source code, and you can install software from source code on any Unix computer. Commercial programs are sometimes released in source code, as are shareware or other low-cost programs.

Source code is basically the programmer's output; the output may be repackaged or changed slightly to work better with individual Unix variants, but the source code is closest to the original work done by the program's developer. Most Unix software is written in the C or C++ programming languages. Though these are very common languages in the computing world, and Unix itself is written in C, you cannot run software directly from source code.

The files that you download from a CD or an archive must be *compiled* before they can be installed and used. Compilation is the process of turning human-readable code—the source code—into machine-readable binary code. Compiling software is largely an automatic process, and the same tasks are used regardless of the type of software being installed.

WARNING Some packages require different installation procedures than the processes described here. If you happen across one of these programs, make sure you know the correct procedure before you start. Installing software incorrectly may cause problems for your entire machine. As always, read the README file or other documentation included with the package before you begin installing. It's also a good idea to check the Web for updates or instruction as well.

The alternative to source code are packages designed for particular Unix variants. Oddly enough, the variants that seem to get the most individualized packages are the variants covered in this book: Linux, FreeBSD, and Solaris. These specialized packages are configured before they are released so that they will install as easily as possible on the particular variant for which they're designed. Solaris packages, for example, are designed to use Solaris's particular directory structure, while Linux packages take advantage of certain features in the Linux kernel or in particular distributions that have their own package formats. FreeBSD packages are called *ports* and work with a set of skeleton files that define a particular port directory architecture.

These variant-based packages are usually installed using a *package management tool*. Package management tools were designed to provide the user with a friendlier, easier interface for software installation. They have become more complex as the Unix world has grown, and some package management tools now have automatic update features, databases of installed software, or extended flags and functions that make managing software a snap. We explain some of the more popular package management tools in the "Software Management for Unix Variants" section of this chapter.

Compiling Software from Source Code

When you find source code packages in a software archive or on a disk, they are usually packaged in the tarball format. As we've noted elsewhere, *tarball* is a nickname for compressed archives created by the `tar` program. You can recognize tarballs because they carry the filename extensions *.tar.gz or *.tgz. The *gz* component of the extension indicates a tarred package that has also been compressed with the `gzip` compression program. The combination of `tar` and `gzip` creates a compact file that can be electronically transferred with a minimum of delay or trouble. As with software packages in other formats, tarballs usually contain documentation and configuration files as well as the code for the program itself.

> **NOTE**   The Zip and StuffIt programs are, respectively, Windows and Macintosh analogues for `tar` and `gzip`. You can usually use the `gunzip` program to unzip files compressed with the Windows version of Zip, but `gunzip` doesn't work very well for stuffed file archives. If at all possible, deal with compressed archive files using the same operating system that was used to compress them in the first place.

To begin working with source code, you must first locate a source code package. There are quite a few packages on the CD-ROM that accompanies this book, so that might be a good place to start. You can also find source code packages at any Unix software archive on the Web or purchase them from commercial software developers or distributors.

Regardless of the source of your packages, you should pick a consistent place to put them after download or transfer from a disk. We suggest using the /tmp directory as the place to start installing source code. Why /tmp? As its name implies, this directory is temporary. While the package is installing, it will create new directories in different locations on the hard disk. Once the program has been correctly installed, you can clean out /tmp without a second thought because no system-critical files are kept there. This is more difficult in directories used for ongoing system purposes, such as /etc or /usr/sbin. Therefore, using /tmp is a good solution, and we encourage you to put uncompiled packages there when you download or transfer them to your hard drive.

TIP   You can also use the /usr/src directory, but you have to be a bit more careful when you clean it out after an installation. Some files need to stay in /usr/src; nothing must stay permanently in /tmp.

Once you have put the source code packages in the /tmp directory, you can begin to install the software. First, unpack the archive by issuing this command at the shell prompt:

```
tar xvfz filename
```

This command decompresses the archive and expands the individual files to their original sizes. Depending on the number of files in the tarball, you may see a few filenames printed to the screen, or you may see a whole list of filenames scrolling past.

When the names stop printing to the screen, issue the command ls. You should see a new subdirectory under /tmp that has a name resembling the program's name. Change to that directory by issuing the command cd *directoryname*, and do another listing with the ls command. You should see a file named README or INSTALL, or something similar. These files are usually named in capitals to make it clear that they are urgent files.

Read the README file by using the more README command or opening the file in your favorite text editor. This file contains last-minute updates or messages from the program's developer. If there are special steps you need to take during installation, they will be listed here. Always follow the directions in the README file, even if they conflict with your normal software installation practices. Some software may require specific behavior during installation to function properly once in place.

No matter what special instructions may be contained in the package's documentation, the process of installing software from source code can be broken down into three general steps. These steps are usually enhanced by specialized programs or files contained in the software file archive. If you find a tarball that, for some reason, doesn't have a README or INSTALL file, try the following steps to install the program. Chances are that you'll install the software successfully.

Configuring the Package

Many packages help you configure the program automatically, through a script file included in the archive that's called `configure`, `configure.pl`, `configure.sh`, or some similar name. The README file will alert you to the actual name of the file, if one exists.

This script will run some tests on your machine to determine your hardware and software configuration, so that the program can be installed to meet your exact specifications. If the program requires certain system files, the `configure` script will check to see whether they exist.

Once the configure script has finished its work, it generates a new file called `Makefile`. A sample `Makefile` is shown in Figure 31.1. It's a good idea to read through any `Makefile` that's created on your system, because error messages will be sent to this file. You can then fix system errors or add required files if necessary, before you actually install the software.

Building the Package

Once the configure script has run successfully and you've addressed any problems reported in `Makefile`, you can begin to compile the software. In Unix terms, a program's compilation is often referred to as its *build*. In this step, you'll prepare the source code for actual installation. The code itself won't perform the tasks required of the program, so you need to run the source code through a *compiler* to translate the code into machine-readable commands.

To begin building the package, issue the command `make` at the shell prompt. `make` invokes the compiler, the program that converts the code into a machine-readable binary. Most programs use the basic `cc` (C Compiler), which is installed by default with almost all Unix variants. If you are compiling Free Software or software that has a strong Free Software component, you'll need to use `gcc` (the Gnu C Compiler). `gcc` is included on the CD-ROM packaged with this book.

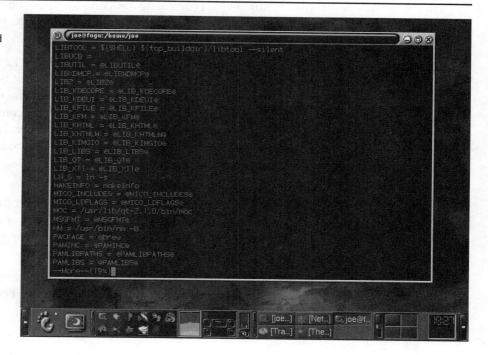

FIGURE 31.1:

A Makefile is generated during the source code installation process.

NOTE   Programs written in other programming languages may require a different compiler; you'll determine that from either the README file, an error statement in Makefile, or the documentation at the software archive or Web page where you obtained the tarball.

---

make uses Makefile as a blueprint for its work. make takes the various source code files included in the archive and runs them through gcc, linking the output into a single binary file that is executable by the computer. When make finishes, you will be returned to the command prompt and can move to the final step of the process.

Installing the Package

When the package has finished compiling, you can install the executable binary file as an actual program. Once the file is installed, you'll be able to invoke the program with its single-word command and any flags that the program requires. You should also be able to call up the program's manual page, which is installed as part of the installation process.

To install the binary file, issue the command `make install` at the shell prompt. This command moves the binary into the proper directory (outside of `/tmp`) and installs any required configuration or documentation files that were included in the archive. You can go into the `/etc` directory and look for configuration files, if used by this program, to adapt the program to your individual needs. If the program's new directory contains a `/doc` subdirectory, check through the files in that directory to see what configurations you need to make.

Once the shell prompt returns to your screen, the program is installed in its new location. You can now use it as you would use any other program already installed on your computer. You may wish to put the new program's directory in your PATH environment variable, if you want to invoke the program without using its complete directory path.

The last step is to clean up. Return to the `/tmp` directory and remove any files left over from the installation process. You can clean `/tmp` out completely, because all the required files for the program have been moved or copied to their permanent locations. Don't leave a lot of junk in `/tmp`.

TIP

You may want to store the original tarball in a source archive on your hard disk, though this isn't necessary. By the time you need it again, a new version may have been released that is better than the version you just installed. The only exception is with code and programs that are no longer being developed; it might be useful to hang onto the tarball just in case you can't find a copy of the software at a later date. If you do save the tarball, consider keeping it in the `/usr/src` directory. It's a good habit to have a single directory where source code is stored.

Software Management for Unix Variants

Though source code should be usable on every Unix variant, this is not always the case. The individual variations between Unix versions, and the adaptations necessary to accommodate those changes, make for source code that is not tailored specifically to any Unix variant and thus may not be 100-percent compatible with your given installation. That is, source code is usable on the majority of different Unices, but it's almost never a perfect fit.

To get the best fit between code and operating system, the user needs to find and install software tailored for a particular operating system. The problem is that such specific software doesn't always exist, or it may be available for several Unix variants, none of which are the one you need. The Unices covered in this book are those for which you're most likely to find specific ports, and each of these operating systems has a unique way of handling software installation.

TIP   Of course, you can install source code on Linux, FreeBSD, and Solaris. If you can find a port for your particular variant, though, use it. It's more likely to work straight out of the box, and you'll probably have to do less configuration than you would with plain source code.

Linux

Linux users have several choices when it comes to dealing with software installation and management. Many Linux users prefer to deal directly with source code, but the majority of Linux users work with package management software for at least part of their software needs. When software is ported to Linux, it's usually ported in the format required by one (or both) of the popular Linux package management programs, not as source code designed for Linux and meant to be installed as source code.

The two major package management programs under Linux are tools created for two of the most popular Linux distributions. The Debian package manager (dpkg) and the Red Hat package manager (rpm) can be used on any Linux distribution—not just Debian or Red Hat. In fact, you can run dpkg on a Red Hat machine or rpm on a Debian machine; there's nothing mutually exclusive about the formats. In this section of the chapter, we explain how to install software with both programs.

TIP   If you run Linux, regardless of the distribution you choose, we suggest installing both of the package managers. It may prove useful when you can find packages in only one Linux-oriented format. However, be aware that a package manager designed for a different distribution may put files in inappropriate directories for your distribution. If you choose to run a package manager that isn't native to your distribution, you'll have to check through the filesystem to learn the location of files installed through the package manager.

dpkg: Debian Package Manager

There is actually more than one Debian package manager, but dpkg is the easiest of the Debian tools to learn and use. dpkg is a command-line tool that handles software installation, upgrades, and removal. (We introduce dselect, a graphical interface to dpkg, in the next section of this chapter.) Note that you must be logged in as root to use dpkg.

Debian packages are widely available. If you are looking in a Linux software archive, you'll know the Debian packages by their *.deb extension. Debian packages use a unique package naming convention. The package name is constructed with the syntax

```
<name>_<version>-<build>.deb
```

Thus, the package name flowerpot_2.3-1.deb indicates that this package contains the first build of the flowerpot program's 2.3 version. The build number identifies the unique compilation of the source code by the program's developers. Most users need to worry about only the version number, not the build number, unless there is a known problem with a particular build.

Installing with dpkg

To install a package with dpkg, first download the *.deb package to your hard drive. Change to the directory where the download package is located, and issue the command

```
dpkg -i <name>_<version>-<build>.deb
```

at the shell prompt. You'll see a number of system messages scroll past on the screen. When the messages stop, the package will be installed in the correct location. You can then delete the original files or store them, as you wish.

Removing with dpkg

You can also use dpkg to remove packages that you no longer wish to keep on your system. The advantage of using dpkg instead of removing files by hand is that dpkg will catch all the documentation and configuration files associated with the program. Removing programs by hand often results in orphan files left on the hard drive.

To remove a package with dpkg, simply issue the command

```
dpkg -r <name>
```

at the shell prompt. You do not need to supply the version number, build, or *.deb suffix when removing the program, simply the program name. The name will be the same as the name used for the original package; although this is usually the same as the program name, sometimes it's different. Keep a record of package names that differ from the program name so that you can remove the packages more easily down the road.

WARNING

By default, **dpkg** does not remove shared files when it deletes a particular program. Shared files are those that are installed with one package, but are used by multiple programs. You can delete shared files when removing a package by issuing the command **dpkg −r −purge** *<name>*, but be aware that, if shared files are found and removed, the other programs that rely on those files might not work properly.

Upgrading with dpkg

You can use **dpkg** when upgrading software, as well. If you download a newer version or build of a program that's already installed on your computer, **dpkg** will install only the files that have changed in the newer version. You won't get duplicate files if some files in the newer package are identical to the files already installed.

dselect: A Graphical dpkg Interface

If you prefer to work with graphical interfaces instead of working at the command line, you might prefer **dselect** for your package management needs. **dselect** is not a separate program; it is merely a front-end to **dpkg**, providing a graphical framework for people who dislike pure text commands. It is a full-screen and menu-driven program, which can be easier to use for some people.

NOTE

dselect also works as a front-end to the **apt-get** program, a Debian tool that can be used to install programs across a network. That is, you can use **apt-get** to install a program directly from a software archive without downloading the program first.

Invoke **dselect** at the command prompt by issuing the command **dselect**. The program will start. Browse through the menus to find various options for installing, removing, configuring, and upgrading Debian packages on your computer. Make your selections with the arrow keys on the keyboard, or use the numbers next to each menu item. dselect will work with packages on your hard drive, on a mounted drive such as a CD-ROM, or across a network. Using dselect is a convenient way to work with Debian packages.

rpm: Red Hat Package Manager

The other dominant package management tool for Linux is Red Hat's rpm program. As with dpkg, using rpm is a simple way to manage the installation and removal of specially configured packages. Unlike dpkg, rpm has a set of advanced tools that check, before installation, whether you already have an earlier version of this package installed or whether you have other software installed that will conflict with the proposed package.

TIP
Although rpm is a text-based tool, there are various graphical interfaces as well. Check your Linux window manager or integrated desktop. The Gnome rpm interface, GnoRPM, is shown in Figure 31.2. If you prefer visual interfaces, give one of these programs a try.

FIGURE 31.2:

GnoRPM is a graphical interface to rpm found in the Gnome integrated desktop.

Red Hat packages are as widely available as Debian packages and, in some archives, are more easily found than the Debian format. Red Hat packages use a unique package naming syntax:

```
<name>-<version number>-<build number>.<architecture>.rpm
```

Thus, the package name `flowerpot-2.3.1-2.i386.rpm` is the 1.2 build of the `flowerpot` program's version 2.3, built for the i386 (Intel) architecture. The *.rpm extension indicates a package configured for use with the `rpm` tool.

Installing with rpm

To install a package with `rpm`, log in as root or assume superuser powers. Issue the command

```
rpm -i <name>-<version>-<build>-<architecture>.rpm
```

at the shell prompt. If you'd prefer to run `rpm` in *verbose mode*, so that you can see the various system messages generated by the installation process, issue this command instead:

```
rpm -ivh <name>-<version>-<build>-<architecture>.rpm
```

The −vh flags will show both the system messages and an installation progress meter, by which the installation's progress is shown as a row of # characters printed across the screen. Note that you won't see many system messages using the −vh flags unless the installation fails. You will see the progress meter with every installation, though, as shown in Figure 31.3.

TIP   If you want to use `rpm` to install a program from a remote location on your network (or from a software archive on the Internet), issue the command `rpm −ivh` `ftp://ftp.archivename.org/directory/path/filename`, including the complete URL for the package you want to install.

Removing with rpm

To remove a package with `rpm`, issue the command

```
rpm -e <name>
```

at the shell prompt. As with dpkg, you don't need to include the version number, build, or architecture. Simply use the name associated with the original package.

FIGURE 31.3:

The rpm package manager has an optional progress meter to track installation.

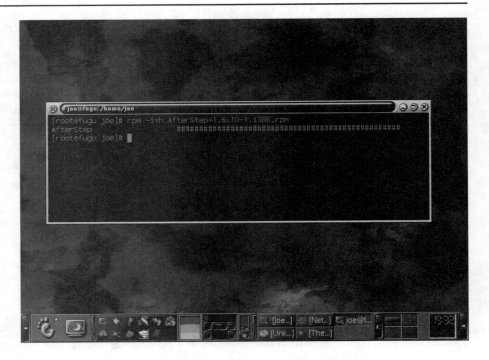

Upgrading with rpm

If you download a newer version of a package you already have installed on your computer, you can use rpm to upgrade the installed package. New files will be installed, and existing files will be upgraded if there are changes in the newer version. To upgrade with rpm, issue the command

```
rpm -U <name>-<version>-<build>-<architecture>.rpm
```

at the shell prompt. rpm will compare the new package with the installed version and make changes as required.

Querying with rpm

One of the most powerful rpm features is the ability to query. rpm maintains a database of all packages installed on the system, and you can query that database through rpm to see whether a particular package is installed or to get various types of information about installed packages. You can also use the query tool to learn whether you need to install additional packages so that a given program will function properly.

The basic syntax for rpm queries is

```
rpm -q <name>
```

issued at the shell prompt. However, rpm queries are most powerful when used with the various flags that can be appended to the -q flag. You can combine any of these flags, as in rpm -qid, to get a complex output with a great deal of information about your machine's software configuration. Sample query output using the -qid flags is shown in Figure 31.4, and the rpm query flags are shown in Table 31.1.

FIGURE 31.4:

You can learn a lot about your software with the rpm query feature.

TABLE 31.1: rpm Query Flags

Flag	Function
-a	Queries all installed packages. The output will contain the full package names for every package installed on the computer.
-f <*filename*>	Identifies all packages containing the string <*filename*> and then queries those packages. This option is especially useful for system libraries and other files that aren't technically part of any program package.
-p <*packagename*>	Queries the package named in <*packagename*> if it is uninstalled and returns query data on the files contained in that package. You must already know the package name for this flag (see −a).
-I	Returns additional information with the standard query output, including package name, release number, size, and description.
-1	Returns additional information with the standard query output, including a complete list of all files contained within the queried package.
-s	Returns additional information with the standard query output, including a report on the current status of all files within the queried package.
-d	Returns additional information with the standard query output, including a list of all the files within the queried package that are documentation files. This may include manual pages, README files, or other installation documents.
-c	Returns additional information with the standard query output, including a list of all the files within the queried package that are configuration files.

TIP   rpm has many more features than the basic tools described here. If you're using Red Hat Linux, you should familiarize yourself with the Red Hat HOWTO document at http://www.linuxdoc.org or the rpm project page at http://www.rpm.org.

FreeBSD

One of the advantages of using FreeBSD is the Ports Collection, a framework built into FreeBSD that handles software packages that have been ported to FreeBSD. If you install a FreeBSD port of a given program, you can take advantage of the various files added to the port that make installation under FreeBSD simpler. When you install pure source code, you have to provide your own tools to replace these files, and this process is generally more involved than using a port.

FreeBSD distinguishes *packages* from *ports*. Ports are the additional material used when installing a particular package, plus the source code for the program. Packages contain a preconfigured version of the software, but may not contain the source code. It's your decision which to install, but we prefer using ports. They offer a bit more flexibility in configuration and installation.

> **NOTE**
>
> What's contained in a port? Several files are always part of every port—skeleton files used to construct the most advantageous environment for software installation. Ports must contain /files, /patches, and /pkg directories, which contain information about the data of the source code files and any additional patches for FreeBSD that are required for the software to run properly, as well as documentation about the particular package for which the port is designed. The port must also include a Makefile (a file familiar from the source code installation process), which determines where the package files will be installed and how the code will be compiled.

Installing a Port

You may already have a port in mind that you want to install. If you installed FreeBSD from a CD-ROM, check that CD for a directory called /usr/ports. This directory should be chock-full of ports for standard Unix programs, and the associated packages should be contained in the /usr/ports/distfiles directory.

Once you've located the port you want to install, change into that port's subdirectory. For this example, assume that you want to install a port for the flowerpot program, which is filed as a miscellaneous port on the CD. Issue the command

```
cd /usr/ports/misc/flowerpot
```

at a shell prompt. Once you are in the port's directory, you can issue regular compilation commands. They will be interpreted contextually by the operating system, so you don't have to repeat the program's name.

Issue the command make at the shell prompt. A number of messages will scroll past; first, FreeBSD determines that this port is not already installed on the system, then FreeBSD works through the file dependencies and patches included in the port. When the system prompt returns, the port will be ready for installation.

Issue the command make install at the shell prompt. You'll see another series of messages as FreeBSD locates required software libraries and moves files to their permanent locations. When the shell prompt returns, the port will be installed and ready for the package's code files.

TIP

If you want to install a port that isn't included on your FreeBSD CD-ROM, create a directory for that port under `/usr/ports/`. When you run `make` or `make install`, FreeBSD will attempt to connect to an external FTP site and download the port and the source files. The rest of the installation should proceed as normal.

Removing a Port

Removing a port is even easier than installing one. To remove a port from your FreeBSD system, change to the directory associated with that port, as in `cd /usr/ports/misc/flowerpot`. When you are in the port's directory, issue the command

```
make deinstall
```

at the shell prompt. You will see a one-line output from the computer telling you that the program is being uninstalled, and then the shell prompt will return. Once you see the shell prompt, the port has been uninstalled, and all related dependencies have been cleaned up.

If, for some reason, you want to reinstall a port that has previously been installed and uninstalled from your system, don't repeat the initial installation process. Instead, change to that port's directory and issue the command

```
make reinstall
```

This will restore the port without duplicating system libraries and dependencies that may have been retained because they were shared files when the original installation was removed.

Finding Ports

If you want to get every single port that has been contributed to the FreeBSD Ports Collection, you can do it with a simple command. Note that this may take some time, so it might be best to set up as an overnight task or at some time when your Internet connection is not already saturated with traffic. If you have an ISP connection that cuts you off after a certain amount of time connected, you may wish to fetch ports in smaller batches.

To fetch every port in the Ports Collection, issue these commands at a shell prompt:

```
cd /usr/ports
make fetch
```

FreeBSD will connect to a software archive and download everything listed as a port. You can also download specific subdirectories of ports by appending the subdirectory's name to the /usr/ports directory path.

TIP
If you are interested in building your own ports for FreeBSD software, consult the Porters' Handbook at `http://www.freebsd.org/porters-handbook/index.html`. This document contains the standard protocol for port creation, as well as some tips on building the most workable ports.

Solaris

Solaris package management and software installation are also simple. Many Unix programs offer Solaris ports, which work better with Solaris than plain source code. (You can, of course, install source code on Solaris; just expect to spend extra time configuring the software, especially the directory locations.)

Solaris packages use the naming syntax

```
name-version-os-processor-directory.gz
```

Thus, the program `flowerpot-2.3-sol7-intel-local.gz` would be the 2.3 version of the `flowerpot` program, ported to Solaris 7 for the Intel chip. This program will install by default into the /local directory.

Installing with pkgadd

You are probably downloading your Solaris package from the Web or from a software FTP archive. Put the downloaded file into the /tmp directory; the installation procedure will place the new program and its related files into new directories, and you can clean out /tmp when the installation is finished.

Move to the /tmp directory with the command cd /tmp. Once in the directory, issue the command

```
gunzip packagename
```

to unpack the files. You'll see a list of filenames scroll up the screen as the archive is unpacked.

When the shell prompt returns, issue the command

```
pkgadd -d packagename
```

The −d flag identifies the device from which the package will be obtained. It can be a directory path or a mount point. Note that you must be logged in as root to use the pkgadd program.

By default, pkgadd installs programs into the /var/spool/pkg directory. If you have downloaded a package that installs into another directory, you may need to check the resulting directory paths and add them to your PATH environment variable so that you can access the program and its related files as needed.

You may experience some trouble if your Solaris installation created directories that are too small. In particular, if too little swap space was defined when Solaris was installed, the /tmp directory may be too small to handle package installation. You can change the size of /tmp by changing the swap space allocation; see your Solaris documentation for the procedure needed by your particular Solaris version.

You might also experience problems if /var, /opt, or /usr/local are too small. You can patch this trouble by using symbolic links, but if it's a consistent problem, you may simply want to reinstall Solaris and configure the directories with enough space. Of course, back up before you do this.

NOTE   You may run into trouble if you're installing a program that requires the gcc libraries to run (most GNU software falls into this category). If you receive a message that reads cannot exec 'as':No such file or directory, make sure that the directory /usr/ccs/bin/ is included in your PATH environment variable so that the as program will be available to pkgadd.

Removing with pkgrm

Deleting unwanted Solaris packages is as easy as installing them. The program used to remove packages is called, obviously enough, pkgrm. To remove a package, issue the command

```
pkgrm filename
```

The program checks for dependencies and shared files before deleting the package.

If you use the command as shown above, pkgrm will run in interactive mode, meaning that you must be there to answer any questions from the program. You can run pkgrm in noninteractive mode by issuing the command

```
pkgrm -n filename
```

but you will lose some control over the package removal process.

When pkgrm finishes, it will return an exit value to the screen. pkgrm exit values are listed in Table 31.2. You may have to reboot the machine after you remove the specified package; the exit value will alert you to that or to other warning messages.

TABLE 31.2: pkgrm Exit Status Values

Exit Value	Meaning
0	Package successfully removed.
1	Fatal error during package removal; process aborted.
2	Warning. **pkgrm** should print an explanatory message.
3	Interruption. Process was interrupted during execution; removal may be incomplete.
4	Administration. Process could not locate specified administration file for named package.
10	Reboot after removal of all packages. If multiple packages are to be removed at one time, do not reboot until all packages are removed.
20	Reboot after removal of this package. You will need to reboot immediately for system changes to take effect.

Keeping Up with Upgrades

The best way to keep up with software upgrades is to browse the Web regularly. For notices about upgrades to your operating system, keep an eye on the Web site maintained by your variant's distributors. You can find a list of these sites in Appendix B: "Documentation and Resources." These sites all have news sections, in which new releases and updates are noted.

If you purchased commercial software, you may be on a mailing list that the company uses to alert its users of new versions or patches. Similarly, if you're involved in the development of a program, you'll know about new patches and releases from the mailing lists and newsgroups used by the development team. You may even be releasing your own patches back to the group.

For Free software and other programs that you've downloaded from the Internet, you'll need to keep up with the sites yourself. Most major programs have sites devoted to news and software downloads, and you should be able to get the latest patches or releases there. Some of these sites are listed in Appendix B, while others will be named in the documentation files that accompany the programs.

You can also learn about new releases if you visit your favorite Unix software archive on a regular basis. For example, Solaris users might find the Sunfreeware.com site a useful regular stop; it's located at `http://smc.vnet.net`, and offers a variety of programs and packages for Solaris installations. Linux users favor archives like Freshmeat (`http://www.freshmeat.net`), which places the newest contributions to the archive on the top page.

If you keep track of your software and its upgrades, you'll always be running the most advanced versions with the best set of features, as well as the most stable releases. (Of course, if you choose to run development releases, some stability will be lost. That's the price you pay for working on the "bleeding edge.") Certainly, upgrades to your operating system are high priority, as are upgrades to programs upon which you rely, such as mail servers or other administrative software. However, you might think that a patch for your favorite first-person-shooter video game is just as important, and we won't argue with you about that.

Summary

Software management is an integral part of system administration. The administrator must be aware of upgrades and new releases of the operating system, as well as upgrades for system software and user software programs. Software that is not regularly upgraded may be more of a security risk, and users may not have access to new features or functions available in an upgraded version of a particular program. Different Unix variants handle software installation and management in different ways. Many programs are released to the Unix community in the source code format, which can be compiled into machine-readable binary files on any Unix variant.

Many commercial programs are released only as precompiled packages, however, and those packages must be obtained in a version that works with the specific Unix variant being used. Once a package has been obtained, it can be installed with variant-specific programs called package managers. Package managers can be used to handle package removal and upgrades as well, or to install programs from remote locations such as Internet software archives. Regardless of the method used to install and manage software on a given system, the administrator should set aside some time for regular Web browsing of software sites to see whether new releases or upgrades are available.

CHAPTER
THIRTY-TWO

32

Getting to Know the Kernel

- What the Kernel Does

- Kernel Development

- Modules vs. Static Kernels

- (Re)Compiling the Kernel under Linux and FreeBSD

- Summary

The *kernel* is the center of the operating system. Although most common computing tasks are handled by utilities such as the shell or other applications and programs, it is the kernel that provides these programs with the infrastructure they need to get the job done. In metaphoric terms, you can think of the kernel as the engine of your car. While the driver interacts with the car by using the pedals, steering wheel, gear shift, and so on, it's the engine that provides the capability for the car to go.

The kernel is responsible for managing the memory space, scheduling tasks for the processor, and providing access to hardware devices. It determines the priority of different commands issued by the user or by other programs, and it decides how much of the system's resources should be devoted to each of those commands. Because its work is so critical to the performance of the computer, the kernel is shielded from direct user access. You need to use shell commands to configure the kernel or to access its power; the shell environment interprets those commands in language the kernel understands, passing them to the kernel for execution.

In this chapter, we provide an example of the kernel in action and explain how kernels are developed. We also show you how to recompile a kernel in Linux and FreeBSD. Solaris users don't have the opportunity to recompile their kernels, so those using Solaris may want to skip over the final sections of the chapter.

What the Kernel Does

It's an interesting concept, but the kernel can be hard to comprehend. How can this mystical, untouchable thing sitting at the core of the computer be responsible for so much? An example of the kernel in action might be helpful.

Consider this scenario: A user starts the Netscape Web browser. How many times have we all started Netscape? From the user's point of view, it's a very simple task—just click an icon, type a command, or select an item from a menu, and the browser appears on the screen. Most users see this as the end of the story, because it happens with every program that's invoked. The action of clicking the icon or selecting the menu item, in the user's mind, is what starts the program.

However, from the operating system's point of view, the story is not so simple. When that icon is clicked or that command is issued, a number of tasks have to be performed before the program can start. First, the mouse click or the keystrokes need to be acknowledged and interpreted. Then, the program must be located on the hard drive. A space must be made for the program in the system memory, and the program must then be read off the hard drive and loaded into that newly created memory space. Finally, the program functions must be interpreted by the processor so that the program will function quickly and smoothly as the user uses it.

Each of these tasks requires action on the part of the computer's processor, and these tasks must be scheduled into a slate of activities that is already full with regular system processes, the requirements of other programs, and the actions of other users. It is the kernel's job to coordinate all of these activities. The kernel can be thought of as a combination of the computer's secretary and the computer's traffic cop.

However, there's more to it than just scheduling. For example, when input comes from the keyboard, the input arrives as electrical signals. Part of the kernel's job is to translate these signals into language that the processor can understand. The same is true for other hardware devices such as video and sound cards, network interfaces, modems, disk drives, printers, and other peripherals attached to the system. In this respect, the kernel is like a United Nations translator, speaking the languages of the various components and translating so that all the devices and peripherals can understand each other well enough to work in tandem.

When you think about this flurry of activity that flows through the kernel, it is quite amazing. The kernel is responsible for a huge portion of the computer's activity. Now, consider that a Unix machine's kernel is handling these processes for dozens—or even hundreds—of users. A picture begins to emerge of the Unix kernel as the most efficient secretary/traffic cop/translator ever to exist, and the user doesn't even have to be aware of its existence.

Kernel Development

Every version of Unix uses a different kernel. This is one of the main points that differentiates the Unix variants. As developers think of new features or functions to add, or ways to deal with existing problems or concerns, the kernel is adapted. Over time, the code bases of the different kernels diverge, leading to variant-dependent code and programming. Also, because at least some of the kernel code needs to be specific to the hardware platform upon which the code is run, there are kernel variants designed for different processor chips that use unique command sets.

Commercial Unices, such as Solaris, are developed by a particular company. All the programmers who work on Solaris and contribute to its kernel, for example, are employees of Sun Microsystems. Decisions about kernel changes at Sun are made at a senior level, and the programmers then work to implement those adaptations.

In the case of the Free Software Unices, such as Linux and FreeBSD, the story is different. Linux uses a very anarchic method of kernel development. The programmers who work on the Linux kernel are largely volunteers, though some are employees of companies that have an interest in the continued development of the kernel. Anyone who is interested in Linux kernel work can contribute code to the kernel project, though there is no guarantee that anyone's code will be added to the next official release. However, even if your code doesn't make it into the official kernel release, nothing is stopping you from releasing your work as a kernel patch or even as a modified full kernel; it's just not official.

> **NOTE** The concept of an *official Linux kernel* is quite basic. In the tradition of the Linux community, only a kernel released directly by Linus Torvalds, the inventor of Linux, can be called official. Even though Linus doesn't work on the kernel very much anymore, he still makes the official releases to keep things consistent.

FreeBSD occupies a middle ground between Solaris's control and Linux's freewheeling marketplace. The FreeBSD kernel is developed by a central team of programmers and is released in source code format. If you want to work on the FreeBSD kernel and make modifications, you're welcome to do so. However, your work will be scrutinized intensely before it is included in an official FreeBSD release, because official development is controlled by the FreeBSD team. This method gives the kernel a measure of consistency, but it lacks the spontaneity and group problem-solving benefits of a community effort.

Modules vs. Static Kernels

There are two ways in which a kernel can run. *Static kernels* have had all the drivers required for all the system's hardware compiled into a single binary file.

Modular kernels have a central kernel binary, but also have some components that are compiled separately and are loaded into the kernel only when needed. Linux, Solaris, and FreeBSD can all use modular kernels, though some Unix variants require static kernels.

All three of the Unix variants covered in this book install a generic kernel when the operating system is first installed on the computer. A generic set of modules is also installed. If you're running Solaris, you'll use this generic kernel and module set, because source code for the kernel is not made available by Sun (and thus the kernel cannot be modified by non-Sun programmers). Linux and FreeBSD users can obtain the kernel source code from a variety of sources, as well as user patches or modified kernels. If Linux or FreeBSD users wish, they can build a customized kernel or run the generic kernel provided at installation.

If you add a new hardware device to your system, you may need to load a kernel module so that the computer can utilize the new device. The first thing you need to do is to identify the module that should be loaded. This is not as easy as it sounds. Sometimes drivers are named after the chips they're built for, while others are named for the device's brand name. Check your system's documentation file to find out which module you need to install; if that doesn't help, you may need to consult the device manufacturer's Web page or see whether there's a third-party Web page that offers hints on appropriate drivers.

For example, we use 3Com EtherlinkII network cards for our network. When we added one of these cards to a Linux machine, we had to do a little research. We found that, to 3Com, these cards are known as the 3c509. A quick check of the `/lib/modules/net` directory, where Linux keeps its kernel modules for network devices, showed a driver called 3c509. Sure enough, this driver worked perfectly with the EtherlinkII card.

Once the driver is located, it needs to be loaded. You'll need to be root to do this. When you're logged in as root, issue the command that loads the module; there are different commands for each operating-system variant, but they all use the same syntax. For Linux, the command to install the 3c509 driver would be

```
insmod 3c509
```

For FreeBSD, it would be

```
kldload 3c509
```

And for Solaris, it would be

```
modload 3c509
```

TIP Manually adding the module is not always necessary. Some systems, especially recent releases of Linux variants, can often detect new hardware and load the appropriate modules automatically.

(Re)Compiling the Kernel under Linux and FreeBSD

FreeBSD and Linux users can recompile the kernel with new modules or kernel code. Solaris users do not have this ability. Although Linux and FreeBSD users do not need to recompile the kernel often, there are several reasons why you may want to do so:

- For whatever reason, you don't like loadable modules. Instead, you want to compile all your hardware drivers into a static kernel.

- Compiling a custom kernel allows you to remove kernel features that you don't want. Thus, custom kernels tend to take up less space in memory than generic kernels.

- A new version of the kernel may have been released, and you want to install it.

NOTE This last scenario is much more likely to be the case under Linux, because FreeBSD doesn't release new kernels unless they also release an updated version of the entire operating system.

For whatever reason, when you've decided to recompile your kernel, you must follow a particular procedure. Luckily, this process is quite simple, which is unusual given how critical the kernel is to the computer's functioning. However, a few of the steps are quite complicated, so some attention is required while you work on the recompilation.

The basic components of the kernel compilation process are these:

1. Download the source code.

2. Unpack the source code into an appropriate directory.

3. Configure the build.

4. Build the kernel.

5. (Optional) Build the modules.

6. Install the kernel.

7. Reboot.

Steps 3 and 6 are the complicated ones. The process is similar, but not identical, in Linux and FreeBSD. The specifics for each operating system are addressed in the next sections.

Recompiling a Linux Kernel

To recompile a kernel under Linux, use the following procedure. Note that you should know exactly why you are compiling the kernel and should have all the relevant code on hand before you begin, so that you don't make a mistake that could crash your computer permanently.

WARNING

Before you install the new kernel, check the files `linux/Documentation/Changes` and `linux/Changes`, which should have been included in the zipped file that you downloaded (or can be found at a friendly FTP site). These files will tell you what's changed in the new kernel—and, more importantly, they will define the minimum requirements for modules and other system requirements. If your system doesn't meet these minimums, do *not* install the new kernel. It won't work, and you'll be frustrated and will probably have to reinstall from scratch.

Linux Kernel Numbering

You will have some choices when you go to download a new kernel for your Linux machine. Linux kernel names are series of numbers, as in 2.2.16. The numbers tell you what kind of kernel this particular download is and whether you want to use it.

- The left number is the major version number. This changes very rarely, and there is always a lot of hoopla when it happens. If Linux goes to a 3.0 kernel in the next few years, it will be surprising.

Continued on next page

- The second number is the series number. Linux kernels are divided into two groups: *production series* and *development series*. An even number in this position means that the kernel is a production kernel and that it is stable for general use. An odd number in the second position means that the kernel is a development kernel and may be buggy or unstable.

- The third number is the minor version number. This changes quite frequently, sometimes as often as monthly or more frequently.

Unless you are a savvy programmer, pick a production series kernel. The stability and uptime are a major benefit over the flakiness of the development kernels. Select a kernel with the highest minor version number you can find, as long as it's a production kernel. This will give you the most recent patches to the kernel code within the stable framework of the production series.

Follow these steps while logged in as root:

1. Download the source code to your hard drive. The most recent kernel releases for Linux, including patches and kernels that aren't official releases, can all be found at `http://www.kernel.org`, the Linux Kernel Archive. The source code will download in the form of a tarball, with a name like `linux-2.2.16.tgz`. (This filename is for kernel version 2.2.16, which was the latest stable release as of the writing of this book.)

2. Move the tarball file to the `/usr/src` directory if you did not download it to that directory directly.

3. Issue the command

   ```
   tar xvfz linux-2.2.16.tgz
   ```

   to untar and decompress the file. As the file untars, a new directory will be created, called `/usr/src/linux-2.2.16`.

4. Move into this directory by issuing the command

   ```
   cd /usr/src/linux-2.2.16
   ```

5. Once in the new directory, issue the command

   ```
   make config
   ```

At this point, you will be asked a series of questions about the features you want to include in your kernel. There are a lot of questions, so settle in for a while.

> **NOTE**
>
> To learn what the major questions will be, consult the Kernel HOWTO document at `http://www.linuxdoc.org/HOWTO/Kernel-HOWTO.html`. We strongly encourage you to read this document before you attempt to recompile a kernel under Linux, because it will explain each step and its consequences in great detail.

> **TIP**
>
> For any option that you don't understand and that isn't addressed in the Kernel HOWTO file, you can respond with a question mark (?) character. This will bring up a help document that explains the question and what sort of information the kernel compilation is looking for. If you're running the X Window System server, try issuing the command `make xconfig` instead. You'll get a handy configuration menu instead of text questions scrolling up the screen.

6. Answer each question as it appears.

7. When you've finished answering all the questions, issue the command

    `make dep`

    A number of messages will scroll up the screen, none of which you really need to read. (Depending on the speed of your system, they may scroll too quickly to read anyway.) This may take some time if you have a slow processor, so plan to have a book or other entertainment nearby. You shouldn't leave the house to see a movie, but you'll probably want something to do while this is happening.

8. When the messages stop scrolling, check to see whether any error messages have printed to the screen. If there aren't any errors, issue the command

    `make clean`

    This command should execute quickly. When it's done, you're ready to build the kernel.

9. To begin building the kernel, issue the command

    `make bZimage`

As with the previous commands, this can take a while. On fast machines, it may be finished in a few minutes; on slower machines, this step may take several hours.

10. (Optional) Once the process has completed (again, assuming that there are no errors), you can build the modules if you enabled loadable module support in the previous configuration questions. To do so, issue the command

    ```
    make modules
    ```

11. (Optional) When the modules are made, install them with the command

    ```
    make modules install
    ```

    You're now ready to install the kernel.

12. Look in the directory `/usr/src/linux-2.2.16/arch/i386/boot` for a file called `bzImage`.

13. Move this file to the `/boot` directory and change its name to something like `/boot/vmlinuz-new`. You can do this all at once with the command

    ```
    mv /usr/src/linux-2.2.16/arch/i386/boot/bzImage➡
    /boot/vmlinuz-new
    ```

14. Next, edit the file `/etc/lilo.conf`. Open this file in a text editor. When you first open it, the file should look something like this:

    ```
    image = /vmlinuz
    label = Linux
    root = /dev/hda1
    ```

15. Add this new section to the `/etc/lilo.conf` file:

    ```
    image = /boot/vmlinuz-new
    label = New
    root = /dev/hda1
    ```

16. Save the file and quit the text editor.

17. Load the new kernel by issuing the command `lilo` at the text prompt.

18. When the shell prompt returns, reboot the computer.

19. When you see the LILO prompt during reboot, type **New** at the prompt and press Enter. The computer will boot with the new kernel.

Once the new kernel is installed, you may need to do extra configuration if some things appear not to be working. For help in diagnosing the problems, you can check the various files in the /proc directory. /proc contains diagnostic reports on the CPU, IRQ interrupts, and other critical hardware interfaces. Each of these files can tell you what the exact settings are for your hardware or what kind of drivers are being used. For example, the interrupts file on one of our Linux machines looks like this:

```
[kate@surimi /proc]$ more interrupts
        CPU0
  0:   41405266        XT-PIC  timer
  1:        1297       XT-PIC  keyboard
  2:           0       XT-PIC  cascade
  5:      590117       XT-PIC  eth0
  8:           1       XT-PIC  rtc
  9:      723049       XT-PIC  eth1
 12:        3666       XT-PIC  PS/2 Mouse
 13:           1       XT-PIC  fpu
 14:     1952020       XT-PIC  ide0
 15:           4       XT-PIC  ide1
NMI:           0
```

These entries show the IRQs that are mapped to specific devices on this machine. Another file, cpuinfo, shows detailed information about this machine's hardware configuration:

```
processor       : 0
vendor_id       : GenuineIntel
cpu family      : 6
model           : 8
model name      : Pentium III (Coppermine)
stepping        : 3
cpu MHz         : 598.196690
cache size      : 128 KB
fdiv_bug        : no
hlt_bug         : no
sep_bug         : no
f00f_bug        : no
coma_bug        : no
fpu             : yes
fpu_exception   : yes
cpuid level     : 2
```

```
wp                    : yes
flags                 : fpu vme de pse tsc msr pae mce cx8 sep mtrr pge mca
                        cmov pat pse36 mmx fxsr xmm
bogomips              : 596.38
```

Such information may not be necessary all the time, but it's quite useful to have it in one place for the times when it is needed.

Recompiling a FreeBSD Kernel

To recompile a kernel under FreeBSD, use the following procedure. Note that you should know exactly why you are compiling the kernel and should have all the relevant code on hand before you begin, so that you don't make a mistake that could crash your computer permanently.

NOTE   Before you begin to work with your kernel, check out the file `/var/run/dmesg.boot`. This file will tell you your current hardware configuration, information you'll need when you begin to work on the kernel. Note that you should check this file soon after a reboot, because it is overwritten with other material as the machine remains up.

The FreeBSD kernel is generally recompiled to build a more customized kernel, not to incorporate new patches or nonofficial code as with the Linux kernel. FreeBSD users will use the code provided with the original FreeBSD installation packages, whether on a CD-ROM or in downloads from the Internet. When a new FreeBSD kernel is released, it's usually as part of a whole new release, and most users will upgrade the entire operating system at that time.

To recompile the FreeBSD kernel, follow this procedure as root:

1. Check for a `/usr/src/sys` directory on your system. This directory was installed at the time the kernel was initially configured, at installation. If you do not have this directory, the kernel source was never installed on your computer. Issue the command `/stand/sysinstall` to run the `sysinstall` program; when the `sysinstall` window appears, select Configure ➢ Distributions ➢ src ➢ sys to make the kernel code available.

2. Move to the appropriate configuration directory. For those running FreeBSD on an x86 Intel architecture machine, issue the command

    ```
    cd /usr/src/sys/i386/conf
    ```

3. Copy the GENERIC file, a basic configuration file, to a blank file. We suggest you use a distinctive name, such as MYMACHINE. It is traditional to name your configuration file after the machine on which it will run. Use the command

    `cp GENERIC MYMACHINE`

TIP

Although we suggest that you use GENERIC in constructing your own kernel configuration file, you can see a kernel configuration that includes all possible options if you look at the LINT file in the same directory as GENERIC. It will take more work if you copy LINT instead of GENERIC, but LINT is a useful document to show you how the various options work together.

---

4. Open the MYMACHINE file in a text editor.

5. Edit the MYMACHINE file as necessary. This file should be edited to contain all the information you want in the new kernel. This process is somewhat complicated; certain elements must be included, and syntax rules must be observed. Make sure to change all references to GENERIC to MYMACHINE.

TIP

The comments and structure of the GENERIC file, which you copied into MYCON-FIG, are somewhat clear, but you can learn more about the general configuration options from the FreeBSD Handbook's section on kernel configuration, located at `http://www.freebsd.org/handbook/kernelconfig-config.html`. We strongly encourage you to read this section before you begin working with the FreeBSD kernel.

---

6. When you have finished editing the configuration file, save it and exit the text editor.

You are now ready to compile and install the kernel. There are different methods for those using a nonupgraded version of FreeBSD and for those who have used FreeBSD tools to upgrade their source tree to FreeBSD 4 or higher.

Users of a Nonupgraded Version of FreeBSD

Regardless of the version number, if you have never upgraded your source tree by running the commands CVSup, CTM, or anoncvs, you can use this method. Those who have used these tools must use the method in the following section.

Compile the new kernel and install it with these commands:

```
/usr/sbin/config MYMACHINE
cd ../../compile/MYMACHINE
make depend
make
make install
```

When the process has finished, the new kernel will be in the root directory, in the file /kernel. The old kernel will be renamed to /kernel.old. Reboot; FreeBSD should start with the new kernel.

If you have problems with the new kernel, you can always return to the previous version, because it is there on your hard drive. Do not delete /kernel.old. To use the old kernel (especially if the new one doesn't boot properly), use the following process:

1. Reboot the machine.

2. As the machine boots, you will see a message reading "booting kernel in ___ seconds" counting down.

3. Press the spacebar while the machine is counting down.

4. At the prompt that appears, issue the command

    unload

5. At the prompt, issue the command

    load kernel.old

6. At the prompt, issue the command

    boot

The old kernel will now boot, and your FreeBSD machine should work just as it did before you upgraded the kernel. You may need to fix the configuration files for the newer kernel, or you may need to consult bug documentation and other resources to check whether there is an intrinsic problem with the kernel you are using.

> **TIP**
>
> FreeBSD builds an extra kernel just in case you have a string of bad kernels, in which case loading /kernel.old won't do you any good. The extra kernel is stored at /kernel.GENERIC and uses the plain GENERIC configuration. However, we know several people who duplicate their desired configuration files and store an extra kernel at /kernel.BACKUP or some similar name. If you take this precaution, you'll always have a clean kernel that you know will work, regardless of the status of the newest or most recently used kernel configuration.

Users Who Have Upgraded Their Source Tree

If you have used the CVSup, CTM, or anoncvs tools to upgrade your FreeBSD source tree to a FreeBSD version 4 or higher, you must use this process to build the new kernel.

Compile and install the new kernel with these commands:

```
cd /usr/src
make buildkernel KERNEL=MYCONFIG
make installkernel KERNEL=MYCONFIG
```

When the process has finished, the new kernel will be in the root directory, in the file /kernel. The old kernel will be renamed to /kernel.old. Reboot; FreeBSD should start with the new kernel.

Summary

The kernel is the core of the Unix operating system. Commands and requests for system resources are filtered through the kernel, which allocates CPU cycles and memory to various programs based on its own priorities. Some commercial Unices have kernels that are changed only when the variant is released with a new version number, but Free variants such as FreeBSD or Linux allow users to recompile their kernels with new modules or patches whenever they like.

Regardless of the Unix variant being used, kernels are either static or modular. Static kernels incorporate all device drivers into the kernel itself, while modular kernels handle device drivers as individual units and load required units only when necessary. FreeBSD and Linux users will probably find themselves using a modular kernel and recompiling that kernel each time a new module needs to be added. Kernel recompilation is a fairly straightforward process, but does require some attention, especially when working with configuration files. Check your distribution's Web site regularly to see whether new kernel patches have been released or to find more information on kernel compilation techniques specific to your Unix variant.

CHAPTER
THIRTY-THREE

Managing Print Services

- Unix and Printers

- BSD Printing: Linux and FreeBSD

- System V Printing: Solaris

- Adding Local Printers

- Adding Network Printers

- Removing a Printer

- Maintaining a Print Queue

- Handling PostScript

- The Common Unix Printing System

- Summary

Perhaps the most frustrating aspect of working with Unix is dealing with printers and print jobs. There are two main ways in which Unix variants handle printing, one based on BSD and one drawn from System V Unix. In addition, each Unix variant may have its own printing quirks or tools. The problem is magnified on a heterogeneous network, where you might have three or four Unix variants (plus some Windows or Macintosh machines) that require access to a network printer.

In this chapter, we review the history of printing under Unix and show you how printing is managed under the Unices covered in this book. Although we explain Unix printing in terms of command-line tools and configuration files, you may have a graphical tool as part of your variant's system administration features that makes configuring printers and print services a much simpler task; Solaris, in particular, handles print administration neatly. We also cover the practical tasks that a system administrator is likely to face: adding local and network printers, managing a print queue, dealing with PostScript, and the like. Finally, we introduce a possible solution to the problems of Unix print management, an attempt to unify the printer tools of all Unix variants.

TIP　　If you are not a system administrator and just want to attach a printer to your standalone Unix computer, we still encourage you to read this chapter. You'll have a better understanding of the general theory behind print management, and if you have problems, you might find the solution here even if it's in a discussion of networked printing.

Unix and Printers

In Chapters 1 and 2: "History and Background of Unix" and "Which Unix?" we described the different branches of the Unix family, which center around the BSD branch and the System V (AT&T) branch. Though many Unix variants now incorporate parts of both Unix ancestors in their code, variant developers must choose one method of printing to implement in their distribution. The combination of the selected method and whatever individual adaptations were added to that particular Unix variant adds to the confusion and frustration surrounding print management with Unix.

No matter which print management method is being used, all print systems are based on a *spool*. Spooling is a method that stacks up print requests, sending multiple requests from multiple users to a printer and organizing those requests through a particular priority pattern. Spooling can be done with a single printer attached to a single computer, or across multiple printers attached to a large network. It is simply a way to handle requests that are made more quickly than the output device can process them. You may also see the term *print queue,* which is just a way to describe the waiting print jobs that are queued up (standing in line).

Unix printer management methods all have the same common features: commands to send a file to the printer, a queueing strategy, server processes that manage file transfer, and a related set of administrative commands that can be used to fix logjams in the queue, change the priority of certain jobs, or cut certain printers or users off from printing services. The differences come in how those features are implemented in each variant.

The main difference between printing under Unix and printing with Windows is that the focus of your activity under Unix will be on managing your print spool, while under Windows your main activity would be installing the printer and getting it to work properly. Unix doesn't require a great deal of fussing up front; with some variants, you can just plug any old printer into the parallel or serial port. It's up to the individual applications to handle the print jobs and how they're transferred to the printer.

NOTE
This is not true for all Unix variants. Some printers work better with Unix than others, especially Linux, and some printers don't seem to work very well at all. Although we don't want to recommend one brand over the other, especially because we haven't tried many of the models out there, we have had very good luck with Hewlett-Packard inkjet printers and the various Unices that we run. (Perhaps this has something to do with Hewlett-Packard having their own Unix variant.) If you decide to buy a new printer, be sure to save the receipt so that if the printer doesn't communicate nicely with your system, you can take it back. Linux users can check compatibility online at the Hardware Compatibility FAQ, located at `http://www.linuxdoc.org/HOWTO/Hardware-HOWTO.html`.

BSD Printing: Linux and FreeBSD

Both FreeBSD and Linux use the Berkeley line printer method of print spooling. BSD handles most printer configuration through the /etc/printcap file, which is used to define both local and remote printers. In /etc/printcap, you will place entries for every printer to which you have access, whether it's local or remote, and define the default printer.

Under BSD print methods, you will send a print job to the spool with the lp command, as in

```
lp filename
```

The file will be sent to the default printer. To send the file to a printer that is not the default, issue the command as

```
lp -P printername filename
```

If you are permitted to use that printer resource and it is defined in your /etc/printcap file, the print job will be sent to that printer's spool.

> **NOTE**   Some Unix variants that use BSD-style printing may require an additional step. You may need to create a directory called /var/spool/PRINTERNAME (replacing PRINT-ERNAME with your printer's actual name) and place an empty document named errs in that file. That will allow the spool to operate correctly. This is not the case in all BSD-based Unix variants, but if you can't seem to get printing working correctly after fiddling with /etc/printcap, try creating this directory and file as an additional attempt to get the print spool functioning correctly. In general, your operating system should create this file as the location of the print spool, but if it isn't created automatically, you should do it yourself. The print spool needs a physical location in the filesystem before it can begin to send jobs to the print resource.

System V Printing: Solaris

Solaris, unlike FreeBSD and Linux, uses the AT&T print spooler mechanism to handle its queue. Although the niceties of print spoolers are far beyond the scope of this book, all you really need to know is that the AT&T method differs from the BSD method in how print requests are handled and defined. The commands are different as well. Luckily, dealing with printer configuration is not that complicated, and as Unix has developed over the last 10 years or so, printing has become easier to deal with.

As they've done with many other administrative tasks, Sun has really streamlined the way in which administrators can deal with their printers and print spools. The key tool for Solaris administrators is the `lpadmin` utility, which works on all versions of Solaris. `lpadmin` is used to add and remove printers from an individual machine or a network.

NOTE Make sure that you have the proper packages installed to enable printing under Solaris. For Solaris versions 2.6 and higher, you will need `SUNWpcr` and `SUNWpcu` for remote printing across a network and `SUNWpsr` and `SUNWpsu` for local printing. Solaris versions earlier than 2.6 require `SUNWlpr`, `SUNWlps`, and `SUNWlpu` for both local and remote printing. These packages should all be on the installation media you received from Sun and were probably installed by default when you installed Solaris. However, if you did not install them at that point, you won't be able to manage printing or attach a printer until the packages are in place.

Adding Local Printers

Most small-network administrators will deal with individual printers more than with networked printers. Certainly, if you have a low-end inkjet printer, it won't be networkable, and you will have to install it as a local printer. Local printers reduce the time needed to print a particular job, because the only print jobs placed into the spool are those generated by the local machine. Local printers are also more affordable than networkable models, and in a small network, there may be only one user machine that requires a printer. Although there are distinct advantages to having some networked printers, it is likely that almost all networks have a good number of local printers along with some shared resources.

The technique for adding local printers varies depending on the Unix you're using and the specific distribution of your Unix variant. Solaris adds local printers using its own utilities, while FreeBSD uses basic BSD printing utilities to configure local printers. Linux deals with local printers much like FreeBSD, though there is some variation among the Linux distributions. If you're using an integrated desktop environment such as KDE or Gnome, you should be able to use the desktop's printer management tools regardless of your Unix variant, as long as you're using a distribution of the desktop that's configured for your operating system. (Clearly, a Solaris Gnome won't be able to handle FreeBSD printers—but then again, a Solaris Gnome wouldn't even install properly on a FreeBSD system.)

Adding a Local Printer with FreeBSD and Linux

Both Linux and FreeBSD use the Berkeley-style print spool method, so you can use the same techniques to add printers on both operating systems. Add local printers under FreeBSD or Linux by editing the /etc/printcap file and creating a new entry for the new printer. When you attach the printer to a port on the computer, note which port you've connected the cable to; under FreeBSD, the first parallel port is /dev/lpt0 and the first serial port is ttyd0.

> **TIP**
>
> You may need to configure your kernel to accept the new printer if you haven't yet added printer support to the kernel. Consult your FreeBSD documentation to see whether printer support was added at the time you installed the operating system; if you need to configure the kernel either for printing or to recognize a new parallel or printer port, see the FreeBSD handbook for help in doing so. The printer setup section is located at http://www.freebsd.org/handbook/printing-intro-setup.html.

Test whether your printer is connected properly by issuing the command lptest. This will send a short file directly to the printer that contains all regular keyboard characters. If the file prints correctly, you have established connection with the printer and can now configure /etc/printcap. If the file doesn't print, you may need to work with your kernel some more.

You'll need to be root to work with lptest. To issue the command, use the syntax

    lptest > *portname*

as in

    lptest > /dev/lpt0

This should work for all parallel port printers.

Once you have established communication with the printer, you can edit /etc/printcap. Here's a sample /etc/printcap entry:

```
lp:\
    :sd=/var/spool/lpd/lp:\
    :mx#0:\
    :sh:\
    :lp=/dev/lp0:\
    :if=/var/spool/lpd/lp/filter:
```

In this entry:

- lp is the name of the printer. lp is usually used as the name of the default printer, but if you want the default printer's name to be something else, there is no reason not to change the name.

TIP

The environment variable PRINTER sets the value of the default printer. If you want to change the default, just change the value of the variable.

- sd is the spool directory where this printer's spooled print jobs will be stored.

- mx#0 is the maximum file size for any given print job; when mx is set to zero, as it is here, the file size is unlimited.

- sh suppresses headers on the printout, so the jobs will just print as sent with no extra pages.

- lp sets the name of the printer device, as noted above.

- if sets the input filter. The input filter formats the text so that it will be correct for the particular printer. This is essentially the printer's driver.

Many other options can be used in the /etc/printcap file. Learn more by reading the printcap manual page, accessed by issuing the command man printcap. The printcap manual page is unusually clear, and you can learn a lot from it.

NOTE

If you've used a graphical printer manager to add and manage your printers (such as Red Hat's printtool), it's probably not a good idea to edit the /etc/printcap file by hand. These printer management programs tend to be very picky about how the text is formatted in the file. If you make entries that don't conform to the program's specifications, the printer may not work.

Adding a Local Printer with Solaris

Add local printers under Solaris with `lpadmin`. The basic process for adding a printer works like this:

```
#  lpadmin [necessary flags]
#  enable [printername]
#  accept [printername]
```

The first command configures the operating system to accept the printer; the second sets the printer to accept print jobs; the third opens the printer queue. If you forget one of these steps, your queue won't work properly; it will either line up print jobs that never get spooled to the printer or refuse to accept new jobs into the queue.

There are a variety of flags for the `lpadmin` command, some of which are shown in Table 33.1. In general, these flags define the name and acceptable content types for the specified printer, as well as control various other options that can make managing print jobs a bit easier. The general syntax of `lpadmin` is

```
lpadmin -p name -D "description" -I type -o banner -o ➡
rate -v port
```

Thus, a sample command might be

```
lpadmin -p bob -D "inkjet" -I simple -o nobanner -o ➡
stty=115200 -v /dev/bpp0
```

This would define the printer **bob** as an inkjet that will accept any type of plain text files (but not PostScript files), will not print a banner page between print jobs, transfers print data at 115,200 baud per second, and is attached to the parallel port.

TABLE 33.1: Flag Options for `lpadmin`

Flag	Function
-p	Printer name. Using this flag will create a new subdirectory in /etc/lp/printers for this printer to hold all configuration information.
-D	Printer description. Visible in printer status reports generated with the `lpstat` command. We recommend that you use the description to show what kind of printer it is, as in *2ndfloorlaser* or *colorinkjet*.
-I	Content type. Options here are −I any, −I simple, and −I postscript. If you plan to send only plain text, select −I simple; otherwise, select −I any.

Continued on next page

TABLE 33.1 CONTINUED: Flag Options for lpadmin

Flag	Function
-o	The option flag, which can be used to toggle banner pages and the rate at which jobs are sent to the printer. You can have multiple −o flags in one lpadmin command. If this is set as −o nobanner, no separating page will print between print jobs. If it is set as −o banner, a page identifying the job will print before the actual document. For x86 machines running Solaris, set the transfer rate as −o stty=115200; if you are running a Sparc as your hardware, you will need to set this rate lower.
-v	Defines the port used by the printer. Under Solaris, the parallel port is /dev/bpp0, the first serial port is /dev/term/a, and the second serial port is /dev/term/b.

Using admintool

You can also use the graphical administration utility admintool to add a new printer to your Solaris system. Open admintool and select Browse ➢ Serial Ports to pick the port to which the printer is attached. Select Edit ➢ Modify and set the baud rate as described in Table 33.1, then set the Template option as Initialize Only – No Connection. Finally, clear the check box next to Service Enable and click OK to save your settings.

Next, select Browse ➢ Printers, then Edit ➢ Add. To add a local printer, select Local Printer. The local printer's information will be displayed, and you can edit name and description as necessary. You can also decide whether to make this printer the default printer. Click OK to save your settings, and exit admintool.

Even though you have used a graphical tool to add this printer, you still need to issue the enable and accept commands described above at a shell prompt. Open a terminal window and issue the following commands:

```
enable [printername]
accept [printername]
```

Adding Network Printers

Sharing printers is one of the great things about having a network. If you have the ability to share a printer between several machines, it reduces the number of individual printers you have to buy or repair. Of course, networkable printers are more expensive than the low-priced and widely available individual printers, but the cost is equal to or less than the cost of buying an individual printer for each person on your network.

Networkable printers are also usually of better quality than individual printers; most networkable printers are laser printers, while affordable individual printers are usually inkjet models. Some networkable printers are specialized or would be far too expensive to buy as individual printers, such as color laser printers, the special plotters used by architects and others who do detailed graphics and technical drawings, or high-quality photographic printers. You can save money by buying just one of these expensive items and making it available across your network so that your users can print to the fancy machine from their desks or to a regular laser printer for their everyday printing needs. Regardless of the type of printers that you have attached to your network, you will use fewer of them and spend less on maintenance if you make them available across a network.

Each Unix handles networked printers a bit differently, but the basic idea is the same: Configure the printer so that it works locally, and then make it available to the network at large. You can limit the machines that have access to any given printer, or you can define the printer as globally available to the entire network. Either way, you have quite a lot of control over your printing resources when you network your printers with Unix.

NOTE   You can limit access to certain printers so that only specified machines may send print jobs to that printer's spool. However, you can't limit individual users to particular printers except by placing their machine names in those printers' configuration files. Still, the user could walk over to another machine and send the print job from there. Be aware that you are limiting only machine access when you define acceptable hosts, not the users themselves.

Adding a Network Printer with FreeBSD

You will need to edit /etc/printcap to add a network printer under FreeBSD. The entry syntax is basically the same as for local printers, though there are a few significant differences. The lp capability must be left blank, as in :lp=:, and a spooling directory must be created and named in the sd entry. Jobs will be kept in that location until they are sent to the printer. The rm entry should contain the name of the printer host, and the printer name should be in the rp entry. Once you've done that, you should be able to send jobs to the remote printer with the `lpr` command, specifying the remote printer as in

```
lpr -P remoteprinter -d documentname
```
Here is a sample `/etc/printcap` entry for a remote printer:

```
lp0:\
    :sd=/var/spool/lpd/lp0:\
    :mx#0:\
    :sh:\
    :rm=surimi:\
    :rp=/var/spool/lpd/lp0:\
    :if=/var/spool/lpd/lp0/filter:
```

Notice the presence of two new parameters (in addition to the parameters described earlier when we showed you an `/etc/printcap` entry for a local printer):

- `rm` is the remote machine that hosts the printer.

- `rp` is the remote print queue—that is, the appropriate directory for this printer's spool on the remote machine.

Again, see the `printcap` manual page for additional options.

Adding a Network Printer with Linux

Adding a network printer under Linux is quite straightforward. Assuming that the remote printer is installed and working properly, you simply need to edit some files on the local computer to recognize and share the remote printer resources. Be sure that you can print from the Linux computer attached to the remote printer to ensure that the printer is truly ready to be shared.

Once your printer is working correctly, open the `/etc/hosts.equiv` file *on the machine to which the printer is attached* in your favorite text editor, or create the file if it does not yet exist. In that file, place the names of all the Linux machines with which you want to share the network printer, one to a line. You'll generally want to include all the machines on your network unless you plan to limit certain printer resources to certain network machines; this may be the case if you have a color laser printer, plotter, or other expensive and complicated printer for which you must limit access to a tightly defined group of machines.

Close the file and restart the printer daemon by issuing the command

```
/etc/init.d/lpd restart
```

This will reboot the printer spool and make the shared printer available to the other specified machines on the network. You can then go to each of the machines for which you've enabled access and configure them so that they will recognize the new printer as one to which they can spool print jobs.

Depending on your Linux distribution, you might have a printer management tool available that makes configuring remote and local printers a lot easier than doing it by hand. In this section, we'll use Red Hat Linux as our example because their printer management tool is representative of such utilities in general. Consult your documentation to see what kind of tools you have available with your distribution.

Red Hat's printtool

The Red Hat printtool is a typical X Window System utility for managing printers. Many Unix variants have a similar tool. If you are running Red Hat Linux, you can invoke printtool from the Red Hat Control Panel or by issuing the command /usr/bin/printtool from the root account.

The main printtool screen is shown in Figure 33.1. Click the Add button to add a new printer; printtool will ask you what kind of printer you want to add. Most likely, you'll choose either Local Printer or Remote Unix (lpd) Queue. Make the appropriate selection and click OK.

When you've made your selection, printtool will display a printer editor window (as seen in Figure 33.2). Fill in the appropriate information in the various fields of this window; then, click the Select button located under Input Filter.

This brings up the Configure Filter window of printtool, as shown in Figure 33.3. Select the brand and model of your printer in the left pane of this window. The default options for that printer will appear in the right pane; most of the time, the defaults are fine, but if they need to be changed, you can do that at this point. Click OK when you've finished, and printtool will automatically edit /etc/printcap to reflect the new printer.

Once your printer has been added, restart the lpd program. You can do this with the drop-down menus in printtool by selecting lpd ➤ Restart; you can also test the printer with the various options in the Test menu. Your printer should now be functioning normally.

FIGURE 33.1:

The Red Hat printtool is representative of graphical printer administration utilities.

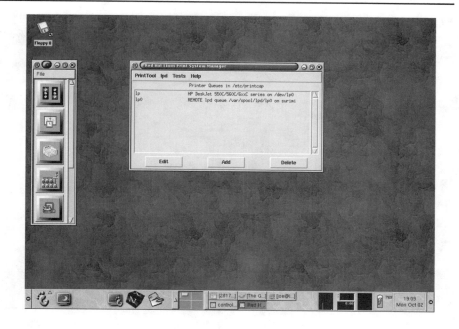

FIGURE 33.2:

Define your new printer's parameters in printtool.

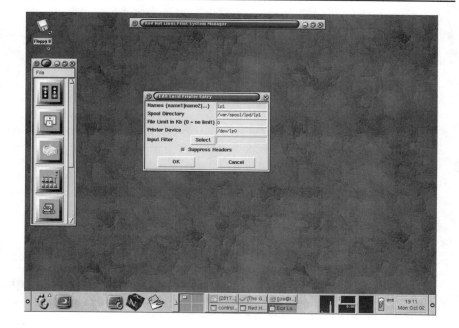

FIGURE 33.3:

printtool supplies a set of default options for a wide variety of printer models.

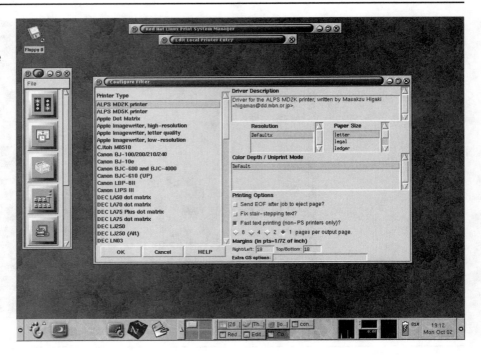

> **TIP**
>
> Whether or not your distribution has its own printer management tool, you may have one available if you're running a window manager or integrated desktop environment. KDE and Gnome, in particular, have good printer management tools that reduce printer configuration to point-and-click. Because we recommend that you try one of these desktop environments anyway, you might add dealing with printers to your list of tasks while you have the desktop installed.

Adding a Network Printer with Solaris

How you add a network printer with Solaris depends on the version of Solaris that you are running. As of Solaris 2.6, the method used to handle remote printers has changed quite a bit. Thus, those running older versions of Solaris will have to use a more complicated command to enable and define a remote printer, while those using newer versions will be able to do it with some new utilities that streamline a lot of the earlier method's quirky flags.

Network Printers with Solaris 2.5 and Earlier

Installing a network printer under earlier versions of Solaris requires the use of two utilities: lpadmin and lpsystem. These commands use the following syntax:

```
#     lpsystem -t s5 [systemname]
#     lpadmin -p [printername] -s ➡
        [systemname]![printername]
```

The first command notifies the operating system that the remote system named exists and that it has a printer attached that uses the System V print spooler. The second command then defines the printer, with the [systemname]![printername] combination used to define the printer as a part of that remote network. Thus, the commands might look like this:

```
#     lpsystem -t s5 solarsystem
#     lpadmin -p juno solarsystem!juno
```

> **NOTE**
>
> If the remote system is not running Solaris, but you are going to use its printer, change the s5 in the lpsystem command to bsd. That will cover both FreeBSD and Linux machines on the remote system, and will tell your Solaris machine to send print jobs using the BSD print spool format.

Network Printers with Solaris 2.6 and Newer

With the 2.6 revision, Sun streamlined Solaris printer management quite a bit. Now, you need to use only the lpadmin command to configure a remote printer; the lpsystem utility is no longer needed. The command takes this syntax:

```
# lpadmin -p [printername] -s [systemname]
```

Thus, you might issue the command lpadmin -p juno -s solarsystem to configure the remote printer juno. With Solaris 2.6 and newer, you do not need to issue the enable and accept commands when working at the command line with lpadmin (though you do need to use them when working with admintool regardless of the Solaris version you have).

Using admintool

You can also use the graphical administration utility admintool to add a network printer to your Solaris system. Open admintool and select Browse ➤ Serial Ports to pick the port to which the printer is attached. Select Edit ➤ Modify and set the baud rate as described earlier in Table 33.1, then set the Template option as Initialize Only – No Connection. Finally, clear the check box next to Service Enable and click OK to save your settings.

Next, select Browse ≻ Printers, then Edit ≻ Add. To add a network printer, select Access to Printer. The network printer's information will be displayed next to Print Client, and you can edit name and description as necessary. The Print Server box should contain the name of the remote system that hosts the networked printer. You can also decide whether to make this printer the default printer. Click OK to save your settings, and exit `admintool`.

Even though you have used a graphical tool to add this printer, you still need to issue the `enable` and `accept` commands described above at a shell prompt. Open a terminal window and issue the following commands:

```
enable [printername]
accept [printername]
```

Removing a Printer

Removing a printer is usually easier than adding one. You should not simply unplug a printer and consider it removed; you need to configure the operating system to recognize that the printer is no longer attached. The methods for doing so are similar under both BSD and System V printing.

Removing a Printer with BSD

To remove a printer under BSD, simply remove its entry from the `/etc/printcap` file. Any related files, such as specific spool directories or other files that deal with only that printer, should also be removed. If you are removing a networked printer, you'll also need to edit the `/etc/printcap` files on any machines that have remote access to the networked printer so that they do not try to access the remote printer when it is no longer available.

Removing a Printer with Linux

If you added a printer to your Linux machine using the printer management tools from either your Linux distribution or your integrated desktop environment, you can use those same tools to remove the printer. Simply reopen the tools and remove the specified printer from the list; some tools will have a Delete or Remove button to click once you've selected the appropriate printer. The utility will then configure all the system files so that the entries relating to that printer are removed.

If you edited your /etc/printcap by hand to add the print resource (whether local or remote), simply remove that entry from /etc/printcap. If necessary, you may also need to remove the /var/spool/*PRINTERNAME* directory by hand. Be sure that, if you remove the /var/spool/*PRINTERNAME* directory, no links remain to that directory in the /etc/printcap file. If links remain, the spool may crash as it searches for a directory that no longer exists. Removing the printer's /etc/printcap entry should take care of that problem.

Removing a Printer with Solaris

To remove a printer under Solaris, issue the command

```
#    lpadmin -x [printername]
```

This will remove the printer from the active printer list and will no longer allow print jobs to be sent to that specified printer. Should you wish to use the printer again, you will need to add it as if it were a new printer.

For those using Solaris versions 2.5 and earlier, you must follow the lpadmin command with a command to remove any local references to the printer as well. Issue the command

```
#    lpsystem -r [printername]
```

to do so.

To remove a printer with admintool, open admintool and select Browse ➤ Printers. Select the printer you want to remove, and then select Edit ➤ Delete from the menus. Click OK to verify the printer's deletion, and exit admintool.

Maintaining a Print Queue

Once you have the printer functioning, whether a network or local printer, you'll need to keep an eye on the print queue. This is generally a low-maintenance task, because the print spool should function without much interaction (just make sure that someone keeps an eye on paper and toner in the printers). To manage the queue, you simply need to issue commands at the shell prompt to learn the status of your various printers; depending on your printer setup, you can view the status of the entire network, or you can look at individual printers. You can also stop or purge individual printers' spools if there is a problem.

Print Queues with FreeBSD and Linux

Managing your print queue with FreeBSD and Linux is straightforward, done with command-line commands. Some sample commands are shown in Table 33.2, and they are all extensions of the basic lp (line printer) command upon which BSD printing is based. Some distributions of Linux (and some third-party FreeBSD tools) offer a graphical interpretation of the output of these commands; some administrators find the graphical output easier to understand, but it is truly a matter of personal preference.

TABLE 33.2: BSD-style Print Queue Commands

Command	Function
lpq -P *printername*	Displays contents of print queue for named printer
lprm *jobnumber*	Stops specified job (get number from **lpq** command)
lprm -	Removes all jobs that belong to you from queue
lprm *user*	Removes all jobs belonging to the specified user from queue (you must be root to remove other people's jobs)
lprm	Removes currently active job, whatever it may be
lpc stop *printername*	Stops named printer and does not print whatever is remaining in queue
lpc start *printername*	Starts named printer and prints everything in queue
lpc disable *printername*	Stops new jobs from being placed in queue for named printer (jobs in queue will be printed)

Print Queues with Solaris

Managing your print queue under Solaris is also quite easy. You just need to remember some basic commands to get reports on the queue status, and most of them are variants on the `lpstat` command, which reports printer status in whatever method you require based on the flags with which you issued the command. Table 33.3 provides the most useful Solaris print queue commands.

TABLE 33.3: Solaris Print Queue Commands

Command	Function
`lpstat -t`	Reports status of entire network's printing system
`lpstat -p` *printername*	Gets printer status for specified printer
`cancel` *jobnumber printername*	Cancels specified job (with job number from the `lpstat` command)
`disable` *printername*	Disables every job in specified printer's queue
`lpadmin -d` *printername*	Sets default printer

Handling PostScript

PostScript is an additional factor in the complexity of Unix printing. *PostScript* is a language that is used to transfer complex documents from a user computer to a printer. For example, a newsletter that Rick composes on his computer, which includes fancy fonts and multiple graphics, can be transferred to Maria's computer for editing, and then to a printer for final production. PostScript encoding keeps everything in place and identical from creation to finish. Any document more complicated than system font in straight lines may use PostScript features, and many high-end printers handle PostScript automatically.

However, Unix doesn't necessarily recognize PostScript on the fly. Unlike other print formats, PostScript files don't start with a simple escape sequence that defines print features for that particular file. Instead, PostScript files begin with a lengthy set of instructions that averages nearly 500 lines—before the actual file to be printed even begins. Needless to say, PostScript files can be very large. Most word processors can't handle the format, so you need a specialized program to work with these files.

You can view PostScript files on a Unix machine with the `ghostview` and `ghostscript` utilities, available at most Unix software archives. Open a

PostScript file in ghostview by issuing the command ghostview &. ghostview opens to an empty window; press the o key to select a PostScript file for display. Figure 33.4 shows a PostScript file as displayed in ghostview. Jump around the document by selecting a page number from the slim window to the right of the button menu.

Printing a PostScript document under Unix requires either a PostScript-enabled printer (an expensive affair) or the ghostscript filter. When you send a document to the printer, the document passes through a series of filters installed at the print server level. If one of those filters is ghostscript, the file will be converted to a language that the destination printer can accept. Output of filtered PostScript files still looks pretty good, if not as perfect as the output to a PostScript-enabled laser printer. Even dot-matrix printers and low-end inkjet or bubble jet printers can produce a reasonable facsimile of PostScript fonts and documents with ghostscript's help, though of course the better the printer technology, the better the printed document.

FIGURE 33.4:

View PostScript documents under Unix with the ghostview utility.

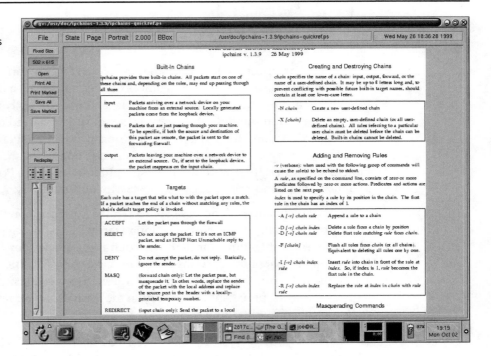

Every printer attached to your network needs to have a driver enabled in ghostscript if the printer is to receive PostScript print jobs. You can determine what drivers are enabled by starting ghostscript (issue the command ghostscript at a shell prompt) and issuing the command devicenames == at the ghostscript prompt. You'll get a long block of text showing all the different drivers enabled in your version of ghostscript, as shown in Figure 33.5. You might be able to pick your driver out of the block, but if you can't, consult the ghostscript documentation or its Makefile for more information about drivers. If you're using a printer manufactured by a major printer corporation—Hewlett-Packard, Epson, Brother, and so on—you should be fine with the installed drivers.

Whether or not you handle PostScript documents regularly, it's a good idea to install ghostview and ghostscript on your system. Some program documentation is available only in PostScript format, or you may receive documents that need to be printed on PostScript-compatible printers. ghostscript doesn't take up much system overhead, and it's a useful print filter to have around.

FIGURE 33.5

Check ghostscript's drivers to see whether it can convert PostScript files for your printer.

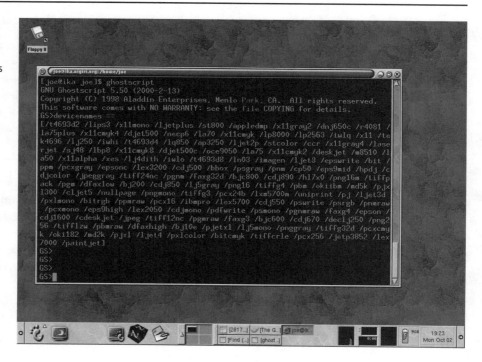

The Common Unix Printing System

Printing is one of the areas in which Unix variants most widely differ. This can be quite annoying, especially if you are managing a heterogeneous network that requires individual configuration on multiple operating systems. Luckily, there is a new development that promises to smooth out these differences and make Unix printing a more sensible and constant issue to manage.

The Common Unix Printing System (CUPS) is a project that aims to create a unified set of print commands and print configuration that will be usable on every Unix variant, regardless of System V or BSD heritage. CUPS is developed by the Easy Software Products corporation, a small company based in Maryland, but is released under the GPL. CUPS is free for use and distribution.

As the backbone of its methodology, CUPS uses the Internet Printing Protocol (IPP) instead of relying on the various print protocols used by different Unices. IPP is based on HTTP (the HyperText Transfer Protocol), which is the protocol used by Web traffic, and was designed to enable remote printing across the Internet. CUPS implements all the required elements of the IPP and most of the optional elements as well. Optional elements not contained in the current release will probably be incorporated through patches or in future releases.

> **NOTE** Some readers may be wondering, "Whatever happened to POSIX Printing?" The POSIX printing standard was an earlier attempt to unify Unix print technology and was promoted by the Institute of Electrical and Electronics Engineers (IEEE). POSIX Printing was a valiant effort, but did not meet with the approval of print and Unix industry leaders. It is no longer an active proposal before IEEE, and the focus has shifted to IPP as a solution for printing under Unix.

CUPS is run as a server, which accepts requests formatted both as System V and BSD commands. The server translates print requests into a common IPP syntax and transfers them to a scheduling module, which then sends the requests to the print queue and, ultimately, to the printer. The CUPS server is configured similarly to the Apache Web server; because many network administrators are running Apache already, the learning curve for CUPS is quite shallow. In fact, the CUPS server can be accessed from the Web to monitor print requests and the queue. CUPS can handle PostScript, image file format, and text files through various filters set up by the administrator.

Most importantly to the administrator, though, CUPS takes the hassle out of working with network printers on a heterogeneous network. Configuration is centralized and simple, and the CUPS interface lets users pick the printers they want to use regardless of how that printer is connected to the network. Print load balancing is also easier because you can divide available printers into classes, so that a print request sent to a color laser printer will print on the first available color laser printer, not on a specified printer that may be occupied with a lengthy job.

The only drawback of CUPS is that it is still quite young. The IPP protocol has not yet been formally accepted by the Internet Engineering Task Force (IETF), though the standard is moving easily through the approval process. The first workable release of CUPS was done in October 1999, and a wide variety of patches and bug fixes have been released as well. CUPS, in its first incarnation, was stable; however, the CUPS 1.1 release adds a number of features requested by users that make print management even easier.

We are watching CUPS with great anticipation. The implications for heterogeneous networks are amazing. The benefits to network administrators should be clear: Less time spent fixing print problems means more time to work on other network issues. In addition, several other features make CUPS a practical and welcome solution to Unix print frustration:

- CUPS uses a Web-based interface to the server, which bolsters the ability to monitor print activity from remote locations, while the encrypted password mechanism protects the server from unauthorized access.

- CUPS supports all types of printers, including USB. (USB support for Solaris printers is forthcoming, and a patch may have been released by the time this book is printed.)

- CUPS is supported under Samba (see Chapter 37: "Integrating Unix with Other Platforms"), and a number of third-party projects take advantage of CUPS for specific programs, such as a KDE interface called KUPS and a generalized print tool for X-using computers called XPP (the X Printing Panel).

- CUPS is included as part of the current Debian Linux release, and the project developers expect CUPS to be part of many other Unix variant releases in the near future.

TIP   Learn more about CUPS at the project Web site, `http://www.cups.org`.

Summary

Printing under Unix is probably the one area in which the least progress has been made toward integrating the ancient Unix strains. Most Unices use either the System V method, as does Solaris, or the Berkeley method, as do FreeBSD and Linux. The two methods handle print management differently, both in the configuration of new printers and in the management of the print spool and various printing jobs.

You can add a new printer under BSD or Linux by editing the /etc/printcap file; under Solaris, you need to use the lpadmin utility. All three Unices also offer graphical printer administration tools, as do the integrated desktop environments and some window managers. System V and Berkeley also handle queue management differently, so you will need to learn a different set of commands if you use both types of Unix on a regular basis. Although the differences between the two methods are significant, there is hope in the development of the Common Unix Printing System (CUPS). CUPS is HTTP-based and promises to remove many of these differences by handling print jobs in much the same way as Web transmissions are handled.

PART VIII

Network Administration

CHAPTER
THIRTY-FOUR

Introduction to Unix Networking

- Basic Networking Concepts

- Basic TCP/IP

- Networking Hardware and Software

- Common Networking Architectures

- Common Networking Concerns

- Summary

This section of the book contains information on networks. We cover the physical aspects of networks, including the computers themselves and the cabling and cards that connect them, as well as the software issues involved in networking, such as the integration of different operating systems on the same network and the protection of network data from external intrusion. The subjects contained in this part of the book range from basic information, such as that covered in this chapter, to more complex concepts, such as the administration of heterogeneous networks and the practical configuration of network devices.

NOTE

In this part of the book, we focus on networks that use 10/100BaseT Ethernet cable. This is the most common type of networking equipment. Although other networking equipment exists and can be found in large networks, such equipment is quite rare for the beginning Unix administrator or the manager of small or home networks. We assume that, if you are new to Unix networking, your first project will be to build a small network in a home or office. For such purposes, using 10/100BaseT cable is the most economical and easiest way to build the network. If you enjoy networking and plan to scale up to truly large networks, you'll need to learn more about networking-specific hardware, such as Cisco routing equipment, that we don't cover here.

In this chapter, we present the basic theories that underlie the remaining chapters in this section. We explain the TCP/IP protocols and other networking concepts. We also show you some common network configurations and discuss the software that powers them. Finally, we conclude by introducing some concerns shared by every network administrator.

Chapter 35: "Network Interfaces and Routing" introduces the practical aspects of building a network. We introduce the variety of hardware devices that goes into building a network, from cards to cables, and show you how to configure them for your specific needs. We then illustrate the difference between an Ethernet network and one that offers dial-up access to its users. Finally, we explain the difference between routers and gateways, and show you how to manage each type of hardware with varying software controls.

Chapter 36: "The Distributed System" is a philosophical chapter. In it, we explain the general concept of client-server architecture, the method upon which most Unix networks and programs are built. We show you how to exploit the benefits of client-server architecture on your own networks, regardless of size, by distributing services across the various computers connected to the network.

Chapter 37: "Integrating Unix with Other Platforms" is a practical chapter written in response to the reality of most networks today. Heterogeneous networks are increasingly common, whether the heterogeneity is found among different Unix variants or in the use of Unix alongside computers running Windows or MacOS. We show you how to handle each type of heterogeneity, and introduce two software packages designed to ease the junctures between Unix and non-Unix operating systems.

Chapter 38: "Network Security" closes out this part of the book with information about the most critical aspect of network administration. If you build a network, you must be concerned about security. If you connect to a network, such as the Internet, you must be concerned about security. We explain some of the common security risks and holes found in many networks, and offer some solutions to keep your data and your users free from harm or malicious use.

Basic Networking Concepts

Before you start working on your own network, it's important to have a grounding in the basic concepts of networking. At its most basic level, a *network* is a group of computers (at least two) connected together. The group can share files and other resources, such as printers or cable modems, through the network connection, which is usually a cable resembling a telephone cord.

Many networks use a *topology,* or layout, which requires a main server machine as well as a number of user machines, as shown in Figure 34.1. The server holds programs that are used by all the user machines and offers those services upon request. This is an efficient use of network resources. Without the central server, copies of each software program would have to be loaded on each user machine. It is simpler to have one copy at a central location and make that server feed the program as necessary.

Server machines are often high-powered and heavy-duty machines with massive amounts of RAM and hard-disk space, but they don't necessarily have to be so imposing. If you are running a small network, you can probably get away with using an older desktop machine as the main server and saving your spending money for the user machines, where significant RAM, faster video cards, and larger hard drives will make more of a difference for the network users.

FIGURE 34.1:

Unix networks are often built on a star topology, with the server at the center.

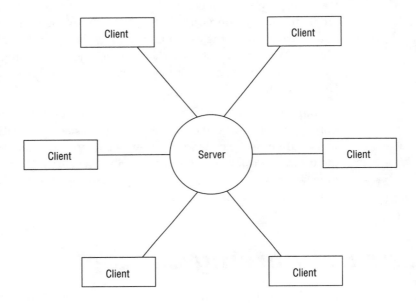

Small networks simply don't place that much stress on a server. When you connect your network to the Internet full time and start running Web servers, or scale your network to a point where you have more than 15 or 20 computers and 75 or 100 users checking their e-mail and using system resources constantly, you'll need to consider other server solutions. For the kind of networks we explain in this part of the book, though, a 486 or basic Pentium-class computer ought to be sufficient.

A network may have a single server or multiple servers. Depending on the kind of traffic generated by the network, the administrator may decide to split certain services onto their own machines. Web traffic is a good example; a popular Web site hosted from a machine on the local network may cause slow traffic through the network itself as the server machine struggles to keep up with both external and internal demands. Moving the Web pages onto a separate machine, along with Web server software such as Apache, divorces the Web requests from the requests made by internal users to the main server. Thus, internal traffic can move more quickly, while external Web requests are also answered more quickly because they are fed to a machine handling only Web traffic.

TIP

Many of the services covered in Part IX: "Administering Services" may be run on individual servers within the network if their traffic threatens to overwhelm the servers with local users' requests.

Basic TCP/IP

The basic *protocol* used in Unix networks is the TCP/IP protocol. A protocol is a standard to which programs must be written; in the case of networking, there are two main protocols. Dial-up connections, such as those made with a modem to an ISP over a phone line, use the PPP (Peer-to-Peer Protocol) protocol. This protocol determines how data is to be sent over a serial connection such as a telephone line.

Networks that don't use telephone lines, however, rely on the TCP/IP (Transmission Connection Protocol/Internet Protocol) protocol. This protocol is the *lingua franca* of the Internet. Every computer connected to the Internet speaks TCP/IP. TCP/IP is actually a suite of protocols that manage how information is transmitted between the various computers on the Internet, a vast pool of computers made up of all sorts of hardware and software. In the early days of the Internet, all computers connected to it ran some flavor of Unix, so it's no surprise that smaller Unix networks work with TCP/IP as well.

Regardless of the type of data being transmitted—whether it's e-mail, graphic files, sound clips, or system commands—TCP/IP can handle it and get the data to its destination without much trouble. Problems with network transmissions can often be traced to a faulty hardware installation or a misconfigured network device, instead of being the fault of the transmission protocol itself. In fact, TCP/IP transmissions are far less susceptible to scrambling or data loss than are PPP transmissions, because the capability of the serial hardware is less than that of the devices used to transmit TCP/IP protocol data.

In this part of the book, we focus on networks that use TCP/IP over Ethernet cable, which is one of the most common network configurations. Ethernet connections are always active. There is no need to use a modem to dial into the server machine, because the network is always in operation (unless you explicitly disable it for some reason). If you have a 24-hour connection to the Internet, such as a cable modem or a DSL connection, on one of your network machines, the Internet is "always on" for everyone on the network. No more do you have to deal with busy signals or share time with your voice telephone line if you have a network and a constant connection.

Ethernet connections using TCP/IP are also significantly faster than dial-up connections using PPP. Although you could build a small network with modems and phone lines, dialing up each machine as needed, it would be a very slow network and prone to data loss. Ethernet cables, in the popular 10BaseT configuration, can transfer data at a rate of 10 million bits per second. In comparison, the fastest modem currently permitted by the U.S. Federal Communications Commission transfers data at only 56,000 bits per second. Thus, Ethernet can be approximately 178 times faster than the fastest dial-up connection; no wonder it's the standard connection for local networks.

Internet Protocol

Every computer that is attached to the Internet network is identified by a particular and unique set of numbers, called an Internet Protocol (IP) address or number. These numbers have that name because their existence and use are determined by the Internet Protocol, the IP part of TCP/IP. Every IP number uses the form

```
aaa.bbb.ccc.ddd
```

where aaa, bbb, ccc, and ddd are numbers between 0 and 255.

IP numbers look somewhat arbitrary, with only the format remaining constant. IP numbers are structured in a specific way, however, which rises from the fact that each IP address is a 32-bit number. A *bit* is the basic unit of information for digital data transfer. Each four-number set in the IP address represents 8 bits, which equals 1 *byte*. Reduced to its binary expression, an IP number has the form

```
xxxxxxxx.xxxxxxxx.xxxxxxxx.xxxxxxxx
```

Each x represents either 0 or 1, because it is binary. Because each segment represents 8 bits, the IP format is sometimes referred to as an *octet format*; you might also hear the comment that IP numbers are *octals*.

Because each of the digits in the octal IP number has two possible values—0 or 1—the full 32-bit number has over four billion possible values. These values can be expressed with the mathematical statement $2e^{32}$. This is a large number to work with, so it's separated into four octets for convenience. An octet has 256 possible values, or $2e^8$.

NOTE

Remember that, in Unix, counting begins from zero. Therefore, the possible values of an IP octet are 0 to 255.

Static and Dynamic IP

As we noted above, every computer connected to the Internet has a unique address called the IP number. There are two ways to assign an IP number: static and dynamic assignment. If the IP number is assigned permanently to a particular computer, that computer has a *static* IP number. If, however, the computer is assigned a different IP number every time it connects to the Internet, that computer has a *dynamic* IP number. Static IPs are ideal because they are easy to work with, but most people have Internet connections that use dynamic IP assignment.

If you have a dial-up connection to the Internet, chances are overwhelming that your Internet provider uses dynamic IP allocation. This is the best solution for ISPs because, though the ISP has control of only a certain set of IP numbers, they can sell access to many more people than they have IP numbers. Because an ISP will never have all their customers connected to the Internet at the same time, they can create multiple accounts for each available IP slot and share the pool of IP numbers as people log in and out of their accounts.

Every time you log into your ISP account, your computer is assigned an IP number from the ISP's pool of available numbers. The number is probably different every time you log in unless you just hit a streak of luck and are assigned the same number twice in a row. The ISP uses a program called DHCP (the Dynamic Host Configuration Protocol) to assign these IP numbers. (We cover DHCP in Chapter 35: "Network Interfaces and Routing.")

NOTE

In some areas, especially in Canada, DHCP is dropping by the wayside in favor of PPPoE (Peer-to-Peer Protocol over Ethernet). This is a new way to handle dynamic IP number allocation. If your ISP uses PPPoE instead of DHCP, it should not affect you unless you're running scripts that are DHCP-specific.

Though dynamic IP numbers are prevalent for dial-up connections, constant-access Internet connections such as cable modems, ISDN, or DSL use static IP numbers. When you open your account with one of these providers, you will be given an IP number that identifies your computer. You can leave your computer connected all the time because you have a "hall pass" to the Internet in your IP number. (If you do leave your connection on all the time, we strongly encourage you to read Chapter 38: "Network Security." Constant Internet connections are an easy target for crackers and other malicious users.)

Networking Hardware and Software

Once you have decided to build a network, you have some shopping to do. At the least, you'll need to purchase a roll of 10/100BaseT Ethernet cable, some jacks to fit the cable, and a crimping tool to fit the jacks onto the cable. You'll probably also need to purchase Ethernet cards for each machine on the network unless your computers already have cards in them. (Some newer machines, especially laptops, have built-in Ethernet capability.)

NOTE   One piece of hardware that we especially like is the small network hub. Available for as little as $30 or $40 (US), the network hub has multiple ports for Ethernet cable plugs. Connect the Ethernet cables from each client and server machine into the hub, and presto! You have a hub topology network (see the "Common Networking Architectures" section of this chapter). There are external hubs and internal hubs, but we recommend the external variety, especially those made by Linksys or 3Com. External hubs have blinking lights that can tell you a lot about the traffic moving across your network; rapid blinks mean that the connection is transporting data, while a darkened light means that, for some reason, that machine is off the network.

If you intend to build a large network or one that will use dedicated servers, you'll also need to investigate new computers. A small network can use regular desktop computers as dedicated servers, but larger networks may require machines built for the server role or specialized routers. These special machines can cost thousands of dollars, and many network administrators have become quite talented at duplicating their features with cheap Pentium machines and a copy of FreeBSD or Linux. We certainly suggest that you start out with a regular desktop machine as a server; if you find that you need a Cisco router or two down the road, you'll have time to save up for them.

When you have connected all the network machines together with the cable and cards, you're ready to begin working with the software configurations required to set up the network. We work through these steps in detail in Chapter 35: "Network Interfaces and Routing." In brief, you'll need to build a table that contains an individual IP address for each computer on the network; the kind of drivers each machine will require for the Ethernet cards; numbers that identify the local network to itself and to the external world; and a domain name and set of system names to use in concert with the numeric addresses.

Network Domain Names and Internet Domain Names

You may use a domain name that you have registered and paid for, or you may use one that is not assigned to you. However, if you use a domain name that you do not own, you won't be able to use it on the Internet. That is, you might build a network around the domain name **amazon**, but you don't own that domain name. You'll have to come up with something else if you want to use your network on the Internet.

We suggest that, if you plan to use your network to handle traffic on the Internet, you pay the fee and register a domain name. It's probably cheaper than all those Ethernet cards you had to buy, and you'll have the security of knowing that nobody else is using your network name. We like the service offered by Register.com, one of the authorized domain name registries that handles .com, .org, and .net as well as more than 20 national top-level domains. Though we have no association with Register.com other than being satisfied customers, we've tried some of the other registries and think that Register.com has the best customer service. In addition, when you purchase a domain name through Register.com, you actually own the domain name. Other registries, Network Solutions in particular, now retain the ownership of the domain name and simply lease it to you.

Network configuration is based on working with several different configuration files, as with most other Unix configuration. The files that deal with TCP/IP configuration are usually collected in the /etc directory; for example, /etc/hosts contains a list of the hostnames used for machines on your network, while /etc/services contains a list of the services you've authorized to run on the network (for either internal or external use). Many Unix variants offer a configuration utility that simplifies some of the TCP/IP setup process, though some variants require that these edits be made with a text editor.

WARNING Be careful if you're editing network configuration files by hand. It's quite easy to delete the wrong line or write down an IP number incorrectly, and you'll save yourself hours of detective work if you start out by taking care.

Once you've set up the servers, you've done the bulk of the work. Now, all that remains is configuring the client machines. This is simpler because you just need to give the client machines information about the central server; when configuring the servers, you had to provide information about every single client machine. When you've finished editing the configuration files on the client machines, you can restart all the computers on the network. If everything has gone smoothly, you'll now be a network administrator.

Common Networking Architectures

In the "Basic Networking Concepts" section of this chapter, we introduced the concept of *network topology*. A topology is simply the layout of the network, comprising both the computers and the way in which they are connected. For example, the term World Wide Web makes reference to the weblike topology of the Internet. There is no central server on the Internet; rather, thousands of computers are interconnected through various subnetworks to make up the whole Internet.

There are a variety of network topologies. The topology used by a particular network is often determined by the type of network in question. Networks can be local area networks (LANs), or they can be wide area networks (WANs). LANs are generally networks that are contained in a particular physical location, whether it be a room or a building. A WAN is generally composed of multiple LANs.

Assume that you are the network administrator for a company that fills the office space of one three-story building. If you have a separate network for the accounting department on the first floor, another network for the legal department on the second floor, and a third network for the administrative offices on the third floor, you have three local area networks. However, you'll probably unite all three of those networks before you connect any of them to the Internet, because computers on all three networks will share the same Internet connection and domain name. Thus, you have both three LANs and one WAN under your management.

Local Area Network Topologies

There are several common topologies for local area networks. Choosing a topology depends on the function of the network, because some architectures are more suited for certain purposes than others. There are three dominant architectures for LANs; because we focus on LANs in this section of the book, it's likely that you'll select one of these topologies when you build your network.

Ring Architecture

From its name, you might expect a ring topology network to be composed of computers and peripheral devices connected by cables, with no clear end. That is, you might think that Computer A has both the beginning and the end of the connection plugged into its case. The *ring* in a ring topology is not a physical ring, though. It is merely a concept, and the name is based on the way in which the central server is constructed.

Even though there is no physical ring in a ring topology, it's a useful concept because there is no single machine that has supremacy over the other machines. Figure 34.2 shows the standard depiction of a ring topology network; the circular line connecting the machines is not a physical cable, but is a depiction of the ring's nonhierarchical structure.

TIP

Do you remember the Dilbert cartoon in which Dilbert successfully confused his boss by claiming that the token had fallen out of the network and thus there was no connectivity? The architecture used at Dilbert's company was a ring topology, often referred to as a *token ring* architecture. There's no actual token to be lost, though; it's just a good way to confuse the Pointy-Haired Bosses.

FIGURE 34.2:

The ring topology's name is misleading, but it is a useful concept.

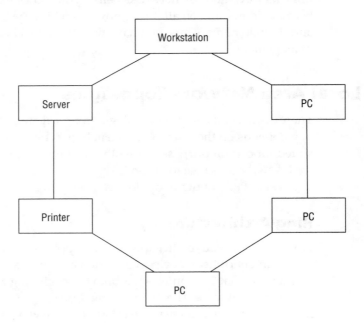

Hub Architecture

Hub topology is popular in large installations. In a hub network, there is a hierarchical system of organization. At the heart of the network lies a main cable called the hub's *backplane*. The backplane is a high-speed cable, usually fiber optic, that can carry a vast amount of data at staggering speeds. From that backplane extend several cables, usually Ethernet cables, to which various *hubs* are connected. These hubs serve smaller clusters of machines and peripherals. Figure 34.3 shows a diagram of a typical hub installation.

Despite its suitability for large networks, the hub topology can be used for smaller networks as well. It's especially useful for situations in which the network is initially small, but the administrators know that the network will become quite large in the future. Hub topologies are easily scaled, because the administrator simply needs to attach more hubs to the high-speed backplane to serve the new users.

The hub topology is useful for both large and small networks.

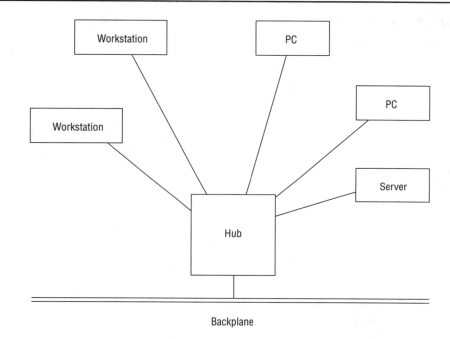

Backplane

In small installations such as the networks we describe in this part of the book, a hub topology is especially useful. We use the hub in our own network, using a single server machine as the backplane. In such a situation, the hub topology is often called a *star topology* because the network's diagram is star-shaped. (Figure 34.1 showed a star topology network.) You can buy hubs designed for small networks at almost all computer or office supply stores, or you can spend thousands of dollars on high-speed and high-capacity hubs.

Bus Architecture

The simplest network architecture is the bus topology. The *bus* is a backbone cable similar to the backplane used in a hub topology. Individual computers and peripherals are connected to the bus, and are given individual identifying numbers similar to the IP numbers used on the Internet network. Figure 34.4 shows the bus architecture.

FIGURE 34.4:

The bus architecture is the simplest network topology.

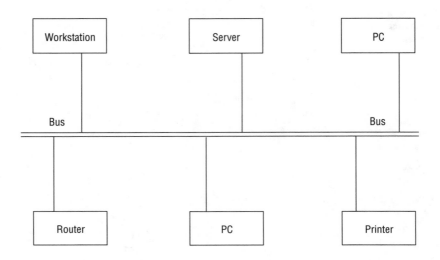

Bus topologies can be constructed so that either individual machines are connected directly to the bus cable or machines are connected to each other in a *daisy chain* architecture. (If you've ever used SCSI peripherals, you've used a daisy chain.) Figure 34.5 shows a bus topology using the daisy chain. The disadvantage to a machine-to-machine chain topology is that the signals along the cable can be degraded or slowed as they pass through each subsequent computer or peripheral. If speed is important to you, we suggest staying away from the daisy chain bus topology.

| NOTE | Consider the type of data you'll be transferring across the network before you pick a topology. In some architectures, the failure of one machine can mean downtime for machines elsewhere on the network. For example, if you are on a daisy chain network and a machine between you and the gateway fails, you may not have access to the rest of the network until that machine is fixed. |

FIGURE 34.5:

Another bus topology
option is the daisy chain.

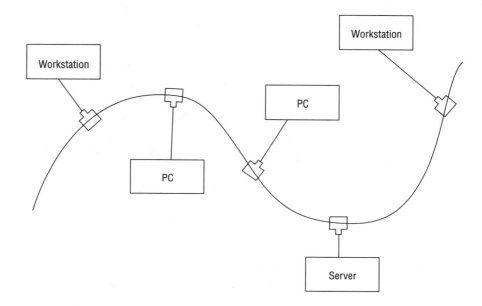

Wide Area Network Topologies

Where local area network topologies are simply methods of connecting sets of computers and peripherals, wide area networks use a different philosophy in their architectures. Designing a wide area network architecture requires a good understanding of the amount of traffic flowing through the WAN. If the individual LANs that make up the WAN never communicate with each other, or there is a low level of traffic, the WAN can be set up in a topology that resembles the LAN hub architecture, as shown in Figure 34.6.

In this architecture, the WAN's backbone (high-speed cable usually providing Internet access) has a number of *routers* connected to it: one router for each LAN. The router is a specialized piece of hardware that does nothing but handle data transfer between computers, and it is used in situations where the expected amount of traffic is quite high. Each LAN's router handles traffic destined for the users of that LAN and the traffic that they send back to the backbone. If the data sent by LAN 1 is destined for LAN 2, the router will sort the data out. If the data is destined for networks outside the WAN, such as the Internet, the backbone transfers that data out beyond the WAN.

For WANs in which the individual LANs often transfer a great deal of data to each other, there is a different topology. The network administrator can build a connection directly between the individual LANs, with an additional router placed between each LAN. In this topology, shown in Figure 34.7, each LAN has the option of transferring data through a router pointed at another LAN in the network or through a router pointed directly at the backbone. Dividing traffic in this way eases congestion on the external backbone and may save money if connection fees are based on the amount of traffic passing through the backbone.

FIGURE 34.6:

A typical WAN topology resembles the LAN hub architecture.

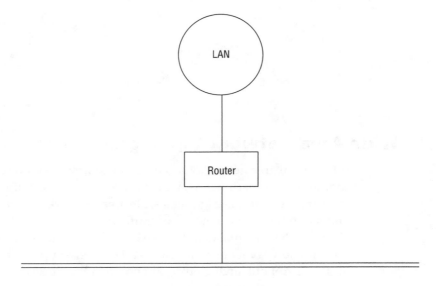

Network Backbone

FIGURE 34.7:

Internal traffic between LANs may flow faster if a separate router is installed.

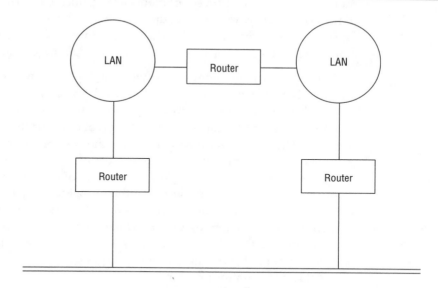

Network Backbone

It's a truism among network administrators that 80 percent of traffic on a network is local, and 20 percent is destined for recipients not on the local network. We think that this rule applies to only very large networks; on the smaller networks with which we're familiar, the numbers are sometimes reversed. The rise of the World Wide Web and the increasing popularity of the Internet have changed the traditional proportions of network traffic.

Common Networking Concerns

Everyone who runs a network, large or small, will have similar concerns. Of course, the administrator of a large network is likely to have more to worry about, but the types of problems encountered are much the same regardless of network size. Among these problems are obvious concerns such as security of data, accessibility, and general up-time. Administrators also worry about less apparent problems, such as hardware compatibility or the encoding systems used by the different operating systems on a heterogeneous network.

Security is such an important networking topic that we've devoted an entire chapter to the subject, Chapter 38: "Network Security." In a capsule version of the material covered there, we can say that security should be the second concern of the network administrator—the first being, of course, whether the network is running. There are several ways in which the network administrator can secure a network. The administrator can require secure software to be used for access, such as the ssh (Secure Shell) program instead of the traditional telnet and rlogin programs. These programs, although widely used, are security risks. The administrator can also implement programs that monitor network access and send out alerts if something untoward happens. The best tool for network security, however, is the administrator's familiarity with normal network operation. If something out of the ordinary happens, a good administrator will notice it almost as quickly as a monitor program.

Accessibility is another important concern for the network administrator. Here, we are using *accessibility* as a term to describe the ability of users to actually use the network. Issues of physical accessibility for the disabled are part of this, but are often associated more with the purchases of adaptive software and hardware. In general, accessibility must be traded off against security issues. A system that is easy to get into, if you're an authorized user, is probably a system that's easy to get into if you're unauthorized. The network administrator generally must discount the complaints of users if the trade-off is an insecure system that can be exploited for malicious use. Yes, it's more of a hassle to use a secure login shell such as ssh, but it also cuts down on potential problems.

Finally, the network administrator must always be concerned with the general function of the network. Are all the machines and peripherals running? If something is offline, why is it not working? Is the backbone itself connecting outside the network? The administrator will quickly become experienced in tracing down problems along the network, whether the problem is a loose cable or net congestion 1000 miles away. Users often complain about network problems when it isn't a network problem at all, and the administrator needs a healthy dose of people skills to handle these situations as well.

Summary

Network administration is a specialized subset of system administration. Network administrators have responsibilities that range from the care of specialized hardware devices to the education and management of users. Networks are constructed using one of two protocols: PPP (Peer-to-Peer Protocol) is used for dial-up connections such as those made to Internet service providers, while TCP/IP (Transmission Connection Protocol/Internet Protocol) is used over large networks such as the Internet or on local networks connected with Ethernet cable.

TCP/IP networks can be either local area networks (LANs), usually contained within a particular physical area, or wide area networks (WANs), composed of several local area networks that share a common connection to external networks such as the Internet. These networks can be constructed with one of several popular topologies, or schematics, including hub, ring, and bus architectures. Once the network is constructed physically, the administrator must configure various files for the network to be recognized by its component computers and by other networks. Then, the administrator must determine various policies and procedures to handle common concerns such as system up-time and security issues.

CHAPTER

THIRTY-FIVE

35

Network Interfaces
and Routing

■ Configuring Network Devices

■ Dial-Up Networking

■ Ethernet Networking

■ Routers and Gateways

■ Small Networks

■ IP Masquerading

■ Summary

In the previous chapter: "Introduction to Unix Networking," we introduced some of the basic concepts that underlie Unix networks large and small. In this chapter, we concentrate on the practical aspects of building Unix networks. We begin by showing you the difference between an Ethernet network and one that offers dial-up access to its users. You may need to provide access for local users, or you might have only dial-up access to the Internet and need to integrate that function into your network's activity.

Next, we introduce the variety of hardware devices that go into building a network and show you how to configure them for your specific needs. Finally, we explain the difference between routers and gateways, and show you how to manage each type of hardware with varying software controls. We also address various networking protocols and show you how to use a single IP number to handle your entire network's behavior on the Internet.

This chapter focuses on the nuts and bolts of Unix networking: configuring network devices and setting up routing. This is not a glamorous topic, but these tasks are necessary prerequisites to any other networking tasks. If the connections between devices are not working, there is no way for data to get from one point to another.

Configuring Network Devices

Before you can set up any network devices, you need to be aware of what kind of devices you're using or plan to use in the future. This is a simple task, even if you're not a networking expert—or if you're completely new to the topic altogether. Networks may involve both types of networking device, but most network administrators will concentrate on one type or the other. For larger networks, different networking device types may be divided into separate LANs or kept on different computers on the network.

For the average user, network devices can be divided into two general types: dial-up networking and Ethernet networking. Dial-up networking uses the *modem* as its network device; Ethernet networking uses the *network interface card (NIC)* as its network device. Those readers who plan to build and manage a small network will probably use both types of devices, especially if you are a home user and have only dial-up access to your Internet provider, but also operate a small local network.

NOTE   Even if you use a permanent Internet connection, such as DSL or a cable modem, it's a good idea to understand how modems work with Unix; you may purchase a laptop that has both a modem and an Ethernet connection, or you might need to configure a user's computer to access your network with a modem. In any event, don't ignore the modem. It may not be the newest technology, but it is certainly not obsolete in the Unix world.

In the next two sections of this chapter: "Dial-Up Networking" and "Ethernet Networking," we show you how to configure these devices under Unix. We explain the basic options for each type and introduce some tools that might help you with your network configurations.

NOTE   Only root can configure network devices. Before you begin any process described in this chapter, log into the root account or assume superuser powers.

Dial-Up Networking

The majority of home-based Internet connections in the United States are dial-up connections. That is, the connection is handled over telephone lines, using regular phone numbers and transmission protocols. If you create an account with a local Internet service provider, chances are very good that your only point of access to their network will be through your modem.

The advantage of dial-up networking is that it uses an easily accessible technology; almost everyone has a phone. Most ISPs have preconfigured software, so that all you have to do is dial up once, and the software makes all the necessary settings. (That's what is on those CD-ROMs that appear in the mail every day and fall out of the pages of your favorite magazines.) Once set up, the dial-up connection is reasonably trouble-free, except for busy signals on the ISP's end.

However, many of the advantages of dial-up networking are reserved for Windows users and, in a few cases, Macintosh users. The Unix-using customer must do quite a bit more work to use the same service that is automatically configured for the Windows user. (See the sidebar "Unix and Your ISP" for more information on choosing an ISP sympathetic to your needs.) This is not to say that you should dump your ISP, though. The only case in which you must change ISPs is if you are using a provider that requires a non-Unix interface, as with America Online; you must use AOL's software to access their network, and they do not provide a Unix variant of their program.

Unix and Your ISP

Depending on where you live, finding a Unix-compatible Internet service provider can be an interesting task. Why should you care? Well, most ISPs are targeted at the Windows user and secondarily at the Macintosh user. Many ISPs, especially the national ones such as the Microsoft Network and America Online, use proprietary software that's available only for the Windows platform; even Mac software may be hard to get. The ironic thing is that many of these ISPs use Unix to run their networks; they just don't make it easy for Unix-using customers. (However, Mindspring/Earthlink is quite receptive to Linux users and has documentation on its Web site for Linux configuration. It should be easy to adapt that information to other variants of Unix.)

There are two main problems here: access and technical support. If the ISP requires that you use their software to access their network, and there's no Unix variant of the software, you can't use the ISP. If you do manage to gain access, but you have a question, the technical support personnel may not know anything about Unix networking. The latter is easier to deal with than the former; you can always read a book, like this one, or consult the Web for answers.

So, how can you find a Unix-friendly ISP? Call around and ask a lot of questions. Here are some of the questions we ask when talking to a new ISP:

- What operating system do you use for your network? (ISPs that run Windows NT are less likely to be helpful for Unix-using customers because these ISPs don't run Unix themselves.)

- Do we have to use proprietary software to connect to our account? Are you sure? (Some ISPs prefer that you use their software, but you can still connect directly through a PPP connection.)

- Are the connections you offer true PPP connections? (If so, you'll be able to connect without their software.)

- Does your technical support staff receive training on operating systems other than Windows? (Although an answer that involves Unix may be rare, you can get a sense of how friendly the ISP is to alternative operating systems.)

Continued on next page

- Do any of your users use Unix? How many? Do you offer technical support or documentation for them? (Some ISPs have internal newsgroups for Unix users; others have no idea whether they have Unix users at all. If the answer is *no,* they simply may not know.)

You probably won't find the perfect Unix ISP, but there's usually a solution in your local calling area.

Dial-Up Hardware

The first thing you need to do when configuring your dial-up connection is to connect your modem. Modems come in two types: external and internal. External modems, as the name implies, are self-contained units that sit outside of your computer and are attached to one of the computer's serial ports with a cable. Internal modems fit into an ISA or PCI bus slot inside your computer, displaying a narrow metal band on the outside of the computer case. The band has a telephone jack, to which you can attach a regular phone line.

Both types of modems have advantages: The internal modem takes up no extra space in your work area; the external modem usually has a series of blinking lights that give you useful information about the status of your network transmissions. You must open your computer case to install an internal modem, which may be daunting to some people. In addition, if you don't have an open bus slot on your motherboard, but you do have an open serial port, you will need to use an external modem. (Those readers who—like Kate—seem to collect serial devices will probably have the reverse situation.) Some people maintain that external modems are more efficient and durable, but we've seen no empirical data that supports this claim. For what it's worth, we've always used internal modems and have had little trouble.

Software Modems

Beware the WinModem! If you are planning to buy a new modem for your Unix personal computer, you must be aware of a real problem in the modem section of your favorite computer supply store. Since the advent of Windows 95, a new subspecies of modem has flooded the market, called the *WinModem* or *software modem.* These modems use operating-system functions to replace some of the work normally performed by the modem's hardware.`

Continued on next page

Software modems are operating-system dependent, and virtually all of them are built with Windows in mind. Although some research has been done on getting these modems to work under some flavors of Unix, right now WinModems are basically useless for the Unix user. This is unfortunate: Software modems occupy the extreme low end of the price spectrum, and appropriate Unix-compatible modems may cost nearly twice as much as a comparable software modem.

You can recognize a software modem by its size. It is smaller than a regular modem, often by half. Software modems are about the size of a tin of mints or a pack of unfiltered cigarettes. Software modems can get away with being so small because they don't use all the pins in the bus slot to which they're attached. You can also identify a software modem while it's still in the box, because they usually have slogans like "Made for Windows 98!" printed on the packaging. If you just can't tell whether the modem you're looking at is a software modem, though, get an iron-clad guarantee that you can return the modem if it doesn't work.

Once you've selected a modem and installed it physically, you need to configure it for operation. If you're using an integrated desktop such as Gnome or KDE, you have a graphical tool that will help you get your connection set up. Some Unix variants have a graphical tool incorporated into the operating system; others require you to follow a text-based process. Graphical tools make the job easier, and they're especially helpful for working with network connections.

Case Study: Kppp

One of the better graphical tools for configuring dial-up is the KDE tool Kppp. It is similar to other graphical configuration tools, such as Gnome's gnome-ppp program or the ezPPP tool, and users of those programs will see the resemblance. We walk you through a Kppp session in this section to highlight the various parts of dial-up network configuration. If you're using KDE, you can use this section as a detailed how-to guide; if you're using another desktop or graphical configuration tool, you'll find that many of the steps are identical in your application.

TIP   Linux users should check out their distribution documentation to see whether they have a graphical network administration tool. Red Hat users, for example, have the netcfg utility, which works much like Kppp.

Before you begin to configure your dial-up connection, you'll need to know some basic information about your ISP account:

- Your login ID and password

- The access phone number for the ISP's modem banks

- The ISP's IP allocation method (static or dynamic)

- IP numbers for the ISP's DNS servers

- The modem's device name

You'll also need to know whether your ISP uses a specific gateway machine (and, if so, what its name and IP number are); whether the ISP uses hardware or software flow control; and any authentication methods used by the ISP. Once you have that information, use the following steps to configure your connection.

1. Open the KDE menu and select Internet ➤ Kppp. The basic Kppp dialog box appears, as shown in Figure 35.1.

FIGURE 35.1:

Using Kppp is a quick way to configure your dial-up connection under KDE.

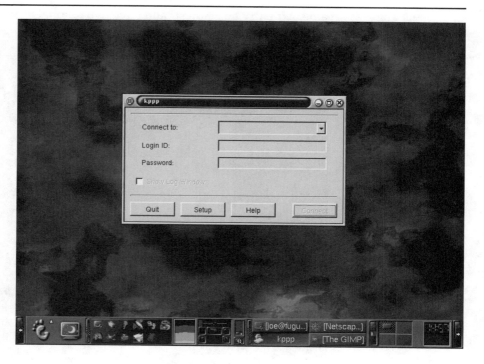

2. Click Setup. The Kppp Configuration screen appears, open to the Accounts tab, as in Figure 35.2.

3. Click the New button to open the New Account dialog box, open to the Dial tab.

4. Enter the local ISP's name, access number, and authentication type (if used). If your ISP does not use authentication, select Script Based.

5. Select the IP tab, shown in Figure 35.3.

6. Select either the Dynamic IP Address or the Static IP Address option. Unless you were told otherwise (and paid for a static IP number), select Dynamic IP Address.

7. (Optional) If you selected Static IP Address, enter your static IP address and the subnet mask address in the appropriate fields.

8. Select the DNS tab, shown in Figure 35.4.

9. Enter the Domain Name Server information from your ISP in the Domain Name text-entry box. You should have two numbers; enter one and click Add, then enter the second and click Add.

FIGURE 35.2:

Set up a new dial-up account on the Kppp Accounts tab.

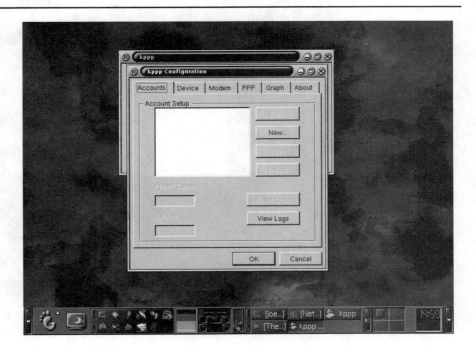

FIGURE 35.3:

Choose your IP settings on the IP tab.

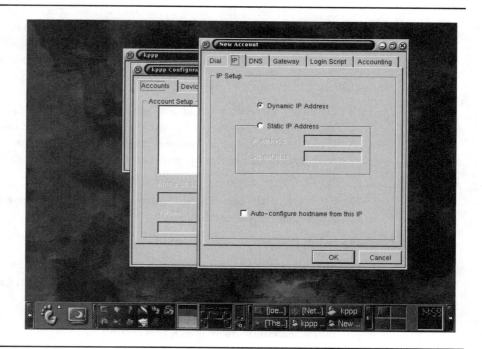

FIGURE 35.4:

Identify the ISP's Domain Name Servers on the DNS tab.

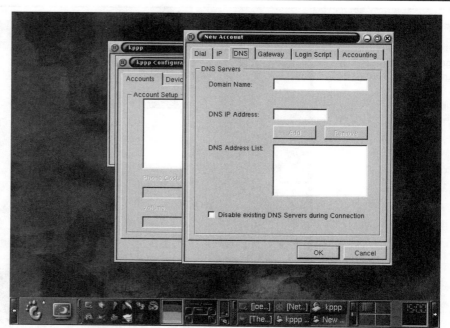

10. (Optional) Select the Gateway tab, shown in Figure 35.5. If your ISP uses a static *gateway machine*, they will tell you. The gateway handles all traffic between the ISP and the Internet; usually, this is handled dynamically. If there is a static gateway, you will be given its IP number. Enter it here.

11. Click the Login Script tab.

12. Edit the login script, which sets up the way in which Kppp passes your login name and password to the ISP. If the ISP doesn't require a text-based login, leave this blank. You may need to write a quick script; if so, see the paragraphs following this numbered list for tips on writing a good login script. A completed script is shown in Figure 35.6.

13. Click OK. The New Account screen closes, and you are returned to the Kppp Configuration dialog box.

14. Select the Device tab, shown in Figure 35.7.

15. Select your modem device from the drop-down window. The exact identification will change from Unix variant to variant; you can usually use /dev/modem, but you may need to use /dev/cua0 for an internal modem, or /dev/ttyS0 or /dev/ttyS1 for an external modem. If you have trouble making a connection, check this setting.

FIGURE 35.5:

If your ISP uses a static gateway to control Internet traffic, identify it here.

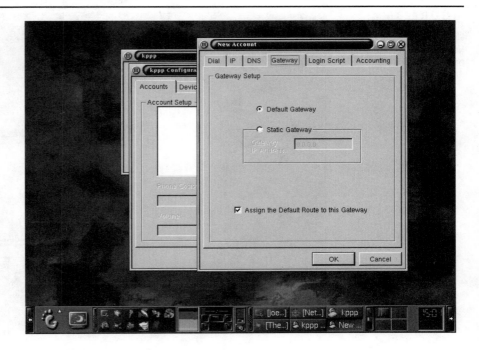

FIGURE 35.6:

Use a login script to pass your username and password to the ISP.

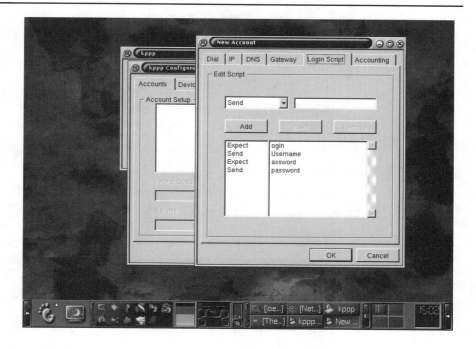

FIGURE 35.7:

Identify your modem configuration on the Device tab.

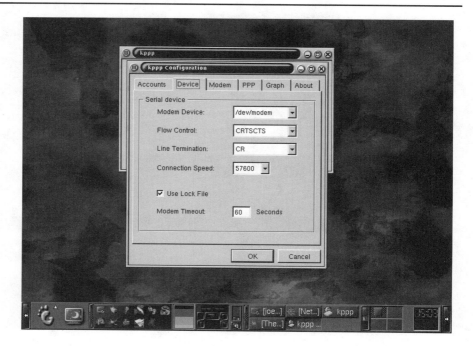

16. Enter other requested information about your modem on this tab.

17. Select the Modem tab. Set the number of seconds that you want the computer to wait before redialing in the Busy Waits box.

18. (Optional) Click the Modem Commands button to open the Edit Modem Commands dialog box, shown in Figure 35.8. If you have a modem with an unusual init string, you will need to change that here. Don't change anything here unless your modem's manual instructs you to do so.

19. Click OK. You will be returned to the Kppp Configuration screen.

20. Click OK. The Kppp Configuration screen closes, and you are returned to the main Kppp dialog box.

21. Click Quit to exit Kppp.

FIGURE 35.8:

If you have an unusual modem, configure it on this screen.

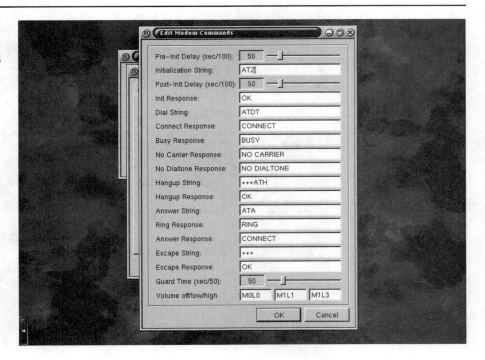

Writing a Login Script

If you need to use a login script for your ISP account, here is a quick script that should get you started. Individual variations with your ISP may require you to edit this script slightly, but it has worked with a wide variety of ISPs and Unix variants. If it doesn't work for you, check with your ISP's help desk to see what you need to do. (This is another good reason to choose a Unix-friendly Internet provider.)

The main thing to remember with a login script is that individual ISPs may capitalize certain components of the script, while others use lowercase letters. You won't know which method your ISP uses, so it's easiest just to avoid the issue altogether. Thus, in this script, you'll see that the initial letters are missing. The basic login script takes this form:

```
Expect      ogin:
Send        <login name>
Expect      assword:
Send        <password>
```

To build this script with Kppp, return to the Login Script tab of the Kppp New Account dialog box and follow these steps:

1. In the upper-right text-entry box, type **ogin:** and click Add.

2. Select Send from the drop-down menu at the upper left.

3. In the text-entry box, type your username and click Add.

4. Select Expect from the drop-down menu.

5. In the text-entry box, type **assword:** and click Add.

6. Select Send from the drop-down menu.

7. In the text-entry box, type your password and click Add.

The completed script appears in the lower box, as you saw in Figure 35.6.

Dial-Up and FreeBSD

Although FreeBSD-specific packages for integrated desktop systems such as KDE and Gnome should handle modem configuration properly, FreeBSD users should know that dial-up networking has changed quite a bit in the latest versions of the operating system. In FreeBSD 4 and later, all dial-up configuration is controlled by the /etc/ppp/ppp.conf file. Simply open that file in a text editor and scroll to the end of the file, where you'll find a set of lines that look like this:

```
papchap:

#
# edit the next three lines and replace the items in caps with
# the values which have been assigned by your ISP:
#

set phone PHONE_NUM
set authname USERNAME
set authkey PASSWORD
```

Replace the all-capital material with the access phone number and your username and password, adding a line above the block to identify this particular configuration. The result might be

```
papchap:

#
# edit the next three lines and replace the items in caps with
# the values which have been assigned by your ISP:
#

LOCALISP:

set phone 555-1212
set authname sallyanne
set authkey m0th3r
```

Save the file and exit the text editor. At the shell prompt, issue the command

```
# ppp -auto LOCALISP
```

The next time you issue a network command, such as doing a `traceroute` or accessing a Web page, the modem should connect to your ISP and log you into your account.

NOTE

Those using FreeBSD versions earlier than 4 may need to configure their dial-up networking by hand; consult the relevant FreeBSD handbook chapters at http://www.freebsd.org/handbook/ to get yourself set up. The Modem and PPP sections will be the most helpful.

Dial-Up and Solaris

Configuring dial-up access under Solaris is a lot trickier than under either Linux or FreeBSD. First, check to see that the UUCP and PPP packages have been installed. (If not, install them with the `packageadd` utility before beginning to configure a dial-up.) If you have the correct packages installed, you can begin to configure Solaris dial-up. Expect to spend a lot of time modifying various configuration and device files.

We have not found a better description of the Solaris dial-up configuration process than that offered by Mike Kempston at his extensive Solaris resources site. His instructions are so clear and useful that we recommend any Solaris user interested in using a dial-up to use his document instead of Solaris documentation. You can find Mike's configuration instructions at `http://www.kempston.net/solaris/connectanyisp.html`.

TIP   While you're there, don't forget to check out Mike's other Solaris resources at `http://www.kempston.net/solaris/index.html`.

Ethernet Networking

If you're not using dial-up networking, it's almost certain that you're using some sort of Ethernet networking. Although there are other types of networks, such as Token Ring, Ethernet has become the most common because of the convenient and inexpensive design of the hardware. New Ethernet network interface cards (NICs) can be had for as little as $20, and used ones can often be found for less than that (or for free, depending on your scrounging skills).

The most common type of Ethernet equipment is 10BaseT or 100BaseT, in which the *T* stands for *twisted pair,* the type of cable being used. Twisted-pair cable is similar to telephone cable and has the same type of modular jack on each end. The only difference is that the Ethernet modular jack is bigger than the phone jack. One end of the cable plugs into the computer's NIC, and the other end attaches to a *hub,* a central switchboard.

Hubs come in a variety of sizes. For example, our home network uses a 5-port hub that we purchased for about $40 at an office supply store. On the other end of the price spectrum, you can buy a 24-port hub that might be suitable for wiring a complete office. Also, hubs can be chained together to provide as many individual ports as are needed. Once all the computers have been connected to the hub with the twisted-pair cable, all that remains is simply to configure and activate the interface to make the network operational. Ironic though it may seem, given the perceived complexity of Ethernet networking, this is actually easier than configuring a dial-up connection under Unix.

Configuring and activating an Ethernet network interface are done in one step with the ifconfig command. ifconfig is a fairly flexible command that can be used to configure an interface, bring it up or down, or simply report information about the interface. It uses the basic syntax

```
ifconfig <interface> [<IP number>] [<options>] [up|down]
```

where items in angle brackets should be replaced with your specific information, and items in square brackets are optional.

Before you can bring up a network interface, you need to know your IP number. If you're part of a larger network, your system administrator may assign you a number; if you are connecting to an ISP that uses static IP numbers, you'll receive that number as part of the sign-up process. However, if you're creating a private network, you can use any numbers you want. Because you may connect to the Internet at some point, though, you should use IP numbers designated for private networks.

IP Numbers and Network Designations

The Internet Protocol divides IP numbers into classes. Class A networks use IP numbers from 0.0.0.0 through 255.255.255.255. Obviously, because this is the entire IP address space, most Class A networks have only a subset of these numbers available to them. An example might be the numbers between 22.0.0.0 and 24.255.255.255 being allocated to a specific network.

In a Class B network, the octet at the farthest left is always the same. An example of a Class B network's IP range might be 123.0.0.0 through 123.255.255.255. Class C networks, like Class B networks, use a constant left octet, but in the Class C network ranges, the second octet is also constant. Thus, 123.231.0.0 through 123.231.255.255 would be an example of a Class C IP range.

Continued on next page

Network classes are distinct from the concept of *private address spaces.* IANA (the Internet Assigned Numbers Authority) has set aside an address space in each network class for IP numbers that will not ever be used by computers connected to the Internet. Thus, these numbers can be used by many different people on many different networks, because these numbers don't have to be used as unique Internet identifiers. For the purposes described in this chapter, you simply need to remember that the IP numbers reserved in the Class C range are 192.168.0.0 through 192.168.255.255.

The IP numbers reserved for private networks in the Class C IP range are 192.168.0.0 through 192.168.255.255. This range offers 65,536 unique IP numbers, which should be more than enough for almost any private network. (If you need more than 65,000 IP numbers, chances are you're not running a private network anymore.) You can use these numbers as part of your internal network freely; even though other private network administrators are using the same numbers on their networks, you won't have a conflict as you would if you were using someone else's non–Class C IP numbers.

For the purposes of this section, assume that you have three computers that you're networking together for a small private system. Using the Class C range, you assign them the IP numbers 192.168.0.1, 192.168.0.2, and 192.168.0.3. Once you have determined the number that will be assigned to each computer, you can configure them. To illustrate the differences in Ethernet configuration, the first machine is a Linux machine, the second is a FreeBSD machine, and the third is a Solaris machine.

NOTE   Avoid giving your computers IP numbers that end in 0 or 255, because these numbers have special meanings in the TCP/IP protocol. Zero is the network address, and 255 is the broadcast address.

Linux, FreeBSD, and Solaris all use different naming conventions to designate network Ethernet interfaces. Linux uses eth*X*, FreeBSD uses ep*X*, and Solaris uses le*X*, where *X* equals a particular device number. So, to configure the Linux machine on this small network, you'd issue the following command at the machine's shell prompt:

```
ifconfig eth0 192.168.0.1 up
```

On the FreeBSD machine, you'd issue the command

```
ifconfig ep0 192.168.0.2 up
```

and on the Solaris machine, you'd issue the command

```
ifconfig le0 192.168.0.3 up
```

All machines should now be up and connected to the network. Look at your Ethernet hub; you should see lights representing each cable connection. If all the lights are showing, it's time to test the connection.

To test the network, try to reach each of the machines from the other machines on the network. On the network's first machine, the Linux computer, issue the command

```
ping 192.168.0.2
```

at the shell prompt. You should receive output that looks like this:

```
PING 192.168.0.2 (192.168.0.2) from 192.168.0.1 :➡
56(84) bytes of data.
64 bytes from 192.168.0.2:icmp_seq=0 ttl=255 time=0.5 ms
64 bytes from 192.168.0.2:icmp_seq=1 ttl=255 time=0.5 ms
64 bytes from 192.168.0.2:icmp_seq=2 ttl=255 time=0.4 ms
64 bytes from 192.168.0.2:icmp_seq=3 ttl=255 time=0.4 ms
64 bytes from 192.168.0.2:icmp_seq=4 ttl=255 time=0.4 ms
64 bytes from 192.168.0.2:icmp_seq=5 ttl=255 time=0.4 ms
64 bytes from 192.168.0.2:icmp_seq=6 ttl=255 time=0.4 ms
64 bytes from 192.168.0.2:icmp_seq=7 ttl=255 time=0.4 ms
```

This output will continue until you press Ctrl+c to stop it. The output shows that network signals are reaching the remote machine and are being sent back to the originating machine. This is exactly what should be happening, and signifies that the connection between the Linux and FreeBSD machine is fine. Repeat the process between every other machine on the network to make sure that messages can be sent and received. When you can successfully ping every machine from every other machine, you have built an operational Ethernet network.

Things are still a bit ungainly, though, because you still need to identify each machine by its IP number. It would be much simpler if each machine had a name, because names are easier to remember than strings of numbers. You may have identified each machine with a name when you installed its operating system, but if you did not, you can still name your machines with the hostname command.

NOTE `hostname` may operate differently from system to system. Check your specific variant documentation to learn how `hostname` will work for you, or consult the manual page by issuing the command `man hostname` at the shell prompt.

Assume that you've named these machines `linux`, `freebsd`, and `solaris`. Once the hostnames have been assigned, you need to set up the machines to recognize each other by name as well as by IP number. Unlike with device configuration, you can control hostname identification by editing the `/etc/hosts` file on each computer.

On the first computer in the network, `linux`, open the `/etc/hosts` file in a text editor and edit the file so that it looks like this:

```
127.0.0.1          linux localhost.localdomain localhost
192.168.0.1        linux localhost
192.168.0.2        freebsd
192.168.0.3        solaris
```

Save the file and exit. On the second computer, `freebsd`, open the `/etc/hosts` file in a text editor and edit the file so that it looks like this:

```
127.0.0.1          freebsd localhost.localdomain localhost
192.168.0.1        linux
192.168.0.2        freebsd localhost
192.168.0.3        solaris
```

Save the file and exit. On the third computer, `solaris`, open the `/etc/hosts` file in a text editor and edit the file so that it looks like this:

```
127.0.0.1          solaris localhost.localdomain localhost
192.168.0.1        linux
192.168.0.2        freebsd
192.168.0.3        solaris localhost
```

Save the file and exit.

Now that all the network machines are identified by name and IP number in the other machines' `/etc/hosts` files, you can use the machine names to identify network computers just as you used IP numbers. This makes the network easier to manage and enables the use of programs that require the use of remote hostnames instead of IP numbers.

DHCP and PPPoE

The Dynamic Host Configuration Protocol (DHCP) is the service used by your ISP to allocate dynamic IP numbers. It's unlikely that you'll need to tinker with your DHCP client settings, because they work automatically with your ISP to obtain a temporary IP number for any given session. You will probably not be affected by DHCP trouble at your ISP's end unless they run out of IP numbers, in which case you won't be able to make a connection.

DHCP servers use a priority protocol to assign a random IP number from a given pool of numbers anytime that a request is made from a client. If you run a DHCP server, you can set a *lease period* for each request. The lease period is the period of time that any given client can use an IP number before the client must break that connection and reregister with the DHCP server for a new IP number. Lease periods vary in duration from very short periods, such as 30 minutes or an hour, up to several billion seconds (which creates a simulated indefinite lease period).

TIP
Some regions, especially in Canada, are turning to an alternative method for assigning dynamic IP numbers. PPPoE (Peer-to-Peer Protocol over Ethernet) is a new method that controls network connections for high-speed hardware devices such as cable modems and DSL. If you have a PPPoE connection, you will probably receive an appropriate client when you install the software provided by your high-speed access provider.

Routers and Gateways

Once your network is working, you'll probably want to connect it to the Internet at some point. Even if you don't want to connect it directly to the Internet, you may need to connect your local network to another network for some reason. Such connections are usually made through a *gateway* machine or device. A gateway is just what its name implies: a machine that connects a network to another network. In the case of small networks, a gateway machine may be a single computer; large networks probably require the use of a dedicated router.

A *router* is a specialized piece of equipment that makes decisions about where to send network traffic, based on a variety of factors. Although ordinary computers can be made to act as routers, most administrators of large networks prefer to use machines designed for the particular tasks unique to routing. At the time we wrote this book—and for many years previously—the most popular routers were those made by the Cisco corporation.

Although they are not computers in the regular sense of the word, routers can take IP addresses just as regular computers can. When you want to connect to the Internet with one of the computers on the network, you can point out a *default route* to the Internet: the router's IP number. This tells the local computer that any traffic not explicitly destined for another machine within the local network should be sent through the gateway. Once that traffic gets to the gateway, the gateway machine will determine where to send the traffic so that it reaches its destination most efficiently. Setting up a default route on each individual networked computer is done with the `route` command and is a good way to memorize your router's IP number. The `route` command is used to update the kernel's IP routing table. The command has a somewhat complicated syntax with multiple options.

NOTE
To demonstrate the `route` command, we need to assume a different network than the one used previously. You can't use Class C private IP numbers unless you use a special function called IP masquerading or NAT (Network Address Translation) for this. We cover IP masquerading below.

Assume that you have a network consisting of several machines with IP numbers ranging from 253.232.15.26 to 253.232.15.30. In addition to these user machines and servers, you also have a dedicated router with the IP address 253.232.15.20. For data from your user machines and servers to reach the Internet, and for Internet traffic to reach your network machines, you need to configure the router as a gateway.

Issue the command

```
route add default gw 253.232.15.20
```

at the shell prompt. With this command, you set the dedicated router as the default gateway for the entire network. Any traffic sent outside the network, or received from machines not on the network, will pass through the router.

NOTE
Because routers handle a lot of traffic, they must be robust machines. They also can fail in ways unknown to most Unix administrators. This is why there are special certifications for routing specialists, and those certifications are often linked to particular hardware platforms such as Cisco routers.

Small Networks

It may be the case that you have a very small network, perhaps one at home or one used for a small business, that is connected to the Internet through a cable modem or a DSL hookup. In this case, the modem itself acts as the router; cable and DSL modems are external modems with complicated hardware inside. Because the modem may not be set up to handle multiple machines, you will need to set up gateway functions on one of your networked computers if you plan to use the Internet connection throughout the network.

WARNING   You may be prohibited by the terms of your agreement from using the cable modem or DSL modem to handle network traffic. Consult your service agreement and the provider's Acceptable Use Policy before you configure any networking services to take advantage of your constant connection.

To set up gateway functions on a network computer, you must first decide which computer to use for that purpose. Assume that you are using the same network as the one for which you created a gateway in the previous example, except that there is no dedicated router. If you decide that the machine 253.252.15.26 is to be the gateway, you can issue a modified `route` command at the shell prompt of that machine, as in

```
route add default eth0
```

This command tells the computer that all nonlocal traffic needs to be sent out through the first Ethernet device (`eth0` under Linux, `ep0` under FreeBSD, and `le0` under Solaris).

In this type of situation, the gateway typically has two NICs: one connected to the external modem and the other connected to the internal network through the hub. One IP address will be assigned to each card, and the card connected to the modem is defined as the default route. Thus, a full setup on this gateway machine under Linux would be done with the following commands:

```
ifconfig eth0 <first IP number> up
ifconfig eth1 <second IP number> up
route add default eth0
```

TIP   You can issue the same commands on a FreeBSD or Solaris gateway machine as long as you use the correct device terminology.

Then, you can configure the other machines in the network to recognize the new gateway machine. To do this, you need to designate the IP number of the second network device (`eth1` in this example) as the default route, by issuing the command

```
route add default gw <second IP number>
```

at the shell prompt of every other computer in the network.

IP Masquerading

One of the most useful tools for small networks is the technique of *IP masquerading*. This is the process through which all local network traffic appears to external machines as if it were coming from a single computer: the gateway machine. The advantage of using IP masquerading is that you need only one "real" IP number for your network; all the other numbers that you use for network computers can be taken from the Class C range for private networks.

> **NOTE**   Native masquerading functions are not available on Solaris. We explain how to set up masquerading under FreeBSD and Linux below.

For example, assume that you have a gateway machine with a static IP number. You received this IP number when you registered a domain name and arranged for the domain to be hosted somewhere, or when you signed up for cable or DSL Internet service. The machine's IP number, 201.121.42.12, has been assigned to one interface on the gateway machine. If you have a cable or DSL modem, that interface carries the IP number. The other interface on the gateway machine carries an IP number from the Class C private network range, such as 192.168.0.1. All the other machines on the network get Class C IP numbers as well. A diagram of this situation is shown in Figure 35.9.

Meanwhile, you've activated masquerade functions on the gateway machine. To the outside world, it appears that all the traffic generated from your network is coming from a single machine: the one identified with the IP number 201.121. 42.12. That machine will keep track of all the traffic sent to the Internet from the individual network machines. If responses come from external machines, the gateway will sort those responses out to the correct machines that initiated the external contact.

FIGURE 35.9:

IP masquerading can help you run an entire network's Internet traffic through a single number.

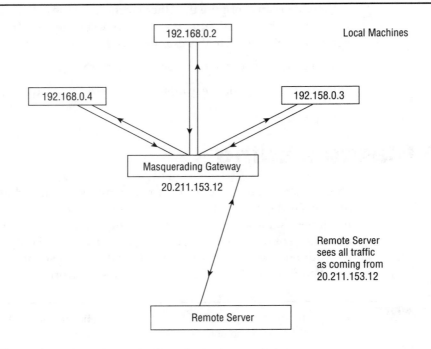

Neither of the methods that follow have any kind of security set up. If you just follow these steps and do not add any security measures, you are wide open and available for exploit. Before you begin to work with IP masquerading, read Chapter 38: "Network Security" and determine what your security plan will be for your entire network.

IP Masquerading with FreeBSD

FreeBSD uses the Network Address Translation Daemon (`natd`) to handle IP masquerading. To set up masquerading on a FreeBSD gateway machine, first make sure you have `natd` installed. Next, build a custom kernel with the following two options included:

```
options IPFIREWALL
options IPDIVERT
```

TIP

See Chapter 32: "Getting to Know the Kernel" for more information on building the FreeBSD kernel.

Open the /etc/services file in your favorite text editor and make sure that the following line is included:

```
natd 6668/divert #Network Address Translation socket
```

Save the file and exit the editor.

Add the following lines to your /etc/rc.firewall script. (If you don't have an /etc/rc.firewall script yet, create a new file with that name and add the following lines to it.)

```
/sbin/ipfw -f flush
/sbin/ipfw add divert natd all from any to any via eth0
/sbin/ipfs add pass all from any to any
```

Save the file and exit the editor.

Add the following lines to the /etc/rc.conf file:

```
natd_enable="YES"
natd_interface="eth0"
```

Save the file and exit the editor.

Once you've edited all the requisite files, issue the following commands at a shell prompt:

```
firewall=client
/etc/rc.firewall
```

Bring up your interfaces and set your routes as explained earlier in this chapter. Your masquerade should be running cleanly, and all outgoing traffic will appear to come from your single IP number.

IP Masquerading with Linux

Under Linux, the process of IP masquerading is a bit simpler. Compile your kernel with masquerade and IP forwarding support.

TIP

If you're using a stock kernel from one of the major Linux distributions, such as Red Hat, Slackware, or Debian, masquerading and forwarding are probably already compiled as modules in your kernel. Don't worry about recompiling unless this process doesn't work.

Bring up your network interfaces, then start the masquerading process by issuing the following commands at the shell prompt:

```
# ipchains -P forward DENY
# ipchains -A forward -I eth0 -j MASQ
# echo 1 > /proc/sys/net/ipv4/ip_forward
```

Next, set up your routes as explained earlier in the chapter. Your masquerade should now be running cleanly.

NOTE

By the time this book is printed (late 2000), the 2.4 version of the Linux kernel may already be available. In 2.4 kernels and later, the `ipchains` method shown here will no longer be the supported method of IP masquerading under Linux. Instead, the Linux kernel will support a new method called `netfilter`, which uses a different mechanism. You don't need to know how `netfilter` is different from `ipchains` to use it, but you do need to know that change is coming, and, if you obtain a copy of Linux that uses a kernel newer than 2.4.0, you'll have to find more recently written documentation to set up IP masquerading properly. The technical Netfilter Hacking HOWTO can be found at `http://netfilter.kernelnotes.org/unreliable-guides/netfilter-hacking-HOWTO.html`. Once the new kernel is released, more user-friendly guides to `netfilter` will likely be available on the Web. Check your favorite Linux news site.

Summary

Whether you have a standalone Unix computer or you administer a network containing dozens of machines, networking issues are important to you. Even the single-computer user will connect to another network at some point, and the techniques used on small local networks are the same as those used across the Internet. Networks are built by connecting computers with hardware, either Ethernet or telephone cable, and with hub devices that split traffic to the various computers connected to the network. Each computer must be configured to recognize the other computers on the network, as well as any gateway machines or routers that monitor traffic in and out of the network.

Configuration differs for dial-up connections to other networks, such as the Internet, and constant connections such as those found on Ethernet networks. The basic principles are the same, however, and once the devices are configured properly, both networks behave in the same manner as they deal with data. One reason for this similarity is that all networks use the unique identifying addresses called IP numbers; however, it is possible to "hide" a complete network behind one IP number so that the small network can handle all its network traffic while appearing as one machine on the Internet. Regardless of how your network is configured, or how many IP numbers you have allocated to that network, you can attach computers running different operating systems to the same network so that they can share resources.

The Distributed System

- Clients and Servers

- Distributing Services across Multiple Machines

- Backing Up Multiple Machines

- The Security Advantage

- Summary

Although the main purpose for many networks is to attach multiple user machines so that they can share resources and data, there are other advantages to network construction. One of the most significant advantages is the ability to distribute programs or data across several machines. This practice allows the system administrator to isolate individual services as necessary or integrate those machines fully into the network. No matter how many services you choose to run, you may find an increase in reliability and speed if you switch from multiple-service machines to a multiple-machine network.

In this chapter, we cover the client-server architecture of most Unix networks. We also show you how to build a distributed network, from the earliest planning stages to full implementation. Then, we explain how best to distribute your various services between the networked machines, and how to back up and manage those machines. Finally, we discuss the security advantages of using a multiple-machine setup for your servers. Regardless of the reasons for which you choose to distribute services across multiple machines, you will probably find that your system as a whole is easier to operate and less prone to successive failures if you create a system that does not rely on a single machine to provide every function required by the network and its users.

NOTE
As we've mentioned elsewhere in this book, you shouldn't run all the servers that are available *just because.* Rather, we encourage you to select the servers that make the most sense for you and your users, and to implement those servers in a tight and well-managed way. One benefit of a multiple-machine network is that you can work on servers individually without the concern that you might inadvertently bring the whole network down as you are working on one portion of it.

Clients and Servers

In Chapter 6: "The X Window System: An Overview," we introduced the concept of *client-server architecture.* The X Window System may not be the best illustration of client-server architecture, though it is certainly a popular implementation of the concept. Client-server mechanisms are integrated into Unix on a variety of levels. If, for example, you use your Web browser to request the home page at `http://www.cnn.com`, your browser acts as a client and makes a request to the

CNN Web server. The server then provides the requested data to your browser, which in turn shows you the news. The basic layout of a client-server architecture network is shown in Figure 36.1.

FIGURE 36.1:

Client-server architecture is based on requests and answers, and is the basis of many popular Unix programs and services.

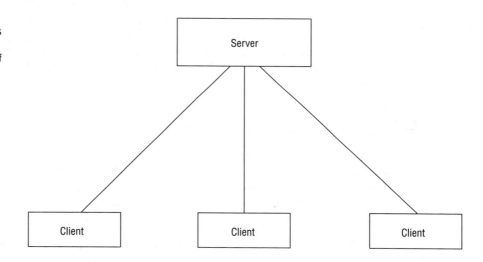

Though external services such as the Web and electronic mail are certainly the most well-known services, they are not the only ones that you might run as a system administrator. The X Window Server is certainly one that you will need to run if you want any sort of graphical display on your network's terminals. You may also want to run a font server to provide access to different fonts to the users on your network, without having to install the fonts individually on each of their machines.

However, though you may use local servers such as X or a font server to provide data and resources to your users, the widely distributed services are the ones that would benefit most from a distributed network of machines. Especially when dealing with the servers that handle Internet traffic, these distributed services can generate a large amount of traffic that may be enough to hamper or even bring down a network. Depending on your Internet connection method and speeds, even a popular mailing list might generate enough messages to significantly slow down your connection if a few of your users are subscribed to it or lists like it.

More likely, if you are running a mail server on the same machine that hosts your filesystem and other services, the load from dealing with the incoming mail will take a disproportionate amount of processor cycles. All other tasks on the system will take a back seat to the incoming e-mail, which can cause sluggishness and other unwanted effects for all users. This is one of the major drawbacks to using multiple-service machines on your network, especially if those machines also hold user accounts and data.

Multiple-Service Machines

The multiple-service machine is a standard part of many networks. In fact, many networks rely on a single server to generate all the responses to multiple client requests from the various user machines connected to the network. This is a reasonably efficient way to begin with your first network or to manage a very small network, but it's not particularly efficient in terms of processor use or security.

The most common multiple-service machine is the one on which the administrator decided to load as many services as possible, whether because she had the packages available or because she felt they were all necessary. We have seen many such machines carrying electronic mail servers, USENET news servers, Web servers, the various INET services, and other server programs, all on one machine. Figure 36.2 shows a representation of such a network. Yes, it's convenient, but at what cost?

A Multiple-Service Case Study

Consider espresso, a machine like the ones described in the previous paragraph. espresso is a reasonably fast and robust machine with a 5GB hard drive and 64MB of RAM. It is connected to the Internet through an aDSL connection, which provides high-speed broadband access (though weighted on the side of speedy downloads, not uploads). espresso's system administrator has loaded five or six different servers onto the machine, because it is the only server he has. The other five machines on the network are all user machines.

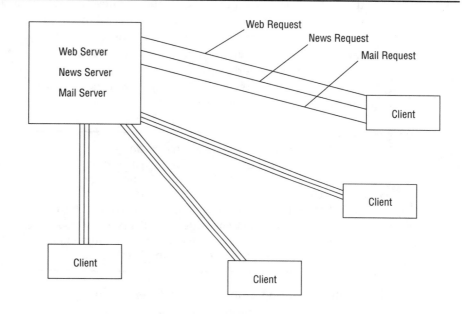

FIGURE 36.2:

Loading multiple servers onto one machine can be convenient, but it may affect speed and performance, and you have one single point of failure.

4 clients, 3 servers = 12 connections

Julia has an account on latte, one of the user machines that is connected to the espresso server. When she gets to work in the morning, she makes several simultaneous requests on her computer.

> **NOTE** No, these are not technically simultaneous requests; that is, she does not make them all at the exact same time. However, they occur very rapidly, within the span of a minute or two. For single-processor servers, that is often close enough to simultaneous to have the same effect.

Julia's regular habit is to log in, and then to check her e-mail, pull up her favorite Web portal, and open her newsreader at the same time. While she shifts between reading the data from each of these requests, she wants all the data there on her desktop immediately.

Each of Julia's morning tasks generates an individual request to a different service hosted on espresso. The e-mail request goes to the sendmail mail server, the Web request is fed to Apache, and the newsreader requests data from the INN news server. Because `espresso` hosts all these services, the requests are all handled by `espresso`'s processor in the order that they were received. If one of these requests generates a particularly complicated process or initiates a fairly large download—perhaps Julia reads a high-traffic mailing list or a graphics-intensive Web portal page—the other requests must wait for the completion of the first request's timeslice before their turn comes.

NOTE   Remember the difference between *timeslicing* and *task-switching*. Unix uses a timeslice method of processor cycle allocation, in which a series of requests is allocated a particular period of CPU time; other operating systems use a task-switching method, in which the first request in a series must be completed before the second request is begun. Even with the more efficient timeslice method, queued Unix requests must share processor time; if a large or complicated process is in the queue, it will take some time to finish because it can access the processor for only short, timed periods.

Julia's morning routine is less efficient simply because her requests must be queued and acted upon at the same time. Now, let's complicate the example by bringing up the topic of *network congestion*. Julia is not the only employee in her company; remember, `espresso` serves five user machines. If each of those other users makes the same requests to the server at the same time, everyone's requests are queued in the same line. Julia's Web request may not be next to her e-mail request in the queue; rather, it may be seven or eight requests back because several of her co-workers' requests arrived between the time `espresso` processed Julia's Web request and her e-mail request.

Tolerance for delay is different for each individual user. What may seem sufficiently quick to one user may be intolerable to another. However, the more users you have issuing requests to a multiple-server machine, the more likely that those users will all be increasingly frustrated as the single server machine works to fulfill all requests.

NOTE   The problem is often exacerbated as annoyed users continue to re-request the same items by clicking Reload or other similar menu items, because the processor sees each of these requests as new individual processes and not as an encouragement to hurry up.

This example should not give you the impression that multiple-server machines are always a bad idea. In fact, for the very small network or the administrator hampered by a lack of money, the multiple-server machine is a good solution. However, as you increase the number of users on your network, you should trace the kinds of requests that they send and consider splitting some high-traffic servers onto their own machines. This will speed up the overall network performance and will make the growing number of users happier.

Distributing Services across Multiple Machines

To avoid the sort of problems experienced by the users of the `espresso` server described in the previous section, the multiple services housed on one machine could be distributed to several different machines on the same network. There are several ways to distribute data and programs across multiple machines; some networks use individual machines for individual services, while others move particular parts of the filesystem onto different machines. Regardless of the method you choose, you need to figure out why you want to distribute services or files, and then come up with a plan to make the distribution as seamless and effective as possible.

In general, you'll be able to tell when you're ready to move to a distributed system. When you review your logs or check your system processes, you'll be able to tell what kind of requests are generating the most system traffic. You may be receiving a lot of Web requests, or you might be handling a deluge of incoming and outgoing e-mail. Any service that generates traffic out of proportion to the other major services is a likely candidate for a new networked machine of its own. The most commonly moved services are Web servers and electronic mail servers, because those two services generate a significant amount of network traffic.

When you begin to design your new multiple-machine server network, you'll have to think about hardware. Luckily, servers don't necessarily have to be flashy machines. You'll probably want your Web server machine to have a faster processor and a large hard drive if you serve a lot of page requests, simply because a faster machine will fulfill those requests faster and get them off your network. An e-mail server doesn't have to be quite as fancy, but you should put a nice big hard drive on an e-mail machine. That way, if you have users who don't delete a lot of their mail right away (or who save large files in their individual mail spools), you won't have to take resources away from other users to serve the hoarders.

TIP

If you're building a firewall or proxy machine (see the next section or Chapter 38: "Network Security"), you don't need a fancy machine at all. Go for something reliable and small; we ran a gateway on a 486 with a small hard drive for several years without trouble. As long as you can run an operating-system kernel that has no known security holes, the machine is sufficient for gateway use.

We suggest starting your multiple-machine server network with a separate machine dedicated to Web service. Web servers are some of the most frequently cracked servers on the Internet, and Web pages are data that users expect to receive quickly without trouble. All the advantages of a distributed system come into play with a Web server machine. So, when you get ready to install Apache because you are about to begin hosting your own domain's Web pages, consider doing so on a separate machine.

After you've worked out the bugs with an Apache machine, we suggest that you next split off your e-mail server. This is especially important if you have a large number of users or a smaller number who are intensive e-mail users. Putting e-mail on a separate machine means that you can devote a larger portion of the hard drive to the incoming mail spool, thus lessening the time you need to spend on harassing your users to delete mail or move it to their /home directories after it's read.

WARNING

If you want to build a POP server so that your users can all log in remotely with graphical mail readers such as Eudora, it's best to place this server on a separate machine. POP servers pass their passwords in clear text, and that's a security risk you don't need on your main filesystem machine, especially if your users' mail passwords are the same as their login passwords.

Other servers don't generate as much traffic and thus don't need their own machines as much as Apache and your e-mail server. However, depending on the way in which you use your network, you may find that it's more logical to put these other servers on their own machines. If you run a small ISP, you'll probably want to put USENET news on its own machine. If you serve a lot of file transfer requests, you might want to put an FTP server on its own machine; however, because so many people use Web browsers to access FTP sites these days, we suggest putting your FTP server on the same machine as the Web server. That way, users making FTP requests from a browser will experience less lag as the request is transmitted to the FTP server. A sample reorganization of espresso's network is shown in Figure 36.3.

FIGURE 36.3:

espresso's administrator might reorganize network services on multiple machines like this.

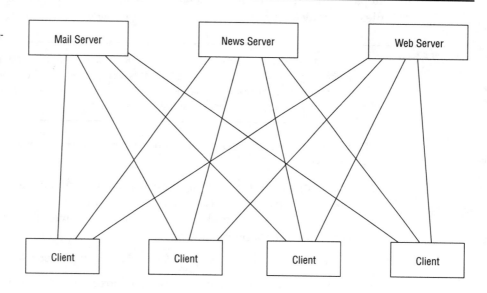

No Server has more than 4 connections

Backing Up Multiple Machines

One task that does become more complicated as you spread services across multiple machines is the process of backing up your files. We've known too many administrators who start to slack off on their backup duties as the number of machines to back up increases. Don't lose track of your backups. The multiple-machine network is one of the best reasons to use cron and at, the automatic scheduling tools introduced in Chapter 28: "System Programming."

You can set up an automatic program that will create backup files without any intervention from you or others on the network, and you will always have a reasonably current backup of the many machines on your network.

The easiest way to back up multiple machines on a network is described in the steps below. Make sure that you have sufficient room to store the multiple backup files; you may even want to set up a separate machine just for storing backups.

WARNING   No matter how you handle the backups, never keep a backup file on the same machine from which it was created. That is, don't keep your Web backup file on the machine that holds the Apache Web server. If the machine crashes or is cracked, you won't have access to the backup files you need to rebuild the service.

To set up automatic backups for your multiple-machine service network, follow this process:

1. Set up `cron` jobs on each machine, using the `crontab -e` tool, that will generate backup archives. The easiest way to build the `/etc/crontab` entry is to use the `tar` command when creating the archives. For example, you could use the following line as an entry in `/etc/crontab`:

    ```
    tar cvf  /backupdir/$HOSTNAME-`date`.tgz /important-dir
    ```

2. Make sure that your entries in `/etc/crontab` on all the server machines point the backup archives to a uniform location on each machine. We suggest a directory called `/backup` to make the location easy to remember.

3. Set up a `cron` job on your central machine that will use the `rsync` command. `rsync` will synchronize all the `/backup` directories on all the relevant machines. A sample entry might be

    ```
    rsync -e ssh -ar espresso:/backup/ /backup/
    ```

    In this example, there are several critical flags:

    *   `-e` designates the method of network connection; we recommend `ssh` for security reasons.

    *   `-a` designates *archive mode,* meaning that everything in `/backup` is saved.

    *   `-r` designates *recursive mode,* meaning that subdirectories will also be synchronized.

Using the syntax of this example means that all files from the named machine (espresso) will be copied to the local machine that issues the rsync command.

4. Repeat this command with crontab -e for every server machine you want to back up to the local machine.

The Security Advantage

Distributing services across multiple machines has a distinct security advantage. If you run a service on an individual machine, you can isolate that machine quickly if a problem occurs. Likewise, you might want to password-protect the individual server so that even users on the same network need to verify their identities before the server will permit access.

Assume that you are running Apache on an individual machine to serve the large number of requests you get for your corporate Web pages. If the Web server gets cracked, you can shut down the Web machine as soon as you notice the intrusion. However, even though your Web server is offline and those pages can't be accessed by anyone outside or inside your network, all other services continue to work, and the security risk is relatively small. If you had been running Apache on a multiple-service machine, however, you might have had to bring down the entire machine to check the system and see what had been affected or compromised. Once the cracker had access to the Web server, he also had access to all the other files on the multiple-server machine because the filesystem was easily accessible.

It makes sense to isolate the servers that are usually called from outside the network and place those servers on individual machines connected to the network. In addition to speeding up the response to individual requests, it also makes those servers easier to seal off against external attacks. You can make the network even more secure if you limit outgoing and incoming access to the server machines so that other computers on the network won't be able to make random connections to the servers.

Reinforcing Multiple-Server Security

Before you begin to consider distributing your various services across multiple machines, we strongly encourage you to read Chapter 38: "Network Security." If you run servers and have traffic robust enough to consider using multiple machines, you probably have a need for extra security precautions. In particular, you should set up firewalls or proxies for your users and your most frequently used services.

If you are using a Unix variant that has the ability to implement firewalls, use it. You can firewall off the ports you aren't using, and you can lock down all ports on a given service machine that aren't used for that service. For example, if you are running an electronic mail server on a given machine, you can lock down all ports not needed by either the server or the connection to the local network. That limits the number of connections made to the e-mail machine; if you see unusual activity in the logs, centering on ports not used by the mail server, you know that something untoward is going on.

We recommend a gateway system, where you place an individual machine at the front door of your internal network. All traffic will pass through the gateway to be routed to the appropriate machine. If you have set up internal rules that define the type of traffic that's permissible on your system, the gateway machine will enforce those rules. See Chapter 38 for more information on gateways, and Figure 36.4 for a diagram of a multiple-server network that uses a gateway (in this figure, we've also shown the effect of locking down the Web server machine in response to a security breach).

You should also consider using proxies in your security regimen. If you set up a proxy, your internal users must pass their requests through an internal guard machine before those requests are sent to the outside world. This helps to shield your internal network machines from any security risks that might occur while the requests are being transmitted to the external world.

TIP
One of the security programs on the CD-ROM included with this book, Dante, is a self-contained proxy package. You can find other useful security software in one of the many Unix file archives on the Web; because security software changes so rapidly in response to real-world needs, you are best served by finding new and effective software to serve your proxy and gatewaying needs.

FIGURE 36.4:

A gateway machine and individual server machines lead to a more secure network that can isolate individual servers in case of trouble.

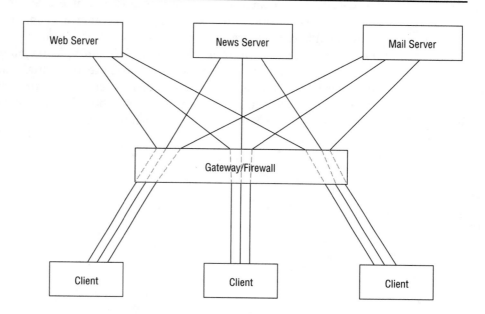

Summary

Although most beginning network administrators load all the servers they wish to run onto a single machine, this is not always the best way to handle multiple servers. The Unix client-server architecture can run successfully whether the servers and clients are on separate machines or on the same computer, but the quality of the connection may vary depending on how heavily the various servers are used and where the requests originate.

In contrast to the single machine running multiple servers, we suggest that any administrator experiencing significant request load consider building a multiple-machine server network. By allocating individual services to individual machines, the administrator can spread out service requests, increase the amount of processor cycles available to an individual service, and organize access to the various services on the network. With various Unix tools such as `cron`, the administrator's work load may not increase significantly even if the number of machines on the network increases by four or five. In addition, multiple machines decrease the security vulnerability of the network because the individual machines can be password-protected. If a server machine is cracked, the administrator can remove it from the network and seal off any potential breaches before the cracker has the opportunity to break into any other machines.

CHAPTER

THIRTY-SEVEN

Integrating Unix with Other Platforms

- Integrating One Unix with Other Unices

- Integrating Unix and Windows

- Integrating Unix and MacOS

- Summary

It is the rare network that has machines all running the same operating system. Even on the smallest networks with which we're familiar, multiple operating systems are at play. Whether it's simply a stray Windows machine or a Macintosh or two, or as complex as a Solaris farm managed by a few Linux servers and a BSD gateway machine, it is a common situation for Unix administrators to find themselves working with heterogeneous networks on a regular basis.

> **NOTE** You might even choose to build a network that uses certain types of machines for their best purposes and other machines for other uses. That's what most Unix administrators do, whether under their own definition of *best* or under a superior manager's definition. Perhaps the most common example is the corporate network that's filled with Windows 98 or NT machines for average users, but that uses Linux or BSD for all the critical servers.

Over the years, several tools have been developed to make working with multiple operating systems a little easier. Certainly, the flexibility and power of the Unix operating systems mean that integrating different Unix variants is not as hard as working with other non-Unix operating systems. Still, different Unices handle identical operations in very different ways; consider the differences between System V printing and Berkeley print management, differences that make integrating Solaris and BSD or Linux machines a bit difficult if you need to share printers across the network. If you need to integrate only different Unix-based operating systems, though, you have a relatively easy path ahead of you.

Those who are working with integrated networks that have radically different operating systems, such as Windows or MacOS, have a bit more work ahead of them. Luckily, the development community has recognized the practical realities of the business software world, and we now have access to two programs that make heterogeneous networks a much more reliable and practical reality. With Samba, you can integrate Windows machines into your Unix-based network (or Unix machines into your NT-based network), share files and print jobs, and manage your network machines on either the Windows or the Unix machines. With `netatalk`, you can use the native AppleTalk networking protocol with kernel-level support on most Unices. Like Samba, `netatalk` allows you to share files and print jobs, and to work nearly seamlessly across the network regardless of the type of machine or operating system being used.

In this chapter, we introduce three major programs that make it easier for you to work with a heterogeneous network, whether it is based solely on Unix or uses other operating systems as well. First, we introduce the Network File System (NFS). NFS acts as a bridge between different Unices, allowing them to mount each others' filesystems remotely and share files across the network. There are some security issues with NFS, but it is far too useful to ignore and is really the only way in which different Unices can coexist happily. We also spend some time discussing Samba, from installation to smooth operation, and show you how to set up Samba so that the network is truly transparent to all your users whether on Windows or Unix. Finally, we introduce `netatalk` and show you how to install it so that you can use Macintoshes on your network without trouble.

Integrating One Unix with Other Unices

Unix machines share resources by sharing files. Remember, everything in Unix is represented as a file, so by sharing files you are able to share the entire contents of a machine if you want to do so. File sharing is an effective way to distribute data to a number of users, regardless of how they are connected to the network. If you have some specialized machines attached to the network, such as servers or machines running particular programs like databases, other machines on the network can access the files on these special machines without having to copy the files directly to their own hard drives.

The unique thing about file sharing over Unix is that directories can be mounted across the network, but will appear as if they are on the local machine. That is, if you are sitting at machine A, you can mount the `/public` directory on machine B and use it as if it were local. When you're finished, just unmount the directory and go on with your business. This is made possible through NFS, the Network File System. NFS is the method used to share files among Unix computers, regardless of the Unix variant installed on any individual computer. NFS is the standard; though it does have some known problems—mostly security-related—there is no better alternative at this point. We recommend that, if you have a network with multiple Unix machines, you run NFS. It makes life a lot simpler.

TIP

You can also use NFS to streamline certain automatic processes. For example, Joe has NFS-mounted his mailbox file on the e-mail server machine to his local workstation. When mail arrives on the server, it triggers the notification (**biff**) program on his workstation and alerts him to new mail. He has his mailreader set to read mail directly from the server. This eliminates the step of downloading mail from the server to the workstation, which might take some time if there are many bulky attachments or there is a lot of mail. File sharing is an efficient way to conserve resources regardless of the size of the network.

Obtaining and Installing NFS

NFS is included with nearly all Unix distributions. It is likely that, when you installed your operating system, NFS was also installed at the same time. If you haven't edited your kernel in any way (especially the case for Linux users), you probably still have NFS available to you. Check the `/etc/init.d` directory for a script called `nfs-server`; the presence of this script means that an NFS server is active and installed on the system. Should you not have NFS or have an old version that needs to be upgraded, you can obtain a copy of NFS at any Unix software archive.

TIP

You'll probably want to install NIS at the same time. NIS is the Network Information System, which serves as a centralized database of important administrative data such as passwords and the `/etc/hosts` file. Although you can run NFS without NIS, the larger your network, the more likely it is that you will appreciate the work NIS does.

Install NFS using the process explained in Chapter 31: "Installing and Managing Software." Once you have it installed, you will need to configure a variety of files and start several daemons before you are able to use NFS. Note that you must install both an NFS server (usually on your main server machine, unless you want to have a separate fileserver machine) and an NFS client on each machine that will access the server and share its files.

NOTE   NFS requires actual, addressable physical disk space to function. You can provide NFS its disk space either by dedicating a separate machine to file serving or by creating a partition devoted to NFS. For security reasons, you probably don't want to install the NFS server on the main partition of your sole server; the security holes in NFS are well-known and easily exploited.

Configuring an NFS Server

If you haven't configured your boot scripts to start up the NFS programs when you boot the system, do so. It will save time when you realize you need a remotely mounted directory and the NFS server isn't running.

NOTE   To mount a remote filesystem, the **nfsd** daemon must be running on the server machine, and the **mountd** daemon must be running on the client machine. Check this with a simple **ps** command before you attempt to mount any directories so that you can start the daemons by hand if necessary.

In Chapter 30: "Disks and Filesystem Management," we introduced the concept of filesystem mounting. Under Unix, any external filesystem must be mounted before it can be used and must be unmounted when you are finished working with it. This is true for filesystems on floppy disks, or on CD-ROM or DVD-ROM drives, and for remotely mounted filesystems accessed through NFS. Unlike the case with CD-ROMs or floppy disks, however, when you mount a directory through NFS, you must do some work on both the client and the server end before you can have the directory.

Assume that you have a user machine, belgium, connected via a network to a server machine, europe. You want to export the /usr/local filesystem from europe to belgium so that you can use the files contained in that directory. To gain access to that directory, you must approve it for mounting on europe before belgium's NFS client can mount it.

To export the /usr/local directory under Linux and FreeBSD, log into europe as root (or assume superuser powers in your favorite manner). Open the file /etc/exports in a text editor, and add the following line:

```
/usr/local              belgium
```

In this entry, `/usr/local` is the filesystem being exported, and `belgium` is the machine that has permission to obtain it. Save the file and exit the editor. Still as root, issue the command

```
exportfs
```

at the shell prompt. This command makes all the directories listed in `/etc/exports` available for export, whether or not they will be accessed immediately.

NOTE   On large networks, the `/etc/exports` file may be quite long. Each time it is edited, you must reissue the command `exportfs` to encompass the new entries as well as the old.

NOTE   As is the case in several other areas, Solaris handles NFS sharing differently. Solaris uses the `/etc/dfs/dfstab` file instead of `/etc/exports`, and entries in that file take the form `share -o rw=belgium -d "Europe Usr Local" /mn/europe/usr/local`. Consult the manual page for `share` to learn more about the syntax for this file.

Mounting Networked File Systems

Return to the client machine, `belgium`, and log into the root account or otherwise assume superuser powers. You first need to make a mount point for the new filesystem; you can do this easily just by creating a new, empty directory called something like `/network` or `/usrlocal`. After the empty directory is created, issue the command

```
mount -t nfs europe:/usr/local /network
```

The NFS client goes to the `europe` NFS server, which checks to see whether `belgium` is eligible to receive the `/usr/local` directory. Because `belgium` is listed in the `/etc/exports` file along with this directory, the NFS server releases the directory. The local client then mounts the remote directory at the new mount point, and you can use the files there as you would use them on `europe`.

Automatic Mounting with /etc/fstab

If you find yourself mounting the same remote directories repeatedly, you may want to use NFS's automatic mounting capabilities. To mount remote directories automatically every time you boot your system, you can use the file /etc/fstab to define those directories. /etc/fstab contains a list of all the directories that should be mounted at boot; most of them are local, but you can place NFS directories here as well. A typical /etc/fstab file looks like this:

```
/dev/hda1    /            ext2    defaults    1 1
/dev/hda5    /ftp         ext2    defaults    1 2
/dev/hdc1    /home        ext2    defaults    1 2
/dev/hdc5    /www         ext2    defaults    1 2
/dev/hda7    swap         swap    defaults    0 0
/dev/fd0     /mnt/floppy  ext2    noauto      0 0
/dev/cdrom   /mnt/cdrom   iso9660 noauto,ro   0 0
none         /proc        proc    defaults    0 0
```

Use /etc/fstab to make your life easier. It can handle much of the drudgery of mounting filesystems and will ensure that you never forget to mount a critical filesystem.

To make an entry in /etc/fstab, you must be root. Open the file in your favorite text editor and make entries for each directory you wish to mount automatically, using the syntax

```
devicename  mountpoint  directorytype options  dump pass
```

Thus, you need to supply the device that contains the desired directory, the location where it will be mounted locally, the type of directory it is, any options such as read-only mode (ro), and its dump and pass numbers, which are used for system-checking purposes only. Save the file and exit; you will need to reboot before the settings in this file take effect.

TIP

Unlike Windows and MacOS, Unix machines do not automatically mount the CD-ROM and floppy drives. If you are used to having those drives available all the time, you should put them into /etc/fstab. Otherwise, you'll have to mount them by hand when you want to use removable media. Some Unix variants automount these devices, which you'll know is the case if they are already in /etc/fstab when you check the file.

NFS Security Issues

There are several known security holes in the Network File System. Because they are so well-known, it is part of most crackers' routine to check for NFS holes and exploit them if found. However, just because these holes exist is no reason to avoid running the very useful NFS altogether; you simply need to take some precautions when you set up your NFS server and mount your directories.

The easiest thing to do is to avoid setting up an NFS server on your firewall or gateway machine. In Chapter 36: "The Distributed System," we showed you how to stagger your various network services across multiple machines for network speed and security. If you do this, and implement the firewalls described in Chapter 38: "Network Security," you will have a relatively safe network. If you then mount the NFS server on your firewall or gateway machine, though, you have reintroduced a security breach. Keep shared files away from any externally accessed machines, and limit your NFS file sharing to other machines on the network. That will cut down on your security exposure.

NFS's main security flaw is that it isn't very good in dealing with password authentication. Removing your server from externally accessible machines is a good start, as is locating and installing all available security patches for your particular Unix variant. Other useful tips include the following:

- Where possible, export filesystems as read-only to avoid the possibility that someone will rewrite the filesystems at their origin.

- Edit your **/etc/exports** file entries so that they export filesystems only to fully qualified domain names, not to single machine names.

- Never place a **localhost** reference in **/etc/exports**.

- Check **/etc/exports** carefully for typing mistakes.

- Don't make changes to **/etc/exports** without running **exportfs** immediately after closing the **/etc/exports** file.

Although these may seem like small steps, they make it much more difficult for crackers to run the common exploits that make NFS vulnerable, such as IP spoofing.

Integrating Unix and Windows

Wouldn't it be nice to use NFS to transfer files between Unix and Windows computers? Unfortunately, you can't. One of the major reasons why Unix and Windows operating systems don't communicate very well is that they each use a different protocol to transfer data. The Windows protocol is called SMB (Session Message Block), and the SMB protocol is not one native to Unix. Although you could spend long hours writing your own conversion scripts, there's no reason to do so.

The program that makes working with mixed Unix-Windows networks a simple job is called Samba. Samba is a suite of programs that allows Unix machines to make use of the SMB protocol, thus enabling file sharing between both kinds of machines. In fact, Samba can even help your Unix servers emulate the attributes of Windows NT servers (with the reliability of Unix) so that Windows client computers can work most efficiently with the servers.

NOTE   The definitive resource for Samba is *Using Samba,* by Robert Eckstein, David Collier-Brown, and Peter Kelly (O'Reilly & Associates, 1999). Though the authors are not part of the Samba development team, the book is so comprehensive that the team has adopted it as the official documentation for the package.

If we didn't have Samba, it would be very difficult to share files across a multiple-operating-system network, and it's likely that Unix (Linux and FreeBSD in particular) would be much less integrated into the everyday life of many corporate and academic mega-networks.

TIP   Depending on your Unix variant, Samba may have been installed when you installed the operating system. We know of a few Linux distributions that install Samba automatically. Check the /etc/init.d directory for the subdirectory /etc/init.d/samba. If it exists, you already have Samba and probably just need to configure it.

Obtaining and Installing Samba

There is a copy of Samba on the CD-ROM that accompanies this book. You may also have a version of Samba on the CD-ROMs that contain your operating system, but—depending on when you purchased this book or obtained your operating-system CD—you'll probably want to download the most current version to take advantage of the latest features. You can get Samba from `http://www.samba.org`, the home of the Samba team. The current version is 2.0.x, which has been available for about a year.

TIP If you like Samba, the developer welcomes contributions of hardware, monetary donations, or pizza. Just remember that Andrew Tridgell (the developer) lives in Australia, so you can't just send him a Domino's delivery. He'd be happy to discuss pizza options with you, though, and some ideas are listed at `http://us4.samba.org/samba/docs/FAQ/#19`. The pizza concept started as a joke, but several people have managed to send Andrew some pizza.

Install Samba as you would any other program, using the methods introduced in Chapter 31: "Installing and Managing Software." Once you have built the program, you'll need to configure it before it can be used. Samba configuration is done with the `/etc/samba/smb.conf` file.

Configuring Samba

Open the `/etc/samba/smb.conf` file in your favorite text editor. This file is quite easy to work with, because it is constructed modularly and the individual entries are laid out clearly. You'll need to have a `[global]` entry regardless of how large your network is and an individual entry for each directory that you want to share with Windows machines on your network.

NOTE In `/etc/samba/smb.conf`, comments are denoted differently than in other programs we've shown you throughout the book. Where most other programs use the hashmark (#) to denote a comment, the `smb.conf` file uses the semicolon (;). Any line beginning with a semicolon is a comment and will not be parsed by the program when it runs.

The global configuration entry defines the network as a whole for your Windows machines. The syntax is quite easy to read, and Samba configuration files in general use English expressions instead of terse abbreviations or acronyms.

One very minimal global configuration for a heterogeneous network might look like this:

```
[global]
      workgroup = NETWORK
      server string = parrot
      encrypt passwords = Yes
      update encrypted = Yes
      log file = /var/log/samba/log
      max log size = 50
      socket options = TCP_NODELAY SO_RCVBUF=8192 ➥
         SO_SNDUP=8192
      dns proxy = No
```

Using this configuration will set the name of the network as NETWORK when the Windows machine's Network Neighborhood folder is opened. You can use anything you want for the network name, though using a descriptive name is better. The value of server string is the name that will appear under the server's icon in the folder. Samba will deliver its logs to /var/log/samba/log (the default), and the log file will contain only the 50 most recent lines. The socket options define the way in which data is transferred across the network, and the dns proxy entry determines whether the server will act as a local DNS proxy server.

Once you have the global entry defined, you need to add an entry for each directory that you want to share with the Windows machines on your network. This may seem overwhelming or not particularly useful, but it does make sense; you may not want to share every directory on the main server with all your user machines. Instead, you can enable the particular directories that you want to share and rest comfortably knowing that nonenabled directories will not be visible to the Windows users on your network.

To enable a particular directory, you need to make an entry in /etc/init.d/samba/conf that takes this form:

```
[public]
      comment = public workspace
         path = /usr/public
         guest ok = yes
         writable = yes
         printable = no
         public = yes
```

This basic syntax defines the name of the shared directory and some parameters for how it is available to network users. The name in the brackets will be shown under the directory's icon in the Network Neighborhood folder on the Windows machine. The `path` entry defines the actual path on the Unix server, while the `guest ok` field determines whether a user can access the directory without her individual username and password. The `writable` and `printable` entries set the permissions on the directory, and the `public` entry determines whether the directory will be visible to users.

TIP

If you want to share documents or programs, but don't want to run the risk of having a user overwrite your data, set the `writable` field to No. This way, users will be able to view or copy the data, but they won't be able to affect the initial files. You might find this especially useful when dealing with configuration files or templates.

Repeat similar entries for each directory that you want to share with your users across the Samba network. If you don't want to share system directories, just don't place an entry into /etc/init.d/samba/conf for that directory. You can also create new directories on the server that are intended for sharing and place copies of sharable files into those directories without removing them from their default locations.

NOTE

Consult the manual page for `smb.conf` if you want to use more complicated entries for your various directories. Access the page by issuing the command `man smb.conf` at the shell prompt, after you've installed Samba.

Starting Samba

When you have finished editing /etc/init.d/samba/conf, you can start Samba and check your network. Restart the Samba server by issuing the command

```
/etc/init.d/samba restart
```

at a shell prompt. The Samba server will restart on the Unix machine with the settings you made in the configuration file, and you should be able to see the Windows machines on your network. However, you probably won't be able to see the Unix machine from your Windows machine right away.

Go to the Windows machine and open the Control Panel. Select the Network option, and click on the Properties tab. Check to be sure that you have the correct gateway and DNS IP numbers entered in those fields; these should be the same IP numbers that are used by the Unix server. This will enable you to share an Internet connection over the Samba connection. When you have the correct IP numbers entered, click the Identification tab.

Enter the Windows machine's name and the network name in the appropriate spaces; you should use the same name for the network that you defined in the global entry of `/etc/init.d/samba/conf`. Click Apply to set your changes, then click OK to exit the Network configuration. If the new network does not appear in Network Neighborhood right away, reboot. The network should appear after rebooting.

NOTE   You may not be used to defining machine names for Windows machines. If you have a consistent naming scheme for your Unix network machines, try to keep the same theme with your Windows machines. You will need a machine name here so that the Unix server can understand your Windows machine as it transfers data across the Samba connection.

Samba and Windows 98

Those administrators who are trying to network Windows 98 machines with Samba should be careful. Windows 98, late versions of Windows 95, and Windows ME use a new password encryption scheme that isn't covered natively by Samba yet. Not only is this password mechanism not included by default in Samba, you may have to hack the Windows Registry to get Samba to work properly.

As with anyone who works with the guts of Windows, hacking the Registry is something we view with caution and not a small amount of dread. We aren't going to tell you how to modify the Registry here, because we think that it's best if you read the documentation before you try to do anything with the Registry. Regardless of your Unix variant, go read the Samba HOWTO document at `http://www.linuxdoc.org/HOWTO/SMB-HOWTO.html`. This document will give you more information on the password issues and show you some basic Registry hacks that might fix the problem.

Continued on next page

You should also read the documentation that was installed along with Samba on your machine. Read ENCRYPTION.txt, Win95.txt, and WinNT.txt to get a better idea of the way in which the password encryption method affects Samba and what you can do to counter its effects.

Don't think that you can't use Samba unless you're running an early version of Windows 95. Samba works just fine with every version of Windows; you just need to hack it a bit if you're using a newer version of the operating system.

Print Sharing with Samba

One of the real advantages of running Samba is that you can use a single printer across the network, whether the print job is coming from a Windows machine or a Unix machine. It's easiest to attach the printer to the Unix server, because printer configuration is a bit easier under Unix. As we mentioned in Chapter 33: "Managing Print Services," print sharing is an effective way to share an expensive printer or printing device between several workstations without having to purchase an identical unit for each workstation that needs access to that kind of resource.

To share a printer attached to a Unix machine with a Windows machine across a Samba connection, you'll need to edit the configuration file again. Open /etc/init.d/samba/conf in your favorite text editor and locate the global configuration entry you created when you set up Samba. At the end of the global entry (but still part of that entry), add the following lines:

```
printing = bsd
    printcap name = /etc/printcap
    load printers = yes
    log file = /var/log/samba/log
    lock directory = /var/lock/samba
```

These lines define the method of printing (BSD instead of System V), the location of the /etc/printcap file used by Berkeley-style printing, and the location of the log and lock files. The third line determines whether printers are loaded onto the network each time the Samba server is restarted.

Once you have finished editing the global entry, you will need to build a new section that configures all your systemwide printer options. Use the following block of code as an example:

```
[printers]
    comment = All Printers
```

```
security = server
path = /var/spool/lpd/lp
browseable = No
printable = Yes
public = Yes
writable = No
create mode = 0700
```

With these lines, you define the overall way in which print jobs are handled on the network. The values of these entries determine the location of the print spool (where jobs from the Windows machines will be sent), the permissions for the print spool, and the printers to which these settings apply.

When you have established the general printer settings, it's time to create individual entries for each networked printer. As with the general Samba configuration, each printer needs its own entry so that it can have individual configuration options. Although the global printer entry defines the overarching way in which jobs are handled, the individual entries show the printer name and path, and other important information that is unique to each printer. To define these entries, use the following format:

```
[ljet]
    security = server
    path = /var/spool/lpd/lp
    printer name = laserjet1
    writable = Yes
    public = Yes
    printable = Yes
    print command = lpr -r -h -P %p %s
```

NOTE The individual printer configuration entries will be different depending on the type of printer being configured. The entry above is suitable for a Hewlett-Packard LaserJet printer, but might not work with other laser printers. To learn which command you need to use with your printer, consult the `lpd` manual page by issuing the command `man lpd` at a shell prompt.

When you have finished configuring your printers, save the file and exit. You'll need to restart the Samba server so that it recognizes the new printers and can make them available to all the machines on the network. To restart the server, issue the command

```
/etc/init.d/samba restart
```

at a shell prompt.

Next, go to the Windows machine and open the Printers folder by selecting Start ➣ Settings ➣ Printers. Locate the new printer and double-click its icon. When the configuration screen appears, configure the new printer as a network printer. You can choose to make it your default or not; if it is not the default, a printer attached to the local machine is likely the default. Click OK to save and exit the Printers folder; you should now be able to select the networked printer from the Print menu of your Windows programs.

TIP
Make an inkjet or other nonnetworkable local printer the default if possible. It's a lot cheaper to print drafts and Web pages on an inkjet than it is on a laser printer. Use the laser for final versions, and share it over the network to amortize its cost.

Printing from Unix to a Windows Printer

To use a printer attached to a Windows machine as a networked printer, you have to work in reverse of the method described above. First, open the Network configuration on your Windows machine by opening the Control Panel and double-clicking the Network icon. Select the network component that you use for the network (probably a network card) from the list, and click the File and Print Sharing button.

In the File and Print Sharing dialog box that appears, click the check box next to I Want to Be Able to Allow Others to Print to My Printer and click OK. You will be returned to the main Network configuration window; click OK to save and exit the tool. The Windows printer is now enabled as a networked printer and will handle external print requests as it would handle local print requests.

Once Windows is configured properly, return to the Unix machine and open whatever printer configuration tool you use. (Working with Windows printers is easiest if you're using a graphical printer administration tool, such as those found in KDE or Gnome.) For example, using the KDE tool, you'd open the printer configuration and select the networked printer option, then set the type as Windows. Click the Browse button and locate the newly networked printer on the network; select it and provide a username and password if prompted. This is the same username and password you use to log onto networking in Windows, not your Unix account name and password. Click Finish to save your changes. Other printer administration tools work in much the same manner.

Integrating Unix and MacOS

Although Samba is immensely useful for administrators with both Windows and Unix machines on the same network, it unfortunately cannot integrate Macintoshes into the same network. Those who have Macs that need to be networked with Unix machines need a different program called `netatalk`. `netatalk` does not use the SMB protocol used by Samba; instead, it uses a kernel-level mechanism that mirrors the native AppleTalk protocol used by MacOS to network between Macintoshes and other Apple computers and peripherals.

TIP

You can obtain the `netatalk` packages from various file archives, though the Web site for the project is located at `http://www.umich.edu/~rsug/netatalk/`. This site contains downloads, a good HOWTO document, and links to other sites with helpful tips. The most up-to-date version can always be obtained here, so it's a good place to start. The current stable version is 1.3.3, with a 1.4 beta version. We recommend sticking with the stable versions, because file and print sharing tend to be important enough to require software with a minimal amount of bugs.

Install `netatalk` using the methods described in Chapter 31: "Installing and Managing Software." The `netatalk` source code has been installed successfully on a wide variety of Unix variants, including all the variants covered in this book. If you find a problem with your particular Unix, check the bug notes and other messages at the `netatalk` Web site; it's possible that a simple configuration change will make the program work properly for you.

NOTE

Before you begin to install `netatalk`, open `Makefile` (found in the directory where you unpacked the code) and set the destination directory with the entry `DESTDIR=/usr/local/atalk`. This is the default, but if you want `netatalk` to install somewhere else, you will need to set the new location in `Makefile`.

`netatalk` versions 1.3.3 and higher support Linux; FreeBSD versions 2.2 and higher contain `netatalk` support; and the current beta version of `netatalk` (1.4b2) supports Solaris 2.4 and higher. See the "Solaris and `netatalk`" section later in this chapter for information on running this beta version with your Solaris installation.

Configuring netatalk

Once netatalk is installed, you will need to configure it. The default configuration files (and all the other netatalk files) may be found in the /etc/netatalk/conf directory, but will need to be copied to your /usr/local/atalk/etc directory before you can use them. You will find several configuration files for netatalk:

- atalkd.conf
- apfd.conf
- AppleVolumes.default
- AppleVolumes.system
- config

atalkd.conf

The atalkd.conf file defines the network interfaces for the Macintoshes so that they can participate in network traffic. You don't really need to have anything in this file, because the atalkd daemon can auto-detect the interface configuration on your network. If you feel more comfortable defining an interface, the only entry you need to include would be eth0 for a Linux or FreeBSD box, or le0 for a Solaris machine.

NOTE   Solaris administrators must place the le0 entry in this file. atalkd won't work properly on Solaris if you leave the atalkd.conf file empty.

The atalkd.conf file is straightforward and quite short. The file is well-commented, so that you can figure out what you might need to do if you want to edit the configuration of atalkd on your system. Here is a sample atalkd.conf file:

```
#
#     Format of lines in this file:
#
#         interface [ -seed ] [ -phase [ 1 | 2 ) ] ➡
#         [ -addr net.node ] [ -net first[-last] ]
#         [ -zone ZoneName ] . . .
#
# -seed only works if you have multi-interfaces. Any
    # missing arguments are automatically configured from
```

```
# the network. Note: lines can't actually be split,
# tho it's a good idea.
#
# Some examples:
#
#    The simplest case is no atalkd.conf. This works on
#    most platforms (notably not Solaris), since atalkd
#    can discover the local interfaces on the machine.
#
#    Very slightly more complicated:
#
#        le0
# or
#        eth0
#    for Solaris/SunOS or Linux.
#
#    A much more complicated example:
#
#        le0 -phase 1
#        le1 -seed -phase 2 -addr 66.6 -net 66-67 ➥
#            -zone "No Parking"
#
#    This turns on transition routing between the le0 and
#    le1 interfaces on a Sun. It also causes atalkd to
#    fail if other routers disagree about its
#    configuration of le1.
#
```

apfd.conf

The apfd daemon controls passwords for remote access over a netatalk connection. As you may recall from Chapter 29: "Managing Users and Groups," password management can be a bit of a security risk unless you take some explicit steps. One of the most common ways to increase the security of your password files is to enable *shadow passwords*.

netatalk supports shadow passwords with the apfd daemon. You will need to alert apfd that you will be using shadow passwords before you build the code; in the etc/afpd/Makefile file, locate the entry beginning with CFLAGS:. In that entry, just before the hashmark denoting entries not to be included, add the phrase -DSHADOWPW. This enables shadow passwords when netatalk is built.

apfd uses the apfd.conf configuration file. As with atalkd.conf, the file is straightforward and well-commented. You should be able to figure out what you need to do with a minimum of effort. A sample apfd.conf file looks like this:

```
#
    # Format of lines in this file:
    #
    #    server [ -tcp ] [ -ddp ] [ -guest ] ➡
    #       [ -loginmesg message ] . . .
    #
# To specify a line with the default server name, use a
    # "-" as the server name.
    #
    # There are a whole plethora of options available. Here
    # they are for your edification:
    #
    #    toggles [-no<option> turns that option off;
    #       -<option> turns it on]:
    #       transports: tcp, ddp, transall
    #       debug: nodebug (can only turn off debug)
    #       auth: cleartxt, afskrb, krbiv, guest, randnum,
    #          rand2num, authall (doesn't include randnum/
    #          rand2num)
    #       passwd: savepassword, setpassword
    #       user volumes: uservolfirst, nouservol (don't
    #          look for ~/.AppleVolumes)
    #
    #    options w/ arguments (-<option> <argument>):
    #       defaultvol, systemvol, loginmesg, guestname
    #       address (binds a server to a specific address)
    #       port (has to be specified if more than one tcp
    #          server is to be served)
    #       ticklevel (sets the tickle interval in seconds)
    #       uampath, nlspath
    #
# Order of precedence:
    #    options in afpd.conf > command-line options >
    #       built-in options
    #
# Some examples:
    #
    #    The simplest case is not to have an apfd.conf.
    #
```

```
#    4 servers w/ names server1-3 and one w/ the
#    hostname. servers 1-3 get routed to different ports
#    with server 3 being bound specifically to address
#    192.168.1.3
#       -
#    server1 -port 12000
#    server2 -port 12001
#    server3 -port 12002 -address 192.168.1.3
#
#    a dedicated guest server, a user server, and a
#    special ddp-only server:
#       "Guest Volume" -nocleartxt -loginmsg "Welcome ➡
#          Guest!"
#       "User Volume" -noguest -port 12000
#       "special" -notcp -defaultvol <path> -systemvol ➡
#          <path>
#
```

AppleVolumes.default

The AppleVolumes.default file is used by netatalk when a known user logs into the network. It tells netatalk how this given user will need to deal with the various volumes and file types on the network. Your users can override the default system settings by creating their own AppleVolumes or .AppleVolumes file in their home directories, but most users won't go to the trouble.

You don't really need to keep much in AppleVolumes.default, except an entry that contains a tilde (~). This designates the user's home directory as the default directory for any network use. You can configure it further if you like, following the comprehensive comments in the configuration file. A sample AppleVolumes. default is shown below:

```
# This file looks empty when viewed with "vi". In fact,
  # there is one '~', so users with no AppleVolumes file
  # in their home directory get their home directory by
  # default.
  #
  #volume format:
  #path [name] [casefold=x] [codepage=y] [options=z,l,j] ➡
  #    [access=a,@b,c,d] [dbpath=path] [password=p]

  #

  #
```

```
# casefold options:
# tolower    -> lowercases names in both directions
# toupper    -> uppercases names in both directions
# xlatelower -> client sees lowercase, server sees upper
# xlateupper -> client sees uppercase, server sees lower
#
# access format:
# user1,@group,user2 -> restricts volume to listed users
#     and groups
#
# miscellaneous options:
# prodos     -> make compatible with appleII clients
# crlf       -> enable crlf translation for TEXT files
# noadouble -> don't create .AppleDouble unless a
#    resource fork needs to be created
#
# codepage=filename  -> load filename from nls directory
# dbpath=path        -> store the database stuff in the #    named
path
# password=password  -> set a volume password (eight
#     characters max)
#
#
~ Home
```

The AppleVolumes files map volumes on the Macintosh machines to paths on the Unix machines. In general, you won't need to edit the AppleVolume files; the syntax is different for Unix and Macintosh files, so if you get it wrong, you'll only see "Unknown Document" messages.

AppleVolumes.system

The longest netatalk configuration file is AppleVolumes.system, a file that maps volumes to paths so that files can be handled appropriately across the network. This file is quite long by default, and you probably won't need to edit it. The syntax in this file is specific, and differs for Unix files and Macintosh files. If you make an edit and are wrong in the syntax, you'll see "Unknown Document" messages when you attempt to open files with that particular format.

Because of the length of the AppleVolumes.system file, we show you only a portion here. Note that the file is set into columns, with the file extension, file type, and program that will execute this type of file as the main components of each entry.

```
# Last Updated July 8, 1999
   #
   #Use at your own risk. No guarantees express or implied.
   #
   # Try to use MacPerl script 'ICDumpSuffixMap' included
   # in /usr/doc to download file mapping list from your
   # Internet Config Preference.
   #
   # inoue@ma.ns.musashi-tech.ac.jp
   #

   .text/plain  "TEXT"  "ttxt"  ASCII Text   SimpleText
   .mf          "TEXT"  "*MF"   Metafont     Metafont
   .sty         "TEXT"  "*TEX"  TeX Style    TeXtures
   .psd         "BBPS"  "8BIM"  PhotoShop    Photoshop
   .pxr         "PXR"   "8BIM"  Pixar Image  Photoshop
   .sea         "APPL"  "????"  Self-Extracting Archive
   .apd         "TEXT"  "ALD3"  Aldus        PageMaker
   .pm3         "ALB3"  "ALD3"  PageMaker 3  PageMaker
   .pm4         "ALB4"  "ALD4"  PageMaker 4  PageMaker
   .pt4         "ALT4"  "ALD4"  PageMaker 4  PageMaker
```

The file continues in this manner for several pages, defining every possible file extension that either the Macintosh or the Unix machines are likely to generate.

config

The `config` file is the general configuration file for `netatalk`. It is very basic, serving only to turn on or off the various modules of `netatalk`. This file is also used to set the AppleTalk name of the server and define how many clients can be connected to the server at one time. Here is a sample `config` file:

```
# Appletalk configuration
   # Change this to increase the maximum number of clients
   # that can connect:
   AFPD_MAX_CLIENTS=5
   # Change this to set the machine's atalk name:
   # ATALK_NAME='echo $(HOSTNAME) | cut -d. fl'
   ATALK_NAME=mymacserver
   # Set which daemons to run:
```

```
PAPD_RUN=no
AFPD_RUN=yes
# Control whether the daemons are started in background
ATALK_BGROUND=yes
```

Starting netatalk

When you have finished with the configuration files, you can start the netatalk server and begin attaching your Macintoshes to the network. To start netatalk, issue the command

```
/etc/init.d/netatalk start
```

at a shell prompt. The server should start cleanly; if it doesn't, error messages will generate to the screen. Any Macintoshes already connected to the network should now appear as part of the network; if you have not connected your Macs yet, do so now. (You may need to reboot netatalk if the machines do not show up right away.)

FreeBSD users should experience almost no problems with netatalk. Because the program was initially written to a BSD standard, you will probably find that netatalk integrates itself seamlessly into your operating system and that, once configured, the Macintoshes on your network will appear and work properly across the network. Solaris and Linux users may have a bit more trouble, and both operating systems are addressed in the remainder of this section.

NOTE   Because netatalk uses the AppleTalk protocol, you will need to consult Apple documentation to learn how to use this protocol if you are not an experienced Macintosh administrator. You will also need to consult Macintosh documentation to make the proper configurations in the Macintosh networking tools.

Solaris and netatalk

If you want to install netatalk on your Solaris machine or network, you have a bit more work to do than the FreeBSD and Linux administrators. Solaris support is just now being implemented into netatalk and is supported only in the current beta version (though when a full, stable 1.4.x release is made, Solaris will be included). Earlier versions may have patches that work reasonably well, but the current beta version is reputed to work much more cleanly. It's expected that the current beta code will go into the stable 1.4.x release.

The major problem with `netatalk` and Solaris involves printing. As we explained in Chapter 33: "Managing Print Services," Solaris uses the System V print spool mechanism. `netatalk` is based on BSD Unix and thus uses the Berkeley print spool mechanism as its default. Administrators using `netatalk` on Solaris need to configure `netatalk` so that it doesn't automatically issue Berkeley-style print management commands. One of the first steps you'll need to take is the installation of LPRng, a module that emulates Berkeley-style printing on the Solaris platform. However, just installing LPRng probably won't handle the problem completely. You'll most likely have to edit the `papd.conf` file to make sure that individual printers are called with `lp` instead of `lpr`. (The 1.4.x version of `netatalk` promises to have easier print management.)

If you have trouble with your network interfaces and find that `netatalk` exits frequently with the message "`atalkd`: can't get interfaces, exiting" you need to edit the `atalkd.conf` file to reflect your correct interfaces. This detail is addressed in the README.SOLARIS file contained with the `netatalk` packages. Of course, read this file early in your `netatalk` career.

`netatalk` does work on Solaris. You may have to do more work with it than your non-Solaris admin friends, but it is possible to run a heterogeneous network with Solaris machines and Macintoshes coexisting nicely. Spend some time tinkering up front, and you should be rewarded with a stable and robust network.

Linux and netatalk

Linux and `netatalk` go together very well. You should be able to install and run `netatalk` quite easily on your Linux system. We have tested it on Debian, Red Hat, and Corel Linux (Debian-based), and haven't had any trouble. If you use a package management system such as those described in Chapter 31: "Installing and Managing Software," Red Hat- and Debian-style formatted packages of `netatalk` are available, and may be of interest to you.

- Get the Red Hat *.rpms at `ftp://contrib.redhat.com/pub/contrib/libc6/SRPMS/`. Search the SRPMS directory for `netatalk-`*`version`*`+ asun`*`version`*`.src.rpm` files; the package contains both `netatalk` and `asun`, the version of `netatalk` released and amended by Adrian Sun.

- Get the Debian *.deb files at `ftp://cgi.debian.org/www-master/debian.org/Packages/stable/net/netatalk.html`.

- If you need source code, visit `ftp://terminator.rs.itd.umich.edu/unix/netatalk/`.

TIP

If you're planning to run `netatalk` on your Linux system, we recommend the Linux `netatalk` HOWTO written by Anders Brownworth. You can find this file at `http://www.thehamptons.com/anders/netatalk`.

Summary

No matter what kind of machines you have on your network, the likelihood that they are all running the same Unix variant and no other operating system is quite small. In fact, the heterogeneous network is a fact of administrative life. Unfortunately, even variants based on the same original Unix flavor don't always work well together, and Unix doesn't integrate seamlessly with non-Unix operating systems.

Luckily, solutions to this problem have been devised and developed by many programmers over the years. For systems with multiple Unix variants, you can use the Network File System to share files and filesystems transparently across the network. Administrators who run networks that contain both Unix and Windows machines can use the Samba program, which translates the Windows file format SMB (Session Message Block) into a format that Unix can work with. Those who run networks that comprise MacOS machines as well as Unix can run the `netatalk` program, which translates between native Unix file format and the AppleTalk protocol. With any of these programs, you can share both files and print jobs, which makes an administrator's life easier and satisfies users who have strong operating-system preferences.

CHAPTER
THIRTY-EIGHT

Network Security

- ■ How Important Is Security to You?

- ■ The Security Mindset

- ■ Internal Security

- ■ External Security

- ■ Intrusion Detection

- ■ Firewalls and Proxies

- ■ Summary

No matter what kind of Unix user you are, you need to be concerned about security. If you are a network administrator, you should be even more aware of issues surrounding network security. Today's Internet is a dangerous place, and even relatively insignificant domains can find themselves under attack on a much more frequent basis than might be imagined.

As we've said in other chapters throughout the book, if you're connected to any external networks—including local Internet service providers, corporate or academic networks, or noncommercial networks—you must be vigilant about security. It does no good to think that connecting to a work network is more secure than connecting to the Internet, because the work network is likely part of the Internet. After all, the Internet is not a single entity; it is a collection of computers and networks, all networked together in a massive intertwining. If you connect to the Internet, you have accepted the security risks in doing so.

In this chapter, we address two sides of the security issue. First, we explain the mental state required of those concerned about security. You will need to decide how important security is to you and your network, and how vulnerable you want to be. Then, we explain the various ways in which you can gird your system against exploits. We show you basic administrative routines and introduce two security packages that you can find on the CD-ROM included with this book.

NOTE Please note that we don't want you to panic. This chapter probably has more doom-and-gloom than any other chapter in the book, but it's there for a reason. You can lose a lot to security violations, both financially and emotionally. However, you shouldn't obsess about becoming perfectly secure. This takes time (and effort) that you probably don't have; the better solution is to get as secure as you can while balancing your time investment and actual security needs. Yes, there are people in the world whose idea of fun is illegally entering into networks or writing malicious programs. Don't let your concern about these people override your enjoyment of Unix.

Hackers vs. Crackers

Before we get further into the chapter, we need to define some terms. A persistent thorn in the side of the Unix community is the use of the word *hacker* to describe someone who illegally breaks into computer systems for fun. Within the Unix world, however, a

Continued on next page

hacker is someone who is simply a clever programmer; the word has been used that way since the dawning of Unix. For example, people who work on the Linux kernel are often called *kernel hackers.*

People who breach security on other networks are called *crackers,* because they "crack into" networks they don't own. Unfortunately, the popular media has this one wrong. Accounts of hackers breaking into military or commercial systems are a common component of media technology coverage, and this annoys people who consider themselves hackers in the proper sense of the word. Ironically, hackers have come up with some of the best anticracker solutions.

In this book, we use *cracker* to refer to someone who is breaking into systems without permission. We encourage you to adopt the correct terminology. Hackers built almost all of the software on the CD-ROM included with this book, and neither the Internet nor the Unix community would exist as we know them today without the (often unpaid) efforts and dedication of the hacker community.

How Important Is Security to You?

Although connecting to the Internet does carry some intrinsic level of risk, the risks involved vary greatly. Risk levels depend on the type of connection that your computer or network has and how you use that connection. To determine what kind of security measures you should take, you first need to evaluate your level of vulnerability. Unfortunately, outside of trying to crack your own machine using some of the many cracker tools available on the Internet, there is no simple process for learning how vulnerable you are. (Well, you could just let yourself be cracked, but that's not the best way to handle it.)

If you have a single Unix computer, or a small local network that accesses the Internet through a dial-up modem, your IP address is likely assigned dynamically each time you log into your ISP, meaning that you have a different IP address every time you dial in. Security risks for this kind of situation are fairly low. You are connected to the Internet for brief sessions, and each time you dial in, you receive a different IP number. This is analogous to visiting New York City on business every other week, but staying in a different hotel room each time. Because it is essentially a moving target, your system presents a level of difficulty to a cracker that probably outweighs its potential usefulness. This does not mean, however, that you should lose interest in security issues, only that whatever decisions you make about security can take these factors into account.

TIP See Chapter 35: "Network Interfaces and Routing" for more information on DHCP and PPPoE, the programs used to assign dynamic IP numbers.

However, if you run a Unix computer or network that is connected to the Internet on a full-time basis through a cable modem, DSL line, or direct connection, you likely have a static IP number, or range of IP numbers, that is assigned directly to your computer. In this case, your computer or network presents an attractive target for crackers. Your system is always locatable and accessible; if a cracker can gain access, your system will be very useful.

Eternal Vigilance

It's tempting to think that your system is insignificant and that nobody would ever want to break into your computer or network. After all, you're just running a couple of FreeBSD boxes and a cable modem, and you don't have anything interesting on your hard drive except Quake—there's not much that anyone could want, right? Unfortunately, this isn't the case. We can tell you from personal experience that this is a bad way to deal with security issues. We run a small, six-computer network attached to the Internet through a broadband connection. Although we had some basic security precautions in place, we had become fairly complacent for reasons similar to those described above. During the writing of this book, we were cracked.

There's no obvious reason why we were selected as a target. We don't handle e-commerce on our site, so we don't have any credit card numbers on file. We don't do a lot of contracted database or programming work, so there were no valuable data files to steal (except the notes for this book, of course). In short, we don't really have anything that makes us an attractive target for crackers, except for one thing.

We have a 24-hour broadband connection to the Internet. This is a valuable item. Many crackers aren't really looking for things to steal from the hard drives of compromised systems. Rather, they're looking for open and available sites from which they can launch attacks on other sites, disguising their true location and shifting blame to an innocent administrator. The person who cracked our site was one of these.

Our cracker was using our system as part of a Denial of Service attack, a method of Internet vandalism that swamps the target site with small electronic messages in an attempt to tie up the target's system in responding to the attack instead of delivering the actual data that the site exists to provide. What's worse is that our cracker was trying a Denial of Service attack against one of our favorite Web sites, run by someone with whom we have both a social and a business relationship!

Imagine our embarrassment when Joe answered the phone and found the system administrator of our friend's site on the other end, asking if we knew anything about the attacks emanating from one of the computers in our house. We were mortified, and we were also quite worried. We learned about the misuse of our system because someone took the time to track it down. How many other systems had been attacked from our domain without our knowledge?

We took down the entire network immediately and set about fixing the problem. Lest you think that embarrassment was the only cost of this attack, we should explain the financial cost as well. We spent about four-and-a-half days repairing damage done by the cracker, obtaining and configuring new hardware, and designing a new security system. All in all, we both lost nearly a week from our income-producing work, both in writing this book and in our other contracts. We figure that the attack cost us several thousand dollars in lost work and expenditure.

The moral of the story is that no matter how insignificant you think you are and no matter how good you think your current security protocol may be, you need to stay on top of what's happening. Complacency is the biggest enemy of security.

The Security Mindset

In many ways, network security is less a practice or set of practices than it is a mindset. That mindset could be described as *rational paranoia.* A properly security-minded administrator is aware of the various threats that exist and takes precautions against them, but also understands the trade-off between security and usability.

Obviously, the most secure network is one with absolutely no points of access. If you can't get into it, you can't harm it. The flip side, though, is that such a system is worthless for most practical purposes. Servers require access to the network; users require access to the network; the administrator requires access to the network.

Each point of access to the network, however, is an increased security risk. A good administrator must balance security against the needs of the system's users and must divide attention among the three main components of a good security policy.

Physical Security

Anyone who has access to the actual computers has access to network functions. Period. All your server machines should be kept in a secure location; user workstations, obviously, cannot be kept apart from their users. In the simplest breach of physical security, someone can just pick up your computer and walk off with it, or open the case and steal the hard drive.

If you administer a network for an organization of some type, you will probably want to keep your servers in a separate, locked room, preferably one with good climate control. (Computers can generate a lot of heat.) Only trusted administrators should have access to the server room. Cleaning should be done by the administrators, not by janitorial staff.

Those who keep their networks at home have different needs. Most houses don't have room for a separate, locked server room, unless you happen to be the Queen of England. Be aware of the people who spend time in your home. Those who live alone need to worry about only their guests; if you keep your servers in a spare bedroom or the linen closet, your guests may never see the machines at all. If you have a family and none of them are interested in Unix, and you have decent passwords, you can probably leave the network accessible. However, if you have family members or frequent guests who may find malicious activity funny or who don't share your commitment to security, find some way to lock your servers away.

Internal Security

Know your users. We can't repeat that often enough. You don't want users using a system nefariously when you're the person in charge. The responsibility for security ultimately lies in your lap, no matter how much you encourage your users to be aware of their own security risks and behaviors.

If you have too many users to know personally, as in a large employer's network, make sure that there are consistent policies in place for computer and network usage. With such policies, you'll have a way to deal with people acting inappropriately even if you don't have the ability to deal with them personally.

You can determine the level of access that each user has to the system by working with individual user permissions. In Chapter 29: "Managing Users and Groups," we explain the concept of user groups. By assigning users to the appropriate groups, you can limit access to given programs to the groups that need it, while other groups don't have the ability to perform those tasks. Limit all your users to the files and programs that they need, and block them from those that they don't.

External Security

When most people think of network security, they think of external security mechanisms. External security deals with outside access to the network, either from individuals or from other programs. Developing an effective external security plan entails the determination of what services will be made available outside the network and then the creation of a plan to handle the security risks presented by those services.

External security is the most risky of the three elements described here, because it deals with the actions of unknown people beyond your control. Luckily, this is also the area that has had the most activity in terms of development and education. You can find third-party programs that will handle the trickier aspects of external security, and it's easy to find scripts and discussions that will help you manage your system.

Internal Security

When it comes down to security issues involving your own users, there are two kinds of misbehavior that you and your users need to avoid. One is caused by bad habits, and the other is caused by bad users. Both can be addressed, though the first is easier to deal with than the second.

The first issue is the inadvertent security problem caused by bad habits. Perhaps your users don't know about effective passwords, or you haven't enforced—or written—policies on network usage. If your users create security problems out of ignorance or sloppy habits, you need to focus on educating your users and enforcing ground rules. If you don't have ground rules, create some and make sure your users are aware of them. Two of the most critical areas for which you should develop policies are file permissions and passwords.

The other issue with internal security concerns bad users who will intentionally use your system for foul purposes. Although you can lock down the system as tightly as possible, the only real answer to bad users is vigilance. Watch your system carefully and be aware of anything unusual. Once you've identified the culprit, get that person off your system and change any systemwide passwords the person may know. The key to this problem is regulation, not education.

File Permissions

When users create files, especially if the files are executable programs, they should do so with the most restrictive permissions that will allow the user to get the work done. As a rule, this means that you should restrict read, write, and (if applicable) execute permission to the user alone. If files need to be shared, they should be shared only within appropriate user groups. Files should be world-readable only as a last resort if there is no other appropriate solution.

TIP   We discuss how to set up groups, and the concept of file permission, in Chapter 29: "Managing Users and Groups."

An administrator can set default file permissions by using the umask command. umask sets the default permission values with which all new files will be created. The umask command uses an octal, or base 8, number as its argument. The number determines the permissions to be set. For example, the command

```
umask 027
```

would give the user (owner of the file) all permissions, the user's group read and execute permissions, and everyone else no permissions at all. Table 38.1 shows the various arguments for umask and their effects on file permissions created with particular arguments. Table 38.2 shows the arguments for umask and how they affect directories created with particular arguments.

TABLE 38.1: umask Arguments for File Permissions

Argument	Mode	Effect on File Permission
077	-rw-------	User may read and write, but nobody else has access to the file.
027	-rw-r-----	User may read and write; user's group may read; no other access.
007	-rw-rw----	User may read and write; group may read and write; no other access.
022	-rw-r--r--	User may read and write; group may read; others may read.
002	-rw-rw-r--	User may read and write; group may read and write; others may read.

TABLE 38.2: umask Arguments for Directory Permissions

Argument	Mode	Effect on Directory Permission
077	drwx------	User may read and write, list filenames in the directory, and delete files from the directory; no other access.
027	drwxr-x---	User may read and write, list filenames, and delete files; group may read and list filenames; no other access.
007	drwxrwx---	User may read and write, list filenames, and delete files; group may read and write, list filenames, and delete files; no other access.
022	drwxr-xr-x	User may read and write, list filenames, and delete files; group may read and list filenames; all others may read and list filenames.
002	drwxrwxr-x	User may read and write, list filenames, and delete files; group may read and write, list filenames, and delete files; all others may read and list filenames.

NOTE

We alluded to this octal form of notation in Chapter 12: "Manipulating Files and Directories." Because we didn't offer a full explanation in that chapter, we include one here. The octal modes are slightly different from those used as arguments for the **chmod** command. If you're interested in learning the octal method for **chmod**, consult the **chmod** manual page by issuing the command **man chmod** at a shell prompt.

As an administrator, you can put the umask command in the default configuration file for your users' default shell. For example, if you're using bash under the Linux operating system on your network, you can add a line to your user configuration file that reads

```
umask 077
```

New users created with this line in the configuration file will have, by default, read and write permission for all files they create, though nobody else will have access to those files.

WARNING These permissions can be overridden by a user with the **chmod** command. Users can also override default permissions by setting their own **umask** arguments in their personal `.bash_profile` files. Odds are, though, that if a user is knowledgeable enough to do this, the user is also aware of the security implications of doing so.

Passwords

In an ideal system, all your users will use *strong passwords*. Strong passwords are those that are not easily guessed and are difficult to decipher using common methods. Strong passwords have some common characteristics:

- They are mixed-case, containing both uppercase and lowercase letters.

- They contain both letters and numbers.

- They are not words found in any unabridged dictionary.

Obviously, there is some tension here. Users want passwords that are easy to remember, but passwords that are easy to remember are also easy to crack. However, if a user has a password that is hard to remember—but is really secure—odds are quite good that the user will just write the password down and leave it in a desk drawer or tape it to the monitor. This is even worse than having a weak password; it's a plain invitation that says, "Use my account! I don't care!"

An easy way around this conundrum is to encourage your users to use a regular word that's easy to remember, but to change it so that it's a bit more secure. Thus, the common word *mother* might become m0th3R, a change that incorporates both uppercase and numeric characters. This technique has its own drawbacks, because some crackers use dictionary programs that include common substitutions like this, but it's better than demonstrably weak passwords such as mother.

Unfortunately, password security is only as good as your users' willingness to help you maintain a secure system. Although there are utilities that scan for weak passwords and require users to change their passwords at a predetermined interval, there is little you can do if a user is determined to use the name of his dog as a password; even if required to change passwords every 30 days, such a user might start with Fido and go to Fido1, Fido2, Fido3, and so on sequentially.

NOTE   If you're interested in such a utility, consult your system documentation. Individual Unix variants handle passwords differently, and what works on our system probably won't work on yours. If you choose a program like this from a software archive on the Internet, make sure that you can use updated dictionaries with it. A password program that runs against a two-year-old crack dictionary is almost useless.

Educating your users on the dangers of weak passwords is the best thing you can do. Explain why you have certain policies and why you enforce them, and what the consequences are if the policies are violated. If you have a persistent problem, as a last resort, you can disable the users' access to the `passwd` command and have your administrators issue new passwords regularly. This is far more trouble than it's worth, and users tend to resent it, so it should be regarded as the atomic bomb of password security.

WARNING   If you use this last method as a way of controlling access to shared files or resources, expect to see a flood of internal e-mail each time the password is changed. Messages like "Could someone post the new database password?" and the resulting flurry of messages containing the password in plain text will completely defeat the purpose of the action. Users are resistant to change, and any attempt at password security must take that reluctance into account.

Malicious Users

If your security breaches are due to malicious users, there are fewer software tricks that you can use. The best advice we can give is that you should be vigilant in scanning your system and reading your system logs. Watch for unusual activity, such as network connections at odd times or files changing that should be static.

Be aware that there are ethical implications involved in watching your users' activities. From some perspectives, such oversight might be interpreted as spying, especially if you're reading private documents. Your users may have a perfectly innocent explanation for suspicious activity; for example, a user may have scheduled a massive download for the middle of the night to get a faster transmission rate and save the network bandwidth during the busy day.

The best policy is to have a clear Acceptable Use Policy. If someone violates it, throw that person off your system. If you want to have the options of reading e-mail, checking personal files, or other activity that would make you uncomfortable or litigious if it happened to you, put those activities in your policy. You should not read someone's e-mail if you have never told your users that you reserve the right to do so. Employers, especially, should have policies in place. You do not want to invoke inadvertently employment law squabbles with an attempt to fix a security problem.

External Security

When most people think of network security, they think of external security: that is, keeping intruders out. Certainly, the threats from external intrusion are problematic. Someone else may use your system and connection free of charge. Even if the intruder you catch is doing nothing more than looking around to see what you have, you may not have caught other intruders who exploited the same entrance into your system to do wrong. No matter how large or small your network is, there are a few basic principles to keep in mind as you determine your external security needs.

Shutting Down All Unnecessary Services

Don't run any services that you don't need. (See Part IX: "Administering Services" for more information on services and determining which services to offer to your users.) If you have no need to run a particular service, such as Apache, don't keep it operational just in case you need it later. Any service that you run must listen on an external port for incoming connections. Any port that is open because it's associated with a service is a security risk.

You can turn the service off without removing it from the system. If you decide you need it later, just turn it back on. In addition to turning the service off, you should also check through your configuration files to ensure that the service is commented out and won't be automatically started at boot-up. For Linux and BSD, check the file /etc/inetd.conf and make sure that unwanted services are commented out. Here's a sample from a typical /etc/inetd.conf file:

```
# These are standard services.
#
#ftp stream tcp nowait root /usr/sbin/tcpd in.ftpd -l -a
#telnet stream tcp nowait root /usr/sbin/tcpd in.telnetd
#
# Shell, login, exec, comsat and talk are BSD protocols.
#
#shell stream tcp nowait root /usr/sbin/tcpd in.rshd
#login stream tcp nowait root /usr/sbin/tcpd in.rlogind
#exec  stream tcp nowait root /usr/sbin/tcpd in.rexecd
#comsat dgram udp wait   root /usr/sbin/tcpd in.comsat
#talk  dgram udp wait nobody.tty /usr/sbin/tcpd in.talkd
#ntalk dgram udp wait nobody.tty /usr/sbin/tcpd in.ntalkd
#dtalk stream tcp wait nobody.tty /usr/sbin/tcpd in.dtalkd
#
# Pop and imap mail services et al
#
#pop-2 stream tcp nowait root /usr/sbin/tcpd ipop2d
#pop-3 stream tcp nowait root /usr/sbin/tcpd     ipop3d
#imap stream tcp nowait root /usr/sbin/tcpd      imapd
```

Each line in this file specifies a particular service and a server to handle that service. Notice that all of these services are commented out, with the initial hash-mark serving as a notice to the computer that the following instructions are not to be performed. Because the services are commented out, they won't operate.

On our network, we have commented out pop-2, pop-3, and imap services. Because we aren't running a mail server on the particular machine from which this sample was taken, we don't need the services. On the machine that does handle mail, we've uncommented pop-3, but left the others commented out.

We have also chosen to comment out the traditional data transfer services: ftp, telnet, rlogin, and rsh. Instead, we've replaced them with the more secure ssh protocol, which runs on its own. We recommend very strongly that you do this as well. ssh is becoming the new standard for network connections, because it is protected by encrypted password verification.

When you've edited /etc/inetd.conf to reflect the services you want to operate and the services you want to comment out, you'll have to restart the inet daemon so that the changes will take effect. `inet` is handled differently depending on the Unix variant you're using, so check your documentation to see what you'll need to do. On a Red Hat Linux system, for example, you'd issue the command `/etc/rc.d/init.d/inet restart`. More generically, you could use the `ps` command to find out the process ID number (PID) of the `inet` process and then issue the command `kill –HUP <PID>`.

Using ssh

In the previous section, we mentioned that we have replaced a number of services with `ssh`, the *Secure Shell*. `ssh` provides a *drop-in replacement* for `telnet`, `rlogin`, `rsh`, and other similar services, meaning that `ssh` can be used straight out of the box with little or no configuration required. The difference between `ssh` and these other services is that `ssh` establishes an encrypted connection between your computer and the remote computer before it sends any data over the network.

If someone is snooping on your network connections, an act possible with a *packet sniffer* program, `ssh` will foil them, because they'll be able to get only encrypted data. This is especially important if you use a password to log into a remote system, as most of these programs do. `ssh` generates a unique cryptographic key for each connection and stores it on your local computer.

NOTE Because of United States export restrictions on cryptographic software, we have not placed any `ssh` software on the CD-ROM that accompanies this book. You can, however, obtain `ssh` in various places on the Internet. True to our GNU roots, we advise you to use OpenSSH, which is a Free Software implementation of the `ssh` protocol. OpenSSH is available at `http://www.openssh.com`. Versions are available for Linux, Solaris, and FreeBSD, as well as for several other Unix variants. We also advise you to read the document "Getting Started With SSH," found at `http://www.tac.nyc.ny.us/~kim/ssh/`. This, and the documentation linked from that page, should get you going with `ssh` without too much trouble.

WARNING Non-US or non-Canadian readers should familiarize themselves with their local cryptography import/export laws before attempting to download any `ssh` software.

Keeping Your Software Up-to-Date

Very few crackers are computer security experts. Most are simply *script kiddies*, a pejorative term used for people (usually male teenagers) who download prewritten cracking programs from the Internet and use them to exploit vulnerable systems. These prewritten programs are designed to target known security flaws in particular operating systems.

Although the people who write these programs know what they're doing—but have chosen to use their abilities for evil, not for good—the people who use them usually don't. (That's why they're using someone else's program, not their own.) You can foil their efforts just by keeping your software upgraded, especially your operating system. Usually, when a security hole in a program or operating system is discovered, people jump on it right away. Updated versions, or small *patches* designed to fix the problem, may be released as soon as 24 hours after the hole is first reported. Keep an eye on Web sites related to your software and your operating system so that you can download patches as soon as they are made available.

Intrusion Detection

Next to keeping crackers out of your system entirely, the best thing is to catch them as soon as possible after they break in. Intrusion detection is an entire area of network security unto itself. With intrusion detection skills and programs, you can keep a constant eye on your ports and system activity and, hopefully, detect intruders before they have a chance to do any harm or misuse your connectivity.

There are a few easy commands that you can use to perform low-level intrusion detection. The first is the common command w. The w command produces output that can tell you a few interesting things, such as the usernames of all people logged into the system, what they're doing, and the current level of system load. For example, if Joe issues the w command on his personal workstation, the output looks like this:

```
1:04pm up 6 days, 4:22, 1 user, load average: 0.03,0.08, 0.08
USER   TTY     FROM    LOGIN@   IDLE   JCPU   PCPU  WHAT
joe    pts/0   :0      11:48am  0.00s  0.10s  0.03s  w
```

This output shows that the user joe is the only user logged into the computer. Notice that the numbers next to load average are very small. The system load will vary from computer to computer, depending on hardware. A load of 1.0 means that there are no idle CPU cycles and that the processor is as busy as it can be, but no tasks have to wait to be executed. Loads higher than 1.0 mean that tasks have to wait until they are executed, while loads below 1.0 mean that the CPU is idle some of the time. Very low loads, such as the ones you see here, indicate that the CPU is idle most of the time. For this machine, that is as it should be. The workstation is a powerful computer with two CPUs, and using a text editor doesn't take up much of the machine's resources.

Were Joe to run this command again and see a spike in the system load, it might make him suspicious. It could be caused by something innocuous; perhaps Kate has logged in from another machine and has started to run a CPU-intensive program, or perhaps an automatic system function has started to run. The other possibility is that the load spike indicates an intruder.

Assume that our intruder (we'll call him Graham) has broken into the computer, but has somehow managed to conceal his presence. We've noticed a spike in the system load, but we can't figure out why it happened. Certainly, when we run w, all we see is ourselves. The next command to try is the top command. top displays a *table of processes* as its output. All the programs that are currently running, and the amount of system resources they're using, are shown in this table. In its normal state, top output looks something like this:

```
1:17pm up 6 days, 4:34, 1 user, load average: 0.10, 0.08, 0.07
60 processes: 59 sleeping, 1 running, 0 zombie, 0 stopped
CPU states: 0.8% user, 3.0% system, 0.0% nice, 96.0% idle
Mem:  257644K av, 226504K used, 31140K free, 60744K shrd,    89180K buff
Swap: 530104K av,    308K used, 529796K free, 84908K cached
```

PID	USER	PRI	NI	SIZE	RSS	SHARE	STAT	LIB	%CPU	%MEM	TIME	COMMAND
20145	joe	11	0	3576	3576	2724	S	0	3.9	1.3	3:29	mult
20008	root	8	0	16488	16M	2872	S	0	2.3	6.3	4:00	X
20446	joe	6	0	864	864	668	R	0	1.1	0.3	0:00	top
20148	joe	2	0	3880	3880	2988	S	0	0.3	1.5	0:00	gnome-ter
1	root	0	0	352	348	272	S	0	0.0	0.1	0:21	init
2	root	0	0	0	0	0	SW	0	0.0	0.0	0:05	kflushd
3	root	0	0	0	0	0	SW	0	0.0	0.0	0:25	kupdate
4	root	0	0	0	0	0	SW	0	0.0	0.0	0:00	kpiod
5	root	0	0	0	0	0	SW	0	0.0	0.0	0:04	kswapd
6	root	-20	-20	0	0	0	SW<	0	0.0	0.0	0:00	mdrecoveryd
6334	bin	0	0	340	324	252	S	0	0.0	0.1	0:00	portmap
6348	root	0	0	0	0	0	SW	0	0.0	0.0	0:00	lockd

```
6349  root 0   0   0    0    0    SW   0   0.0  0.0  0:00  rpciod
6358  root 0   0   516  512  428  S    0   0.0  0.1  0:00  rpc.statd
6400  root 0   0   504  500  404  S    0   0.0  0.1  0:04  syslogd
6409  root 0   0   724  720  304  S    0   0.0  0.2  2:01  klogd
```

The table refreshes itself every few seconds, so you can see the programs as they use system resources in something that approaches real-time transmission.

While top is running, you can give it various one-letter commands. To see an entire list of commands, type h while you're running top. For our purposes here, we just want to use the P command. P will sort the list in order of CPU usage, so that the process using the most CPU time will be placed at the top of the list. This should tell us who's using all those CPU cycles and causing the system load to spike.

w and top are very common system commands, and most clever crackers (or at least ones who are copying the methods of the clever crackers) will employ some method or other to conceal their presence on your system. For example, they may replace your login program with a new version that doesn't advertise their illicit presence to programs like w or top. Still, we mention these tools because they give you a good way to see what's happening on your system, and that's a good habit to develop.

Logs

Another way to learn what's happening on your system is to make a habit of browsing through the various log files on your machine. Many processes, particularly servers, record their activity in one or more system logs. These logs are usually located in the /var/log directory, but some servers create logs in other places. For example, the Apache Web server might create a log in /var/apache/log. Most of the time, you can configure default log locations in the server's configuration files. Also, check your system documentation to make sure that you're looking in the right place for log files.

Logs are fairly easy to read. Here is part of the /var/log/messages file from one of our Linux workstations:

```
Aug 13 08:46:06 localhost gdm[14296]: gdm_auth_user_remove:➥
Ignoring suspicious looking cookie file /home/joe/.Xauthority
Aug 13 08:46:06 localhost gnome-name-server[19677]:➥
input condition is: 0x10, exiting
Aug 13 11:48:07 localhost PAM_pwdb[20009]: (gdm)➥
```

```
session opened for user joe by (uid=0)
Aug 13 11:48:08 localhost gnome-name-server[20113]: starting
Aug 13 11:48:08 localhost gnome-name-server[20113]:➡
name server starting
Aug 13 12:16:45 localhost kernel: parport0: PC-style at 0x378➡
   [SPP,PS2]
Aug 13 12:16:47 localhost kernel: parport0: Printer,➡
HEWLETT-PACKARD DESKJET 610C
Aug 13 12:16:47 localhost kernel: lp0: using parport0 (polling).
Aug 13 13:01:15 localhost PAM_pwdb[6676]:➡
   (login) session closed for user root
Aug 13 13:44:30 localhost PAM_pwdb[20456]:➡
   (su) session opened for user root by joe(uid=501)
```

The most interesting and useful lines in this segment of the log are the lines that note new sessions that have been opened:

```
Aug 13 11:48:07 localhost PAM_pwdb[20009]: (gdm)➡
session opened for user joe by (uid=0)
```

and

```
Aug 13 13:01:15 localhost PAM_pwdb[6676]: (login)➡
session closed for user root
Aug 13 13:44:30 localhost PAM_pwdb[20456]: (su)➡
session opened for user root by joe(uid=501)
```

Because Joe was the person who opened the session for root (a session required because Joe used the su command so that he could read logs, because only root may read the logs), he has no need to be suspicious of these entries. If we saw entries for users we didn't recognize, or entries with our usernames at times we know we weren't using the computer, it would be reason for concern.

TIP Check your logs regularly and accustom yourself to their normal appearance. You'll be rewarded with a better understanding of your system as well as an opportunity to catch intrusion early.

Intrusion Detection Software

Even if you scour your logs frequently, you can still miss a cracker. Most crackers now run *log scrubber* programs that edit the log files and eliminate entries that might draw suspicion. To detect crackers at a more subtle level, you'll need to turn to intrusion detection software. We've placed one such program on the book's CD-ROM, a program called AIDE.

AIDE (the Advanced Intrusion Detection Environment) is a program that creates a database of information about various files on your system. After the database is built, you can use it to verify that these files are the same ones used to build the database. This is very useful. Imagine that a cracker replaces your login program, usually found in /bin/login, with a login program that's been hacked to allow undetected entries. No matter how clever that cracker is, he can't change certain things about the new software he installs on the system. He can't, for example, duplicate the exact size of the binary file he is replacing. AIDE uses this piece of information, along with other data points, to create a "fingerprint" for each file.

The normal procedure for using AIDE is to install it on a new machine before that machine is connected to the network for the first time. The database should be created at this time and should include files that are not expected to change over the course of the machine's life. For example, files that change frequently—such as log files—should not be included in the database.

Once the database has been created, the administrator can run periodic checks. AIDE will compare the information in the database to the corresponding files currently on the computer. If any of these files have been altered, AIDE will alert the administrator, who can then investigate the discrepancy further.

AIDE is included on the CD-ROM accompanying this book. You can install it using the process explained in Chapter 31: "Installing and Managing Software." Once it's installed, you'll need to edit the configuration file located at /etc/aide. conf. The default /etc/aide.conf file is printed below; the file's comments make it quite easy to figure out what you need to do to get AIDE configured properly for your system.

```
    #AIDE conf

# Here are all the things we can check - these are the
# default rules
#
#p:     permissions
#i:     inode
#n:     number of links
#u:     user
#g:     group
```

```
#s:      size
#b:      block count
#m:      mtime
#a:      atime
#c:      ctime
#S:      check for growing size
#md5:    md5 checksum
#sha1:   sha1 checksum
#rmd160: rmd160 checksum
#tiger:  tiger checksum
#R:      p+i+n+u+g+s+m+c+md5
#L:      p+i+n+u+g
#E:      Empty group
#>:      Growing logfile p+u+g+i+n+S
# You can alse create custom rules - my home made rule
# definition goes like this
# MyRule = p+i+n+u+g+s+b+m+c+md5+sha1
# Next decide what directories/files you want in the
# database

/etc p+i+u+g #check only permissions, inode, user and
             #group for etc
/bin MyRule  #apply the custom rule to the files in bin
/sbin MyRule #apply the same custom rule to the files
             #in sbin
/var MyRule !/var/log/.* #ignore the log dir it changes
             #too often
!/var/spool/.* #ignore spool dirs they change too often
```

You should also add a line to specify where the database should be put once it has been created, as in

```
database_out = /root/aide.db
```

Once you've set up your configuration the way you want it, create the database by using the command `aide - init`. This will create the database file as `/root/aide.db`. You should then move the database to some place where it can't be altered, such as a diskette. If the database is too big for a diskette, consider burning it onto a CD-ROM, or use a Zip disk. If you can't get the database onto some sort of removable medium, put a copy on another machine, preferably not connected to the network. You need a copy that is not going to be tampered with by crackers.

When the file has been moved, you need to reedit /etc/aide.conf and specify the location where you'll be reading the database. If you burned the AIDE database to a CD-ROM, you'll be reading it from the drive mounted at /mnt/cdrom (or applicable mount point for your Unix variant). Linux users can add the line

```
database = /mnt/cdrom/aide.db
```

to the file. You can then check the filesystem against the database by issuing the command aide - check. Any irregularities should be detected at that time.

TIP There are many more configuration options, and if you choose to run AIDE, we suggest that you read the manual pages for AIDE and /etc/aide.conf by issuing the commands man aide and man aide.conf.

PortSentry

When crackers are getting ready to attack a given system, they usually start by running a *port scan*. This is a procedure in which a program attempts to connect to various ports on your system in sequential order. It's a simple way to see which ports are open and which might be vulnerable to crack attempts.

PortSentry is a program that detects these scans and will respond to them as they are happening. We did not put PortSentry on the CD-ROM, but it is available on the Web at http://www.psionic.com/abacus/portsentry. PortSentry is free, in the *free beer* sense, so you don't have to pay to use it. The PortSentry folks have some other good security programs as well, so take a look around the site. We do recommend that you read the Web page and the PortSentry documentation before you attempt to install and use the program.

Port Scanners

One good way of safeguarding your system is to use the crackers' own tools against your own network. A *port scanner* is a good tool for doing this. There are a lot of port scanners out there, and they all have different features. Which one you use is up to you. Do a search on *portscan* at a good Unix software archive such as http://www.freshmeat.net, and you should find up-to-date choices.

Ideally, you should run a port scanner from a computer outside your network. The best way to see your external vulnerabilities is from outside, as they will appear to the cracker. Finding an external machine from which to run your scan may be troublesome. Probably the best solution is to befriend another Unix administrator and trade services.

Firewalls and Proxies

Most Unix systems have the ability to *firewall,* or block access to, various service ports. Linux, for example, can block access to certain ports in response to a port connection, the originating address of the signal, its destination, or its protocol. Other systems have their own methods of controlling port access.

Unfortunately, the way in which port access is handled can vary quite a bit from Unix to Unix. Linux uses a utility called ipchains (though by the time this book is published, a new kernel release will implement a process called netfilter), FreeBSD uses the ipfw utility, and Solaris uses the Service Access Facility. We won't discuss these programs in detail here, because each works differently, and they are all specific to your particular hardware configuration.

Whatever method your Unix variant uses to handle port access, you will need to implement that method with a consistent firewall policy in mind. How you set up your firewall has a lot to do with how you set up your network. The most typical setup is an internal network that connects to the Internet through a single *gateway* machine. All traffic entering or leaving the network must pass through this gateway. Assuming that this is the machine with the firewall on it, all incoming and outgoing traffic will be subjected to the rules about what kind of packets may enter or leave the local network.

The exact firewall rules for any particular network will vary quite a bit, depending on the kinds of services that you need to provide for your users and the types of connections that you expect to receive from outside the network. In general, though, here are a few rules of thumb for a good firewall policy:

- For incoming connections, block all ports except the ones that are needed for legitimate incoming connections. For example, if you expect people to log into your system from remote machines, you should leave port 22 open for ssh connections. If you want to allow access to a POP e-mail server so that your users can get their local mail at a remote location, you should leave port 110 open. In general, though, using POP servers is not a good idea because passwords and usernames are transmitted without encryption.

- Allow outgoing connections only from ports with numbers greater than 1024. These are the so-called *unprivileged* ports. The only exception you should make here is if you have a server that needs to connect to a remote peer server; some mail and news servers might need this function. In this case, allow that outgoing traffic to be directed only to a specific port on a specific machine. Do not allow general outgoing traffic on these ports.

- Do not allow any X Window System connections outside your network. Block both outgoing and incoming traffic on ports 6000–6063.

TIP

For an excellent and detailed discussion of firewall building, we cannot recommend *Linux Firewalls,* by Robert Ziegler (New Riders/Macmillan, 1999) highly enough. Though this book is specific to Linux and the `ipchains` program, the principles developed in the book should transfer easily to other systems as well.

OpenBSD

For the ultimate in Unix security, check out OpenBSD. The distribution's page is at `http://www.openbsd.org`. OpenBSD is, as you might suspect from the name, a BSD variant like FreeBSD. OpenBSD's focus is security. The OpenBSD developers have performed a line-by-line security audit of the operating system's source code; although no operating system is perfect, OpenBSD is about as crack-proof as any OS can be. OpenBSD is an excellent choice if you need an operating system that will integrate your firewalls tightly and securely.

Proxies

Proxies are programs that perform *port forwarding*. That is, a proxy is a machine that stands between a client and a server. The client connects to the proxy as if it were a server, and then the proxy connects to the server as if it were a client. The proxy then relays the information from the server back to the client. The security advantages of this method should be evident. Clients in your internal network never need to connect to machines outside the network, because the proxy does all the connecting for them.

We have included on the CD-ROM a proxy program called Dante. Dante implements the SOCKS proxy protocol. To use Dante, extract and build the package as explained in Chapter 31. Once Dante is built, you will need to run the shell script `socksify` (included as part of the installation process), which will add SOCKS support to your system libraries. There are also two system configuration files: `/etc/socks.conf` for the client functions and `/etc/sockd.conf` for the server functions. Configuration options are included in the documentation provided in the Dante packages.

WARNING Read all the documentation included in the packages carefully before you attempt to use Dante. Dante affects your system at a very basic level, and you should understand what it is doing before you try to use it.

Summary

No matter what kind of network or computer you are running, you should be aware of the various security risks inherent in computer use. Security risks range from the most prosaic concerns of physical access to those exploited by sophisticated programming designed to take advantage of hidden flaws. Administrators should balance their security needs against the needs of their users, because the most secure systems are those to which nobody has access. As a computer's connections increase, whether to a local network or a worldwide network such as the Internet, chances for security breaches also increase.

An administrator who is interested in strengthening the security of a given computer or network must be dedicated to vigilant surveillance of that machine or set of machines. Physical concerns can be alleviated with locked doors, while internal security relies more on knowing one's users and educating them on appropriate system use. Attacks from outside the network are hardest to control, but can be minimized through the use of security-oriented programs that scan open ports or report unusual activity. Fear of security breaches should not keep a person or a network off the Internet or isolated from any network contact; precautions should be taken just as one would receive immunizations before traveling to a region with known diseases, but the travel itself need not be avoided.

PART IX

Administering Services

CHAPTER
THIRTY-NINE

39

Selecting a Suite of Services

- What Is a Service?

- Why Not Run All of Them?

- What Are Your Needs?

- A Word about Security

- Managing Services

- Summary

The final section of this book is Part IX: "Administering Services." In this section, we explain the technical, security, and social aspects of running various server functions, including servers for e-mail, Web, and other remote access services. Whether you run your own network or use these services on someone else's network, the chapters in this part of the book can give you a broader understanding of the functions many take for granted when they boot up a computer.

In this chapter, we provide an overview of services in general. We divide the Unix-using population into several categories and explain how each category might choose to allocate system resources. Finally, we give you a general idea of server management, including installation, configuration, and removal.

What Is a Service?

When we talk about *services*, we refer to functions that utilize the Unix server-client architecture. That is, a service is a function that is available to one or more clients, whether those clients are other programs, computers, or human users. For example, if you pull up Netscape and enter the URL of a Web page you'd like to view, Netscape contacts the hosting computer's Web service as a client, requesting the given URL. We cover client-server architecture in detail in Chapter 36: "The Distributed System."

Services are generally used to distribute or gather information. In this chapter, we focus on services that are usually used across multiple networks. Although they are not specifically *Internet services*, they do provide data for the most common Internet functions: electronic mail, Web pages, USENET news articles, and file transfer. However, other services are used extensively within local networks to handle local issues, such as NFS (the Network File Server), covered in Chapter 30: "Disks and Filesystem Management." If you're running the X Window System, you're running a server; you're also running its partner, the X Font Server.

Why Not Run All of Them?

Because servers can be run locally or on a broader scale, but have no required minimum or maximum number of users, it is up to the system administrator to select the servers that will be run on a given network. In addition, the administrator can determine who will have access to any given service; in theory, you could run an entire suite of Internet services that were usable only on the interior network. (It's actually quite common, though the reality is that services are used both for external access and for internal purposes.)

So, why not run all the services you can? It's a reasonable question. Running a lot of services means that you can offer your users many more functions and that you can handle more of your own Internet traffic rather than relying on a commercial provider. You may have a really magnificent hardware setup, and running multiple constant processes may not be an issue for you. You could even decide to run a large number of services *just because*. All of these are quite common answers—and they're not necessarily wrong.

WARNING   If you currently have constant Internet access, as with a cable modem, ISDN, or DSL service, check the terms of your user agreement before you install any services that will utilize the Internet connection. Some of these services—including the popular @Home cable modem—prohibit end users from running servers through their networks. You may be required to switch to a business-oriented plan, even if you're not a business, if you want to run services through a consumer connection.

The first thing you must consider when deciding what to run is what you really need. If you are the only user of your standalone Unix computer, chances are you won't need to run servers designed for networks. If you run a small network, but your users all connect to external POP servers (run by commercial ISPs or by their employers) for their e-mail, you might not need to run a mail server on your local machine. If you're running an e-commerce enterprise out of your garage, you'll need a Web server. Only you can determine what are your basic server needs.

NOTE   If you're anything like us, the *just because* answer really struck a chord with you. People who are interested in running Unix networks are usually the sort of people who plug in strange equipment to see what it does and how it works. However, we can't recommend installing and running every server you can get your hands on. Each service you run is constantly operating, placing (sometimes significant) demands on your system resources. If you run enough servers, you won't be able to accomplish anything from a user account because the services have brought system speed to a near-halt. We recommend running the basics that you really need; you can always add more services later.

What Are Your Needs?

The services you need depend on the kind of user or administrator you are. The person running a single computer that connects to the Internet via a dial-up service provider has different needs than the person who administers a 40-machine distributed network for a popular Web site, or the person who manages a large multipurpose and heterogeneous corporate network. Once you figure out what you do with your computer, you're halfway to deciding what services you need to run to accomplish your goals.

The Hobbyist

Hobbyist is not a pejorative term. We use this term to describe users who do not administer networks professionally (see Chapter 27: "What Is System Administration?"). Rather, the hobbyist works with Unix for fun. This category ranges from the single user with one computer running Linux, to the family with multiple accounts on a two-computer network, to the hard-core hobbyist with five or six dedicated machines.

In general, though, the hobbyist runs a network with three or fewer machines, sharing access to the Internet through IP masquerading rather than having dedicated IP numbers for each machine. Hobbyists rely on a commercial Internet service provider to handle e-mail and news. If you fall into this category, here are our suggestions:

- Turn off all services that may have been installed by default with your Unix variant. Some variants automatically install a full suite of services, assuming that you'll use them.

- If you run a multiple-computer network, keep NFS. If you have a single computer and no plans for a network, turn it off.

- If you have a multiple-computer, multiple-OS system, install Samba (if it isn't already installed) for the Windows computers and `netatalk` for the Macintosh computers.

The Worker

Workers are those who run Unix machines for small-scale business needs. If you have a home business and run a network for that purpose, you're a worker. If you work for someone else, you are probably a worker only if you are in charge of the entire system and the company itself is fairly small. (System administrators at larger companies, especially companies where administrative duties are divided up among a staff, should see the next section.)

Workers' needs change based on the functions the network provides. In general, workers will need to manage file and print sharing, and will probably have to provide some sort of interface between the intranet and the Internet. Whether the business uses a commercial ISP, as the hobbyist does, or has a faster connection with less customer service will affect the services that the worker uses. If you are a worker, consider these suggestions:

- Make sure to enable Samba or `netatalk`, depending on your network's heterogeneity.

- You probably won't need a business news server, so you can turn off INN or C News.

- Enable Apache if your business's Web presence is hosted in-house. If your pages are housed by a Web hosting company, you can turn off Apache.

- An electronic mail server is a good idea, especially if your company's employees are using their personal addresses (or Web freebies such as Hot-Mail) to do company business.

NOTE It is never a good idea to use your work e-mail address to handle personal correspondence. Although it may seem logical to think that your e-mail belongs to you, if you're using a computer or connection from work, your e-mail probably is the legal property of your employer. There have been several cases where courts have issued subpoenas for employer-owned computers that employees were using at home, and many more cases where people have been fired for using corporate Internet resources for personal use. Keep your personal and work lives completely separate, even by buying an additional computer if you have to.

The Specialist

If you're a specialist, you already know what you need. Specialists are people who need specific tools to complete specific tasks. Usually, specialists are those whose work responsibilities are particular segments of system administration, such as e-mail or Web services. Other specialists are those who do a lot of programming, whether at work or on their own time.

No matter what kind of specialist you are, you demand a lot from your computer and know how to get it. You don't need us to tell you what services to run or how to configure them most appropriately. Just keep an eye on security and consider broadening your skills a bit by learning a new service if you find one that's appealing.

A Word about Security

As we noted in Chapter 38: "Network Security," you should be aware of the security risks involved any time you install a program that allows external access to your computer. Almost by definition, the services described in this part of the book are based on external access for various functions. Therefore, if you plan to run servers, you need to be vigilant about your security program.

WARNING   Any service that you run represents a security risk. Although this sounds scary, don't let it stop you from running services. Just make a commitment to security and to keeping on top of the latest security news. Use the material presented in Chapter 38 to help you build a security program, and keep abreast of the news reported on the security sites listed in Appendix B: "Documentation and Resources."

The services covered in these chapters each operate on traditional ports. One of the most common cracker programs is a *port scanner*, which will check all the ports on the target machine. If a weakness is found, the cracker can utilize that weak port to make an entry and use your computer as a base for illicit activity. Running services leaves those ports open because the services require them. Do not run services if you are not willing to be on the constant lookout for security risks, intrusions, and new patches that will help you maintain a secure system.

That said, we don't think you should avoid running services altogether. They're useful, and they are some of the major features for which people use Unix in the first place. Just be careful: Install only the services you need, be aware of their normal activity, and investigate anything suspicious at once.

WARNING   Those who run 24-hour constant connections, such as cable modems or DSL, should be particularly vigilant about their security and unauthorized activity on their systems. We cannot stress highly enough that you should read Chapter 38 and use its information to help you construct an effective security program for your particular system.

Managing Services

In general, services work like any other program that you'd run on your Unix machine. The process of installation is the same: Install the packages, configure the software, and then configure your system to recognize and work with the new program.

NOTE   Some versions of server software will automatically install initialization scripts during installation. Check the **/etc/init.d** file before you start configuring the system yourself, just to see whether a script has already been placed in the directory. It's annoying to learn, after you've spent some time writing a script by hand, that the installation program already handled it for you.

Removal of services is almost like removal of any other kind of program, with one exception. With services, you need to decide whether you are going to delete the service or just turn it off. In most cases, we recommend that you leave the service installed. Circumstances change, and you may find yourself wanting to run a Web server even though you'd never envisioned such a thing a few months previously. (Upgrading your Internet connection type often has this effect.)

The next two sections of the chapter explain the methods you'll need to use to deactivate services, based on your operating system. Once you've made the appropriate edits, you can delete the service if you want. If you don't want to delete it, just leave it exactly as it is. The next time you want to activate that service, all its initialization and configuration scripts will be intact—you simply need to reenter the service into the appropriate start-up file to make it active again.

Turning Off Services: FreeBSD and Linux

With FreeBSD and Linux, there are two ways a service can be started. (Solaris uses a different method.) In FreeBSD and Linux, services can be started either from inetd or from init, and each has a different method for turning off services.

- To remove service references for services started from inetd, you will need to remove entries from the /etc/services and /etc/inetd.conf files. We cover inetd in Chapter 43: "Remote Access (inet) Services," and you can learn how to configure those files in that chapter.

- To remove service references for services started from init, as with some versions of Linux, you'll need to decide whether you want to keep the service. If you plan to delete the service, remove its initialization script file from the /etc/init.d directory. If you just want to turn off the service, delete its symbolic link in the /etc/rcX.d directory, where X is the number of the run-level directory containing the symbolic links.

- If you are using FreeBSD or some Linux variants (most notably Slackware), you will find a set of scripts in /etc with names like rc.web, rc.mail, and so on. Those scripts are run at init, and to turn off the service, you will need to remove the script or copy it to a different location. We recommend moving the script out of /etc, but keeping it around in case you want to run the service at a later date.

Turning Off Services: Solaris

Solaris uses a different set of tools to control access to network functions, accessed with the Service Access Facility (SAF) tool. The SAF controls Solaris's *port monitors*, small programs that watch over each port and detect requests for connection. The monitors make real-time decisions about whether the request meets the requirements for entry on that port; if requirements are met, the monitor hands the request to the appropriate service.

The two SAF commands you'll use to turn off Solaris services on the operating-system level are sacadm and pmadm. Use sacadm to add and remove the monitors on ports associated with services, and use pmadm to associate or disassociate a monitor with a given service. You can also use pmadm to add or remove services themselves. The syntax for sacadm and pmadm is somewhat arcane and complex enough that newcomers to Solaris shouldn't mess around with it. If you're running Solaris and you want to turn off services, check the documentation for each individual service. If you downloaded Solaris packages for the service, the documentation contained within those packages will probably tell you how to handle turning the service off; you can leave the port monitors active if you like.

> **WARNING** Because of the enormously complicated and system-dependent nature of this procedure, we don't recommend that casual Solaris users experiment with it. If you're more experienced with Solaris, Sun recommends that you learn about the Service Access Facility by reading the second edition of the *Solaris Advanced System Administrator's Guide,* by Janet Winsor (Macmillan Technical Publishing).

Summary

For Unix users to use particular network functions, a service for the function must be installed. Such servers make use of the Unix client-server architecture, answering requests from clients and managing data. The most familiar servers are those used for Internet activity, such as e-mail or Web browsing, but servers are used for a variety of other functions, such as print and file sharing or remote login access.

Deciding which services to run can be confusing. The best way to choose services is to determine what functions you need and then install services to meet those needs. Running more services than necessary will drain your system resources and slow down your computer. If you don't want to run certain services, you can turn them off, but you don't need to delete the service from your computer. You may decide to run the service at a later date, and if you've retained old initialization scripts and packages, it will save some time at that point.

CHAPTER
FORTY

Electronic Mail

- How Electronic Mail Works

- An Overview of Mail Services

- sendmail

- Postfix

- Exim

- qmail

- smail

- Setting Up POP and IMAP Services

- Summary

If you decide to set up a network and provide services that transfer data to and from the Internet, the first server you'll install will probably be an electronic mail server. E-mail is the core function of many Internet-connected networks, and is rapidly becoming the business and personal communication method of choice. A network that doesn't offer electronic mail to its users may not have those users very long.

Electronic mail is transferred in a more complicated manner than most people think. It relies on a series of servers and directory searches, all of which take place in the blink of an eye. These servers exist on the sending machine, the receiving machine, and many machines between the originator and the ultimate destination. Although many users think that e-mail is sent directly between the sender's mail client and the recipient's mail client, that is not the case.

Much of the work of electronic mail transfer is done by the mail server, also called the *mail transfer agent (MTA)*. A variety of MTAs are available for you to run, ranging from the small and relatively insecure to the large, impenetrable, and multifeatured. There are quite a few other server options along that spectrum as well. You can try out a few different MTAs until you find a transfer agent that works for you, but they are complicated enough to install and configure that many administrators just live with the one they picked first. That doesn't have to be the case, though, because moving to a more streamlined mail server may be easier than continuing to maintain and upgrade the complicated one.

In this chapter, we show you how electronic mail is transferred across the Internet. Tracing the progress of one e-mail message, we introduce the various components of electronic mail transfer and show you how more domains are involved in a single message's route than most people understand. Next, we introduce a variety of mail transfer agents and explain their features, installation methods, and configuration. Although you may choose to use a mail transfer agent that is not listed in this chapter, the servers described here are a good representation of the kinds of servers you're likely to find elsewhere.

Finally, we explain how to set up a POP or IMAP mail server. If your users prefer to work from a graphical environment—whether a Unix environment or a Windows or MacOS environment—they will probably need to use a POP or IMAP protocol mail client. These clients connect to your mail server using a particular protocol and download the user's mail to the local machine. This is an increasingly popular way to handle electronic mail, and it may be right for your network as well.

How Electronic Mail Works

Electronic mail is one of the most frequently used applications on the Internet and within local networks. With electronic mail, you can send messages nearly instantaneously, whether to the office next door or to a friend on the other side of the world. However, even though most people with an Internet connection send and receive electronic mail every day, very few of them know how e-mail actually works.

The Software Components

Electronic mail transfer is handled by a suite of programs. First, there is the *user agent*, sometimes called a mail user agent (MUA). This is what most people think of when they think about electronic mail software, because it's the client program. A wide array of e-mail clients is available, with a multitude of choices, regardless of the operating system you are using. Unix users tend to cluster around the shell-based electronic mail readers Pine, `elm`, and `emacs`, because these programs offer extra features such as individualized mail sorting and various composition features.

> **TIP**
>
> Pine uses the `pico` text editor, covered in Chapter 19: "`pico`, `joe`, and `jed`." `elm` uses the `vi` editor by default, but can be configured to use whatever editor you prefer. `vi` is introduced in Chapter 17: "The `vi` Editor."

Those Unix users who prefer to use a graphical environment such as the integrated desktops KDE or Gnome may use the graphical mail clients that are packaged with those desktops, or may find other graphical mail clients that suit their needs. If you run a heterogeneous network, your Windows users might like Eudora or Simeon as a graphical mail client—or even Microsoft Outlook, though we can't recommend Outlook.

> **WARNING**
>
> We aren't bashing Outlook simply because it's a Microsoft product. Rather, it's a security choice. Most of the e-mail viruses that make the evening news are Outlook-based viruses, written to exploit the Outlook program alone. People who receive these viruses but don't use Outlook to read their mail are less affected; people who read their mail with a shell-based text mail client don't have any issues with Windows-based viruses. If you run a network that includes Windows machines, consider banning Outlook and enforcing the use of a POP or IMAP mail client such as Eudora or Simeon.

The second component of electronic mail delivery is the *mail transfer agent (MTA)*. An MTA runs behind the scenes and is a server program, like the other programs described in this section of the book. If an MTA runs properly, most users will never even know that it exists. We describe some common MTAs in this chapter, including sendmail, Postfix, and qmail. The transfer agent receives outgoing messages from local mail clients and transmits them to the local network or Internet, while simultaneously receiving incoming mail from the network or Internet and sorting it into individual mail spools for each recipient. MTAs are responsible for getting the mail where it needs to be; they function like the postal service, where the mail client is like a local post office.

The third component of electronic mail delivery is the *delivery agent* itself. Delivery agents are part of the operating system, and there is not a wide range of choices as with mail clients and transfer agents. Delivery agents receive incoming mail from the transfer agent and deliver the message to its final destination, the user's personal mail spool. You don't need to worry much about delivery agents, because they work automatically and don't have much configurability on the administrative end.

The Process

To understand how these elements of mail transfer software work together to get your e-mail to its destination, here is an example. Assume that you have written an e-mail to your friend Page, who has an e-mail account at HushMail.

> **TIP**   HushMail, http://www.hushmail.com, is a free Web-based electronic mail service that offers encrypted e-mail. This service became quite popular after a well-publicized series of cracks into the Hotmail system in 1999. If you need to use a Web-based e-mail service, we recommend HushMail.

First, you must compose your message. Open your favorite e-mail client—perhaps Pine—and start a new message, placing Page's e-mail address in the To: field. Write your note to Page; when you're finished, select the Send option. (In Pine, it's Ctrl+x.) Your mail client takes the finished message and delivers it to the local network's mail transfer agent.

On this network, the local transfer agent is qmail. qmail receives the message from your client and notes that it is to be delivered outside the local network.

Were it a local message, sent to someone with the same domain name as you, `qmail` would simple shuttle the message to that person's incoming mail spool. However, because Page has an account at another domain, `qmail` must send the message across the Internet.

If you have an Internet connection that is not always on, your network's mail agent will queue up all outgoing mail and send it when the connection is active. Likewise, the mail agent will download all incoming mail when the connection is alive. If your message passes through a machine whose connection is down, it will be delayed.

Once `qmail` determines that the message is destined for another domain, it checks the To: header to get that domain's name from the recipient's e-mail address. In this case, it takes the `@hushmail.com` segment of Page's e-mail address as the intended receiving domain. `qmail` then looks up the *MX record* for `hushmail.com`.

An MX (Mail eXchanger) record is part of the domain's entry on a *Domain Name Server* machine, and it indicates where messages for that domain should be sent. Electronic mail messages are never sent directly from the originating domain to the recipient domain; instead, they are sent through intermediate hops. The MX record tells the sending transfer agent which intermediate site should receive the message first on its way to its ultimate destination.

Once the MX record has been consulted and the first intermediate site is known, the transfer agent on your network sends the message to that site. The MTA at that site looks up the MX record for the ultimate recipient domain and sends the message to the next intermediate hop, and so on. Eventually, the message arrives at its intended destination, `hushmail.com`. Depending on how far away geographically the destination is from the originating site, the message may travel through as many as 15 or 20 hops, or as few as 3 or 4. When `hushmail.com` receives the message, its transfer agent recognizes the address as its own.

The HushMail transfer agent then checks to see whether the e-mail address you specified for Page actually exists on their system. If it does, the message is placed in Page's incoming mail directory: usually `/var/spool/mail/$USER` or, in this case, `/var/spool/mail/page`. The message remains in that spool until Page checks for new mail and reads, downloads, or deletes the message. Should Page respond to you, the message will follow the same path in reverse.

An Overview of Mail Services

Mail services are a bit more complicated than some of the other servers that we discuss in this part of the book. The reason for this complication is that, when we talk about *mail servers,* we are talking about two separate types of programs:

- The mail server that accepts incoming electronic mail from the Internet

- The mail server to which your system's users connect to obtain their electronic mail

Although these two types of programs are very tightly related, they are distinctly different kinds of servers and should not be confused.

Electronic mail that travels over the Internet is handled by the Simple Mail Transport Protocol (SMTP). When your system receives electronic mail from the Internet, the sending site makes an SMTP connection to your site. Your SMTP server will verify that the intended recipient actually exists on your system and then will accept the mail message.

NOTE   Some older Unix systems might be configured to use the Unix-to-Unix Copy Protocol (UUCP), but recent advances in security and other considerations have made this protocol largely obsolete.

Once the SMTP server on your site accepts the message, it is deposited into a spool directory designated for that user. The standard location is `/var/spool/mail/$USER`, where $USER is the user ID of the person on the system to whom the mail was addressed. The message then sits in that spool directory until it is either read, using a local mail client that is configured to read mail directly from the spool, or downloaded, using a POP or IMAP server.

TIP   Encourage your users to download or delete their mail frequently. The incoming mail directory, `/var/spool/mail`, contains mail for everyone on the system in the same directory, simply divided into $USER subdirectories at the lowest level. If readers do not save or delete their mail when it's read, the messages remain in `/var/spool/mail`. Enough readers leaving enough undeleted messages in that spool will fill it, and no new incoming mail will be received. If your readers read mail directly from the spool, as with the shell-based mail readers Pine or `elm`, this is especially important. When users save messages with these readers, they are saved to the user's home directory and removed from `/var/spool/mail`.

POP (the Post Office Protocol) and IMAP (the Internet Message Access Protocol) are two slightly different protocols that accomplish essentially the same thing. That is, a user using a POP or IMAP mail client connects to the mail server and downloads his mail to his local machine (the IMAP protocol usually leaves a copy of the message on the server). Most modern graphic electronic mail programs, whether designed for Unix, Windows, or Macintosh machines, can download mail using one of these protocols. Popular POP and IMAP mail readers include Eudora, Microsoft Outlook, and Simeon.

The advantage of using a POP or IMAP server to distribute your users' electronic mail is that the user never needs to log directly into the mail server. This is a good thing from a security standpoint. However, each user who receives mail on your system still needs to have an account on the mail server, even if it's never accessed directly. This is because each user needs to have a separate spool directory, each user needs to be a valid user so that the SMTP server can authenticate mail for that person, and the POP or IMAP server will require the user to provide the password to her mail server account before downloading mail.

NOTE   Assuming that you don't want your users to log into shell accounts on the mail server, you should configure your `adduser` program to set each user's default shell on the mail server machine to either `/bin/false` (which will completely disallow logins) or `/usr/bin/passwd` (which will allow logins only for the purpose of changing passwords).

So, if you wish to set up mail services for your system, you must first install and configure an SMTP server. Then, you need to install a POP or IMAP server for users who want to download their mail remotely. Because POP and IMAP are controlled from the `inet` daemon, you must configure these services in the `/etc/inetd.conf` file. (This generally involves only uncommenting the relevant lines.) Learn more about the `inet` daemon in Chapter 43: "Remote Access (`inet`) Services."

Finally, you must ensure that every user on your system has an individual account on the mail server and make whatever security arrangements you think are necessary to protect the mail server machine from unauthorized entry. In particular, turn off any features that permit electronic mail to be relayed through your mail server. If you permit relaying, whether intentionally or not, your server is a valuable resource to those who send unsolicited commercial e-mail, which is a waste of everyone's time and money.

NOTE The mail servers described in this section of the chapter should all work as drop-in replacements for sendmail. You will need to configure your system to recognize the replacement server instead of sendmail if your Unix variant expects sendmail to be used as the local transfer agent. Do so by making the file /usr/lib/sendmail a symbolic link to the executable binary of your chosen replacement, then restarting the mailer daemon.

sendmail

The sendmail mail server is the granddaddy of mail transport agents. Now in version 8, sendmail has been around for years. It is comprehensive, will meet any mail transfer need you or your users have, has relatively few bugs because it's been under development for so long, and is the heavyweight option for mail software. The downside is that it is a very, very complicated program. Configuring sendmail—before you can even begin to run it—requires a 28-page FAQ. sendmail is not for the faint of heart or the newbie; it really is an advanced server and is best suited for large-scale networks that require the most bulletproof mail server possible.

NOTE Even then, large-scale networks often opt for mail servers other than sendmail because of the complicated way in which sendmail must be managed. See the "qmail" section later in this chapter.

We treat sendmail with a great deal of respect, but choose not to run it on our own systems. Instead, we run Postfix and are considering a switch to qmail. sendmail is overkill for small systems like ours, which don't receive a great deal of e-mail. Were we running an ISP, or managing networks for a major company or academic institution, sendmail might be a more appropriate answer. We include it here to introduce you to the most commonly used mail transport agent on the Internet, but we do not recommend that you use sendmail as your first MTA. Start with one of the mail servers listed in subsequent sections; if you find that one of those MTAs is not appropriate for your needs, consider sendmail—but only after doing your homework and learning how this complicated program works.

Installing and Configuring sendmail

Get the latest version of sendmail directly from the sendmail project at
http://www.sendmail.org. The current release is 8.11.1, which includes bug
fixes for the 8.11.0 version. Be sure you get the version with patches so that you
are running the most secure version of sendmail possible. Install the software
using the methods explained in Chapter 31: "Installing and Managing Software."

WARNING

Before you install and compile sendmail, read the "Compiling Sendmail" document at http://www.sendmail.org/compiling.html. This lengthy document
describes the various ways in which you can install sendmail and configure it during
compilation. There is an extensive listing of known quirks with almost every Unix
variant, as well as a set of manual pages and other data. Reading this file will help
you to avoid problems that may make it impossible for you to send or receive mail.

TIP

The easiest way to compile sendmail is to use the script Build, which you invoke
by issuing the command sh Build in the directory where you've placed sendmail. This script auto-probes your hardware and determines the configuration so
that the Makefile is generated appropriately.

When sendmail is installed, you can begin to configure it. Configuring sendmail is a lengthy and involved process that may seem quite intimidating: It is.
The configuration files are contained in the directory /etc/mail/cf. The configuration files all use the suffix .cf, and they must be parsed through the m4 program
to be edited properly. Thus, you'll need to install m4 and learn how to work with
it before you can configure sendmail. Those readers interested in learning to configure sendmail should consult the sendmail configuration README file
located at http://www.sendmail.org/m4/cf-readme.txt.

Postfix

Postfix is a newer mail server that is rapidly gaining adherents. Postfix is easier to
configure than sendmail or Qmail, but is still quite efficient, secure, and stable
under high loads. You can run Postfix on almost any kind of network configuration without a great deal of fuss. Several basic sample configurations are even

provided in the Postfix FAQ, so you can get your mail server running without a lot of homework to figure out the appropriate configuration.

Installing and Configuring Postfix

Obtain Postfix at almost any Unix software archive or directly from the Postfix development team at `http://www.postfix.org`. Install it with the methods described in Chapter 31: "Installing and Managing Software." When you have finished with the installation, you can begin to configure the server for your particular network.

Postfix configuration is done with the file `/etc/postfix/main.cf`. Although this is a lengthy file, few edits need to be made for the vast majority of sites running Postfix. Typical configurations can accept most of the defaults. The `/etc/postfix/main.cf` file is extensively commented, and you should not have much trouble understanding what each section of code is intended to do.

There are, however, some specific configurations that you'll need to make to get Postfix working. The first edit you'll need to make is to define your domain name so that Postfix knows what mail it should accept. Open the configuration file in a text editor and locate the line

```
myhostname = <your server's name here>
```

Change the `<your server's name here>` entry to your mail server's fully qualified domain name, such as `mail.mydomain.com`. If you've given the mail server another name, such as `george`, you'd need to enter `george.mydomain.com`. Check to be sure that the angle brackets are deleted.

WARNING   This entry is used as a basic parameter for many other configuration options and for Postfix operation in general, so be sure you enter the correct machine name and that you include the entire domain name. If you don't, Postfix won't work.

Next, look for the `/etc/postfix/main.cf` entry that defines the domain name that will be attached to outgoing mail. This entry is

```
mydomain = <your domain name here>
```

Replace the placeholder text and the brackets with your domain name. Do not include any machine names; just use the domain and the top-level extension, as in `mydomain.com`.

To configure the outgoing domain name further, locate the entry that reads

```
myorigin = <either $myhostname or $mydomain>
```

If you choose the variable $myhostname, mail sent from your domain will carry a return address that specifies the machine from which the mail was sent. That is, if user ellen sends mail from the machine topaz on your network, her return address will be shown as ellen@topaz.*yourdomain*.com. If you choose the variable $mydomain instead, her return address will be shown as ellen@*yourdomain*.com. The $mydomain option is more common, though the choice is yours.

The last configuration that you must make for Postfix to run is to define the various names by which your mail server is known, so that Postfix will accept mail intended for your network regardless of how the server name is configured. Locate the line

```
mydestination =  <list of destinations here>
```

and edit the placeholder text so that it contains any aliases that your mail server machine might have. A typical list would look something like this:

```
mydestination = $myhostname, localhost.$mydomain,➡
$mydomain, mail.$mydomain
```

Of course, replace these placeholders with the actual machine names on your system and add any others that might be required due to your configuration. Editing this line properly means that any of these address configurations will be accepted as valid on incoming mail and that those messages will not be returned to the sender as invalid.

The remainder of /etc/postfix/main.cf deals with virtual domains, junk filtering, and address rewriting. These are somewhat advanced topics and probably won't be of interest to a majority of administrators. With the basic setup outlined above, you should be able to use the default values in these other entries without worry.

Starting Postfix

Once you have finished configuring /etc/postfix/main.cf, save the file and exit the text editor. Now you can start Postfix, which is usually done by issuing the command

```
/usr/bin/postfix
```

as root. (If you happen to have a System V init script for Postfix, run that instead.) Make sure that port 25, the default SMTP port, is open to incoming connections. You should now be able to receive mail for your system, and it should be delivered to the appropriate /var/spool/mail/$USER directory for each user.

TIP

Postfix documentation, such as the comments in /etc/postfix/main.cf, is exhaustive and useful. The Postfix FAQ is a lengthy document that contains several sample Postfix configurations—standalone machine, networked machines, Postfix on a firewall or inside an intranet, and so on—as well as a good list of troubleshooting solutions. You can find the FAQ at http://postfix.sparks.net/faq.html.

Exim

The Exim mail server is an English program, developed at Cambridge as a replacement for smail (described below). Like smail, Exim is released under the GNU Public License and is freely available. However, Exim incorporates some features that were never part of the smail distribution, including address verification and some spam filtering tools. Exim is small, takes up a limited footprint on a machine, and has low CPU overhead. It's a good alternative for small networks that don't deliver a huge amount of mail, though it's been tested in production environments as well.

Exim is becoming increasingly popular. Many administrators who once used smail and liked having a GPL mail server on their system replaced smail with Exim because of its increased security and its ease of administration. Exim even comes as the default mail transfer agent on some Unix variant distributions, and it has been picked up by some major sites that transfer thousands of messages per day over Exim.

Obtaining and Installing Exim

You can get the latest version of Exim from the Exim project site, http://www. exim.org. The latest version is 3.16. The Exim team recommends that you stay away from versions 2.0.*x* and earlier, because they were essentially beta versions; the 3.0 and higher versions have much improved security and other tools.

Install Exim as you would install any other Unix software package, using the methods introduced in Chapter 31: "Installing and Managing Software." Be sure to read any text files included in the Exim package, especially the README file. This file will contain any last-minute changes to the package, as well as offer helpful guidance in getting Exim compiled and configured on your system.

> **WARNING**   Before you begin to install Exim, create a new local configuration file with the name `Local/Makefile`. When you unzip the packed Exim file after downloading, you'll find a template in the `/src/EDITME` file; you can just copy the `/src/EDITME` file to the correct location. Read through this `Makefile` before you build the package, because you may need to make some edits before installation.

Exim is configured through a single file that runs at boot, which uses both regular entries and macros to handle its settings. The syntax for Exim configuration is tricky, and we suggest that, should you want to install Exim and configure it to run on your system, you consult the Exim FAQ at the Exim project Web site. The FAQ explains each configuration option and shows you the correct syntax for enabling or disabling the options.

> **NOTE**   The default configuration file for Exim is located at `/src/configure.default`. This file is copied into the actual configuration file location (which changes, depending on the Unix variant being used) at the time of installation. You can review this file if you want to know a default configuration that has since changed, or you can copy it from the `/src` location into the current configuration file location if you've edited the file and you don't like your changes.

Testing and Monitoring Exim

When you have finished working with the configuration and building the server, you can test your installation by issuing the command

```
exim -bV
```

at the shell prompt. If you've made mistakes, Exim will return error messages specifying what the problem was. If there were no problems, you'll see output containing the version number and build date.

Next, test to see whether Exim can recognize your local users and remote domains. First, issue the command

```
exim -v -bt <username>
```

placing your local user ID in the *username* field. Exim should return a message showing that it found the local user's mailbox. Test for remote identification by issuing the command

```
exim -v -bt <remote address>
```

using a remote e-mail address of your own, if possible. Exim should return a message confirming that it found the remote address. Once both of these tests return positive results, try opening your mail client and sending messages to yourself, both locally and remotely.

For ongoing diagnostics, you'll find Exim logs in several locations, each serving a different function. The main log works as the logs in other mail servers do, by recording each message received and sent. There is also a reject log, a panic log, and a process log. The most critical of these is probably the panic log, because it records instances when Exim crashed and what was happening at that time. By keeping an eye on the panic log, you'll have a better understanding of any flaws on your system that may contribute to mail server failure.

qmail

The qmail mail server is a young program that has, despite its relatively recent creation, been adopted by many high-volume sites as well as small networks. qmail is a secure and reliable mail server that is easy to administer and offers a lot of features that users can manipulate without involving the mail administrator. qmail is compatible with many of the sendmail standard habits, so it's easy to migrate a mail system from sendmail to qmail.

NOTE

qmail is so robust that it's the mail server of choice for sites that run unbelievable amounts of data through the server on a constant basis. eGroups (http://www.egroups.com) is a Web-based mailing list site that transmits millions of messages each day; it runs qmail. Hotmail (http://www.hotmail.com), a Web-based free e-mail service owned by Microsoft, runs qmail. Microsoft has tried to migrate Hotmail to Microsoft Exchange, their own mail server, but Exchange hasn't yet been able to handle the volume of mail generated by more than 32 million users. Many major universities and large ISPs also use qmail.

Installing and Configuring qmail

qmail can be installed on any Unix variant, including all the variants covered in this book. We've placed a copy of qmail on the CD-ROM included with this book, or you can download the most recent version from the qmail site at http://cr.yp.to/qmail.html. The current version is 1.03.

Before you install qmail, consult the file INSTALL in the qmail package. Though installation of qmail follows most of the rules explained in Chapter 31: "Installing and Managing Software," there are some changes you must make and options you must select to install qmail properly. Follow the instructions in INSTALL to get your qmail server up and running.

You'll find good documentation included with the qmail package. Manual pages are installed in the /var/qmail/man directory, and there are quite a few HOWTO pages in /var/qmail/doc. There is a good FAQ at the qmail site (http://cr.yp.to/qmail/faq.html) and other valuable information at that site, including a set of graphics that show you exactly how qmail transfers particular kinds of messages. For those readers who are visual learners, these graphics are highly useful.

The INSTALL file will show you how to configure qmail so that it will work on your system. You can move on to more advanced topics, such as working with virtual domains, receiving mail for another valid host, and managing a very large network's incoming mail, with the tips in the FAQ. The FAQ also contains good information on mail monitoring and network administration.

Mailing Lists and qmail

One of the most useful features of `qmail` is the ability for individual users to set up and manage their own mailing lists. This takes some burden from you as an administrator because you won't have to add or delete lists, or list members, from central files. Instead, your users can decide the name of their lists, the people who will be on the list, and how the list will be managed.

To set up a user-managed mailing list under `qmail`, log into your user account. Create a file called `.qmail-`*listname* in your home directory, replacing *listname* with a simple name for your list that does not include spaces or special characters. In that file, enter all the e-mail addresses of the people who will be on this mailing list, one address to each line. Save the file and exit the text editor. Now, when mail is sent to the e-mail address *youruserid-listname@yourdomain*`.com`, `qmail` will automatically send a copy to everyone listed in the `.qmail-`*listname* file in your home directory.

To make sure that you receive bounces and other administrative messages at your e-mail address (and that bounces are not sent to the mail administrator), issue the command `touch .qmail-`*listname*`-owner` to create an empty file called `.qmail-`*listname*`-owner` in your directory, which identifies you as the list owner.

There is no limit to the number of mailing lists that can be managed by an individual user on your system. However, because the subscription and deletion of users must be done by hand, there is an effective limit on the amount of time any user will probably want to spend maintaining mailing lists. The `qmail` developer, Dan Bernstein, suggests the `ezmlm` package as an alternative; `ezmlm` supports automatic subscriptions, archives, and other useful features. It is installed globally, but is used by individual users in much the same way as the regular `qmail` mailing lists described above. You can learn more about `ezmlm` at `http://cr.yp.to/ezmlm.html`.

smail

The `smail` mail server is the GNU Foundation's mail server program. It hasn't been upgraded in a very long time and has significant security holes because it permits mail relays without authorization. We cannot recommend that you run `smail`, even though we support most GNU software; it just isn't secure enough to place on a machine connected to the Internet.

Most sites that have run `smail` in the past are now running `exim`, `qmail`, or some other small and robust mail server program. Relatively few have switched to `sendmail`, because `smail` was initially intended as a smaller replacement for `sendmail`. If you're interested in a Free mail server, you'll have to look somewhere other than the GNU Foundation. It's unfortunate that `smail` is not currently being developed, because it served a useful purpose.

Setting Up POP and IMAP Services

POP and IMAP services are very simple to set up on Unix. In general, one need only install the IMAP package. The IMAP package, often included with your Unix distribution or available from a Unix software archive, usually includes support for both the IMAP and POP protocols. Once the package is installed, using the regular Unix software installation methods described in Chapter 31: "Installing and Managing Software," granting access to the POP or IMAP service is simply a matter of uncommenting the relevant lines in `/etc/inetd.conf` to make the service operational.

In the `/etc/inetd.conf` file, as introduced in Chapter 43: "Remote Access (`inet`) Services," you should see a section of code that looks like this:

```
# Pop and imap mail services et al
#
#pop-2   stream  tcp nowait root /usr/sbin/tcpd ipop2d
#pop-3   stream  tcp nowait root /usr/sbin/tcpd ipop3d
#imap    stream  tcp nowait root /usr/sbin/tcpd imapd
```

Simply uncomment the line corresponding to the service you wish to use by opening the file in a text editor and deleting the hashmark at the start of the appropriate line.

NOTE   POP2 is an older version of the POP protocol. Most recent mail programs support the newer POP3 version. We suggest that, if possible, you use POP3 in preference to POP2. Use POP2 only if you have some very compelling reason why you should support an older mail client program.

If you choose to use the POP3 service, for example, the code would look the same as above, but the second line would not have a hashmark:

```
# Pop and imap mail services et al
  #
  #pop-2  stream  tcp nowait root /usr/sbin/tcpd ipop2d
  pop-3   stream  tcp nowait root /usr/sbin/tcpd ipop3d
  #imap   stream  tcp nowait root /usr/sbin/tcpd imapd
```

At this point, you can restart `inetd`, and your users should have access to their mail through any POP or IMAP client that they wish to use.

POP or IMAP?

Are you better off using a POP or an IMAP server? It is largely a question of preference. IMAP is the more flexible of the two: It allows you to set up shared mailboxes, for example, and IMAP mail clients can perform more operations on messages. However, the flexibility comes at the price of complexity.

POP3 is the simpler of the protocols and is supported by almost all common mail software. The conventional wisdom in the Unix mail world at this time is that most people should use POP3 servers, because the mail clients are slightly easier to use and support. However, administrators who use POP3 servers should plan to migrate to IMAP servers in the not-too-distant future. Considering the nature of the software world, though, the conventional wisdom can change abruptly. You shouldn't have too much trouble supporting and upgrading whatever protocol you choose to implement for your mail server.

Summary

Installing an electronic mail transfer agent, or server, is probably one of the first activities of a new network administrator. Users rely on electronic mail for both personal and business communication, and a network that does not offer e-mail may lose users in favor of a network that does. Electronic mail is transferred between networks through the combined work of several software programs: a mail user agent (MUA) or mail client, a mail transfer agent (MTA) or server, and a delivery agent. The first two may be chosen from a wide array of user clients and servers, while the third is usually a function of your Unix operating-system variant.

Once a message is composed and sent by a user agent, the transfer agent determines whether the message has a local or remote destination. Local messages are promptly placed in the recipient's personal mail spool, while remote message destinations are checked using an MX record, part of the Domain Name Service. The message is then sent to the first of a series of intermediate servers between the originating and receiving machines. When the recipient domain's transfer agent receives the mail, the message is placed in the recipient's mail spool.

There are several mail transfer agents, from which the network administrator can choose the one best suited for her use. The most widely used mail transfer agent is `sendmail`, though it is large and difficult to configure. Many network administrators have chosen to switch to smaller, more easily managed servers such as `qmail`, Exim, or Postfix. Regardless of the agent you choose, you may want to install a server that will provide electronic mail for download using the POP or IMAP protocols if your users prefer graphical environments that require a POP or IMAP mail client.

CHAPTER
FORTY-ONE

41

USENET News

- How USENET Works

- Administering a Sound USENET Site

- INN

- Summary

Although it may not be the first priority of many Unix system administrators, running a USENET feed is one distinguishing mark of a full-service system. Though the Web has taken over much of the incidental information-seeking that characterized USENET's early years, USENET is still a valuable part of the Internet, and users who cannot obtain news service from their Internet provider are often willing to pay a third party to obtain reliable USENET access.

Administering a news server can be as simple or as complicated as you'd like. At the easy end, you simply need to set up a couple of servers, define a default set of newsgroups, and obtain an upstream newsfeed provider. At the more complicated end, you need to set up the same servers, define a more complex set of newsgroups, run programs that will obtain updated lists of newsgroups on a regular basis, obtain at least one—though usually three or four—upstream feeds, and define filters that will delete spam before it hits your news spool.

NOTE

Most administrators fall into the middle ground between these two. We happen to know a lot of people who operate on the complicated end of the equation, but they're professional news administrators who happen to care deeply about USENET administration. Because we also care about USENET, we tend toward recommending more involvement with your news server than toward recommending a *laissez-faire* method of running news.

Regardless of how you decide to run your news service, when you choose to provide USENET access to your users, you are participating in one of the oldest Internet protocols. News has been around for many years, and protocols haven't changed much from the early days. There is a more hierarchical naming structure now, and there is far more traffic across the multitude of newsgroups than the early Internet carried as a whole, but the simple mechanism of posts and responses remains familiar to those—like us—who have been on USENET far longer than we like to think.

How USENET Works

If you've never used USENET, you might think that news works in the same way that the Web does, where a file exists in a central location and is accessed by multiple clients, or in the way that e-mail works, where an individual file is sent directly across the Internet to its recipient. This, however, is not the case. News uses a distributed dispersal mechanism, codified in the NNTP protocol.

USENET is a giant conglomeration of *newsgroups,* which are divided into *hierarchies.* A hierarchy is a group of newsgroups that fall—loosely—under the category defined by the hierarchy name. Therefore, groups in the us.* hierarchy are groups related to the United States, while groups in the staroffice.* hierarchy are groups related to the StarOffice integrated office suite released by Sun.

Table 41.1 shows some of the dominant hierarchies. Note that the first eight hierarchies are collectively known as the Big Eight, because they are internationally available and are generally considered the core USENET groups. Within each of these hierarchies, there are various subhierarchies, often going down two or three levels until the actual groups are named. Table 41.2 shows some of the many national hierarchies; many of these hierarchies carry groups that duplicate Big Eight and alt.* groups, but are used in the local language instead of in English, the USENET *lingua franca.*

TABLE 41.1: Selected USENET Hierarchies

Hierarchy	Purpose
comp	Computer-related groups, both hardware and software
humanities	Groups covering topics in the humanities, such as literature and music
misc	Groups that don't fit elsewhere in the Big Eight
news	Groups about USENET
rec	Groups focused on recreational topics, such as sports, television, and crafts
sci	Scientific groups, often intended for professionals instead of enthusiasts
soc	Groups about society, such as individual cultures and lifestyles
talk	Mostly unmoderated groups about hot-button issues, such as gun control and abortion
alt	Groups on a variety of topics, created using a less restrictive process than that in the Big Eight
biz	Business-related groups
christnet	Groups on Christian topics

Continued on next page

TABLE 41.1 CONTINUED: Selected USENET Hierarchies

Hierarchy	Purpose
clarinet	Moderated groups available by subscription only, which contain syndicated material from the Associated Press, Reuters, and other press agencies
free	A completely open hierarchy where anyone may create a group on any desired topic
k12	Groups targeted at United States students and teachers at the kindergarten, primary, and secondary levels

TABLE 41.2: Selected Regional and National USENET Hierarchies

Hierarchy	Region or Nation
ar	Argentina
at	Austria
aus	Australia
be	Belgium
bermuda	Bermuda
ch	Switzerland
chile	Chile
chinese	China (and Chinese language)
cym	Wales (and Welsh language)
cz	Czech Republic
de	German language
dk	Denmark
es	Spain
esp	Spanish language
finet	Finland (and Finnish language)
fj	Japan (and Japanese language)

Continued on next page

TABLE 41.2 CONTINUED: Selected Regional and National USENET Hierarchies

Hierarchy	Region or Nation
fr	French language
han	Korean (and Hangul language)
hk	Hong Kong
hun	Hungary
ie	Ireland
is	Iceland
il	Israel
israel	Israel
it	Italy (and Italian language)
japan	Japan
malta	Malta
nigeria	Nigeria
no	Norway (and Norwegian language)
nz	New Zealand
pl	Poland (and Polish language)
pt	Portugal (and Portuguese language)
relcom	Commonwealth of Independent States (and Russian language)
se	Sweden
si	Slovenia
sk	Slovakia
tw	Taiwan (and Chinese language)
ukr	Ukraine
wales	Wales (and English and Welsh languages)
za	South Africa

A typical newsgroup name is something like

```
rec.arts.tv.mst3k.misc
```

The first component is the top-level hierarchy, and the remaining components are used to narrow the focus of the group's name until the particular topic of the group is reached. In this case, the group is contained in the general `rec.*` hierarchy, and the rest of the name indicates that it is part of a lower-level television hierarchy devoted to the *Mystery Science Theatre 3000* television show. This particular group is the miscellaneous discussion group devoted to the show; it happens to have a partner group, `rec.arts.tv.mst3k.announce`, which is *moderated* and carries only important announcements about the show.

NOTE A moderated newsgroup does not permit direct posts from readers to the group. Instead, posts are e-mailed to the group's moderator(s), who then decide whether the post is permissible on the moderated group. Most moderated groups have well-stated descriptions of what is permissible and what is not; other groups, such as those with the `*.announce.*` component in their names, are moderated so that only announcements (no discussion) will be posted. Groups are moderated for different reasons, whether from a desire to focus discussion narrowly on a topic or to remove completely unrelated posts from the spool, and can use different methods to moderate, whether it is a majority-rules voting panel or a *robomoderator* (a software program that parses incoming posts according to a defined protocol). Moderated groups are neither better nor worse than unmoderated groups; they simply present a different kind of USENET experience.

The Process

Assume that you have found a group that you're interested in reading or that you want to participate in. Because you've merely found a reference to this group on a Web page or in a book, you want to see whether the group is as exciting as the name promises. To see what's in the group, you'll need to use a newsreader, a client program that connects to the local news server and obtains the messages for that particular group.

A variety of newsreaders are available for Unix users, both the traditional shell-based programs, such as `nn`, `trn`, and `tin`, and the graphical programs included with integrated desktop environments or window managers. We find that the shell-based programs are far more powerful and allow you to manage your groups more effectively, but there are many adherents to graphical news clients. We're particularly fond of the threaded newsreader `trn`.

As you read the posts in the group, you are looking at documents that are stored locally on your news server. News articles are transported across the Internet in a way different from much other data transfer. When you make a USENET post, it is stored in the outgoing spool on your local news server. At a predetermined interval, your news server uploads all the outgoing messages to its *upstream feed,* another news server at a different location. That server then distributes the messages across the Internet. Eventually, every news server that receives articles for this particular newsgroup will have a copy of your message.

The protocol that underlies transfer of news messages is NNTP (the Net News Transfer Protocol). The NNTP protocol is defined as a TCP, or stream, process that runs on port 119. NNTP itself is not a news server or a news client, but the method by which data is transferred between servers and servers, or between servers and clients.

Figure 41.1 shows a graphical representation of this mechanism.

There is no central server somewhere on the Internet that holds all the USENET messages. Messages are distributed and downloaded from various servers, depending on the subscription list for that server. That is, if your server receives messages for three hierarchies from your upstream provider, you cannot pass on messages for any other hierarchies to your downstream peers. To get messages for those hierarchies, your downstream peers will need to arrange a feed from some other source. In Figure 41.2, you can see the complicated nets that are required to get full newsfeeds on a local server.

FIGURE 41.1:

USENET articles are distributed in a diffuse manner.

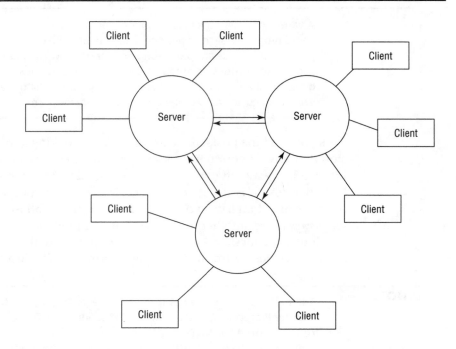

News articles are identified with a long string of alphanumeric characters and the originating news server's name. Each article carries a unique Message-ID number, which looks like this:

```
finding_970997403@qucis.QueensU.CA
```

This particular Message-ID identifies a posting called "FAQ: How to find people's E-mail addresses," which is regularly posted to the `news.announce.newusers` newsgroup. You can use the Message-ID of any given post to locate it on the news spool or to search in a Web archive such as that maintained by Deja at `http://www.deja.com`.

FIGURE 41.2:

It is likely that a given news server obtains newsfeeds from a variety of upstream sources.

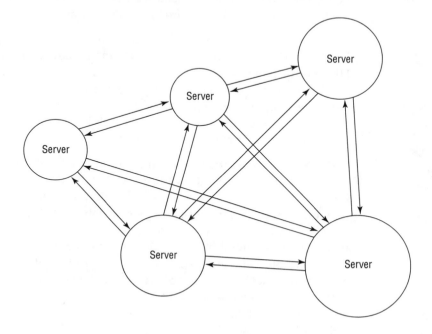

<table>
<tr><td>NOTE</td></tr>
</table>

Deja used to be a much more useful resource than it is now. It offered reasonably complete archives of postings to the Big Eight, `alt.*`, and several other hierarchies, going back well into the mid-1990s. Unfortunately, Deja chose to take down the older archives in late 1999, and now you can use the Deja archives to search for only USENET posts that have been made since early 1999. Although Deja is still helpful, it is nowhere near the resource it used to be. Most USENET regulars hope that Deja will reconsider removing the archives or that they'll make the data available to another provider.

Retaining Posts

Once any given post has been received by a local news server, the post remains available to readers on that system for a length of time determined by the news administrator. When the time period has ended, the message *expires* and is deleted from the system. Depending on the number of groups carried locally and the type of those groups, expire times range from one day to a month or more.

It is generally recommended that announce groups and groups dealing with USENET administration, such as `news.announce.newgroups`, expire monthly. High-traffic hierarchies such as `rec.*` or `soc.*` may need to expire weekly, and some hierarchies may require a daily expire period. The `misc.jobs.*` groups are particularly large, and you may not want to carry them; most people offering jobs also post their offerings in the big Web-based services such as `http://www.monster.com` and `http://www.dice.com`.

These fast-expire groups are usually found in the `alt.binaries.*` hierarchy. We don't think that any news administrator should carry these groups, because they will overwhelm your news spool with huge amounts of binary data. In addition, the data posted in these groups is usually posted illegally; the groups are simply cesspools of copyright violation. For example, a quick scan of `alt.binaries.*` shows pirated copies of Microsoft Office, hundreds of scanned pictures from Penthouse and Hustler, and other copyrighted data that is being released over the Internet without the copyright holder benefiting from the transmission. Although it's a remote possibility, if you knowingly permit posts containing illegally transmitted data to pass through your server, you might be liable for copyright violation yourself.

NOTE
If the copyright violation issue doesn't move you, consider this: A full USENET feed (all Big Eight and `alt.*` groups) will contain about a gigabyte of data a day. Assuming that you don't expire everything daily, you'll need a multiple-gigabyte drive just to handle news—a decidedly low priority compared to regular network needs and e-mail transfer. If you're on any sort of metered-bandwidth connection, it's ridiculous to pay for software and porn that you won't use.

Creating Newsgroups

The process for creating a newsgroup differs depending on the hierarchy in which you want the group to exist. For the Big Eight hierarchies (`rec`, `org`, `soc`, `bio`, `misc`, `humanities`, `talk`, and `sci`), there is a strict procedure involving a formal Request for Discussion, a minimum discussion period, and a formal automated vote controlled by an impartial volunteer. The entire process takes about three or four months, but is the best alternative for topics with significant existing traffic that should be available worldwide. The relevant newsgroups for Big Eight newsgroup creation are news.announce.newgroups and news.groups.

Starting a group in the alt.* hierarchy is quite different. New alt.* groups are proposed and discussed in alt.config, though discussion in alt.config is not necessarily required. Anyone can send out a newgroup message for an alt.* group, though it may be negated because anyone can send out an rmgroup command to remove the group. Good news administrators do not accept newgroup or rmgroup commands for alt.* automatically.

To start a group in a local or national hierarchy, locate the individual hierarchy's configuration group and find out what the procedure is for that hierarchy. In the uk.* (United Kingdom) and it.* (Italy) hierarchies, for example, a voting process similar to that used in the Big Eight is used. In other local and national hierarchies, there is no formal process.

Administering a Sound USENET Site

The biggest factor in maintaining a sound USENET site is whether you prevent your users, and others, from using your site to act against the best interest of the network. That is, if your site is a haven for spammers and people who consistently flood unrelated newsgroups with commercial e-mail or junk posts, or if you have an open port that lets unauthorized users inject USENET posts at your site without your knowledge, you won't be a good citizen.

It's easy to fix these problems, though. You can set up a strict set of user policies and abide by them, which will fix most of your problems with user behavior. If users don't follow the rules, you can pull their access. You can also lock down your ports so that people can't hook onto your network and use your access to post junk, which will carry your own IP address as the originating location. Unfortunately, though it's reasonably simple to address these concerns, many news administrators don't. Many sites simply don't seem to care, and their users make USENET a more difficult place to exchange ideas.

Arranging a Newsfeed

There are several ways to obtain a newsfeed for your local news server. The easiest way is to ask a friend, if your friends happen to be news administrators who run a clean server and are willing to share their data with you. (Not all your friends will be able to do so; many commercial or academic sites prohibit their employees from providing downstream feeds without formal permission or a paid contract.)

If you don't have pals who are news administrators with friendly dispositions, you can always purchase a feed. How much this service will cost depends on what kind of groups you want in this feed. If you're looking for a full feed with thousands of groups, you'll require quite a bit of bandwidth from your upstream provider, and they'll probably charge you accordingly. Feeds of single hierarchies are usually much more affordable.

TIP   Check with your upstream Internet access provider. If you have a local ISP, they may feed you both local and international groups. Larger ISPs or connection providers may be able to offer you a feed of hierarchies you didn't even know you wanted, or they might be limited to the Big Eight and a few regional hierarchies.

Most news servers accept multiple newsfeeds, whether to increase redundancy—and thus limit the number of articles that might be lost in transit—or to obtain hierarchies that aren't available through their main feed. It's worth searching around for feeds of hierarchies that you really want. Just remember that, in newsfeeds more than in almost any other form of data transfer on the Internet, location counts. If you have the ability to get a feed from someone geographically close to you, choose that feed over a distant feed if possible. You'll get articles faster with less degradation.

Keeping Your Newsgroups Updated

To offer your users the most accurate list of groups possible, you need to keep your *active file* updated. The active file is a list of all current valid groups in all hierarchies. Even if you don't carry all these groups, you should have an accurate list of what is valid. This will help your users find and post to the most appropriate groups instead of to groups that either are inappropriate or were created incorrectly and thus are not carried on well-formed sites.

Continued on next page

If you are using INN (see the section on INN below), you can use the utility `actsync` and the server `actsyncd` to set up an automated synchronization with a trusted upstream site. This utility will obtain the active file from that site on a regular basis (defined by you) and replace your current active file with the newer one.

It is quite difficult to maintain an active file by hand, especially if you're not a full-time news administrator. There are over 35,000 active newsgroups; even if you carry only a tiny fraction of that number, there will still be 35,000 groups in your active file. You won't be able to process every `newgroup` and `rmgroup` command that appears at your site, and you may be tempted to put `newgroup`s and `rmgroup`s on automatic approval. Don't do this; instead, get a copy of the active file from a trusted site.

User Policies

When you offer news access to your users, you should make it clear that on USENET, unlike most other areas of the Internet, the old rules of netiquette still apply. Point your users to established USENET FAQs and other documentation, and let them know that you do not permit the posting of off-topic messages, unsolicited commercial material, or massive crosspostings to unrelated groups. Newsgroups generally have charters and other documents that define the kinds of posts that are on topic and those that are not; most newsgroups do not permit commercial postings or binary material.

If you receive messages saying that your users have posted inappropriately, research the situation before you rush to a decision. Usually, a complaint to the news administrator means that your user posted something inappropriate or is posting without complying with the charter of a particular group. However, some people fly off the trigger very quickly where USENET is concerned and will complain about posts that aren't really a problem at all. Warn your user for borderline cases, and reserve pulling their access to USENET (or to your entire system) for instances where a truly blatant transgression has happened.

INN

If you are going to offer USENET news to your users, you need to run a news server. One of the most popular and reliable news servers is called INN, the Inter-NetNews program. INN is an NNTP news server that is capable of handling multiple input streams, thus processing incoming and outgoing news articles at a rate much higher than that reached by other news servers. INN manages all aspects of article traffic, including forwarding, receiving, organizing, and expiring.

INN is highly configurable and is reasonably easy to administer and maintain. In addition, the documentation for INN is easy to understand and is extremely detailed. You shouldn't run across any problems that aren't covered in the exhaustive documentation, whether in the FAQ or in the documentation included with the INN package.

Obtaining and Installing INN

You can get INN at many Unix software archives. You can always find the latest official release at `ftp://ftp.vix.com/pub/inn`. The current release is 1.7.2.

WARNING If you are looking in a software archive and you find INN version 1.5.1, pass it by. It has a security hole that can be patched, but why bother with patching if you can obtain a secure version in 1.7.2?

Any patches that are released for INN will be located at `ftp://ftp.isc.org/isc/inn/unoff-patches`. You can also find some neat add-ons at `ftp://ftp/isc/org/isc/inn/unoff-contrib` if you're interested in expanding the functions in your installation of INN.

INN will run on most popular Unix variants, including the Unices covered in this book. If you have the functions `socket()` and `select()`, INN will work with little reconfiguration. You will need to have a significant amount of RAM on the machine where you run INN, because INN is explicitly designed to eat up memory as it runs. After a few days of operation, an INN process may require several megabytes of memory all to itself. The faster processor you have, the better.

To install INN, first unpack the compressed archive package you downloaded from the Internet. In that package, you'll find a file called `Install.ms`. Read this file first and follow its instructions explicitly. This file is extremely well-written and will walk you through INN configuration and installation without much trouble. The "First Time Installation" section is particularly helpful.

Installing INN on Linux

Linux administrators should obtain the Linux-specific INN package from `ftp://sunsite.unc.edu/pub/Linux/system/News`; look for the most recent version. This package will have the regular `Install.ms` file as well as some Linux-specific installation tips. The package also includes a preconfigured `config.data` file that should work out of the box.

Installing INN on Solaris

Although Solaris administrators can install INN without trouble, you should be sure that you are running all the current TCP patches if necessary. Solaris 2.x and higher have known trouble with TCP, and patches are available from Sun. Solaris 7 is reputed to have incorporated many of these patches into the operating system, but if you find trouble with INN on a Solaris 7 system, you might need to check your TCP/IP throughput and see whether it is lower than it should be.

Installing INN on FreeBSD

FreeBSD administrators can install and run INN as described in the regular `Install.ms` file. However, there is an alternative. Vincent Archer, an INN administrator, has written an autoconfiguration package specifically for FreeBSD systems. You can get it at `ftp://ftp.frmug.org/pub/news/autoconf-inn.1.5.1.tar.gz`.

To install this package, download and untar the autoconfiguration package in your INN 1.5 source directory. You'll see new subdirectories for `configure` and `config`. Use the regular source code installation method outlined in Chapter 31: "Installing and Maintaining Software," using `configure`, `make`, and `make install` to install the autoconfiguration package.

Configuring and Running INN

Once you have installed INN properly, you really don't have that much work to do. First, you'll need to run the `rc.news` script to start the `innd` daemon. The daemon will monitor incoming articles and sort them to the correct directories, expire articles that have reached their end on your system, and perform all the other basic administrative tasks of maintaining a news spool.

Managing Newsfeeds

For `innd` to handle your incoming newsfeed correctly, you'll need to set up the `newsfeeds` configuration file. This file tells `innd` what groups you carry; what articles are already on your system; and other important information that will determine what is kept from the feed or sent on to your downstream feeds, and what is discarded. A sample entry in `newsfeeds` looks like this:

```
feed1/newsfeed.myisp.com\

    :*,!alt.*/!alt\
    :Tf,Wnm:
```

In the first line, `feed1` is an alias for the feed that comes from `newsfeed.myisp.com`. You need to specify the full domain name of the upstream feed provider, because INN will not send an article back to a site where it has already been. The domain name will be in the `Path:` header of the article, so INN will compare that header to the various entries in `newsfeeds` to see whether an article should be sent upstream.

In the second line, we've defined the feed so that you will receive all articles from `newsfeed.myisp.com` except for articles posted or crossposted to the `alt.*` hierarchy. To do this, we've used the negation operator (`!`) instead of listing all the hierarchies that will be accepted. This is much shorter and saves space in the file.

The final feed defines how the posts will be configured when you get them. The `Tf` component means that you're receiving a file feed, which is the method used for almost every newsfeed on the Internet. You will probably never have a feed that isn't a file feed. The `Wnm` component means that the Message-ID and name of every article sent to the upstream site will be logged in a particular file, usually `/var/spool/news/out.going/feed1`.

Why would you send articles to an upstream site that provides your newsfeed? Well, if anyone on your site ever posts articles to USENET, you'll need to send those posts upstream so that they'll be distributed to all the other news servers that make up USENET. In addition, if you receive multiple feeds, you may be able to provide articles to one upstream provider, which that provider doesn't already receive from its own feed sources. USENET traffic works in both directions; you need to configure the transmission so that it meets your requirements regardless of which way the articles are flowing.

Setting Expirations

In the `expire.ctl` file, you'll decide how long each group's posts will be retained on your system. As we explained above, you'll probably need to set different expires for different kinds of groups. Administrative and local groups can be retained for quite a while, but high-traffic groups will need to be expired much more quickly to keep their posts from overwhelming your hard disk. A sample `expire.ctl` entry looks like this:

```
/remember/:21
    *:A:1:7:21
    akr.*:A:1:14:28
```

The first line tells `innd` that, no matter when the article expires, history data about the article should be kept for 21 days. This will allow you to look back and see whether an article was received and expired.

The second line is the core of your `expire.ctl` file. It says that, no matter what other configuration you have, every article is retained for at least 1 day (24 hours from receipt). The default expiration time is 7 days, which will apply to any article that doesn't have an `Expires:` header that self-defines a different expiration. Finally, regardless of any `Expires:` header, no article on your system will be kept for longer than 21 days. This line covers articles in every hierarchy on your system that doesn't have its own specific entry in the `expire.ctl` file.

The third line is an example of one of these specific entries. This particular line controls how articles in the `akr.*` hierarchy are handled on this site.

akr.* is the local hierarchy for Akron, Ohio (US). We just picked it out of the canonical hierarchy list, but we're sure it's a great hierarchy. Many local hierarchies have a wonderful sense of community.

According to this entry, posts in the akr.* groups are set to expire after 14 days unless they have a different Expires: header and after 28 days regardless of any Expires: header that may exist.

You can cover your entire newsfeed through a single entry like the second line in this example, or you can set different rules for different hierarchies. It all depends on what hierarchies and groups you decide to carry. Note that you can set rules for subhierarchies by including the relevant components of the hierarchy name in the entry, as in misc.jobs.*

Managing Groups

Each group that you carry will have its own subdirectory in your News directory. One question that most new news administrators ask is, "Do I need to manually build a new directory each time I decide to carry a new group?" The answer is No; each time your server receives an article for a newsgroup you don't carry yet, innd will create a new directory for that group. If you want to edit your active file by hand, you can use some specific INN commands: newgroup, rmgroup, and changegroup. These commands will add or remove groups to or from your active file, or will change the status of a particular group from moderated to unmoderated.

NOTE Don't use these commands to get groups "right" for your system. The configuration in the active file must match the configuration of the group as it is canonically set; that is, if you define a group as moderated on your system, but it is unmoderated, your users won't be able to post to the group. Refer to the sidebar "Keeping Your Newsgroups Updated" earlier in this chapter.

You should clean up your news spool once every four to six weeks by issuing the command

```
makehistory -buv
```

This command will check for articles that should have been deleted upon expiration, but that for some reason got lost in the spool and are still available.

You'll find that INN cleans up after itself pretty well if you have appropriate expires set in your configuration. As long as you keep an accurate active file, you won't experience a work overload from INN. It's likely that dealing with the human side of news will take more of your time than dealing with the software in INN.

Summary

One of the Internet services frequently offered by network administrators is USENET access. USENET is the segment of the Internet that carries news, a conglomeration of articles sorted into a hierarchical arrangement of newsgroups. There are a multitude of newsgroup hierarchies, ranging from the canonical and internationally available Big Eight to the smallest of local or language-based hierarchies. You can choose to offer all the hierarchies you can get or just a small subset that meets your users' interests.

When you decide to offer USENET access, you'll need to install a news server that runs according to the NNTP protocol. One of the best news servers is INN (InterNetNews). Once you have INN installed, you need to configure your newsfeeds, which are streams of articles that are fed to you from an upstream provider. You may have multiple newsfeeds, and you may offer newsfeeds to sites downstream of you. After you set up your feeds, you should decide how often articles will expire on your site. Some hierarchies should be retained for a lengthy period of time, such as one month; other hierarchies will need to be expired frequently, perhaps as often as daily or twice a day. Regardless of how you set up your newsfeeds and expirations, you will need to monitor your users to be sure they are posting in appropriate groups and are adhering to each individual group's rules of conduct.

CHAPTER
FORTY-TWO

World Wide Web Services

- Getting and Installing Apache

- Configuring Apache

- Other Web Servers

- Summary

If you want to serve Web pages from your network, you must run a Web server. The Web server, as with the other services described in this section of the book, is software designed to respond to client requests for data formatted in a particular manner. For Web pages, the format is HTML (HyperText Markup Language), and the protocol used to transfer those pages is HTTP (HyperText Transfer Protocol).

TIP

Both the HTML and HTTP standards are developed and administered by the W3C (the World Wide Web Consortium). The W3C is based simultaneously in France and at MIT, and is the professional home of Tim Berners-Lee. Berners-Lee has the best answer to "What do you do?" of anyone we can think of, because he can say, "I invented the World Wide Web. What do you do?"

The most popular Web server is the Apache server. Apache is used by more Web sites (six million at last count) than any other server software throughout the world. Its closest competitor, Microsoft's Internet Information Server (IIS), serves less than half the number of sites served by Apache. In fact, Apache is often touted as the biggest success story of the Free Software community, because Apache is released under the GNU Public License and is free to download as well as Free in the programming sense.

In this chapter, we introduce the Apache server, and show you how to install and configure it for a typical small Web site. If you run a very large network, chances are that you have a dedicated Web administrator whose entire job is working with Apache (or another server) and whose scope of knowledge far outpaces what we can cover in this chapter. Still, if you run a network—whether you're the sole administrator or not—your users will probably want Web space to serve their own pages. These days, it's almost as important to know how to run a Web server as it is to know how to run an e-mail server. At the end of the chapter, we introduce you to some other Web server alternatives. Although Apache is certainly the 10-ton gorilla of the Web server world, there are robust alternatives that might suit your needs better.

Getting and Installing Apache

Getting Apache is easy. We've included it on the CD-ROM that accompanies this book; if you're reading this book more than a few months after its publication date, we suggest that you also check the Apache Web site at `http://www.apache.org/httpd.html` to see whether a more updated version is available. As of the writing of this chapter, the current stable version (the one on the CD) is 1.3.12. If you have an earlier version available to you, we suggest that you upgrade. New features in the 1.3.12 version make a significant difference in this version compared to earlier versions of Apache.

Apache makes available packaged versions of the server software that are designed for individual Unix variants. Many of these variant-specific packages are available at `http://www.apache.org/dist/binaries/`, including binary packages for the three Unix variants covered in this book as well as for many other Unix variants, both commercial and Free. Make sure you download a package appropriate for your operating system if one is available, because it will be much simpler to install, configure, and run a version of Apache that works seamlessly with the unique directory structure of your chosen Unix.

Once you have the Apache package, install it as you would install any other source code package, using the method explained in Chapter 31: "Installing and Managing Software." As with most server software, you must be root—or have assumed superuser powers in some other manner—to install the software.

TIP

Linux users may be able to find packages formatted for the Red Hat or Debian package managers at their favorite Linux software archives. However, these formatted packages are primarily useful for casual users. If you plan to run a serious Web server, you need to locate and compile Apache from source code. Although this is a judgment call, many of the modules don't install particularly well from formatted packages, and you won't save any time.

The package will install into the `/etc/apache` directory in most cases. Some Unix variants will use the term `httpd` instead of `apache`, so if you can't find Apache files on your system, check for an `httpd` directory and see whether the files are there.

Once the software is installed, we strongly encourage you to take a moment before you begin to configure the server. The documentation contained with the Apache packages, located at `/usr/doc/apache` after installation, is some of the best software documentation that we've found. The files are clear and easy to understand, even if you've never run a Web server. In addition to the documentation, the configuration files themselves are well-commented and helpful. Of course, you won't learn enough about Apache just by reading the comments in the configuration files, but you'll learn a lot.

TIP

We also suggest that you read Chapter 25: "Regular Expressions," because Apache administration is far easier if you understand how regular expressions work.

The Apache Software Foundation

If you're wondering who invented Apache, the answer is somewhat complex. The original team was the Apache Group, who wanted to build a Web server that was completely Free Software and would be released under the GNU Public License. However, by 1999, Apache had become so wildly popular that the loose organization of the typical Free Software project was no longer sufficient for the Apache team.

Thus, at the end of 1999, the Apache Software Foundation was established as a full not-for-profit organization under United States law. The Foundation has the ability to receive donations and disburse them to benefit Apache, as well as the right to act as a legal entity when entering into contracts or other legal action in the US legal system. Apache is certainly not the first development project to construct a nonprofit foundation—the GNU folks have their own foundation, as well—but it is notable because Apache's success was the impetus for the more structured aspects of a formal corporation.

The Apache Software Foundation's Web site is `http://www.apache.org`, from which you can reach sites for each of the programs that the Foundation supports: the Apache Web server, projects designed to incorporate Java and XML into Apache programs, efforts to include Perl-based modules in Apache (a mechanism known as `mod_perl`), and other standards-based development efforts. Additional documentation and news alerts are available at the Apache site, as well.

Configuring Apache

Apache is configured through the /etc/apache/httpd.conf file, which is a well-commented file. You can learn a lot about Apache configuration from reading the comments, though—as the comments themselves point out—you won't learn everything you need just from reading httpd.conf. However, when you're in the middle of configuring your Web server, a well-commented configuration file is a wonderful thing to have.

> **TIP**
>
> Remember that, on some Unix variants, you will find this file at /etc/httpd/conf/httpd.conf instead of in the /etc/apache directory.

We show you the complete Apache configuration file below, with comments interspersed throughout at especially important points. You'll see the various comments included by the Apache team; this is the Linux version of the file, but the FreeBSD and Solaris versions are almost identical, so you will be able to work with one of those flavors of Apache without too much conversion from this file.

```
## httpd.conf - Apache HTTP server configuration file
##
#
# Based upon the NCSA server configuration files
# originally by Rob McCool.
#
# This is the main Apache server configuration file.  It
# contains the configuration directives that give the
# server its instructions. See
# <URL:http://www.apache.org/docs/> for detailed
# information about the directives.
#
# Do NOT simply read the instructions in here without
# understanding what they do.  They're here only as
# hints or reminders.  If you are unsure consult the
# online docs. You have been warned.
#
# After this file is processed, the server will look for
# and process /usr/conf/srm.conf and then
# /usr/conf/access.conf unless you have overridden these
# with ResourceConfig &/or AccessConfig directives here.
```

```
#
# The configuration directives are grouped into three
# basic sections:
#  1. Directives that control the operation of the
# Apache server process as a whole (the 'global
# environment').
#  2. Directives that define the parameters of the
# 'main' or 'default' server, which responds to requests
# that aren't handled by a virtual host. These
# directives also provide default values for the
# settings of all virtual hosts.
#  3. Settings for virtual hosts, which allow Web
# requests to be sent to different IP addresses or
# hostnames and have them handled by the same Apache
# server process.
#
# Configuration and logfile names: If the filenames you
# specify for many of the server's control files begin
# with "/" (or "drive:/" for Win32), the server will use
# that explicit path.  If the filenames do *not* begin
# with "/", the value of ServerRoot is prepended — so
# "logs/foo.log" with ServerRoot set to
# "/usr/local/apache" will be interpreted by the server
# as "/usr/local/apache/logs/foo.log".
#
### Section 1: Global Environment
#
# The directives in this section affect the overall
# operation of Apache, such as the number of concurrent
# requests it can handle or where it can find its
# configuration files.
#
# ServerType is either inetd, or standalone.  Inetd mode
# is only supported on Unix platforms.
ServerType standalone

# ServerRoot: The top of the directory tree under which
# the server's configuration, error, and log files are
# kept.
#
# NOTE!  If you intend to place this on an NFS (or
# otherwise network)mounted filesystem then please read
```

```
# the LockFile documentation available at
#<URL:http://www.apache.org/docs/mod/core.html#lockfile>
# and you will save yourself a lot of trouble.
#
# Do NOT add a slash at the end of the directory path.
ServerRoot "/etc/httpd"


# The LockFile directive sets the path to the lockfile
# used when Apache is compiled with either
# USE_FCNTL_SERIALIZED_ACCEPT or
# USE_FLOCK_SERIALIZED_ACCEPT. This directive should
# normally be left at its default value. The main reason
# for changing it is if the logs directory is NFS
# mounted, since the lockfile MUST BE STORED ON A LOCAL
# DISK. The PID of the main server process is
# automatically appended to the filename.
LockFile /var/lock/httpd.lock
```

Don't change this entry, but be aware of it. A file existing at this location means that Apache is active. If the Web server crashes, you'll need to remove this file before you can restart Apache; Apache will then create a new lock file when it begins running again.

```
# PidFile: The file in which the server should record
    # its process identification number when it starts.
    #
    PidFile /var/run/httpd.pid


    # ScoreBoardFile: File used to store internal server
    # process information. Not all architectures require
    # this.  But if yours does (you'll know because this
    # file will be created when you run Apache) then you
    # *must* ensure that no two invocations of Apache share
    # the same scoreboard file.
    ScoreBoardFile /var/run/httpd.scoreboard


    # In the standard configuration, the server will process
    # this file, srm.conf, and access.conf in that order.
    # The latter two files are now distributed empty, as it
    # is recommended that all directives be kept in a single
    # file for simplicity.  The commented-out values below
    # are the built-in defaults.  You can have the server
```

```
# ignore these files altogether by using "/dev/null"
# (for Unix) or "nul" (for Win32) for the arguments to
# the directives.
#
#ResourceConfig conf/srm.conf
#AccessConfig conf/access.conf

# Timeout: The number of seconds before receives and
# sends time out.
Timeout 300

# KeepAlive: Whether or not to allow persistent
# connections (more than one request per connection).
# Set to "Off" to deactivate.
KeepAlive On

# MaxKeepAliveRequests: The maximum number of requests
# to allow during a persistent connection. Set to 0 to
# allow an unlimited amount. We recommend you leave this
# number high, for maximum performance.
MaxKeepAliveRequests 100

# KeepAliveTimeout: Number of seconds to wait for the
# next request from the same client on the same
# connection.
KeepAliveTimeout 15

# Server-pool size regulation.  Rather than making you
# guess how many server processes you need, Apache
# dynamically adapts to the load it sees -- that is, it
# tries to maintain enough server processes to handle
# the current load, plus a few spare servers to handle
# transient load spikes (e.g., multiple simultaneous
# requests from a single Netscape browser).
#
# It does this by periodically checking how many servers
# are waiting for a request.  If there are fewer than
# MinSpareServers, it creates a new spare.  If there are
# more than MaxSpareServers, some of the spares die off.
# The default values are probably OK for most sites.
MinSpareServers 5
MaxSpareServers 20
```

```
# Number of servers to start initially -- should be a
# reasonable ballpark figure.
StartServers 8

# Limit on total number of servers running, i.e., limit
# on the number of clients who can simultaneously
# connect -- if this limit is ever reached, clients
# will be LOCKED OUT, so it should NOT BE SET TOO LOW.
# It is intended mainly as a brake to keep a runaway
# server from taking the system with it as it spirals
# down...
MaxClients 150

# MaxRequestsPerChild: the number of requests each child
# process is allowed to process before the child dies.
# The child will exit so as to avoid problems after
# prolonged use when Apache (and maybe the libraries it
# uses) leak memory or other resources.  On most
# systems, this isn't really needed, but a few (such as
# Solaris) do have notable leaks in the libraries. For
# these platforms, set to something like 10000 or so; a
# setting of 0 means unlimited.
#
# NOTE: This value does not include keepalive requests
# after the initial request per connection. For example,
# if a child process handles an initial request and 10
# subsequent "keptalive" requests, it would only count
# as 1 request towards this limit.
MaxRequestsPerChild 100

# Listen: Allows you to bind Apache to specific IP
# addresses and/or ports, in addition to the default.
# See also the <VirtualHost> directive.
#Listen 3000
#Listen 12.34.56.78:80

# BindAddress: You can support virtual hosts with this
# option. This directive is used to tell the server
# which IP address to listen to. It can either contain
# "*", an IP address, or a fully qualified Internet
# domain name. See also the <VirtualHost> and Listen
# directives.
```

```
#BindAddress *

# Dynamic Shared Object (DSO) Support
#
# To be able to use the functionality of a module which
# was built as a DSO you have to place corresponding
# `LoadModule' lines at this location so the directives
# contained in it are actually available _before_ they
# are used. Please read the file README.DSO in the
# Apache 1.3 distribution for more details about the DSO
# mechanism and run `httpd -l' for the list of already
# built-in (statically linked and thus always available)
# modules in your httpd binary.
#
# Note: The order is which modules are loaded is
# important.  Don't change the order below without
# expert advice.
#
# Example:
# LoadModule foo_module modules/mod_foo.so
#LoadModule mmap_static_module modules/mod_mmap_static.so
LoadModule vhost_alias_module modules/mod_vhost_alias.so
LoadModule env_module         modules/mod_env.so
LoadModule config_log_module  modules/mod_log_config.so
LoadModule agent_log_module   modules/mod_log_agent.so
LoadModule referer_log_module modules/mod_log_referer.so
#LoadModule mime_magic_module  modules/mod_mime_magic.so
LoadModule mime_module        modules/mod_mime.so
LoadModule negotiation_module modules/mod_negotiation.so
LoadModule status_module      modules/mod_status.so
LoadModule info_module        modules/mod_info.so
LoadModule includes_module    modules/mod_include.so
LoadModule autoindex_module   modules/mod_autoindex.so
LoadModule dir_module         modules/mod_dir.so
LoadModule cgi_module         modules/mod_cgi.so
LoadModule asis_module        modules/mod_asis.so
LoadModule imap_module        modules/mod_imap.so
LoadModule action_module      modules/mod_actions.so
#LoadModule speling_module     modules/mod_speling.so
LoadModule userdir_module     modules/mod_userdir.so
LoadModule alias_module       modules/mod_alias.so
LoadModule rewrite_module     modules/mod_rewrite.so
```

```
LoadModule access_module        modules/mod_access.so
LoadModule auth_module          modules/mod_auth.so
LoadModule anon_auth_module     modules/mod_auth_anon.so
LoadModule db_auth_module       modules/mod_auth_db.so
LoadModule digest_module        modules/mod_digest.so
LoadModule proxy_module         modules/libproxy.so
#LoadModule cern_meta_module    modules/mod_cern_meta.so
LoadModule expires_module       modules/mod_expires.so
LoadModule headers_module       modules/mod_headers.so
LoadModule usertrack_module     modules/mod_usertrack.so
#LoadModule example_module      modules/mod_example.so
#LoadModule unique_id_module    modules/mod_unique_id.so
LoadModule setenvif_module      modules/mod_setenvif.so
#LoadModule bandwidth_module    modules/mod_bandwidth.so
#LoadModule put_module          modules/mod_put.so

# Extra Modules
LoadModule perl_module          modules/libperl.so
#LoadModule php_module          modules/mod_php.so
LoadModule php3_module          modules/libphp3.so

#  Reconstruction of the complete module list from all
# available modules (static and shared ones) to achieve
# correct module execution order. [WHENEVER YOU CHANGE
# THE LOADMODULE SECTION ABOVE UPDATE THIS, TOO]
ClearModuleList
#AddModule mod_mmap_static.c
AddModule mod_vhost_alias.c
AddModule mod_env.c
AddModule mod_log_config.c
AddModule mod_log_agent.c
AddModule mod_log_referer.c
#AddModule mod_mime_magic.c
AddModule mod_mime.c
AddModule mod_negotiation.c
AddModule mod_status.c
AddModule mod_info.c
AddModule mod_include.c
AddModule mod_autoindex.c
AddModule mod_dir.c
AddModule mod_cgi.c
AddModule mod_asis.c
```

```
AddModule mod_imap.c
AddModule mod_actions.c
#AddModule mod_speling.c
AddModule mod_userdir.c
AddModule mod_alias.c
AddModule mod_rewrite.c
AddModule mod_access.c
AddModule mod_auth.c
AddModule mod_auth_anon.c
AddModule mod_auth_db.c
AddModule mod_digest.c
AddModule mod_proxy.c
#AddModule mod_cern_meta.c
AddModule mod_expires.c
AddModule mod_headers.c
AddModule mod_usertrack.c
#AddModule mod_example.c
#AddModule mod_unique_id.c
AddModule mod_so.c
AddModule mod_setenvif.c
#AddModule mod_bandwidth.c
#AddModule mod_put.c

# Extra Modules
AddModule mod_perl.c
#AddModule mod_php.c
AddModule mod_php3.c

# ExtendedStatus: controls whether Apache will generate
# "full" status information (ExtendedStatus On) or just
# basic information (ExtendedStatus Off) when the
# "server-status" handler is called. The default is Off.
#
#ExtendedStatus On

### Section 2: 'Main' server configuration
#
# The directives in this section set up the values used
# by the 'main' server, which responds to any requests
# that aren't handled by a <VirtualHost> definition.
# These values also provide defaults for any
# <VirtualHost> containers you may define later in the
```

```
# file.
#
# All of these directives may appear inside
# <VirtualHost> containers, in which case these default
# settings will be overridden for the virtual host being
# defined.

# If your ServerType directive (set earlier in the
# 'Global Environment' section) is set to "inetd", the
# next few directives don't have any effect since their
# settings are defined by the inetd configuration. Skip
# ahead to the ServerAdmin directive.

# Port: The port to which the standalone server listens.
# For ports < 1023, you will need httpd to be run as
# root initially.
Port 80
```

If you change the port on which Apache listens for requests, you'll need to publicize that port for people to know where your Web pages are. Browsers make requests to port 80 by default. However, if you want to test a site before you make it public, set this to something high such as 8080; just be sure to change it back when you're done.

```
# If you wish httpd to run as a different user or group,
  # you must run httpd as root initially and it will
  # switch.
  #
  # User/Group: The name (or #number) of the user/group to
  # run httpd as. On SCO (ODT 3) use "User nouser" and
  # "Group nogroup". On HPUX you may not be able to use
  # shared memory as nobody, and the suggested workaround
  # is to create a user www and use that user. NOTE that
  # some kernels refuse to setgid(Group) or
  # semctl(IPC_SET) when the value of (unsigned)Group is
  # above 60000; don't use Group nobody on these systems!
  User nobody
  Group nobody

  # ServerAdmin: Your address, where problems with the
  # server should be e-mailed.  This address appears on
```

```
# some server-generated pages, such as error documents.
ServerAdmin root@localhost
```

Change this entry to reflect the address to which you want the server to send you critical administrative messages. Many administrators like to get this mail at root@*yourmachine.name,* but you may want to have it sent to a particular user address instead.

```
# ServerName: allows you to set a host name which is
    # sent back to clients for your server if it's different
    # than the one the program would get (i.e., use "www"
    # instead of the host's real name).
    #
    # Note: You cannot just invent host names and hope they
    # work. The name you define here must be a valid DNS
    # name for your host. If you don't understand this, ask
    # your network administrator. If your host doesn't have
    # a registered DNS name, enter its IP address here. You
    # will have to access it by its address (e.g.,
    # http://123.45.67.89/) anyway, and this will make
    # redirections work in a sensible way.
    #
    ServerName localhost
```

If you make no other changes to this file, you must replace localhost with your own server's name. Otherwise, Apache won't work. You can leave localhost here for testing purposes, but you'll be able to answer only requests from the machine on which Apache is installed—not even requests from within the same network.

```
# DocumentRoot: The directory out of which you will
    # serve your documents. By default, all requests are
    # taken from this directory, but symbolic links and
    # aliases may be used to point to other locations.
    DocumentRoot "/home/httpd/html"
```

You can leave this as it is, or you can change it to /var/www, which is what we usually do. Don't change it to anything other than /var/www, because using a non-standard directory as the DocumentRoot can lead to a major security risk. This is an important setting, because it defines how Apache will show files to the external world. The directory defined in this entry becomes the root directory in Apache's eyes, and—at least through Apache—none of the directories above this directory exist. This is a security technique designed to block off your system files from anyone trying to hack through Apache into your network.

```
# Each directory to which Apache has access, can be
    # configured with respect to which services and features
    # are allowed and/or disabled in that directory (and its
    # subdirectories).
    #
    # First, we configure the "default" to be a very
    # restrictive set of permissions.
    <Directory />
        Options FollowSymLinks
        AllowOverride None
    </Directory>

    # Note that from this point forward you must
    # specifically allow particular features to be enabled -
    # so if something's not working as you might expect,
    # make sure that you have specifically enabled it below.
    #
    # This should be changed to whatever you set
    # DocumentRoot to.
    <Directory "/home/httpd/html">

    # This may also be "None", "All", or any combination of
    # "Indexes", "Includes", "FollowSymLinks", "ExecCGI", or
    # "MultiViews". Note that "MultiViews" must be named
    # *explicitly* -- "Options All" doesn't give it to you.
        Options Indexes Includes FollowSymLinks

    # This controls which options the .htaccess files in
    # directories can override. Can also be "All", or any
    # combination of "Options", "FileInfo", "AuthConfig",
    # and "Limit"
        AllowOverride None

    # Controls who can get stuff from this server.
        Order allow,deny
        Allow from all
    </Directory>

    # UserDir: The name of the directory which is appended
```

```
                    # onto a user's home directory if a ~user request is
                    # received.
                    UserDir public_html

                    # Control access to UserDir directories.  The following
                    # is an example for a site where these directories are
                    # restricted to read-only.
                    #
                    #<Directory /home/*/public_html>
                    #    AllowOverride FileInfo AuthConfig Limit
                    #    Options MultiViews Indexes SymLinksIfOwnerMatch
                    #        IncludesNoExec
                    #    <Limit GET POST OPTIONS PROPFIND>
                    #        Order allow,deny
                    #        Allow from all
                    #    </Limit>
                    #    <Limit PUT DELETE PATCH PROPPATCH MKCOL COPY MOVE
                    #        LOCK UNLOCK>
                    #        Order deny,allow
                    #        Deny from all
                    #    </Limit>
                    #</Directory>
```

If you want users to be able to maintain their own Web pages, uncomment the section above. Note the path name for users' directories: /home/*/public_html. This means that, for user jane, Apache will look in /home/jane/public_html for documents. Browser clients will be able to access jane's file at the URL http:// www.*domainname*/~jane. (Note also the use of the wildcard character * to cover all possible values in that field.)

```
  # DirectoryIndex: Name of the file or files to use as a
     # pre-written HTML directory index.  Separate multiple
     # entries with spaces.
     DirectoryIndex index.html index.htm index.shtml index.cgi

     # AccessFileName: The name of the file to look for in
     # each directory for access control information.
     AccessFileName .htaccess

     # The following lines prevent .htaccess files from being
     # viewed by Web clients.  Since .htaccess files often
     # contain authorization information, access is
```

```
# disallowed for security reasons.  Comment these lines
# out if you want Web visitors to see the contents of
# .htaccess files.  If you change the AccessFileName
# directive above, be sure to make the corresponding
# changes here.
#
# Also, folks tend to use names such as .htpasswd for
# password files, so this will protect those as well.
<Files ~ "^\.ht">
    Order allow,deny
    Deny from all
</Files>

# CacheNegotiatedDocs: By default, Apache sends "Pragma:
# no-cache" with each document that was negotiated on
# the basis of content. This asks proxy servers not to
# cache the document. Uncommenting the following line
# disables this behavior, and proxies will be allowed to
# cache the documents.
#CacheNegotiatedDocs
#
# UseCanonicalName:  (new for 1.3)  With this setting
# turned on, whenever Apache needs to construct a self-
# referencing URL (a URL that refers back to the server
# the response is coming from) it will use ServerName
# and Port to form a "canonical" name.  With this
# setting off, Apache will use the hostname:port that
# the client supplied, when possible.  This also affects
# SERVER_NAME and SERVER_PORT in CGI scripts.
UseCanonicalName On

# TypesConfig describes where the mime.types file (or
# equivalent) is to be found.
TypesConfig /etc/mime.types

# DefaultType is the default MIME type the server will
# use for a document if it cannot otherwise determine
# one, such as from filename extensions. If your server
# contains mostly text or HTML documents, "text/plain"
# is a good value.  If most of your content is binary,
# such as applications or images, you may want to use
# "application/octet-stream" instead to keep browsers
```

```
# from trying to display binary files as though they are
# text.
DefaultType text/plain

# The mod_mime_magic module allows the server to use
# various hints from the contents of the file itself to
# determine its type.  The MIMEMagicFile directive tells
# the module where the hint definitions are located.
# mod_mime_magic is not part of the default server (you
# have to add it yourself with a LoadModule [see the DSO
# paragraph in the 'Global Environment' section], or
# recompile the server and include mod_mime_magic as
# part of the configuration), so it's enclosed in an
# <IfModule> container. This means that the
# MIMEMagicFile directive will only be processed if the
# module is part of the server.
<IfModule mod_mime_magic.c>
    MIMEMagicFile share/magic
</IfModule>

# HostnameLookups: Log the names of clients or just
# their IP addresses e.g., www.apache.org (on) or
# 204.62.129.132 (off). The default is off because it'd
# be overall better for the net if people had to
# knowingly turn this feature on, since enabling it
# means that each client request will result in AT LEAST
# one lookup request to the nameserver.
HostnameLookups Off

# ErrorLog: The location of the error log file. If you
# do not specify an ErrorLog directive within a
# <VirtualHost> container, error messages relating to
# that virtual host will be logged here.  If you *do*
# define an error logfile for a <VirtualHost> container,
# that host's errors will be logged there and not here.
ErrorLog /var/log/httpd/error_log

# LogLevel: Control the number of messages logged to the
# error_log. Possible values include: debug, info,
# notice, warn, error, crit, alert, emerg.
LogLevel warn

# The following directives define some format nicknames
```

```
# for use with a CustomLog directive (see below).

LogFormat "%h %l %u %t \"%r\" %>s %b \"%{Referer}i\"
"%{User-Agent}i\"" combined
LogFormat "%h %l %u %t \"%r\" %>s %b" common
LogFormat "%{Referer}i -> %U" referer
LogFormat "%{User-agent}i" agent

# The location and format of the access logfile (Common
# Logfile Format). If you do not define any access
# logfiles within a <VirtualHost> container, they will
# be logged here.  Contrariwise, if you *do* define per-
# <VirtualHost> access logfiles, transactions will be
# logged therein and *not* in this file.
CustomLog /var/log/httpd/access_log common

# If you would like to have agent and referer logfiles,
# uncomment the following directives.
#
#CustomLog /var/log/httpd/referer_log referer
#CustomLog /var/log/httpd/agent_log agent

# If you prefer a single logfile with access, agent, and
# referer information (Combined Logfile Format) you can
# use the following directive.
#
#CustomLog /var/log/httpd/access_log combined

# Optionally add a line containing the server version
# and virtual host name to server-generated pages (error
# documents, FTP directory listings, mod_status and
# mod_info output etc., but not CGI generated
# documents). Set to "EMail" to also include a mailto:
# link to the ServerAdmin. Set to one of:  On | Off |
# EMail
ServerSignature On

# Aliases: Add here as many aliases as you need (with no
# limit). The format is Alias fakename realname
#
# Note that if you include a trailing / on fakename then
# the server will require it to be present in the URL.
```

```
# So "/icons" isn't aliased in this example, only
# /icons/"..
Alias /icons/ "/home/httpd/icons/"

<Directory "/home/httpd/icons">
    Options Indexes MultiViews
    AllowOverride None
    Order allow,deny
    Allow from all
</Directory>

# ScriptAlias: This controls which directories contain
# server scripts. ScriptAliases are essentially the same
# as Aliases, except that documents in the realname
# directory are treated as applications and run by the
# server when requested rather than as documents sent to
# the client. The same rules about trailing "/" apply to
# ScriptAlias directives as to Alias.
ScriptAlias /cgi-bin/ "/home/httpd/cgi-bin/"

# "/home/httpd/cgi-bin" should be changed to whatever
# your ScriptAliased CGI directory exists, if you have
# that configured.
<Directory "/home/httpd/cgi-bin">
    AllowOverride None
    Options ExecCGI
    Order allow,deny
    Allow from all
</Directory>

# Redirect allows you to tell clients about documents
# which used to exist in your server's namespace, but do
# not anymore. This allows you to tell the clients where
# to look for the relocated document. Format: Redirect
# old-URL new-URL

# Directives controlling the display of server-generated
# directory listings.

# FancyIndexing: whether you want fancy directory
# indexing or standard
IndexOptions FancyIndexing
```

```
# AddIcon* directives tell the server which icon to show
# for different files or filename extensions.  These are
# only displayed for FancyIndexed directories.
AddIconByEncoding (CMP,/icons/compressed.gif) x-compress x-gzip
AddIconByType (TXT,/icons/text.gif) text/*
AddIconByType (IMG,/icons/image2.gif) image/*
AddIconByType (SND,/icons/sound2.gif) audio/*
AddIconByType (VID,/icons/movie.gif) video/*
AddIcon /icons/binary.gif .bin .exe
AddIcon /icons/binhex.gif .hqx
AddIcon /icons/tar.gif .tar
AddIcon /icons/world2.gif .wrl .wrl.gz .vrml .vrm .iv
AddIcon /icons/compressed.gif .Z .z .tgz .gz .zip
AddIcon /icons/a.gif .ps .ai .eps
AddIcon /icons/layout.gif .html .shtml .htm .pdf
AddIcon /icons/text.gif .txt
AddIcon /icons/c.gif .c
AddIcon /icons/p.gif .pl .py
AddIcon /icons/f.gif .for
AddIcon /icons/dvi.gif .dvi
AddIcon /icons/uuencoded.gif .uu
AddIcon /icons/script.gif .conf .sh .shar .csh .ksh .tcl
AddIcon /icons/tex.gif .tex
AddIcon /icons/bomb.gif core
AddIcon /icons/back.gif ..
AddIcon /icons/hand.right.gif README
AddIcon /icons/folder.gif ^^DIRECTORY^^
AddIcon /icons/blank.gif ^^BLANKICON^^

# DefaultIcon: which icon to show for files which do not
# have an icon explicitly set.
DefaultIcon /icons/unknown.gif

# AddDescription: allows you to place a short
# description after a file in server-generated indexes.
# These are only displayed for FancyIndexed directories.
# Format: AddDescription "description" filename
#
#AddDescription "GZIP compressed document" .gz
#AddDescription "tar archive" .tar
#AddDescription "GZIP compressed tar archive" .tgz
```

```
# ReadmeName: the name of the README file the server
# will look for by default, and append to directory
# listings.

# HeaderName: the name of a file which should be
# prepended to directory indexes.
#
# The server will first look for name.html and include
# it if found. If name.html doesn't exist, the server
# will then look for name.txt and include it as
# plaintext if found.
ReadmeName README
HeaderName HEADER

# IndexIgnore: a set of filenames which directory
# indexing should ignore and not include in the listing.
# Shell-style wildcarding is permitted.
IndexIgnore .??* *~ *# HEADER* README* RCS CVS *,v *,t

# AddEncoding: allows you to have certain browsers
# (Mosaic/X 2.1+) uncompress information on the fly.
# Note: Not all browsers support this. Despite the name
# similarity, the following Add* directives have nothing
# to do with the FancyIndexing customization directives
# above.
AddEncoding x-compress Z
AddEncoding x-gzip gz tgz

# AddLanguage: allows you to specify the language of a
# document. You can then use content negotiation to give
# a browser a file in a language it can understand.
# Note that the suffix does not have to be the same as
# the language keyword -- those with documents in
# Polish (whose net-standard language code is pl) may
# wish to use "AddLanguage pl .po" to avoid the
# ambiguity with the common suffix for perl scripts.
AddLanguage en .en
AddLanguage fr .fr
AddLanguage de .de
AddLanguage da .da
AddLanguage el .el
AddLanguage it .it
```

```
# LanguagePriority: allows you to give precedence to
# some languages in case of a tie during content
# negotiation. Just list the languages in decreasing
# order of preference.
LanguagePriority en fr de


# AddType: allows you to tweak mime.types without
# actually editing it, or to make certain files to be
# certain types. For example, the PHP3 module (not part
# of the Apache distribution - see http://www.php.net)
# will typically use:
<IfModule mod_php3.c>
  AddType application/x-httpd-php3 .php3
  AddType application/x-httpd-php3-source .phps
</IfModule>


# The following is for PHP/FI (PHP2):
<IfModule mod_php.c>
  AddType application/x-httpd-php .phtml
</IfModule>


AddType application/x-tar .tgz


# AddHandler: allows you to map certain file extensions
# to "handlers", actions unrelated to filetype. These
# can be either built into the server or added with the
# Action command (see below)
#
# If you want to use server side includes, or CGI
# outside ScriptAliased directories, uncomment the
# following lines.
#
# To use CGI scripts:
#
#AddHandler cgi-script .cgi


# To use server-parsed HTML files
#
AddType text/html .shtml
AddHandler server-parsed .shtml


# Uncomment the following line to enable Apache's send-
```

```
# asis HTTP file feature
#
#AddHandler send-as-is asis

# If you wish to use server-parsed imagemap files, use
#AddHandler imap-file map

# To enable type maps, you might want to use
#
#AddHandler type-map var

# Action: lets you define media types that will execute
# a script whenever a matching file is called. This
# eliminates the need for repeated URL pathnames for
# oft-used CGI file processors.
# Format: Action media/type /cgi-script/location
# Format: Action handler-name /cgi-script/location


# MetaDir: specifies the name of the directory in which
# Apache can find meta information files. These files
# contain additional HTTP headers to include when
# sending the document
#
#MetaDir .web

# MetaSuffix: specifies the file name suffix for the
# file containing the meta information.
#
#MetaSuffix .meta

# Customizable error response (Apache style) these come
# in three flavors
#
#     1) plain text
#ErrorDocument 500 "The server made a boo boo."
# n.b.  the (") marks it as text, it does not get output
#
#     2) local redirects
#ErrorDocument 404 /missing.html
#  to redirect to local URL /missing.html
```

```
#ErrorDocument 404 /cgi-bin/missing_handler.pl
# N.B.: You can redirect to a script or a document
# using server-side-includes.
#
#      3) external redirects
#ErrorDocument 402
http://some.other_server.com/subscription_info.html
# N.B.: Many of the environment variables associated
# with the original request will *not* be available to
# such a script.
#
# The following directives modify normal HTTP response
# behavior. The first directive disables keepalive for
# Netscape 2.x and browsers that spoof it. There are
# known problems with these browser implementations.
# The second directive is for Microsoft Internet
# Explorer 4.0b2 which has a broken HTTP/1.1
# implementation and does not properly support keepalive
# when it is used on 301 or 302 (redirect) responses.
#
BrowserMatch "Mozilla/2" nokeepalive
BrowserMatch "MSIE 4\.0b2;" nokeepalive downgrade-1.0
force-response-1.0

# The following directive disables HTTP/1.1 responses to
# browsers which are in violation of the HTTP/1.0 spec
# by not being able to grok a basic 1.1 response.
#
BrowserMatch "RealPlayer 4\.0" force-response-1.0
BrowserMatch "Java/1\.0" force-response-1.0
BrowserMatch "JDK/1\.0" force-response-1.0

# If the perl module is installed, this will be enabled.
<IfModule mod_perl.c>
  Alias /perl/ /home/httpd/perl/
  <Location /perl>
    SetHandler perl-script
    PerlHandler Apache::Registry
    Options +ExecCGI
  </Location>
</IfModule>
```

mod_perl is a Perl interpreter that runs as part of Apache. This is helpful, especially if you run a lot of Perl scripts that generate dynamic Web pages. By using mod_perl, you can avoid having to run the main Perl interpreter every time you get a request for a Perl-generated dynamic page.

```
# Allow http put (such as Netscape Gold's publish
    # feature) Use htpasswd to generate
    # etc/httpd/conf/passwd. You must unremark these two
    # lines at the top of this file as well:
    #LoadModule put_module          modules/mod_put.so
    #AddModule mod_put.c
    #
    #Alias /upload /tmp
    #<Location /upload>
    #     EnablePut On
    #     AuthType Basic
    #     AuthName Temporary
    #     AuthUserFile /etc/httpd/conf/passwd
    #     EnableDelete Off
    #     umask 007
    #     <Limit PUT>
    # require valid-user
    #     </Limit>
    #</Location>

    # Allow server status reports, with the URL of
    # http://servername/server-status
    # Change the ".your_domain.com" to match your domain to
    # enable.
    #
    #<Location /server-status>
    #     SetHandler server-status
    #     Order deny,allow
    #     Deny from all
    #     Allow from .your_domain.com
    #</Location>

    # Allow remote server configuration reports, with the
    # URL of  http://servername/server-info (requires that
    # mod_info.c be loaded). Change the ".your_domain.com"
    # to match your domain to enable.
    #
```

```
#<Location /server-info>
#     SetHandler server-info
#     Order deny,allow
#     Deny from all
#     Allow from .your_domain.com
#</Location>

# Allow access to local system documentation from
# localhost
Alias /doc/ /usr/doc/
<Location /doc>
  order deny,allow
  deny from all
  allow from localhost
  Options Indexes FollowSymLinks
</Location>

# There have been reports of people trying to abuse an
# old bug from pre-1.1 days.  This bug involved a CGI
# script distributed as a part of Apache. By
# uncommenting these lines you can redirect these
# attacks to a logging script on phf.apache.org.  Or,
# you can record them yourself, using the script
# support/phf_abuse_log.cgi.
#
#<Location /cgi-bin/phf*>
#     Deny from all
#     ErrorDocument 403
http://phf.apache.org/phf_abuse_log.cgi
#</Location>

# Proxy Server directives. Uncomment the following lines
# to enable the proxy server:
#
#<IfModule mod_proxy.c>
#ProxyRequests On
#
#<Directory proxy:*>
#     Order deny,allow
#     Deny from all
#     Allow from .your_domain.com
#</Directory>
```

```
# Enable/disable the handling of HTTP/1.1 "Via:"
# headers. ("Full" adds the server version; "Block"
# removes all outgoing Via: headers) Set to one of: Off
# | On | Full | Block
#
#ProxyVia On

# To enable the cache as well, edit and uncomment the
# following lines:
# (no cacheing without CacheRoot)
#
#CacheRoot "/var/cache/httpd"
#CacheSize 5
#CacheGcInterval 4
#CacheMaxExpire 24
#CacheLastModifiedFactor 0.1
#CacheDefaultExpire 1
#NoCache a_domain.com another_domain.edu
joes.garage_sale.com
#</IfModule>
# End of proxy directives.

### Section 3: Virtual Hosts
```

A *virtual host* is a secondary domain name. For example, if your domain is mydomain.com, but you want to host the second domain myotherdomain.org, you can add it in this section. You can use the configurations in this section of the document to define a second set of Web pages that will be served by the virtual domain.

```
# VirtualHost: If you want to maintain multiple
    # domains/hostnames on your machine you can setup
    # VirtualHost containers for them. Please see the
    # documentation at
    # <URL:http://www.apache.org/docs/vhosts/> for further
    # details before you try to setup virtual hosts. You may
    # use the command line option '-S' to verify your
    # virtual host configuration.

    # If you want to use name-based virtual hosts you need
    # to define at least one IP address (and port number)
    # for them.
    #
```

```
#NameVirtualHost 12.34.56.78:80
#NameVirtualHost 12.34.56.78
#
# VirtualHost example:
# Almost any Apache directive may go into a VirtualHost
# container.
#
#<VirtualHost ip.address.of.host.some_domain.com>
#     ServerAdmin webmaster@host.some_domain.com
#     DocumentRoot /www/docs/host.some_domain.com
#     ServerName host.some_domain.com
#     ErrorLog logs/host.some_domain.com-error_log
#     CustomLog logs/host.some_domain.com-access_log common
#</VirtualHost>

#<VirtualHost _default_:*>
#</VirtualHost>
```

Other Web Servers

For many reasons, some administrators choose not to run Apache as their Web server software. Perhaps they don't need a multifeatured system like Apache, which may have too many options for a small network that serves only a limited number of static pages. Other administrators might prefer a server that is targeted toward one particular kind of traffic or that is designed for security or speed instead of for multiple types of requests. Still other administrators might just want to use a newer server because they enjoy supporting developers in their work.

Regardless of the reasons for which you might want to run a Web server that isn't Apache, you have quite a few choices of Web servers to run. A few of the most popular non-Apache Web servers are introduced in this section, and most of them are built to run on multiple Unix platforms. Only one—kHTTPd—is platform-specific, because it requires the Linux kernel to operate. The others, however, have run successfully on a myriad of Unix variants.

boa

The boa Web server is a GNU Public License program that is designed for speed and security. Unlike many other Web servers, boa runs without forking processes to handle traffic requests; instead, multiple requests are handled internally. This mechanism allows boa to withstand a barrage of requests and still provide pages within a quick response time. Unofficial benchmarking has shown that boa can handle thousands of hits per second on a Pentium and several dozen hits per second on a 386, according to the boa development team.

Although boa is being developed on the Linux platform, it has run successfully on other Unix variants, including FreeBSD and Solaris. It installs like any other source code package and should not present a problem for those using non-Linux Unices. boa has been under development since 1991, though it languished for some years until a new development team took it over. The current release is 0.94.8.3, and the current team says that development will renew with the 0.95 version.

> **NOTE**
>
> Learn more about boa at the project Web site, `http://www.boa.org`. The site offers downloads and complete documentation, including an installation guide. The `boa.conf` file, boa's main configuration file, is well-commented and should be easy to configure to your system's needs.

dhttpd

The second in this array of less well-known Web servers is called dhttpd. This server is written for several Unix variants, mostly the ones covered in this book. It is very small and designed only for personal Web use; that is, if you plan to offer pages that will be popular places to visit, you probably don't want to use dhttpd. However, if you just want to run something so that you can offer a personal Web page or two, but you don't think that the world will be clicking its mouse to your door, dhttpd might be the right option. It certainly requires less space and fewer CPU cycles than Apache.

One advantage of dhttpd is that the developer has made it possible for this server to be run from user space. You don't have to be root to run this Web server, which may be of use if you have a user account on a machine that doesn't supply Web space to its users. Instead, you can compile and run dhttpd in your user account, allocating it to a very high port number unlikely to be used by any "official" processes on the system.

You can use this user-account Web server to publicize pages from your account; be sure, though, that only your files intended for the public have their permissions set for that purpose. Running a Web server from your user account means all your files are vulnerable to public view, especially if you haven't established appropriate file permissions. Be sure you have a file called index.html in your Web directory; if no index.html file exists, most Web servers will serve a file listing of the directory in which the server is running. If that's your personal directory, all your personal files will be named in public and, if the permissions are set incorrectly, available to the world. Imagine the havoc someone could cause if your mail directory were publicly available.

WARNING

Alert your system administrator before you run a Web server off your personal account. Web may be disabled on your network for a practical security reason, and running a personal Web server may violate your agreement with the provider—whether it is an employment, academic, or commercial account. We do not encourage the use of *stealth servers* through user accounts against the terms of any usage agreement.

dhttpd supports page caching and customized error messages (such as 404 pages that report "Page not found"). It is available both in a stable release version (the current version is 1.02) and a beta version, which offers more functions, but also probably has more bugs than the stable version. The current beta version is 1.10; note that this beta version was released in summer 1997. We do not know whether dhttpd is still being developed, but the stable version is still usable.

NOTE

Download dhttpd from one of the several Unix file archives that carry it or directly from the project Web page at http://uts.cc.utexas.edu/~foxx/dhttpd/. The site doesn't carry much other than the download and a handy Web button to display if you use the server, so you'll have to puzzle through installation and con- figuration with the documentation provided in the package itself.

fhttpd

Another small Web server program, released under the GNU Public License, is called fhttpd, which stands for File/HyperText Transport Protocols Daemon. fhttpd is designed to be fast and streamlined without as much configuration as Apache, but to be as robust as possible in transferring both files and HTML documents.

NOTE   Most Web servers are targeted toward HTML documents (though Web servers can usually handle file transfer as well), while file transfer is reserved for FTP (File Transfer Protocol) clients. fhttpd attempts to bridge that gap.

---

fhttpd is currently in version 0.4.2, meaning that it is still beta software. However, the developer claims that it is quite robust and secure, with no major security holes since version 0.3 or so. It will run on almost any Unix variant, including the three covered in this book. In a useful touch, the developer has provided an unusually complete Makefile, in which there are lines for different Unices. Though the default configuration is designed for Linux, if you are running a different Unix, all you need to do is comment out the Linux lines by placing a hashmark at the start of the line and uncomment the lines relating to your particular variant. This is a nice feature that is, unfortunately, not widespread.

NOTE   To learn more about fhttpd—which might be a good solution for the small network that doesn't serve much Web traffic, but does serve files in about the same amount as HTML pages—you can consult the project Web site at http://www.fhttpd.org. The documentation on the site is very well organized, with a step-by-step installation guide and a complete list of options for the configuration file fhttpd.conf.

Jigsaw

If you want to run a Web server that is guaranteed to comply with every component of the HyperText Transfer Protocol standard, you should run Jigsaw. The Jigsaw server is developed by the W3C (the World Wide Web Consortium), which administers the HTTP protocol. Jigsaw was created to act as the production server for W3C programmers and is designed to implement every aspect of the protocol as it evolves.

Jigsaw is unique among Web servers in that it's written in Java, making it platform-independent. Although it's designed as an experimental server for the W3C's purposes, it's robust and strong enough to be run as a regular server by the ordinary Web administrator. The server is intended primarily for programmers who are interested in working with various Java servlets as part of a modular server, instead of being intended for administrators who simply want to run the thing. If you like working with Java, though, and you'd like to run a fully compliant Web server, Jigsaw might be the right server for you. We certainly support software that is fully compliant with established protocols wherever possible.

NOTE

Obtain Jigsaw and its detailed documentation at the W3C's site, `http://www.w3c.org/Jigsaw/`. You can read the FAQ, the programmers' guide, and the code itself at the site, or you can download the server. The current version of Jigsaw is 2.1.2, which is an unstable release. The 2.0 version is the latest stable release.

Protocol-Compliant Browsers

If you're going to use Jigsaw because it's compliant with the HTTP standard, why not use a compliant browser on the client side? The Opera browser will display only pages written in HTML compliant with the current version of the HTML protocol. We think Opera is a fantastic browser; the downside is that many, many pages on the Web are not HTML-compliant.

In particular, pages written with Netscape Composer and Microsoft FrontPage generate noncompliant HTML, and Opera will simply refuse to show those pages. However, if you're willing to browse a limited set of pages, Opera might be the right idea for you. Check out the project's Web page at `http://operasoftware.com`. Note that you'll have to pay for the browser if you choose to use it.

kHTTPd

Linux users have an unusual Web server option in the kHTTPd program. This server works in a manner completely different from other Web servers: It is kernel-based.

This means that kHTTPd runs as a kernel module instead of as a regular program, lending stability and speed to its operation.

kHTTPd, because of its method of operation, can be used to serve only static Web pages. Such pages—those saved as files in a public directory that remain the same every time they are pulled up and are generally saved as HTML-formatted text—form the bulk of personal Web pages on the Internet and are probably still a significant portion of corporate Web pages. (Not everyone is interested in adopting the flashy animation-based Web designs, especially those designers interested in serving those users who must use adaptive Web browsers.) You would need to run kHTTPd in conjunction with a more fully featured Web server, such as Apache, if you need to serve dynamic pages as well as static ones. However, if your site is completely static, using kHTTPd might be the appropriate way to handle those requests.

NOTE   The current version of kHTTPd is 0.1.6b, which integrates into the 2.3.14 Linux kernel. You can get the kHTTPd kernel module at the project's Web site, http://www.fenrus.demon.nl/.

WN

The WN Web server is a robust and feature-loaded server that, while offering many of the same features as Apache, takes up much less space on the server machine. One of the main features offered by WN is the ability to serve particular pages to client requests, based upon whom the client is, with a simple direction mechanism. WN also has robust navigational tools that make it easier for the Web administrator to direct clients to the appropriate pages without a great deal of fuss.

WN supports many of the current trends in Web page design and administration, such as Server Side Includes (SSI). WN also works with SSL (the Secure Socket Layer protocol), which underlies secure monetary transactions on the Web, such as those made with credit cards. You can use WN to do almost anything that Apache can do, but WN has a smaller footprint.

WN installs either in the traditional Unix software way or through a Perl script that will handle most of the installation tasks automatically. The current stable version is 2.2.9, and the current beta version is 2.3.11. In keeping with the Linux kernel numbering tradition, WN versions with an even middle number are stable, while odd middle numbers denote unstable beta releases. WN should run on almost any Unix variant with a minimum of variant-specific configuration.

> **NOTE**
>
> The WN Web pages are located at `http://hopf.math.nwu.edu/`. This is one of the better project development sites available, because it offers both downloads and an extensive set of documentation.

Summary

To provide Web pages to the Internet community, you must run a Web server. The server answers requests generated by individual browsers, which act as clients to the server. The most popular Web server in the world is Apache, a Free Software program released under the GNU Public License. Apache will run on almost every known Unix variant, and is easy to install and configure. Most of Apache's default configurations reflect the way in which many Web administrators run their sites, so there is relatively little configuration for you to do. However, should you want to configure Apache closely, the developers have provided clear comments in the relevant files.

If you don't want to run Apache, several other Web servers are available for Unix administrators. Each of these servers is developed with slightly different goals in mind; some are targeted at speed, while others are designed for security or low traffic. Regardless of the kind of Web service you want to offer from your network, there is a Web server that is right for the job.

CHAPTER
FORTY-THREE

43

Remote Access (inet) Services

If you're connected to the Internet, you're probably running services on your network. Even if this involves just a couple of services such as an electronic mail server and a Web server, you are offering some services to remote users or people on the Internet. Those services respond to external requests with a particular kind of data stream, whether it's a Web page or a complete file.

Although you can run some Internet services independently of each other (in particular, Apache and INN or other Web and USENET news servers), it can be a tedious procedure to start each service by hand when you boot the computer or when the service is called by an external request. In fact, if you rely on starting services by hand, you may not be able to answer every external request because you may not be aware of those requests arriving.

What's needed is a process that notices incoming requests, determines the service that should answer a particular request, and turns on the appropriate service in response. Luckily, such a process exists. It's called inet, and it manages your various Internet services from one central location. With inet, you can install your services and then let them run automatically under inet's guidance without having to involve yourself with the individual services so that they run properly.

NOTE   A variety of services run under the inet umbrella. In this chapter, we introduce you to the major programs started through inet. Some of these programs are standard Internet software; other inet programs used to be popular, but have now been superseded, whether because of security risks or just because something better has been developed. However, even if a program is listed here that you shouldn't run, you should still know what it is and how it works. As with a lot of software, some programs out there rely on these older inet-based programs or at least on your knowledge of how these programs worked. In the interest of backward compatibility—both technological and intellectual—we cover those programs here.

---

inetd: The Internet Supervisor

The inet program acts as a bridge between external client requests and your network's servers. If a request is made for a Web page or a file held on your network, inet determines which server receives the request. Configuring inet beyond the default settings allows you to set up your network so that servers run only upon demand, instead of running constantly. This will save your network some overhead, because you don't lose CPU cycles to services that run even when they're not being called by clients.

Quite a few services are controlled by inet; in fact, any server that receives external requests can be run through inet. The inet daemon, inetd, runs at boot like many other daemons. It is configured to listen for incoming requests on a wide range of ports—unlike servers, which are usually configured to listen on only one or two specific ports—that are defined in the file /etc/services. When inet receives a client request, inet invokes the appropriate server and turns the request over to the server when it is fully started.

NOTE   inetd does not answer any of the client requests itself; it is a one-way port of entry into the system. Instead, inetd manages traffic and lets the individual servers handle responses.

You don't have to put every externally directed server program under the control of inetd. However, it's a convenient place to put servers that may not represent the bulk of your incoming data requests. You probably don't want to put your mail server or news server into inetd, because those programs must run constantly and check their upstream providers on a timed and regular basis.

TIP   You might not want to put your Web server under inetd's control, though it could be useful if you rarely serve Web pages, but still want to have a Web server running. If you place your Web server under inetd, people requesting your pages will experience a slower response than if you were running the server constantly; however, you will have faster network speeds internally, because the server won't run unless prompted. It's a trade-off that depends on your priorities. Note that Apache specifically suggests that you not do this, but it shouldn't break httpd should you try it.

Configuring inetd

inetd requires two separate configuration files. Actually, there is one configuration file and one file that associates ports and services. The /etc/inetd.conf file contains information about servers, their protocols, and what to do when a request is detected for that particular server, while the /etc/services file contains a table of active ports and the servers associated with them. You need to set up both files to use inetd.

/etc/inetd.conf

The inet daemon, inetd, is configured with the /etc/inetd.conf file. We have shown you several configuration files throughout this book, and the /etc/inetd.conf file is similar to those files. It contains a variety of entries that may or may not be commented out and some active entries that define the work of the daemon controlled by the file. Like the Apache configuration file, /etc/inetd.conf is heavily commented. There are far more options that are commented out than there are active options, which is not a bad thing. There are relatively few active entries in /etc/inetd.conf.

Below, we show you a sample /etc/inetd.conf file for a Debian or Red Hat Linux system. Note the comments that explain what each service is, and note how the services are grouped into sections of similar kinds of programs. Although you can edit this file to reflect your actual inet needs, don't remove any of the commented lines. You may need them later in a different network configuration. If you want to remove a service from inetd's control, just comment out its entry.

```
# inetd.conf  This file describes the services that will be
#   available through the INETD TCP/IP super server.  To
#   re-configure the running INETD process, edit this file,
#   then send the INETD process a SIGHUP signal.
#
# Version:    @(#)/etc/inetd.conf    3.10  05/27/93
#
# Authors:    Original taken from BSD UNIX 4.3/TAHOE.
# Fred N. van Kempen, <waltje@uwalt.nl.mugnet.org>
#
# Modified for Debian Linux by Ian A. Murdock
# <imurdock@shell.portal.com>
#
# Modified for RHS Linux by Marc Ewing <marc@redhat.com>
#
# <service_name> <sock_type> <proto> <flags> <user>
# <server_path> <args>
#
```

```
# Echo, discard, daytime, and chargen are used primarily
# for testing.
#
# To re-read this file after changes, just do a 'killall
# -HUP inetd'
#
#echo    stream    tcp    nowait    root  internal
#echo    dgram udp    wait    root  internal
#discard stream    tcp    nowait    root  internal
#discard dgram udp    wait    root  internal
#daytime stream    tcp    nowait    root  internal
#daytime dgram udp    wait    root  internal
#chargen stream    tcp    nowait    root  internal
#chargen dgram udp    wait    root  internal
#time    stream    tcp    nowait    root  internal
#time    dgram udp    wait    root  internal
#
# These are standard services.
#
#ftp stream tcp nowait root /usr/sbin/tcpd in.ftpd -l -a
#telnet stream tcp nowait root /usr/sbin/tcpd in.telnetd
#
# Shell, login, exec, comsat and talk are BSD protocols.
#
#shell stream tcp nowait root /usr/sbin/tcpd in.rshd
login stream tcp nowait root /usr/sbin/tcpd in.rlogind
#exec stream tcp nowait root /usr/sbin/tcpd in.rexecd
#comsat dgram udp wait root /usr/sbin/tcpd in.comsat
#talk dgram udp wait nobody.tty /usr/sbin/tcpd in.talkd
#ntalk dgram udp wait nobody.tty /usr/sbin/tcpd in.ntalkd
#dtalk stream tcp wait nobody.tty /usr/sbin/tcpd ➥
#    in.dtalkd
#
# Pop and imap mail services et al
#
#pop-2 stream tcp nowait root /usr/sbin/tcpd ipop2d
pop-3 stream tcp nowait root /usr/sbin/tcpd ipop3d
#imap stream tcp nowait root /usr/sbin/tcpd imapd
#
# The Internet UUCP service.
#
#uucp stream tcp nowait uucp /usr/sbin/tcpd ➥
```

```
#    /usr/lib/uucp/uucico  -l
#
# Tftp service is provided primarily for booting.  Most
# sites run this only on machines acting as "boot
# servers." Do not uncomment this unless you *need* it.  #
#tftp dgram udp wait root /usr/sbin/tcpd in.tftpd
#bootps dgram udp wait root /usr/sbin/tcpd bootpd
#
# Finger, systat and netstat give out user information
# which may be valuable to potential "system crackers."
# Many sites choose to disable some or all of these
# services to improve security.
#
#finger stream tcp nowait nobody /usr/sbin/tcpd ➥
#    in.fingerd
#cfinger stream tcp nowait root /usr/sbin/tcpd ➥
#    in.cfinger
#systat stream tcp nowait guest /usr/sbin/tcpd ➥
#    /bin/ps -auwwx
#netstat stream tcp nowait guest /usr/sbin/tcpd ➥
#    /bin/netstat -f inet
#
# Authentication
#
# identd is run standalone now
#
#auth stream tcp wait root /usr/sbin/in.identd ➥
#    in.identd -e -o
## End of inetd.conf
```

The file gets longer as more services are added, but it can be quite short if you don't start a lot of services through inet. Entries in /etc/inetd.conf take a particular syntax:

```
service  socket  protocol  flags  user  path  filename
```

These components vary from entry to entry, but most entries use all of them. If there is an error in one of the fields, the entry will be invalid, and the service won't start as needed. The various fields are shown in Table 43.1.

TABLE 43.1: `/etc/inetd.conf` Entry Syntax

Field	Purpose
service	Defines the service being configured in this entry.
socket	Defines the socket type used for this service. Socket types correspond with the TCP and UDP protocols, with `stream` being associated with TCP entries and `dgram` (datagram) being associated with UDP entries. Stream sockets handle continuous data flow, while datagram sockets deal with discrete data packets.
protocol	Defines the protocol being used. `/etc/inetd.conf` requires an explicit statement of protocol even though the socket type usually indicates the protocol in use. May be TCP or UDP.
flags	Defines the manner in which datagram sockets handle incoming connections. May be `wait` or `nowait`.
user	Defines the user under whose control the server operates. If the server runs as root, it will use the root privileges and environment. Some servers run as individual users, such as Apache, which usually runs as `nobody`.
path	Defines the directory path for the actual server program location.
filename	Defines the actual filename of the program, which is used by `inetd` to invoke the server.

Whenever you edit the `/etc/inetd.conf` file, you must restart the `inet` daemon for it to function properly. Do this by issuing the command

```
/etc/init.d/netbase restart
```

at a shell prompt. The `netbase` script restarts several daemons devoted to networking, including `inetd`.

/etc/services

The `/etc/services` file lists all servers running on the network and the port upon which each server listens for incoming connections. The file is quite long, and we include only a small portion here (though it's long, it is a short segment of the full file). The part we've selected contains entries for the various Internet-related services, including those that we cover at the end of this chapter.

```
# Network services, Internet style
    #
    # Note that it is presently the policy of IANA to assign
```

```
# a single well-known port number for both TCP and UDP;
# hence, most entries here have two entries even if the
# protocol doesn't support UDP operations.
# Updated from RFC 1700, ``Assigned Numbers'' (October
# 1994).  Not all ports are included, only the more
# common ones.

tcpmux      1/tcp     # TCP port service multiplexer
echo        7/tcp
echo        7/udp
discard     9/tcp     sink null
discard     9/udp     sink null
systat      11/tcp    users
daytime     13/tcp
daytime     13/udp
netstat     15/tcp
qotd        17/tcp    quote
msp         18/tcp    # message send protocol
msp         18/udp    # message send protocol
chargen     19/tcp    ttytst source
chargen     19/udp    ttytst source
ftp-data    20/tcp
ftp         21/tcp
fsp         21/udp    fspd
ssh         22/tcp    # SSH Remote Login Protocol
ssh         22/udp    # SSH Remote Login Protocol
telnet      23/tcp
# 24 - private
smtp        25/tcp    mail
# 26 - unassigned
time        37/tcp    timserver
time        37/udp    timserver
rlp         39/udp    resource  # resource location
nameserver  42/tcp    name  # IEN 116
whois       43/tcp    nicname
re-mail-ck  50/tcp    # Remote Mail Checking Protocol
re-mail-ck  50/udp    # Remote Mail Checking Protocol
domain      53/tcp    nameserver # name-domain server
domain      53/udp    nameserver
mtp         57/tcp    # deprecated
bootps      67/tcp    # BOOTP server
bootps      67/udp
```

```
bootpc      68/tcp    # BOOTP client
bootpc      68/udp
tftp        69/udp
gopher      70/tcp    # Internet Gopher
gopher      70/udp
rje         77/tcp    netrjs
finger      79/tcp
www         80/tcp    http   # WorldWideWeb HTTP
www         80/udp    # HyperText Transfer Protocol
link        87/tcp    ttylink
kerberos    88/tcp    kerberos5 krb5  # Kerberos v5
kerberos    88/udp    kerberos5 krb5  # Kerberos v5
supdup      95/tcp
# 100 - reserved
hostnames   101/tcp   hostname  # usually from sri-nic
iso-tsap    102/tcp   tsap  # part of ISODE.
csnet-ns    105/tcp   cso-ns # also used by CSO name server
csnet-ns    105/udp   cso-ns
# unfortunately the poppassd (Eudora) uses a port which
# has already been assigned to a different service. We
# list the poppassd as an alias here. This should work
# for programs asking for this service.
# (due to a bug in inetd the 3com-tsmux line is
# disabled)
#3com-tsmux 106/tcp   poppassd
#3com-tsmux 106/udp   poppassd
rtelnet     107/tcp   # Remote Telnet
rtelnet     107/udp
pop2        109/tcp   pop-2      postoffice # POP version 2
pop2        109/udp   pop-2
pop3        110/tcp   pop-3  # POP version 3
pop3        110/udp   pop-3
sunrpc      111/tcp   portmapper # RPC 4.0 portmapper TCP
sunrpc      111/udp   portmapper # RPC 4.0 portmapper UDP
auth        113/tcp   authentication tap ident
sftp        115/tcp
uucp-path   117/tcp
nntp        119/tcp readnews untp # NewsTransferProtocol
ntp         123/tcp
ntp         123/udp   # Network Time Protocol
netbios-ns  137/tcp   # NETBIOS Name Service
netbios-ns  137/udp
```

```
netbios-dgm 138/tcp    # NETBIOS Datagram Service
netbios-dgm 138/udp
netbios-ssn 139/tcp    # NETBIOS session service
netbios-ssn 139/udp
imap2       143/tcp    imap # Interim Mail Access Proto v2
imap2       143/udp    imap
snmp        161/udp    # Simple Net Mgmt Proto
snmp-trap   162/udp    snmptrap  # Traps for SNMP
cmip-man    163/tcp    # ISO mgmt over IP (CMOT)
cmip-man    163/udp
cmip-agent  164/tcp
cmip-agent  164/udp
xdmcp       177/tcp    # X Display Mgr. Control Proto
xdmcp       177/udp
nextstep    178/tcp    NeXTStep NextStep # NeXTStep window
nextstep    178/udp    NeXTStep NextStep  # server
bgp         179/tcp    # Border Gateway Proto.
bgp         179/udp
prospero    191/tcp    # Cliff Neuman's Prospero
prospero    191/udp
irc         194/tcp    # Internet Relay Chat
irc         194/udp
smux        199/tcp    # SNMP Unix Multiplexer
smux        199/udp
at-rtmp     201/tcp    # AppleTalk routing
at-rtmp     201/udp
at-nbp      202/tcp    # AppleTalk name binding
at-nbp      202/udp
at-echo     204/tcp    # AppleTalk echo
at-echo     204/udp
at-zis      206/tcp    # AppleTalk zone information
at-zis      206/udp
qmtp        209/tcp    # The Quick Mail Transfer Protocol
qmtp        209/udp    # The Quick Mail Transfer Protocol
z3950       210/tcp    wais  # NISO Z39.50 database
z3950       210/udp    wais
ipx         213/tcp    # IPX
ipx         213/udp
imap3       220/tcp    # Interactive Mail Access
imap3       220/udp       # Protocol v3
rpc2portmap 369/tcp
rpc2portmap 369/udp    # Coda portmapper
```

```
codaauth2    370/tcp
codaauth2    370/udp    # Coda authentication server
ulistserv    372/tcp    # UNIX Listserv
ulistserv    372/udp
ldap         389/tcp    # Lightweight Dir. Access Protocol
ldap         389/udp    # Lightweight Dir. Access Protocol
https        443/tcp    # MCom
https        443/udp    # MCom
snpp         444/tcp    # Simple Network Paging Protocol
snpp         444/udp    # Simple Network Paging Protocol
saft         487/tcp    # Simple Asynchronous File Transfer
saft         487/udp    # Simple Asynchronous File Transfer
npmp-local   610/tcp    dqs313_qmaster # npmp-local / DQS
npmp-local   610/udp    dqs313_qmaster # npmp-local / DQS
npmp-gui     611/tcp    dqs313_execd # npmp-gui / DQS
npmp-gui     611/udp    dqs313_execd # npmp-gui / DQS
hmmp-ind     612/tcp    dqs313_intercell # HMMP Indication
hmmp-ind     612/udp    dqs313_intercell # HMMP Indication
#
# UNIX specific services
#
exec         512/tcp
biff         512/udp    comsat
login        513/tcp
who          513/udp    whod
shell        514/tcp    cmd    # no passwords used
syslog       514/udp
printer      515/tcp    spooler  # line printer spooler
talk         517/udp
ntalk        518/udp
route        520/udp    router routed   # RIP
timed        525/udp    timeserver
tempo        526/tcp    newdate
courier      530/tcp    rpc
conference   531/tcp    chat
netnews      532/tcp    readnews
netwall      533/udp    # -for emergency broadcasts
uucp         540/tcp    uucpd   # uucp daemon
afpovertcp   548/tcp    # AFP over TCP
afpovertcp   548/udp    # AFP over TCP
remotefs     556/tcp    rfs_server rfs # remote filesystem
klogin       543/tcp    # Kerberized `rlogin' (v5)
```

```
kshell       544/tcp   krcmd  # Kerberized `rsh' (v5)
kerberos-adm 749/tcp   # Kerberos `kadmin' (v5)
#
webster      765/tcp   # Network dictionary
webster      765/udp
swat         901/tcp   # Samba Web Administration Tool
```

As you can see in this segment of the /etc/services file, the file is divided into columns. Each entry uses the following syntax:

```
servicename    port:protocol  other information
```

The port number is usually the standard port for that particular server, though you can assign a different port; however, if you don't publicize that port, external clients won't be able to access the service. The protocol entry identifies the particular protocol needed to start the service: TCP (Transmission Control Protocol) or UDP (Unix Datagram Protocol). Note that many services have entries for both protocols. The final segment of the entry is for other information, which might include a comment or an alias for the service.

You don't need to make many manual entries into /etc/services. When you install a new server, chances are that its configuration and installation will make an /etc/services entry automatically. However, if you use nonstandard ports or want to make sure that there is a reference for a particular server, you'll need to edit this file by hand.

xinetd: An inet Alternative

Recent distributions of Linux, such as Red Hat 7, have begun to use the program xinetd (the extended Internet daemon) as a replacement for inetd. Use of xinetd is similar to that of inetd, but the configuration system is different.

NOTE　　Although we haven't seen xinetd running on any non–Red Hat systems, there is no reason why it couldn't be used on other Unix variants.

The main xinetd configuration file is /etc/xinetd.conf. In this file, you can define sections that configure each service, just as the entries in /etc/inetd.conf do. The main difference, apart from format, is that xinetd has more options. Here's a sample /etc/xinetd.conf file:

```
# Simple configuration file for xinetd
  #
  # Some defaults, and include /etc/xinetd.d/

  defaults
  {
      instances           = 60
      log_type            = SYSLOG authpriv
      log_on_success      = HOST PID
      log_on_failure      = HOST RECORD
  }


  includedir /etc/xinetd.d
```

The last line tells xinetd to include all the files in the /etc/xinetd.d directory. If you issue an ls command for that directory, you'll get the following output:

```
finger   imaps   ipop3   ntalk   rexec   rsh     talk    tftp
imap     ipop2   linuxconf-web pop3s  rlogin  rsync   telnet
```

As you can see, each service covered by inet has a file in this directory. It is not necessary to split the files out like that; you can put the configuration blocks directly into /etc/xinetd.conf, but many administrators prefer to have the various services represented by separate files because it makes maintenance easier. These files show the various settings for that particular service. Here's the telnet file, as an example:

```
# default: on
  # description: The telnet server serves telnet sessions;
  # it uses unencrypted username/password pairs for
  # authentication.
  service telnet
  {
        flags           = REUSE
        socket_type     = stream
        wait            = no
        user            = root
        server          = /usr/sbin/in.telnetd
        log_on_failure  += USERID
  }
```

The imap program has a similar file:

```
# default: off
   # description: The IMAP service allows remote users to
   # access their mail using an IMAP client such as Mutt,
   # Pine, fetchmail, or Netscape Communicator.
   service imap
   {
        socket_type          = stream
        wait                 = no
        user                 = root
        server               = /usr/sbin/imapd
        log_on_success       += DURATION USERID
        log_on_failure       += USERID
        disable              = yes

   }
```

Note the disable = yes option. This shows that the imap service is disabled by default. You can add this line to any configuration file in the /etc/xinetd.d directory to disable a service or change the option to disable = no to enable it.

There are many other options that you can use if you choose to replace inetd on your Linux system with xinetd. For example, you can use these configuration files to control access to the various services controlled by xinetd. If you have xinetd installed on your system, read the manual pages associated with xinetd.conf (type man xinetd.conf at a shell prompt) for a complete list of features.

Running Services from inetd

Although you can run almost any service from inetd, a few services are traditionally called "inet services." These include programs that manage remote access to your network, programs that transfer data, and programs that provide information about your network and its users. Many of these programs are familiar because they have been an integral part of the Unix (and thus the Internet) community for many years.

Unfortunately, many of these popular programs also carry significant security risks. Because they are so old—and because they were developed in the days before constant vigilance and patching were necessary to defeat a determined cracker—their faults are well-known and thus easily exploited to gain illegal access to a network. Although we cover some of these programs in this chapter, there are often more secure ways to handle the same kind of activity; you may wish to limit the use of a particular program such as `rlogin` or `telnet` to machines within your network, or you might replace all remote access programs with the secure SSH protocol.

Connection-Based Services

The most well-known services traditionally run through the `inet` daemon are those that provide remote access to the network. These programs can be invoked on one machine to open the login process on another machine, whether the two machines are on the same local network or connected through the Internet, though they are thousands of miles apart.

For many years, the `telnet` and `rlogin` programs were the standard remote access programs, and both are still used widely today. However, `telnet` and `rlogin` are not particularly secure programs, and they are quite easy to use in an unauthorized access attempt. We recommend that you keep your use of `telnet` and `rlogin` to machines within your local network, if you use these programs at all. Instead, you should use SSH for remote access to your network, which uses a randomly generated seed for an encrypted access key. With SSH, you can make it very difficult to break into your network without an authorized password and key.

TIP	Learn more about SSH's security aspects in Chapter 38: "Network Security."

telnet

The `telnet` protocol relies on the TCP/IP protocol, which defines how data is dispersed over the Internet. TCP/IP is one of the most widely used protocols in all networking and has been dominant for years. As part of the TCP/IP implementation, `telnet` was developed to handle remote logins in a way consonant with the TCP/IP protocol. Once established, a `telnet` connection maintains an open channel through which TCP/IP-compliant data can flow in both directions, allowing you to work on a remote Unix machine and issue commands as if you were logged directly into that computer.

`telnet` is quite useful both locally and across larger networks such as the Internet, because you can do a great deal of work without needing to be physically present at the computers on which you're working. Many other programs rely on `telnet` to establish a protocol-compliant channel for data; if you use programs like this, check to see whether a more secure version has been developed or whether you can change a configuration to use SSH instead. Data, including usernames and passwords, sent over a `telnet` connection is sent in plain text and is not secure at all.

Like all the programs described in this chapter, `telnet` requires both a client and a server to establish a connection. The `telnet` client is installed by default with almost every Unix variant we know of; if you type `telnet` at the shell prompt and don't get a response, either you (or your system administrator) have turned off `telnet` or it was never installed, which is generally a deliberate choice.

The `telnet` server is managed by the `inet` daemon and runs only when an incoming `telnet` connection is noticed on the relevant port, usually port 23. The `telnet` server is not necessarily part of the default installation of most Unix variants, but you can obtain a copy at almost any Unix file archive and install it using the process explained in Chapter 31: "Installing and Managing Software."

The server will run under the process `in.telnetd`, with the TCP protocol and a stream socket. You do not need to configure a `telnet` server beyond installing it, because it doesn't check the incoming request against any parameters. (This is part of the reason why `telnet` is an insecure answer to remote access.)

rlogin

Like `telnet`, `rlogin` is used to start a terminal session on a remote machine. The command is issued with the syntax

    rlogin *user@remote.host.name*

or

    rlogin -1 *user remote.host.name*

If no username is specified, you will be logged into the remote machine under the username you're currently using on the local machine. (Obviously, if no such username exists on the remote machine, the attempt will fail.)

The server that responds to rlogin requests is called rlogind, and it runs under the inet daemon. rlogind uses two kinds of authentication, based either on privileged port numbers or on the Kerberos protocol, and the choice between the two is made by the administrator when rlogind is installed.

Users can specify the Kerberos-based secure session when making the remote connection, by using the klogin command instead of rlogin.

It is fairly easy to overpower the privileged port authentication of rlogind, so we recommend that—if you must run rlogin—you choose to require the klogin version, which is more secure. However, running SSH is probably still a better bet.

You may find that rlogin and rlogind are available with the Unix distribution you're using. They are standard tools, and many programs still suggest their use. If you don't have an rlogin/rlogind package, you can obtain one at any Unix file archive. Just be aware that passwords are passed as plain text instead of in an encrypted manner when rlogind accepts an rlogin connection. It's a security issue you might not be comfortable with.

rsh

The rsh program executes a specified command on a remote machine. You can use rsh, for example, to start a script or process on another machine without logging into that machine. To gain access to the remote machine, your current machine and account must be permitted through an entry in the hosts.equiv file on the remote machine.

rsh requests are answered by the daemon rshd, which runs under inet and starts when an rsh request is received by the remote inet daemon. rshd listens for incoming requests on port 514 and uses a privileged-ports method of authentication: If the incoming request does not originate from a port in the range of 512 to 1023, the request is denied, and the connection is aborted.

Although rsh can be useful, it is not secure. You should disable rsh in your /etc/inetd.conf file and in /etc/services. If someone needs to run Unix commands remotely, you should require a secure login using an encrypted scheme, such as the connections made with SSH. However, if you're using SSH, be sure to disable rsh in the /etc/sshd file as well.

Data Transfer Services

Perhaps the most used service that traditionally runs under the inet daemon is FTP, the File Transfer Protocol program. FTP is used to send and receive files over the Internet or smaller networks, using a specialized protocol that ensures the files arrive complete and without damage. Using FTP is faster than transferring files by download from the Web and more reliable than sending files through e-mail. A number of FTP clients are available, both for Unix and for other operating systems such as Windows and MacOS. FTP is one of the protocols that has aged best from the early days of the Internet to the complicated computing world of today; regardless of other advances in networking technology, file transfer has remained relatively stable.

Although you and your users can run any sort of FTP client that will work with the particular operating system that you're using, all FTP clients send their requests to the FTP daemon, ftpd. To serve FTP requests from your network, you need to run one of the several ftpd programs that are available for Unix. Once you have downloaded and installed the FTP daemon, it will begin to listen for FTP connections on port 21.

FTP verifies users against the regular user configuration and password files. If a user has an account on your system, he may use the same account name and password to access his files via FTP; however, he will have the same access he would have if he logged into his regular user account. To place a certain set of files in a separate directory so that anyone may access them, you'll need to enable *anonymous FTP* on your system.

When someone logs in using anonymous FTP, she is asked to send her regular e-mail address as the password. If this request is answered honestly, this can be a good way to monitor usage of your anonymous FTP service. However, anything will satisfy the daemon, so you might not get valid e-mails from any of your visitors. Anonymous FTP utilizes a wholly separate filesystem, from which visitors cannot access your regular filesystems or data. Anonymous FTP is configured differently in each FTP server variant, so you'll need to consult your daemon's documentation to learn what to do.

TIP

Two of the most popular FTP servers for Unix are WU-FTPD and ProFTPD. Learn more about the WU server at http://www.wu-ftpd.org and about ProFTPD at http://www.proftpd.org. There is little practical difference between the two, so try both and see which you like best.

Information Services

Several information-related services run under `inet`. These services may report on individual users or provide information about the network as a whole. The two services described in this section, `finger` and `netstat`, are two of the most popular `inet`-based information services. `finger` lets you know whom individual users are, how they're connected to the system, how long they've been connected, and what they're doing. `netstat` provides minute-by-minute information about each of your network interfaces, how they are handling packets, and what kind of information they are transmitting.

> **WARNING**   Although these services may seem innocuous, they can be used to get information about your system as a whole, which could be a useful item for someone attempting to break into your system illegally. If you want the kind of information provided by these services, consider limiting them to your network alone and not permitting external requests.

finger

The `finger` program used to be a popular way to learn more about a particular user on a network, whether or not the network was local. To use `finger`, you issue the command

```
finger user@machine.domain
```

at a shell prompt. `finger` then produces output containing information from the initial configuration of the user account, as well as the content of the user's individual `.project` and `.plan` files if those files exist. The output also shows whether the user is logged in and how long that particular login session has lasted.

Useful as this information might be, `finger` is a very insecure program. Not only does it display information about open and idle connections, as well as personal contact information for the fingered user, `finger` is vulnerable to *worms*, cracker programs that slip into a system at a soft point and make their way throughout the local network. Though versions of `finger` are available that have closed off the most egregious security risks, no reliable system we know uses `finger` anymore.

WARNING   If you administer a system that permits `finger` requests, especially from outside the network, turn `finger` off. Even if you think it's not such a big deal to provide personal information about your users, note that `finger` also shows what machines your users use to log into the network and what machines they connect to once logged in. This can be very useful information to a cracker, because those other machines may not have very rigid security procedures in place and could serve as comfortable hosts for illegal activity.

netstat

The `netstat` program is used to display output showing the status of various network devices. You can use `netstat` to learn the size of various queues, see what state particular processes are in, or see how packets are being transferred through individual servers. It's a useful program if you're interested in how your network interfaces are working at any given moment.

Issuing the command `netstat` without any arguments will produce a lengthy output of data, one line for each individual network interface. The output does not end, but will pause until a new set of packet traffic is piped through a defined interface and then print a new line. The `netstat` output is much more useful if you use some of the myriad options available with the program, which produce a limited output tailored to your actual needs. Table 43.2 contains some of the most popular `netstat` options.

NOTE   `netstat` is implemented slightly differently on different Unix variants. The options available to BSD users are not all the same as the options available to Solaris users, which aren't quite the same as the Linux options, and so on. However, most of the options in Table 43.2 should work regardless of the Unix variant on which you're using `netstat`.

TABLE 43.2: netstat Options

Flag	Function
-e	Displays the user under which the specified service is running
-a	Prints all sockets, both listening and answering sockets
-v	Causes output to print in verbose mode, including "complaints" about active sockets that are not configured
-o	Displays information on timers set on various sockets
-i	Shows all networking interfaces in a table using the same format as the ifconfig -e command
-n	Shows interfaces as numerical addresses instead of resolving machine names
-c	Prints output continuously until you interrupt or kill the process
-M	Includes output about masqueraded sessions (servers using unofficial network addresses, as explained in Chapter 38: "Network Security")

Miscellaneous Services

Many other services run under inet and may or may not be active on your particular system. If you page through /etc/services or /etc/inetd.conf and see a comment that refers to a service you find intriguing, you should be able to find more information on that service's manual page.

TIP   If you don't have the relevant man page installed on your system, try searching Google (http://www.google.com) or some other metacrawler Web search engine with the search terms "*command* manual page." This usually gives good results.

One inet program that many people keep on their systems just because it's fun and easy to use is talk or one of talk's variants.

NOTE   On many systems, the program that's invoked with the `talk` command is actually `ntalk` or (new `talk`). `ntalk` fixed some annoying bugs with the original `talk` program.

`talk` is a Stone-Age chat program that's limited to two people. When you issue the command

`talk user@domain.name`

a split screen appears, with a horizontal line running directly through the middle of the screen. The person who was named in the invocation will receive a message alerting him that you want to talk, and he must issue the command

`talk you@your.domain.name`

to enable the connection.

Once the connection is established, you type your comments in the top half, and the comments of your `talk` partner show up in the bottom half. It's somewhat confusing at first, but it begins to make sense after a while. We admit that we have a soft spot for `talk`, because when we were both first on the Internet years and years ago, `talk` was the only chat option, and we've both logged many hours in this basic, but functional, program.

Summary

No matter how many services you run, it's likely that you'll appreciate the convenience and reliability of an automated manager. On Unix systems, the `inet` program and its daemon, `inetd`, act as a gateway between incoming client requests and the servers that run on your network. When `inetd` senses an incoming request, it determines which service should answer and directs the request to that service. If the service is not currently running, `inetd` invokes the service and brings it up before the request is sent. Thus, requests to servers handled through `inetd` may be processed more slowly than requests to servers that are constantly running, but there is a savings on network CPU cycle usage because you do not have a wide variety of infrequently used services constantly available.

You can run almost any service that answers external requests through `inet`. `inet` is configured with two files: /etc/services, which associates particular ports with individual servers, and /etc/inetd.conf, which defines how each server will respond to a request when it arrives. Some of the more popular services run through `inet` include connection-based services such as `telnet`, `rlogin`, `rsh`, and sometimes SSH; data transfer services such as the FTP daemon `ftpd`; information services such as `finger` or `netstat`; and miscellaneous services, including `talk` and its variants. Some of these services are quite old in Unix terms and may not incorporate current security standards. You are advised to check out the security risks of any particular service before you run it.

APPENDIX

A

Common Unix Commands

We use the following conventions for the entries in this appendix:

- Items in square brackets, such as [*option*], are optional.

- Items in angle brackets, such as *<filename>*, must be replaced with an actual file or program name, deleting the angle brackets.

- Items separated by a pipe, | , are mutually exclusive.

- If the pipe is placed within square brackets, it denotes an optional choice; for example, if the entry shows syntax with the component [x | y], you can select x, y, or none.

- If the pipe is placed within curly braces, such as {x | y}, you are required to choose either x or y.

NOTE

We provide the most common uses of these commands. Many of these commands have a more extended syntax that permits other constructions. When in doubt, consult the relevant manual page for the appropriate options.

---

adduser

adduser is used to create a new user account. It uses the syntax

    adduser [*options*] *username*

Options for adduser include

- -c (Includes a comment when creating the account)

- -d (Specifies the user's home directory)

- -e (Specifies an expiration date for this account)

- -M (Use if you do not want to create a home directory for this user)

- -p (Specifies the initial password for the account)

WARNING

You should require your users to change their passwords immediately.

- -s (Specifies the user's default shell environment if they do not want to use the default shell)

apropos

Use `apropos` to search for a specified file on the computer (not just in your user account), using a keyword. It is usually used for help in finding a man page. `apropos` uses the syntax

```
apropos <keyword>
```

at

`at` is used to schedule a one-time command execution for a later time. It uses the syntax

```
at [options] <time>
```

One of `at`'s most useful options is the −f flag, which directs `at` to take input from a file rather than from the standard input.

NOTE   `at` normally takes its input from standard input. If you simply give the command `at <time>` you will be presented with an `at>` prompt at which you can enter shell commands to be executed at the time you've specified.

You can also use `at` with a redirection operator, as in

```
at <time> < <command>
```

If your job is more complex, you can put the commands in a file and invoke the file using the −f flag, as in

```
at -f <command file> <time>
```

bash

Use the `bash` command to invoke the GNU Bourne Again Shell environment. `bash` takes the syntax

```
bash [<command>]
```

The `bash` command starts a Bourne Again Shell interpreter. If a command is given as an argument, the command (usually the name of a script) is run in the Bourne Again Shell environment.

cat

cat is used to print the contents of a specified file to the screen. It uses the syntax

    cat [options] <file(s)>

There are several options for cat, including

- -n (cat will number the lines of output)

- -s (cat collapses consecutive blank lines into one single blank line)

TIP

One useful cat application is to concatenate several files into one new file, using the command cat <file 1> <file 2> <file 3> >> <new file>. This will combine a variety of shorter files into one long file, which is easier to work with.

---

cd

Use cd to change directories in the Unix filesystem. It uses the syntax

    cd [directory]

If no directory is specified when you issue the command, cd changes to your home directory.

cfdisk

This command is used to partition a hard disk. It is similar to fdisk, but with a slightly friendlier interface.

chmod

Use chmod to change file permissions. This command can be issued only by root or by the file's owner. chmod takes the syntax

    chmod [u|g|a] {+|-} {r and/or w and/or x} <filename>

NOTE

chmod assumes that you want to assign global permission if you do not specify any other level of permission. Therefore, if the u, g, or a options are not included when you issue the command, chmod will use a by default.

---

chmod options include

- u (Grants permissions only to the owner of the file)
- g (Grants permissions to the user's groups)
- a (Grants global permissions, including access permissions for those outside the local network)
- + (Notifies chmod that you are going to change the permissions on the specified file)
- - (Notifies chmod that you are going to remove an existing permission from the specified file)
- r (Assigns the *read* file permission, giving read-only access)
- w (Assigns the *write* file permission, giving both read and edit permissions)
- x (Assigns the *execute* file permission, granting the ability to run the file if it is an executable binary, as well as read and edit permissions)

chmod can be difficult to comprehend the first few times you use it. Here are the most commonly used chmod commands:

```
chmod a+r <filename>
```

This command gives read permission on the specified file to all users.

```
chmod g+rw <filename>
```

This command gives read and write permission on the specified file to the user's group.

```
chmod a-x <filename>
```

This command removes execute permission from all users. If you issue this command, follow it up with another command that grants execute permission to those people who should be able to execute the file (such as the user).

chown

Use chown to change the ownership of a given file. chown uses the syntax

```
chown <user> <filename>
```

You must use chown as root; otherwise, it can be executed only by the owner of the specified file.

cp

cp is used to copy a specified file to a new location. It uses the syntax

```
cp <file 1> <file 2>
```

file 1 is the file to be copied, and file 2 is the name of the new file.

WARNING Be careful with cp. If you use an existing file's name for file 2, the contents of that file will be replaced with the contents of file 1.

---

crontab

The crontab command is used to maintain cron files for automated system administration, by editing the /etc/crontab file. crontab takes the syntax

```
crontab [-u <user>] {-l|-r|-e}
```

crontab options include

- -u (Specifies a particular user to issue the command. The default, if no other user is specified, is the user issuing the command. If you edit /etc/crontab as root, this will be set to the root account.)

- -l (Prints the /etc/crontab file to the screen)

- -r (Clears the entire existing /etc/crontab file)

- -e (Edits the /etc/crontab file with the current entry)

date

date sets, or prints to the screen, the current time and date. date takes the syntax

```
date [options]
```

Issuing the date command with no argument will cause the current date and time to be printed to the screen.

To set the date, you must be root. Issue the date command with the −s option, and set the time using two-digit numbers for the day, month, and year. Set the time using the 24-hour clock. Thus, to set the date to 10 seconds past 1:20 A.M., November 27, 1933, you would issue the command

```
date −s 2711330120.10
```

dd

Use dd to copy a specified file to another location. dd is usually used to make a copy of a file on a removable disk, because it streams the data directly to the new location without formatting it in any way. dd takes the syntax

```
dd if=<input file> of=<output file>
```

The *output file* component is usually the device name of the floppy disk drive or the drive to which you are transferring the file.

declare

declare is used to declare and assign a particular type to a variable. declare takes the syntax

```
declare [options] VAR[=<value>]
```

declare's options are

- -i (Declares the variable is an integer)

- -r (Declares the variable is read-only)

- -a (Declares the variable is an array)

NOTE   You can declare a variable type only if you are using the **bash** shell in version 2 or later.

diff

Use diff to compare the contents of two specified files. Any differences found will be printed to the screen. It uses the syntax

```
diff <file 1> <file 2>
```

diff compares the files by checking each character in file 1 against each character in file 2. If there are a lot of differences, as in a case where the two files are not versions of the same document or script, the diff output will be lengthy, and it is best to pipe it to another file.

du

The du command's output shows the amount of disk space used by a particular user, or used by a specified file or directory. du takes the syntax

```
du [options] <file or directory name>
```

Options for du include

- -b (Prints the size in bytes)
- -c (Prints a full listing of each directory and its size, ending with a grand total of space taken on the disk)
- -h (Reports in familiar sizes, such as kilobytes or megabytes)
- -k (Prints the size in kilobytes, even if the directory or file occupies more than a megabyte of space)
- -m (Prints the size in megabytes, even if the directory or file occupies less than a megabyte of space)
- -S (Ignores the size of subdirectories and counts only the size of top-level directories)
- -s (Displays the total size only of the directory [and subdirectories] in which the command is issued)

echo

echo prints a requested string to the screen. echo uses the syntax

```
echo [options] <string>
```

To have echo print a trailing new (blank) line, issue the command without options. To get output without a new line, issue the command as

```
echo -n <string>
```

exit

The exit command is used to end a shell process. exit takes the syntax

```
exit [<value>]
```

In script programming, <value> is a number used to denote the status of the process upon ending. Normally, 0 (zero) represents success, and anything else represents failure.

export

The export command makes a specified variable available to the shell environment. export takes the syntax

```
export <variable>[=<value>]
```

For example, if you wish to set the value of the EDITOR variable to pico and make that variable's new value available to the shell environment, you would issue the command

```
export EDITOR="pico"
```

exportfs

Use the exportfs command to export a network filesystem with NFS. exportfs takes the syntax

```
exportfs [options]
```

Options for exportfs include

- -a (Exports all filesystems named in /etc/exports)

- -r (Reexports all previously exported filesystems)

- -u (Unexports one or more named filesystems)

expr

The expr command provides numerical evaluation of a given expression. expr uses the syntax

```
expr <expression>
```

TIP

If you have not declared your variables to take a certain type (see declare), the expr command is needed so that, for example, "1+1" is interpreted as the arithmetic value "2", rather than as the string "1+1". If you are using typed variables and have declared your variables as integers, the expr command is unnecessary.

fdisk

The fdisk command invokes an interactive disk partitioning program. fdisk takes the syntax

```
fdisk <device>
```

WARNING fdisk is an interactive program. It is also a potentially destructive one. See its doc-umentation before attempting to use it.

---

fsck

The fsck command is used to check the integrity of a filesystem. fsck uses the syntax

```
fsck [options] <filesystem>
```

fsck has several options, including

- -t (Specifies filesystem type)

- -A (Checks all filesystems; uses the /etc/fstab file as a guide)

- -N (Dry run: shows only what would be checked, but doesn't actually check it)

- -R (When checking all filesystems using the –A option, skips the root filesystem [see note below for the reason behind this option])

- -V (Verbose mode)

- -a (Automatically makes all necessary repairs in the filesystem being checked)

- -r (Converse of –a; makes repairs interactively, prompting for approval of each repair)

NOTE Filesystems must not be mounted, or must be mounted *read-only*, before they can benefit from the fsck command. The -R option exists so that the root filesystem can remain mounted *read-write* while all other filesystems are checked using fsck -A.

---

grep

The grep command searches a specified input source for characters or numbers matching a specified pattern. grep uses the syntax

```
grep [options] <pattern> [filename]
```

There are a wide variety of options for grep, and it is best to consult the manual page to see what options are enabled on your system.

TIP   grep is pronounced "grep," not "gee-rep."

---

grep can use the output of another process as its input. To do so, construct a command using the | character. For example, if you wanted to grep the output of an ls command for the character string mail, you would issue the command

```
ls -x | grep -e mail
```

The pipe causes the output of the ls command to be run through grep before reporting to the screen.

groups

The groups command is used to display the names of all groups to which a user belongs. groups takes the syntax

```
groups [<username>]
```

If you provide another user's name in the *<username>* field, groups will report the group memberships of that user. Without that argument, groups will report your group memberships.

gzip and gunzip

The gzip command is used to compress a specified file or set of files. The gunzip command is used to expand a file compressed with gzip. They both take a similar syntax:

```
gzip  <filename>
gunzip <filename>
```

head and tail

Use the head command to see the first few lines of a specified file, and use the tail command to see the last few lines of the specified file. They use the same syntax:

```
head <filename>
tail <filename>
```

ifconfig

The ifconfig command is used to configure network devices under Linux. ifconfig uses the syntax

```
ifconfig [<device>] [options] [up|down]
```

If no options are given in the command, ifconfig displays all active devices. The <device> component is the path name of any network device, such as ppp0 or eth0. Options for ifconfig include

- -a (Causes ifconfig to display all devices, regardless of status)
- netmask <address> (Allows the specified IP number to be entered as a netmask)
- <address> (Assigns <address> as the device's IP number)

init

The init command invokes the init daemon, initd. initd is usually used to change the runlevel under Linux. init uses the syntax

```
init <runlevel>
```

where <runlevel> is one of the following: 0, 1, 2, 3, 4, 5, 6, or s.

- 0 (shut-down)
- 1 (single user mode)
- 2–5 (locally defined)
- 6 (reboot)
- s (single user mode)

insmod

The insmod command is used to insert a kernel module for a modular kernel. insmod may be issued only as root. It takes the syntax

```
insmod <module name>
```

For example, the command

```
insmod 3c509
```

loads the driver module for the 3Com 3c509 network card into the kernel.

kill

The `kill` command is used to send a signal to an active process. `kill` takes the syntax

```
kill [-s <signal>] <process ID>
```

`kill` can take a number of signal numbers as arguments to the `-s` flag. If no signal is specified, SIGTERM (signal 15) is used.

A complete list of valid `kill` signals can be seen by issuing the command

```
kill -l
```

less

Use the `less` command to view a specified file in page-sized chunks. `less` takes the syntax

```
less <filename>
```

Use the spacebar to advance to the next page, and the b key to view the previous page.

ln

The `ln` command creates a link to a specified file; the link can be either a hard link or a symbolic link. `ln` takes the syntax

```
ln [options] <linked-to file> <name of link>
```

Options for `ln` include

- `-s` (Creates a symbolic link)
- `-b` (Makes a backup file of the linked file in addition to creating the link)
- `-v` (Produces verbose output, listing the name of the file before making the link)

locate

The `locate` command is used to find the path to a specified program on the hard drive. `locate` uses the syntax

```
locate [filename]
```

logout

The `logout` command is used to end a user's session. `logout` is simply issued as a single command at the shell prompt:

```
logout
```

lpc

The `lpc` command is a line printer control program. `lpc` takes the syntax

```
lpc [command [arguments]]
```

Two important `lpc` commands are

- `help` (Prints a short description of each command)
- `abort` (Terminates an active spooling daemon)

`lpc` accepts various arguments, including

- `all` (Terminates all spools)
- `printer` (Terminates a particular spool)
- `clean` (Removes temporary files and data from spool directories)
- `disable` (Turns a spool off)
- `down` (Turns a spool off and prints a message saying that the spool is off)
- `message` (Message to be printed)
- `enable` (Turns a spool on)
- `exit` (Quits `lpc`)
- `quit` (Same as `exit`)
- `start` (Starts a print queue and spooling daemon for the designated printer)
- `restart` (Turns the designated queue off and on again)

lpq

The `lpq` command is used to view queued jobs in a print spool. `lpq` takes the syntax

```
lpq [-1] [-P<printer>] [<job number>] [<user>]
```

The main lpq option is the −1 flag, which generates an extended format display for output.

For example, the command

```
lpq -1 -Plp
```

will generate a long format view of information for all jobs in the queue for printer lp. The command

```
lpq pete
```

will display one-line information for all queued print jobs owned by user pete.

lpr

The lpr command is used to send a job to a print spool. lpr takes the syntax

```
lpr [options] [<file>]
```

Two common lpr options are

- -P<printer> (Specifies a printer name)
- -#<number> (Prints a specified number of copies)

For example, to send the file foo.txt to the print spool for printer lp, you would issue the command

```
lpr -Plp foo.txt
```

To send the same file to the same print spool, but to print three copies, you would issue the command

```
lpr -Plp -#3 foo.txt
```

lprm

The lprm command removes a job from a line printer's spool. lprm takes the syntax

```
lprm [-P<printer>] [-] [<job number>] [<user>]
```

For example, to remove all jobs owned by user harry from the printer lp's spool, you would issue the command

```
lprm -Plp - harry
```

To remove job number 13 from the spool for printer lp, you would issue the command

```
lprm -Plp 13
```

TIP   Job numbers for specific jobs can be obtained from the output of the `lpq` command.

ls

The `ls` command produces output that lists the contents of a directory. `ls` takes the syntax

    ls [options] [directory]

If no directory is specified, `ls` lists the contents of the current directory. Options for `ls` include

- `-l` (Lists directory contents in long format, giving additional information about file size and other file characteristics)

- `-a` (Lists all files in the directory, including those that begin with a leading dot)

- `-i` (Lists files showing their inode, or disk index, numbers)

- `-R` (Lists all subdirectories of the current directory and all files within those subdirectories)

- `-t` (Lists directory contents sorted by the time of the last modification to the file)

make

The `make` command is used in installing new software. It is a front end to the C compiler and linker. `make` takes the syntax

    make [options]

The various options available for `make` are defined in the `Makefile`. Common options include `dep`, which causes dependencies to be configured, and `install`, which causes the binary file(s) to be placed in the appropriate directory.

man

The `man` command displays the manual page for a specified command or program. `man` uses the syntax

    man [options] <name of command or program>

Options for man include

- -p (Specifies the pager to use with the manual page; the default is less)
- -a (Finds all manual pages that match the string *<name>*)
- -h (Prints a one-line help message and exits man)
- -K (Searches for *<name>* in the text of all manual pages, as well as in the title)

mkdir

The mkdir command creates a new directory with the specified name, using the syntax

```
mkdir <directory name>
```

mke2fs

The mke2fs command is a Linux utility that creates an ext2 (Linux native format) filesystem and formats a specified filesystem or partition. mke2fs takes the syntax

```
mke2fs [options] <device>
```

Options for mke2fs include

- -b (Specifies block size in bytes; valid block sizes are 1024, 2048, and 4096 bytes per block)
- -c (Checks for bad blocks while formatting)
- -n (Dry run: doesn't actually create the filesystem, but reports what it would have done if it did)
- -v (Runs in verbose mode)

more

more shows the specified file in page-size chunks, using the syntax

```
more <filename>
```

Use the spacebar to move forward one page in the file.

mount

The mount command is used to mount a filesystem and make the data on that device available for use. mount uses the syntax

```
mount -t <fs type> <device> <mount point>
```

The arguments to mount are

- *<fs type>* (The type of filesystem to be mounted; e.g., ext2, msdos, iso9660)
- *<device>* (The path name of the filesystem to be mounted; e.g., /dev/hda3 in the case of a physical drive or remote:/usr/local in the case of a network filesystem)
- *<mount point>* (The name of an existing but empty local directory; e.g., /mnt/floppy)

mv

The mv command is used to move a specified file to a new location and uses the syntax

```
mv <old> <new>
```

The entry *<old>* is the filename of the file that will be moved to the location specified in *<new>*. If *<new>* is a filename, the file is renamed. If *<new>* is a directory name, the file is moved to the new directory with the same filename.

netstat

The netstat command displays the status of various network functions. netstat uses the syntax

```
netstat [options]
```

If the command is issued without an option, netstat displays all open network sockets. Other options for netstat include

- -e (Reports the user ID of each socket user)
- -r (Displays the complete routing table)

passwd

The passwd command is used to change the login password for a given account. passwd uses the syntax

```
passwd [<user>]
```

If issued as root, passwd can be used to change any user's password or user information. If not logged in as root, you can use passwd to change only your own password or user information.

ping

The ping command tests network connections; it sends small packets of data to a specified remote machine and reports the time taken for the packets to return. ping uses the syntax

```
ping [options] <remote machine>
```

Options for ping include

- -c (Specifies the number of data packets to be sent. If you do not use this, ping continues to send packets until you press Ctrl+c to stop.)
- -i (Specifies the number of seconds to wait between each packet; the default is 10 seconds.)

ps

The ps command produces output showing a list of all current processes, the amount of time they have been running, and the amount of CPU time they consume. ps uses the syntax

```
ps [options]
```

Options for ps include

- -a (Shows all processes running on the computer, including those of other users)
- -x (Includes processes without a controlling terminal: that is, background processes that were not manually started by you or another user)
- -u (Displays all processes sorted by user ID)

pwd

The pwd command prints the full path of the current directory. Issue the command

```
pwd
```

at a shell prompt to learn where you are in the filesystem.

read

The read command instructs the computer to take input from the standard input (usually the keyboard). read uses the syntax

```
read $VAR
```

This command is used in script programming. The construction read $VAR will take a line from the standard input and assign it to variable $VAR.

rm

The rm command is used to delete a specified file. rm takes the syntax

```
rm [options] <filename>
```

Options for rm include

- -i (Interactive mode, requesting confirmation for each file to be deleted)

Use the -i flag with rm. It prevents files from being deleted inadvertently, especially if you use the wildcard *. For example, the command rm conf* will remove all files beginning with the characters *conf,* whether you intended to remove all those files or not. Using -i forces you to approve each file's deletion, and you can stop the deletion process before you lose critical files.

- -r (Recursive mode, deleting all subdirectories of the current directory as well as the files they contain)
- -f (Force mode, ignoring all warnings that rm issues to itself)

The -r and -f flags are often combined, as in the command rm -rf <file-name>, as a shortcut to remove entire filesystems. This should be done only with extreme caution, however, especially when root. The command rm -rf *.* will remove every single file from your filesystem. *Do not do this.*

rmdir

The rmdir command deletes the specified directory. rmdir uses the syntax

```
rmdir <directory name>
```

If you issue an rmdir command for a directory that is not empty, rmdir prints an error message and exits.

route

The route command is used to view or manipulate the IP routing table. route takes the syntax

```
route [options] <target>
```

Options for route include

- -v (Verbose mode)

- -n (Shows numerical addresses instead of host names [useful if you can't get to your DNS server])

- add (Adds a route)

- del (Deletes a route)

- -net (Specifies target is a network)

- -host (Specifies target is a host)

- netmask (Specifies netmask to be used if target is a network)

- default (Makes this route the default, to be used if no other route matches)

- gw (Routes packets through a gateway. The gateway can be an interface or a host. If the interface is a host, this option is normally used in conjunction with the default option. [See examples below.])

For example, if you wish to add a static route to the host designated by the IP number 192.168.0.1, you would issue the command

```
route add -host 192.168.0.1
```

To send all traffic to the network that uses the addresses 192.168.0.1 through 192.168.0.255 through the eth1 interface, you would issue the command

```
route add -net 192.168.0.0 dev eth1
```

If you wish all network traffic not matching other routes to be sent through the
eth0 interface, issue the command

```
route add default eth0
```

To send all network traffic, not matching other routes, through the gateway
machine numbered 192.168.0.1, issue the command

```
route add default gw 192.168.0.1
```

rsync

The rsync command is used to synchronize files or directories across a network.
rsync uses the syntax

```
rsync [options] <source> <destination>
```

There are several options for the rsync command:

- -e (Used to choose method of transport [rsh or ssh]; the default is rsh)
- -a (Archive mode; preserves all file attributes)
- -r (Recursive mode; copies files in all subdirectories)
- -u (Update mode; copies over files only if the source file's timestamp is
  more recent than the destination's)
- -R (Specifies the use of relative path names)
- -v (Verbose mode)
- -b (Backup mode; makes backups of old files before overwriting)
- -n (Dry run; shows what would have been transferred, but doesn't actually
  do the transferring)
- -z (Compresses data for transfer [good for slow connections])
- --delete (Deletes files on the receiving side that don't exist on the sending
  side)
- --exclude (Excludes a subdirectory from the recursive transfer)

For example, if you want to transfer the file /foo/bar from the local machine to
a remote machine using the rsh protocol, you would issue the command

```
rsync /foo/bar remote:/foo/bar
```

To perform the same action, but use the SSH protocol instead, you'd use the command

```
rsync -e ssh /foo/bar remote:/foo/bar
```

To copy the contents of the local directory /foo, and all of its subdirectories, to the remote directory /foo, you would issue this command:

```
rsync -e ssh -ruv /foo/ remote:/foo/
```

Note that, if a file on the receiving machine is newer than the corresponding file on the sending machine, the file is not copied. rsync will use verbose mode.

To perform the same action without copying the subdirectory /foo/bar, use this command:

```
rsync -e ssh -ruv /foo/ remote:/foo/ --exclude bar/
```

set

The set command displays a list of environment variables with their current values. Issue the command

```
set
```

at a shell prompt to see the output.

setenv

The setenv command is used to change an environment variable under the C Shell. setenv uses the syntax

```
setenv(VAR=<value>)
```

sh

The sh command invokes the Bourne Shell. sh takes the syntax

```
sh [<command>]
```

The sh command starts a Bourne Shell interpreter. If a command is given as an argument, the command (usually the name of a script) is run in the Bourne Shell environment.

shutdown

The `shutdown` command halts all processes and shuts down the computer. `shutdown` uses the syntax

```
shutdown [options] <time> [<warning message>]
```

There are several components to the `shutdown` command:

- *<time>* (The time until the machine shuts down. It has three options: now; +*<m>*, where *<m>* is the number of minutes to wait before shutting down; and *<hh>*:*<mm>*, which is the time at which shut-down will commence in hours and minutes.)

- *<warning message>* (A message to be sent to all users alerting them of impending shut-down)

`shutdown` options include

- `-h` (Causes `shutdown` to halt or stop the system)

- `-r` (Causes the computer to reboot, instead of turning off)

The most common `shutdown` command is

```
shutdown -h now
```

sort

The `sort` command is used to sort items in a file, either numerically or alphabetically. It then prints the sorted output to the screen. `sort` uses the syntax

```
sort <filename>
```

ssh

The `ssh` command invokes a secure shell, which is a secure replacement for `rsh`, `rcp`, `rlogin`, and other remote-shell commands. `ssh` takes the syntax

```
ssh [-l <login name>] [hostname] [command]
```

NOTE   `ssh` provides encrypted data connections either for interactive logins or for running commands on a remote system. At its most basic, `ssh` can be used as a replacement for `telnet`. `ssh` can, however, be made to perform extremely complex behaviors such as port forwarding and virtual private networking. Excellent documentation is available on the World Wide Web. You might also want to investigate the `scp` program, which is a secure replacement for the FTP protocol.

startx

The startx command is used to start the X Window System. startx is simply invoked at the command line as

    startx

Although command-line arguments to startx do exist, these parameters are better configured using the .xinitrc file.

su

The su command is used to change user identities. It is primarily used by administrators to access superuser powers or maintain a particular user account. su takes the syntax

    su [-] [<username>]

If the - character is used, the new user identity's environment variables will be used. If the - character is not used, you will be in the new user's account, but using your own environment variables.

Use su to issue root commands with the syntax

    su -c <command>

This construction allows you to issue a command as root without having to leave your user account.

tar

The tar command creates or extracts an archive file, often referred to as a *tarball*. tar is issued with the syntax

    tar [options] <file 1> <file 2>... <file N>

or

    tar [options] <directory 1> <directory 2>... <dir. N>

Options for tar do not use the hyphen, as most other flags do. Options include

- c (Creates an archive from the specified files)
- x (Extracts the files from the specified archive)
- f (Compresses the specified file)

- z (Decompresses the specified file, using the `gunzip` protocol)
- v (Verbose output)

test

The `test` command is used to evaluate a specified condition. `test` uses the syntax

    test <condition>

or

    [<condition>] (Square brackets interpreted literally here)

or

    test [options] <target>

Options for test include

- -e (File exists.)
- -f (File exists and is a regular file.)
- -d (Target exists and is a directory.)
- -s (File exists and is not empty.)

   The `test` command will return `"true"` (0) if the expression being tested is true. Expressions may be of the following forms:

- `test ( $VAR = "hello" )`, in which the variable $VAR is equal to the string `"hello"`
- `test ($VAR -eq 3)`, in which the variable $VAR is equal to integer 3
- `[ $VAR -eq 3 ]`, in which the variable $VAR is equal to integer 3
- `test -e /var/run/myPID`, in which the file /var/run/myPID exists
- `[ -e /var/run.myPID]`, in which the file /var/run/myPID exists

top

The `top` command is used to display the table of processes. `top` takes the syntax

    top [options]

Options for top include

- d (Specifies the interval between updates)

- p (Displays only the process with this PID. This option can be given up to 20 times to create abridged process tables.)

- q (Causes top to refresh without any delay. Be careful with this option, because this can really eat up CPU time.)

- i (Ignores idle or zombie processes)

TIP top can also use a number of interactive commands. A description of those commands can be seen by typing h while top is running.

---

touch

The touch command updates the timestamp on a specified file. touch uses the syntax

```
touch <filename>
```

If the filename given does not match an existing file, touch creates an empty file with that filename.

traceroute

The traceroute command locates the route that packets travel from one host to another. traceroute uses the syntax

```
traceroute [options] <remote machine>
```

Options for traceroute include

- -n (Displays IP numbers of only machines, not hostnames)

- -w (Sets the time [in seconds] that traceroute will wait for a response before timing out)

ulimit

The ulimit command controls the resources available to processes started by the shell environment. ulimit uses the syntax

```
ulimit [options [limit]]
```

Options for ulimit include

- -S (Sets and uses the soft resource limit, which sends a warning if a process goes over the specified limit)

- -H (Sets and uses the hard resource limit, which will not permit a process to go over the specified limit)

- -a (Reports all current limits to the screen)

- -c (Sets the maximum size of core files)

- -d (Sets the maximum size of a process's data segment)

- -t (Sets the maximum amount of CPU time, in seconds, that a process can use)

- -f (Sets the maximum size of files created by the shell)

- -p (Sets the pipe buffer size)

- -n (Sets the maximum number of open file descriptors)

- -u (Sets the maximum number of user processes)

- -v (Sets the size of virtual memory)

umask

The umask command is used to set default permissions for any newly created file. umask takes the syntax

```
umask [-S] [<mode>]
```

If you use the −S option, the command will show the current file creation mask.

NOTE   The mode can be either an octal number or a symbolic string like that used for the chmod command.

---

umount

The umount command is used to unmount a filesystem. umount uses the syntax

```
umount [options] <filesystem>
```

The <filesystem> component can be a device name, such as /dev/hda1, or a directory name, such as /usr/local.

umount can also be used to unmount every filesystem listed in /etc/mtab at the same time with the -a flag, as in

```
umount -a
```

useradd

The useradd command (may be called adduser on some systems) is used to create a new user account. useradd takes the syntax

```
useradd [options] <username>
```

Options for useradd include

- -c (Adds a comment)
- -d (Specifies the user's home directory)
- -e (Specifies the date the account expires)
- -p (Specifies the user's initial password)
- -s (Specifies the user's default shell)
- -u (Specifies the user's user ID)

For example, if you wish to create an account for the user harry, using the default values listed in the file /etc/default/useradd, you would issue the command

```
useradd harry
```

To create an account for harry where his user ID number will be 501, issue the command

```
useradd -u 501 harry
```

To create an account for harry where his user ID number will be 501 and his default shell will be the tcsh shell, issue the command

```
useradd -u 501 -s /bin/tcsh harry
```

userdel

The userdel command (called deluser on some systems) is used to delete a user account. userdel takes the syntax

```
userdel [-r] <username>
```

The most common option for userdel is the -r flag, which deletes the user's account and all files in the user's home directory.

w

The w command shows a list of users currently logged into system. w takes the syntax

    w [options]

Options for w include

- -h (Specifies to not print header information)
- -s (Short format)
- <user> (Shows information about the specified user only)

wc

The wc command counts the number of words in a specified file. wc uses the syntax

    wc [options] <filename>

Options for wc include

- -c (Counts the characters [bytes] of the file instead of the words)
- -l (Counts lines in the file instead of words)
- -L (Prints the length of the longest line)

whereis

The whereis command finds a file or program on the hard disk. whereis uses the syntax

    whereis [options] <filename>

Options for whereis include

- -b (Searches only for binaries with the given filename)
- -m (Searches only for manual pages with the given filename)
- -s (Searches only for source code packages with the given filename)

which

The `which` command finds a given program on the hard disk. `which` uses the syntax

```
which [options] <programname>
```

If you issue the command with the –a flag, `which` will find all matching executables in the list of directories specified in the PATH environment variable.

APPENDIX

B

Documentation and Resources

- Introducing Unix

- Getting Started

- Unix Desktop Environments

- Using the Shell

- Using Text Editors

- Shell Programming

- Basic System Administration

- Network Administration

- Administering Services

- On the CD

This appendix contains a selective set of Web resources that expand on information presented in this book. Although we did not set out to create an exhaustive reference to Unix Web sites, we did choose some sites that had a similar goal, so you'll find a few listings in here that are essentially link collections. Other listings are targeted to a specific issue or problem, while many others are official pages for individual programs or projects.

NOTE As with any Internet resource, these sites may be under construction, down, or no longer maintained. We do not verify the accuracy of the information presented, though we've picked sites we feel to be reputable.

We have covered only Web resources; there are many mailing lists and newsgroups that cover much of the same material, often with a faster turnaround. However, it's easier to locate specific material on the Web, and Web information is thus more reliable when printed in an actual paper book. We are voracious readers of mailing lists and newsgroups, however, and encourage you to seek out those resources as well.

Introducing Unix

In Part I: "Introducing Unix," we offered a brief history of the Unix operating system, introduced a number of Unix variants, and explained the concepts of Free Software and Open Source. We also provided a basic tutorial for beginning Unix users. In this section of the appendix, we list some Web resources that will give you more in-depth explanations of these concepts.

History of Unix

As we explained in Chapters 1 and 2: "History and Background of Unix" and "Which Unix?" we think it's important for Unix users to understand the history behind the operating system. Here are a few links that offer different perspectives on Unix's development.

http://www.uwsg.iu.edu/usail/library/history.html

This site offers links to a small selection of Unix history documents. Most of the Unix history information on the Web is found in repeated copies of the documents linked here; we provide this URL because it gathers all of these frequently found pages at one location.

http://www.cs.bgu.ac.il/~omri/Humor/unix-history.html

Okay, maybe it didn't happen *exactly* like this. This page is a humorous retelling of the Unix saga, which is quite amusing if you know what really happened. Just don't rely on this as the Official Story.

http://www.rs6000.ibm.com/resource/unix_history.html

This is IBM's interpretation of the early Unix years. Because IBM was intimately involved in the development of Unix, it's interesting to see their take on the project.

Unix Variants

We covered three major Unix variants in this book, all of which run on the x86 personal-computer processor chip and are available at no cost (or a low charge for nondownloaded versions). Other commercial variants are covered in Appendix C: "Other Types Of Unix." Here are links to the most major sites for the Unices covered in this book.

http://www.linux.org

Linux Online is an excellent place to start learning about Linux. Although there is an immense amount of documentation and information available on this site, there are also well-managed sets of links and download information. The site also offers its own editorial content.

http://www.freebsd.org

The home site for the FreeBSD project offers downloads and documentation, of course, but also has a great set of external links and a robust bug inventory. You can find information here on user groups, mailing lists, and other FreeBSD community initiatives, as well.

http://www.sun.com/solaris/index.html

Because it's a commercial venture, Sun Solaris's Web page is clearly different from the Linux and FreeBSD sites listed above. However, you'll find much of the same material available here: documentation, external links, and media references. Source code is free to download, but (as with Linux and FreeBSD) if you want Solaris on CD-ROM, you'll have to pay. You can also purchase a service contract directly from Sun if you like.

Free Software and Open Source

Probably the most significant philosophical issue in the Unix world today is that of Free and Open Source software. We explained some of the reasoning behind this movement in Chapter 2: "Which Unix?" Here are some Web sites that contain the original documents sparking the discussion, as well as up-to-date news and information.

http://www.gnu.org

Home of both the Free Software Foundation and the GNU project, this site handles the ideological and philosophical side of Free Software as well as the software itself. Here you'll find documentation and downloads for all GNU software, as well as a bit of humor and some other interesting stuff. At the Free Software Foundation page (`http://www.fsf.org/fsf/fsf.html`), you'll find information on how to support the group if you so desire.

http://www.opensource.org/

This site is more information-oriented than the GNU site. You can find a series of articles designed to encourage the use of Open Source software, as well as a plethora of information to help the media report on Open Source issues more accurately. The site also offers a FAQ and a set of links to other Open Source/Free Software sites.

http://www.tuxedo.org/~esr/writings/

This site contains links to all of Eric Raymond's writings. The reason we've listed the site is that this is where you'll find the highly influential triad of articles that kicked off the Open Source movement: "The Cathedral and the Bazaar," "Homesteading the Noosphere," and "The Magic Cauldron."

http://www.salon.com/tech/fsp/index.html

Andrew Leonard is writing a book about Free Software, and it's being serialized at Salon. Leonard is interested in people and culture as well as in technology, and he has a good grasp of what makes Unix/Linux/BSD folks tick. We encourage you to check this site often, because all of Salon's Open Source coverage is linked here in addition to Leonard's book.

Getting Started

In Chapter 3: "Some Basic Unix Concepts" and Part II: "Getting Started," we covered the ground-level information necessary to use a Unix system. If you need more review at the basic level, here are some links that might help.

http://www.linuxnewbie.org

Despite its name, this site isn't solely for Linux newbies. Much of the information here can be translated to other Unix variants. One of the most useful things on the site is the "newbie-ized" help files; for those who find man pages and HOWTO documents a bit too confusing because they assume too much prior knowledge, these files might be the perfect answer.

http://lithos.gat.com/docview/unix-5.html

New to shell commands? Do you have users who need a really basic primer on shell use? Check out *Unix Tips for Your Mom*. It's not rocket science, but it is a useful thing to print out and leave near the keyboard of any new Unix user. (Disclaimer: We know moms—and dads—who could kick our butts at anything Unix-y.)

Unix Desktop Environments

In Part III: "Unix Desktop Environments," we addressed the concept of the X Window System and the various programs developed to take advantage of X and bring a windowed, graphic interface to the Unix computer. These links will provide additional information about X itself, and about the window managers and integrated desktops that rely on X to run.

X Window System

The X Window System is mind-bogglingly complex, and you won't learn everything you need to know from Chapters 6 and 7: "The X Window System: An Overview" and "Advanced X Techniques." You won't even learn everything from the Web, despite the vast amount of information out there. Still, there are some good resources for X information, and we've listed a few of them here.

http://www.x.org

This is the home site for the X Consortium, the group that develops and maintains the standard for the X Window System. There's not a lot of basic help-oriented information here, but you will certainly get a better understanding of what the X Consortium does and how large the project really is, as well as an understanding of the future of graphics on Unix and Unix-derived platforms.

http://www.xfree86.org

Throughout the book, we stressed the Unix variants that run on personal-computer chips as well as on larger architectures. If you're running an x86 processor, you're probably using the XFree86 implementation of the X Window System. At this site, you'll find a useful FAQ and detailed information on how XFree86 works with specific chip architectures.

http://www.rahul.net/kenton/xsites.framed.html

As we said at the beginning of this section, there is a lot of X information on the Web. Thank goodness for Kenton Lee, who has compiled a definitive list of X Web resources from the most basic FAQ to specification documents for developers.

http://www.apl.jhu.edu/~larry/unix/unixdocs/xwindows/customx.html

When you're ready to start customizing your X Window System installation, this is the place to start. (Warning: You really need to know what you're doing before you tackle X configuration.) The document provides specific information on editing X configuration files, as well as hints on recovering from a failed customization. (Those of you running the twm window manager may find the "Customizing twm" section to be of interest.)

Window Managers

As we explained in Chapter 8: "Window Managers," X offers the ability to run multiple sessions in a graphic environment. There are a variety of Unix window managers available; here are some resources for the managers we described in Chapter 8.

http://www.uwo.ca/its/doc/hdi/x11/x4-twm.html

Although designed for staff and students at the University of Western Ontario, this site offers the best tutorial we've seen for twm. Learn how to use twm most effectively, configure its appearance, and perform useful tasks.

http://www.fvwm.org/

The home of the FVWM project, this site offers documentation and downloads, as well as new buttons not included in the current release, icons, and sounds. You can report a bug or look through the bug archive, or subscribe to an fvwm mailing list.

http://icewm.sourceforge.net/

IceWM's page offers downloads and documentation, as well as links to other sites that offer Ice-friendly items. Note that IceWM will run KDE and Gnome themes, even though IceWM is not an integrated desktop. The site also provides tips on configuring IceWM to resemble other window managers or the KDE desktop.

http://blackbox.alug.org/

As with other project home sites, the BlackBox site offers downloads and documentation. It also offers new tools and themes, as well as information on integrating KDE and BlackBox to work together smoothly. There are archives for mailing-list posts, previous releases, and screenshots from those releases.

http://www.windowmaker.org/

The WindowMaker site offers updates, downloads, news items, and documentation. Now that WindowMaker is part of the GNU project, you can expect the same level of detail in its documents as other GNU pages provide.

http://www.afterstep.org/

The AfterStep home is a sophisticated site with a great amount of information. Of course, there are downloads and documentation, as well as bug fixes, source code, and themes.

http://www.enlightenment.org/

The Enlightenment site offers downloads, patches, documentation, screenshots, and all the other features of a good project site. Enlightenment's news reports are updated less frequently than other window manager sites, but work does continue on the window manager itself.

KDE

We covered KDE, the K Desktop Environment, in Chapter 9: "KDE." Two major resources for KDE information are listed here. You should be able to find links to updated and useful information from the main KDE project page, because it is updated frequently.

http://www.kde.org

This is the home site for the KDE project. As with other project sites, it contains downloads and documentation. It also has a well-maintained news section and a wide variety of KDE programs that were contributed by volunteers. One of the best features about the site is that it's translated into many languages, and not just the standard French and German translations one usually sees. Check here first for new releases and information.

http://kde.themes.org

This is the KDE-specific section of `themes.org`, which houses themes for a wide variety of Unix desktop and window manager programs. At the time we wrote this chapter, there were nearly 225 KDE themes available, as well as instructions for creating your own KDE themes (which you can upload to `themes.org` if you want to share them).

Gnome

We covered Gnome in Chapter 10: "Gnome." As with KDE, the main Gnome site is a good way to find updated links and information.

http://www.gnome.org

The home site for Gnome offers downloads and documentation. It also has a frequently updated news section, and places the most recent stories and newest software offerings on the front page of the site. You can download programs that aren't part of the official Gnome release, as well as obtain patches and upgrades.

http://gtk.themes.org/

As with KDE, `themes.org` has a special section for Gnome desktop themes. At the time we wrote this, there were 261 themes available for Gnome. Note that KDE 2 and higher should be able to use these themes as well, because the new release has support for The Gimp ToolKit widgets.

Using the Shell

As we explained in Part IV: "Using the Shell," we've focused on the `bash` shell in this book. However, other shells are available that may suit your needs more easily. The link below offers a good comparison between various Unix shells, and the remainder of this section contains links both for `bash` and for the shells covered in Chapter 15: "Other Shells."

http://pluto.phys.nwu.edu/~zhaoyj/learn/Unix-system/ch13.htm

This page offers to help you decide "Which Unix Shell Is Best for You?" by comparing the features and drawbacks of seven popular shells. If you're completely confused by the plethora of choices available to you for shell environments, we suggest that you read through this article and take some of its comments to heart. (Then, of course, we recommend that you choose `bash` until you're comfortable with shells in general, but the author of this article makes some good points in favor of other shells.)

bash

Although there's quite a bit about bash on the Web, you really need only two documents to start with. The bash manual and the bash FAQ are excellent complements that should give you a good start on any solution.

http://www.gnu.org/manual/bash-2.02/html_chapter/bashref_toc.html

This is the bash manual, direct from the GNU project. If you have a question about bash, it's probably answered here. Some people find this document to be a bit on the technical and dry side, but it's pretty easy to figure out once you get used to the style.

http://www.faqs.org/faqs/unix-faq/shell/bash/

If you couldn't find answers to your questions in the bash manual, try the bash FAQ. It's thorough, and used in conjunction with the bash manual, it ought to help you solve almost any bash problem you have.

http://cnswww.cns.cwru.edu/~chet/bash/bashtop.html

An additional bash resource, the Bash Home Page contains links to the FAQ and manual listed above, as well as various other documents relating to the effective use of bash.

Other Shells

If you don't want to use bash, or you are interested in the other shells and their individual features, try these resources to learn more about the shells covered in Chapter 15. These links are mostly to the shell's manual pages; luckily, they're all written rather well and are thus comprehensible.

http://cres.anu.edu.au/manuals/korn.html

This is the basic Korn Shell manual. ksh is quite popular, but works just differently enough from bash that a good reference is necessary.

http://terra.rice.edu/unix.web/geo.csh.html

The manual for the C Shell. If you're familiar with the C programming language, you'll probably find this familiar.

http://www.frognet.net/help/manpages/docs/tcsh.html

Another manual page, this is for the tcsh shell. This page has the same layout as the other manual pages, which makes comparison between shells simpler.

http://www.zsh.org/

The Z Shell project has its own site, but it's limited to a list of mirror sites. Once you select the mirror closest to you, you'll be sent to an FTP archive. The archive contains downloads and FAQs, but in the regular FTP format. Use your Web browser if you want to view the files with the least amount of hassle.

http://www.focusresearch.com/gregor/psh/

The Perl Shell's page offers downloads and change logs, as well as a link to the psh mailing lists. Because psh is so new, there is relatively little here. We don't recommend psh as a primary shell yet, but it's fun to have around for a change of pace.

Using Text Editors

In Part V: "Using Text Editors," we reviewed some of the most popular text editors available for Unix. In this section of the appendix, you'll find links to resources for ed, vi, and GNU Emacs, as well as links for additional text and graphical editors covered in Part V.

ed

Chapter 16: "The ed Editor," addressed the simple line editor ed. There are relatively few Web resources for this editor, but the following two links ought to answer most of your ed questions.

http://www.sao.nrc.ca/imsb/rcsg/documents/basic/node119.html

This document, part of a more comprehensive treatment of Unix, provides some basic ed commands and offers hints on performing routine tasks with the editor.

http://www.neosoft.com/neosoft/man/ed.1.html

The official ed manual pages are a bit more comprehensive than the previous source, though not by much—ed itself isn't that complicated. Use the manual to learn all the things that ed can do, because everything it's capable of is included in the manual.

vi

In Chapter 17: "The vi Editor," we introduced the vi text editor and showed you how to create and edit text with its arcane commands. Here are a few links to expand your knowledge of this popular, though often challenging, text editor.

http://www.smu.edu/smunet/docs/vi/vi_faq1.html

This document is the vi FAQ, which offers help for vi beginners and advanced users. It also explains some shortcuts and tricks, and offers some fun activities as well as noting known bugs.

http://www.thomer.com/thomer/vi/vi.html

Thomer Gil has created the vi Lovers' Home Page, which is a paean to all things vi. He has documentation, a comprehensive set of vi links, macros, and tutorials. If you're wondering about whether you should use vi, Thomer may convince you to do so.

GNU Emacs

Chapter 18: "GNU Emacs" was an introduction to this complicated and polarizing text editor: You'll either love it or hate it. Here are some resources that will provide additional information and assistance.

http://www.gnu.org/software/emacs/emacs.html

The official GNU site for GNU Emacs, this document contains basic help information, installation help, and references to other sources of assistance. It also provides a bit of historical background for the package.

http://www.emacs.org/

This site in progress is basically a fan site for GNU Emacs. Currently, the site contains downloadable packages, but there are plans to provide much more information about the editor. Look in on this site from time to time; it has the potential to be a useful part of Web `emacs` resources.

Other Text Editors

In Chapter 19: "`pico`, `joe`, and `jed`," we covered three additional text editors that have their own fan bases, despite having less popularity than the three editors mentioned in the previous sections. Below are some additional resources for these editors.

http://www.indiana.edu/~uitspubs/b103/

Although the frames seem like a bit of overkill for the amount of information contained here, this is a useful site for basic `pico` information. The site explains common tasks, and offers some tips for more streamlined and effective use of the `pico` editor. Ignore references to Indiana's own machine networks.

http://www.rochester.edu/ATS/Documentation/joeeditor.html

Designed for employees and students in the University of Rochester library, this is the most comprehensive introduction to `joe` that we've found on the Web. Useful and straightforward explanations make using `joe` a piece of cake.

http://www.cs.cmu.edu/~jeliza/work/jed-intro.html

This site offers a quick reference card for `jed` commands, as well as a few tips on configuring the editor. There's not a lot of in-depth documentation here, but the reference would be a useful thing to print and tape up somewhere near your monitor if you use `jed` a lot.

Graphical Editors

The editors described so far in this section of the appendix have all been text based. The next three links are for the graphical text editors covered in Chapter 20: "Graphical Text Editors." These editors have most of the features of a text editor, but have the graphical interface familiar to users of word processors.

http://www.mit.edu/afs/sipb/project/gnome/doc/GXedit/manual.txt

This is the user's guide for GXedit, the graphical text editor that is part of the Gnome development project. It is a straightforward guide to GXedit's features, and pays special attention to encryption and scripting.

http://www.trylinuxsd.com/KDEtour/Applications/kedit/

If you've chosen KDE as your desktop, you'll have KEdit as your default graphical text editor. This is the user's guide for KEdit, which covers installation, the menu system, and basic editor functions.

http://nedit.org/

If you read Chapter 20, you know that we really like NEdit. This is the NEdit project's home site, which contains downloads and documentation, as well as screenshots and troubleshooting assistance.

Shell Programming

Part VI: "Shell Programming" focused on this important skill. We explained shell programming in the bash shell, though you can write shell scripts for any shell environment. These resources will help you move into writing increasingly complex scripts.

http://www.washington.edu/computing/unix/shell.html

This page is a simple introduction to the shell environment concept, with some emphasis on how scripts operate within shells.

http://www.oase-shareware.org/shell/

Ah, SHELLdorado! Heiner has organized a marvelous resource for shell scripters, including an archive of sample scripts, articles about scripts and shells, and a variety of documentation. It's easy to find what you need, and the information presented here is all useful.

http://www.uwsg.iu.edu/edcert/session3/shell/

If you want to see what you'd learn about shell scripts in an actual university Unix course, consult this page. The scripting sequence is part of a course developed to support the Unix System Administration Educational Certification, so you know you're getting information that you really need.

Basic System Administration

We covered basic system administration in Part VII: "Basic System Administration." The resources listed here deal with much the same information, but presented slightly differently. We've found that, with system administration, repeated bashing on the head is the best way to get the information ingrained in the brain.

http://www.uwsg.indiana.edu/usail/

Do you learn best following a self-paced course? Try this site from Indiana University, which is a comprehensive Unix system administration course. It covers installation, routine tasks, dealing with services and peripherals, and other useful topics.

http://www.washington.edu/R870/

Here's another course site, this one from the University of Washington. These notes are from an actual course taught by Dave Dittrich and contain sample problems for you to work through. The beauty of this course is that it's based on real-life system administration issues, not on some mythical system where nothing ever goes wrong.

http://www.linuxdoc.org/LDP/lame/LAME/linux-admin-made-easy/book1.html

If you're running a Linux system, you shouldn't be without *Linux System Administration Made Easy*. This is a guide written for those who are contemplating becoming a Linux systems administrator or who find themselves in that position. Although this guide is Linux specific, those running other Unix variants may find it helpful as well.

Network Administration

Once you internalized the information needed for basic system administration, it was time to move to Part VIII: "Network Administration" to learn how to handle multiple computers on one network. These resources are good places to learn more.

http://www.ee.siue.edu/~bnoble/classes/anet/links.html

This is a great place to start. Brad Noble has pulled together a strong set of network administration links, divided neatly into sections covering LAN administration, security, scripting, and various online references.

http://www.dhcp-handbook.com/dhcp_faq.html

If you're running DHCP, you'll find this FAQ to be useful. It covers multiple access topics, subnets, laptops, and other questions common to the new user of DHCP.

http://www.linuxdoc.org/LDP/nag/nag.html

Although some of the information is out of date (it was last edited in 1996), the *Network Administrator's Guide* is an excellent resource for those interested in networking with Linux computers. The content is released under an Open Source license; though you can purchase this book at almost any bookstore, the entire book is also available online.

Heterogeneous Networks

A growing proportion of Unix networks include non-Unix machines. We covered heterogeneous networks in Chapter 37: "Integrating Unix with Other Platforms." Whether you want to attach a Windows computer or a Macintosh to your network, these resources can help.

http://www.samba.org

The main site for Samba information contains documentation, news stories, archives of past announcements, and software downloads. If you're interested in networking between Unix and Windows machines, you need Samba.

http://www.umich.edu/~rsug/netatalk/

For those who want to integrate Macintoshes into a heterogeneous network, there is `netatalk`, a Samba equivalent for MacOS that uses the Appletalk protocol to manage file and print sharing. This page offers a FAQ, a set of links, and downloads.

http://www.rit.edu/~pcm6519/linux.html

If you have (or are planning to get) a cable modem and want to use it as a router and print server for a heterogeneous network consisting of Linux and Windows machines, check this site. It is written for Red Hat Linux users, but the general philosophy should be applicable to other Unix variants.

Security

If you think it won't happen to you, you might be right. However, if you think it can't happen to you, you're wrong. We covered Unix security in Chapter 38: "Network Security," but things change so rapidly in this field that we encourage you to make a regular habit of reading security-oriented Web pages.

http://www.alw.nih.gov/Security/Docs/network-security.html

This is a wonderful overview of Unix networks and how they should be protected against invasion or attack. The author concentrates on firewalls and gateways, with some reference to other methods of control.

http://www.softpanorama.org/Security/sos.shtml

If you're running Solaris, you need to check this site. The author links Solaris security articles from across the Web and provides his own tips. His focus tends to be on e-commerce, but it's a useful site for anyone running Solaris.

http://securityportal.com/lasg/

Like the *Network Administrator's Guide* described above, the *Linux Administrator's Security Guide* is an Open Source document that will help you install and run Linux securely. It is routinely updated and includes information on a wide variety of Linux security topics.

http://www.cert.org/

Keep on top of what's happening by reading the CERT page. CERT is the organization responsible for identifying security risks, such as e-mail viruses, known exploitable software bugs, and other critical information. (You can also use the CERT page to check out suspicious rumors that often end up to be hoaxes.)

Administering Services

In Part IX: "Administering Services," we covered the basics of the common Unix servers: electronic mail, World Wide Web, USENET, and remote access. This section of the appendix contains links to official sites and other helpful Web pages for the various servers and topics covered in Part IX.

Electronic Mail

The most basic server package is an electronic mail server. In Chapter 40: "Electronic Mail," we provided an overview of several popular mail servers and explained how e-mail works from a system administrator's point of view. Here you'll find links to sites covering the mail servers we addressed in that chapter.

http://www.sendmail.org/

Maintained by the Sendmail Consortium, this site contains documentation and downloads. You'll find a lot of information on security here as well, in addition to FAQs and installation/troubleshooting guides. Those of you running Sun Solaris should read http://www.sendmail.org/sun-specific/ to see the latest information on porting sendmail to the Solaris platform.

http://www.linuxdoc.org/LDP/nag/node198.html

This chapter of the Linux *Network Administrator's Guide* (see above) focuses on the installation and operation of smail. Configuration is covered as well. Although smail is certainly not as popular as other mail servers, you can use the *Network Administrator's Guide* as a good resource should you choose to run smail.

http://cr.yp.to/qmail.html

This is the main site for the Qmail project. Here you'll find links to site mirrors, downloads, and documentation. There is also information on mailing lists and other important resources for effective Qmail administration.

http://www.postfix.cs.uu.nl/start.html

The home site for Postfix contains links to documentation and downloads, as well as information on Postfix-related mailing lists and mentions in the press. It also offers links to general e-mail administration guides.

USENET News

It's not uncommon for people to begin running their own Unix systems to run a customized USENET newsfeed. We covered USENET administration in Chapter 41: "USENET News." Here are links for INN information, as well as information about USENET in general.

http://www.isc.org/products/INN/

This is the home site for the INN project, the robust news server described in Chapter 41. Here you'll find documentation and downloads, as well as a series of links and update reports.

http://www.landfield.com/usenet/usenet.html

If you're new to USENET, please read the FAQs and documents linked through this site before you decide whether to run a news server (or even whether to participate in USENET at all). USENET is an independent culture with its own history, and there are many pitfalls—as well as benefits—for those who choose to run their own USENET servers instead of reading news from someone else's server.

World Wide Web

When it comes to solid Web server administration, the low-cost and secure solution is Apache. We covered Apache in detail in Chapter 42: "World Wide Web Services." Here are some sites that provide further information and assistance.

http://www.apache.org

This site is the best place to start, because it is the home of the Apache Software Foundation. Here you'll find downloads, documentation, a well-defined set of external links, and updated news about Apache. You won't find a great deal of practical information for your individual problems, but this is a good site to keep in mind for updates and new features.

http://www.irt.org/articles/js180/index.htm

Once you've installed Apache and familiarized yourself with its default appearance, you may want to customize your server. This article offers some tricks and more detailed information on Apache customization, taking the server's modularity as the jumping-off point for modification.

http://www.apache-ssl.org/

Interested in secure Web server technology? Check out the work of the Apache-SSL project, which seeks to combine the flexibility of Apache with the Secure Socket Layer technology that ensures private transfer of critical information.

Remote Access Services

In Chapter 43: "Remote Access (inet) Services," we covered a variety of services that you'd use to control remote access to your Unix computer. Below are several links to sites that expand upon that chapter or provide additional information.

http://www.securityfocus.com/focus/sun/articles/inetd1.html

This is the first in a series of articles focusing on Sun Solaris's implementation of the inetd file. Recommended reading for Solaris users, and moderately interesting for non-Solaris folks.

http://www.uwsg.iu.edu/security/inetd.html

This site offers tips on configuring inetd as securely as possible. The inetd file can be the source of unexpected security breaches, so it's wise to adopt the strategy given here and use TCP wrappers as an additional layer of defense.

http://hoth.stsci.edu/man/man1/telnet.html

This page contains the man page for telnet. It's primarily written for users, not for system administrators, but it's a good way to find obscure flags that will streamline your telnet time. (Because telnet is a security risk, the less time spent in a telnet session the better.)

http://www.employees.org/~satch/ssh/faq/ssh-faq.html

Here you'll find the detailed and comprehensive FAQ for ssh, the Secure Shell technology. The FAQ includes information on specifications, installation, troubleshooting, and other common questions. As we noted in several places in the book, we think ssh is the common-sense security solution for remote access and recommend this FAQ as a good place to start learning about the concept.

http://www.ssh.org/

This page contains the latest details about the development of ssh. You can also download the latest versions of the client and server software, and keep up with the latest ssh news.

On the CD

Reference sites for most of the programs included on the CD can be found in previous sections of this appendix. This section contains documentation references for programs on the CD that are not listed elsewhere.

http://gcc.gnu.org

This is the main site for the GNU gcc libraries. There are several documents available here, including an installation FAQ. You can also download new versions or link back to the main GNU pages.

http://www.perl.org/

This site is the home of the Perl Mongers, a nonprofit advocacy group devoted to the support and spread of the perl programming language. The site contains links to documentation and downloads, mentions of perl in the media, and other useful tools. You can also purchase perl-oriented clothing and other merchandise to support the Perl Mongers' goals.

http://www.gimp.org/

At this site, home of The GIMP (GNU Image Manipulation Program), you can find downloads, documentation, and a collection of images created in The GIMP. There are also handy tutorials and a good set of external links.

APPENDIX
C

Other Types of Unix

- AIX

- BSD

- HP-UX

- IRIX

- OSF/1

- SCO Unix

- SunOS

- System V

- Xenix

In this book, we focused on Unix variants that run on personal computers using the x86 chip architecture. Even though these Unices have made some inroads into the corporate and academic computing environments, they are still not the norm. Many companies and academic institutions invested heavily in mainframe Unix systems in the 1970s and 1980s, and continue to use those systems today. Given the immense financial investment in hardware and software contracts, plus the cost of training employees on a new system, it is unlikely that the mainframe Unices will disappear any time soon.

In this appendix, we introduce some of the other flavors of Unix. They are all commercial Unices, meaning that you cannot download them or purchase them cheaply (at a cost nearly equal to the cost of producing the disks). They are designed for large installations, not for personal use. If you're interested in running your own Unix computer, you probably won't use one of these variants; if you use Unix at work or at school, chances are pretty good that you'll encounter a Unix listed here at one time or another. Regardless of how you encounter these Unices, however, you'll find that most of the commands and concepts introduced in this book will carry over to that variant. Unices are more similar than they are different. Remember that you can always install programs that you like in your own home directory, if the administrator does not want those programs installed globally. They should work in the same way regardless of where they are installed, with the exception of some compilers or servers.

NOTE   Most Unices are variants of the two major Unix strains: System V and BSD.

AIX

AIX is IBM's Unix, written to run on the RS/6000 systems that IBM markets. (RS/6000 systems have been both mainframes and RISC systems.) AIX is based on System V, but also uses some BSD components. Although commercial Unices are somewhat similar (because of their common roots), AIX is considered to be a bit different from the other Unices, possibly because of the blend of System V and BSD, but also because of the tight integration between IBM hardware and the AIX operating system.

The current release of AIX is 4.3.3. IBM continues to develop and market AIX, with a particular emphasis on e-commerce solutions. Due to IBM's current emphasis on Linux-based solutions, AIX developers are beginning to integrate the Linux system interface into AIX so that the same programs and processes can be run on both platforms. In fact, the next generation of AIX will be called AIX 5L, with the L signifying the close relationship between Linux and AIX.

Those using AIX will soon realize that it does not, by preference, use the regular sort of system programming that is common to other Unix variants (and the sort described in this book). Rather, it uses a utility called SMIT (System Management Interface Tool). SMIT provides a menu interface to the superuser. From these menus, the superuser can select any administrative commands that need to be given. SMIT builds up a series of commands as a script and then runs the script, which is stored in the `smit.script` file. The actions are then recorded in `smit.log`, which is analogous to the various logs kept in the `/var/log` directory.

NOTE You can use regular system administration practices on an AIX system. However, the authors of the AIX FAQ note that, "You can also do things the normal way, but it is unfortunately difficult to know when the normal way works."

http://www.ibm.com/servers/aix/

The home site for IBM AIX. Most of the information here is either marketing material or links to commercial services, though IBM does link external, noncommercial material such as the AIX FAQ.

http://www.faqs.org/faqs/aix-faq/

The AIX FAQ (Frequently Asked Questions) developed by posters to the `comp.unix.aix` newsgroup. It covers installation, compilers, third-party products, and other points of importance.

http://www.thp.uni-duisburg.de/cuaix/cuaix.html

An archive of posts to `comp.unix.aix`, covering a variety of topics relevant to administering AIX systems.

BSD

BSD is one of the earliest forms of Unix, as we explained in Chapter 1: "History and Background of Unix." Originally developed by the University of California at Berkeley, BSD is now controlled by a private company, BSDI (Berkeley Software Design, Inc.). Though it was once a single effort, BSD is now divided into four variants: BSD/OS, a commercial BSD sold by BSDI; FreeBSD, used in this book, which focuses on simple installation and use; NetBSD, another free variant, which supports almost all known hardware platforms; and OpenBSD, also free, which concentrates on security.

BSD/OS

BSD/OS is currently being marketed as part of the BSDi Internet Server package, which includes specific software targeted at Internet solutions such as NAT (an IP number pool management program), various network administration tools, and traffic analysis utilities. The Internet Server package also includes a utility that makes it possible to run Linux programs on the BSD platform, a useful tool for some system administrators. The current release is 4.1.

BSD/OS 4.1 has been developed with an eye toward Internet server use, so the features it provides tend to be slanted toward the enterprise system and not the individual user. For example, one of the useful tools available in version 4.1 is a packet management tool, which controls the rate at which packets enter and leave the server, based on the IP number of the packet's destination. This smoothes out traffic over a limited-bandwidth Internet connection. You can learn more about BSD/OS at http://www.bsdi.com.

TIP   A particularly readable set of documentation pages specifically about BSD/OS 4.1 is available as a PDF file at http://www.BSDI.COM/products/internet/release-notes/.

NetBSD

NetBSD has been developed to be as portable as possible. This means that many *application programming interfaces (APIs)* from other operating systems are incorporated into the NetBSD code and that NetBSD is written so that it will work on as many different hardware platforms as possible. The reason for this development direction is to make Free Software available to as many users as possible, without the limitations imposed by either hardware or financial requirements. Though it may seem that incorporating so many diverse requirements would lead to messy code, the NetBSD developers pride themselves on a clean and compact code base that will be usable years from now without big sections of *legacy code* that have never been removed.

NetBSD supports most of the currently popular protocols and hardware. It has built-in support for wireless and wired networking using at least eight different protocols. It also supports multiple filesystem types and file-sharing protocols. NetBSD claims to have the fewest security bugs on file at independent bug tracking sites such as `http://www.securityfocus.com`. NetBSD even offers operating-system emulation for nine other operating systems (including most of the Unix variants described in this appendix) so that programs written for those platforms will run transparently on the NetBSD system.

The current release is NetBSD 1.4.2. Learn more about this variant at `http://www.netbsd.org`, where you will find downloads, documentation, and a wide variety of helpful links and files. The NetBSD community is strong and vocal, as well, and there are links to community gathering spots at the main site.

OpenBSD

If you are concerned about security, OpenBSD is the Unix variant for you. OpenBSD was developed in an attempt to build the most secure Unix possible, and the developers have largely succeeded. They claim that no remote hole has been found in over three years on the default downloadable install version and that only one local hole has been found in the past two years. (For those who don't follow operating-system security news, this rate of success is phenomenal.)

The OpenBSD developers want to build the most robust and reliable operating system possible. They make all their development notes available to anyone who's interested, and they incorporate only new code that is released under either the Berkeley license or the GNU Public License. This means that, when someone installs OpenBSD, every component of the operating system has its code available to the end user.

However, the main attraction of OpenBSD is its focus on security. More than any other Unix, OpenBSD has fully integrated support for the latest cryptographic tools including Kerberos, key engines, and the various cryptographic IP tools. OpenBSD is also available to the world—despite its strong cryptographics—because the project is based in Canada, which has no cryptography export restrictions. OpenBSD is built to run on as many different hardware platforms as possible so that users need not be restricted by their hardware.

The current release version is 2.7; you can download the source from the Web, or you can order a double CD version through the mail. The OpenBSD project's Web site is located at `http://www.OpenBSD.org`, where you will find documentation and patches, as well as a bug reporting system and other useful tools.

HP-UX

HP-UX, as the name implies, is the Hewlett-Packard Unix. It is designed to run on HP RISC systems and is primarily based on System V, with some BSD features. The current version of HP-UX is HP-UX 11. It is a 32- or 64-bit operating system, an upgrade from previous 32-bit-only versions of the OS.

HP-UX is a commercial Unix designed for large-scale operations. It handles extremely large files without an excessive amount of disk swapping, and it can support up to 4TB of RAM and 8TB of shared memory. (A gigabyte is 1024MB of information, whereas a terabyte is 1024GB of information.) Hewlett-Packard suggests that HP-UX be used for data warehousing or large-scale Web servers, or for any situation where large volumes of data are handled at the same time. HP-UX is not really a Unix designed for single users or small networks, especially since it is written for hardware that is not affordable for the vast majority of people.

You are likely to encounter HP-UX only if you use Unix at work and work at a large corporation, academic institution, or technology company. HP-UX is seen as fast and reliable, though—as with most commercial Unices—it is expensive and proprietary. Still, for the right kinds of systems, HP-UX is a very good choice.

http://www.devresource.hp.com/STK/hpux_faq.html

The official HP-UX FAQ from Hewlett-Packard. The document covers questions about upgrading from previous versions of HP-UX, and information on new features and configuration.

http://www.faqs.org/faqs/hp/hpux-faq/index.html

The FAQ for the newsgroup `comp.sys.hp.hpux`. The document addresses config-uration, software, utilities, the X Window System, and other relevant topics. Extensive resources for other HP-UX information are also included.

IRIX

IRIX is the Unix that runs on Silicon Graphics MIPS systems, which are high-end multiple-processor machines. It is especially favored by people doing high-end graphics work, though it is not so popular as a general Unix variant for multiple-function purposes. The current release is IRIX 6.5.x.

IRIX has an unusually large base of support in military and aeronautical insti-tutions. NASA (the United States National Aeronautics and Space Administra-tion) uses IRIX at the Ames Research Center to support its research in climate change and computational fluid dynamics, as well as in other highly processor-intensive models. IRIX is also being used by Boeing and Lockheed Martin as they develop a new fighter plane for the United States military. Such types of work rely heavily on accurate representation of technical scale drawings, and IRIX reli-ably delivers the accuracy needed in those situations.

Like HP-UX, IRIX is not designed for the small network or single-user installa-tion. You'd need to purchase Silicon Graphics hardware to run IRIX, and those machines are priced at a corporate and governmental purchase rate, not an indi-vidually affordable rate. Still, if you enjoy computer graphics and have the oppor-tunity to try an IRIX system, you will probably be amazed at the clarity and accuracy of the operating system.

http://www.sgi.com/developers/technology/irix/index.html

The IRIX site at Silicon Graphics. You can get ordering information, documenta-tion, and some technical support here, though you may need to buy a service plan if you require detailed support directly from SGI. There is quite a bit of information in the online Supportfolio.

http://www-viz.tamu.edu/~sgi-faq/

This site offers all the user-created FAQs for SGI equipment and software. The IRIX FAQ is the SGI-admin FAQ, but if you're running IRIX, you'll probably need to look at the graphics, hardware, and security FAQs as well.

OSF/1

You won't see OSF/1 running as itself any more. The Open Software Foundation stopped developing and releasing OSF/1 in 1994, though Digital Unix is based heavily on the OSF/1 code. When Digital was acquired by Compaq, the Digital Unix OS began being developed under the Compaq Tru64 Unix name.

Tru64 Unix is a scalable 64-bit operating system that is designed to work with Compaq's Alpha series of servers. It is designed to work closely with Windows, so administrators using an NT network for their users may find Tru64 to be a good option for servers and other non-end-user installations on the network. Tru64 features an "out of the box maintenance" array of utilities and applications, including a graphical system event manager and both a Java and a Web-based interface for remote system administration. Tru64 has been adopted by a variety of well-known companies, including Mindspring/Earthlink, one of the United States' largest Internet providers.

There are still some legacy installations of Digital Unix and even of OSF/1, even though it hasn't been available since 1994. The FAQ listed below, maintained by users of the `comp.unix.osf.osf1` USENET newsgroup, offers some information about Digital's Unix and about the original OSF/1 Unix. However, most networks that ran either OSF/1 or Digital Unix have changed to another Unix or adopted Tru64, so it is unlikely that you'll run across one of these older Unices unless you happen upon a system that hasn't been upgraded in a few years.

http://www.UNIX.digital.com/unix/index.html

The home site of Compaq's Tru64 Unix. Compaq offers documentation, news releases, and some technical support.

http://www.faqs.org/faqs/dec-faq/Digital-UNIX/index.html

The FAQ for `comp.unix.osf.osf1`. It addresses installation, software, peripherals, networking, and other topics. Useful for those who find themselves running Digital Unix, because there is no longer a great deal of information available on the OS.

SCO Unix

SCO Unix is marketed as UnixWare by the Santa Cruz Operations company (SCO). UnixWare is an operating system designed for the Intel platform, unlike many of the other Unices described in this appendix, which are designed for proprietary (and expensive) hardware. The company has targeted small- and medium-sized businesses for some time, offering the robust Unix platform to companies that can't afford the high-end hardware, but still want a commercial Unix.

SCO Unix uses a variety of unique tools for system administration and management. Like Solaris, it provides a comprehensive administration utility, called `scoadmin`. UnixWare is scalable and quite fast, supporting a wide variety of x86-based configurations. It is System V based and, in fact, is probably the one Unix currently available that is closest to the AT&T development tree. The current release is UnixWare 7.

TIP

If you are interested in commercial Unices, we recommend that you give SCO Unix a try. You can get a free license for noncommercial use of the operating system; you will need to purchase the CD set from SCO, which will cost you about $50 US. (Like Solaris, SCO is one of the higher-cost "free" licenses.) Still, if you're interested in learning more about the kinds of Unices that run in commercial settings, you can learn a lot from SCO Unix.

SCO Unix has been in the news lately, because SCO has just been acquired by Caldera, a leading Linux distribution provider. What this means for Unix users is that Caldera will now begin to develop an integrated Unix/Linux operating system, taking the best from both systems. They hope to build a powerful and robust operating system that will fit easily into the business computing world. Interesting news should continue to appear on the Caldera/SCO merger, and the result of the operating-system integration promises to have a significant effect on the Unix world in general.

http://www.sco.com/unix/

The home page for SCO Unix. You will find a variety of information here, from product brochures to documentation. You can also order CD sets and books directly from SCO.

http://www.aplawrence.com

Tony Lawrence has compiled an excellent set of resources for Unix administrators in general and SCO Unix in particular. You should be able to find almost every Web and FTP resource for SCO Unix from this page, including documentation written for those new to SCO and those who have been hacking it for years.

SunOS

Before Sun switched its development emphasis to Solaris, SunOS was the Unix that shipped with all Sun hardware. SunOS is still being used in places, but most Sun customers have made the change to Solaris. SunOS was primarily BSD-based, with some System V enhancements, and was the first Unix to incorporate such now-standard elements as NFS.

There is still quite a bit of information available about SunOS and its administration, though a good portion of that information is devoted to integrating SunOS with the earliest versions of Solaris. There is a small market for those who enjoy purchasing used Sun hardware, and the earlier hardware runs SunOS (though some configurations cannot handle Solaris). It is unlikely that you'll find a SunOS installation, because Sun's customers were all upgraded to Solaris several years ago, and Sun no longer supports SunOS directly.

http://gsbjfb.uchicago.edu/howto/sunos.faq.html

The FAQ for `comp.sys.sun.admin`. The FAQ is quite dated, having been revised last in 1995, about the time that SunOS administrators began switching to Solaris. However, if you need SunOS reference material, this is a good place to start.

http://www.sun.com

Sun doesn't offer direct SunOS support any more, though you might be able to find answers with the site's search engine.

System V

If BSD is the matriarch of a line of Unix variants, AT&T's Unix is the granddaddy of the rest of the variants. Currently released as System V, AT&T Unix is part of almost all other Unix variants and is the most frequently ported Unix. AT&T no longer retains total control of System V, responsibility for the operating system having first passed to Unix International (UI), a consortium of companies involved with commercial Unix. Upon the end of UI, control of AT&T Unix passed to Unix System Laboratories, an entity now owned by Novell. However, System V is no longer being developed as a unique operating system. Sun's Solaris is the most direct descendant of System V and incorporates much of the final System V release, SVR4.

We provide no links for SVR4 (Unix System V, release 4) because there is almost nothing available on the Web for SVR4 users, except for discussions about porting newer Unix programs to machines running SVR4. If you're working on a true SVR4 system, we recommend *UNIX in a Nutshell*, by Arnold Robbins (third edition, O'Reilly & Associates, 1999) or *UNIX Unleashed*, by Robin Burk and Salim Douba (MacMillan, 1999).

Xenix

Oddly enough, in the late 1970s, Microsoft developed its own variant of Unix, called Xenix. Microsoft eventually licensed Xenix to SCO (Santa Cruz Operations). It's unlikely that you'll run across Xenix unless you run it yourself, though there are still quite a few Xenix diehards out there who appreciate its streamlined operation. We include it here mostly because it's a historical amusement to realize that Microsoft was once a developer of a PC-based Unix.

http://www.unicom.com/pw/sco-xenix

The FAQ for `comp.unix.xenix.sco`. It answers general questions as well as those targeted at peripherals, networking, and interoperability between Xenix and MS-DOS.

Glossary

A

Acceptable Use Policy (AUP) Acceptable Use Policies are used by Internet service providers (ISPs), employers, schools, and other third-party entities that provide individual users with access to the Internet. An AUP defines the behavior that is and is not acceptable, usually banning activities that are harmful to the Internet as a whole (such as spam or illegal entry to other computers).

Aliases

1. A parameter in a shell configuration file such as $HOME/.bash_profile that causes one command line to be used as a synonym for another.

2. A condition where a machine may have multiple names (usually denoted in the /etc/hosts file).

3. A mail configuration file such as /etc/aliases that defines local users to handle system mail (i.e., postmaster may be an alias for user hank).

Anonymous FTP A way to obtain files from an Internet file server without needing a user account on that server. To log into an FTP server anonymously, use the word anonymous as your user ID and your electronic mail address as the password. This will identify you to the administrator.

Applet A small program that may be run, for example, over the Web or in a Gnome or KDE panel. Applets are often written for Web applications in the Java programming language, but not all desktop applets are written in Java.

Archive Files Files that are created as a method of bundling a number of separate files. Usually created with the tar command.

Argument In a command, any additional input given that affects the behavior of the command. Arguments can be targets, flags, options, or similar items.

Array Variables Variables that have as their value a list of elements.

B

Backplane

1. Part of the motherboard that carries the computer's processor and other electronic circuitry.

2. A high-speed cable that carries data to the various computers connected in a hub topology network.

Bang An exclamation point character (!). Used as a negation character, as in !=, an expression meaning *does not equal*.

Buffer A space that is designated in system memory. Many programs use buffers to provide fast access to program data.

Build

1. The process of compiling and linking a program; e.g., to *build* a piece of software.

2. A particular binary package, compiled and linked in a particular way; e.g., the Solaris *build* of Apache.

(

Case Sensitive A system is said to be *case sensitive* if capital letters are not considered equal to their lowercase counterparts. Thus the word *hello* would not be considered the same as the words, *Hello, HELLO,* or *HeLlO.* Unix systems are almost always case sensitive, whereas, for example, early DOS systems are not.

Client-Server Architecture A method of constructing networks so that resources are housed on a central server machine and accessed by remote clients. More specifically, the server accepts incoming network connections from the clients.

Command Interpreter A program, such as the bash shell or the Perl interpreter, that translates a language's commands into instructions that the computer's processor can understand.

Command Shell The command shell is a program that acts as a translator between the operating-system kernel and the user. The shell provides the command-line interface common to Unix systems. A variety of command shells are available for Unix and Unix-derived operating systems; in this book, we focus on the bash shell.

Command Syntax The particular format in which a command must given for it to be understood by the command interpreter.

Command-Line Interface An interface to an operating system where input is received in the form of typed commands.

Comments Elements of a program that are ignored by the command interpreter or compiler. Comments exist for the purpose of making programs more comprehensible to human programmers.

Compilers A compiler is a platform-specific program that converts code written in the C programming language to the language understood by that particular platform's native command language. The use of compilers permits programmers to write one non-platform-specific version of a program that will be usable on all platforms once compiled.

Configuration Files Text files that contain operating parameters for a particular program. By altering the parameters in a configuration file, it is possible to change the behavior of that program.

Cookie A small bit of information delivered by a server when a request is made by a server. Typically used in the context of Web pages, a cookie is a piece of identifying information placed on your hard drive when you make a request with a client program. The cookie will speed access to the server with later requests, because its existence notifies the server that you have already been permitted to have data from that server.

Cracker A security breaker. One who gains unauthorized access to networks and machines, often for the purpose of data theft or as a means of cloaking the source of attacks on other networks. Crackers are often incorrectly called *hackers* in the popular media.

D

Daemon A program that runs constantly and that performs commands and other actions automatically. A daemon may respond to incoming data or provide data from another process. Most servers run daemons, and many other programs use a daemon to manage their activity.

The term is not religious in intent. Daemons are mythological beings that are attendants to other, greater, personages; in the Unix sense, they do the work.

Daisy Chain A network arrangement in which computers are connected to each other in a chain, instead of each computer being connected directly to a server or a backplane cable. SCSI devices also use the daisy chain topology.

See also *Backplane* and *Topology*.

Datagram Usually called a *packet*, a datagram is a small, self-contained unit of data that is transferred across a network. A data-

gram carries enough identifying data that it can be passed from originating to recipient machine without any intervening requests for address information.

See also *User Datagram Protocol (UDP)*.

Delivery Agent Part of the electronic mail transfer array of programs. The delivery agent handles the transmission of an individual message from the local mail server to the recipient's incoming mail spool, usually located at `/var/spool/mail/$USER`.

See also *Mail Transfer Agent* and *Mail User Agent*.

Device A piece of hardware, though not usually the CPU or motherboard. A device may be internal or external and is run through a program called a *device driver,* which tells the operating system how to handle the hardware. Devices may be disk drives, peripherals, cards, or other similar equipment.

See also *Peripheral Devices*.

Disk A random access storage medium that consists of a thin plastic center coated with a magnetic medium. Disks can be fixed (hard disks) or removable (floppy disks or diskettes).

See also *Optical Disk*.

Display Manager The component of a graphical user interface that is responsible for maintaining data about display servers, and for handling login and logout functions.

Display Server An alternative term used to describe the server providing X Window System access to a graphical user interface.

Dot Files Under most Unix command shells, files that begin with a leading dot character are not visible in a directory listing (unless the -a option to 1s is used). Such files are usually used to store configuration parameters or data for specific programs.

E

Environment Variables Variables that are available to all programs running on the system. Such variables taken together influence the environment under which all programs run. Variables are made available to the environment by use of the export command.

Escape Character Another term for the backslash character, \. When using regular expressions for pattern matching, the escape character is used to force the regular meaning of a particular character usually used as a metacharacter.

See also *Metacharacter*.

Escape Sequence A character or string of characters that cause a modification to normal processing behavior. Escape sequences are usually seen in the use of regular expressions, where one desires to treat literally a character that normally functions as a metacharacter.

Exit Status A number that is returned on the completion of a process that reports the success or failure of that process. Normally, an exit status of 0 (zero) denotes success, while anything else denotes failure; however, this behavior can be customized by the programmer.

F

File Permissions File metadata that controls the set of users on the system that have access to the specified file. There are three types of permission: read, write, and execute; and three classes of users to whom these permissions can apply: the file's owner, the file's owning group, and all users. The root user has all permissions to all files.

File Tree The display used by some graphical file managers to show the various files and directories on a given filesystem. In the file tree, individual directories and their subdirectories are shown in a nested hierarchical manner. This is the method used by Windows Explorer.

Filesystem

1. The format used by an operating system to manage files and directories (e.g., the ext2 filesystem).

2. The files and directories on a computer considered as an organized whole.

3. Any subset of item 2 (e.g., the home/ filesystem).

Firewall A networking construct that prevents unauthorized users from accessing a local network. Firewalls are usually installed on gateway machines and serve as a security precaution. They examine incoming packets to see whether the packets should be forwarded to a local machine.

See also *Gateway* and *Proxy Server*.

Flag An option to a command that may change the behavior of that command. Flags are usually preceded by a dash character.

Flow Control In programming, those statements that can cause the program to alter the sequence of its own execution in response to a given condition. Flow control can be conditional or iterative.

Free Hog Slice Under Solaris, a temporary disk partition used to hold otherwise unallocated disk space.

Free Software As defined by the Free Software Foundation, Free Software is any software that is licensed in such a way that it

- Allows the program to be used by anyone for any reason

- Allows the program to be modified by anyone

- Allows the program to be redistributed by anyone

- Requires that derivative work be licensed under the same conditions

Function Calls In programming, the act of invoking either a native function of the programming language or a user-defined function is known as *calling the function.*

G

Gateway A computer that serves as the connection point between a local network and a larger network such as the Internet. Gateways are used as security mechanisms and may have a variety of security programs installed, such as proxies or firewalls. A gateway machine may be either a traditional computer or a dedicated piece of specialized hardware, such as a router.

GPL (GNU Public License) Software license developed by the Free Software Foundation for the GNU project. The GPL implements the tenets of the FSF's definition of *Free Software.*

Graphical Text Editor A text editor that uses graphical functions such as mouse clicks to perform editing functions.

Graphical User Interface An interface to an operating system that uses graphical elements such as windows and buttons, and takes input from pointing devices such as a mouse. Distinct from a command-line interface, which takes input only from the keyboard. Unix has both command-line and graphical user interfaces. In fact, using graphical terminal emulator programs, it is even possible to use both interfaces simultaneously.

Group A particular subset of a system's user base that has a common set of permissions to files owned by that group. Groups are defined in the /etc/group file.

H

Hacker A clever, or inspired programmer. Often one who programs for the love of the art form, rather than one who programs purely for employment purposes.

Hashmark The # character. Hashmarks are usually used in programming to identify a comment, which is intended for human readers and is not a line that should be executed by the computer.

See also *Comments*.

Heterogeneous In computer terms, a heterogeneous network is one that contains machines running at least two different operating systems. A network containing a Linux machine and three FreeBSD machines is heterogeneous, as is a network containing Macintoshes, Windows PCs, and a couple of Sparcs running Sun Solaris. The opposite of heterogeneous is *homogeneous*.

Hexadecimal Notation A method of noting binary numbers that uses base-16 notation. Hexadecimal notation uses the numbers 0 to 9 and the letters A to F to represent the numbers 10 to 15. One hexadecimal digit represents four binary bits of data.

Homogeneous A homogeneous network is one where all machines connected to the network are running the same operating system. An all-Debian Linux network would be homogeneous. Mixed networks are called *heterogeneous* networks.

Hub

1. A piece of hardware into which individual computers are plugged to form a network or share a resource.

2. A networking topology in which all networked computers are attached to a central server.

I

Integer Any positive, negative, or zero number that does not include a fractional component. Thus 1, 0, and –1 are all integers, whereas 1.1, –1 ½, and 0.3333 are not.

Integrated Desktop Environment Software suites such as Gnome and KDE that provide an overall graphical environment, as well as a suite of programs that operate under that environment.

Internet Protocol (IP) The protocol by which small packets of information are delivered across the Internet or other networks. Packet destinations are identified by a unique number. The Internet Protocol is half of the standard TCP/IP protocol.

See also *IP Number* and *Transmission Control Protocol (TCP)*.

Interprocess Communication The method through which individual processes communicate with each other and take action on those communications, without human interaction. Scripts that provide input to other scripts or other Unix commands are communicating in an interprocess manner that does not require human input to complete the task.

Intrusion Detection The craft of detecting the presence and activities of crackers despite their efforts to conceal it, using a variety of techniques including file comparison, log tracking, and the tracing of individual signatures unique to each cracker.

IP Classes IP numbers are divided into three separate classes. These classes are used to distinguish particular kinds of networks from other types of networks. The classes are defined in the Internet Protocol.

- Class A networks use 0.0.0.0 to 255.255.255.255. This is the entire address space, so an individual network will have only a particular sequence of numbers allocated to that network.

- Class B networks use a constant leftmost octet and are assigned individual numbers below that top-level network number, such as 102.1.2.3 and 102.4.5.6.

- Class C networks use constant octets in the two left positions and are assigned individual numbers below those top-level hierarchy numbers, such as 18.25.1.2 and 18.25.3.4.

See also *Private Address Space.*

IP Masquerading The use of a single valid IP number to serve as the main interface with the Internet, while other computers cluster behind that valid IP number and use private IP numbers to handle data transfer within the network. IP masquerading started as a Linux trick used to place networks on the Internet without obtaining a multitude of valid (and expensive) IP numbers. It is now supported by several other Unix variants.

IP Number The unique identifying number assigned to a computer that is part of the Internet. IP numbers are used for a wide variety of data transfer, in accordance with the Internet Protocol. Although each individual computer attached to the Internet is required to have an individual number, these numbers may be assigned dynamically by an Internet service provider or other access point that has more clients than numbers available.

K

Kerberos An encryption mechanism that permits the safe transmission of data across a network. Kerberos creates an encrypted session key that your client presents as its proof of entry before the session is opened. Many security programs are Kerberos-based; it is one of the more secure transmission technologies available.

Kernel The portion of the operating system that provides functions at the lowest level. The kernel is responsible for scheduling tasks for the processor, managing memory, and coordinating input to and output from the various hardware devices.

Key Bindings Functions triggered by a single keystroke or key combination. Key bindings are most often associated with text editors such as GNU Emacs, but are also used in graphical user interfaces and operating systems in general.

L

Launcher An icon or button on a desktop (usually in a panel pertaining to a particular desktop environment) that causes a particular program to start.

Lease Period The time that any given machine may use an IP number assigned from a pool of available IP numbers. The lease period is defined in the DHCP server by the network administrator.

Line Editor A text editor such as ed that processes text one line at a time. Line editors have been largely replaced by full-screen editors such as vi and graphical editors such as NEdit.

Load A measure of how busy a processor is. A load of one means that there are no idle processor cycles, but no tasks need to wait for a free cycle. A load of less than one means the processor is idle some of the time. A load of more than one means that some tasks must wait for free processor time.

Load Average Shown in output from the w command, the load average shows the system load at present, 30 seconds ago, and 60 seconds ago.

Log A file that records the activity of a particular process or set of processes. Log files are vital tools for the system administrator.

Log Scrubber A cracker tool that edits log files to conceal the cracker's activity.

M

Macro

1. In a text editor, a series of complex operations performed on a chunk of text with a single command or key binding.

2. In programming, the substitution of a short command for a more complex operation. (For example, in C, one can create a macro by using the preprocessor command "#define".)

Mail Transfer Agent The server component of an electronic mail client-server application. A mail transfer agent is also called a mail server. A variety of mail transfer agents are available, though the most popular (and most complex) mail server is sendmail.

Mail User Agent The user component of an electronic mail client-server application. A mail user agent is also called a mail client, and there are both text-based and graphical mail clients. Some of the more popular mail user agents are Pine and elm, two shell-based mail clients, and Eudora and KMail, two graphical mail clients.

Makefile In source code packages, the file that contains instructions for the make utility, which in turn provides instructions to the compiler.

Manual Page The portion of the Unix online manual that pertains to a single command or function. (Note that *page* is something of a misnomer, because these sections can sometimes be quite lengthy.)

Message of the Day (MOTD) A message from the system administrator that is displayed to all users at login. Usually kept in the file /etc/motd.

Metacharacter A character that is used to represent a particular programming construct instead of being used for its actual meaning. Metacharacters are found in shell programming and some text editors.

Metakey A key that is pressed in combination with other keys to execute a particular command. Found in graphical user interfaces, the traditional metakeys are Ctrl, Alt, and Esc. In many graphical interfaces, you can define your own key combinations using these metakeys and other keyboard actions.

Modular Kernel A kernel that is compiled with a variety of modules, each one affecting a particular system activity or function. The Linux kernel is a modular kernel. To add new functions to the operating system, the kernel is recompiled with one or more additional modules.

Modularity The condition of having complex functions handled by combinations of small, simple elements. Many Unix programs are designed to be small, simple, and multipurpose. They can then be used in varying combinations and configurations to build complex function chains.

Mount To make a disk partition (either local or networked) an active part of the filesystem.

Usually accomplished by means of the mount command or the /etc/fstab file.

Multitasking Being able to perform multiple tasks at the same time. There are two types of multitasking.

See also *Task Switching* and *Time Slicing*.

MX (Mail eXchange) Record Part of the Domain Name Service (DNS) record for a particular host or domain. The MX record defines the actual IP address of the machine that receives electronic mail for that domain. If the address changes, but the MX record is not updated, mail will not be delivered.

N

Nesting In programming, the practice of containing one block of code inside another, especially if the blocks are flow control structures of the same type (often referred to as *nested loops*). Nested structures are usually indicated visually by indenting the internal block, like this:

```
outer block {
    outer block statement 1
    outer block statement 2
    outer block statement 3
        inner block {
        inner block statement 1
        inner block statement 2
        inner block statement 3
    }
}
```

Network A conglomeration of individual computers: as few as two or as many as a thousand (or more). Networks are used to share resources, provide quick transmission of data, and assist administrators in monitoring and maintaining individual machines. The Internet is simply a giant network made up of other networks.

Network Congestion The condition that occurs when there is too much traffic over a network's connections to handle all requests and responses in a timely fashion. If network congestion occurs regularly on a local network, it is an indicator that the network might be better served if particular servers were placed on their own machines instead of sharing a single machine with a single connection to the network.

Network File System (NFS) The service that permits remote directories to be mounted across a network as if they were local. With NFS, you can use data from a central server without even knowing the data is not present on your local machine. NFS is a convenient way for administrators to manage large amounts of data that is needed by users at various points on the network. There are, however, security risks inherent in using NFS, though there is not a better alternative for local Unix-based networks.

Network Information Service (NIS) A mechanism that manages the various names and addresses of machines on a local network. Developed by Sun, the Network Information Service is now available for users on all Unix platforms. It is commonly installed at the same time as the Network File System.

O

Open Source As defined by the Open Source Initiative, Open Source software must allow free redistribution and availability of source code, but may restrict modifications to the original source provided that it allows for the distribution of patches.

Operating System An operating system is the software that runs behind the scenes and allows the user to operate the machine's hardware, stop and start programs, and set the various parameters under which the computer operates. We discuss the Unix operating system in this book, along with other Unix-derived operating systems such as Linux, FreeBSD, and Sun Solaris. Other popular operating systems designed for personal use include Microsoft's Windows 98 and Apple's MacOS.

Operator A programming element that may perform assignment, mathematical operations (addition, subtraction, etc.), comparison, negation, etc.

Optical Disk A disk that is made of a hard plastic and etched by laser with many invisible facets. The facets contain data and can be read by the laser contained within a CD-ROM or DVD-ROM drive. Some systems have drives that are capable of both reading data from and writing data to optical disks.

See also *Disk*.

P

Package Management Tool A program that allows for easy installation of software packages. Popular package management tools include Red Hat's RPM, and Debian's apt-get and dpkg.

Packages A method of software distribution. Most software is too complex to be distributed as a single file, so *packages* of the multiple files that need to be distributed are made. These can be in the form of source code, which may need to be compiled, or in packages that are designed to be used by a package management system such as Red Hat's RPM or Debian's dpkg.

Packet
See *Datagram.*

Packet Sniffer A program that intercepts all traffic on a network. Packet sniffers are a common cracker tool, which is why network traffic should be encrypted whenever possible.

Partition A physical section of a (usually fixed) disk. FreeBSD uses the term *slice,* and Solaris uses the term *volume,* to refer to the same concept.

Patch A file that contains modifications to a source code package. Using the patch utility, these files can be used to update a source code package. This is especially useful to people using slow Internet connections, because patch files are typically much smaller than the packages they modify, and thus much faster and easier to download.

Path A string of directory names that describes an exact location within the filesystem. Unix paths can be either absolute, in which case they begin with a leading slash, or relative to the current directory, in which case they don't.

Peripheral Devices Hardware devices such as printers or keyboards that can be detached from the machine.

Pipe A method for passing information from one process to another. Pipes can be used to send the output from one process to be used as the input for another process. For example, you might issue the command

```
cat /etc/services | more
```

which would send the output of the cat command as the input for the more command. Thus, you could read through the /etc/services file in page-sized units.

Point-to-Point Protocol (PPP) The protocol that governs how data will be transmitted between two computers using a serial connection (often a telephone line). PPP is the basis for many ISP software programs. If you set up a connection between your Unix machine and your local Internet provider, it will likely be a PPP connection.

Port To port a piece of software is to rewrite it for a different platform. For example, Corel decided to release WordPerfect Suite 2000, a popular Windows 95/98 integrated office suite, for the Linux platform. To do so, they had to port the program to Linux.

Port Forwarding The process of making a port on one machine synonymous with a port on another machine. Programs may then use the local port as if it were the remote port. SSH is a good tool for this.

Port Scanner An automated series of individual data bursts, called packets, sent from a remote site to determine whether any ports on your local network are open and accessible. A tool routinely used by crackers searching the Internet for exploitable machines that can be used as home base for illegal activity such as Denial of Service attacks or other nefarious schemes.

Positional Parameter A character, usually @, used in shell programming. The positional parameter helps the script track which variable is currently being used in the script.

Print Queue The print jobs waiting to be sent to the printer. If the printer is networked, the queue may hold jobs from various machines on the network and can be quite long. Jobs in the queue are held in the print spool.

See also *Spool.*

Private Address Space IP numbers set aside for machines that will not be connected to the Internet. Because they will not be used to identify particular computers, these numbers can be reused by many different people on a wide range of networks. The IP numbers reserved in the Class C range as private address space are 192.168.0.0 to 192.168.255.255.

See also *IP Classes* and *IP Masquerading.*

Process Running programs. Every program that is currently active is considered a process and is given a process ID number (PID) by the system. You can view the process table (the list of processes) using the ps command.

Process Identification Number (PID) The unique number assigned to every running process on your machine. The PID can be used to manage individual processes, as with the kill command. Learn the PIDs of the active processes on your machine with the ps or top commands.

Protocol An accepted method for handling information on a network. The use of protocols ensures that information will be handled in a uniform way regardless of the individual program being used. Protocols are described on a series of papers known as RFCs (requests for comments), which are maintained by the Internet Engineering Task Force (IETF). You can look up an RFC by going to the IETF's Web page at http://www.ietf.org/rfc.html.

Proxy Server A server that acts as intermediary between a local network and an external network such as the Internet. If a proxy is in use, a request from the local network's user will be passed through the proxy on its way to the destination. The destination machine will see the request as if it had originated with the proxy server, not from the actual originating machine. Proxy servers are part of a complete security program and are usually housed on the gateway computer.

Q

Queue A list of commands or other requests waiting to be processed. There are a variety of queues on a Unix system, including those for print jobs and various servers.

R

README File The most important file in any software package, especially in source code packages. The README file contains information on the package, especially with regard to the package's installation.

Recursive Acronym An acronym that contains itself. For example, GNU is an acronym for GNU's Not Unix. Likewise PINE, the name of a popular mail program, is an acronym for Pine Is Not Elm. Recursive acronyms are inspired by recursive programming functions, which are functions that call themselves. For example, a very simple (and useless) recursive function might look like this:

```
function {
    function()
    }
```

In other words, a recursive function is one where the function itself is part of its own definition.

Redirection Operators Shell operators that can change the destination of the input or output stream. For example, if a program nor-

mally sends its output to the terminal screen, that output can be redirected into a file by appending > <filename> to the program. Common redirection operators are

- >, used for output redirection

- <, used for input redirection

- |, used as a pipe

Regular Expression A text expression, usually involving metacharacters, that can match one or more literal text strings.

Rescue Kit A very stripped-down version of an operating system and some tools (such as a text editor) that can fit onto a diskette. A rescue kit allows a system administrator to boot a broken machine and perform operations on it so that it may be fixed.

Return Value
See *Exit Status.*

Root The superuser's login name. Also used as shorthand for *the person who has ultimate control over the machine.* A popular Unix T-shirt mimics the American Milk Producers' advertising campaign, asking "Got Root?"

Router A machine that routes incoming data to the appropriate destination. A router may be software on a central or gateway computer, or it may be an individual piece of hardware. Packets of data may pass through one or more routers on their trips across local networks or larger networks such as the Internet. The router uses the packet destination's identifying IP number to determine where the packet should be sent next.

Run Control Files Another name for configuration files or dot files.

Runlevels The System V init procedure allows the administrator to define several alternative configurations that can be started directly from the init program. These alternate configurations are called runlevels, and they are normally numbered 1 through 6, with 1 being *single user*, 6 being *reboot*, and 2–5 being user-definable.

S

Script Kiddie A particularly irritating form of cracker, script kiddies are usually young computer users who don't understand the systems they crack, but rather use prewritten cracking tools downloaded off the Internet.

Scripts Programs that are usually short and in an interpreted language, such as Perl or bash.

Service A general term for the server part of a client-server application. Most frequently, the term is used for applications that are used for Internet activity. In Part IX: "Administering Services," we introduce some of the most popular services: electronic mail, World Wide Web, USENET news, and others.

Shadow Passwords A security precaution in which user passwords are not stored in the /etc/passwd file. Instead, the passwords are encrypted and stored in a different file, usually /etc/shadow. Originally a practice usable only on a Linux system, many other Unix variants now allow the practice, including Solaris and FreeBSD.

Shell
See *Command Shell.*

Shell Account An account that allows the user access to a command shell. It is no longer common to obtain a shell account from an Internet service provider, though some ISPs still offer shell accounts.

Shell Command A command recognized by the shell's command interpreter. The term is used to differentiate commands issued at the shell prompt from commands issued in a graphical user environment by the click of a mouse or other peripheral device.

Shell Environment Those characteristics of a particular system's or user's unique shell setup. The shell environment can be altered using run control files and environment variables.

Shell Prompt The signal that the shell gives to the user that it is ready to accept input. The prompt is configurable, but usually shows the machine name and sometimes the user's name.

Signal The data sent to or by a given process that alerts the operating system of a desired action. A variety of signals are sent and received in the execution of any given Unix process.

Slice
See *Partition.*

Software Modem Also known as a Win-Modem. A software modem is smaller than a regular modem because it uses software commands to perform many of the tasks for which the larger hardware was once needed. Software modems are Windows-specific and cannot be used on computers running Unix variants. Unfortunately, they are often much less expensive than traditional modems, but they are useless purchases for the Unix user.

Source Code The raw programming instructions that make up a particular program. The source code must be compiled or interpreted before it can be understood by the machine.

Spool The manner in which data is handled as it waits for further action. Unix computers produce a number of spools. The most familiar are the mail spool, in which incoming electronic mail is stored until the recipient reads it with a mail client program, and the print spool, in which waiting print jobs are stored until the printer is free to process them.

Standard A written description to which a program or a system must conform if it is to be considered compliant. For example, the X Window System is a standard. It describes how such a system would operate. XFree86 is an implementation of that standard, in that it is a piece of software that functions in the way described by the X standard.

Standard Input The particular input stream that a given program uses under normal circumstances. Often the keyboard.

Standard Output The particular output stream that a given program uses under normal circumstances. Often the terminal screen.

Statement Any command that constitutes a step in a program. A statement can be imperative, such as `echo "hello"`, one of assignment, such as `x=10`, or one of flow control that usually contains an element of evaluation, such as `if X, then Y`.

Static Kernel A kernel that must be recompiled if new information is required. Many commercial Unices use a static kernel, which cannot be recompiled by the local administrator.

See also *Kernel* and *Modular Kernel*.

Stream Editor A text editor that processes text as it passes through the editor in a stream of data. Stream editors are rare, and only the programs `sed` and `awk` are examples of currently used stream editors. They are primarily useful in programming contexts.

Strings Combinations of characters, both alphabetical and numerical. Text processing, among other things, is done largely by manipulating strings.

Subshell A new shell process spawned by an existing shell process. Subshells can be used to perform a single task or run a process without rendering the initial shell process immobile.

Superuser The most powerful user on the system. The superuser has all permissions to every file on the system. The superuser has the power to start or stop any process, shut down the system (or even completely destroy it), and add or delete users. Every Unix system must have a superuser.

Symbolic Link A file that serves as a pointer to another file. For example, on some systems, the file /bin/sh is a symbolic link to the file /bin/bash. This means that any script that is designated to run under the Bourne Shell will instead be run under the bash shell.

System Administrator The person responsible for the overall running of the system. The system administrator may design networks, install hardware and software, maintain user accounts, maintain statistics about the system, engineer security, and do just about anything else you can think of.

System Calls Programming functions that make a direct request to functions provided by the operating-system kernel.

T

Tarball Any set of files (usually a software package) collected together using the Unix tar utility and often compressed using the gzip program.

Task Switching Task switching is the version of multitasking used by personal operating systems, such as Windows and MacOS. With task switching, the operating system allows each running process to complete a particular task before the next process is permitted to use system resources. Task switching is the opposite of *time slicing*.

TCP/IP The combination of the Transmission Control Protocol and the Internet Protocol. Because both protocols are required for the safe and complete transmission of data across a network, the two are usually covered in the single term TCP/IP.

See also *Internet Protocol (IP)* and *Transmission Control Protocol (TCP)*.

Text-Mode Editor A text editor that processes text as a complete file, instead of one line at a time like a line editor. Text-mode editors are usually full-screen editors such as pico or vi, but are not graphical, and require the use of arrow keys and key combinations instead of mouse clicks.

Time Slicing Time slicing is the version of multitasking used by multiple-user operating systems, such as Unix and its variants. With time slicing, each running process has access to the system resources for a certain defined period of time. When the time is over, the next process gains access, and so on. Time slicing is the opposite of *task switching*.

Timestamp File metadata that identifies the last time the file was modified. Timestamps are used both by humans and by other processes to sort or identify files based on the access or modification data.

Topology The way in which a network is constructed. A given network's topology can also be called its *architecture*. There are several typical network topologies:

> **Hub or bus:** Each networked computer is attached to a backplane cable that transfers data throughout the network.

> **Daisy chain:** Each computer is attached to the next computer, with the main server merely being one computer on the chain. If

the first and last computers on the chain are connected, it is a ring topology; if they are not, it is a daisy chain.

Star: Each networked computer is attached directly to a central server.

Transmission Control Protocol (TCP)

The protocol that is used to reassemble a series of packets after they have been delivered using the Internet Protocol. With the TCP protocol, it is possible to split up large accretions of data, such as a file, into small individual packets to transfer the data across the Internet or other network more quickly.

See also *Internet Protocol (IP).*

U

Unices   The commonly used plural form of Unix. Although not particularly grammatically pleasing, this is the term used by most Unix administrators and programmers. For some reason, the term *Linuces* has not caught on for plural versions of Linux.

User Accounts   The identification of, and allocation of resources to, users on the system. At the very minimum, a user account requires an entry in the /etc/passwd file. User accounts are normally created using the useradd or adduser programs.

User Datagram Protocol (UDP)   A protocol used for data transfer that manages the receipt of discrete packets and reassembles the packets at the receiving end of the connec-

tion. One of the two protocols from which you may choose when editing /etc/initd.conf.

See also *Datagram.*

Username (User ID)   A word that identifies a user on the system. Synonymous with *login name* and *login ID.*

V

Variable   A name that can serve as a container for a value. For example, the variable $EDITOR will always define the user's default text editor, regardless of the value, which is the name of whatever editor the user prefers.

Verbose Mode   Many programs have a mode that prints out a great deal of information about what the program is doing at any particular time. Such modes are called *verbose* and are usually used for debugging network configurations and the like. Some programs even support multiple levels of verbosity.

Virtual Desktops   A feature of several window managers and integrated desktop environments. A virtual desktop appears as a completely separate desktop, upon which you can open various windows and work with programs as if you were running a separate login session. Some programs permit you to work with as many as 256 virtual desktops at one time, each with a different set of activities.

Virtual Host

1.   A configuration of a mail transfer agent that makes the MTA willing to accept

electronic mail destined for a domain other than the domain on which the server is installed. This is a way to expand the range of a particular network's presence without having to establish a separate mail server for the second domain.

2. A way in which a domain can be represented on the Internet without having a physical presence. Many companies will sell virtual hosting packages for a reasonable price.

Visual Editor   In contrast to a line or stream editor, an editor that allows interactive editing, usually including such features as direct interactive cursor movement, direct editing of the text in place, and the like. Visual editors include vi, GNU Emacs, pico, and jed. A case could be made that the visual editors should also include the graphical editors, but conventionally, the term refers to text-mode editors.

Volume
See *Partition*.

W

Widgets   Elements of graphical programming. Most graphically based programs have a need for a common set of elements. Items such as windows, scroll bars, buttons, and pop-up menus are needed in just about all graphic programming. Programmers often create libraries of these elements so that they need not be recoded every time a new pro-

gram is created. These libraries are referred to as *widget sets*.

Wildcard   An element of regular expressions. A metacharacter that can stand in for any other character.

Window Manager   The element of the graphical user interface that is responsible for the overall look and feel of the screen.

Worms   A type of computer virus that enters the system at a vulnerable point and moves around inside the computer until it finds the proper location from which to execute its intended purpose.

X

X Window System   Any graphical user interface that conforms to the X Windows standard as described by the X Consortium (http://www.x.org). The current version of the standard is X11R6.

x86 Processor   An x86 processor is a chip built by Intel, or to Intel's specifications, that falls into the x86 chip family. This family includes the 386 and 486 chips, now nearing obsolete status, as well as the various Pentium chips. All three Unices used in this book have been ported to the x86 processor platform; Linux and FreeBSD were written intentionally for the x86 platform.

INDEX

Note to Reader: In this index, **boldfaced** page numbers refer to primary discussions of the topic; *italics* page numbers refer to figures.

G

J

M

V

Y

Z

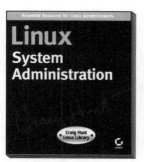

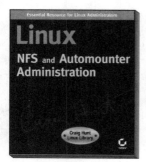

What's on the CD

The CD-ROM included with this book contains an array of software released under various Open Source/Free Software licenses. Combined with the programs usually included with any given Unix or Unix-derived distribution, these programs comprise a strong set of software that should give you a robust and easily administered Unix machine.

NOTE Licenses for the software contained on the CD are included with each package in a digital version. Note that all software is provided without warranty, and that by installing and using a given package, you accept its license terms.

Updated versions of these packages may have been released since the printing of this book. We encourage you to visit each program's Web site (listed in Appendix B) to see whether there is a newer version of the program or whether known bugs have been reported and patches released to fix them.

System Requirements

- A computer (PC) with at least a 486 processor chip
- A working installation of any Unix variant
- A working installation of the X Window System
- At least 64MB of RAM (and as much as you can afford)
- A hard drive, preferably with at least 500MB to 1GB free
- A CD-ROM drive
- Sound and video cards
- A monitor capable of 256 colors or grayscale

Programs Included

gcc (GNU C Compiler): Install this first, because most of the packages we've included are GNU programs (or have significant GNU contribution) and require the gcc libraries to function. We provide both binary packages and source code; if you have no compiler installed on your system, put the binary files into an executable directory.

bash: The default shell environment used in this book; the shell programming covered in Part VI: "Shell Programming" is bash-based.